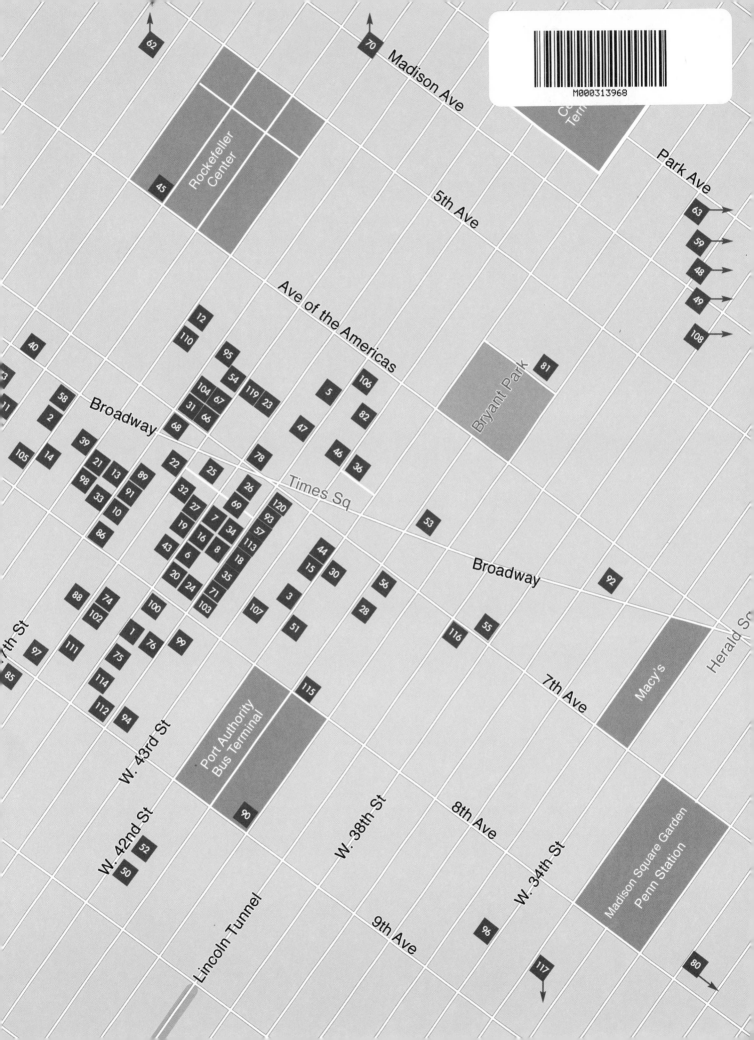

The Playbill® Broadway Yearbook

Tenth Annual Edition
2013-2014

Robert Viagas
Editor

Amy Asch
Assistant Editor

Frank Dain
Production Coordinator

Kesler Thibert
Art Director

Brian Mapp   Joseph Marzullo   Monica Simoes
Photographers

PLAYBILL®
BOOKS

APPLAUSE
THEATRE & CINEMA BOOKS

The Playbill Broadway Yearbook: Tenth Annual Edition, June 1, 2013–May 31, 2014
Robert Viagas, Editor

ISBN 978-1-4803-8546-7
ISSN 1932-1945

Published by PLAYBILL® BOOKS
525 Seventh Avenue, Suite 1801
New York, NY 10018
Email: yearbook@playbill.com
Internet: www.playbill.com

Exclusively distributed by Applause Theatre & Cinema Books
An Imprint of Hal Leonard Corporation
7777 West Bluemound Road
Milwaukee, WI 53213

Trade Book Division Editorial Offices
33 Plymouth St., Montclair, NJ 07042

Printed in the United States of America

Book design by Kesler Thibert
Cover photo of the Belasco Theatre interior by Brian Mapp

www.applausebooks.com

Preface to the Tenth Edition

On days when those of us here at Playbill are researching long-ago shows, long-ago theatres and long-ago show folk for a program feature or a news story, we stop and wish: If only we'd been publishing *The Playbill Broadway Yearbook* back in the '60s or the '40s or the '20s! We'd have everything we'd need right at our fingertips.

Imagine if we'd had a firsthand account of the opening night from the cast of the original *Show Boat*, gotten candid dressing room shots of Mary Martin and Cyril Ritchard in *Peter Pan*, recorded the exercise regimen of the original cast of *The Pajama Game*, seen how the stage crew went about their business on *The Band Wagon*, heard Noël Coward's witticisms when he visited his friends at *The King and I*, or known the backstage rituals of the *Ziegfeld Follies*? We'd know not only who was in every show and what the show looked like, we'd know what was on the minds of the people working on the show: how they had fun, and how they managed the joy and stress of working on Broadway every day.

Researchers of the future will have it a little easier: this is the tenth edition of the *Yearbook*, meaning that for the 2004-05 season and everything after that, we've got those bases covered for the shows of our own lifetimes. We continue to fulfill publisher Philip Birsh's original vision of creating a high-school type yearbook for Broadway, one that would include not just the actors, but everyone involved in putting on a show, from the writers to the stagehands to the behind-the-scenes people in support groups like Broadway Cares, the Broadway League and the various unions and professional organizations. And all with an emphasis on people—more than 10,000 of them are listed our index; and photos—more than 4000 of them, many taken by our staff and existing no place else.

A lot has changed since 2004. Back then stage folks were obsessed with the no-carb Atkins Diet; *Rent, Spamalot* and *The Producers* were still drawing crowds; Stephen Sondheim had a (mostly) new musical and Cy Coleman was planning several.

Of course, some things haven't changed at all. Ten years ago Broadway was marveling at Jefferson Mays playing multiple roles (in *I Am My Own Wife*) and Kenny Leon was directing a starry revival of *A Raisin in the Sun*. Among the long-running hits that year were *Phantom of the Opera, Chicago, The Lion King, Wicked* and *Mamma Mia!*, all of them still with us as of this writing.

David Gewirtzman, an original *Yearbook* staffer who has moved on to other things here at Playbill, continues, as a labor of love, to custom-design the Alumni and Transfer Student logos that appear in nearly each chapter.

Over the past decade, the *Yearbook* has recorded Broadway's reaction to strikes, blizzards, protests, Tony controversies and endless construction projects. Old landmarks have vanished, like McHale's, Colony Records and Roseland. Some have been renovated and born anew, like the TKTS booth, the Times Square pedestrian mall and the Sondheim Theatre (which replaced Henry Miller's Theatre).

And the *Yearbook* is constantly evolving. Kesler Thibert took over as art director, introducing a cleaner, sharper look to the book. We

YOUR 2013-2014 YEARBOOK COMMITTEE
Standing (L-R): Joseph Marzullo, David Gewirtzman and Amy Asch.
Seated (L-R): Brian Mapp, editor Robert Viagas and Frank Dain.
Not pictured: Art director Kesler Thibert, photographer Monica Simoes

Photo: Michael Gioia

try to add or improve something each year. In Volume 7 we added plot summaries, which have been very popular. This year we added a map to the inside of the covers—not just a traditional map of the Times Square theatre district but a map that includes all the places mentioned in the *Yearbook*, from the great old theatres to the locations named in the plays themselves, and the places where the actors hang out, and where they held their cast parties, special events and press get-togethers.

The current yearbook covers a season in which there was a bumper crop (twelve) of new Broadway musicals, but no clear blockbuster. Seemingly sure-fire shows like *Big Fish* fizzled, and late-season shows with first-class pedigrees like Jason Robert Brown's *Bridges of Madison County* and Woody Allen's *Bullets Over Broadway* found themselves struggling more than they expected. In the end the awards all went to a small-scale musical comedy *A Gentleman's Guide to Love & Murder*, which had not been selling out for most of the season (that changed after the Tonys) and the SRO went up at a jukebox musical about the life and career of Carole King, *Beautiful*. One of the biggest musical hits of the season wasn't even considered a musical: *Lady Day at Emerson's Bar & Grill*, Audra McDonald's tour-de-force salute to singer Billie Holiday, which was judged a "play with music" despite a score of 16 songs.

This year's Scrapbook correspondents include everyone from actors to stage managers to understudies. Our correspondents include three Tony nominees: Nick Cordero of *Bullets Over Broadway*, Charl Brown of *Motown*, and Lena Hall of *Hedwig and the Angry Inch*. Lena did her Scrapbook page the week after she was nominated, and she went on to win the award as Best Featured Actress in a Musical on Tony night.

On her Scrapbook page Hall writes about a private exchange of passive-aggressive "love" notes she maintains—in twisted character—with Neil Patrick Harris' Hedwig. Cordero writes about what it was like to get his first note from that show's librettist, Woody Allen. Brown tells what it felt like to be interviewed on the Tony red carpet.

Jason Dirden, who plays suitor George Murchison in *Raisin in the Sun*, tells what it was like for the mostly African-American cast to perform the classic for our first African-American president, Barak Obama, and the First Lady. And Paul Whitty, the bearded music shop owner in *Once*, shares his memory of meeting Vice President Joe Biden backstage, and also the advice Whitty's mother gave him that led to his winning a role in that show.

The cast of this year's Tony-winning Best Musical *A Gentleman's Guide* submitted a candid backstage photo of how star Jefferson Mays dealt with the grueling holiday performance schedule at Christmas time. Ryann Redmond, a member of the ensemble in the musical *If/Then*, shared her favorite selfie with the show's star, Idina Menzel.

Supernatural ensemble member Stephanie Fieger tells how her production of *Macbeth* managed to avoid that Shakespeare play's famous Curse. Conrad Kemp, who played Benvolio opposite Orlando Bloom in *Romeo and Juliet*, explains how the show's Juliet, Condola Rashad, handled it when she found herself onstage in the last scene without the knife needed to bring the play to its conclusion. Dominic Brewer, who understudied Mark Rylance in *Twelfth Night*, shares a company memo in which management tried to convince the all-British acting company that the extra hour of sleep they'd get during the switchover to Standard Time had been arranged especially for them.

Carmen Ruby Floyd, one of the stylish performers in *After Midnight*, shares what dance icon Shirley MacLaine told the cast when she came backstage. Kevin Duda who plays singer Neil Sedaka in *Beautiful*, recounts a ghostly encounter he endured in the elevator of the Sondheim (nee Henry Miller's) Theatre.

And those are just a handful of the stories, secrets, photos and tips packed into this year's *Playbill Broadway Yearbook*. Think of it as a giant blog that covers all of Broadway from the inside.

So here's to ten years of the *Yearbook*. The best compliment we receive is people wishing we'd started it a century sooner. Amen to that.

In the meantime we've already begun work on the eleventh edition. See you in 2015!

Robert Viagas
June 2014

Special Thanks

Special thanks to Amy Asch, Frank Dain, Brian Mapp, Joseph Marzullo, Monica Simoes, Kesler Thibert, David Gewirtzman, Pam Karr, Matt Blank, Andrew Gans, Adam Hetrick, Jean Kroeper Murphy, O. Paul Corley Jr., Heidi Giovine, Richard D. Kaye, William Mitchell, Susan Sunday, Stephanie Wallis and Debra Candela Novack, whose help made this year's edition possible.

We also thank the Tenth Edition *Yearbook* Correspondents who shared their stories with such wit and insight: Eric Anderson, Shirine Babb, Whitney Bashor, Dominic Brewer, Charl Brown, James Brown-Orleans, Laurel Casillo, Sara Chase, Lauren Cohn, Jill Cordle (for the fourth time), Kaleigh Cronin, Stephen DeRosa, Jason Dirden, Kevin Duda, Michael Fatica, Stephanie Fieger, Russell Fischer, Carmen Ruby Floyd, Shalita Grant, Lena Hall, Leah Hofmann, the company of *A Gentleman's Guide to Love and Murder*, Conrad Kemp, Nikki Kimbrough, Caitlin Kinnunen, Derek Klena, Cody Scott Lancaster, James Latus, Winnie Lok, Jessica Love, Michael J. Lutch, Lesli Margherita, Luke Marinkovich, Ellyn Marie Marsh, Tom McGowan, Chris McBurney, Vasthy Mompoint, Alex Morf, Brian O'Brien, Stephen Pilkington, Ryann Redmond, Christopher Rice, Rachel Rincione, Adam Roberts, Michael McCorry Rose, Tory Ross (for the third time), Colin Ryan, Pat Shortt, Karina Smirnoff, Sarah Solie, Bobby Steggert, Bill Timoney, Molly Tynes, Marisha Wallace, Paul Whitty, Cody Williams and Conwell Worthington III.

And we thank the folks on each show who shared their pho-

Photographer Joan Marcus, who took production photos for many of the Broadway shows in this book, was honored with a Special 2014 Tony Award for Lifetime Achievement. *The Playbill Broadway Yearbook* adds its congratulations and thanks.

Photo: Joan Marcus

tographs and other artwork that lent extra sparkle to the Scrapbook pages: Eric Anderson, Dominic Brewer, Danny Burstein, Kaleigh Cronin, Jeremy Daniel, Stephanie Fieger, Leah Hofmann, Conrad Kemp, Nikki Kimbrough, Cody Scott Lancaster, Winnie Lok, Lesli Margherita, Ellyn Marie Marsh, Debra Messing, Vasthy Mompoint, Joe Perrotta, Ryann Redmond, Michael McCorry Rose, Colin Ryan, Paul Whitty, Cody Williams, and others.

Also the Broadway press agents who helped set up interviews and photo sessions and helped track down the names of all the people in the crew photos: especially Chris Boneau, Adrian Bryan-Brown, Michael Hartman, Richard Kornberg, Jeffrey Richards, Keith Sherman, Marc Thibodeau, Philip Rinaldi, Sam Rudy, Rick Miramontez, Leslie Baden Papa, Matt Polk, and their respective staffs.

Plus Joan Marcus, Paul Kolnik, Carol Rosegg, Chuck Kennedy, Evgenia Eliseeva, Jenny Anderson, Jeremy Daniel, Max Dodson, T. Charles Erickson, Simon Annand, Chad Batka, Jacob Cohl, Nathan Johnson, Brigitte Lacombe, Stephen Lovekin, Walter McBride, Matthew Murphy, Johan Persson, Richard Phibbs, Deen Van Meer, Cylla von Tiedemann, and all the fine professional photographers whose work appears on these pages.

And, most of all, thanks to the great show people of Broadway who got into the spirit of the Yearbook and took time out of their busy days to pose for our cameras. There's no people like them.

Frequently-Asked Questions

Which Shows Are Included? *The Playbill Broadway Yearbook 2013-2014* covers the Broadway season that ran, as per tradition, from June 1, 2013 to May 31, 2014. Each of the seventy-one shows that played at a Broadway theatre under a Broadway contract during that time are spotlighted in this edition. That includes new shows that opened during that time, like *Aladdin*; shows from last season that ran into this season, like *Kinky Boots*; older shows from seasons past that closed during this season, like *Spider-Man: Turn Off the Dark*; and older shows from seasons past that ran throughout this season and continue into the future (and into the next *Yearbook*), like *Wicked*.

How Is It Decided Which Credits Page Will Be Featured? Each show's credits page (which PLAYBILL calls a "billboard page") changes over the year as cast members come and go. We use the opening-night billboard page for most new shows. For most shows that carry over from the previous season we use the billboard page from the first week in October.

Occasionally, sometimes at the request of the producer, we use a billboard page from another part of the season, especially when a major new star joins the cast.

What Are "Alumni" and "Transfer Students"? Over the course of a season some actors leave a production; others take their place. To follow our yearbook concept, the ones who left a show before the date of the billboard page are listed as "Alumni"; the ones who joined the cast are called "Transfer Students." If you see a photo appearing in both "Alumni" and "Transfer Students" sections, it's not a mistake; it just means that they went in and out of the show during the season and were not present on the billboard date.

What Is a "Correspondent" and How Is One Chosen? We ask each show to appoint a Correspondent to record anecdotes of backstage life at their production. Sometimes the show's press agent picks the Correspondent; sometimes the company manager, the stage manager or the producer does the choosing. Each show gets to decide for itself. A few shows

decline to provide a correspondent, fail to respond to our request, or miss the deadline. Correspondents bring a richness of experience to the job and help tell the story of backstage life on Broadway from many different points of view.

Who Gets Their Picture in the *Yearbook*? Anyone who works on Broadway can get their picture in the *Yearbook*. That includes actors, producers, writers, designers, assistants, stagehands, ushers, box office personnel, stage doormen and anyone else employed at a Broadway show or a support organization. PLAYBILL maintains a database of headshots of all Broadway actors and most creators. We send our staff photographers to all opening nights and all major Broadway-related events. We also offer to schedule in-theatre photo shoots at every production. No one is required to appear in the *Yearbook*, but all are invited. A few shows declined to host a photo shoot this year or were unable to provide material by our deadline. We hope the ones that are still running will join us in 2015.

TABLE OF CONTENTS

Timeline 2013-2014

Opening Nights, News Headlines and Other Significant Milestones of the Season

June 9, 2013 At the 67th Annual Antoinette Perry "Tony" Awards, *Kinky Boots* is named Best Musical and *Vanya and Sonia and Masha and Spike* is named Best Play.

June 26, 2013 The TKTS discount ticket booth at the north end of Times Square marks 40 years in business.

Summer 2013 City workers tear up the stretch of Broadway between 42nd and 47th Streets as part of a multi-year streetscape project that will include repaving Times Square. Construction continues throughout the season.

The Richard Rodgers Theatre gets a $3.5 million facelift, including a complete interior repainting and restoration of the original proscenium and murals, by EverGreene Architectural Arts.

Statues of four female performing arts paragons are removed (for cleaning and restoration) from their niches above 46th Street where they have stood since 1929: Ethel Barrymore for drama, Marilyn Miller for musicals, Mary Pickford for film and Rosa Ponselle for opera. They will be returned in early spring.

Also this summer: The song ends for the clutch of music stores that drew musicians to the western end of the block of 48th Street between Seventh Avenue and Avenue of the Americas for more than six decades. Most of the stores, where you could buy everything from 76 trombones to big banjos, were owned by Sam Ash Inc. They moved to 34th Street to make way for demolition and development of that block in the northeast quadrant of the Theatre District.

July 14, 2013 Luis Bravo's dance revue *Forever Tango* returns to Broadway for the second time for a limited run, featuring rotating guest stars, including two from the TV series "Dancing with the Stars."

July 14, 2013 Also today, thousands crowd Times Square and conduct a sit-in at the TKTS booth to protest the not-guilty jury decision in

President Barak Obama (top, center) and First Lady Michelle Obama (far right) vist backstage with the cast of *A Raisin in the Sun*. See April 11.

Official White House Photo by Chuck Kennedy

the Florida trial of George Zimmerman, who had been accused of second-degree murder in the shooting of black teen Trayvon Martin.

July 17-18, 2013 The logo of boxer Mike Tyson's one-man show *Undisputed Truth* appears on the marquee of the Imperial Theatre as Tyson tapes the performances there for an HBO special.

July 24, 2013 The music of the Beatles returns to Broadway in the concert-style musical *Let It Be.*

July 29, 2013 Mark Hotton pleads guilty to wire fraud in the case of *Rebecca—The Musical*, a Broadway production that collapsed in 2012 when it was discovered that an investor brought aboard by Hotton did not actually exist. Hotton agrees to forfeit $500,000 and to pay an additional $500,000 to his victims, with additional sentencing and possible jail time to come.

July 31, 2013 *Avenue Q* celebrates ten years since its Broadway opening night. The production moved in 2009 to Off-Broadway, where it is still running.

August 8, 2013 Zachary Levi and Krysta Rodriguez star in *First Date*, an original musical about an oddly matched contemporary couple on a blind date. A Broadway debut for the songwriting team of Alan Zachary and Michael Weiner.

August, 15, 2013 The musical biography *Soul Doctor* tells the story of Shlomo Carlebach, a rabbi who became a 1960s celebrity when he set religious texts to folk and rock music.

August 15, 2013 Also today, Daniel Curry, one of the actors playing the title role in *Spider-Man Turn Off the Dark* during stunt scenes, is injured when his leg becomes entangled in scenery. The rest of the performance is cancelled, but the show goes on as scheduled the next night.

August 24-25, 2013 First Lady Michelle Obama attends performances of *The Trip to Bountiful* and *Motown* with her daughters, Sasha and Malia.

September 15, 2013 The 66th Annual Tony Awards broadcast, aired in June 2012, wins four Emmy Awards: for Outstanding Music Direction (Elliot Lawrence, music director), Outstanding Original Music and Lyrics ("If I Had Time," lyrics by Adam Schlesinger, music by David Javerbaum), Outstanding Special Class Program, and Outstanding Technical Direction, Camerawork, Video Control for a Miniseries, Movie or a Special. It represents the second most awards of any show, tied with HBO's "Boardwalk Empire."

September 19, 2013 Orlando Bloom and Condola Rashad star in the title roles of *Romeo and Juliet*, a lavish revival that is the first of four Shakespeare plays to open on Broadway this fall.

September 26, 2013 Cherry Jones plays Amanda and Zachary Quinto plays Tom in a revival of Tennessee Williams' *The Glass Menagerie.*

September 27, 2013 The Off-Broadway hit musical *Natasha, Pierre & The Great Comet of 1812* moves to a tent named Kazino in a vacant lot on 45th Street in the thick of the Broadway theatre district. It runs until March 2.

September 29, 2013 The iconic Shubert Theatre, home to *A Chorus Line, Babes in Arms, Can-Can, A Little Night Music, Spamalot, Matilda* and dozens more classic shows, celebrates its 100th anniversary, as does the accompanying Shubert Alley, the unofficial heart of the Broadway theatre district.

October 6, 2013 Norbert Leo Butz stars in *Big Fish*, Andrew Lippa's lavish musical about a man who goes in search of the truth about his tall-tale-telling father.

October 10, 2013 Mary Bridget Davies offers a remarkable impersonation of a rock legend in the concert musical *A Night With Janis Joplin.*

October 10, 2013 Also today, another 1960s icon, the real-life Paul McCartney, uses Twitter to gather a flash mob in Times Square to hear songs from his new album, "New."

Photo: Robert Viagas

Times Square was a construction site from summer 2013 to the end of the season as the city repaved the entire plaza. See Summer 2013.

Timeline 2013-2014

October 16, 2013 Another classic Broadway house celebrates its centenary: the Booth Theatre, built in tandem with the Shubert, which has hosted numerous classics including original productions of *That Championship Season, The Elephant Man* and *Sunday in the Park With George.*

October 17, 2013 Roger Rees stars as a father determined to clear his son's name in a revival of Terence Rattigan's *The Winslow Boy.*

October 20, 2013 The courtroom drama *A Time To Kill* is Rupert Holmes's adaptation of John Grisham's best-seller about a black man on trial for killing his daughter's white rapists.

October 20, 2013 Also on this date *The Lion King* becomes the first Broadway show in history to record earnings of $1 billion. The Disney show, which opened in November 1997, has been sold out, or nearly so, for most of its 16-year run.

biographical solo show *700 Sundays*, which is taped for television.

November 17, 2013 Jefferson Mays plays eight patrician murder victims in the new musical comedy *A Gentleman's Guide to Love and Murder,* which also provides the Broadway debut for a raft of new talent including ingénues Lauren Worsham and Lisa O'Hare, and the songwriting team of Robert L. Freedman and Steven Lutvak.

November 21, 2013 Ethan Hawke and Anne-Marie Duff star in Lincoln Center Theater's revival of *Macbeth,* featuring Daniel Sunjata as Macduff and Brian d'Arcy James as Banquo. It is the second production of the tragedy on Broadway in 2013, and the fourth Shakespeare play on the Broadway boards simultaneously, the first such syzygy since 1987.

November 24, 2013 *No Man's Land/Waiting for Godot*: Another repertory offering, starring Ian

Rock of Ages and the upcoming *Rocky.*

December 2, 2013 Also today, the 1960s rock group The Rascals cancels the Broadway return of its concert show, *The Rascals: Once Upon a Dream,* just two weeks before the planned opening night, blaming scheduling conflicts.

December 5, 2013 NBC-TV's live broadcast of *The Sound of Music,* officially retitled *The Sound of Music Live!,* stars Carrie Underwood, Stephen Moyer, Audra McDonald, Laura Benanti and Christian Borle. Despite extensive web debate before and after the broadcast about Underwood's fitness for the lead role, the $9 million production is a ratings smash, seen by a reported 18.6 million people. Within days NBC announces plans to broadcast a live musical every holiday season.

Dec. 29, 2013 For the week ending today, *Wicked* sets the all-time Broadway record for a single week's box office receipts: $3,201,333, the first time any Broadway show has earned more than $3 million in a single week. Now in the eleventh year of its run, the musical broke its own record of $2.9 million set the week ending December 30 the previous year, due to holiday crowds paying higher ticket prices, especially for premium seating. The starry revival of *Betrayal* also sets the all-time weekly record for a non-musical, $1,442,087. Weekly records for individual theatres are broken by many other shows as well.

January 4, 2014 The most expensive musical in Broadway history closes with the biggest loss in Broadway history. *Spider-Man: Turn Off the Dark* ends its run of 182 previews and 1,066 performances at a loss reported between $60 million and $80 million. Nevertheless, Theatre District restaurateur Joe Allen tells *The New York Times* that he will not add the show's window card to the notorious Wall of Flops at his eponymous 46th Street eatery, explaining "Any show that plays for three years on Broadway, providing steady employment to members of the theater community and pumping money into the local economy, is no failure in my book."

January 9, 2014 The Broadway League publishes its annual survey of the Broadway audience, covering the 2012-2013 season. Among the interesting findings: Women made up 68 percent of all audiences. Nearly a quarter of all tickets—23 percent—were bought by international tourists, the highest yearly proportion on record. And a total of 66 percent of tickets were bought by tourists from the U.S. and abroad combined. The average age of Broadway theatregoers fell slightly to 42.5 from 43.5 the season before. The average Broadway theatregoer saw four shows a year. Hardcore fans who saw 15 or more shows a year comprised only 5 percent of the audience—but they bought 31 percent of all tickets. The Broadway audience was overwhelmingly white (78 percent) and fairly wealthy, with an average annual household income of $186,500.

January 12, 2014 The life and songbook of pop singer/composer Carole King form the back-

Members of the original cast of *Hello, Dolly!* gather at Sardi's to mark the show's 50th anniversary, organized by Richard Skipper (far right). See January 19.

Photo: Joseph Marzullo

October 24, 2013 Mary-Louise Parker plays the feckless matriarch of an upstate New York family that suddenly finds itself penniless in Sharr White's original drama, *The Snow Geese.*

October 27, 2013 Daniel Craig, Rachel Weisz and Rafe Spall form the fractured romantic triangle in a revival of Harold Pinter's time-reversed drama, *Betrayal.*

October 30, 2013 *Wicked* notches its tenth anniversary on Broadway.

November 3, 2013 The musical revue *After Midnight,* first seen as part of Off-Broadway's "Encores!" series, features stylishly-staged classic tunes from the Harlem Renaissance.

November 7, 2013 The concert show *Il Divo–A Musical Affair* features four international singers performing pop and showtunes in quasi-operatic style.

November 10, 2013 Mark Rylance leads a British troupe performing Shakespeare's *Richard III* and *Twelfth Night* (styled "*Twelfe*" in ads) in repertory with live musicians on a candlelit stage. Other Elizabethan touches include men playing the women's roles, and a post-show dance interlude.

November 13, 2013 Comedian Billy Crystal toplines a return engagement of his 2004 auto-

McKellen, Patrick Stewart, Shuler Hensley and Billy Crudup alternating nights in the Beckett and Pinter modern classics. Includes the second Pinter play to open on Broadway in the space of a month.

November 27, 2013 The animated Disney film *Frozen* opens to positive reviews for its score, co-written by Robert Lopez (*Avenue Q, Book of Mormon*), and cast of voice actors, including Broadway's Idina Menzel, Josh Gad, Jonathan Groff, Santino Fontana and Ciarán Hinds.

November 28, 2013 The annual Macy's Thanksgiving Day Parade marches out performances by *Matilda, Motown, A Night With Janis Joplin, Kinky Boots* and *Pippin.* Some users of Twitter tweet their objections to the sight of *Kinky Boots'* cross-dressers on a family TV show. Librettist Harvey Fierstein defends the show in a statement widely covered in the press. It reads, in part, "I'm so proud that the cast of *Kinky Boots* brought their message of tolerance and acceptance to America's parade."

December 2, 2013 Michael Hartman announces he will close his press agency, Broadway's second largest, in January to take a job as CEO of Amy's Ice Creams in his native Texas. Among his orphaned clients: *Wicked,*

Timeline 2013-2014

bone of the biographical *Beautiful: The Carole King Musical*, starring Jessie Mueller in the title role. Claiming she's unable to watch her first marriage fall apart on stage, King herself declines to attend the opening.

January 16, 2014 *Machinal*, Sophie Treadwell's expressionistic 1928 drama about a woman trapped by life, gets its first Broadway revival, starring Rebecca Hall. Opening night becomes memorable when the turntable carrying the 30,000-pound set becomes stuck, and the show's technical supervisor, head of the scene shop and stagehands, including volunteers from other theatres, labor to get it going again. When that fails, they spend the rest of opening night turning the set with old-fashioned muscle power so the show can go on.

January 19, 2014 Members of the original cast of *Hello, Dolly!* gather at Sardi's to celebrate the 50th anniversary of the show's opening.

January 19, 2014 Also today, Craig Zadan and Neil Meron, producers of the hit live TV broadcast of *The Sound of Music* in December 2013, announce that they will follow it up with a live broadcast of Broadway's *Peter Pan* in December 2014. Speculation begins over who will play Peter, Hook, et al.

January 23, 2014 Debra Messing and Brían F. O'Byrne play the heirs to neighboring Irish farms in *Outside Mullingar*, John Patrick Shanley's drama (his first dealing with his Irish background) about people who take too long to reveal their hearts.

January 23, 2014 Also today, dozens of Broadway celebrities perform cameos in a YouTube video, "Russian Broadway Shut Down," protesting Russian persecution of gays in connection with the upcoming Olympic Games (www.youtube.com/watch?v=QBDJG x8ck0c#t=49). Fans play a game of their own, trying to spot and name them all.

January 26, 2014 The original cast album of *Kinky Boots* wins the Grammy Award for Best Musical Theatre Album.

January 27, 2014 The Theater Hall of Fame at the Gershwin Theatre inducts actors Ellen Burstyn and Cherry Jones; directors Lynne Meadow, George C. Wolfe and Jerry Zaks; playwright Lorraine Hansberry, designer David Hays and producer Cameron Mackintosh.

January 27, 2014 Also today, the Broadway Green Alliance, an industry-wide initiative to develop environmentally-friendly best practices on Broadway, turns five years old.

January 26 to February 2, 2014 Broadway from Times Square to Herald Square is renamed "Super Bowl Boulevard" in honor of the football championship game being played miles away at MetLife Stadium in East Rutherford, New Jersey between two teams not from New York. Attractions include a simulated toboggan run at 41st Street and a chance to pose for photos next to the game's trophy. A section of Times Square itself is covered with artificial turf so fans can placekick a football into a net. The promotion coincides with a week of bitter cold as a so-called

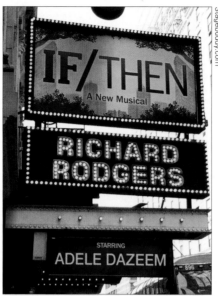

When John Travolta mispronounced Idina Menzel's name on the Oscars, internet Photoshoppers had a field day. See March 2.

Polar Vortex sends frigid arctic air into the Northeast. On Sunday, February 2, the day of the game itself, *Waiting for Godot* stars Ian McKellen, Patrick Stewart, Billy Crudup and Shuler Hensley hand out free hot chocolate to ticketholders outside the Cort Theatre near the upper end of Super Bowl Boulevard.

February 1, 2014 As Woody Allen prepares for his return to Broadway with the musical *Bullets Over Broadway*, a controversy erupts in print when his adopted daughter, Dylan Farrow, publishes a letter accusing Allen of having molested her when she was a child. Allen denies it. Theatregoers on social media are left wondering whom to believe and whether there is a moral dimension involved in buying tickets to his show.

February 2, 2014 Beloved stage and screen actor Philip Seymour Hoffman is found dead of a heroin overdose just two years after earning a Tony nomination for playing Willy Loman in a revival of *Death of a Salesman*.

February 6, 2014 Major League Baseball becomes a Broadway producer with the debut of Eric Simonson's *Bronx Bombers*, a drama in which famed catcher-turned-coach Yogi Berra (Peter Scolari) dreams that he's in conference with all the greats of Yankees history.

February 6, 2014 Also today, an underground explosion on 49th Street causes power outages that affect area Broadway shows. Reduced power leads to the cancellation of the first preview of *Rocky*, which had been set for February 11.

February 13, 2014 Sky, a wire fox terrier who won Best in Show at the February 11 Westminster Kennel Club competition, does a walk-on at *Kinky Boots*.

February 20, 2014 Marsha Norman and Jason Robert Brown adapt Robert James Waller's 1992 bestselling romance novel *The Bridges of*

Madison County as a musical. Kelli O'Hara plays the isolated and long-neglected farm wife who spends four days in a torrid affair with a hunky National Geographic photographer, played by Steven Pasquale.

March 2, 2014 At the annual Academy Awards ceremony, Robert Lopez, co-composer of *Avenue Q* and *Book of Mormon*, wins the Best Song Oscar for "Let It Go" (co-written with Kristen Anderson-Lopez) from Disney's *Frozen*, which is sung in the film by Tony-winner Idina Menzel. Introducing her performance of the song on the telecast, John Travolta garbles Menzel's name as something like "Adele Dazeem." Clips of the flub go viral on the web, and *The Washington Post* reports that the notoriety doubles ticket sales for her Broadway musical, *If/Then*, which is about to start previews.

March 6, 2014 Fresh off the hugely ballyhooed finale of his hit cable TV series "Breaking Bad," actor Bryan Cranston makes his Broadway debut with *All the Way*, a portrait of President Lyndon B. Johnson and his political struggles to pass the Civil Rights Act of 1964 and get through the next election.

March 6, 2014 Also today, producers of the forthcoming revival of *On the Town* announce that it will be play at the playhouse formerly known as the Foxwoods Theatre, which will be renamed the Lyric Theatre. The 42nd Street space opened in 1998 as the Ford Center, was renamed Hilton in 2005, and then the Foxwoods in 2010, in each case named for a sponsor.

March 6, 2014 Also today, *Mamma Mia!* surpasses *Rent* to become the ninth longest running show in Broadway history.

March 8, 2014 Lifetime TV airs an adaptation of *The Trip to Bountiful*. Cicely Tyson and Vanessa Williams reprise their roles from the Tony-winning 2013 revival.

March 13, 2014 A musical adaptation of the Oscar-winning boxing film *Rocky* has an original score by Lynn Ahrens and Stephen Flaherty (buttressed by two pieces of music from the films) and book by Thomas Meehan based on Sylvester Stallone's screenplay. Andy Karl plays the palooka with a shot at the title. Much is written about the Act II moment when the first eight rows of the audience are evacuated to the stage so the boxing ring set can move out into the middle of the theatre for the climactic fight.

March 16, 2014 Passersby on 44th Street do a double-take upon seeing *Funny Girl* on the marquee of the St. James Theatre. The TV series "Glee" is shooting a sequence there in which co-star Lea Michele is appearing in an imagined revival of the musical.

March 20, 2014 Disney Theatricals goes all out on a stage extravaganza based on the animated musical film *Aladdin*. Trunk songs by Alan Menken and Howard Ashman, and additional lyrics by Chad Beguelin, enhance the movie's songs by Menken & Ashman and Menken with Tim Rice. Special effects and magic are crowned by a flying carpet that really seems to fly.

Spring 2014 The Nederlander Organization reconfigures the orchestra section of the venerable Palace Theatre for the incoming rap musical *Holler If You Hear Me.* Rows A-J now rise stadium-style to the front mezzanine. Rows K-Z will be used as a National Museum of Hip-Hop performance space, bringing the seating capacity of this one-time vaudeville mecca from 1740 down to 1120.

March 23, 2014 Producer Cameron Mackintosh presents the second Broadway revival of *Les Misérables,* freshly restaged by Laurence Connor and James Powell. This version stars Ramin Karimloo as Jean Valjean, Will Swenson as Javert, Caissie Levy as Fantine and Nikki M. James as Eponine.

March 24, 2014 Four-time Tony-winning playwright Terrence McNally marks a half century on the Great White Way with his 20th Broadway show, *Mothers and Sons,* starring Tyne Daly alongside Frederick Weller and Bobby Steggert who are said to portray the first married gay couple to appear on a Broadway stage.

March 30, 2014 *If/Then,* an original new American musical by Tom Kitt and Brian Yorkey, explores two different possible life paths taken by a divorced woman. Idina Menzel plays Liz and Beth, with a supporting cast of friends and lovers including Anthony Rapp, LaChanze, Jenn Colella and James Snyder.

March 31, 2014 The New York State Legislature gives theatre producers a huge leg up by voting a 25 percent refundable tax credit to investors who originate plays and musicals in New York State.

April 2, 2014 The Library of Congress adds the original cast recording of *Sweeney Todd,* the 1979 musical by Stephen Sondheim and Hugh Wheeler, to the National Recording Registry.

April 3, 2014 Denzel Washington stars in a revival of Lorraine Hansberry's *A Raisin in the Sun,* also featuring Anika Noni Rose and LaTanya Richardson Jackson, the latter of whom replaced Diahann Carroll during rehearsals.

April 3, 2014 Three long-running Broadway shows start playing Thursday matinees, breaking Wednesday's long-time monopoly on midweek afternoon shows. The Thursday club consists of *Phantom of the Opera, Mamma Mia!* and *Cinderella.* Come May, *Matilda* will join them.

April 3, 2014 Also today, pop singer Carole King surprises the cast of the musical biography *Beautiful* by appearing onstage during their post-show appeal for the annual "Easter Bonnet" fundraiser for Broadway Cares/Equity Fights AIDS. It is the first time King sees the show after spending months avoiding doing so, which *The New York Times* termed "a confounding mystery of the Broadway season." King then auctions off a performance of her song "You've Got a

Friend," raising $30,000.

April 6, 2014 Will Eno's new American play *The Realistic Joneses* stars Tracy Letts, Toni Collette, Michael C. Hall and Marisa Tomei as neighbors who discover they have a lot more in common than they thought.

April 7, 2014 Roseland dance hall, a Broadway theatre district landmark since 1919, closes its doors for the final time. Pop singer Lady Gaga is the final concert attraction at the venue, where generations came to dance to live music. Roseland is considered to be the inspiration for

Pop star Carole King (second from right) surprises the cast of *Beautiful— The Carole King Musical* at curtain call after spending months avoiding doing so. See April 3.

Photo: Stephen Lovekin/Getty Images for *Beautiful*

the film *Queen of the Stardust Ballroom* and the musical *Ballroom.*

April 9, 2014 Producers announce cancellation of the planned Off-Broadway transfer of the musical *A Night With Janis Joplin,* which closed on Broadway February 9 and had been announced to reopen at the Gramercy Theatre April 10. Unspecified "production issues" are blamed.

April 10, 2014 Film director/writer/actor Woody Allen returns to Broadway with a musical adaptation of his movie comedy, *Bullets Over Broadway,* about a hard-bitten 1920s gangster who discovers his one weakness: he falls in love with the stage. Susan Stroman directs and choreographs a cast that includes Marin Mazzie, Zach Braff and Brooks Ashmanskas. The show uses period pop music in lieu of an original score.

April 11, 2014 President Barack Obama and First Lady Michelle Obama attend a performance of *A Raisin in the Sun.*

April 13, 2014 Multiple Tony-winner Audra McDonald incarnates blues singer Billie "Lady Day" Holiday in the play with music *Lady Day at Emerson's Bar and Grill,* which had been presented Off-Broadway in 1987 with another actress in the title role, Lonette McKee.

April 14, 2014 The Off-Broadway play *The Flick* wins the Pulitzer Prize for Drama.

April 16, 2014 Revival of John Steinbeck's drama *Of Mice and Men,* about two migrant workers whose dream of owning their own farm is threatened when one of them unintentionally commits a terrible crime. The production stars James Franco and Chris O'Dowd.

April 17, 2014 James Lapine's stage adaptation of playwright/director Moss Hart's classic autobiography, *Act One,* stars Santino Fontana,

Tony Shalhoub and Andrea Martin.

April 20, 2014 Sutton Foster stars in a revival of the 1997 Off-Broadway Jeanine Tesori/Brian Crawley musical *Violet,* about a disfigured young woman on an odyssey to see a faith healer whom she is certain will restore her looks. This production is based on one presented as part of City Center's "Encores! Off-Center" series in 2013.

April 20, 2014 Daniel Radcliffe, star of the Harry Potter films and seen more recently on Broadway in *Equus* and *How to Succeed,* stars in Martin McDonagh's *Cripple of Inishmaan,* about a remote Irish village turned upside-down by the arrival of a Hollywood film crew.

April 21, 2014 A 79-year-old woman barricades herself in her brownstone and refuses to be moved to a nursing home in the new drama, *The Velocity of Autumn,* starring Estelle Parsons and Stephen Spinella.

April 22, 2014 Neil Patrick Harris stars in the Broadway debut of the musical *Hedwig and the Angry Inch,* about a transsexual East German punk singer who has a good reason to be furious with the world.

April 23, 2014 Harvey Fierstein's play *Casa Valentina* explores a real-life 1960s Catskill bungalow colony that catered to a very special clientele—heterosexual men who liked to dress up as women. The cast includes John Cullum and Patrick Page. It's Fierstein's third currently-running Broadway show, along with *Newsies* and *Kinky Boots.*

April 23, 2014 The 450th anniversary of William Shakespeare's birth gets a low-key celebration on Broadway.

April 24, 2014 The Tony-winning 1998 revival of *Cabaret,* directed by Sam Mendes and Rob Marshall, and starring Alan Cumming as the Emcee, gets a revival of its own.

May 12, 2014 Broadway's *The Phantom of the Opera* welcomes its first black Phantom when Norm Lewis steps into the title role.

May 25, 2014 HBO airs Ryan Murphy's film adaptation of Larry Kramer's play *The Normal Heart,* with some actors from the Tony-winning 2011 Broadway production.

May 31, 2014 After a dip in 2012-13, Broadway box-office receipts rebounded to a record $1.269 billion in 2013-14, and attendance rose from 11.57 million to 12.21 million, just shy of the record 12.33 million tickets sold in 2011-2012, according to figures released by The Broadway League. The average Broadway ticket price crossed the $100 mark for the first time, rising $5.50 to $103.92. New and continuing productions ran a total of 1496 playing weeks.

June 8, 2014 The 68th Annual Tony Awards are given at Radio City Music Hall. *All the Way* is named Best Play and *A Gentleman's Guide to Love & Murder* is named Best Musical.

—Robert Viagas

Head of the Class

Trends, Extraordinary Achievements and Peculiar Coincidences of the Season

Most Tony Awards to a Musical: Tie: *A Gentleman's Guide to Love & Murder* and *Hedwig and the Angry Inch* (4 each).

Most Tony Awards to a Play: *A Raisin in the Sun* (3).

Shortest Run: *Il Divo* (6 performances, limited run).

Long Runs Say Farewell: *Spider-Man: Turn Off the Dark* (1066 performances after a record 182 previews), losing the most money in Broadway history, an estimated $60 million. *Annie* revival, 487 performances.

Top Price for a "Premium" Ticket: $477 for *The Book of Mormon*.

Stars You Could Have Seen on Broadway This Season: Fantasia Barrino, Orlando Bloom, Sierra Boggess, Zach Braff, Norbert Leo Butz, Victoria Clarke, Toni Collette, Chuck Cooper, Daniel Craig, Bryan Cranston, Billy Crystal, John Cullum, Alan Cumming, Tyne Daly, Fran Drescher, Tovah Feldshuh, Sutton Foster, James Franco, Stephen Fry, Michael C. Hall, Rebecca Hall, Neil Patrick Harris, Ethan Hawke, Carly Rae Jepsen, Cherry Jones, LaChanze, k.d. lang, Adriane Lenox, Tracy Letts, Norm Lewis, Marin Mazzie, Jefferson Mays, Audra McDonald, Ian McKellen, Idina Menzel, Debra Messing, Jessie Mueller, Chris O'Dowd, Kelli O'Hara, Patrick Page, Mary-Louise Parker, Tonya Pinkins, Billy Porter, Zachary Quinto, Daniel Radcliffe, Anthony Rapp, Condola Rashad, Mark Rylance, Christopher Sieber, Tony Shalhoub, Tom Skerritt, Patrick Stewart, Marisa Tomei, Denzel Washington, Rachel Weisz, Michelle Williams and Vanessa Williams, among many more.

Female Singers So Memorably Impersonated, You Felt Like You Actually Saw Them: Billie Holiday, Carole King, Janis Joplin.

Fall Bardapalooza: With *Macbeth, Richard III, Romeo and Juliet* and *Twelfth Night*, fall 2013 marked the first time that four Shakespeare plays were on Broadway simultaneously since May 1987. (Chicago Civic Shakespeare Society produced a record nine in rep in March 1930.)

Awards They Should Give: #1 Best New Showtune: Our nominees: "Time Stops" in *Big Fish*; "The Last One You'd Expect" in *Gentleman's Guide*; "Falling Into You" from *The Bridges of Madison County*; "My Nose Ain't Broken" from *Rocky*; "What the Fuck" from *If/Then*; "In Love With You" from *First Date*.

Costume Effect of the Year: Men in Women's Clothing: *Casa Valentina, Chicago, Gentleman's Guide, Hedwig, Kinky Boots, Macbeth, Matilda, Richard III, Twelfth Night*. Honorable Mention: Lena Hall in male drag in *Hedwig*.

Scenic Element of the Year: Star Drops: *Act One, Aladdin, Big Fish, Bridges of Madison County, Bullets Over Broadway, Les Misérables, Lion King, Rocky, Snow Geese, Violet*. Honorable Mention for a star mirror effect: *If/Then*. Dishonorable Mention for taking place outdoors at night and discussing constellations, but *not* having a star drop: *Realistic Joneses*.

Runner Up for Scenic Element of the Year: A smaller false proscenium inside the real one: *After Midnight, Beautiful, Bridges of Madison*

County, Gentlemen's Guide, Violet, Waiting for Godot.

Prop of the Year: Live Dogs: *Annie, Bullets Over Broadway, Kinky Boots*, Lady Day at Emerson's Bar & Grill, Twelfth Night**. *One night only.

Awards They Should Give: #2 Best Special Effect: Our nominees: The flying carpet in *Aladdin;* A boxing ring rolls out over the first eight rows of the orchestra in *Rocky*; A tree grows to indicate passage of time in *Big Fish*; The ghost of Banquo pops up in *Macbeth*; Jefferson Mays gets his head cut off but appears immediately as another (alive) character in *Gentleman's Guide*.

Multiple Characters: Mark Rylance and company in rep with *Twelfth Night* and *Richard III*. Ian McKellen, Patrick Stewart, Billy Crudup and Shuler Hensley in rep with *No Man's Land* and *Waiting for Godot*. Tony Shalhoub and Andrea Martin playing three characters each in *Act One*. Jefferson Mays playing eight roles in *Gentleman's Guide*.

Most Performers Playing a Single Role: Six actresses alternated in the title role of *Matilda* from December 23, 2013 to January 6, 2014.

Put That on Your Resume: Unusual Character Names: Skszp in *Hedwig*, Johnnypateenmike and Babbybobby in *Cripple of Inishmaan*, Svec in *Once*, Buzzard Pole and Ant Hill Lady in *Lion King*, The Holy Hippie in *Soul Doctor*, Medda Larkin in *Newsies*, Corna DeKobb and Mayor Naise in *Big Fish*, Lady Salome D'Ysquith Pumphrey in *Gentleman's Guide*, Sir Toby Belch in *Twelfth Night*.

Broadway's Longest Runs

By number of performances
(2,500 or more).
Asterisk (*) indicates show still running as of May 31, 2014. Totals are for original runs except where otherwise noted.

**The Phantom of the Opera* 10,959
Cats 7485
*Chicago (Revival) 7285
*The Lion King 6878
Les Misérables 6680
A Chorus Line 6137
Oh! Calcutta! (Revival) 5959
Beauty and the Beast 5461
**Mamma Mia!* 5223
Rent 5123
*Wicked 4406
Miss Saigon 4092
*Jersey Boys 3548
42nd Street 3486
Grease 3388
Fiddler on the Roof 3242
Life With Father 3224
Tobacco Road 3182
Hello, Dolly! 2844
My Fair Lady 2717
Hairspray 2641
Mary Poppins, 2619
Avenue Q 2534
The Producers 2502

Swallowed Raw, Scrambled, Smashed on a Head or Whooshed up with Worcestershire Sauce: Eggs! *Cabaret, Cripple, Raisin, Rocky*.

Bees! *Gentlemen's Guide, Outside Mullingar, Spider-Man*.

Awards They Should Give: #3 Best New Rendition of an Old Song in a Revival or Jukebox Musical: Our nominees: "Me and Bobby McGee" in *Janis Joplin*; "Peckin'" and "Women Be Wise" in *After Midnight*; "The Rain It Raineth Every Day" in *Twelfth Night*; "Up on the Roof" in *Beautiful*; "Bring Him Home" in *Les Misérables*, "The Hot Dog Song" in *Bullets Over Broadway*; "God Bless the Child" in *Lady Day*.

Fire in a Crowded Theatre: Productions that used open flame (including candles and matches to light cigarettes) for dramatic effect: *Bridges of Madison County, Casa Valentina, Glass Menagerie, If/Then, Les Misérables, Macbeth, Phantom of the Opera, Pippin, Realistic Joneses, Romeo and Juliet, A Time to Kill, Twelfth Night/Richard III*.

Women Stifled by Their Husbands: *Beautiful, Betrayal, Bridges of Madison County, Casa Valentina, Glass Menagerie, Machinal, Once*.

***Gentleman's Guide* or *Richard III*?** Ambitious man murders all the relatives who stand in his way to a rich inheritance.

***A Night with Janis Joplin* or *Beautiful*?** Curly redheaded 1960s female pop singer wows 'em with her mad skillz.

***Once* or *Bridges of Madison County*?** Soulful, artistic man conducts a brief, bittersweet romance with an unhappy married woman who speaks with a foreign accent, and is devoted to her children. Their love is doomed, but after singing several solos he comes away with fresh inspiration.

Awards They Should Give: #4 Best Acting Ensemble: Our nominees: the cast of *After Midnight*; the cast of *Twelfth Night*; the cast of *Gentleman's Guide*, the cast of *Godot/No Man's Land*; the cast of *Raisin in the Sun*.

Courtroom Scenes: *Chicago, Gentleman's Guide, Les Misérables, Machinal, A Time To Kill*.

Disfigured or Mutilated Main Character: *Cripple of Inishmaan, Hedwig, Phantom, Violet, Wicked*. Honorable Mention: *Rocky*, whose nose finally gets broken in Act II.

Nightclub Show Within a Show: *After Midnight, Bullets Over Broadway, Cabaret, Casa Valentina, Janis Joplin, Kinky Boots, Lady Day, Once, Soul Doctor*.

Coups de Théâtre: The slamming door scene in *Gentleman's Guide*. Love at first sight in *Big Fish*. President Johnson uses every political trick he knows to win passage of the Civil Rights Act in *All the Way*. The first moment Audra McDonald starts singing in character as Billie Holiday in *Lady Day*. Mark Rylance becomes tongue-tied as Olivia in *Twelfth Night*. Lena Hall transforms into a woman in *Hedwig*. Kelli O'Hara chooses to stay with her family in *Bridges of Madison County*. Tony Shalhoub writhes in discomfort caused by fawning adoration in *Act One*. The opening office scene in *Machinal*. Jessie Mueller plays the first Carole King hit in *Beautiful*.

Act One

First Preview: March 20, 2014. Opened: April 17, 2014.
Still running as of May 31, 2014.

PLAYBILL®

Dramatization of playwright Moss Hart's 1959 autobiography about his poverty-stricken upbringing in the Bronx, his introduction to theatre through an eccentric aunt, and his determination to elbow his way into the glamorous world of Broadway during the 1920s. Act Two of Act One is occupied with Hart's budding collaboration with the older and even more eccentric playwright George S. Kaufman, and the painful and protracted gestation of their first hit together, the Hollywood satire Once in a Lifetime.

CAST

(in order of speaking)

Moss Hart	SANTINO FONTANA
Moss Hart/Barnett Hart/	
George S. Kaufman	TONY SHALHOUB
Moss Hart/	
Bernie Hart	MATTHEW SCHECHTER
Aunt Kate/Frieda Fishbein/	
Beatrice Kaufman	ANDREA MARTIN
Lillie Hart/Helen*	MIMI LIEBER
Belle/Mrs. Rosenbloom	DEBORAH OFFNER
Augustus Pitou/Jed Harris	WILL LeBOW
Irving Gordon/Pianist	STEVEN KAPLAN
Eddie Chodorov	BILL ARMY
Phyllis/May*	CHARLOTTE MAIER
Mrs. Henry B. Harris	AMY WARREN
Wally/Charles Gilpin/	
Max Siegel	CHUCK COOPER
Priestly Morrison/Sam Harris/	
Pianist	BOB STILLMAN
Joseph Regan/Jerry*	MATTHEW SALDIVAR

Continued on next page

Continued on next page

LINCOLN CENTER THEATER AT THE VIVIAN BEAUMONT

André Bishop
Producing Artistic Director

Adam Siegel
Managing Director

Hattie K. Jutagir
Executive Director of
Development & Planning

presents

ACT ONE

A Play Written and Directed by
James Lapine

From the autobiography by
Moss Hart

with (in alphabetical order)

Bob Ari   Bill Army   Will Brill   Laurel Casillo

Chuck Cooper   Santino Fontana   Steven Kaplan   Will LeBow

Mimi Lieber   Charlotte Maier   Noah Marlowe   Andrea Martin

Greg McFadden   Deborah Offner   Lance Roberts   Matthew Saldivar

Matthew Schechter   Tony Shalhoub   Jonathan Spivey

Wendy Rich Stetson   Bob Stillman   Amy Warren

Beowulf Boritt	Jane Greenwood	Ken Billington	Dan Moses Schreier
Sets	Costumes	Lighting	Sound

Louis Rosen	Rick Steiger	Daniel Swee
Original Music	Production Stage Manger	Casting

Jessica Niebanck	Jeff Hamlin	Linda Mason Ross	Philip Rinaldi
General Manager	Production Manager	Director of Marketing	General Press Agent

With special appreciation to Christopher Hart

Lead sponsor: Jerome L. Greene Foundation

Sponsored by American Express

LCT also gratefully acknowledges these generous contributors to ACT ONE:
The Blanche and Irving Laurie Foundation · The New York Community Trust - Mary P. Oenslager Foundation Fund
Florence and Robert Kaufman · Laura Pels International Foundation for Theater · Judi and Douglas Krupp
The Frederick Loewe Foundation · National Endowment for the Arts

This play was commissioned by LCT with a gift from Ellen and Howard Katz.

Special thanks to The Harold and Mimi Steinberg Charitable Trust for supporting new American plays at LCT.

American Airlines is the official airline of Lincoln Center Theater.

ACT ONE was developed in part at Vineyard Arts Project, Edgartown, MA.

LCT wishes to express its appreciation to Theatre Development Fund for its support of this production.

4/17/14

Santino Fontana (L) as Moss Hart and Tony Shalhoub as George S. Kaufman

Photo: Joan Marcus

Act One

Cast Continued

David Allen/Dore Schary/George* .....WILL BRILL
Roz/Mary ....LAUREL CASILLO
Ensemble...........BOB ARI, NOAH MARLOWE,
    GREG McFADDEN, LANCE ROBERTS,
JONATHAN SPIVEY, WENDY RICH STETSON

Once in a Lifetime

TIME
1914–1930
PLACE
New York and environs

Assistant Stage Managers ....JANET TAKAMI,
    CHRISTOPHER R. MUNNELL

UNDERSTUDIES

For Moss Hart: STEVEN KAPLAN

For Moss Hart/Barnett Hart/George S. Kaufman,
    Augustus Pitou/Jed Harris: BOB ARI

For Moss Hart/Bernie Hart: NOAH MARLOWE

For Frieda Fishbein: AMY WARREN

For Irving Gordon, Eddie Chodorov, David Allen/
    Dore Schary/George: JONATHAN SPIVEY

For Phyllis: LAUREL CASILLO

For Phyllis/May, Mrs. Henry B. Harris, Roz/
    Mary: WENDY RICH STETSON

For Wally/Charles Gilpin/
    Max Siegel: LANCE ROBERTS

For Priestly Morrison/Sam Harris,
    Joseph Regan/Jerry: GREG McFADDEN

MOSS HART

In 1959, at the peak of his career as one of Broadway's legendary playwright-directors, Moss Hart published his riveting autobiography *Act One*. A sensation upon its publication, *Act One* became an instant classic, remaining on *The New York Times* bestseller list for almost a year. The memoir, a rags-to-riches story of a young playwright striving to make it in the theater, inspired generations of playwrights, directors and actors to seek a career in the theater.

Born in 1904, Moss Hart was raised in the Bronx and Brooklyn and as a teenager worked as an office boy for the theatrical producer Augustus Pitou. It was while working for the producer that Hart, under a pseudonym, wrote a play produced by Pitou called, variously, *The Hold-Up Man* or *The Beloved Bandit*. Hart's first big success, his collaboration with playwright-director George S. Kaufman on his own original play about Hollywood, *Once in a Lifetime*, opened on Broadway in 1930. The two men went on to collaborate on a series of plays including *Merrily We Roll Along* (1934); *You Can't Take It With You* (for which they won the Pulitzer Prize, the film version by Frank Capra won the Academy Award for Best Picture in 1939) and the musical *I'd Rather Be Right*, with a score by Richard Rodgers and Lorenz Hart (both in 1937); *The Fabulous Invalid* (1938); *The American Way* and *The Man Who Came to Dinner* (both in 1939); and their final collaboration *George Washington Slept Here* (1940). During this period Hart also collaborated with Irving Berlin on the musical *Face the Music* (1933) and the revue *As Thousands Cheer* (1933); adapted the book for the musical *The Great Waltz* (1934); and wrote the book to Cole Porter's score for the musical *Jubilee* (1935). Hart wrote the book for the 1941 musical *Lady in the Dark*, which he also directed, with a score by Kurt Weill and Ira Gershwin, and was the playwright and director of *Winged Victory*, a tribute to the Air Force (1943), *Christopher Blake* (1946), *Light Up the Sky* (1948) and *The Climate of Eden* (1952). As a director, he had successes with *Junior Miss* (1941), *Dear Ruth* (1944), Irving Berlin's *Miss Liberty* (1948) and *Anniversary Waltz* (1954). His film work includes the screenplays for *Gentleman's Agreement* (1947 Academy Award for Best Picture), *Hans Christian Andersen* (1952), *A Star Is Born* (1954) and *Prince of Players* (1955), among others. In 1956, Hart directed Lerner and Loewe's *My Fair Lady*, one of the greatest successes in musical theater history, for which he won both the Tony and New York Drama Critics Awards for Best Director. It was equally well-received in London in 1958. Hart collaborated with Lerner and Loewe a second time, on the musical *Camelot* (1960). In 1946, Hart married the actress and singer Kitty Carlisle, with whom he had two children, Christopher and Catherine. After *Camelot*, Hart moved his family to Palm Springs for health reasons. He had begun work on what he called a "comedy of manners" when he was stricken suddenly with heart failure in 1961.

Bob Ari
Ensemble

Bill Army
Eddie Chodorov

Will Brill
David Allen, Dore Schary, George

Laurel Casillo
Miss Hester Worsley, Ingenue, Roz, Mary

Chuck Cooper
Wally, Charles Gilpin, Max Siegel, Langston Hughes

Santino Fontana
Moss Hart

Steven Kaplan
Irving Gordon, Pianist

Will LeBow
Augustus Pitou, Jed Harris, Slimowitz, Alexander Woollcott

Mimi Lieber
Lillie Hart, Helen; Choreographer

Charlotte Maier
Mrs. Borofsky, Phyllis, Aline MacMahon, May

Noah Marlowe
Ensemble

Andrea Martin
Aunt Kate, Frieda Fishbein, Beatrice Kaufman

Greg McFadden
Ensemble

Deborah Offner
Lady Caroline, Belle, Mrs. Rosenbloom Ida, Edna Ferber

Act One

Lance Roberts
Ensemble

Matthew Saldivar
Sir John, Joseph Regan, Jerry, Harpo Marx

Matthew Schechter
Moss Hart, Bernie Hart

Tony Shalhoub
Moss Hart, Barnett Hart, George S. Kaufman

Jonathan Spivey
Ensemble

Wendy Rich Stetson
Ensemble

Bob Stillman
Mr. Borofsky, Priestly Morrison, Gilpin's Manager, Sam Harris, Pianist

Amy Warren
Mrs. Henry B. Harris, Muriel Liston, Dorothy Parker

James Lapine
Playwright, Director

Beowulf Boritt
Sets

Jane Greenwood
Costumes

Ken Billington
Lighting

Dan Moses Schreier
Sound

Louis Rosen
Original Music

Wes Grantom
Associate Director

Deborah Hecht
Vocal & Dialect Coach

André Bishop
Lincoln Center Theater
Producing Artistic Director

Photo: Brian Mapp

FRONT OF HOUSE
Front Row (L-R): Monika Koziol, Diana Lounsbury, Barbara Hart, Amy Yedowitz
Middle Row (L-R): Eleanor Rooks, Denise Bergen, Rheba Flegelman, Jeff Goldstein, Farida Asencio
Back Row (L-R): Judith Fanelli, Nick Andors, Catherine Thorpe, Douglas Charles

Photo: Brian Mapp

WARDROBE
Front (L-R): Lauren Gallitelli, Melanie Olbrych, Amelia Haywood
Back (L-R): John Robelen (Wardrobe Supervisor), Judy Kahn, Edmund Harrison
Not Pictured: Jennifer Griggs, Erin Brooke Roth

Photo: Brian Mapp

Photo: Courtesy of the production

COMPANY MANAGEMENT
Matthew Markoff,
Jessica Fried

HAIR & WIGS
(L-R): Jun Kim, Yolanda Ramsey (Hair Supervisor), Enrique Vega

Photo: Brian Mapp

STAGE MANAGEMENT
(L-R): Tommy Grassey, Karen Evanouskas (Production Assistant), Rick Steiger (Production Stage Manager), Janet Takami (Assistant Stage Manager), Christopher R. Munnell (Assistant Stage Manager)
Not pictured: Mark A. Stys, Edward Wasserman

2013-2014 AWARDS

TONY AWARD
Best Scenic Design of a Play
(Beowulf Boritt)

OUTER CRITICS CIRCLE AWARD
Outstanding Featured Actress in a Play
(Andrea Martin)

Act One

CREW

(L-R): Frank Linn, Ray Skillin, Kevin McNeill, William Nagle (Production Carpenter), John Weingart (Production Flyman), Patrick Merryman (Production Electrician), Brant Underwood, Joe Pizzuto, Karl Rausenberger (Production Propertyman), Jeff Ward, Victor Seastone, Rudy Wood, Adam Smolenski, Marc Salzberg (Production Soundman), Andrew Belits, Mark Dignam

LINCOLN CENTER THEATER

ANDRÉ BISHOP
Producing Artistic Director

ADAM SIEGEL
Managing Director

HATTIE K. JUTAGIR
Executive Director of Development
& Planning

ADMINISTRATIVE STAFF

GENERAL MANAGER ....JESSICA NIEBANCK
Associate General Manager ....Meghan Lantzy
General Management Assistant ....Laura Stuart
Facilities Manager ....Alex Mustelier
Associate Facilities Manager ....Michael Assalone
GENERAL PRESS AGENT ....PHILIP RINALDI
Press Associate ....Amanda Kaus
Press Assistant ....Emily McGill
PRODUCTION MANAGER ....JEFF HAMLIN
Associate Production Manager ....Paul Smithyman
DEVELOPMENT
Associate Director of Development ....Rachel Norton
Manager of Special Events and Advisor,
    LCT Young Angels ....Karin Schall
Grants Writer ....Neal Brilliant
Manager, Patron Program ....Sheilaja Rao
Assistant to the Executive Director of
    Development & Planning ......Raelyn R. Lagerstrom
Development Associate/LCT Young Angels &
    Special Events ....Jenny Rosenbluth-Stoll
Development Assistant/Patron Program &
    LCT Young Angels ....Sydney Rais-Sherman
DIRECTOR OF FINANCE ....DAVID S. BROWN
Controller ....Susan Knox
Finance Assistant ....Kristen Parker
Systems Manager ....Stacy Valentine
IT Support Assistant ....Allotey Peacock
DIRECTOR OF MARKETING ..LINDA MASON ROSS
Associate Director of
    Marketing ....Ashley Dunn Gatterdam
Digital Marketing Associate ....Rebecca Leshin
Marketing Assistant ....David Cannon
DIRECTOR OF EDUCATION ....KATI KOERNER
Associate Director of Education ....Alexandra Lopez
Education Projects Manager ....Jennifer Wintzer
Executive Assistant ....Barbara Hourigan
Office Manager ....Mike Adank

Messenger ....Esau Burgess
Reception ....Kira Rice, Michelle Metcalf

ARTISTIC STAFF

ASSOCIATE DIRECTORS ......GRACIELA DANIELE,
                                    NICHOLAS HYTNER,
                                    JACK O'BRIEN,
                                    SUSAN STROMAN,
                                    DANIEL SULLIVAN
RESIDENT DIRECTOR ....BARTLETT SHER
DRAMATURG and DIRECTOR,
    LCT DIRECTORS LAB ....ANNE CATTANEO
CASTING DIRECTOR ....DANIEL SWEE, CSA
MUSICAL THEATER ASSOCIATE
    PRODUCER ....IRA WEITZMAN
ARTISTIC DIRECTOR/LCT3 ....PAIGE EVANS
Artistic Administrator ....Julia Judge
Casting Associate ....Camille Hickman
LCT3 Associate ....Natasha Sinha
Lab Assistant ....Alice Pencavel

HOUSE STAFF

HOUSE MANAGER ....RHEBA FLEGELMAN
Production Carpenter ....William Nagle
Production Electrician ....Patrick Merryman
Production Soundman ....Marc Salzberg
Production Propertyman ....Karl Rausenberger
Production Flyman ....John Weingart
House Technician ....Linda Heard
Chief Usher ...................................M.L. Pollock
Box Office Treasurer ....Fred Bonis
Assistant Treasurer ....Robert A. Belkin

SPECIAL SERVICES

Advertising, Marketing, Digital ....SpotCo
Principal Poster Artist ....James McMullan
Counsel ....Charles H. Googe Jr., Esq.;
    Carolyn J. Casselman, Esq.; and Caroline Barnard, Esq.
    of Paul, Weiss, Rifkind, Wharton & Garrison
Immigration Counsel ....Theodore Ruthizer, Esq.;
                                        Mark D. Koestler, Esq.
    of Kramer, Levin, Naftalis & Frankel, LLP
Labor Counsel ....Michael F. McGahan, Esq.
    of Epstein, Becker & Green, P.C.
Auditor ....Lauren Cresci, C.P.A.
                                        Lutz & Carr, L.L.P.
Insurance ....Jennifer Brown of DeWitt Stern Group
Production Photographer ....Joan Marcus
Video Services .... Fresh Produce Productions/Frank Basile
Blogger-in-Residence ....Brendan Lemon

Consulting Architect ....Hugh Hardy,
                            H3 Hardy Collaboration Architecture
Construction Manager ....Yorke Construction
Payroll Service ....Castellana Services, Inc.
Merchandising .... Marquee Merchandise, LLC/
                                        Matt Murphy
Lobby Refreshments ....Sweet Hospitality Group
Database Consulting ....SGP International

STAFF FOR *ACT ONE*

COMPANY MANAGER .... MATTHEW MARKOFF
Assistant Company Manager ....Jessica Fried
Associate Director ....Wes Grantom
Associate Set Designer ....Alexis Distler
Associate Costume Designer ....Daniel Urlie
Associate Lighting Designer ....John Demous
Associate Sound Designer ....Joshua Reid
Props Supervisor ....Buist Bickley
Props Assistant ....Bridget Santaniello
Hair and Wig Designer ....Tom Watson
Hair Supervisor ....Yolanda Ramsey
Hair Assistants ....Jun Kim, Enrique Vega
Make-up Designer ....Jon Carter
Wardrobe Supervisor ....John Robelen
Dressers ....Artie Brown, Lauren Gallitelli, Jennifer Griggs,
    Edmund Harrison, Amelia Haywood, Melanie Olbrych
Choreographer ....Mimi Lieber
Production Assistants ....Mark A. Stys, Edward Wasserman
Children's Guardian ....Jenna Bauman
Children's Tutoring ....On Location Education

Vocal & Dialect Coach ....Deborah Hecht

Fight Director ....Thomas Schall

CREDITS

Scenery by Show Motion, Inc. Costumes by Eric Winterling, Inc., Cosprop, Angels the Costumiers, Western Costume, United American Costume Company. Shirts by CEGO. Distressing by Izquierdo Studio. Lighting equipment from PRG Lighting. Sound equipment by Masque Sound. Yamaha Disklaviers provided courtesy of Yamaha Artist Services, New York, and Faust Harrison Pianos. "Always," Music and Lyrics by Irving Berlin. This selection is used by special arrangement with Rodgers & Hammerstein: an Imagem Company, on behalf of the Estate of Irving Berlin, www.irvingberlin.com. All Rights Reserved.

Visit www.lct.org

Act One
SCRAPBOOK

Photos: Courtesy of Laurel Casillo

Correspondent: Laurel Casillo, "Miss Hester Worsley," "Roz," "Ingenue," "Mary."

Memorable Fan Letter: Diana, our usher extraordinaire, sent the cast authentic Western Union telegrams on opening night, just like Moss Hart received when *Once in a Lifetime* opened on Broadway!

Opening Night Parties and/or Gifts: Chris and Catherine Hart gave each cast member a beautiful signed, framed cartoon from the New Yorker.

The cast of *Act One* in rehearsal on the stage of the Vivian Beaumont Theater. That's Tony Shalhoub standing center with Santino Fontana to his right and director/playwright James Lapine to his left.

André Bishop gave us each a Tiffany key chain inscribed with "Act One" and James Lapine gave us all a cast photo album.

Most Exciting Celebrity Visitor: Joan Rivers came to LCT to see the wonderful *City of Conversation* downstairs. Cast member Amy Warren invited her to come to our opening night party, and our beautiful dresser Lauren helped her crash! She rode to the party on the cast bus and entertained everyone on the way, wishing us well!

Mascot: George S. Penguin, an inflatable friend with a Kaufman-style wig and glasses, who hangs around backstage. You never know where he'll pop up next!

Favorite Backstage Photo: Our favorite backstage photos are of our mascot, George S. Penguin. (See below, left.)

Most Memorable Audience Reaction: We did a matinee performance for around 900 school kids who all applauded at the end of the play when Moss receives a hug from his father. They were an amazing, energetic crowd. The way they applauded at the end of the show was electric!

Worst Audience Behavior: Cell phones, sleeping, "Eating their young" (inside joke).

Unique Pre-Show Announcement: "Get [understudy Bob] Ari ready. I can't get the comb-over!"—Will LeBow. Our stage manager, Rick Steiger, always gives a "pre-boarding flight" announcement at the five-minute call for "passengers to begin boarding" the theatre seats on our set.

In-Theatre Gathering Place: The greenroom.

Memorable Ad-Lib: "You look GREAT!" or "You would never know"—Will Brill as Davey to Mrs. Henry B. Harris, survivor of the Titanic.

Memorable Directorial Note: "Bill, can you make Alan Campbell's entrance a little less...Gloria Swanson?"

Memorable Stage Door Fan Encounter: One night, one of our fans had printed headshots of a lot of cast members. I asked how he got them and he said, "Google." That's a dedicated fan.

Company In-Jokes: "The toaster in the corner." 'Minnie Ha-Ha." (These are from some hilarious jokes by the AMAZING Andrea Martin.)

Embarrassing Moments: "Uuuuuh...Irving ... Dore!"—An infamous skipped line on opening night. "Falling down steps coming out of the theatre."—Noah Marlowe

Favorite Off-Site Hangout: The Smith or Atlantic Grill—yum!

Favorite Snack Foods: Fudge! For energy! We all love Adam "Mo" Smolenski's baked goods!!

Favorite Therapy: Sleep. Or Mo's baked goods!

Company Catchphrase: "Journey."

Nicknames: "Franco Santorini." "Tubby Munchkins."

Fastest Costume Change: At the end of the show, Tony Shalhoub goes from Kaufman to Lawrence Vail to Hart to Lawrence Vail to Father within ten minutes time!!!

Who Wore the Heaviest/Hottest Costume: The men in the show have some amazing wool suits, but I think Hester Worsley's 20-pound skirt at the top of show has them all beat!

Who Wore the Least: Will LeBow as Jed Harris. "Is it true he was naked when you first arrived!?"

Ghostly Encounters Backstage: One of our cast members was tapped on the shoulder three times, then again five minutes later. We're not sure if it was a prankster or a ghost!

Coolest Thing About Being in This Show: Seeing how proud Moss Hart's kids looked when they saw how the audience reacted to their father's story.

Be-wigged company mascot George S. Penguin with *Yearbook* correspondent Laurel Casillo.

A pensive Andrea Martin in her dressing room waiting for her next entrance.

After Midnight

First Preview: October 18, 2013. Opened: November 3, 2013.
Still running as of May 31, 2014.

A musical revue in the stylish spirit of the 1920s-30s Harlem Renaissance at its peak. Originated at the Off-Broadway "Encores!" series under the title Cotton Club Parade, *the show is notable for its vibrant cast of young dancer/singers, colorful costumes by trendy designer Isabel Toledo making her Broadway debut, an orchestra consisting of 16 musicians from the Jazz at Lincoln Center All-Stars, and staging that captures the playfulness of jazz-age choreography.*

CAST

FANTASIA BARRINO
DULÉ HILL
ADRIANE LENOX
JULIUS "iGLIDE" CHISOLM
VIRGIL "LIL'O" GADSON
JARED GRIMES
KARINE PLANTADIT
DORMESHIA SUMBRY-EDWARDS

MARIJA ABNEY
PHILLIP ATTMORE
EVERETT BRADLEY
CHRISTOPHER BROUGHTON
TAELER ELYSE CYRUS
C.K. EDWARDS
CARMEN RUBY FLOYD
BAHIYAH HIBAH
ROSENA M. HILL JACKSON
MONROE KENT III
ERIN N. MOORE
CEDRIC NEAL

Continued on next page

Continued on next page

"Peckin'" with Everett Bradley (front) and members of the Company

Photo: Matthew Murphy

BROOKS ATKINSON THEATRE
UNDER THE DIRECTION OF JAMES M. NEDERLANDER AND JAMES L. NEDERLANDER

SCOTT SANDERS PRODUCTIONS   WYNTON MARSALIS   ROY FURMAN   CANDY SPELLING
STARRY NIGHT ENTERTAINMENT   ALLAN S. GORDON/ADAM S. GORDON   JAMES L. NEDERLANDER
HAL NEWMAN   ROBERT K. KRAFT   CATHERINE and FRED ADLER
ROBERT APPEL   JEFFREY BOLTON   SCOTT M. DELMAN
JAMES FANTACI   TED LIEBOWITZ   STEPHANIE P. McCLELLAND
SANDY BLOCK   CAROL FINEMAN

IN ASSOCIATION WITH
MARKS-MOORE-TURNBULL GROUP   STEPHEN & RUTH HENDEL   TOM KIRDAHY

PRESENT

AFTER MIDNIGHT

CONCEIVED BY
JACK VIERTEL

SPECIAL GUEST STAR
FANTASIA BARRINO

FEATURING
DULÉ HILL

WITH
ADRIANE LENOX

KARINE PLANTADIT   DORMESHIA SUMBRY-EDWARDS
JULIUS "iGLIDE" CHISOLM   VIRGIL "LIL'O" GADSON   JARED GRIMES

MARIJA ABNEY   PHILLIP ATTMORE   EVERETT BRADLEY   CHRISTOPHER BROUGHTON
TAELER ELYSE CYRUS   C.K. EDWARDS   CARMEN RUBY FLOYD   DANIELLE HERBERT
BAHIYAH HIBAH   ROSENA M. HILL JACKSON   DAVID JENNINGS   MONROE KENT III
ERIN N. MOORE   CEDRIC NEAL   BRYONHA MARIE PARHAM   JUSTIN PRESCOTT   T. OLIVER REID
DESMOND RICHARDSON   ALLYSA SHORTE   MONIQUE SMITH   DANIEL J. WATTS

MUSIC DIRECTION
THE JAZZ AT LINCOLN CENTER ALL-STARS
ARTISTIC DIRECTOR, WYNTON MARSALIS

KURT BACHER   ART BARON   ADAM BIRNBAUM   DAN BLOCK
JAMES BURTON III   JAMES CHIRILLO   ANDY FARBER   ALVESTER GARNETT
GREGORY GISBERT   WAYNE GOODMAN   MARK GROSS   BRUCE HARRIS
ALPHONSO HORNE   GODWIN LOUIS   JENNIFER VINCENT   JAMES ZOLLAR

| SCENIC DESIGN | COSTUME DESIGN | LIGHTING DESIGN | SOUND DESIGN |
| JOHN LEE BEATTY | ISABEL TOLEDO | HOWELL BINKLEY | PETER HYLENSKI |

| HAIR DESIGN | CASTING | ASSOCIATE DIRECTOR | MUSIC CONTRACTOR | TECHNICAL SUPERVISOR |
| CHARLES G. LaPOINTE | LAURA STANCZYK, C.S.A. | SARA EDWARDS | SEYMOUR RED PRESS | NEIL A. MAZZELLA |

| PRODUCTION STAGE MANAGER | ADVERTISING & MARKETING | PRESS REPRESENTATIVE | MARKETING & PRESS OUTREACH | GENERAL MANAGEMENT |
| KIM VERNACE | SPOTCO | O&M CO. | LINDA STEWART | BESPOKE THEATRICALS |

SELECTED TEXT BY
LANGSTON HUGHES

MUSIC SUPERVISOR/ADDITIONAL ARRANGER/CONDUCTOR
DARYL WATERS

DIRECTED AND CHOREOGRAPHED BY
WARREN CARLYLE

BASED ON THE PRESENTATION BY NEW YORK CITY CENTER *ENCORES!* AND JAZZ AT LINCOLN CENTER

11/3/13

After Midnight

Cast Continued

BRYONHA MARIE PARHAM
T. OLIVER REID
DESMOND RICHARDSON
MONIQUE SMITH
DANIEL J. WATTS

SWINGS
DANIELLE HERBERT, DAVID JENNINGS,
JUSTIN PRESCOTT, ALLYSA SHORTE

DANCE CAPTAIN
JUSTIN PRESCOTT

ASSISTANT DANCE CAPTAIN
BAHIYAH HIBAH

UNDERSTUDIES
For Fantasia Barrino: DANIELLE HERBERT
For Julius "iGlide" Chisolm: JUSTIN PRESCOTT
For Virgil "Lil'O" Gadson:
JUSTIN PRESCOTT, DANIEL J. WATTS
For Jared Grimes:
PHILLIP ATTMORE, DANIEL J. WATTS
For Dulé Hill:
DAVID JENNINGS, T. OLIVER REID
For Adriane Lenox: DANIELLE HERBERT
For Karine Plantadit: BAHIYAH HIBAH
For Dormeshia Sumbry-Edwards:
ERIN N. MOORE, ALLYSA SHORTE

THE JAZZ AT LINCOLN CENTER ALL-STARS
Conductor: DARYL WATERS
Associate Conductor: JAMES BURTON III

Woodwinds .... KURT BACHER, DAN BLOCK,
ANDY FARBER, MARK GROSS,
GODWIN LOUIS
Trumpets .... GREGORY GISBERT,
BRUCE HARRIS, ALPHONSO HORNE,
JAMES ZOLLAR
Trombones .... ART BARON,
JAMES BURTON III, WAYNE GOODMAN
Tuba .... WAYNE GOODMAN
Piano .... ADAM BIRNBAUM
Guitar .... JAMES CHIRILLO
Bass .... JENNIFER VINCENT
Drums .... ALVESTER GARNETT

MUSICAL NUMBERS

Opening .... Dulé Hill
"Daybreak Express" .... The Jazz At Lincoln Center All-Stars & The Company
  By Duke Ellington
  Transcription by David Berger
"Happy As the Day Is Long" .... Daniel & Phillip
  By Ted Koehler & Harold Arlen
  Arrangement by Duke Ellington
  Transcription & additional orchestrations by Chris Crenshaw
"Between the Devil and the Deep Blue Sea" .... Carmen, Rosena, & Bryonha
  By Ted Koehler & Harold Arlen
  Arrangement by Richard DeRosa
"I've Got the World on a String" .... Dulé Hill & The Company
  By Ted Koehler & Harold Arlen
  Arrangement by Duke Ellington
  Transcription by Mark Lopeman
  Additional orchestration by David Berger
"Women Be Wise" .... Adriane Lenox
  By Sippie Wallace
  Transcription by Mark Lopeman
"Braggin' in Brass" .... The Jazz At Lincoln Center All-Stars
  By Duke Ellington, Henry Nemo & Irving Mills
  Transcription by David Berger
"I Can't Give You Anything But Love" .... Fantasia Barrino
  By Dorothy Fields & Jimmy McHugh
  Arrangement by David Berger
"Peckin'" .... Phillip, Christopher, C.K., Desmond, Daniel & Everett
  By Harry James & Ben Pollack
  Arrangement by Duke Ellington
  Transcription by Mark Lopeman
"Diga Diga Doo" .... Everett, Cedric, Monroe, & T. Oliver
  By Dorothy Fields & Jimmy McHugh
  Arrangement by the Mills Brothers & Duke Ellington
  Transcription & additional orchestration by Chris Crenshaw
"East St. Louis Toodle-oo" .... Virgil "Lil'O" Gadson, Karine Plantadit, Monique,
  By Duke Ellington & Bubber Miley   Marija, Erin, Bahiyah, & Taeler
  Transcribed by David Berger
"Stormy Weather" .... Fantasia Barrino
  By Ted Koehler & Harold Arlen
  Arrangement by David Berger
  Vocal Arrangements by Daryl Waters
"The Skrontch" .... Dormeshia Sumbry-Edwards & The Company
  By Duke Ellington, Henry Nemo & Irving Mills
  Arrangement by Duke Ellington
  Transcription by Chris Crenshaw

Continued on next page

Fantasia Barrino

Dulé Hill

Adriane Lenox

Marija Abney

Phillip Attmore

Everett Bradley

Christopher Broughton

After Midnight

"Hottentot Tot" ....Julius "iGlide" Chisolm & Virgil "Lil'O" Gadson
　By Dorothy Fields & Jimmy McHugh
　Transcription by Mark Lopeman

"Ain't it De Truth?" ....Dulé Hill, Everett, Cedric, Monroe & T. Oliver
　By E.Y. Harburg & Harold Arlen

"Raisin' the Rent"/"Get Yourself a New Broom" ....Dormeshia Sumbry-Edwards,
　By Ted Koehler & Harold Arlen　　　　　　　　　　　　　　　　　Phillip & Daniel
　Arrangement by Duke Ellington
　Transcription by Mark Lopeman & Chris Crenshaw
　Additional orchestration by David Berger

"Zaz Zuh Zaz" ....Fantasia Barrino, Everett, Monroe, Cedric & T. Oliver
　By Cab Calloway & Harry White

"Creole Love Call" ....Carmen & The Jazz At Lincoln Center All-Stars
　By Duke Ellington
　Transcription by David Berger

"Go Back Where You Stayed Last Night" ....Adriane Lenox
　By Sidney Easton & Ethel Waters
　Arrangement by Dick Hyman

"The Mooche" ....Desmond, Taeler, Bahiyah & Marija
　By Duke Ellington & Irving Mills
　Transcription by David Berger

"On the Sunny Side of the Street" ....Fantasia Barrino, C.K. & Christopher
　By Dorothy Fields & Jimmy McHugh
　Arranged by Quincy Jones
　Transcribed by Chris Crenshaw

"The Gal From Joe's" ....Carmen, Rosena & Bryonha
　By Duke Ellington & Irving Mills

"Black and Tan Fantasy" ....Karine Plantadit
　By Duke Ellington & Bubber Miley
　Transcriptions by David Berger & Chris Crenshaw

Tap Mathematician / "It Don't Mean a Thing" ....Jared Grimes &
　By Duke Ellington　　　　　　　　　　　　The Jazz At Lincoln Center All-Stars
　Transcribed & Adapted by Chris Crenshaw

"Cotton Club Stomp" ....The Company
　By Duke Ellington, Harry Carney & Johnny Hodges
　Arrangement by Bob Wilber

"Freeze and Melt" ....Dulé Hill, Carmen, Rosena,
　By Dorothy Fields & Jimmy McHugh　　　　　　　　Bryonha & The Company
　Arrangement by Duke Ellington
　Transcription by Dan Block

"Rockin' in Rhythm" ....The Jazz At Lincoln Center All-Stars
　By Duke Ellington, Irving Mills & Harry Carney
　Transcription by David Berger

Julius "iGlide" Chisolm

Taeler Elyse Cyrus

C.K. Edwards

Carmen Ruby Floyd

Virgil "Lil'O" Gadson

Jared Grimes

Danielle Herbert

Bahiyah Hibah

Rosena M. Hill Jackson

David Jennings

Monroe Kent III

Erin N. Moore

Cedric Neal

Bryonha Marie Parham

Karine Plantadit

After Midnight

Justin Prescott

T. Oliver Reid

Desmond Richardson

Allysa Shorte

Monique Smith

Dormeshia
Sumbry-Edwards

Daniel J. Watts

Kurt Bacher
Woodwind

Art Baron
Trombone

Adam Birnbaum
Piano

Dan Block
Woodwind

James Burton III
Trombone

James Chirillo
Guitar/Banjo

Andy Farber
Woodwinds

Alvester Garnett
Drums

Gregory Gisbert
Trumpet

Wayne Goodman
Trombone/Tuba

Mark Gross
Woodwind

Bruce Harris
Trumpet

Alphonso Horne
Trumpet

Godwin Louis
Woodwind

Jennifer Vincent
Bass

James Zollar
Trumpet

Jack Viertel
Conceiver

Warren Carlyle
*Director/
Choreographer*

Wynton Marsalis
Jazz at Lincoln
Center
*Music Direction,
Producer*

Daryl Waters
*Musical Supervisor/
Additional Arranger/
Conductor*

John Lee Beatty
Scenic Design

Isabel Toledo
Costume Design

Howell Binkley
Lighting Design

Peter Hylenski
Sound Design

Charles G. LaPointe
Hair and Wig Design

Laura Stanczyk, CSA
Laura Stanczyk
Casting
Casting

Seymour Red Press
Music Coordinator

Sara Edwards
Associate Director

After Midnight

Jason Sparks
Assistant Choreographer

Neil A. Mazzella
Hudson Theatrical Associates
Technical Supervisor

Maggie Brohn
Bespoke Theatricals
General Management

Amy Jacobs
Bespoke Theatricals
General Management

Devin Keudell
Bespoke Theatricals
General Management

Nina Lannan
Bespoke Theatricals
General Management

Scott Sanders
Scott Sanders Productions
Producer

Roy Furman
Producer

Candy Spelling
Producer

Michael Shulman
Starry Night Entertainment
Producer

Allan S. Gordon
Producer

Adam S. Gordon
Producer

James L. Nederlander
Producer

Robert K. Kraft
Producer

Catherine Adler
Producer

Scott M. Delman
Producer

Stephanie P. McClelland
Producer

Carol Fineman
Producer

Stephen Hendel
Producer

Ruth Hendel
Producer

Tom Kirdahy
Producer

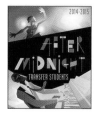

Toni Braxton

Bobby Daye

Kenny "Babyface" Edmonds

Christopher Jackson

k.d. lang

Jay Staten

Vanessa Williams

2013-2014 AWARDS

TONY AWARD
Best Choreography
(Warren Carlyle)

DRAMA DESK AWARDS
Outstanding Musical Revue
Outstanding Choreography
(Warren Carlyle)

OUTER CRITICS CIRCLE AWARD
Outstanding Choreographer
(Warren Carlyle)

FRED & ADELE ASTAIRE AWARDS
Outstanding Choreography
of a Broadway Show
(Warren Carlyle)

Outstanding Female Dancer
in a Broadway Show (Tie)
(Dormeshia Sumbry-Edwards)
(Karine Plantadit)

Outstanding Male Dancer
in a Broadway Show
(Jared Grimes)

After Midnight

ORCHESTRA
The Jazz at Lincoln Center All-Stars

CREW
Front Row (L-R): George Vamvoukakis, Kimberlee Imperato, Ilona Fusco, Bobbi Morse, Megan J. Schneid (Stage Manager), Kate Sorg (Dresser), Cody Renard Richard (Assistant Stage Manager), Jeffrey Johnson, Jessica Reiner
Middle Row (L-R): Debbie Vogel, Fred Velez, Clifford Herbst, Tara McCormack, Anthony Fusco, Marc Schmittroth, Sam Brooks (Dresser), Reeve Pierson (Assistant Company Manager), Diane Needleman
Back Row (L-R): Ben Horrigan (Automation Operator), Joseph P. DePaulo (House Propman), Joe Maher (Flyman), Thomas A. Lavaia (House Carpenter), Matthew C. Gratz, Kim Vernace (Production Stage Manager), Manuel Becker (House Electrician), Kurt Fischer, TJ McEvoy, Vangeli Kaseluris (Dresser), Mike Attianese, Vivienne Crawford, Jesse Galvan, Doug Gaeta (Company Manager), Peter Attanasio (Treasurer), Jillian Gloven, Barry Lee Moe (Hair Supervisor), Jessie Mojica

After Midnight

STAFF FOR *AFTER MIDNIGHT*

GENERAL MANAGEMENT
BESPOKE THEATRICALS
Maggie Brohn
Amy Jacobs Devin Keudell Nina Lannan
Associate General Manager ....David Roth

COMPANY MANAGER
Doug Gaeta
Assistant Company Manager ....Reeve Pierson

PRODUCTION MANAGEMENT
HUDSON THEATRICAL ASSOCIATES
Neil A. Mazzella, Sam Ellis, Geoff Quart,
Irene Wang, Caitlin McInerney

GENERAL PRESS REPRESENTATIVE
O&M CO.
Rick Miramontez
Ryan Ratelle   Michael Jorgensen

CASTING
LAURA STANCZYK CASTING
Laura Stanczyk, CSA
Nicholas Petrovich, Ilana Bolotsky, Carrie Watt,
Chrystal Vassilyadi

PRODUCTION STAGE MANAGER ...KIM VERNACE
Stage Manager ....Megan J. Schneid
Assistant Stage Manager ....Cody Renard Richard
Artist in Residence ....Ruben Toledo
Assistant Choreographer ....Jason Sparks
"Tap Mathematician" Choreography ....Jared Grimes
Associate Scenic Designer ....Kacie Hultgren
Associate Costume Designer ....Cathy Parrott
Assistant Costume Designer ....Aileen Abercrombie
Associate Lighting Designer ....Ryan O'Gara
Assistant Lighting Designer ....Brandon Baker
Associate Sound Designer ....Keith Caggiano
Associate Sound Designer ....Jesse Stevens
Assistant Hair/Wig Designer ....Elizabeth Printz
Assistant to the Hair/Wig Designer ..Gretchen Androsavich
Makeup Designer ....Cookie Jordan
Production Carpenter ....Paul Wimmer
Automation Operator ....Ben Horrigan
Production Electrician ....Keith Buchanan
Production Sound ....Phil Lojo

Dulé Hill

Production Props Supervisor ....Buist Bickley
Moving Light Programmer ....Timothy Rogers
Wardrobe Supervisor ....Jesse Galvan
Dressers ....Sam Brooks, Kimberly Butler-Gilkeson,
Jeffrey Johnson, Vangeli Kaseluris,
Jessica Reiner, Kate Sorg
Hair Supervisor ....Barry Lee Moe
Assistant Hair Supervisor ....Jessie Mojica
Gentlemen's Grooming ....BBRAXTON
Music Copying ....Emily Grishman Music Preparation/
Emily Grishman, Katharine Edmonds
Costume Shoppers ..Isabelle Simone, Amanda Dobrzeniecki
Costume Studio Assistant ....Will Lowry
Production Assistants ....Alex Hajjar, Ginny Parker
SDC Observer ....Kasey RT Graham
Physical Therapy ....PhysioArts
Production Photographer ....Kyle Froman
Advertising ....SpotCo/Drew Hodges, Tom Greenwald,
Ilene Rosen, Stephen Santore, Jason Vanderwoude
Marketing ....SpotCo/Nick Pramik,
Kristen Rathbun, Julie Wechsler
Online/Digital Interactive ....SpotCo/
Kyle Young, Steven Tartick
Press Associates ..Sarah Babin, Molly Barnett, Scott Braun,
Jaron Caldwell, Philip Carrubba, Jon Dimond,
Joyce Friedmann, Yufen Kung, Chelsea Nachman,
Marie Pace, Pete Sanders, Andy Snyder
Press Interns ....Nancy Alligood, Patrick Lazour
Accountant ....Fried & Kowgios CPAS LLP/
Robert Fried CPA,
Comptroller ....Galbraith & Company/Kenny Noth
General Management
Office Manager ....Michael Demniak
General Management Interns ....Sarah Bedo,
Allison Tiagonce
Insurance ....AON Albert G. Ruben
Insurance Services, Inc./Claudia B. Kaufman
Banking ....City National Bank/Michele Gibbons
Payroll ....Checks and Balances Payroll Inc.
Travel Agent ....Tzell Travel/The "A" Team, Andi Henig
Legal Counsel ....Davis Wright Tremaine LLP/
M. Graham Coleman
Merchandising ....Broadway Merchandising, LLC/
Adam S. Gordon, David Eck
Opening Night Coordination ....Serino/Coyne,
Suzanne Tobak
Opening Night Creative Consultant ....Susan Holland

Fantasia Barrino

After Midnight rehearsed at the Foxwoods Theatre

CREDITS
Scenery constructed by Hudson Scenic Studio, Inc. Lighting
and sound equipment by Production Resource Group.
Costumes by Tricorne Inc., Giliberto Designs, Scafati
Theatrical Tailors, Artur & Tailors, Katrina Patterns, Cego.
Knitwear by Kate Sorg. Dance shoes by T.O. Dey,
Worldtone, LaDuca and Capezio. Custom textiles by Hurel,
Bischoff. Millinery by Rodney Gordon, JJ Hat Center, Top
Hats of America, Patricia Underwood, Worth & Worth by
Orlando Palacios. Gloves by Cornelia James. Fantasia's shoes
by Edmund Castillo. Jewelry by Erickson Beamon. Fur by
Fur & Furgery. Piano provided by Steinway & Sons. Drums
provided by D'Amico Drums.

SPECIAL THANKS/SPONSORS
Swarovski, Patricia Fellows, John Coles.
Hair products provided by ARROJO.
Makeup provided by M•A•C.
Special thank you to Steven Rivellino.

NEDERLANDER

Chairman ....**James M. Nederlander**
President ....**James L. Nederlander**

Executive Vice President
Nick Scandalios

Vice President	Senior Vice President
Corporate Development	Labor Relations
Charlene S. Nederlander	**Herschel Waxman**

| Vice President | Chief Financial Officer |
| **Jim Boese** | **Freida Sawyer Belviso** |

STAFF FOR THE BROOKS ATKINSON THEATRE
Theatre Manager ....Susan Martin
Treasurer ....Peter Attanasio
Associate Treasurer ....Elaine Amplo
House Carpenter ....Thomas A. Lavaia
Flyman ....Joe Maher
House Electrician ....Manuel Becker
House Propman ....Joseph P. DePaulo
House Engineer ....Reynold Barriteau

Adriane Lenox

Photos: Matthew Murphy

After Midnight
SCRAPBOOK

Correspondent: Carmen Ruby Floyd, Ensemble

Opening Night Parties and/or Gifts: Umbrellas, shot glasses, keychains, mugs w/ spoon—all with *After Midnight* logos, magnets, candy, smell-goods, macaroons, survival kits, jewelry, champage and small bottles of alcohol tied to a little red balloon.

Most Exciting Celebrity Visitor and What They Did/Said: Liza! said "I've never seen

anything like it. It's the best!" Shirley MacLaine graciously met/spoke with everyone and took pictures as well. She asked to speak to Warren because she wants to join the cast.

Favorite In-Theatre Gathering Place: Dulé's Room, aka Kenny Leon Lounge.

Special Backstage Rituals: Before half hour, prayer circle on stage and tap battles.

Most Memorable Audience Reaction: When Host says "That's the evening, daddy'" the audience screams "NO!!" and "Awhhh"

because they don't want the show to end, of course.

Worst Audience Behavior: Front row center audience member speaking on telephone; and off-beat clapping.

Unique Pre-Show Announcement: Well, the announcer is none other than our sultry bass vocalist Monroe Kent III...that's unique!

Memorable Ad-Lib: Fantasia's "Yes Sir" and anything Adriane Lenox does!!

"Gypsy of the Year" Presentation: "The Sepia Beauty," conceived and directed by T. Oliver Reid.

Memorable Press Encounter: We performed for the POTUS and FLOTUS at the Waldorf-Astoria for the United Nations Reception.

Memorable Stage Door Fan Encounter: The man from South Africa who came three times in one weekend. And Miss Charlotte, who seems to always be at the stage door. We'd only been open for two weeks and she had seen it five times. I just saw her again last night!

Memorable Directorial Note: "Elegance Elegance" "Very Expensive you can't afford

me sexual attractive handsome and beautiful you can't have me!" It's actually a song!

Company In-Jokes: May not be appropriate for print.

Embarrassing Moments: Dormeshia wore her blue tap shoes in the all white finale. Phillip's tap shoe came off during "Happy As the Day Is Long." Whenever Carmen, Bryonha or Rosena's balloon doesn't pop.

Favorite Moment During Each Performance: "Freeze and Melt"—the band, the performers and the audience have a heavenly good time.

Favorite Off-Site Hangout: Glass House.

Favorite Snack Foods: Candy provided by Miss Viv.

Favorite Therapies: PT and laughter.

Catchphrases Only the Company Would Recognize: Found Som'n. Freeze that toe.

Nickname: Spanky Brytastic.

Fastest Costume Change: Daniel and Phillip from Opening to "Happy As the Day..." and Jared into the finale.

Who Wore the Heaviest/Hottest Costume?: Carmen's "Creole Love Call" gown.

Who Wore the Least?: Marija, Taeler, Bahiyah—Feather Ladies.

**What Did You Think of the Web Buzz on

Your Show?: Overwhelmingly fantastic. They love it.

Ghostly Encounters Backstage: The motion-sensor paper towel dispenser dispenses when no one is near it.

Coolest Thing About Being in This Show: Crazy talent; the music; the legacy; the 90 minutes; everything!!

Other Stories: After we did our first runthough at the theatre, we were all so overwhelmed we

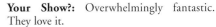

Photos: Courtesy of the production

began to scream and shout for joy. Then the band started to play "church praise chords" as the entire company, creative team and crew danced, stomped, clapped to this blessed music for three minutes straight! We had arrived as a family.

T. Oliver was supposed to get the Gypsy Robe but declined the offer so it would go to Rosena, saying he had his moment and it's her turn now.

1. Having fun (clockwise from top) Julius "iGlide" Chisolm, Christopher "Spanky" Broughton, Art Baron (trombone player), C.K. Edwards.
2. Lovely in white: Daniel J. Watts, Rosena M. Hill Jackson, Phillip Attmore.
3. Getting limber pre-show with (L-R): Erin N. Moore, Dulé Hill, Taeler Elyse Cyrus.
4. Filming B Roll of "Between the Devil and the Deep Blue Sea" (L-R): Rosena M. Hill Jackson, Bryonha Marie Parham, and *Yearbook* correspondent Carmen Ruby Floyd.
5. Backstage with one of the Feather Ladies, Bahiyah Hibah.

Aladdin

First Preview: February 26, 2014. Opened: March 20, 2014.
Still running as of May 31, 2014.

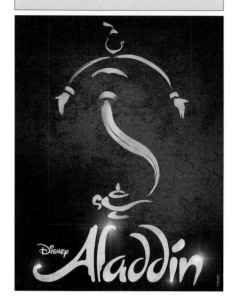

Stage adaptation of Disney's 1992 animated film musical about a Middle Eastern "street rat" who falls in love with a princess and tries to win her heart with the help of a sassy, wisecracking genie he conjures by rubbing a magic lamp. This extravaganza is filled with Disney-style magic and special effects, notably a flying carpet. The film score is augmented with trunk songs and several more numbers written or rewritten specially for this production.

CAST
(in order of appearance)

Genie	JAMES MONROE IGLEHART
Jafar	JONATHAN FREEMAN
Iago	DON DARRYL RIVERA
Aladdin	ADAM JACOBS
Jasmine	COURTNEY REED
Sultan	CLIFTON DAVIS
Babkak	BRIAN GONZALES
Omar	JONATHAN SCHWARTZ
Kassim	BRANDON O'NEILL
Shop Owner	BOBBY PESTKA
Razoul	DENNIS STOWE
Henchmen	ANDREW CAO, DONALD JONES, JR.
Prince Abdullah	JAZ SEALEY
Attendants	TIA ALTINAY, KHORI MICHELLE PETINAUD, MARISHA WALLACE
Spooky Voice	BRANDON O'NEILL
Fortune Teller	MARISHA WALLACE

Continued on next page

Continued on next page

Disney Theatrical Productions
under the direction of
Thomas Schumacher
presents

BROADWAY'S NEW MUSICAL COMEDY

Music by **ALAN MENKEN** *Lyrics by* **HOWARD ASHMAN and TIM RICE** *Book and Additional Lyrics by* **CHAD BEGUELIN**

Based on the Disney film written by RON CLEMENTS, JOHN MUSKER, TED ELLIOTT & TERRY ROSSIO and directed and produced by JOHN MUSKER & RON CLEMENTS

Starring
ADAM JACOBS

JAMES MONROE IGLEHART   **COURTNEY REED**

BRIAN GONZALES   **BRANDON O'NEILL**   **JONATHAN SCHWARTZ**

CLIFTON DAVIS   **DON DARRYL RIVERA**

MERWIN FOARD   **MICHAEL JAMES SCOTT**

and

JONATHAN FREEMAN
as "Jafar"

TIA ALTINAY MIKE CANNON ANDREW CAO LAURYN CIARDULLO JOSHUA DELA CRUZ
YUREL ECHEZARRETA DAISY HOBBS DONALD JONES, JR. ADAM KAOKEPT NIKKI LONG STANLEY MARTIN
BRANDT MARTINEZ MICHAEL MINDLIN RHEA PATTERSON BOBBY PESTKA KHORI MICHELLE PETINAUD ALEKS PEVEC
ARIEL REID JENNIFER RIAS TRENT SAUNDERS JAZ SEALEY DENNIS STOWE MARISHA WALLACE BUD WEBER

Associate Producer	*Technical Supervision*	*Production Supervisor*
ANNE QUART	GEOFFREY QUART/ HUDSON THEATRICAL ASSOCIATES DAVID BENKEN	CLIFFORD SCHWARTZ

Production Managers	*Associate Director*	*Associate Choreographer*	*Casting*
MYRIAH BASH EDUARDO CASTRO	SCOTT TAYLOR	JOHN MacINNIS	TARA RUBIN CASTING ERIC WOODALL, CSA

Dance Music Arrangements	*Music Coordinator*	*Fight Direction*
GLEN KELLY	HOWARD JOINES	J. ALLEN SUDDETH

Sound Design	*Hair Design*	*Makeup Design*	*Illusion Design*
KEN TRAVIS	JOSH MARQUETTE	MILAGROS MEDINA-CERDEIRA	JIM STEINMEYER

Costume Design	*Lighting Design*
GREGG BARNES	NATASHA KATZ

Scenic Design
BOB CROWLEY

Orchestrations
DANNY TROOB

Music Supervision
Incidental Music & Vocal Arrangements
MICHAEL KOSARIN

Directed and Choreographed by
CASEY NICHOLAW

The premiere of *Aladdin* was produced by The 5th Avenue Theatre in Seattle, WA. David Armstrong, Executive Producer & Artistic Director;
Bernadine C. Griffin, Managing Director; Bill Berry, Producing Director.

3/20/14

Adam Jacobs and
Courtney Reed

Photo: Deen Van Meer

The Playbill Broadway Yearbook 2013-2014

Aladdin

MUSICAL NUMBERS

ACT I

"Arabian Nights"*	Genie, Company
"One Jump Ahead"†	Aladdin, Ensemble
"Proud of Your Boy"*	Aladdin
"These Palace Walls"	Jasmine, Female Attendants
"Babkak, Omar, Aladdin, Kassim"*	Babkak, Omar, Aladdin, Kassim, Jasmine, Ensemble
"A Million Miles Away"	Aladdin, Jasmine
"Diamond in the Rough"	Jafar, Iago, Aladdin
"Friend Like Me"*	Genie, Aladdin, Ensemble
Act One Finale	
("Friend Like Me" Reprise* / "Proud of Your Boy" Reprise)	Genie, Aladdin

ACT II

"Prince Ali"*	Babkak, Omar, Kassim, Genie, Ensemble
"A Whole New World"†	Aladdin, Jasmine
"High Adventure"*	Babkak, Omar, Kassim, Ensemble
"Somebody's Got Your Back"	Genie, Aladdin, Babkak, Omar, Kassim
"Proud of Your Boy" (Reprise II)*	Aladdin
"Prince Ali" (Sultan Reprise)	Sultan, Company
"Prince Ali" (Jafar Reprise)†	Jafar
Finale Ultimo	
("Arabian Nights" Reprise / "A Whole New World" Reprise†)	Company

Music by Alan Menken. *Lyrics by Howard Ashman. †Lyrics by Tim Rice.
All other lyrics and additional lyrics by Chad Beguelin.

ORCHESTRA

Conductor: MICHAEL KOSARIN
Associate Conductor/Keyboards:
    ARON ACCURSO
Assistant Conductor/Keyboards:
    ANNBRITT duCHATEAU
Reeds: TODD GROVES, CHARLES PILLOW,
    MARK THRASHER
Trumpets: DON DOWNS (lead),
    TONY KADLECK, SCOTT HARRELL
Trombone: GARY GRIMALDI
Bass Trombone: ERNIE COLLINS

French Horn: DAVID PEEL
Bass: DICK SARPOLA
Drums: JOHN REDSECKER
Percussion: MICHAEL ENGLANDER
Guitar: KEVIN KUHN
Violins: SUZANNE ORNSTEIN (Concertmaster),
    MINEKO YAJIMA
Cello: ROGER SHELL
Music Coordinator: HOWARD JOINES
Music Preparation: ANIXTER RICE MUSIC
    SERVICE
Electronic Music Programming: JEFF MARDER

Cast Continued

Voice of the Cave	BRANDON O'NEILL
Ensemble	TIA ALTINAY, ANDREW CAO, JOSHUA DELA CRUZ, YUREL ECHEZARRETA, DAISY HOBBS, DONALD JONES, JR., ADAM KAOKEPT, NIKKI LONG, STANLEY MARTIN, BRANDT MARTINEZ, RHEA PATTERSON, BOBBY PESTKA, KHORI MICHELLE PETINAUD, ARIEL REID, TRENT SAUNDERS, JAZ SEALEY, DENNIS STOWE, MARISHA WALLACE, BUD WEBER

STANDBYS

For Jafar/Sultan .... MERWIN FOARD
For Genie/Babkak ...... MICHAEL JAMES SCOTT

SWINGS

MIKE CANNON, LAURYN CIARDULLO,
MICHAEL MINDLIN, ALEKS PEVEC,
JENNIFER RIAS

UNDERSTUDIES

Aladdin: JOSHUA DELA CRUZ,
    TRENT SAUNDERS, BUD WEBER
Jafar: DENNIS STOWE
Genie: DONALD JONES, JR.
Jasmine: TIA ALTINAY, LAURYN CIARDULLO
Kassim: YUREL ECHEZARRETA, JAZ SEALEY
Omar: ANDREW CAO, MICHAEL MINDLIN
Babkak: MARISHA WALLACE
Sultan: DENNIS STOWE
Iago: ADAM KAOKEPT, MICHAEL MINDLIN

DANCE CAPTAINS

NIKKI LONG, MICHAEL MINDLIN

FIGHT CAPTAIN

MICHAEL MINDLIN

The cast of *Aladdin* performs "Arabian Nights."

Photo: Deen Van Meer

Aladdin

Adam Jacobs
Aladdin

Jonathan Freeman
Jafar

James Monroe Iglehart
Genie

Courtney Reed
Jasmine

Brian Gonzales
Babkak

Brandon O'Neill
Kassim, Spooky Voice, Voice of the Cave

Jonathan Schwartz
Omar

Clifton Davis
Sultan

Don Darryl Rivera
Iago

Merwin Foard
Standby for Jafar/Sultan

Michael James Scott
Standby for Genie/Babkak

Tia Altinay
Attendant, Ensemble

Mike Cannon
Swing

Andrew Cao
Henchman, Ensemble

Lauryn Ciardullo
Swing

Joshua Dela Cruz
Ensemble

Yurel Echezarreta
Ensemble

Daisy Hobbs
Ensemble

Donald Jones, Jr.
Henchman, Ensemble

Adam Kaokept
Ensemble

Nikki Long
Ensemble, Dance Captain

Stanley Martin
Ensemble

Brandt Martinez
Ensemble

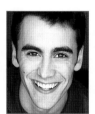
Michael Mindlin
Swing, Dance Captain, Fight Captain

Rhea Patterson
Ensemble

Bobby Pestka
Shop Owner, Ensemble

Khori Michelle Petinaud
Attendant, Ensemble

Aleks Pevec
Swing

Ariel Reid
Ensemble

Jennifer Rias
Swing

Trent Saunders
Ensemble

Jaz Sealey
Prince Abdullah, Ensemble

Dennis Stowe
Razoul, Ensemble

Marisha Wallace
Attendant, Fortune Teller, Ensemble

Bud Weber
Ensemble

Aladdin

Alan Menken
Music

Howard Ashman
Lyrics

Tim Rice
Lyrics

Chad Beguelin
Book, Additional Lyrics

Casey Nicholaw
Director, Choreographer

Bob Crowley
Scenic Design

Gregg Barnes
Costume Design

Natasha Katz
Lighting Design

Ken Travis
Sound Design

Michael Kosarin
Music Supervision, Incidental Music, Vocal Arrangements

Danny Troob
Orchestrations

Glen Kelly
Dance Music Arrangements

Howard Joines
Music Coordinator

Josh Marquette
Hair Design

Milagros Medina-Cerdeira
Make-up Design

Jim Steinmeyer
Illusion Design

Jeremy Chernick
Special Effects Design

J. Allen Suddeth
Fight Direction

Scott Taylor
Associate Director

John MacInnis
Associate Choreographer

Tara Rubin
*Tara Rubin Casting
Casting*

Geoffrey Quart
Hudson Theatrical Associates
Technical Supervision

David Benken
Technical Supervision

Clifford Schwartz
Production Supervisor

Thomas Schumacher
Disney Theatrical Productions

David Armstrong
The 5th Avenue Theatre
Executive Producer and Artistic Director

Bernadine C. Griffin
The 5th Avenue Theatre
Managing Director

Bill Berry
The 5th Avenue Theatre
Producing Director

2013-2014 AWARDS

TONY AWARD
Best Performance by an Actor
In a Featured Role in a Musical
(James Monroe Iglehart)

DRAMA DESK AWARD
Outstanding Featured Actor in a Musical
(James Monroe Iglehart)

Photo: Deen Van Meer

Adam Jacobs as Aladdin in The Cave of Wonders.

Aladdin

FRONT OF HOUSE
Kneeling (L-R): Meghan Duffy, Kasey Perlinger, Jacob Pincus, David Apolo, Standley McCray, Jessica Pilla, Sarah Crounse, Luis Mora, Michelle Ruggieri, Leticia Lemos, Bryan Plummer, Jason Blanche
Standing (L-R): James McKenna (Head Usher), Jeryl Costello (Guest Relations Manager), Laura Speidell, Kellie Murphy, Fred Velez, Trey Harrington, Allison Weaver, Joshua Garcia, Lori Ramirez, Lauren Glennon, Brian Newell, Kirsten Johnson, Thomas Trimble, Karina Orozco, Alexander Allen, Tania Velez, Brandon Cintron, John M. Loiacono (Theatre Manager)

HAIR/MAKE-UP
(L-R): Scott Smith (Hair/Make-up Assistant),
Brandalyn Fulton (Hair/Make-up Assistant),
Gary Martori (Hair/Make-up Supervisor), Cheryl Thomas

MANAGEMENT
Seated (L-R): Patrick Wetzel (Production Assistant),
Jimmie Lee Smith (Stage Manager)
Standing (L-R): Holly R. Coombs (Assistant Stage Manager), Jason Trubitt (Assistant Stage Manager), Clifford Schwartz (Production Stage Manager), Alexis Shorter (Assistant Stage Manager)

BOX OFFICE
Seated (L-R): Michael Campanella, Lisa Kenny, Eric Moroney
Standing (L-R): Peter Kane, Andrew Grennan (Box Office Treasurer), Anthony Oliva (Assistant Treasurer), Charlie Luff, Michael Schiavone

SECURITY
Belvin Williams
(DTG Security Host)

DOORMAN
Julez Seino-Davis

MANAGEMENT
Matthew Kurtis Lutz
(Asst. Stage Manager)

Aladdin

STAFF FOR *ALADDIN*

COMPANY MANAGER ....MICHAEL BOLGAR
Assistant Company Manager ....Christopher Taggart
PRODUCTION STAGE
    MANAGER ....CLIFFORD SCHWARTZ
Stage Manager ....Jimmie Lee Smith
Assistant Stage Managers ....Jason Trubitt,
    Holly R. Coombs, Matthew Kurtis Lutz
Dance Captains ....Nikki Long, Michael Mindlin
Fight Captain ....Michael Mindlin
Production Assistants ....Mitchell Anderson,
    Nathan Brewer, Lisa Jaeger,
    Patrick Wetzel, Will Murdock

DISNEY ON BROADWAY PUBLICITY

SENIOR PUBLICIST ....DENNIS CROWLEY
Associate Publicist ....Michael Strassheim

Associate Scenic Designer ....Ros Coombes
Associate Scenic Designer ....Bryan Johnson
UK Scenic Assistants ....Justin Nardella,
    Charles Quiggen, Jaimie Todd, Adam Wiltshire
U.S. Scenic Assistants ....Gaetane Bertol,
    Denny Moyes, Joanie Schlafer
Projection Consultant ....Daniel Brodie
Projection Programmer ....Patrick Southern
Associate Costume Designer ....Sky Switser
Assistant Costume Designers ....Rachel Attridge,
    Dana Burkhart, Stephen Stratton
Costume Assistant ....Bernadette Banner
Costume Interns ....AC Gottlieb, Ricky Lurie
Associate Lighting Designer ....Aaron Spivey
Assistant Lighting Designer ....Ken Elliott
Moving Light Programmer ....Sean Beach
Lighting Intern ....James Roderick
Associate Sound Designer ....Alexander Hawthorn
Assistant Fight Director ....Ted Sharon
Fight Direction Associate ....Mitchell McCoy
Associate Make-Up Designer ....Amy Porter
"Diamond in the Rough" Animation ....Dave Bossert
Technical Supervision ....Geoffrey Quart
Associate Technical Supervisor ....Gerald Frentz

Technical Associate ....Irene Wang
Technical Supervision ....David Benken
Associate Technical Supervisor ....Rose Palombo
Production Carpenter ....John McPherson
Head Carpenter ....Drew Siccardi
Assistant Head Carpenter ....Tony Goncalves
Fly Man ....John Fullum
Deck Automation ....Steve Stackle
Fly Automation ....David Helck
Deck Hands ..Brett Daley, Gary Matarazzo, Cody Siccardi,
    Josh Tocco, Joseph Valentino
Production Electrician ....Jimmy Maloney
Console Operator ....Brad Robertson
Head Spot Operator ....Joseph P. Garvey
Moving Light Technician ....Andy Catron
Pyro Technician ....Kevin Strohmeyer
Spot Operator ....Christopher Passalacqua
Production Sound ....Lucas Indelicato
Sound Mixer ....Gabe Wood
Sound Engineer ....Marie Renee Foucher
Sound Technician ....William Romanello
Co-Production Props Supervisors ....Tim Abel,
    Jerry Marshall
Head Props ....Victor Amerling
Props ....Alan Cabrera, James Maloney III,
    John Saye, John Taccone
Special Effects Assistant ....Ben Hagen
Wardrobe Supervisor ....Rick Kelly
Assistant Wardrobe Supervisor ....Cecilia Cruz
Dressers ....Meredith Benson, Tom Bertsch,
    Gary Biangone, Douglas Earl, Margiann Flanagan,
    Barry Hoff, Carrie Kamerer, Ritchy McFadden,
    Leslie Moulton, Ryan Oslak, Mike Piscitelli,
    Bonnie Prather, Jaime Samson,
    Stacey Sarmiento, Amanda Zane
Hair and Makeup Supervisor ....Gary Martori
Assistant Hair and Makeup Supervisor .....Cheryl Thomas
Hair and Makeup Assistants ....Brandalyn Fulton,
    Scott Smith
Associate Music Director ....Aron Accurso
Assistant Music Director ....Annbritt duChateau
Electronic Music Programming ....Jeff Marder
Music Coordinator ....Howard Joines
Rehearsal Musicians .....John Redsecker, Brendan Whiting
Additional Orchestrations ....Doug Besterman,
    Ned Ginsburg, Larry Hochman
Music Preparation ....Russ Anixter, Donald Rice
Music Intern ....Henry Lewers
Associate to Mr. Menken ....Rick Kunis
Vocal Consultant ....Liz Caplan Vocal Studios, LLC
Physical Therapy ....PhysioArts
Orthopedist ....David S. Weiss, M.D./
    NYU Langone Medical Center

Advertising ....Serino/Coyne, Inc.
Production Photography ....Deen Van Meer,
    Cylla von Tiedemann
Production Travel ....Jill L. Citron
Payroll Managers ....Anthony DeLuca, Cathy Guerra
Corporate Immigration Counsel ....Michael Rosenfeld

TARA RUBIN CASTING

Tara Rubin CSA, Eric Woodall CSA
Merri Sugarman CSA, Kaitlin Shaw CSA
Lindsay Levine CSA, Scott Anderson

SPECIAL EFFECTS DESIGNER

Jeremy Chernick

CREDITS

Scenery by Hudson Scenic Studio, Inc.; Daedalus Design
and Production, Inc.; Proof Productions, Inc.; Tom Carroll
Scenery Inc.; and Gordon Aldred. Lighting equipment by
PRG Lighting. Additional projection animation by Gabriel
Aronson. Automation by Hudson Scenic Studio, Inc. Props
by Jerard Studio, the Paragon Innovation Group, Proof
Productions Inc., the Rabbit's Choice, Eric Buss, Tony
Clark. Sound equipment by Masque Sound. Video
projections provided by Sound Associates, Inc. Magic carpet
by Tait Towers Scene Shop. Illusion effects by William
Kennedy MagicEffect. Special effects equipment by J&M
Special Effects. Show curtain by Arquepoise Ltd. Soft goods
by iWeiss. Costumes by Arel Studio; Carelli Costumes Inc.;
Jennifer Chapman; J. Doug James Millinery; Donna
Langman Costumes; Eric Winterling Inc.; Jan Parran; Jeff
Fender Studio; Lynne Baccus; Lynne Mackey Studio; Killer;
Monica Vianni; Parsons-Meares, Ltd.; Polly Kinney;
Rodney Gordon Inc.; Tricorne; Seamless Costumes. Special
thanks to Bra*Tenders for undergarments and hosiery.
Custom shoes by Jitterbug Boy, LaDuca, T.O. Dey Shoe
Company. Wigs by Hudson Wigs. Makeup supplied by
Alcone. Brushes by Karen.

American Tourister is a proud partner of *ALADDIN*.

Makeup provided by M•A•C.

Hair care provided by ORIBE HAIR CARE.

SONG EXCERPTS (used by permission)

"Mambo," music by Leonard Bernstein. "Beauty and
the Beast," "Belle," "Part of Your World" and "Under the
Sea," music by Alan Menken, lyrics by Howard Ashman.

Genie:
James Monroe Iglehart

Photo: Cylla von Tiedemann

Jafar:
Jonathan Freeman

Photo: Deen Van Meer

Aladdin

Photo: Brian Mapp

CREW

Sitting Front (L-R): Holly R. Coombs (Stage Manager), Tom Bertsch (Dresser), Bonnie Prather (Dresser), Amanda Zane (Dresser), Carrie Kamerer (Dresser), Meredith Benson (Dresser), Leslie Moulton (Dresser), Travis Ryder (Dresser), Tim Abel (Props), Gabe Wood (Sound),
Kneeling (L-R): Alexis Shorter (Stage Manager), Patrick Wetzel (Stage Manager), Barry Hoff (Dresser), Ritchy McFadden (Dresser), Douglas Earl (Dresser), Andy Catron (Electrics), John Saye (Props)
Standing (L-R): Cecilia Cruz (Wardrobe), Jimmie Lee Smith (Stage Manager), Marie Renee Foucher (Sound), Josh Tocco (Carpenter), Alan Cabrera (Props) Jay Cole (Wardrobe), William Romanello (Sound), Christopher Passalacqua (Electrics), Jaime Samson (Dresser), Brad Robertson (Electrics), Chris McInerney (Electrics), Jason Trubitt (Stage Manager)
Standing Back (L-R): Michael Bolgar (Company Manager), Christopher Taggart (Company Manager), John McPherson (Carpenter), Mike Meury (Carpenter), James Maloney III (Props)

"Colors of the Wind," music by Alan Menken, lyrics by Stephen Schwartz.

ALADDIN previously performed at the Ed Mirvish Theatre in Toronto, Ontario.

ALADDIN rehearsed at the New 42nd Street Studios.

DISNEY THEATRICAL PRODUCTIONS

President & Producer ....Thomas Schumacher
EVP & Managing Director ....David Schrader

Creative & Production

Executive Music Producer ....Chris Montan
VP, Creative Development ....Ben Famiglietti
VP, Production ....Anne Quart
Director, Production ....Mimi Intagliata
Director, Labor Relations ....Scott Kardel
Associate Director ....Jeff Lee
Production Supervisor ....Clifford Schwartz
Sr. Manager, Creative Development ....Jane Abramson
Dramaturg & Literary Manager ....Ken Cerniglia
Sr. Manager, Labor Relations ....Stephanie Cheek
Sr. Manager, Education & Outreach ....Lisa Mitchell
Sr. Production Manager ....Myriah Bash
Production Manager ....Eduardo Castro
Production Manager......................Michael Height
Production Manager ....Thomas Schlenk
Associate Production Manager ....Kerry McGrath

Marketing, Sales & Publicity

SVP, Marketing & Sales ....Andrew Flatt
VP, Sales, CRM & Partnerships.............Bryan Dockett
VP, Marketing ....Robin Wyatt
Director, Synergy & Partnership ....Kevin Banks
Director, Worldwide Publicity ....Michael Cohen
Director, Sales & Ticketing ....Nick Falzon
Director, Licensed Brands ....Gary Kane
Sr. Manager,
    Publicity & Communications ....Lindsay Braverman
Sr. Manager, Data Modeling &
    Consumer Insights ....Craig Trachtenberg
Design Manager ....James Anderer
Design Manager.................................Eric Emch
Marketing Manager, *Newsies* ....Lauren Daghini

Manager, Sales & Ticketing ....Erin Dooley
Manager, Digital Marketing & Social Media ...Greg Josken
Sales Manager, Groups & Tourism ....Nicholas Faranda
Manager, Sales & Ticketing ....Jenifer Thomas
Manager, Digital Marketing ....Peter Tulba
Marketing Manager, *Aladdin* ....Jason Zammit
Asst. Manager Synergy & Partnership ....Cara Epstein
Publicity Associate ....Brendan Padgett

Domestic

VP, Domestic ....Jack Eldon
Director, Domestic Touring ....Michael Buchanan
Director, Regional Engagements ....Scott A. Hemerling
Director, Regional Engagements ....Kelli Palan
Manager, Domestic Touring & Planning ....Liz Botros
Manager, Theatrical Licensing ....David R. Scott

International

SVP, International ....Ron Kollen
VP, International, Australia ....James Thane
VP, International, Europe ....Fiona Thomas
Director, International Production ....Felipe Gamba

Business & Legal Affairs

SVP, Business & Legal Affairs ....Jonathan Olson
VP, Business & Legal Affairs ....Seth Stuhl
Counsel ....Naila McKenzie
Sr. Paralegal ....Jessica White

Finance & Operations

VP, Finance/Business Development ....Mario Iannetta
VP, Operations ....Dana Amendola
Director, Finance ....Joe McClafferty
Director, Accounting ....Brigitte Pascual
Manager, Technical Services & Support ...Michael Figliulo
Manager, Accounting ....Adrineh Ghoukassian
Manager, Finance ....Mikhail Medvedev
Project Manager ....Ryan Pears
Manager, Finance ....Liz Jurist Schwarzwalder
Manager, Production Accounting ....Arlene Smith
Senior Business Planner ....Jennifer August
Senior Technical Support Engineer ......Kevin A. McGuire
Senior Technical Support Engineer ....Noel Moore Jr.
Production Accountant ....Angela DiSanti

Production Accountant ....Jessica Bochman
Assistant Production Accountant ....Isander Rojas

Human Resources

Director, Human Resources ....Marie-Pierre Varin
Manager, Human Resources ....Jewel Neal
Manager, Human Resources &
    Labor Relations ....Valerie Hart

Administrative Staff

Kelly Archer, Zachary Baer, Caley Beretta, Elizabeth Boulger, Amanda Cole, Jubie Deane, Leah Diaz, Adam Dworkin, Christina Francis, Sarah Funk, Phil Grippe, Frankie Lynn Harvey, Andrew Hollenbeck, Christina Huschle, Sarah Kenny, Julie Lavin, Colleen McCormack, Will Murdock, Misael Nunez, Tim Parker, Marisa Perry, Jessica Petschauer, Matt Quinones, Meaghan Shea, Suzanne Sheptock, Bri Silva, Lee Taglin, Anji Taylor

---

DISNEY THEATRICAL MERCHANDISE

Vice President ....Steven Downing
Sr. District Manager, Retail Strategy & Ops ...Alyssa Somers
Merchandise Manager ....Michael Dei Cas
Merchandise Manager ....Neil Markman
Associate Buyer ....Violet Burlaza
Corp. Sales &
    Product Development Manager ....Ellete Poulin

Disney Theatrical Productions
guestmail@disneytheatrical.com

Staff for the New Amsterdam Theatre

Theatre Manager ....John M. Loiacono
Guest Relations Manager ....Jeryl Costello
Box Office Treasurer ....Andrew Grennan
Assistant Treasurer ....Anthony Oliva
Chief Engineer ....Dan Milan
Lead Engineer ....Jason Gordon
Engineer ....Charlie Lembo
Security Manager ....Carl Lembo
Head Usher ....James McKenna
Lobby Refreshments ....Sweet Hospitality
Special Thanks ....Sgt. Arthur J. Smarsch,
                                        Det. Adam D'Amico

Aladdin
SCRAPBOOK

Opening night's curtain call at the New Amsterdam with the cast and, in front (L-R): Michael Kosarin (Conductor), Glen Kelly (Dance Music Arrangements), Chad Beguelin (Librettist/Lyricist), Casey Nicholaw (Director), Alan Menken (Composer), Bob Crowley (Scenic Design) and Natasha Katz (Lighting Design).

Correspondent: Marisha Wallace "Attendant," "Fortune Teller," "Ensemble"

Opening Night Gifts: Large prints of our costume designs from the show!

Most Exciting Celebrity Visitors: Ben Vereen. He said he had not been moved so much by a show in years. And Whoopi Goldberg. She said to me, "Don't I know you?" and I said, "No, but I think we share a kindred spirit." I told her we may be cousins and she said, "Yeah, your OLD cousin!" She's hysterical and she loved the show!

Favorite In-Theatre Gathering Place: In the fourth floor stairway for birthday parties or one of the Disney conference rooms for a fried chicken princess birthday!

Actor Who Performed the Most Roles in This Show: Michael Mindlin: 14 tracks

Special Backstage Rituals: Cast prayer at five minutes to "places." Saturday Night Dance Party: we all go on stage when the Entr'acte starts playing and dance together right before "Prince Ali."

Most Memorable Audience Reaction: Standing ovation after "Friend Like Me"—all three tiers of the house!

How Does the Cast and Audience Handle the Special Effects?: If we told you we would have to kill you... #disneymagic

Unique Pre-Show Announcement: Dollar Saturday! If you can't love yourself, how the heck you gonna love somebody else... Can I get an amen up in here?!

Memorable Ad-Lib: "She stole...my things!"—Bud Weber.

Memorable Press Encounter: *Vanity Fair* spread with Casey and all the girls.

Memorable Stage Door Fan Encounter: I was trying to sneak out the stage door without signing autographs to catch an early train and someone yelled, "Marisha!!!" from down the street. I thought it was someone I knew, so I turned around. It was a group of NYU students who wanted to meet me and tell me how much they enjoyed my performance. Needless to say, I missed my train and signed their Playbills. They earned it for calling me out.

Memorable Directorial Note: "You guys are the best cast alive...there are some better dead ones!"

Embarrassing Moments: One of my shoes came off during the "BOAK" dance number and I had to dance the rest of the song with one shoe. Meanwhile, the cast was dancing by in slow motion laughing at the orange LaDuca in the middle of the stage.

Jonathan Freeman as Jafar, wearing the heaviest costume in the show.

Favorite Moment During Each Performance: Singing the iconic line from the movie, "Still I think he's rather tasty!," and my entrance as the Phoenix in "Prince Ali." Offstage: our cast potlucks we had in Toronto...good food...great bonding.

Favorite Off-Site Hangout: Schnipper's

Favorite Snack Food: Wasabi almonds

Favorite Therapies: Physical therapy and Popeye's Chicken.

Mascot: Jimmie Lee.

Catchphrases Only the Company Would Recognize: "Broadway's hard!" "Wayzzzzz!" "Take it from the Schlomo!" "Your Actors!"

Best In-House Parody Lyrics: "Make way for the prince of peace! He turned the water to wine. Healed seven people... not nine. And he's always on time. He's the prince of peace!"

Understudy Anecdote: WERK!!! (yelled from the back of the house).

Nicknames: Miss Brandt! Yurel Eriffolota! Security! Deacon! Captain of the Dance!

Fastest Costume Change: 14 seconds. Jafar has one-sec changes in the wedding.

Who Wore the Heaviest/Hottest Costume: Jafar. His robe weighs a ton. (See picture, left.)

Who Wore the Least?: Donald...just pants and a dream.

Ghostly Encounters Backstage: Olive Thomas is the *Follies* girl ghost who lives in the theatre. She can make unusual things happen if she's feeling frisky.

Coolest Thing About Being in This Show: It's my first Broadway show and it's a Disney classic! I get to work with an amazing cast each day and retell this story for the masses! It is truly pure Disney magic!

Best Day: Recording the cast album!

All the Way

First Preview: February 10, 2014. Opened: March 6, 2014.
Still running as of May 31, 2014.

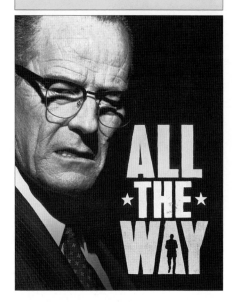

PLAYBILL

ALL THE WAY

Portrait of Lyndon Baines Johnson, the small-time Texas politician who rose to become senator and vice president, and then, upon the assassination of John F. Kennedy, president of the United States. The play covers the eleven months from the assassination to Johnson's winning his own term in 1964, as he engaged enemies and friends alike in a series of political arm twists and knife fights to win passage of the 1964 Civil Rights Act. The title comes from his campaign slogan, "All the way with LBJ." The production is notable as the Broadway debut of Bryan Cranston, lately of the TV series "Breaking Bad," as LBJ.

CAST

(in order of speaking)

President
    Lyndon Baines Johnson ....BRYAN CRANSTON
Lady Bird Johnson, *First Lady*; Katharine Graham,
    Washington Post publisher; Rep. Katharine
    St. George, *R-NY* ....BETSY AIDEM
Walter Jenkins, *top aide to LBJ*; Rep. William
    Colmer, *D-MS* ....CHRISTOPHER
                  LIAM MOORE
Secretary; Lurleen Wallace; Muriel Humphrey;
    Sen. Maurine Neuberger, *D-OR* .....SUSANNAH
                  SCHULMAN
Sen. Hubert Humphrey, *D-MN* ....ROBERT
                  PETKOFF
Sen. Richard Russell, *D-GA* .....JOHN McMARTIN
J. Edgar Hoover, *FBI director*;
    Sen. Robert Byrd, *D-WV* ...MICHAEL McKEAN

Continued on next page

Continued on next page

NEIL SIMON THEATRE

UNDER THE DIRECTION OF JAMES M. NEDERLANDER AND JAMES L. NEDERLANDER

Jeffrey Richards   Louise Gund   Jerry Frankel

Stephanie P. McClelland   Double Gemini Productions   Rebecca Gold
Scott M. Delman   Barbara H. Freitag   Harvey Weinstein   Gene Korf
William Berlind   Luigi Caiola   Gutterman Chernoff   Jam Theatricals
Gabrielle Palitz   Cheryl Wiesenfeld   Will Trice

present

The Oregon Shakespeare Festival and
American Repertory Theater production of

BRYAN CRANSTON

in

ALL THE WAY

BY **ROBERT SCHENKKAN**

Eric Lenox Abrams   Betsy Aidem   J. Bernard Calloway   Rob Campbell   Brandon J. Dirden
James Eckhouse   Peter Jay Fernandez   Christopher Gurr   William Jackson Harper
Michael McKean   John McMartin   Christopher Liam Moore   Robert Petkoff
Ethan Phillips   Richard Poe   Roslyn Ruff   Susannah Schulman   Bill Timoney   Steve Vinovich
Tony Carlin   Gina Daniels   Danny Johnson   Monette Magrath

SCENIC DESIGN	COSTUME DESIGN	LIGHTING DESIGN	COMPOSER/SOUND DESIGN
Christopher Acebo	Deborah M. Dryden	Jane Cox	Paul James Prendergast

PROJECTION DESIGN	PROJECTION CONSULTANT	HAIR & WIG DESIGN	SOUND CONSULTANT
Shawn Sagady	Wendall K. Harrington	Paul Huntley	Peter Fitzgerald

CASTING	DRAMATURG	PRODUCTION STAGE MANAGER	TECHNICAL SUPERVISION
Telsey + Company William Cantler, CSA	Tom Bryant	Matthew Farrell	Hudson Theatrical Associates

PRESS REPRESENTATIVE	ADVERTISING	COMPANY MANAGER	GENERAL MANAGEMENT
Irene Gandy/Alana Karpoff	AKA	Alexandra Agosta	Richards/Climan, Inc.

ASSOCIATE PRODUCERS
Rob Hinderliter & Dominick LaRuffa Jr.   Michael Crea   PJ Miller

DIRECTOR

BILL RAUCH

First performed at Oregon Shakespeare Festival. Bill Rauch – Artistic Director
Subsequently performed at the American Repertory Theater at Harvard University
Diane Paulus, Artistic Director, Diane Borger, Producer
ALL THE WAY was developed, in part, with assistance from The Orchard Project, a program of The Exchange *(exchangenyc.org)*

3/6/14

(L-R): Bryan Cranston as LBJ and Robert Petkoff as Hubert Humphrey

Photo: Evgenia Eliseeva

All the Way

Brandon J. Dirden as the
Rev. Martin Luther King, Jr.

Cast Continued

Robert McNamara, *Secretary of Defense*; Sen. James
    Eastland, *D-MS*; Rep. William Moore
    McCulloch, *R-OH*; Gov. Paul B.
    Johnson, Jr., *D-MS* ....JAMES ECKHOUSE
Rev. Martin Luther King, Jr.,
    SCLC president ....BRANDON J. DIRDEN
Rev. Ralph Abernathy, *SCLC secretary-treasurer*;
    Butler ....J. BERNARD CALLOWAY
Stanley Levison, *SCLC advisor*; Rep. John
    McCormack, *D-MA*; Seymore Trammell, *District
    Attorney in Alabama*; Rev. Edwin King, *MFDP
    organizer* ....ETHAN PHILLIPS
James Harrison, *SCLC accountant*; Stokely
    Carmichael, *SNCC organizer* ....WILLIAM
                                 JACKSON HARPER

Cartha "Deke" DeLoach, *FBI deputy director*;
    Rep. Howard "Judge" Smith, *D-VA*;
    Sen. Everett Dirksen, *R-IL*;
    Gov. Carl Sanders, *D-GA* ....RICHARD POE
Coretta Scott King; Fannie Lou Hamer,
    SNCC organizer ....ROSLYN RUFF
Gov. George Wallace, *D-AL*; Rep. James Corman,
    D-CA; Joseph Alsop, *journalist*; Sen. Mike
    Mansfield, *D-MT*; Walter Reuther, *president of
    UAW* ....ROB CAMPBELL
Roy Wilkins, *NAACP executive director*; Shoeshiner;
    Aaron Henry, *MFDP delegate* ....PETER JAY
                                          FERNANDEZ
Bob Moses, *COFO co-director*; David Dennis,
    CORE leader, MS ....ERIC LENOX ABRAMS
Rep. Emanuel Celler, *D-NY*; White House
    Aide/Butler ....STEVE VINOVICH
Sen. Strom Thurmond, *D-SC*; White House
    Aide/Butler ....CHRISTOPHER GURR
Sen. Karl Mundt, *R-SD*; White House Aide/
    Butler ....BILL TIMONEY

SCLC: Southern Christian Leadership Conference;
MFDP: Mississippi Freedom Democratic Party;
SNCC: Student Nonviolent Coordinating
Committee; NAACP: National Association for the
Advancement of Colored People; COFO: Council
of Federated Organizations; CORE: Congress of
Racial Equality

UNDERSTUDIES

For Sen. Hubert Humphrey, J. Edgar Hoover,
    Sen. Robert Byrd, Sen. Richard Russell,
    Cartha "Deke" Deloach, Rep. Howard "Judge"

Smith, Sen. Everett Dirksen, Gov. Carl Sanders,
    Rep. Emanuel Celler, White House Aide,
    Butler: TONY CARLIN
For Coretta Scott King,
    Fannie Lou Hamer: GINA DANIELS
For Gov. George Wallace, Rep. James Corman,
    Sen. Mike Mansfield, Walter Reuther,
    Walter Jenkins, Rep. William Colmer:
    CHRISTOPHER GURR
For Bob Moses, David Dennis, Rev. Ralph
    Abernathy, White House Butler, Rev. Martin
    Luther King, Roy Wilkins, Aaron Henry,
    Shoe Shiner, James Harrison, Stokely Carmichael:
    DANNY JOHNSON
For Lady Bird Johnson, Katharine Graham,
    Rep. Katharine St. George, Secretary, Lurleen
    Wallace, Muriel Humphrey, Sen. Mundt, White
    House Aide, Maid: MONETTE MAGRATH
For Robert McNamara, Sen. James Eastland,
    Rep. William Moore McCulloch, Sen. Strom
    Thurmond, Gov. Paul Johnson, White House
    Aide, Butler: BILL TIMONEY
For President Lyndon Baines Johnson, Stanley
    Levison, Rep. John McCormack, Seymore
    Trammel, Rev. Edwin King: STEVE VINOVICH

SETTING

Washington, DC; Atlantic City; Atlanta; Mississippi.

TIME

November, 1963-November, 1964

Bryan Cranston
*President Lyndon
Baines Johnson*

Eric Lenox Abrams
*Bob Moses/
David Dennis*

Betsy Aidem
*Lady Bird Johnson/
Katharine Graham/
Katharine St. George*

J. Bernard Calloway
*Ralph Abernathy/
Butler*

Rob Campbell
*George Wallace/
James Corman/
Mike Mansfield/
Walter Reuther*

Tony Carlin
Understudy

Gina Daniels
Understudy

Brandon J. Dirden
Martin Luther King, Jr.

James Eckhouse
*Robert McNamara/
James Eastland/
William Moore
McCulloch/ Paul B.
Johnson, Jr.*

Peter Jay Fernandez
*Roy Wilkins/
Shoeshiner/
Aaron Henry*

Christopher Gurr
*Strom Thurmond/
Butler*

**William Jackson
Harper**
*James Harrison/
Stokely Carmichael*

Danny Johnson
Understudy

Monette Magrath
Understudy

All the Way

Michael McKean
J. Edgar Hoover/
Robert Byrd

John McMartin
Richard Russell

Christopher Liam
Moore
Walter Jenkins/
William Colmer

Robert Petkoff
Hubert Humphrey

Ethan Phillips
Stanley Levison/
John McCormack/
Seymore Trammell/
Edwin King

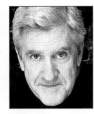
Richard Poe
Cartha DeLoach/
Howard Smith/
Everett Dirksen/
Carl Sanders

Roslyn Ruff
Fannie Lou Hamer/
Coretta Scott King

Susannah Schulman
Secretary/
Lurleen Wallace/
Muriel Humphrey

Bill Timoney
Karl Mundt/Butler

Steve Vinovich
Emanuel Celler/
Butler; u/s LBJ

Robert Schenkkan
Author

Bill Rauch
Director

Christopher Acebo
Scenic Design

Deborah M. Dryden
Costume Design

Jane Cox
Lighting Design

Wendall K.
Harrington
Projection
Consultant

Paul Huntley
Hair & Wig Design

Bernard Telsey
Telsey + Company
Casting

Neil A. Mazzella
Hudson Theatrical
Associates
Technical
Supervision

David R. Richards
Tamar Haimes
Richards/Climan, Inc.
General
Management

Jeffrey Richards
Producer

Jerry Frankel
Producer

Stephanie P.
McClelland
Producer

Carl Moellenberg
Double Gemini
Productions
Producer

Wendy Federman
Double Gemini
Productions
Producer

Rebecca Gold
Producer

Scott M. Delman
Producer

Barbara H. Freitag
Producer

Harvey Weinstein
Producer

Gene Korf
Producer

Luigi Caiola
Producer

Jay and Cindy Gutterman
Producers

Cathy Chernoff
Producer

Arny Granat
Jam Theatricals
Producer

All the Way

Steve Traxler
Jam Theatricals
Producer

Gabrielle Palitz
Producer

Cheryl Wiesenfeld
Producer

Will Trice
Producer

2013-2014 AWARDS

TONY AWARDS
Best Play
Best Performance by an Actor
in a Leading Role in a Play
(Bryan Cranston)

**NY DRAMA CRITICS'
CIRCLE AWARD**
Best American Play

DRAMA DESK AWARDS
Outstanding Play
Outstanding Actor
in a Play
(Bryan Cranston)

DRAMA LEAGUE AWARD
Outstanding Production
of a Play

**OUTER CRITICS CIRCLE
AWARDS**
Outstanding New
Broadway Play
Outstanding Actor in a Play
(Bryan Cranston)

THEATRE WORLD AWARD
(Bryan Cranston)

STAGE MANAGEMENT
(L-R): Jeff Brancato (Production Assistant),
James Latus (Assistant Stage Manager),
Matthew Farrell (Production Stage Manager),
Sarah Perlin (Production Assistant)

WARDROBE
Front (L-R): Jessica Dermody (Wardrobe Supervisor),
Jamie Englehart, Emily Merriweather, Polly Noble
Back (L-R): Bryen Shannon, Timothy Greer

STAGE DOOR
(L-R): Dawn Edmonds, Janine Peterson, Rey Concepcion

HAIR
Tim Bohle (Hair Dresser)

BOX OFFICE
(L-R): Erich Stollberger, Guy Bentley

CREW
Front (L-R):
Timothy A. Perry
(Production Carpenter),
Ed Chapman
(Production Sound Engineer,
Stuart Metcalf
(Production Props),
Mitchell Christenson
(Deck Audio)
Back (L-R):
Ron Schwier (Associate
Production Electrician),
Danny Viscardo (House
Propman), Stephen Vessa
(Follow Spot Sub),
James Travers, Sr.
(House Electrician)

All the Way

FRONT OF HOUSE

Seated (L-R): Christopher Langdon, Maria Collado, Joanne DeCicco, Rosaire Caso, Jane Publik, Gracelyn Darbasie
Standing (L-R): Angel Diaz, Tom Tassiello, Michelle Schechter, Evelyn Olivero, Marisol Olavarria, Sharon Hauser, Gwen Barbee, Mariea Crainiciuc, Robyn Corrigan, Michelle Smith, Eddie Cuevas, Kim Raccioppi, John Cuevas, Joann Thomas, Kaitlyn Spillane, Sean M. Coughlin (Theatre Manager)

Photo: Brian Mapp

STAFF FOR *ALL THE WAY*

GENERAL MANAGEMENT
RICHARDS/CLIMAN, INC.
David R. Richards   Tamar Haimes
Michael Sag   Kyle Bonder
Jenny Peek   Rachel Welt

COMPANY MANAGER
Alexandra Agosta

PRODUCTION MANAGEMENT
HUDSON THEATRICAL ASSOCIATES
Neil A. Mazzella   Sam Ellis
Caitlin McInerney   Irene Wang

GENERAL PRESS REPRESENTATIVE
JEFFREY RICHARDS ASSOCIATES
Irene Gandy   Alana Karpoff
Christopher Pineda   Thomas Raynor   Steven Strauss

CASTING
TELSEY + COMPANY
Bernard Telsey CSA, Will Cantler CSA, David Vaccari CSA, Bethany Knox CSA, Craig Burns CSA, Tiffany Little Canfield CSA, Rachel Hoffman CSA, Justin Huff CSA, Patrick Goodwin CSA, Abbie Brady-Dalton CSA, David Morris, Cesar A. Rocha CSA, Andrew Femenella CSA, Karyn Casl CSA, Kristina Bramhall, Conrad Woolfe, Rachel Nadler, Rachel Minow, Sean Gannon, Scott Galina

PRODUCTION STAGE MANAGER ....Matthew Farrell
Stage Manager ....James Latus
Associate Director......................Emily Sophia Knapp
Assistant Company Manager ....Kendall Booher
Dialect Coach ....Rebecca Clark Carey
Associate Scenic Designer ....Steven Kemp
Associate Costume Designer ....Sarah Smith
Associate Lighting Designer ....Porsche McGovern
Assistant Sound Designer ....Kevin Heard
Associate Projection Designer ....Michael Clark
Production Electrician ....Jimmy Maloney
Associate Production Electrician ....Ron Schwier
Production Carpenter ....Timothy A. Perry

Production Props..............................Eric Castaldo
Production Sound Engineer ....Ed Chapman
Followspot Operator ....John Kelly
Moving Light Programmer ....Jay Penfield
Watchout Projection Programming ....Paul Vershbow
Advance Production Carpenter ....Donald Oberpriller
Advance Production Video ....Christopher Kutz
Wardrobe Supervisor ....Jessica Dermody
Dressers ....Jamie Englehart, Timothy Greer,
Emily Merriweather, Bryen Shannon
Wig Supervisor ....Cynthia Demand
Hair Dresser ....Tim Bohle
Production Assistants ....Jeff Brancato,
Sarah Perlin, Laura Wilson
Assistant to Mr. Cranston ....Georgette Timoney
Transportation and Security for
Mr. Cranston ....Squared Away Services
Advertising ....AKA/Scott Moore, Elizabeth Furze,
Bashan Aquart, Melissa Marano, Sam Gates,
Jacob Matsumiya, Jamaal Parham, Janette Roush
Website Design/
Online Marketing Strategy ......AKA/Sarah Borenstein,
Ryan Greer, Flora Pei
Interactive Marketing
Service ....Broadway's Best Shows/
Andy Drachenberg, Lindsay Hoffman
General Management Interns ....Elliot Miranda,
Harriet Taylor, Katie Titley
Banking..................Signature Bank/Thomas Kasulka,
Margaret Monigan, Mary Ann Fanelli
Insurance ....DeWitt Stern Group/
Peter Shoemaker, Anthony Pittari
Accountants ....Fried & Kowgios CPAs LLP
Comptroller ....Elliott Aronstam
Production Legal Counsel ....Lazarus & Harris LLP/
Scott R. Lazarus, Esq.; Robert C. Harris, Esq.
Payroll ....Castellana Services, Inc.
Merchandise ....Max Merchandise
Production Photographer ....Evgenia Eliseeva
Travel ....Tzell Travel/Andi Henig
Housing ....Road Concierge/Lisa Morris

CREDITS
Scenery built by Hudson Scenic Studio. Lighting provided

by Hudson Sound & Light. Sound and video equipment from Sound Associates. Costumes executed by Eric Winterling Inc., Tricorne and A.R.T. Costume Shop. Glasses by Clearlight Optical. Mr. Cranston's prosthetics by KNB EFX. Make-up coordinators, Greg Nicotero and Carey Jones. Sculptor, David Grasso. Special thanks to Bra*Tenders for undergarments and hosiery. Tuba provided by Jon Baltimore Music Company, Inc.

SPECIAL THANKS
Jeannette Hawley; A.R.T. Costume Shop; Christine Smith-McNamara; Merilee Barrera; Gail Brassard; Ray at Ray's Ragtime; Bobby From Boston Vintage Clothing; David Woolard; Sarah Holden; Rachel Padula Shufelt; Renee Blair and Ruth Goerger; museum specialists at the LBJ Library and Museum in Austin, TX.; the entire A.R.T. staff; Marcy Kamler; Ian Merrigan.

All the Way rehearsed at Roundabout Theatre Company

NEDERLANDER

Chairman ....**James M. Nederlander**
President ....**James L. Nederlander**

Executive Vice President
Nick Scandalios

Vice President   Senior Vice President
Corporate Development   Labor Relations
Charlene S. Nederlander   **Herschel Waxman**

Chief Financial Officer
Freida Sawyer Belviso

STAFF FOR THE NEIL SIMON THEATRE
Theatre Manager ....Sean M. Coughlin
Treasurer......................................Eddie Waxman
Associate Treasurer ....Marc Needleman
House Carpenter ....John Gordon
Flyman ....Michael Bennet
House Electrician ....James Travers, Sr.
House Propman ....Danny Viscardo
House Engineer ....John Astras

All the Way
SCRAPBOOK

Correspondent: Bill Timoney, "Sen. Karl Mundt" "Butler"

Opening Night Parties and/or Gifts: Our stage management staff—Matthew, James, Laura, Jeff and Sarah—put together an amazing opening night gift. Every member of the company received a mysterious box, like the anonymous box in *All the Way* that FBI Director J. Edgar Hoover mails to Coretta Scott King containing audiotapes of her husband with other women. Inside these boxes were reams of audiotape, along with gloves to avoid leaving fingerprints, and a bound handbook titled "Legal Handbook for FBI Special Agents." Written as an instruction manual with pictures of Hoover (actor Michael McKean), the book is actually a scrapbook of candid photos taken during our rehearsal process, with a scowling, disapproving Hoover haunting every page! It was a spectacular gift!

Most Exciting Celebrity Visitors: Helen Mirren wowed the company when she came backstage with her husband Taylor Hackford to visit Bryan (Hackford directed them in a movie together). Diane Lane charmed everyone backstage. A steady stream of notable celebs from both politics and media have trekked backstage. But the most exciting visitors were two men who are depicted in *All the Way*: Civil Rights activists Bob Moses and Rev. Edwin King. Both men have seen the show more than once. Both have come backstage to compliment and share their insight with the cast.

Real-Life Politician Story: When New York Senator Charles Schumer met Michael "J. Edgar Hoover" McKean backstage after the show, the Senator blurted out, "You were on 'Laverne & Shirley!'" Michael replied, "You need to see 'This Is Spinal Tap.'"

Favorite In-Theatre Gathering Place: Stage left wings.

Special Backstage Rituals: Peter Jay Fernandez ("Roy Wilkins") leads a non-denominational pre-show prayer circle just before the show starts.

Most Memorable Audience Reaction: As Bryan began his Broadway Cares/Equity Fights AIDS post-curtain speech one night, a young lady in the balcony yelled, "Mr. White!" (Bryan played "Walter White" on TV's "Breaking Bad.") The audience laughed... and then roared when Bryan responded with his "Heisenberg" alter ego's signature phrase: "Say my name!"

Worst Audience Behavior: None. They've all been great. Even the legions of "Breaking Bad" fans—many seeing a Broadway show for the first time—have been awesome! One night, a woman in the balcony unfurled a large Texas state flag—an unusual sight at a Broadway show. Many of the cast responded to her display of Lone Star patriotism with the "Hook 'Em Horns" hand signal during the company bow.

At the curtain call on opening night (front L-R:) director Bill Rauch, Bryan Cranston and playwright Robert Schenkkan.

Memorable Ad-Lib: During one of our first preview performances, John McMartin paraphrased his line "...now take a tranquilizer and get yourself some sleep" and out came "...now take an APPETIZER and get yourself some sleep." It's become the cast's rallying slogan.

Memorable Stage Door Fan Encounter: One "Breaking Bad" fan suggested Bryan play LBJ for one performance wearing his "Heisenberg" signature yellow Hazmat suit. We think the fan was kidding. We think.

Memorable Directorial Note: During the notes session before the final preview, ensemble performer Bill Timoney cracked up the cast when he raised his hand and said with a straight face, "During the curtain call bows, Bryan's always going last. Is he going to keep doing that? Because it feels like we're getting into a rut." Director Bill Rauch masterfully held a straight face while the company laughed and then responded, "Bryan will keep it fresh."

Company In-Jokes: The audience can't hear it, but, when Ethan "Johnny" Phillips as Edwin King greets Brandon Dirden as Dr. Martin Luther King, he always uses a variation of the character's name—Doc Martin, Lucky Luther...

Embarrassing Moments: "Fly-itis." So many of our male cast have accidentally walked out onto the stage with their zippers down that we now obsessively check our zippers as we make our entrances.

Favorite Moment During Each Performance: The curtain call. Audiences love this show, and it's wonderful to feel them express it.

Favorite Off-Site Hangout: The Cosmic Diner down the block on the corner of West 52nd and 8th Avenue. The prices are more like a midtown restaurant than a Jersey diner, but pre-show or post-curtain, it's just so damn convenient!

Favorite Snack Foods: Wigs supervisor Cindy keeps a bowl of Whole Foods veggie chips on the shelf next to her backstage station. She refills it daily. During one performance, Bryan looked around the stage left wings as he was about to make an entrance and saw everyone in the wings munching on those

chips. He quipped, "At least you're getting your vegetables."

Favorite Therapy: There are containers of Ricola cough drops in both wings. The crew has to re-stock the supply constantly. Runner-up: Throat Coat Tea is a presence in most of our dressing rooms.

Mascot: The quick-change dressing room area backstage right has a frequent visitor—a rat. Although he has sent dressers Jamie and Polly scurrying more than once, Jamie has affectionately named it "Splinter."

Catchphrases Only the Company Would Recognize: "Rusty Sack-Saw." In a preview performance, Senator Dick Russell's line "....just after you cut his balls off with a rusty hacksaw" came out "...with a rusty SACK-saw." Afterward, Michael McKean called it a "highly specialized surgical instrument." Several in the company have chosen "Rusty Sack-Saw" as their porn name. Runner-up: "Seat Them Now!"

Understudy Anecdote: Danny Johnson understudies several roles, including Dr. Martin Luther King, Jr. Actor Brandon Dirden (who plays MLK) has been on "baby-watch" awaiting the birth of his first child, so Danny knew he was on deck. Sure enough, Brandon's wife Crystal went into labor on a Friday evening and baby Chase arrived during Saturday's matinee. Danny went on for Brandon both shows that Saturday, delivering flawless performances!

Fastest Costume Change: Ethan "Johnny" Phillips exits stage left as LBJ's tailor, and re-enters stage right seconds later as Civil Rights activist Stanley Levison, and he does it without benefit of a backstage telephone booth. But the best costume change happens onstage: with the help of actors Betsy "Lady Bird" Aidem and Christopher Liam Moore (LBJ aide "Walter Jenkins"), Bryan gets out of bed and changes into his best presidential suit in front of the audience.

Who Wears the Heaviest/Hottest Costume: Our play takes place in 1964 America. There are twenty of us in the cast, and none of us escapes wool.

Who Wore the Least: Susannah Schulman wears a sexy slip as Dr. King's motel lover. But Bryan Cranston wears the crown of "most naked man on TV" from his numerous "in-his-skivvies" scenes on "Breaking Bad" and "Malcolm in the Middle." Those who attend *All the Way* to see Mr. Cranston in his underwear in person are not disappointed.

Coolest Thing About Being in This Show: *All the Way* is an important new play about America. But it's very cool to be on the stage as audiences discover that the show is also funny and vastly entertaining!

Annie

First Preview: October 3, 2012. Opened: November 8, 2012.
Closed January 5, 2014 after 38 Previews and 487 Performances.

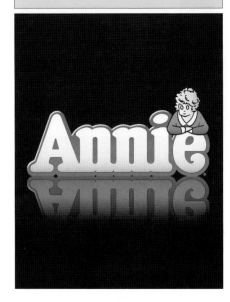

Red-headed moppet Annie suffers through life at an oppressive Depression-era orphanage run by the tyrannical Miss Hannigan. Through a lucky break Annie is chosen to spend Christmas with billionaire Oliver Warbucks, who develops a strong affection for the child and decides he wants to adopt her. She resists, insisting that her parents are alive somewhere. Miss Hannigan and her crooked brother Rooster concoct a scheme to pretend to be Annie's folks, with the aim of collecting money from Warbucks and then killing Annie. Their plot is foiled and Annie is saved—only to learn that the FBI has discovered her parents are no longer living. Warbucks steps up and adopts Annie, at last becoming her "Daddy Warbucks."

CAST

(in order of appearance)

Annie	TAYLOR RICHARDSON, SADIE SINK
Molly	EMILY ROSENFELD
Pepper	GABY BRADBURY
Duffy	TAYLOR RICHARDSON, SADIE SINK
July	AMAYA BRAGANZA
Tessie	TYRAH SKYE ODOMS
Kate	BROOKLYN SHUCK
Miss Hannigan	FAITH PRINCE
Bundles	JEREMY DAVIS
Apple Seller	JANE BLASS
Dog Catcher	GAVIN LODGE
Asst. Dog Catcher	RYAN VANDENBOOM
Stray Dog	MIKEY
Sandy	SUNNY
Lt. Ward	DENNIS STOWE
Eddie	JEREMY DAVIS

Continued on next page

₦ PALACE THEATRE

UNDER THE DIRECTION OF
STEWART F. LANE, JAMES M. NEDERLANDER AND JAMES L. NEDERLANDER

Arielle Tepper Madover   Roger Horchow   Sally Horchow   Roger Berlind   Roy Furman
Debbie Bisno   Stacey Mindich   James M. Nederlander
Jane Bergère/Daryl Roth   Eva Price/Christina Papagjika

PRESENT

THE MUSICAL
Annie

BOOK BY	MUSIC BY	LYRICS BY
Thomas Meehan	**Charles Strouse**	**Martin Charnin**

BASED ON THE COMIC STRIP "LITTLE ORPHAN ANNIE" BY HAROLD GRAY
"ANNIE" AND "LITTLE ORPHAN ANNIE" USED BY PERMISSION OF TRIBUNE MEDIA SERVICES, INC.

STARRING

Faith Prince   Anthony Warlow

AND

Taylor Richardson   Sadie Sink

WITH

Brynn O'Malley   Clarke Thorell   J. Elaine Marcos

AND

Gaby Bradbury   Amaya Braganza   Skye Alyssa Friedman
Tyrah Skye Odoms   Emily Rosenfeld   Brooklyn Shuck

Ashley Blanchet   Jane Blass   Mary Callanan   Jeremy Davis   Merwin Foard   Joel Hatch
Danette Holden   Fred Inkley   Amanda Lea LaVergne   Gavin Lodge   Desi Oakley
Keven Quillon   David Rossetti   Sarah Solie   Dennis Stowe   Ryan VanDenBoom

SCENIC DESIGN	COSTUME DESIGN	LIGHTING DESIGN	SOUND DESIGN
David Korins	Susan Hilferty	Donald Holder	Brian Ronan
PROJECTION DESIGN	**HAIR DESIGN**	**ANIMAL TRAINER**	**CASTING**
Wendall K. Harrington	Tom Watson	William Berloni	Telsey + Company Patrick Goodwin, CSA
MUSIC DIRECTOR & VOCAL ARRANGEMENTS	**ORCHESTRATIONS**	**DANCE MUSIC ARRANGEMENTS**	**MUSIC COORDINATOR**
Todd Ellison	Michael Starobin	Alex Lacamoire	Patrick Vaccariello
ADVERTISING & MARKETING	**PRESS REPRESENTATIVE**	**SPONSORSHIP**	**EXECUTIVE PRODUCER**
Serino/Coyne	Boneau/Bryan-Brown	Rose Polidoro	101 Productions, Ltd.
PRODUCTION STAGE MANAGER	**PRODUCTION MANAGER**	**ASSOCIATE CHOREOGRAPHER**	**COMPANY MANAGER**
Rachel A. Wolff	David Benken	Rachel Bress	Heidi Neven

CHOREOGRAPHY BY

Andy Blankenbuehler

DIRECTED BY

James Lapine

ORIGINALLY PRODUCED BY THE GOODSPEED OPERA HOUSE
MICHAEL P. PRICE, EXECUTIVE PRODUCER
ORIGINAL CAST RECORDING BY SHOUT! BROADWAY

7/29/13

Clarke Thorell as Rooster Hannigan and Faith Prince as Miss Hannigan dream of "Easy Street."

Photo: Joan Marcus

Annie

MUSICAL NUMBERS

ACT I

OVERTURE
"Maybe" ....Annie
"It's the Hard Knock Life" ....Annie, Orphans
"It's the Hard Knock Life" (Reprise) ....Orphans
"Tomorrow" ....Annie
"We'd Like to Thank You" ....Annie, Ensemble
"Little Girls" ....Miss Hannigan
"Little Girls" (Reprise) ....Miss Hannigan
"I Think I'm Gonna Like It Here" ....Annie, Grace, Ensemble
"N.Y.C." ....Oliver Warbucks, Grace, Annie, Lily, Ensemble
"Easy Street" ....Miss Hannigan, Rooster, Lily
"You Won't Be an Orphan for Long" ....Oliver Warbucks, Grace, Annie, Ensemble

ACT II

ENTR'ACTE
"Maybe" (Reprise) ....Annie
"You're Never Fully Dressed Without a Smile" ....Bert Healy, The Boylan Sisters
"You're Never Fully Dressed Without a Smile" (Reprise) ....Orphans
"Easy Street" (Reprise) ....Miss Hannigan, Rooster, Lily
"Tomorrow" (Reprise) ....Annie, Oliver Warbucks, F.D.R., Cabinet
"Something Was Missing" ....Oliver Warbucks
"Annie" ....Grace, Ensemble
"I Don't Need Anything But You"* ....Annie, Oliver Warbucks, Grace, Ensemble
"Maybe" (Reprise) ....Annie
"New Deal for Christmas" ....Annie, Oliver Warbucks, Grace, Orphans, Ensemble

(L-R): Taylor Richardson and Sadie Sink, the two new Annies.

Photo: Jade Albert

ORCHESTRA

Conductor: TODD ELLISON
Associate Conductor: JOEY CHANCEY
Reed 1: DAVID NOLAND
Reed 2: DAVID YOUNG
Reed 3: KENNY DYBISZ
Reed 4: RONALD JANELLI
Lead Trumpet: TREVOR NEUMANN
Trumpets: SCOTT WENDHOLT,
EARL GARDNER
Trombone: MARK PATTERSON
Bass Trombone: JEFF NELSON
Guitar/Banjo: SCOTT KUNEY
Bass: DAVE KUHN
Drums: ERIC POLAND

Percussion: JOE NERO
Piano/Keyboard: JOEY CHANCEY
Keyboard 2/Accordion: MAGGIE TORRE
Violin: JUSTIN SMITH
Cello: DIANE BARERE
Music Coordinator: PATRICK VACCARIELLO
Music Copying: Emily Grishman Music
Preparation - EMILY GRISHMAN/KATHARINE
EDMONDS
Keyboard Programmer: RANDY COHEN

Additional Orchestrations by DOUG
BESTERMAN*
and ALEX LACAMOIRE

Cast Continued

Sophie the Kettle ....AMANDA LEA LaVERGNE
Grace Farrell ....BRYNN O'MALLEY
Drake ....JOEL HATCH
Mrs. Greer ....JANE BLASS
Mrs. Pugh ....MARY CALLANAN
Cecile ....ASHLEY BLANCHET
Annette ....SARAH SOLIE
Oliver Warbucks ....ANTHONY WARLOW
Star to Be ....ASHLEY BLANCHET
Rooster Hannigan ....CLARKE THORELL
Lily ....J. ELAINE MARCOS
Bert Healy ....JEREMY DAVIS
Fred McCracken ....JOEL HATCH
Jimmy Johnson ....DENNIS STOWE
Sound Effects Man ....KEVEN QUILLON
Bonnie Boylan ....SARAH SOLIE
Connie Boylan ....AMANDA LEA LaVERGNE
Ronnie Boylan ....ASHLEY BLANCHET
Ickes ....GAVIN LODGE
Perkins ....JANE BLASS
Hull ....JEREMY DAVIS
Morganthau ....DENNIS STOWE
F.D.R. ....MERWIN FOARD
Howe ....KEVEN QUILLON
Judge Brandeis ....GAVIN LODGE

UNDERSTUDIES

For Annie: TAYLOR RICHARDSON, SADIE SINK
For Warbucks: MERWIN FOARD, JOEL HATCH
For Miss Hannigan: JANE BLASS,
    MARY CALLANAN, DANETTE HOLDEN
For Grace: AMANDA LEA LaVERGNE,
    DESI OAKLEY
For Rooster: JEREMY DAVIS, DAVID ROSSETTI
For Lily: ASHLEY BLANCHET, DESI OAKLEY
For Duffy: TAYLOR RICHARDSON, SADIE SINK
For Kate: TYRAH SKYE ODOMS
For Molly: BROOKLYN SHUCK
For Sandy: MIKEY

SWINGS

DANETTE HOLDEN, FRED INKLEY,
DESI OAKLEY, DAVID ROSSETTI

DANCE CAPTAIN

DAVID ROSSETTI

Standby for the roles of Annie, Duffy, Pepper, July and
Tessie: SKYE ALYSSA FRIEDMAN

Anthony Warlow is appearing with the permission of
Actors' Equity Association.

SETTING

New York City, December 1933

Annie

Faith Prince
Miss Hannigan

Anthony Warlow
Oliver Warbucks

Taylor Richardson
Annie/Duffy

Sadie Sink
Annie/Duffy

Brynn O'Malley
Grace Farrell

Clarke Thorell
Rooster Hannigan

J. Elaine Marcos
Lily

Gaby Bradbury
Pepper

Amaya Braganza
July

Skye Alyssa
Friedman
*Standby for Annie,
Duffy, Pepper, July,
Tessie*

Tyrah Skye Odoms
Tessie; u/s Kate

Emily Rosenfeld
Molly

Brooklyn Shuck
Kate; u/s Molly

Sunny
Sandy

Ashley Blanchet
*Cecile, Star to Be,
Ronnie Boylan*

Jane Blass
*Apple Seller,
Mrs. Greer, Perkins*

Mary Callanan
Ensemble

Jeremy Davis
*Bundles, Bert Healy,
Hull, Eddie*

Merwin Foard
F.D.R.

Joel Hatch
*Drake, Fred
McCracken*

Danette Holden
*Swing;
u/s Miss Hannigan*

Fred Inkley
*Swing; u/s F.D.R.,
Drake*

Amanda Lea
LaVergne
*Connie Boylan,
Sophie the Kettle;
u/s Grace*

Gavin Lodge
Ensemble

Desi Oakley
*Swing; u/s Grace,
Lily*

Keven Quillon
*Sound Effects Man,
Howe*

David Rossetti
Swing; u/s Rooster

Sarah Solie
*Annette,
Bonnie Boylan*

Dennis Stowe
*Lt. Ward, Jimmy
Johnson,
Morganthau*

Ryan VanDenBoom
Asst. Dog Catcher

Mikey
*Stray Dog;
u/s Sandy*

Thomas Meehan
Book

Charles Strouse
Music

Martin Charnin
Lyrics

James Lapine
Director

Annie

Andy
Blankenbuehler
Choreographer

Todd Ellison
*Music Director/
Vocal Arrangements*

David Korins
Set Design

Susan Hilferty
Costume Design

Donald Holder
Lighting Design

Brian Ronan
Sound Design

Wendall K.
Harrington
Projection Design

Tom Watson
Hair Design

Ashley Ryan
Make-up Design

William Berloni
Animal Trainer

Michael Starobin
Orchestrations

Alex Lacamoire
*Dance Music,
Arrangements*

Patrick Vaccariello
Music Coordinator

Rick Sordelet
Fight Director

Rachel Bress
*Associate
Choreographer*

Bernard Telsey
Telsey + Company
Casting

Rachel A. Wolff
*Production Stage
Manager*

Charles Underhill
Stage Manager

Mary Kathryn Flynt
*Assistant Stage
Manager*

David Benken
*Production
Management*

Wendy Orshan
101 Productions, Ltd.
General Manager

Arielle Tepper
Madover
Producer

Roger Horchow
Producer

Sally Horchow
Producer

Roger Berlind
Producer

Roy Furman
Producer

Debbie Bisno
Producer

Stacey Mindich
Producer

James M.
Nederlander
Producer

Jane Bergère
Producer

Daryl Roth
Producer

Photo: Joan Marcus

Anthony Warlow
as Oliver Warbucks

Annie

CREW
Front Row (L-R): Ron Hiatt, Graziella Zapata, Angela Simpson, Jesse Hancox, Roseanna Sharrow, Stuart Metcalf, Mary Kathryn Flynt (Assistant Stage Manager), Heidi Neven, James Cariot, Rachel A. Wolff (Stage Manager)
Second Row (L-R): Taylor Michael, Polly Noble, Meredith Benson, Amanda Grundy, Dustin Harder, Scott Westervelt, Jill A. Valentine, Bryan Odar, Patrick Eviston, Scott Anderson, Michael Carey, Shannon Slaton
Stairway (L-R): Hector Lugo, Mia Mel Rose, Douglas Earl, Cecilia Cruz, Ryan Oslak, Barry Hoff, Brendan O'Neal, Julienne Schubert-Blechman, Joshua Gericke

USHERS
(L-R): Maria Agurto, Lorraine O'Sullivan

Eva Price
Producer

Christina Papagjika
Producer

Lilla Crawford
Annie

Madi Rae DiPietro
July

Georgi James
Pepper

Junah Jang
Tessie

Jane Lynch
Miss Hannigan

Matt Wall
Dog Catcher, Ickes, Judge Brandeis

Jaidyn Young
Standby for Annie, Pepper, Duffy, July, Tessie

Jenni Barber
Grace Farrell

Tessa Grady
Star to Be, Cecile, Ronnie Boylan

Justin Greer
Lt. Ward, Jimmy Johnson, Morgenthau

Alexandra Matteo
Swing; u/s Grace, Lily

Shina Ann Morris
Connie Boylan, Sophie the Kettle

Justin Petterson
F.D.R.

Ron Raines
Oliver Warbucks

Sam Strasfeld
Sound Effects Man, Howe

Matt Wall
Lt. Ward, Jimmy Johnson, Morgenthau

Kirsten Wyatt
Lily

Annie

STAFF FOR *ANNIE*

GENERAL MANAGEMENT
101 PRODUCTIONS, LTD.
Wendy Orshan   Jeffrey M. Wilson
Elie Landau
Chris Morey
Ron Gubin

COMPANY MANAGER
Heidi Neven
Associate Company Manager: Roseanna Sharrow

GENERAL PRESS REPRESENTATIVE
BONEAU/BRYAN-BROWN
Adrian Bryan-Brown   Jim Byk
Emily Meagher   Michelle Farabaugh

PRODUCTION MANAGEMENT
BenRo PRODUCTIONS
David Benken, Rose Palombo

CASTING
TELSEY + COMPANY
Bernard Telsey CSA, Will Cantler CSA,
David Vaccari CSA,
Bethany Knox CSA, Craig Burns CSA,
Tiffany Little Canfield CSA, Rachel Hoffman CSA,
Justin Huff CSA, Patrick Goodwin CSA,
Abbie Brady-Dalton CSA,
David Morris, Cesar A. Rocha CSA,
Andrew Femenella CSA,
Karyn Casl CSA, Kristina Bramhall,
Conrad Woolfe, Amelia Nadler

Associate Director ....Wes Grantom
Production Stage Manager ....Rachel A. Wolff
Stage Manager ....Charles Underhill
Assistant Stage Manager ....Mary Kathryn Flynt
Assistant to the Company Managers ......Caitlin Clements
Fight Captain ....David Rossetti
Associate Scenic Designer ....Rod Lemmond
Assistant Scenic Designer ....Amanda Stephens
Associate Costume Designer ....Tricia Barsamian
Assistant Costume Designers ....Rebecca Lasky,
Anna Lacivita
Associate Lighting Designer ....Michael P. Jones
Assistant Lighting Designer ....Carolyn Wong
Associate Sound Designer ....Cody Spencer
Associate Projection Designers ....Daniel Brodie,
Michael Clark
Moving Light Programmer ....Richard Tyndall
Moving Lighting Tracking ....Sarah Bullock
Projection Programmer ....Paul Vershbow
Projection Researchers ....Mary Recine, Anya Klepikov,
Susan Hormuth
Projection Graphics ....Bo G. Eriksson

FIGHT DIRECTOR
Rick Sordelet

Head Carpenter ....Patrick Eviston
Automation Carpenters ....Mike Carey, Bryan Odar
Production Electrician ....Jimmy Maloney
Head Electrician ....Vince Goga
Assistant Electrician ....Jesse Hancox
Production Sound ....Nicholas Borisjuk

(L-R): Faith Prince
(Miss Hannigan) and
Emily Rosenfeld (Molly)

Photo: Joan Marcus

Head Sound Engineer ....Shannon Slaton
Production Props ....Jerry Marshall
Assistant Properties Supervisor ....Stuart Metcalf
Wardrobe Supervisor ....Scott Westervelt
Assistant Wardrobe Supervisor ....Angela Simpson
Dressers ....Meredith Benson, Cecilia Cruz, Barry Hoff,
Hector Lugo, Polly Noble, Ryan Oslak,
Julienne Schubert-Blechman
Costume Interns ......Bernadette Banner, Amanda Shafran
Hair Supervisor ....Thomas Augustine
Hair Assistants ....Josh Gericke, Mia Mel Rose
Makeup Designer ....Ashley Ryan
Assistant Makeup Designer ....Eli Aguirre
Animal Trainer ....William Berloni
Animal Handler ....Dustin Harder
Vocal Coach ....Deborah Hecht
Music Coordinator ....Patrick Vaccariello
Music Department Production
Assistant ....Scott Wasserman
Physical Therapist ....PhysioArts, Jennifer Green,
Ryanne Glasper
Keyboard Programmer ....Randy Cohen
Technical Production Assistant ....Morgan Holbrook
Production Assistants ....Michelle Heller, Derric Nolte,
Ellen Mezzera, Taylor Michael, Max Pescherine
Head Child Guardian ....Jill A. Valentine
Child Guardian ....Amanda Grundy
Children's Tutoring ....On Location Education/
Alan Simon, Jodi Green
Tutors ....Lisa Chasin, Irene Karasik
Producer's Associate ....Holly Ferguson
ATM Productions Staff...............Sam Levy, Allie Keller
Producers' Apprentice ....John Mara, Jr.
Strouse IP CEO ....Ben Strouse
Executive Producer ....Carolyn Rossi Copeland
Assistant to Mr. Strouse ....Katy Wadsworth
Assistants to Mr. Korins ....Stephen Edwards,
Emily Inglis, Sarah Wreede
Legal Counsel ....Lazarus & Harris LLP/
Scott Lazarus, Robert C. Harris, Emily Lawson
Accountant ....Fried & Kowgios, LLP
Comptroller ....Galbraith & Co./
Sarah Galbraith, Kenny Noth
Advertising ....Serino/Coyne/
Nancy Coyne, Angelo Desimini, Tom Callahan,
Matt Upshaw, Lauren Houlberg, Christina Hernandez
Interactive Marketing ....Situation Marketing/
Damian Bazadona, Chris Powers, Jeremy Kraus,
Maris Smith, Mollie Shapiro
101 Productions, Ltd. Staff.................Beth Blitzer,
Kit Ingui, Kathy Kim, Mike McLinden
Michael Rudd, David van Zyll de Jong
101 Productions, Ltd. Interns ....Simon Pincus,
Sarah Springborn

Production Photographer ....Joan Marcus
Insurance ....DeWitt Stern Group, Inc.
Immigration ....David King, Lisa Carr
Opening Night Coordination ....Serino Coyne/
Suzanne Tobak
Merchandising ....Creative Goods/Pete Milano
Banking ....City National Bank/Anne McSweeney
Payroll Services ....Checks and Balances
Theatre Displays ....King Displays, Inc.
Group Sales ....Nederlander Group Sales

www.anniethemusical.com

CREDITS
Scenery provided by PRG Scenic Technologies, Proof Productions Inc., Daedalus Design & Production Inc. Props provided by Gerrard Studios, Tom Carroll Scenery. Video projection system engineered and provided by Worldstages. Costume construction by Eric Winterling, Inc.; Tricorne, Inc.; Arel Studio, Inc.; Giliberto Designs; and Maria Ficalora Knitwear. Custom fabric printing by Gene Mignola, Inc. Custom fabric painting and distressing by Hochi Asiatico. Custom fur pieces by Fur & Furgery. Millinery by Lynne Mackey Studio and Arnold Levine, Inc. Custom footwear by LaDuca Shoes and Worldtone Dance. Undergarments and hosiery by Bra*Tenders. Newsreel footage by Historic Films Archive LLC. Orthotics by Chic Silber.

SPONSORSHIPS
The PEDIGREE® Brand, Sergeants

SPECIAL THANKS
Dave Auster, Beverly Randolph, David van Zyll de Jong, Helen Uffner Vintage Clothing and Illisa's Vintage Lingerie, Lizzie Levin, Al Roker Entertainment, Thirteen, the PEDIGREE Brand, Arren Spence, Judy Grant, Tracie Brennan, Al Roker, Shana Scott, Bruce Kallner, Sabrina Lopez, Charles Compagnone, Justin Black

Annie rehearsed at New 42nd Street Studios.

NEDERLANDER

Chairman ....**James M. Nederlander**
President ....**James L. Nederlander**

Executive Vice President
Nick Scandalios

Vice President   Senior Vice President
Corporate Development   Labor Relations
Charlene S. Nederlander   **Herschel Waxman**

Vice President   Chief Financial Officer
Jim Boese   **Freida Sawyer Belviso**

STAFF FOR THE PALACE THEATRE
Theatre Manager ....Austin Nathaniel
Treasurer ....Cissy Caspare
Assistant Treasurer ....Richard Aubrey
Carpenter ....Thomas K. Phillips
Flyman ....Robert W. Kelly
Electrician ....Eddie Webber
Property Master ....Steve Camus
Engineer ....Rob O'Connor
Chief Usher ....Gloria Hill

Annie
Scrapbook

Correspondent: Sarah Solie, "Annette"

Most Vivid Memory of the Final Performance: It felt like opening night! The house was so enthusiastic and responsive.

Memorable Quote from Farewell Stage Speech: There was no farewell speech. We treated it like a normal show.

Memorable Note, Fax or Fan Letter in the Final Weeks: Anthony Warlow, our original Warbucks, sent us some humorous and touching emails from Down Under in the last few days of the run.

Most Exciting Celebrity Visitors and What They Did/Said: Our most memorable visitor was David (Big Papi) Ortiz of the Boston Red Sox. Even the diehard Yankees fans were impressed. Everyone was very honored to meet Congresswoman Gabby Giffords. Also notable were David Grohl of Foo Fighters and Heidi Klum.

Favorite In-Theatre Gathering Place: Brynn O'Malley's dressing room.

Which Actor Performed the Most Roles in This Show?: It goes without saying that our swings performed the most roles. However, in the nightly cast, Gavin Lodge performed the most roles (12) and had the most costume changes: dock worker, dog catcher, Hoovervillian, Bergdorf shopper, random passerby, chef, chauffeur, valet, beggar, Santa Claus, Secretary of the Interior Harold Ickes and Judge Brandeis.

Special Backstage Rituals: I tap-danced in the wings every night before my entrance as the Salvation Army bell ringer. Gavin, along with dressers Hector and Ryan, would also do a few backup vocals while doing the costume change at the top of "NYC."

I also had a high-five moment in the wings at the same point of every show with Jerry Marshall, head of props. He actually wrote it into his show cues for subs, so that even if he was not there, the moment lived on.

Most Memorable Audience Reactions: I loved it when the audience applauded when Warbucks and Annie said "I love you" to each other in Act II. It happened rarely, but when it did, it always had a strong impact on me. It happened in our final show. There were also times when young audience members were not shy about warning Annie not to go with the Mudges (Lily St. Regis and Rooster) when they came to claim her at the Warbucks mansion. Some kids even screamed and cried. One night during the reprise of "Tomorrow" in the Washington cabinet scene, the audience began to clap along...on beats 1 and 3. Not

exactly the kind of tune that elicits rhythmic clapping, but...OK!

Worst Audience Behavior: There was a man sitting in one of the boxes one night who actually removed his shoes and put his feet up on the railing. At one performance, a man in the front row tried to distract our dog, Sunny, during the Hooverville scene.

Unique Pre-Show Announcement: Our pre-show announcement was given by Sandy the dog, and interpreted by a voiceover from cast member Joel Hatch.

Memorable Ad-Lib: One night Jane Lynch (as Miss Hannigan) said, "Don't get up" to FDR. That line stuck around for a while. I also recall her calling the orphans "little pig droppings" on occasion. We also loved it when Sunny (Sandy) would sing (howl) along with Annie during "Tomorrow." Dustin Harder, our dog trainer, was not pleased about this however. :-)

Memorable Directorial Note: James Lapine very often reminded us to play to the people in the balcony.

Embarrassing Moments: The 8-foot-tall stuffed giraffe in the Christmas scene fell over one night. Many of us had trouble maintaining composure. I do not admit to being one of these people. During one performance, a folding stool in Hooverville collapsed under ensemble member Jane Blass as she sat on it. Embarrassing for her; hysterical for everyone else.

Favorite Moment During Each Performance: My favorite moment was with nearly everyone on stage at the end of the

"Star to Be" solo in "NYC" as the orchestra swelled and the Roxy sign flew in overhead. It just doesn't get more Broadway than that.

Favorite Off-stage Hangout: Pretty much everyone liked Langan's. Haven rooftop bar was also a fave.

Public Relations: Best Story from the Ushers and Front-of-House Staff: A patron introduced herself to our house manager, Austin Nathaniel, during a matinee walk in. She told him how excited she was to see the show because she had taken her daughter to the original Broadway production of *Annie* in 1977! She introduced Austin to her family: her daughter, granddaughter, and her beautiful four-year-old GREAT GRAND DAUGHTER! It was her great granddaughter's very first time at a Broadway show. Four generations keeping a Broadway tradition alive at *Annie*. That's what makes this show so special.

Mascots: The dogs, of course: Sunny, Mikey and Casey King Kong

"Carols for a Cure" Carol: We recorded "Children, Go Where I Send Thee." It was arranged by assistant conductor Joey Chancey.

Catchphrases Only the Company Would Recognize: "Look at the people, look at the people." "Boom cack." "No dog in the cart." "It is BALLOONS!"

Who Wore the Heaviest/Hottest Costume?: Gavin Lodge, as Santa. Gavin is the answer to many *Annie* questions.

Who Wore the Least?: I did, as the Roxy Girl in "NYC."

Ghostly Encounters Backstage: Some people reported faucets turning on by themselves and I think our original PSM, Peter Lawrence, had a sighting in the balcony. Ensemble member Ryan VanDenBoom was alone in the dressing room one night and thought he heard a voice call, "Judy." (Ms. Garland???)

Coolest Thing About Being in This Show: Everyone says, "Never work with dogs or kids." Well, I think that was the coolest part about doing the show.

Sweethearts Within the Company: I won't divulge that, but I will say that there were two weddings and two babies born during the production.

Company In-Jokes: "So that's a change?" "So the dog is cut?"

1. Orphans entertain the summer crowd at *Broadway in Bryant Park*.
2. Cast members welcome the summer with an afternoon party at Magnolia Bakery. (L-R): Madi Rae DiPietro, Brooklyn Shuck, Sadie Sink, Jaidyn Young, Tyrah Skye Odoms, David Rossetti, Taylor Richardson, Emily Rosenfeld and Georgi James.

The Assembled Parties

First Preview: March 21, 2013. Opened: April 17, 2013.
Limited Engagement. Closed July 28, 2013 after 28 Previews and 119 Performances.

PLAYBILL®

THE ASSEMBLED PARTIES

Richard Greenberg's new drama is a portrait of four generations in the life of an Upper West Side Manhattan Jewish family. Over the course of two Christmases (that's right) two decades apart, they come together, break apart, then come together again in a new and unexpected way, bound by a palatial 14-room apartment on Central Park West, a ruby necklace that may or may not be genuine, and a love (or hate) for the central character, Julie.

CAST

(in order of appearance)

Julie	JESSICA HECHT
Jeff	JEREMY SHAMOS
Ben	JONATHAN WALKER
Mort	MARK BLUM
Shelley	LAUREN BLUMENFELD
Faye	JUDITH LIGHT
Scotty/Tim	JAKE SILBERMANN
Timmy	ALEX DREIER
Voice of Hector	GABRIEL SLOYER

TIME

Act One: Christmas Day 1980
Act Two: Christmas Day 2000

PLACE

A fourteen-room apartment on Central Park West

Manhattan Theatre Club
Samuel J. Friedman Theatre

ARTISTIC DIRECTOR
Lynne Meadow

EXECUTIVE PRODUCER
Barry Grove

PRESENTS

THE **ASSEMBLED PARTIES**

BY
Richard Greenberg

WITH

Jessica Hecht   Judith Light   Jeremy Shamos

Mark Blum   Lauren Blumenfeld

Alex Dreier   Jake Silbermann   Jonathan Walker

SCENIC DESIGN	COSTUME DESIGN	LIGHTING DESIGN	ORIGINAL MUSIC & SOUND DESIGN
Santo Loquasto	**Jane Greenwood**	**Peter Kaczorowski**	**Obadiah Eaves**

HAIR & WIG DESIGN	PRODUCTION STAGE MANAGER	CASTING
Tom Watson	**Barclay Stiff**	**Nancy Piccione**

DIRECTED BY
Lynne Meadow

ARTISTIC PRODUCER
Mandy Greenfield

GENERAL MANAGER
Florie Seery

DIRECTOR OF ARTISTIC DEVELOPMENT	DIRECTOR OF MARKETING	PRESS REPRESENTATIVE
Jerry Patch	**Debra Waxman-Pilla**	**Boneau/Bryan-Brown**

PRODUCTION MANAGER	ARTISTIC LINE PRODUCER	DIRECTOR OF DEVELOPMENT
Joshua Helman	**Lisa McNulty**	**Lynne Randall**

The Assembled Parties was commissioned through the U.S. Trust New American Play Commissioning Program.
Special thanks to the Harold and Mimi Steinberg Charitable Trust for supporting Manhattan Theatre Club.
Manhattan Theatre Club wishes to express its appreciation to Theatre Development Fund for its support of this production.

6/3/13

(L-R): Jessica Hecht, Jonathan Walker and Jeremy Shamos

Photo: Joan Marcus

Continued on next page

The Assembled Parties

Cast Continued

Stage Manager ....KELLY BEAULIEU

UNDERSTUDIES
For Ben/Mort: TONY CARLIN
For Timmy: STEPHEN McGAHAN
For Scotty/Tim/Jeff: JED ORLEMANN
For Julie/Faye/Shelley: LORI WILNER

Jessica Hecht
Julie

Judith Light
Faye

Jeremy Shamos
Jeff

Mark Blum
Mort

Lauren Blumenfeld
Shelley

Alex Dreier
Timmy

Jake Silbermann
Scotty/Tim

Jonathan Walker
Ben

Tony Carlin
u/s Ben/Mort

Stephen McGahan
u/s Timmy

Jed Orlemann
u/s Scotty/Tim/Jeff

Lori Wilner
u/s Julie/Faye/ Shelley

Richard Greenberg
Playwright

Lynne Meadow
Director/ Artistic Director Manhattan Theatre Club

Santo Loquasto
Scenic Design

Jane Greenwood
Costume Design

Peter Kaczorowski
Lighting Design

Obadiah Eaves
Original Music & Sound Design

Tom Watson
Hair & Wig Design

Barry Grove
Executive Producer Manhattan Theatre Club

2013-2014
THE TRANSFER
STUDENT

Remy Auberjonois
Jeff

Photos: Joan Marcus

(L-R): Jake Silbermann
and Judith Light

(L-R): Alex Dreier
and Jake Silbermann

(L-R): Judith Light
and Jessica Hecht

The Assembled Parties

CREW
Front Row (L-R): Andrew Braggs, Richard Klinger, Jeremy Von Deck, Andrew Belits, John Fullum
Middle Row (L-R): Jodi Jackson, Kelly Beaulieu (Stage Manager), Leah Redmond (Wardrobe Supervisor), Vaughn Preston
Back Row (L-R): Louis Shapiro (Sound Engineer), Jeff Dodson (Master Electrician), Chris Wiggins (Head Carpenter), Barclay Stiff (Production Stage Manager), Timothy Walters (Head Propertyman)

FRONT OF HOUSE
First Row (L-R): Patricia Polhill
Second Row (L-R): Lyanna Alvarado,
Sarah Crounse
Third Row (L-R): Bridget Leak, Jaime Burgos
Fourth Row (L-R): Wendy Wright, Jim Joseph
Fifth Row: Richard Ponce, Ed Brashear,
Christine Snyder
Top: Jackson Ero

The Assembled Parties

Beautiful: The Carole King Musical

First Preview: November 21, 2013. Opened: January 12, 2014.
Still running as of May 31, 2014.

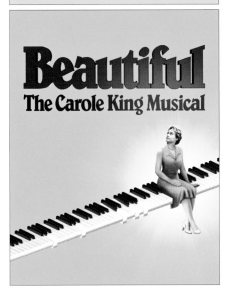

Musical biography of 1960s pop songwriter Carole King, focusing on her evolution from self-effacing studio composer to self-confident concert performer. Starting with King's first hit at age 17, the story follows her rocky marriage to lyricist Gerry Goffin, which is contrasted with the relationship of rival tunesmiths Barry Mann and Cynthia Weil. The story concludes with King's divorce and her blossoming with the 1971 solo album "Tapestry," one of the best-selling records ever. Along the way King performs "So Far Away," "You've Got a Friend," "I Feel the Earth Move" and other hits, including the title song.

CAST

(in order of appearance)

Carole King .... JESSIE MUELLER
Genie Klein .... LIZ LARSEN
Betty .... REBECCA LaCHANCE
Neil Sedaka .... KEVIN DUDA
Lucille .... CARLY HUGHES
Don Kirshner .... JEB BROWN
Gerry Goffin .... JAKE EPSTEIN
The Drifters .... E. CLAYTON CORNELIOUS,
DOUGLAS LYONS, ARBENDER J. ROBINSON,
JAMES HARKNESS
Cynthia Weil .... ANIKA LARSEN
Barry Mann .... JARROD SPECTOR
The Shirelles .... ASHLEY BLANCHET,
ALYSHA DESLORIEUX, CARLY HUGHES,
RASHIDRA SCOTT
Janelle Woods .... RASHIDRA SCOTT
Little Eva .... ASHLEY BLANCHET

Continued on next page

STEPHEN SONDHEIM THEATRE

Paul Blake   Sony/ATV Music Publishing

Jeffrey A. Sine   Richard A. Smith   Mike Bosner

Harriet N. Leve/Elaine Krauss   Terry Schnuck   Orin Wolf   Patty Baker/Good Productions   Roger Faxon
Larry Magid   Kit Seidel   Lawrence S. Toppall   Fakston Productions/Mary Solomon
William Court Cohen   John Gore   BarLor Productions   Matthew C. Blank   Tim Hogue
Joel Hyatt   Marianne Mills   Michael J. Moritz, Jr.   StylesFour Productions   Brunish & Trinchero

AND

Jeremiah J. Harris

PRESENT

Beautiful
The Carole King Musical

BOOK BY

Douglas McGrath

WORDS AND MUSIC BY

Gerry Goffin & Carole King   Barry Mann & Cynthia Weil

MUSIC BY ARRANGEMENT WITH

Sony/ATV Music Publishing

STARRING

Jessie Mueller

Jake Epstein   Anika Larsen   Jarrod Spector
Jeb Brown   Liz Larsen

Ashley Blanchet   E. Clayton Cornelious   Josh Davis   Alysha Deslorieux   Kevin Duda
James Harkness   Carly Hughes   Sara King   Rebecca LaChance   Douglas Lyons
Chris Peluso   Gabrielle Reid   Arbender J. Robinson   Rashida Scott   Sara Sheperd   Melvin Tunstall

SCENIC DESIGN	COSTUME DESIGN	LIGHTING DESIGN	SOUND DESIGN
Derek McLane	Alejo Vietti	Peter Kaczorowski	Brian Ronan

CASTING BY	WIG & HAIR DESIGN	MAKE-UP DESIGN
Stephen Kopel, CSA	Charles G. LaPointe	Joe Dulude II

ORCHESTRATIONS, VOCAL AND MUSIC ARRANGEMENTS	MUSIC SUPERVISION AND ADDITIONAL MUSIC ARRANGEMENTS
Steve Sidwell	Jason Howland

PRODUCTION STAGE MANAGER	PRODUCTION MANAGEMENT	MUSIC COORDINATOR
Peter Hanson	Juniper Street Productions, Inc.	John Miller

EXECUTIVE PRODUCERS	PRESS REPRESENTATIVE	GENERAL MANAGER
Sherry Kondor	O&M Co.	The Charlotte Wilcox Company
Christine Russell		

CHOREOGRAPHED BY

Josh Prince

DIRECTED BY

Marc Bruni

1/12/14

(L-R): Jessie Mueller as Carole King, Anika Larsen as Cynthia Weil, Jarrod Spector as Barry Mann, and Jake Epstein as Gerry Goffin.

Photo: Joan Marcus

Beautiful: The Carole King Musical

MUSICAL NUMBERS

ACT I

"So Far Away"	Carole King
"Oh Carol"	Neil Sedaka
"1650 Broadway Medley"	Ensemble
"It Might as Well Rain Until September"	Carole King
"Be-Bop-A-Lula"	Ensemble
"Some Kind of Wonderful"	Carole King, Gerry Goffin and The Drifters
"Happy Days Are Here Again"	Cynthia Weil
"Take Good Care of My Baby"	Gerry Goffin and Carole King
"Who Put the Bomp"	Barry Mann
"Will You Love Me Tomorrow"	Carole King
"He's Sure the Boy I Love"	Cynthia Weil and Barry Mann
"Will You Love Me Tomorrow"	The Shirelles
"Up on the Roof"	Gerry Goffin and The Drifters
"On Broadway"	The Drifters
"The Locomotion"	Little Eva and Ensemble
"You've Lost That Lovin' Feeling"	Barry Mann and The Righteous Brothers
"One Fine Day"	Janelle, Backup Singers and Carole King

ACT II

"Chains"	Carole King and Ensemble
"Walking in the Rain"	Barry Mann and Cynthia Weil
"Pleasant Valley Sunday"	Marilyn Wald, Gerry Goffin and Ensemble
"We Gotta Get Out of This Place"	Barry Mann
"Will You Love Me Tomorrow" (Reprise)	Carole King
"Uptown"	"Uptown" Singer and Ensemble
"It's Too Late"	Carole King
"(You Make Me Feel Like) A Natural Woman"	Carole King and Ensemble
"Beautiful"	Carole King and Company

Photo: Joan Marcus

Jessie Mueller (R) as Carole King with her backup singers at the recording session for "(You Make Me Feel Like) A Natural Woman" for the *Tapestry* album.

Cast Continued

The Righteous Brothers	JOSH DAVIS, KEVIN DUDA
"One Fine Day"	
Backup Singers	ASHLEY BLANCHET, ALYSHA DESLORIEUX, CARLY HUGHES
Nick	JOSH DAVIS
Marilyn Wald	SARA KING
"Uptown" Singer	ALYSHA DESLORIEUX
Lou Adler	KEVIN DUDA

UNDERSTUDIES

For Carole King: REBECCA LaCHANCE,
SARA SHEPERD
For Gerry Goffin: JOSH DAVIS, CHRIS PELUSO
For Cynthia Weil: SARA KING,
REBECCA LaCHANCE
For Barry Mann: KEVIN DUDA, CHRIS PELUSO
For Don Kirshner: KEVIN DUDA,
CHRIS PELUSO
For Genie Klein: SARA SHEPERD
Dance Captain: SARA SHEPERD

SWINGS

CHRIS PELUSO, GABRIELLE REID,
SARA SHEPERD, MELVIN TUNSTALL

ORCHESTRA

Conductor: JASON HOWLAND
Associate Conductor: JEFF TANSKI
Reeds: DAVID MANN, DAVE RIEKENBERG
Trumpet/Flugel: TREVOR NEUMANN
Trombone/
Bass Trombone: JENNIFER WHARTON
Guitars: JOHN BENTHAL, DILLON KONDOR
Bass: ZEV KATZ
Drums: CLINT deGANON
Percussion: JOE PASSARO
Keyboards: JASON HOWLAND, JEFF TANSKI,
NICK CHENG
Music Coordinator: JOHN MILLER
Assistant to John Miller:
JENNIFER COOLBAUGH

Jessie Mueller
Carole King

Jake Epstein
Gerry Goffin

Anika Larsen
Cynthia Weil

Jarrod Spector
Barry Mann

Jeb Brown
Don Kirshner

Liz Larsen
Genie Klein

Ashley Blanchet
*Ensemble, Shirelle,
Little Eva*

Beautiful: The Carole King Musical

E. Clayton Cornelious
Ensemble, Drifter

Josh Davis
Ensemble, Righteous Brother, Nick; u/s Gerry Goffin

Alysha Deslorieux
Ensemble, Shirelle

Kevin Duda
Ensemble, Neil Sedaka, Righteous Brother, Lou Adler; u/s Barry Mann, Don Kirshner

James Harkness
Ensemble, Drifter

Carly Hughes
Ensemble, Lucille, Shirelle

Sara King
Ensemble, Marilyn; u/s Cynthia Weil

Rebecca LaChance
Ensemble, Betty; u/s Carole King, Cynthia Weil

Douglas Lyons
Ensemble, Drifter, Stage Manager

Chris Peluso
Swing; u/s Gerry Goffin, Barry Mann, Don Kirshner

Gabrielle Reid
Swing

Arbender J. Robinson
Ensemble, Drifter

Rashidra Scott
Ensemble, Shirelle, Janelle

Sara Sheperd
Swing, Dance Captain; u/s Carole King, Genie Klein

Melvin Tunstall
Swing

Douglas McGrath
Book

Gerry Goffin
Words and Music

Carole King
Words and Music

Barry Mann
Words and Music

Cynthia Weil
Words and Music

Marc Bruni
Director

Josh Prince
Choreographer

Jason Howland
Music Supervision and Additional Music Arrangements

Derek McLane
Scenic Design

Alejo Vietti
Costume Design

Peter Kaczorowski
Lighting Design

Brian Ronan
Sound Design

Stephen Kopel
Casting

Charles G. LaPointe
Wig and Hair Design

Joe Dulude II
Make-up Design

Ana Rose Greene, Guy Kwan, Joseph DeLuise, Hillary Blanken Juniper Street Productions
Production Manager

Steve Sidwell
Orchestrations, Vocal and Music Arrangements

Sherry Kondor
Executive Producer

Christine Russell
Executive Producer

Beautiful: The Carole King Musical

John Miller
Music Coordinator

Alison Solomon
Associate Choreographer

Ross Evans
Associate Director

Charlotte Wilcox
The Charlotte Wilcox Company
General Manager

Paul Blake
Producer

Jeffrey A. Sine
Producer

Richard A. Smith
Producer

Mike Bosner
Producer

Harriet N. Leve
Producer

Elaine Krauss
Producer

Terry Schnuck
Producer

Orin Wolf
Producer

Patty Baker
Good Productions
Producer

Larry Magid
Producer

Kit Seidel
Producer

Dan Stone
Fakston Productions
Producer

Mary Solomon
Fakston Productions
Producer

John Gore
Producer

Barbara Freitag
Barlor Productions
Producer

Loraine Alterman Boyle
Barlor Productions
Producer

Matthew C. Blank
Producer

Joel Hyatt
Producer

Marianne Mills
Producer

Michael J. Moritz, Jr.
Producer

John Styles
StylesFour Productions
Producer

Dave Clemmons
StylesFour Productions
Producer

Corey Brunish
Brunish & Trinchero
Producer

Brisa Trinchero
Brunish & Trinchero
Producer

Jeremiah J. Harris
Producer

2013-2014
Beautiful
Transfer Students

Yasmeen Sulieman
Swing

Daniel Torres
Swing

Alan Wiggins
Ensemble, Drifter

Beautiful: The Carole King Musical

2013-2014 AWARDS

TONY AWARDS
Best Performance by an Actress
in a Leading Role in a Musical
(Jessie Mueller)

Best Sound Design of a Musical
(Brian Ronan)

DRAMA DESK AWARDS
Outstanding Actress
in a Musical
(Jessie Mueller)

Outstanding Featured Actress
in a Musical
(Anika Larsen)

Outstanding Sound Design
of a Musical
(Brian Ronan)

Photos: Brian Mapp

MANAGEMENT
(L-R): Jon Krause
(Stage Manager),
Peter Hanson
(Production Stage Manager),
Stacey Zaloga
(Assistant Stage Manager)

HAIR
(L-R): Patricia Marcus (Hair Supervisor), Rich Fabris (Hairdresser),
Jennifer Mooney Bullock (Assistant Hair Supervisor)

DOOR MAN
Carl Meade

BOX OFFICE
Front: Carol Nitopi
Back (L-R): Ronnie Tobia, Carlos Morris

FRONT OF HOUSE
Front Row (L-R): Travis Navarra, Molly McQuilkin (Assistant House Manager),
Johannah-Joy G. Magyawe (House Manager), Jessica Alverson, Barbara Kagan
Middle Row (L-R): Nicole Ramirez, Sarah Pauley, Karen Murray, Alix Golden, Jessica Carollo
Back Row (L-R): Tara Murphy, Eric Byrd, Adrian Ruz

Beautiful: The Carole King Musical

CREW
Kneeling (L-R): Adam Blood (Assistant Electrician/Lead Follow Spot Operator), Dorion Fuchs (Spot Operator), Nelson Vaughn (Props),
Mike Norris (Deck Automation), John H. Paull III (Head Propmaster)
Standing (L-R): Louis Igoe (Sound Engineer), Nick Borisjuk (Assistant Sound Engineer), Ron Martin (Head Electrician),
Donald "Buck" Roberts (Assistant Carpenter), Erik Hansen (Head Carpenter), Andrew Forste (House Props), Michael Pilipski (Production Propmaster)

WARDROBE
Front Row (L-R): Natalie Ferris (Dresser), Shana Albery (Assistant Wardrobe Supervisor)
Back Row (L-R): Kyle Wesson (Wardrobe Supervisor), Tara Delahunt (Dresser), Lisa Isley (Dresser), Charles Catanese (Dresser), Meghan Gaber (Dresser)

Beautiful: The Carole King Musical

STAFF FOR
BEAUTIFUL — THE CAROLE KING MUSICAL

GENERAL MANAGEMENT
CHARLOTTE WILCOX COMPANY
Matthew W. Krawiec
Dina S. Friedler   Ryan Smillie
Margaret Wilcox   Stephen Donovan   Melissa Sinaly
Ariana Orfanella

COMPANY MANAGER
Scott M. Ellis

ASSISTANT COMPANY MANAGER
Claire Trempe

GENERAL PRESS REPRESENTATIVE
O&M Co.
Rick Miramontez
Molly Barnett   Chelsea Nachman

CASTING
Stephen Kopel, CSA

PRODUCTION MANAGEMENT
JUNIPER STREET PRODUCTIONS
Hillary Blanken   Guy Kwan
Ana Rose Greene   Joseph DeLuise

Production Stage Manager .... Peter Hanson
Stage Manager .... Jon Krause
Assistant Stage Manager .... Stacey Zaloga
Dance Captain .... Sara Sheperd
Associate Director .... Ross Evans
Associate Choreographer .... Alison Solomon
Associate Scenic Designer .... Erica Hemminger
Assistant Scenic Designers .... Shoko Kambara,
Aimee Dombo
Associate Costume Designer .... Rory Powers
Assistant Costume Designer .... Leon Dobkowski
Associate Lighting Designer .... John Viesta
Assistant Lighting Designers .. Gina Scherr, Keri Thibodeau
Moving Light Programmer .... Josh Weitzman
Associate Sound Designer .... Cody Spencer
Production Carpenter .... Fred Gallo
Head Carpenter .... Erik Hansen
Advance Flyman .... Geoffrey Vaughn
Deck Automation .... Scott "Gus" Poitras
Assistant Carpenter .... Jack Anderson
Production Electricians ..... Randall Zaibek, James Fedigan
Head Electrician .... Ron Martin
Assistant Electrician/
Lead Follow Spot Operator .... Adam Blood
Advance Electrician .... Nicholas Partin
Production Propmaster .... Michael Pilipski
Head Propmaster .... John H. Paull III
Assistant Propmaster .... Diego Irizarry
Advance Sound .... Michael "Fodder" Carrico
Sound Engineer .... Louis Igoe
Assistant Sound Engineer .... Nick Borisjuk
Wardrobe Supervisor .... Kyle Wesson
Assistant Wardrobe Supervisor .... Shana Albery
Dressers .... Charles Catanese, Tara Delahunt,
Meghan Gaber, Lisa Isley
Hair Supervisor .... Patricia Marcus
Assistant Hair Supervisor .... Jennifer Mooney Bullock
Hairdresser .... Rich Fabris
Keyboard Programmer .... Billy Jay Stein
Assistant Synthesizer Programmer .... Hiro Iida

Music Preparation Services ..... JoAnn Kane Music Service/
Russ Bartmus, Mark Graham
Production Assistants ..... Lucy Kennedy, Hannah Sullivan,
Beverly Sotelo, Nick Eilerman,
Sammi Cannold, Amy Beckwith
Dialect Designer .... Amy Stoller
Legal Counsel .... Sendroff & Baruch/Jason Baruch
Accountant .... FK Partners LLP/Robert Fried
Comptroller .... Galbraith & Company/Heather Allen
Advertising .... Serino/Coyne/Nancy Coyne,
Greg Corradetti, Tom Callahan, Robert Jones,
Drew Nebrig, Ben Skinner, Vinny Sainato
Marketing .... Serino/Coyne/Leslie Barrett,
Diana Salameh, Mike Rafael, Andrea Cuevas
Interactive Marketing .... Situation Interactive/
Damian Bazadona, Tom Lorenzo,
Jeremy Kraus, Lisa Cecchini, Nina Donnard
Payroll Services .... Checks + Balances/Anthony Walker
Production Photographer .... Joan Marcus
Banking .... City National Bank/Stephanie Dalton
Insurance Broker .... Reiff and Associates, LLC/
Regina Newsom
Group Sales .... Group Sales Box Office/
Broadway.com/Groups
Merchandise .... The Araca Group
Information Management
Services .... Marion Finkler Taylor
Travel Services ... Tzell Travel/Andi Henig, Alan Braunstein

MUSIC CREDITS
"Be Bop a Lula" by Tex Davis and Gene Vincent. Sony/ATV Songs LLC (BMI) and Three Wise Boys Music LLC (BMI). **"Beautiful"** by Carole King. Colgems-EMI Music Inc. (ASCAP) **"Chains"** by Gerry Goffin and Carole King. Screen Gems-EMI Music Inc. (BMI). **"Happy Days Are Here Again"** by Milton Ager and Jack Yellen. EMI Robbins Catalog Inc. (ASCAP). Special lyrics by Douglas McGrath and Cynthia Weil. **"He's Sure the Boy I Love"** by Barry Mann and Cynthia Weil. Screen Gems-EMI Music Inc. (BMI). **"I Go Ape"** by Neil Sedaka and Howard Greenfield. Screen Gems-EMI Music Inc. (BMI) and Universal/BMG (BMI). **"It Might As Well Rain Until September"** by Gerry Goffin and Carole King. Screen Gems-EMI Music Inc. (BMI). **"It's Too Late"** by Carole King and Toni Stern. Colgems-EMI Music Inc. (ASCAP). **"Little Darlin'"** by Maurice Williams. Cherio Corporation (BMI) 100%. **"The Locomotion"** by Gerry Goffin and Carole King. Screen Gems-EMI Music Inc. (BMI). **"Love Potion #9"** by Jerry Leiber and Mike Stoller. Sony/ATV Tunes LLC (ASCAP). **"Oh Carol"** by Neil Sedaka and Howard Greenfield. Screen Gems-EMI Music Inc. (BMI) and Universal/BMG (BMI). **"On Broadway"** by Barry Mann, Cynthia Weil, Jerry Leiber and Mike Stoller. Screen Gems-EMI Music Inc. (BMI). **"One Fine Day"** by Gerry Goffin and Carole King. Screen Gems-EMI Music Inc. (BMI). **"Pleasant Valley Sunday"** by Gerry Goffin and Carole King. Screen Gems-EMI Music Inc. (BMI). **"Poison Ivy"** by Jerry Leiber and Mike Stoller. Sony/ATV Tunes LLC (ASCAP). **"So Far Away"** by Carole King. Colgems-EMI Music Inc. (ASCAP). **"Some Kind of Wonderful"** by Gerry Goffin and Carole King. Screen Gems-EMI Music Inc. (BMI). **"Splish Splash"** by Bobby Darin and Jean Murray. EMI Unart Catalog Inc. (BMI), Trio Music Co. Inc. (BMI) and Alley Music Corp. (BMI). **"Stupid Cupid"** by Neil Sedaka and Howard Greenfield. Screen Gems-EMI Music Inc. (BMI) and EMI Longitude Music (BMI). **"Take Good Care of My Baby"** by Gerry Goffin and Carole King. Screen Gems-EMI Music Inc. (BMI). **"There Goes My Baby"** by Jerry Leiber, Mike Stoller, Ben King, George Treadwell and Lover Patterson. Sony/ATV Songs LLC (BMI). **"Up on the Roof"** by Gerry Goffin and Carole King. Screen Gems-EMI Music Inc. (BMI). **"Walking in the Rain"** by Barry Mann, Cynthia Weil and Phil Spector. Screen Gems-EMI Music Inc. (BMI), EMI Blackwood Music Inc. obo Mother Bertha Music (BMI). **"We Gotta Get Out of This Place"** by Barry Mann and Cynthia Weil. Screen Gems-EMI Music Inc. (BMI). **"Who Put the Bomp"** by Barry Mann and Gerry Goffin. Screen Gems-EMI Music Inc. (BMI). **"Will You Love Me Tomorrow"** by Gerry Goffin and Carole King. Screen Gems-EMI Music Inc. (BMI). **"Yakkety Yak"** by Jerry Leiber and Mike Stoller. Sony/ATV Tunes LLC (ASCAP). **"(You Make Me Feel Like a) Natural Woman"** by Gerry Goffin, Carole King and Gerald Wexler. Screen Gems-EMI Music Inc. (BMI). **"You've Lost That Lovin' Feeling"** by Barry Mann, Cynthia Weil and Phil Spector. Screen Gems-EMI Music Inc. (BMI), EMI Blackwood Music Inc. obo Mother Bertha Music (BMI).

CREDITS
Scenery fabrication by PRG-Scenic Technologies, a division of Production Resource Group, LLC, New Windsor, NY. Show control and scenic motion control featuring Stage Command Systems® by PRG-Scenic Technologies, a division of Production Resource Group, LLC, New Windsor, NY. Additional scenery built, painted and electrified by Show Motion, Inc., Milford, CT. Lighting equipment from PRG Lighting. Audio equipment from PRG Audio. Ladies costumes by Tricorne, Inc.; Euroco Costumes, Inc.; Shana Albery; Claudia Diaz Costume Shop; Roberta Hamelin and John Cowles; Krostyne Studio; and By Barak LLC. Men's tailoring by Arel Studio, Inc. Custom knitwear by CC Wei. Props provided by Prop N Spoon LLC. Make-up provided by M•A•C.

SPECIAL THANKS
Martin Bandier, Jimmy Asci, Steven Banks, Caroline Barnard, Mark Bennett, Charles H. Googe Jr., George Lane, Jane Read Martin, Patricia Masera, Ellen Pilipski, Bruce Scavuzzo, George Sheanshang, Joshua Pilipski Pulos, Greg Holland, Carole Shorenstein Hays

To learn more about the production, please visit
www.beautifulonbroadway.com

Rehearsed at New 42nd Street Studios
and Chelsea Studios.

STEPHEN SONDHEIM THEATRE
SYDNEY BEERS   GREG BACKSTROM
General Manager   Associate Managing Director

VALERIE D. SIMMONS
Operations Manager

Katharine Croke, Assistant Managing Director

STEPHEN SONDHEIM THEATRE STAFF
House Manager .... Johannah-Joy G. Magyawe
Assistant House Manager .... Molly McQuilkin
Treasurer .... Jaime Perlman
House Carpenter .... Steve Beers
House Electrician .... Josh Weitzman
House Properties .... Andrew Forste
Assistant Treasurers .... Andrew Clements,
Carlos Morris, Ronnie Tobia
Engineer .... Deosarran
Security .... Gotham Security
Maintenance .... Juan Hernandez
Lobby Refreshments by .... Sweet Hospitality Group

Beautiful: The Carole King Musical
SCRAPBOOK

Correspondent: Kevin Duda, "Neil Sedaka"

Opening Night Party: Our opening night was held at Cipriani and was HUGE. Tons of music industry folks including Sting, Sara Bareilles, Phil Collins, Darlene Love, plus Katie Couric, Jerry Seinfeld, Thomas Roberts and many more!

Most Exciting Celebrity Visitors: Gloria Estefan came back and raved about Jessie's performance and the show as a whole. We also had Tom Hanks and Rita Wilson, Ben Vereen, Tommy Mottola, Jon Hamm, Jennifer Westfeldt, Simon Cowell and Stacy London!

Celebrity Gifts: Some great gifts have come backstage at the Sondheim. Rhea Perlman and Danny DeVito sent back goodies. Whoopi Goldberg sent cookies. Hugh Jackman sent us the sweetest note after seeing the show. He remains such a great supporter of musical theatre and Broadway in general. We were all Wolverine fans after that!

Favorite In-Theatre Gathering Places: The dressing rooms at the Sondheim are quite awesome, being a newer building. During the show, the cast can mostly be found hanging out in the stage-level dressing room of Liz Larsen or the greenroom, where we get to visit and hang with our amazing crew!

Actor Who Performed the Most Roles in This Show: I get this award. I play Sedaka, Righteous Bro and Lou.

Special Backstage Ritual: On Sundays, during the backstage singing for "Beautiful" at the end of the show, the stage left contingent does the Electric Slide. Seriously… try it. It works out strangely well. Mr. Lyons tosses his shoes into the basket before his final change… if he makes it.

Most Memorable/Worst Audience Reaction: Admittedly, we do have a catchy score. That leads to a LOT of singing along. I've listed this under "most memorable" and "worst" because it depends on who you ask in the cast.

Photo: Stephen Lovekin/Getty Images for *Beautiful*

After seeing *Beautiful*, for the first time, Carole King (front, right) joins Jessie Mueller (left) for a duet during curtain call while Liz Larsen and *Yearbook* correspondent Kevin Duda look on.

Memorable Ad-Libs: Chris Peluso and Rebecca LaChance who cover Gerry and Carole (our leading duo) were thrown on with not much rehearsal (LaChance with NONE in San Fran) —so the ad libs they HAD to use were extremely entertaining. But their performances are amazing! More memorable: off-stage, Jeb Brown seems to ad-lib his way through life. And does it brilliantly.

Memorable Stage Door Fan Encounter: One of the best moments, during a new show like this, is when fans show up with new merchandise to sign and we had NO idea we even had that thing. Case in point: we recently started selling souvenir programs and we hadn't seen them, until a fan showed up with one. We all spent WAY too long looking through some poor fan's purchase. Of course, we ran and bought our own immediately.

Memorable Directorial Note: Marc Bruni was

amazing and everyone loved this process with him. But, Doug Lyons introduced him to the term "trick bag" (look it up in the Urban Dictionary) and Marc memorably tried to use it during a notes session. It was his only bump along the journey.

Favorite Rehearsal: We had already done our out-of-town try-out in San Francisco for ten weeks in the Fall of 2013, so coming back to NYC rehearsals was just to touch up some spots and make a few changes here and there. The best surprise was to walk into that rehearsal room on Day One and have Carole King standing there. It was a complete surprise to everyone. She was so gracious and wonderful, meeting us all and answering any questions we had about our characters.

Favorite Off-Site Hangouts: This cast is very partial to BXL on 43rd, as well as Glass House Tavern, The Long Room, and Frames for Broadway Bowling! And I can't forget right here at the Sondheim for our Third Thursday party! The brainchild of Anika Larsen, we invite a different Broadway cast to come and hang with us after the third Thursday show. So far, we've enjoyed the companies of *Book of Mormon, Kinky Boots, Once* and *Bridges of Madison County*. But don't worry—you'll get your invite.

Favorite Snack Foods: You could put hay in the greenroom and it would get eaten. Seriously, this cast LOVES to eat. Josh Davis is the mix-master with organic juices flowing. Liz Larsen keeps us never wanting for snacks with all of the eats in her stage-level dressing room. On top of the Third Thursday party, there's also "Cheese Club" which takes place on the fourth Sunday night. The group (Stacey, Tara, Lisa, Pat, Nick, Louis, Liz, Jessie, Alysha, Ashley, Doug, Shep, Gabs, Rebecca, Gus, Josh, Molly & Joy) explores new and different types of cheeses. But…the first rule of "Cheese Club" is "you don't talk about cheese club." I've already said too much.

Favorite Therapy: We are so thankful that Jessica from

Photo: Joseph Marzullo

Jessie Mueller gets a visit from Whoopi Goldberg backstage at the Stephen Sondheim Theatre.

Beautiful: The Carole King Musical
SCRAPBOOK

Neurosport takes care of our bodies with PT weekly. For the voice, it's a fairly large tea-drinking cast and the fact that we are in a "certified green building" here in NYC, we get the cleanest air. (Which NONE of us are used to!) Sara King can sometimes be seen doing crazy yoga poses in nooks and crannies. And, even though we don't dance constantly, you'll find PT rollers/balls (heh heh...balls) in every dressing room.

Pit Stop: Best Story from the Orchestra: Jason Howland, our Musical Supervisor and Music Director, loves a good subtle joke during a show or backstage. There is this great "train whistle" during "Locomotion" that somehow has made it to be the last thing you hear in the curtain call music. And, because it's the last thing heard, sometimes they have a little fun with it. Enough said.

Public Relations: O&M Co., our press team, is awesome! They always set us up for success and manage to keep us entertained whenever they visit!

Mascot: Jason Howland was Doug Lyons's Secret Santa this year and gave him a gorgeous aquarium which sits on Doug's dressing room spot. He bought four black fish and named them James, Alan, Douglas and E. Clay, a.k.a. "The Drifters." Seems right.

Tales from the Put-In: Peter Hanson (PSM) runs a fantastic ship and has made it so that, so far (fingers crossed), we haven't had to do any put-ins. Ask me this question when we are in year four.

Nicknames: Anika Larsen is ";" ("semi-colon") because of her near-death surgery story when we first started rehearsals (Google it!). Sara Sheperd (our Dance Captain) is "Shep,"

More backstage visitors: Front (L-R): Jarrod Spector, Liz Larsen and Jeb Brown Back (L-R): Jessie Mueller, Jennifer Westfeldt, Jon Hamm, James Harkness, Jake Epstein, Sara King

Gabrielle Reid, our female swing, is "Gabs."

Fastest Costume Change: Pretty sure Jessie's first costume change is the fastest. She goes from Carnegie Hall (a.k.a. Carole at 30) to The Klein Home (a.k.a. Carole at 16) in about 30 seconds. The Shirelles (Carly, Rashidra, Alysha and Ashley) drop layers extra fast for their rehearsal-to-stage transition. Also, Ashley Blanchet technically has the fastest on-stage change from Little Eva to Locomotion Eva. Both are awesome feats of stagecraft!

Who Wore the Heaviest/Hottest Costumes: The Drifters have to underdress their "On Broadway" costumes under their "Up on the Roof" costumes—so that makes those probably the heaviest. Hottest goes to Jarrod, Jessie, Anika and Jake in their "Vermont" entrance clothes—where they dress for the falling snow.

Who Wore the Least: Sara King as that hussy, home-wrecker Marilyn, wears a nightie when she spoils the show.

Web Buzz: Our show was a real unknown entity before we came in, so a lot of the buzz was geared towards "how are they gonna tell the story using

Photos: Joseph Marzullo

the music?" We were all relieved to read a lot of great press about the show which simultaneously praised not only Jessie on her magical portrayal of Carole King, but also for our creative team: Doug McGrath who wrote such a sharp story around these monstrous hits, Bruni who was able to give it style and class, and Josh Prince, who took the movement of the period that you thought you knew, and turned it all around to make it fresh and exciting. The Internet was very kind to us, initially calling us another "jukebox" musical, but settling on the very apropos feat of being a play with these substantial musical moments.

Ghostly Encounters Backstage: Personal story here: your contributor had stayed late one night at the theatre, walked up to the stage door and realized that I had forgotten something in my dressing room. I noticed the old "Henry Miller" sign, which hangs over our security desk at the stage door, as I returned to the elevator to go back downstairs. I murmured, under my breath, "Wow, I wonder what Henry Miller thinks of his sign being relegated to the stage door?" And the elevator bounced. And stopped. I was stuck. I screamed for about five minutes and finally, Adolf, our head of security, came to my rescue and pried the doors open. I have NEVER said Henry Miller's name in this theatre again.

Coolest Thing About Being in This Show: We get to hear these amazing songs as the soundtrack to our workplace. They never get old. We just recorded the cast album and now these amazing arrangements by Jason Howland and orchestrations by Steve Sidwell will live on forever!

Recording the cast album (L-R): Carly Hughes, Ashley Blanchet, Alysha Deslorieux, Rashidra Scott

Recording the cast album (L-R): Douglas Lyons, Alan Wiggins, James Harkness, E. Clayton Cornelious.

Betrayal

First Preview: October 1, 2013. Opened: October 27, 2013.
Limited Engagement. Closed January 5, 2014 after 29 Previews and 83 Performances.

PLAYBILL

Pinter's drama about a love triangle formed when a man conducts a love affair with his best friend's wife. The story is told more or less in reverse chronology, beginning in 1977 with a reunion of the wife and her former lover, and moving backward to the affair's end, the apparent discovery of the affair, the full flowering of the affair and finally the affair's beginning in 1968. The final scene contains revelations that raise questions about the entire rest of the story.

CAST

Robert ....DANIEL CRAIG
Emma ....RACHEL WEISZ
Jerry ....RAFE SPALL
Waiter ....STEPHEN DeROSA

Rafe Spall appears with the support of Actors' Equity Association pursuant to an exchange program between American Equity and UK Equity.

UNDERSTUDIES

For Robert: ANTONY HAGOPIAN
For Emma: LUCY TAYLOR
For Jerry: ALEX MOGGRIDGE

SCENE 1
1977. A Pub. Spring.

SCENE 2
1977 Later. Jerry's House. Study. Spring.

SCENE 3
1975. Flat. Winter.

Continued on next page

Continued on next page

---

⑤ ETHEL BARRYMORE THEATRE

243 West 47th Street
A Shubert Organization Theatre

Philip J. Smith, *Chairman*   **Robert E. Wankel,** *President*

SCOTT RUDIN   BARRY DILLER   ELI BUSH   JON B. PLATT   ROGER BERLIND
SCOTT M. DELMAN   ROY FURMAN   JOHN GORE   STEPHANIE P. MCCLELLAND
SONIA FRIEDMAN / TULCHIN BARTNER   THE ARACA GROUP   RUTH HENDEL
HENI KOENIGSBERG   DARYL ROTH

EXECUTIVE PRODUCERS
JOEY PARNES   S.D. WAGNER   JOHN JOHNSON

PRESENT

DANIEL CRAIG
RACHEL WEISZ
RAFE SPALL

DIRECTED BY
MIKE NICHOLS

A PLAY BY
HAROLD PINTER

BETRAYAL

SCENIC DESIGN IAN MACNEIL   COSTUME DESIGN ANN ROTH
LIGHTING DESIGN BRIAN MACDEVITT   SOUND DESIGN SCOTT LEHRER
ORIGINAL MUSIC JAMES MURPHY   VIDEO DESIGN FINN ROSS
HAIR, WIGS & MAKEUP CAMPBELL YOUNG & LUC VERSCHUEREN
UK CASTING ANNE MCNULTY   US CASTING CINDY TOLAN
PRODUCTION STAGE MANAGER JILL CORDLE   COMPANY MANAGER PENELOPE DAULTON
PRODUCTION MANAGEMENT AURORA PRODUCTIONS
PRESS REPRESENTATIVE BONEAU/BRYAN-BROWN

10/27/13

Daniel Craig
as Robert

Rachel Weisz
as Emma

Rafe Spall
as Jerry

Photos: Brigitte Lacombe

Betrayal

Photo: Brigitte Lacombe

Daniel Craig and
Rachel Weisz

Scenes Continued

SCENE 4
1974. Robert and Emma's House.
Living Room. Autumn.

SCENE 5
1973. Hotel Room. Venice. Summer

SCENE 6
1973 Later. Flat. Summer.

SCENE 7
1973 Later. Restaurant. Summer

SCENE 8
1971. Flat. Summer.

SCENE 9
1968. Robert and Emma's House.
Bedroom. Winter.

Daniel Craig
Robert

Rachel Weisz
Emma

Rafe Spall
Jerry

Stephen DeRosa
Waiter

Antony Hagopian
u/s Robert

Alex Moggridge
u/s Jerry

Lucy Taylor
u/s Emma

Harold Pinter
Playwright

Mike Nichols
Director

Ian MacNeil
Scenic Design

Ann Roth
Costume Design

Brian MacDevitt
Lighting Design

Scott Lehrer
Sound Design

James Murphy
Original Music

Finn Ross
*Projection/Video
Design*

Campbell Young
Campbell Young
Associates
*Hair, Wigs &
Make-up Design*

Luc Verschueren
Campbell Young
Associates
*Hair, Wigs &
Make-up Design*

Gene O'Donovan
Aurora Productions
*Production
Management*

Ben Heller
Aurora Productions
*Production
Management*

Scott Rudin
Producer

Barry Diller
Producer

Betrayal

(L-R) Rafe Spall and Daniel Craig

Photo: Brigitte Lacombe

Jon B. Platt
Producer

Roger Berlind
Producer

Scott M. Delman
Producer

Roy Furman
Producer

John Gore
Producer

Stephanie P. McClelland
Producer

Sonia Friedman
Producer

Norman Tulchin
Tulchin/Bartner
Producer

Michael Rego, Hank Unger, Matthew Rego
The Araca Group
Producer

Ruth Hendel
Producer

Heni Koenigsberg
Producer

Daryl Roth
Producer

Joey Parnes
Executive Producer

S.D. Wagner
Executive Producer

John Johnson
Executive Producer

Photo: Brian Mapp

CREW
Front Row (L-R): Rafe Spall (Actor), David Stollings (Sound)
Middle Row (L-R): Matt Maloney (House Electrician), Kathryn L. McKee (Assistant Stage Manager), Laura Beattie (Dresser), Valarie Shea (Props), Andrea Gonzalez (Dresser), Daniel Craig (Actor), Anthony Ferrer (Props)
Back Row (L-R): Brian Dawson (Electrics), Joseph Hickey (Dresser), Jason Clark (Carpenter), Jill Cordle (Production Stage Manager), Philip Feller (House Props), Carmel Vargyas (Hair & Make-up), Morgan R. Holbrook (Stage Manager), Linda Lee (Wardrobe Supervisor), Stephen DeRosa (Actor), Mike Cole (Security), Penelope Daulton (Company Manager)

Betrayal

FRONT OF HOUSE
Front Row (L-R): John Barbaretti, Sherry McIntyre,
Dan Landon (House Manager)
Second Row (L-R): Alexandra Zavilowicz, Lori McElroy,
Carmen Walker, Kim Pollard
Third Row (L-R): Julie Smith
Fourth Row (L-R): David McElroy, John Dancy
Back Row (L-R): Julia Pazimino, Julie Lugo, Justin Roman

BOX OFFICE
Diane Heatherington,
Chuck Loesche

STAFF FOR *BETRAYAL*

SCOTT RUDIN PRODUCTIONS
Robert Hoffman   Marjon Javadi   Chris McEwen
Daniel Piepenbring   Melody Ramnath   David Rogers
Jason Sack   Dan Sarrow   Jason Shrier

GENERAL MANAGEMENT
JOEY PARNES PRODUCTIONS
Joey Parnes
S.D. Wagner   John Johnson
Jillian Robbins

COMPANY MANAGER
Penelope Daulton

PRODUCTION MANAGEMENT
AURORA PRODUCTIONS, INC.
Gene O'Donovan   Ben Heller   Chris Minnick
Jarid Sumner   Anthony Jusino   Anita Shah
Liza Luxenberg   Rachel London   David Cook
Bridget Van Dyke   Melissa Mazdra   Cat Nelson

PRESS REPRESENTATIVE
BONEAU / BRYAN-BROWN
Chris Boneau   Jim Byk   Kelly Guiod

SCENIC DESIGN SUPERVISION
Edward Pierce

MUSIC CREDITS
Music performed and arranged by
James Murphy and Jeremy Turner.

Production Stage Manager ....Jill Cordle
Stage Managers ...Morgan R. Holbrook, Kathryn L. McKee
Assistant Director ....Colleen O'Donnell
Management Associate ....Jillian Robbins
Casting Associate ....Adam Caldwell, CSA
Associate Costume Designer ....Matthew Pachtman
Research Assistant to Ms. Roth ....Debbe DuPerrieu
Associate Lighting Designer ....Jen Schriever
Associate Sound Designers .....Drew Levy, Alex Neumann
Associate Projection Designer ....Brian Beasley

Assistant Scenic Designers ....Nick Francone,
     Stephen Davan, Jennifer Price Fick
Assistant Lighting Designers ....Joel E. Silver,
     Peter Hoerburger
Model Construction ....Akiko Kosaka,
     Robert Sweetnam, Jerome Martin
Production Carpenter ....Jason Clark
Production Properties ....Kathy Fabian, Mike Smanko
Production Electrician ....Dan Coey
Automation ....Erik Yans
Head Props ....Neil Rosenberg
Head Electrician ....Brian Dawson
Head Sound ....David Stollings
Moving Light Programmer ....Michael Hill
Watchout Programmer ....Peter Acken
Video Technician ....Christopher Kurtz
Wardrobe Supervisor ....Linda Lee
Mr. Craig's Dresser ....Andrea Gonzalez
Ms. Weisz's Dresser ....Laura Beattie
Mr. Spall's Dresser ....Joseph Hickey
Hair Supervisor ....Carmel Vargyas
Film Editor ....Bill Henry
Music Editor ....Suzana Peric
Film/Video Research &
     Clearance ....Search Works Research
     Roxanne Mayweather
Film/Video Research ....Mridu Chandra
Production Assistants ....Shelley Miles, Greg Tate
Legal Counsel ......Loeb & Loeb, LLP, Seth Gelblum, Esq.
Accountant ...Marks Paneth & Shron, Mark A. D'Ambrosi,
     Patricia M. Pedersen, Ruthie Skochil
Advertising ....Serino/Coyne, Inc., Scott Johnson
Creative Advertising Design &
     Website ....BLT Communications, Inc.
Banking.....................................City National Bank
     Stephanie Dalton, Michele Gibbons
Insurance ....AON / Albert G. Ruben,
     George Walden, Claudia B. Kaufman
Opening Night Coordinator ......The Lawrence Company
     Michael Lawrence
Payroll Services ....Castellana Services, Inc.
     Lance Castellana, James Castellana, Norman Sewell
Immigration ....Traffic Control Group
Production Photographer ....Brigitte Lacombe

CREDITS
Scenery and scenic effects built, painted and automated by
Show Motion, Inc. Milford, Connecticut. Automation and
show control by Show Motion, Inc. using the AC2
Computerized Motion Control System. Lighting equipment
from PRG Lighting. Sound and video equipment from
Sound Associates, Inc. Props by Paper Mache Monkey,
Jeremy Lydic, R. Ramos Upholstery and SFDS. Ms. Weisz's
costumes by Lynne Baccus. Men's tailoring by Leonard
Logsdail. Custom beading by Douglas Esselmann.

Rehearsed at the New 42nd Street Studios and the Clark
Studio Theatre at Lincoln Center for the Performing Arts.

www.BetrayalBroadway.com

 THE SHUBERT ORGANIZATION, INC.
Board of Directors

Philip J. Smith	**Robert E. Wankel**
Chairman	President
Wyche Fowler, Jr.	**Diana Phillips**
Lee J. Seidler	**Michael I. Sovern**

Stuart Subotnick

Chief Financial Officer ....Elliot Greene
Sr. Vice President, Ticketing ....David Andrews
Vice President, Finance ....Juan Calvo
Vice President, Human Resources ....Cathy Cozens
Vice President, Facilities ....John Darby
Vice President, Theatre Operations.............Peter Entin
Vice President, Marketing ....Charles Flateman
Vice President, General Counsel ....Gilbert Hoover
Vice President, Audit ....Anthony LaMattina
Vice President, Ticket Sales ....Brian Mahoney
Vice President, Creative Projects ............D.S. Moynihan
Vice President, Real Estate ....Julio Peterson

Staff for The Ethel Barrymore
House Manager ....Dan Landon

Betrayal
SCRAPBOOK

Correspondent: Stephen DeRosa, "Waiter"

Memorable Note, Fax or Fan Letter: When movie stars are on Broadway you can expect a LOT of fan mail coming to the theatre. What amazed me was that Daniel and Rachel often received caricatures done by fans. Some quite elaborate and framed. Lovely gesture, but a bit too much.

Opening Night Parties and Gifts: Our opening was incredibly star studded, attended by the likes of Steven Spielberg, Julia Roberts and Bruce Springsteen, just to name a few. Mike Nichols gave engraved flasks to the cast. And the producers gave engraved silver key chains for the flat in Kilburn where the affair from the play takes place.

Most Exciting Celebrity Visitor and What They Did/Said: There were so many celebrity guests who came to see our show I can't name them all. But for me, getting to meet Barbra Streisand AND Madonna?!?!?! Yes, DeRosa, some dreams can come true.

Favorite In-Theatre Gathering Place: Notes were always in Rachel's dressing room, but the boys relaxed after the show on the steps in the alleyway with a beer and a smoke.

Special Backstage Rituals: Nightly there are many. Particularly Rachel counting to 20 on one breath. Or Rafe sitting in the Pub. Or Daniel's occasional primal scream. There's Lucky Friday and Sunday Brunch. But I was most proud of Saturday Night on Broadway! Where, at half hour I, DeRosa, ran around the theatre dressed as a character from a different Broadway show each night. (See photos on this page.) Anything for a laugh....

Favorite Backstage Antics: Magic snowflakes on stage right.

Most Memorable Audience Reaction: Complete silence after the final curtain for almost a minute. Even when the curtain rose, they took a breath before applauding, then flew to their feet. It first happened on November 21, but happened a few more times after.

Most Memorable Audience Behavior: During a preview a woman got into an aggressive altercation with another patron; she was then escorted to the lobby. Within the same week, in same seat locations, a patron violently threw up. (Are these seats cursed?)

The-Show-Must-Go-On Moment: During one show, the set malfunctioned and after a half hour of deliberation the cast and crew

rallied and we performed the show with limited sets moved on and off by crew members. The audience stayed with the show and the story was told as beautifully as ever despite the prolonged scene changes. A true "show must go on" moment in the Broadway tradition.

Memorable Stage Door Fan Encounter: When a crazed fan chased our prop man down the street thinking he was Daniel Craig.

Memorable Directorial Note: "More Carol Channing."

Favorite Moment During Each Performance: Pre-show dance party on the third floor.

Favorite Snack Foods: KIND bars. Clementines.

Mascot: MIKE COLE.

Catchphrase Only the Company Would Recognize: "Smash the Gary!!"

Coolest Thing About Being in This Show: Everything!!

Yearbook correspondent Stephen DeRosa all dressed up for Saturday Night on Broadway, letting loose his:
1. Inner Annie.
2. His Dolly Levi.
3. The Mustache Guild (clockwise from L): Morgan R. Holbrook (Stage Manager), Kathryn L. McKee (Stage Manager), correspondent Stephen DeRosa, Jill Cordle (Production Stage Manager).
4. His merry murderess from *Chicago*.
5. And his animal nature for *The Lion King*.

Big Fish

First Preview: September 5, 2013. Opened: October 6, 2013.
Closed December 29, 2013 after 34 Previews and 98 Performances.

New musical based on the 2003 film of the same title about a young man who sets out to discover how much truth there was to the tall tales his traveling-salesman father has been telling all his life about his amazing childhood, the courtship of his wife, his time in a circus, his military exploits in wartime, and his alleged encounters with a giant, a witch, a mermaid and other magical creatures large and small—including a monster catfish.

CAST

Edward Bloom	NORBERT LEO BUTZ
Will Bloom	BOBBY STEGGERT
Sandra Bloom	KATE BALDWIN
Young Will	ZACHARY UNGER
(at Wed. and Sat. matinees)	ANTHONY PIERINI
Josephine Bloom	KRYSTAL JOY BROWN
Karl	RYAN ANDES
Amos Calloway	BRAD OSCAR
Don Price	BEN CRAWFORD
The Witch	CIARA RENÉE
Jenny Hill	KIRSTEN SCOTT
Girl in the Water	SARRAH STRIMEL
Dr. Bennett	JC MONTGOMERY
Zacky Price	ALEX BRIGHTMAN
Dancing Fire	BRYN DOWLING
The Alabama Lambs	ROBIN CAMPBELL, LARA SEIBERT
Mayor	TALLY SESSIONS
Fisherman	CARY TEDDER

Continued on next page

NEIL SIMON THEATRE

UNDER THE DIRECTION OF JAMES M. NEDERLANDER AND JAMES L. NEDERLANDER

Dan Jinks   Bruce Cohen   Stage Entertainment USA
Roy Furman   Edward Walson   James L. Nederlander
Broadway Across America/Rich Entertainment Group   John Domo

IN ASSOCIATION WITH

Parrothead Productions   Lucky Fish   Peter May/Jim Fantaci   Harvey Weinstein/Carole L. Haber
Dancing Elephant Productions   CJ E&M   Ted Liebowitz   Ted Hartley   Clay Floren   Columbia Pictures

PRESENT

BigFish

BOOK BY
John August

MUSIC & LYRICS BY
Andrew Lippa

Based on the novel *Big Fish* by Daniel Wallace
and the Columbia Pictures film screenplay by John August

STARRING

Norbert Leo Butz   Kate Baldwin   Bobby Steggert

AND

Krystal Joy Brown   Anthony Pierini   Zachary Unger
Ryan Andes   Ben Crawford   Brad Oscar

WITH

JC Montgomery   Ciara Renée   Kirsten Scott   Sarrah Strimel

Preston Truman Boyd   Bree Branker   Alex Brightman   Joshua Buscher
Robin Campbell   Bryn Dowling   Jason Lee Garrett   Leah Hofmann   Synthia Link
Angie Schworer   Lara Seibert   Tally Sessions   Cary Tedder   Ashley Yeater

SCENIC DESIGN **Julian Crouch**	COSTUME DESIGN **William Ivey Long**	LIGHTING DESIGN **Donald Holder**	SOUND DESIGN **Jon Weston**
PROJECTION DESIGN **Benjamin Pearcy for 59 Productions**	WIG AND HAIR DESIGN **Paul Huntley**	MAKE-UP DESIGN **Angelina Avallone**	CASTING **Tara Rubin Casting**
DANCE MUSIC ARRANGEMENTS **Sam Davis**	MUSIC COORDINATOR **Michael Keller**		VOCAL ARRANGEMENTS & INCIDENTAL MUSIC **Andrew Lippa**
ADVERTISING & INTERACTIVE MARKETING **SpotCo**	PRESS REPRESENTATIVE **The Hartman Group**	ASSOCIATE DIRECTOR **Jeff Whiting**	ASSOCIATE CHOREOGRAPHER **Chris Peterson**
PRODUCTION MANAGEMENT **Aurora Productions**	PRODUCTION SUPERVISOR **Joshua Halperin**	COMPANY MANAGER **David van Zyll de Jong**	GENERAL MANAGER **101 Productions, Ltd.**

ORCHESTRATIONS
Larry Hochman

MUSIC DIRECTION
Mary-Mitchell Campbell

DIRECTION AND CHOREOGRAPHY BY
Susan Stroman

The producers wish to express their appreciation to the Theatre Development Fund for its support of this production.

10/6/13

Norbert Leo Butz and Zachary Unger (C) and Company in "Be the Hero."

Photo: Paul Kolnik

Big Fish

MUSICAL NUMBERS

ACT I

By the Banks of a River
"Prologue" ....Orchestra
Outside the Rehearsal Dinner
Will's Bedroom
"Be the Hero" ....Edward and Company
The Swamp
"The Witch" ....The Witch, Edward and Company
Wedding Reception
Doctor's Office in NYC/Doctor's Office in Alabama
Central Park
"Stranger" ....Will
The Backyard
"Two Men" ....Sandra
Ashton Town Square
"Ashton's Favorite Son" ....Company
A Cave
"Out There on the Road" ....Edward, Karl, Jenny Hill and Company
The Calloway Circus
"Little Lamb From Alabama" ....Sandra and Alabama Lambs
"Time Stops" ....Edward and Sandra
"Closer to Her" ....Amos, Edward and Company
Auburn University
"Daffodils" ....Edward and Sandra

ACT II

Scout Campsite
"Red, White and True" ....Sandra, Edward and Company
Edward and Sandra's Bedroom
"Fight the Dragons" ....Edward and Young Will
"Showdown" ....Will, Edward and Company
"I Don't Need a Roof" ....Sandra
Jenny Hill's House
Ashton Town Square
"Start Over" ....Edward, Don, Amos, Karl and Company
Hospital
"What's Next" ....Will, Edward and Company
"How It Ends" ....Edward
The River's Edge
"Be the Hero" (Reprise) ....Will

ORCHESTRA

Conductor: MARY-MITCHELL CAMPBELL
Associate Conductor: SHAWN GOUGH
Reeds: CHARLES PILLOW,
RICHARD WALBURN
Trumpet: DYLAN SCHWAB
French Horn: DAVID BYRD-MARROW
Violin: CENOVIA CUMMINS
Viola: LIUH-WEN TING
Cello: SUMMER BOGGESS

Keyboard 1: DAVID GARDOS
Keyboard 2: SHAWN GOUGH
Guitars: JIM HERSHMAN, ALEC BERLIN
Bass: BRIAN HAMM
Drums: PERRY CAVARI
Percussion: BILLY MILLER
Music Coordinator: MICHAEL KELLER
Synthesizer Programmer: JAMES ABBOTT
Music Preparation: Kaye-Houston Music

Cast Continued

Wedding Guests, New Yorkers, Citizens of Ashton,
Circus Performers ....BREE BRANKER,
ALEX BRIGHTMAN, ROBIN CAMPBELL,
BRYN DOWLING, JASON LEE GARRETT,
LEAH HOFMANN, JC MONTGOMERY,
CIARA RENÉE, ANGIE SCHWORER,
KIRSTEN SCOTT, LARA SEIBERT,
TALLY SESSIONS, SARRAH STRIMEL,
CARY TEDDER

SWINGS
PRESTON TRUMAN BOYD,
JOSHUA BUSCHER, SYNTHIA LINK,
ASHLEY YEATER

UNDERSTUDIES
For Edward:
BEN CRAWFORD, TALLY SESSIONS
For Sandra:
KIRSTEN SCOTT, LARA SEIBERT
For Will:
ALEX BRIGHTMAN, CARY TEDDER
For Josephine:
BREE BRANKER, LARA SEIBERT
For Karl:
PRESTON TRUMAN BOYD, TALLY SESSIONS
For Amos:
PRESTON TRUMAN BOYD, TALLY SESSIONS
For Don:
PRESTON TRUMAN BOYD,
JOSHUA BUSCHER
For Dr. Bennett:
PRESTON TRUMAN BOYD,
JOSHUA BUSCHER
For Zacky:
JOSHUA BUSCHER, CARY TEDDER
For The Witch:
BRYN DOWLING, SYNTHIA LINK
For Girl in the Water:
SYNTHIA LINK, ASHLEY YEATER
For Jenny:
BRYN DOWLING, SYNTHIA LINK
For Mayor:
PRESTON TRUMAN BOYD,
JOSHUA BUSCHER

DANCE CAPTAINS
JOSHUA BUSCHER, ASHLEY YEATER

FIGHT CAPTAIN
JOSHUA BUSCHER

LOCATION
ALABAMA

Big Fish

Norbert Leo Butz
Edward Bloom

Kate Baldwin
Sandra Bloom

Bobby Steggert
Will Bloom

Krystal Joy Brown
Josephine Bloom

Anthony Pierini
Young Will

Zachary Unger
Young Will

Ryan Andes
Karl

Ben Crawford
Don Price

Brad Oscar
Amos Calloway

JC Montgomery
Dr. Bennett

Ciara Renée
The Witch

Kirsten Scott
Jenny Hill

Sarrah Strimel
Girl in the Water

Preston Truman Boyd
Swing

Bree Branker
Ensemble

Alex Brightman
Zacky Price

Joshua Buscher
Dance Captain, Swing

Robin Campbell
Ensemble

Bryn Dowling
Ensemble

Jason Lee Garrett
Ensemble

Leah Hofmann
Ensemble

Synthia Link
Swing

Angie Schworer
Ensemble

Lara Seibert
Ensemble

Tally Sessions
Mayor

Cary Tedder
Ensemble

Ashley Yeater
Dance Captain, Swing

Andrew Lippa
Music & Lyrics

John August
Book

Susan Stroman
Director/ Choreographer

Daniel Wallace
Novel

Julian Crouch
Scenic Design

William Ivey Long
Costume Design

Donald Holder
Lighting Design

Paul Huntley
Wig & Hair Design

Big Fish

Benjamin Pearcy
59 Productions
Projection Design

Mary-Mitchell
Campbell
*Music Director/
Conductor*

Larry Hochman
Orchestrations

Sam Davis
*Dance
Arrangements*

Michael Keller
Music Coordinator

Jeremy Chernick
Special Effects

Thomas Schall
Fight Director

Kate Wilson
Dialect Coach

Jeff Whiting
Associate Director

Chris Peterson
*Associate
Choreographer*

Shawn Gough
*Associate Music
Director/Conductor*

Joshua Halperin
*Production
Supervisor*

Tara Rubin
Tara Rubin Casting
Casting

Gene O'Donovan
Aurora Productions
*Production
Management*

Ben Heller
Aurora Productions
*Production
Management*

Wendy Orshan
101 Productions, Ltd.
*General
Management*

Dan Jinks
Producer

Bruce Cohen
Producer

Joop van den Ende
Stage Entertainment
USA, Inc.
Producer

Roy Furman
Producer

Edward Walson
Producer

James L.
Nederlander
Producer

John Gore
Broadway Across
America
Producer

Mindy Rich
Rich Entertainment
Group
Producer

Bob Rich
Rich Entertainment
Group
Producer

John Domo
Producer

Wendy Federman
Lucky Fish
Producer

Ricardo F. Hornos
Lucky Fish
Producer

Carl Moellenberg
Lucky Fish
Producer

Mary Beth O'Connor
Lucky Fish
Producer

Lou Spisto
Lucky Fish
Producer

Peter May
Producer

Harvey Weinstein
Producer

Carole L. Haber
Producer

Antonio Marion
Dancing Elephant
Productions
Producer

Big Fish

Kate Baldwin sings "I Don't Need a Roof" to Norbert Leo Butz.

Photo: Paul Kolnik

Michael J. Moritz, Jr.
Dancing Elephant Productions
Producer

Van Dean & Kenny Howard
Dancing Elephant Productions
Producer

Vincent Palumbo
Dancing Elephant Productions
Producer

Byeong Seok Kim
CJ E&M
Producer

Ted Hartley
Producer

Clay Floren
Producer

BOX OFFICE
Erich Stollberger, Dawn Bentley

STAGE MANAGEMENT
(L-R): Jason Brouillard (Stage Manager), Joshua Halperin (Production Supervisor), Rachel Miller Davis (Assistant Stage Manager)

COMPANY MANAGEMENT
Katie Pope, David van Zyll de Jong

Photos: Brian Mapp

FRONT OF HOUSE
Front Row (L-R): Marisol Olavarria, Gracelyn Darbasie, Dorothy Marquette, Robyn Corrigan, Daisy Irizarry, Jean Manso, Jane Publik
Middle Row (L-R): Sean M. Coughlin (Theatre Manager), Helen-Michell Schecter, Christopher Langdon, Evelyn Olivero, Joseph V. Melchiorre, David Eschinger, Kim Raccioppi, Joanne Decicco
Back Row (L-R): Dana Diaz, Mariea Crainiciuc, Eddie Cuevas, Joann Thomas, Marion L. Mooney

Big Fish

Photo: Brian Mapp

CREW

Front Row (L-R): Danny Viscardo (House Propman), Rob Ward (Assistant Properties Supervisor), John J. Kelly, Ron Schwier (Head Electrician/Associate Production Electrician), David Elmer, Brian Munroe (Production Carpenter), Sean McGrath
Back Row (L-R): James Cariot (Properties Supervisor), Chuck Fields, Mitch Christenson, Scott Mecionis, Stephen Vessa, Timothy A. Perry (Automation Carpenter/Deck), Michael Bennet (Flyman), Tommy Schultz, Charles Grieco, Carin Ford (Sound Engineer), John Gordon (House Carpenter)

STAFF FOR *BIG FISH*

GENERAL MANAGEMENT
101 PRODUCTIONS, LTD.
Wendy Orshan   Jeffrey M. Wilson
Elie Landau   Ron Gubin   Chris Morey

COMPANY MANAGEMENT
David van Zyll de Jong   Katie Pope

PRESS REPRESENTATION
THE HARTMAN GROUP
Michael Hartman   Wayne Wolfe   Colgan McNeil

PRODUCTION MANAGEMENT
AURORA PRODUCTIONS, INC.
Gene O'Donovan   Ben Heller
Chris Minnick   Jarid Sumner   Anita Shah
Anthony Jusino   Liza Luxenberg   Rachel London
David Cook   Bridget Van Dyke
Melissa Mazdra   Cat Nelson

CASTING
TARA RUBIN CASTING
Tara Rubin CSA, Eric Woodall CSA
Merri Sugarman CSA, Kaitlin Shaw CSA
Lindsay Levine CSA, Scott Anderson

Production Supervisor ....Joshua Halperin
Stage Manager ....Jason Brouillard
Assistant Stage Manager ....Rachel Miller Davis
Assistant Company Manager ....Katie Pope
Assoc. Director/Asst. Choreographer ....Jeff Whiting
Resident Choreographer/Director ....Chris Peterson
Stroman Productions Producer ....Scott Bishop
Dance Captains ....Joshua Buscher, Ashley Yeater
Fight Captain ....Joshua Buscher
Associate Scenic Designer ....Frank McCullough
Assistant Scenic Designers...Lauren Alvarez, Stephen Davan
Associate Costume Designer ....David Kaley
Assistant Costume Designer ....Sarah Cubbage
Costume Assistants ....Angela Harner, Stephanie Levin
Costume Intern ....Whitley S. Floyd
William Ivey Long Studio Director ....Donald Sanders
Associate Wig & Hair Designers ....Edward J. Wilson,
Giovanna Calabretta

Associate Makeup Designer ....Jorge Vargas
Associate Lighting Designer ....Caroline Chao
Assistant Lighting Designer ....Heather Graff
Moving Light Tracking .. Aaron Porter, Porsche McGovern
Assistant to the Lighting Designer ....Eunjung Choi
Associate Sound Designer ....Jason Strangfeld
Assistant Sound Designer ....Sean Foote
Projection Animator ....Lawrence Watson

FIGHT DIRECTOR
Thomas Schall

PUPPETRY DESIGN
Will Pike

SPECIAL EFFECTS DESIGN
Jeremy Chernick

Puppetry Assistants ....Jessica Scott, Pat McNichol
Special Effects Assistant ....Ben Hagen
Production Carpenter ....Brian Munroe
Automation Carpenter (Deck) ....Timothy A. Perry
Automation Carpenter (Fly) ....David Elmer
Production Electrician ....Jimmy Maloney
Head Electrician/
    Associate Production Electrician ....Ron Schwier
Assistant Electricians ....Renee Alaksa, Joel Dunham
Automated Lighting Programmer ....Richard Tyndall
Video Programmer ....Zach Peletz
Video Technician ....Daniel Mueller
Production Sound Engineer ....Phil Lojo
Associate Production Sound Engineer ......Charlie Grieco
Sound Engineer ....Carin Ford
Deck Audio ....Jason Strangfeld
Production Properties Coordinator ....Peter Sarafin
Properties Supervisor ....James Cariot
Assistant Properties Supervisor ....Rob Ward
Wardrobe Supervisor ....Douglas Petitjean
Assistant Wardrobe Supervisor ....Deirdre LaBarre
Dressers/Wardrobe Staff........Irma Brainard, Scotty Cain,
Fran Curry, Tracey Diebold, Karen Eifert, Maggie Horkey,
Raven Jakubowski, Samantha Lawrence, Erick Medinilla,
Jeannie Naughton, John Rinaldi, Roy Seiler, Mark Trezza
Hair Supervisor ....Edward J. Wilson
Assistant Hair Supervisor ....Steven Kirkham
Hairdressers ....Eric Hatch, Daniel Koye

Associate Music Director/Conductor ....Shawn Gough
Additional Orchestrations ....Bruce Coughlin
Additional Drum Arrangements ....Perry Cavari
Music Copying ....Kaye-Houston Music/
Anne Kaye, Doug Houston
Music Coordinator ....Michael Keller
Electronic Music Programmer ....James Abbott
Music Department Production Assistant ......David Reiser
Music Assistant to Mr. Lippa ....Daniel Green
Personal Assistant to Mr. Lippa ....Robb Nanus
Music Department Intern ....Roberto Sinha
Physical Therapy ....PhysioArts
Orthopaedist ....David S. Weiss, M.D./
NYU Langone Medical Center
Production Assistants ....Colyn Fiendel, Sarah Helgesen,
Mark A. Stys, Andrew J. White
Dialogue Coach ....Kate Wilson
Stilt Consultant ....Mark Mindek
Unicycle Consultant ....Kyle Peterson
Child Guardian ....Felicia Velasco
SDC Observer ....Amber Mak
Legal Counsel ....Levine Plotkin & Menin, LLP/
Loren Plotkin, Susan Mindell, Cris Criswell
Accountant ....Marks, Paneth & Shron LLP/
Christopher Cacace, Jana Jevnikar
Advertising ....SpotCo/Drew Hodges, Ilene Rosen,
Tom Greenwald, Nick Pramik, Kyle Young,
Stephen Sosnowski, Beth Watson, Corey Schwitz
Marketing and Promotions ....SpotCo/Kristen Rathbun,
Julie Wechsler, Emily Hammerman, Sara Barton
Assistant to the General Managers ....Michael Rudd
101 Productions, Ltd. Staff...Beth Blitzer, Mark Gagliardi,
Rebecca Habel, Richard Jones, Kathy Kim, Steve Supeck
101 Productions, Ltd. Interns ....Lionel Christian,
Justin Coffman, Benjamin Lowy,
Geoffrey Weiss, Jenna Wisch
Production Photographer ....Paul Kolnik
Press Representative Staff ....Nicole Capatasto,
Tom D'Ambrosio, Whitney Holden Gore, Bethany Larsen,
Emily McGill, Leslie Papa, Matt Ross, Frances White
Insurance ....DeWitt Stern Group, Inc.
Merchandising ....Creative Goods/Pete Milano
Banking ....City National Bank/Anne McSweeney
Travel ....The A Team at Tzell Travel/Andi Henig
Housing..Road Rebel Entertainment Touring, ABA-IDEAL

Big Fish

Tutoring Services ....On Location Education
Tutor ....Christine Carino
Payroll Services ....Checks and Balances
Assistant to Mr. Jinks ....Chase Clements
Assistant to Mr. Cohen ....Jessica Leventhal

STAGE ENTERTAINMENT USA, INC.

CEO ....Bill Taylor
Vice President of Sales & Marketing ....Michele Groner
CFO & Director of Business Affairs.......Adam Silberman
Associate Producer ....Eric Cornell
Asst. Marketing Manager ....Whitney Britt
Executive Assistants ....Katrin Kausek, Allyson Backus
Production Assistant ....Scott Hedley

Rehearsed at the New 42nd Street Studios

CREDITS

Scenery and scenic effects built, painted and electrified by Show Motion, Inc., Milford, CT. Automation and show control by Show Motion, Inc., Milford, CT, using the AC2 Computerized Motion Control System. Prop units and hand props fabricated by Tom Carroll Scenery, Daedalus Production and Design, Jerard Studios, Craig Grigg, Jeremy Lydic, Buist Bickley, Anna Light, James Cariot, Rob Ward and Peter Sarafin. Military backpacks supplied by Jim Korn

and KSI NYC. Lighting equipment and sound equipment provided by PRG, Secaucus, NJ. Projection equipment provided by Sound Associates, Yonkers, NY. Costumes constructed by Tricorne, Inc., Jennifer Love Costumes, Timberlake Studios Inc., Artur & Tailors, Euroco Costumes Inc., Katrina Patterns, Scafati Tailors. Specialty costumes by Spandexman, Custom Uniform Company, Varsity Sports Apparel, Jerard Studio, Maria Ficalora Knitwear, Ltd. Shoes by LaDuca Shoes, Celebrity Dance Shoes, Capezio, Sansha. Millinery by Rodney Gordon Ltd., Arnold S. Levine, Inc. Fabric painting and printing by Jeff Fender Studio, Inc., Dyenamix. Undergarments provided by Bra*Tenders.

Andrew Lippa plays Yamaha pianos.

Guitars courtesy of Gibson Brands, Inc.

SPECIAL THANKS

Dave Auster, Ashley Berman, Kit Ingui, Stuart Levy, Walt Kiskaddon, Lory Yan, Jim Aquino, Michael Lynton, Amy Pascal, Andrea Giannetti, Bill Rosenfield, Gary Gunas, John Logan, George Cohen, Ben Jehoshua, Michael Passaro, Nick Nantell, David Bloch, Gene Elm - Amalgamated Vintage, Alice Lindholm - Right to the Moon Alice, Sara Kay, Stephen Schwartz, Mike McLinden, Justin Black, Mike Martinez, Lou Raizin, Eileen LeCario, Suzanne Bizer

Chairman ....James M. Nederlander
President ....James L. Nederlander
Executive Vice President
Nick Scandalios

Vice President•   Senior Vice President•
Corporate Development   Labor Relations
Charlene S. Nederlander   **Herschel Waxman**

Chief Financial Officer
Freida Sawyer Belviso

STAFF FOR THE NEIL SIMON THEATRE

Theatre Manager ....Sean M. Coughlin
Treasurer..Eddie Waxman
Associate Treasurer ....Marc Needleman
House Carpenter ....John Gordon
Flyman..Michael Bennet
House Electrician ....James Travers, Sr.
House Propman ....Danny Viscardo
House Engineer ....John Astras

ORCHESTRA
Front Row (L-R): Liuh-Wen Ting, Jim Hershman, Cenovia Cummins
Middle Row (L-R): Shawn Gough, Rick Walburn, Tim McCarthy, Barbara Merjan, Billy Miller, Dylan Schwab
Back Row (L-R): Charity Wicks-Depinto, Alec Berlin, Brian Hamm, David Gardos, Jennifer DeVore

HAIR/WIG
Front: Edward J. Wilson (Hair Supervisor)
Back (L-R): Steven Kirkham (Assistant Hair Supervisor), Jason Demers, Eric Hatch (Hairdressers)

WARDROBE
Front Row (L-R): Mark Trezza, Douglas Petitjean (Wardrobe Supervisor), Samantha Lawrence, Scotty Cain, Katie Chick, Jeannie Naughton
Back Row (L-R): Deirdre LaBarre (Assistant Wardrobe Supervisor), Raven Jakubowski, Ali Maher Barclay, Fran Curry, John Rinaldi, Maggie Horkey, Amy Nielson, Terry LaVada
Not pictured: Roy Seiler, Erick Medinilla

Big Fish
SCRAPBOOK

Correspondent: Leah Hofmann, Ensemble

Memorable Note, Fax or Fan Letter: Our cast has received several notes from fans expressing how much the story of *Big Fish* has deeply moved them, even helping mend loss in their own lives. It is clear that *Big Fish* offers very relatable, universal themes of forgiveness, legacy and love.

Opening Night Parties and/or Gifts: Our very own Ryan Andes, a.k.a. Karl the Giant, made hand-crafted brass fish pendants for the entire cast and creative team. Talk about a one-of-a-kind catch! (See photo on next page!)

Most Exciting Celebrity Visitors: Geoffrey Rush, Hugh Jackman, John Lithgow and Anna Wintour (in her sunglasses) were all very exciting, but Kristin Chenoweth joined us backstage after she hugged her friend Norbert. Through her happy tears she exclaimed, "You know, you really should have people pay for the ticket as they leave the theater. You'll get more money that way."

Favorite In-Theatre Gathering Place: It's the Wardrobe room, home to the (in)famous Wine and Cheese gatherings on select Thursday evenings.

Actor Who Performed the Most Roles in This Show: Cary Tedder, with 17 costume changes (most cast members have at least 13-14 changes). Cary plays 15 characters every night.

Special Backstage Rituals: As Norbert and Kate sing "Daffodils" onstage, Bree Branker helps out the crew by riding the circus tricycle to its backstage home while dodging three elephant butts.

Favorite Backstage Photo: I enjoy the photo (on the next page) of Bree Bear with Zachary Unger as the Little Clown. And I don't think any explanation is needed.

Most Memorable Audience Reaction: Our production definitely brings out the "ugly cry" in some people, most often the male audience members. As Norbert says in our Broadway

Cares Collection speech, "*Big Fish*: the show where middle-aged men come to cry like little girls at *Wicked*."

Worst Audience Behavior: I recall someone bringing their baby and sitting in the front row. At least she was a very cute baby.

Unique Pre-Show Announcement: Instead of a verbal announcement, we used to have an instrumental cacophony of ringing cell phones that escalated and ended with a "PLOP!" into our onstage theatrical river.

Memorable Ad-Lib: During one night of our Chicago out-of-town tryout, Norbert as Edward Bloom admired all of the beautiful

red-haired characters walking past him in the college scene, and he added, "There are a lot of redheads at this school." Then he read the university sign, realizing, "Oh, duh. I get it. Auburn University." The audience roared, and the line was added into the script.

Memorable Press Encounter: Before we started rehearsals again in August, Norbert Leo Butz, Kate Baldwin, Susan Stroman and William Ivey Long were joined by the ensemble women for a *Vanity Fair* photo shoot at the Martha Graham Studio. It had been a couple months since we had all seen each other in Chicago. Before we got dressed, I remember an impromptu run-through of our tap number, "Red, White and True," in front of the mirrors. I was excited that I remembered the dance steps and felt honored to be included with this fantastic group of performers.

Memorable Stage Door Fan Encounter: I always love when stage door fans ask if I'm Kate Baldwin. Don't know if Kate would feel the same...:-)

Memorable Directorial Note: "If I could lock you all in an ivory tower, and let you out in time for the show, I would."——Stro before opening night.

Company In-Joke: "Mr. Callowaaaaaay."

Embarrassing Moments: In honor of SNOB (aka Saturday Night on Broadway), the ensemble men stormed out of the stage door in their skivvies one night at five minutes to places

1. (L-R): Julian Crouch, Norbert Leo Butz, Andrew Lippa, Susan Stroman and Kate Baldwin at the curtain call on opening night.
2. (L-R): *Yearbook* Correspondent Leah Hofmann and Bree Branker's tribute to the charity Movember.
3. Jason Lee Garrett gets a hand from his dresser, Roy Seiler.
4. Leah Hofmann as "Corna DeKobb" and Tally Sessions as "Mayor Naise."

Big Fish
SCRAPBOOK

in hopes of giving our neighbors at *Jersey Boys* a little "pre-show" chant and dance. Unbeknownst to them, Susan Stroman was also outside the stage door. She quickly and lovingly scolded the boys to get back inside for the show. "Ah! Mom's here!" shouted cast member Alex Brightman. Unfortunately/thankfully it was all caught on video by the *Jersey Boys* stage crew.

Favorite Moment During Each Performance: Personally, my favorite moment onstage is as the Popcorn Gal falling in love with the Magician across the circus, the entire sequence performed within the slow-motion during the song "Time Stops." As for the offstage moment, I love exercising with Lara Seibert in our elephant butt puppets.

Favorite Off-Site Hangout: I always seem to find someone from the cast at Chipotle on Eighth Avenue. Otherwise, Kirsten Scott, a.k.a. Jenny Hill, offers a lovely humble abode and hangout at her nearby apartment.

Favorite Snack Foods: Did I mention Chipotle?

Favorite Therapy: Amy's Bread Birthday Cake.

Pit Stop—Best Story From the Orchestra: We don't get to see them very much, as they are located upstage in our unique bandstand, but we do have the pleasure of watching our musical director Mary-Mitchell Campbell on the monitor. And she is one talented lady, often conducting the entire orchestra and performing a hip hop dance at the same time.

Public Relations—Best Story from the Ushers and Front-of-House Staff: One time we heard that during the show a group of female patrons were mixing Red Bulls and vodka while sitting in their seats at the back of the house. Those ladies know how to party!

Mascot: Mudgie the Cat. Unfortunately, Mudgie's role in *Big Fish* was severely

diminished as the show moved from Chicago to Broadway. I guess that's showbiz, kid (or kitten).

Catchphrases Only the Company Would Recognize: "New Game." "Much Respect." "Mom's Here!" (Wait—I already told you that one.)

Best In-House Parody Lyrics: In our opening number, "Be the Hero of Your Story" turns into "Be the Weirdo of Your Story."

Tales from the Put-In: That would be the absence of a put-in for Ben Crawford going on as Edward Bloom mid-show in early October. Stellar.

Understudy Anecdote: I don't know about you all, but I'm always impressed by the stilt skills of our boys Preston Truman Boyd and Tally Sessions who understudy Karl the Giant. Talk about being multi-"tall"ented.

Nicknames: Bree Bear, Mayor Naise, Big Busch and Corna DeKobb. Then there's Clown Robin, always sung to the jingle of the restaurant chain "Red Robin."

Fastest Costume Change: All of them. But all joking aside, it's Bryn Dowling twirling/transforming centerstage into the Dancing Fire with the help of her fellow showgirls.

Who Wore the Heaviest/Hottest Costume: I'd like to think it's my western bustle and skirt for the musical number "Showdown," but I believe Bree Branker wins this one with the bear costume.

Who Wore the Least: Hands down, it's Sarrah Strimel as the Mermaid. And no complaints from any parties involved. She looks incredible.

Web Buzz: This has been the first production I have been involved with that utilizes to such

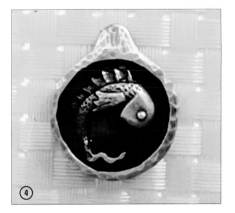

extent the power of social media. Whether on Facebook, Twitter or Instagram, it's encouraging to read the support and compliments of our fans, and the impact the show has had on their lives. It was great to see how excited people were when we opened or when we announced our cast album. The social media offers an easy forum for people who may not have the chance to write a formal note and send it to the powers that be. It truly catapults the idea of "word-of-mouth" advertising. It will be intriguing to see where the pros and cons of social media advertising take Broadway shows in the future.

Coolest Thing About Being in This Show: This is a remarkable, passionate company of creative artists. And now we can all say that we were in the original company of a Susan Stroman Broadway Musical. Pretty cool.

Fan Club Info: John August is our genius book writer, not to mention a top-notch Hollywood

screenwriter. (He also wrote the screenplay for the movie *Big Fish*.) From day one he has been our cheerleader, and he never ceases to support us. You can follow him and his brilliance on Twitter and Instagram, @johnaugust. You can also follow us on the *Big Fish* on Broadway Facebook page, Twitter and Instagram @bigfishbroadway.

1. Things get a little "hairy" backstage as Lara Seibert and Ryan Andes adjust their precious wigs (with a little help from their friends).
2. Backstage with Zachary Unger (Little Dot Clown) and Bree Branker (Bree Bear).
3. Kirsten Scott prepares to go on as the Fish Bowl Juggler.
4. Hand-crafted brass fish pendant, the opening night gift from Ryan Andes (Karl the Giant).

The Book of Mormon

First Preview: February 24, 2011. Opened: March 24, 2011.
Still running as of May 31, 2014.

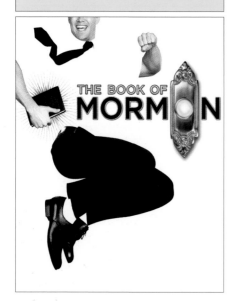

PLAYBILL®

Elder Price, the smartest, most devout and most handsome young Mormon in missionary school, is stunned to find himself assigned, not to Orlando, Florida, as he had prayed, but to a small, miserable village in Africa. He's also shocked to find himself partnered with his dorkiest missionary classmate, Elder Cunningham. Things go from bad to worse—until Cunningham starts making up his own additions to the Mormon Bible.

CAST

(in order of appearance)

Mormon ....JASON MICHAEL SNOW
Moroni ....MATT LOEHR
Elder Price...............................MATT DOYLE
Elder Cunningham ....CODY JAMISON STRAND
Missionary Training Center Voice ...LEWIS CLEALE
Price's Dad ....LEWIS CLEALE
Cunningham's Dad ..............K.J. HIPPENSTEEL
Mrs. Brown ....ANASTAĆIA McCLESKĒY
Guards ....TERREN WOOTEN CLARKE,
                                 JOHN ERIC PARKER
Mafala Hatimbi....................MICHAEL POTTS
Nabulungi ....ASMERET GHEBREMICHAEL
Elder McKinley ....MATT LOEHR
Joseph Smith ....LEWIS CLEALE
General.....................................RYAN ALLEN
Doctor ....TOMMAR WILSON
Mission President ....LEWIS CLEALE
Ensemble....................SCOTT BARNHARDT,
        JACOB ben WIDMAR, DARLESIA CEARCY,
                        TERREN WOOTEN CLARKE,
        CHRISTIAN DELCROIX, K.J. HIPPENSTEEL,

Continued on next page

𝄖 EUGENE O'NEILL THEATRE

A JUJAMCYN THEATRE

JORDAN ROTH, *President*
ROCCO LANDESMAN, *President Emeritus*
PAUL LIBIN, *Executive Vice President* JACK VIERTEL, *Senior Vice President*

ANNE GAREFINO   SCOTT RUDIN

ROGER BERLIND   SCOTT M. DELMAN   JEAN DOUMANIAN
ROY FURMAN   IMPORTANT MUSICALS   STEPHANIE P. McCLELLAND
KEVIN MORRIS   JON B. PLATT   SONIA FRIEDMAN PRODUCTIONS

EXECUTIVE PRODUCER STUART THOMPSON

PRESENT

THE BOOK OF MORMON

BOOK, MUSIC AND LYRICS BY

TREY PARKER, ROBERT LOPEZ AND MATT STONE

WITH

MATT DOYLE   CODY JAMISON STRAND

ASMERET GHEBREMICHAEL   MATT LOEHR   MICHAEL POTTS

LEWIS CLEALE   RYAN ALLEN   SCOTT BARNHARDT   JACOB ben WIDMAR
NYK BIELAK   GRAHAM BOWEN   DARLESIA CEARCY   TERREN WOOTEN CLARKE
CHRISTIAN DELCROIX   DELIUS DOHERTY   JEFF HEIMBROCK   K.J. HIPPENSTEEL
TYSON JENNETTE   CLARK JOHNSEN   MATTHEW MARKS   ANASTAĆIA McCLESKĒY
JOHN ERIC PARKER   CHRISTOPHER RICE   BRIAN SEARS   KYLE SELIG   ALLISON SEMMES
JASON MICHAEL SNOW   LAWRENCE STALLINGS   MAIA NKENGE WILSON
TOMMAR WILSON   CANDICE MARIE WOODS

SCENIC DESIGN	COSTUME DESIGN	LIGHTING DESIGN	SOUND DESIGN
SCOTT PASK	ANN ROTH	BRIAN MacDEVITT	BRIAN RONAN

HAIR DESIGN	ORCHESTRATIONS	CASTING	PRODUCTION STAGE MANAGER
JOSH MARQUETTE	LARRY HOCHMAN & STEPHEN OREMUS	CARRIE GARDNER	KAREN MOORE

DANCE MUSIC ARRANGEMENTS	MUSIC DIRECTION	MUSIC COORDINATOR	ASSOCIATE PRODUCER
GLEN KELLY	CIAN McCARTHY	MICHAEL KELLER	ELI BUSH

MARKETING DIRECTOR	PRESS REPRESENTATIVE	PRODUCTION MANAGEMENT	GENERAL MANAGEMENT
STEVEN CARDWELL	BONEAU/ BRYAN-BROWN	AURORA PRODUCTIONS	STP/DAVID TURNER

MUSIC SUPERVISION AND VOCAL ARRANGEMENTS

STEPHEN OREMUS

CHOREOGRAPHED BY

CASEY NICHOLAW

DIRECTED BY

CASEY NICHOLAW AND TREY PARKER

10/1/13

Syesha Mercado as Nabulungi and
Ben Platt as Elder Cunningham

Photo: Joan Marcus

The Book of Mormon

Cast Continued

CLARK JOHNSEN, ANASTAĆIA McCLESKĒY,
JOHN ERIC PARKER, BRIAN SEARS,
JASON MICHAEL SNOW,
LAWRENCE STALLINGS,
MAIA NKENGE WILSON, TOMMAR WILSON,
CANDICE MARIE WOODS

UNDERSTUDIES
For Elder Cunningham: BRIAN SEARS
For Missionary Training Center Voice/Price's
Dad/Joseph Smith/Mission President:
JACOB ben WIDMAR, GRAHAM BOWEN,
CHRISTIAN DELCROIX
For Mafala Hatimbi: TYSON JENNETTE,
JOHN ERIC PARKER
For Nabulungi: ALLISON SEMMES,
CANDICE MARIE WOODS
For Elder McKinley: SCOTT BARNHARDT,
GRAHAM BOWEN, BRIAN SEARS
For the General: DELIUS DOHERTY,
TYSON JENNETTE, JOHN ERIC PARKER

Standbys for Elder Price:
K.J. HIPPENSTEEL, KYLE SELIG
Standby for Elder Cunningham: NYK BIELAK

SWINGS
GRAHAM BOWEN, DELIUS DOHERTY,
JEFF HEIMBROCK, TYSON JENNETTE,
MATTHEW MARKS,
CHRISTOPHER RICE, ALLISON SEMMES

Resident Dance Captain: GRAHAM BOWEN
Assistant Dance Captain: SCOTT BARNHARDT

ORCHESTRA
Conductor: CIAN McCARTHY
Associate Conductor: ADAM BEN-DAVID

Keyboards: CIAN McCARTHY,
ADAM BEN-DAVID
Guitars: JAKE SCHWARTZ
Bass: DAVE PHILLIPS
Drums/Percussion: SEAN McDANIEL
Reeds: BRYAN CROOK
Trumpet: RAUL AGRAZ
Trombone: RANDY ANDOS
Violin/Viola: ENTCHO TODOROV

Music Coordinator: MICHAEL KELLER
Keyboard Programmer: RANDY COHEN
Copyist: Emily Grishman Music Preparation

Matt Doyle
Elder Price

Cody Jamison Strand
Elder Cunningham

Asmeret
Ghebremichael
Nabulungi

Matt Loehr
Elder McKinley

Michael Potts
Mafala Hatimbi

Lewis Cleale
*Missionary Training
Center Voice/Price's
Dad/ Joseph Smith/
Mission President*

Ryan Allen
General

Scott Barnhardt
Ensemble

Jacob ben Widmar
Ensemble

Nyk Bielak
*Standby Elder
Cunningham*

Graham Bowen
*Swing, Resident
Dance Captain*

Darlesia Cearcy
Ensemble

Terren Wooten Clarke
Ensemble

Christian Delcroix
Ensemble

Delius Doherty
Swing

Jeff Heimbrock
Swing

K.J. Hippensteel
*Ensemble; Standby
Elder Price*

Tyson Jennette
Swing

Clark Johnsen
Ensemble

Matthew Marks
Swing

The Book of Mormon

Anastácia McCleskĒy
Ensemble

John Eric Parker
Ensemble

Christopher Rice
Swing

Brian Sears
Ensemble

Kyle Selig
Standby Elder Price

Allison Semmes
Swing

Jason Michael Snow
Ensemble

Lawrence Stallings
Ensemble

Maia Nkenge Wilson
Ensemble

Tommar Wilson
Ensemble

Candice Marie Woods
Ensemble

Trey Parker
Co-Director, Book, Music, Lyrics

Robert Lopez
Book, Music, Lyrics

Matt Stone
Book, Music, Lyrics

Casey Nicholaw
Co-Director and Choreographer

Scott Pask
Scenic Design

Ann Roth
Costume Design

Brian MacDevitt
Lighting Design

Brian Ronan
Sound Design

Stephen Oremus
Music Director/ Vocal Arranger/ Co-Orchestrator

Larry Hochman
Co-Orchestrator

Josh Marquette
Hair Design

Randy Houston Mercer
Makeup Design

Carrie Gardner, C.S.A.
Casting

Glen Kelly
Dance Arrangements

Michael Keller
Music Coordinator

Jennifer Werner
Associate Director

John MacInnis
Associate Choreographer

Gene O'Donovan
Aurora Productions
Production Management

Ben Heller
Aurora Productions
Production Management

Karen Moore
Production Stage Manager

Michael P. Zaleski
Assistant Stage Manager

Brian Usifer
Associate Music Supervisor

Cian McCarthy
Music Direction

David Turner
General Manager

The Book of Mormon

Anne Garefino
Producer

Scott Rudin
Producer

Roger Berlind
Producer

Scott M. Delman
Producer

Jean Doumanian
Producer

Sonia Friedman
Sonia Friedman
Productions, Ltd.
Producer

Roy Furman
Producer

Stephanie P.
McClelland
Producer

Kevin Morris
Producer

Jon B. Platt
Producer

Stuart Thompson
Executive Producer

Will Blum
*Standby for Elder
Cunningham*

Kevin Duda
*Cunningham's Dad,
Ensemble*

Brian Tyree Henry
General

Carly Hughes
*Mrs. Brown,
Ensemble*

David Hull
Ensemble

Nikki M. James
Nabulungi

Stanley Wayne
Mathis
Mafala Hatimbi

Benjamin Schrader
Ensemble

Michael James Scott
Doctor, Ensemble

Stephen Christopher
Anthony
Mormon, Ensemble

Daxton Bloomquist
Swing

Daniel Breaker
Mafala Hatimbi

Rob Colletti
*Standby for Elder
Cunningham*

Kevin Duda
*Cunningham's Dad,
Ensemble*

Camille
Eanga-Selenge
Swing

Marja Harmon
*Mrs. Brown,
Ensemble*

Phyre Hawkins
Ensemble

Brian Tyree Henry
General

A.J. Holmes
*Standby for
Elder Cunningham*

Bre Jackson
Ensemble

Nikki M. James
Nabulungi

Syesha Mercado
Nabulungi

The Book of Mormon

Darius Nichols
Ensemble

Ben Platt
Elder Cunningham

Nic Rouleau
Elder Price

Nick Spangler
*Cunningham's Dad,
Ensemble*

Nichole Turner
Ensemble

Derrick Williams
General

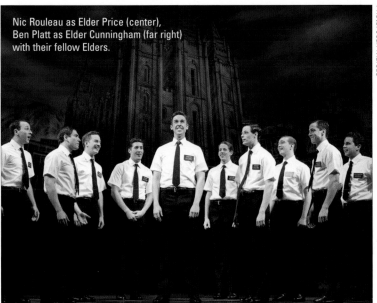

Nic Rouleau as Elder Price (center),
Ben Platt as Elder Cunningham (far right)
with their fellow Elders.

Photo: Joan Marcus

Photos: Brian Mapp

FRONT OF HOUSE
Front Row (L-R): Lorraine Wheeler (Usher), Giovanni Monserrate (Director), Verna Hobson (Usher), Claire Newhouse (Usher), Raymond Millan (Usher), Ying Le, Danelly Santana, Irene Vincent (Usher)
Back Row (L-R): Saime Hodzic (Head Usher), Mili Vela (Director), Dorothy Lennon (Ticket Taker), Sandra Palmer (Usher), Gregory Brito, Michael Composto (Associate Theatre Manager), John Nascenti (Usher), Bruce Lucoff (Usher)

WARDROBE
(L-R): Mia Bednowitz, Michael Harrell (Dresser), Veneda Truesdale (Dresser), Fred Castner (Assistant Wardrobe Supervisor), Tasha Cowd, Dolly Williams (Production Wardrobe Supervisor), James Martin, Williams Gunn, Jamie Friday, Melanie McClintock, D'Ambrose Boyd (Dresser)

The Book of Mormon

Photo: Brian Mapp

CREW

Front Row (L-R): Christopher Beck (Head Propertyman), Jason McKenna (Sound Engineer), Mary McGregor (House Sound Engineer), Jake Mooney (Carpenter), Scott Dixon (Fly Automation), Andrew Lanzarotta (Deck Automation), Drayton Allison (Head Electrician), Mike Martinez (Production Carpenter), Chris Sloan (Production Sound Engineer)
Middle Row (L-R): Guy Patria (Carpenter), Kevin Maher (Flyman), Damian Caza-Cleypool (Lead Front Electrics), Todd J. D'Aiuto (Head Electrician), Gregory Fedigan (Propertyman), Kevin Crawford
Back Row (L-R): Mitchell Kerr, Donald E. Robinson (Head Carpenter)

STAFF FOR *THE BOOK OF MORMON*

GENERAL MANAGEMENT
STUART THOMPSON PRODUCTIONS
Lily Alia   Gregg Arst   Megan Curren
Kevin Emrick   Michele Haberman
Nick Lugo   Shaun Moorman
Marshall Purdy   Jillian Ruben   Julie Schneider
Caitlyn Thomson   Zachary Spitzer
Matthew L. Wright

ASSOCIATE GENERAL MANAGER
Adam J. Miller

COMPANY MANAGER
James Lawson

PRODUCTION MANAGEMENT
AURORA PRODUCTIONS
Gene O'Donovan   Ben Heller
Chris Minnick   Jarid Sumner   Anita Shah
Anthony Jusino   Liza Luxenberg   Rachel London
David Cook   Bridget Van Dyke
Melissa Mazdra   Cat Nelson

PRESS REPRESENTATIVE
BONEAU/BRYAN-BROWN
Chris Boneau   Jim Byk
Christine Olver   Michelle Farabaugh

MAKEUP DESIGNER
Randy Houston Mercer

ASSOCIATE DIRECTOR
Jennifer Werner
Steve Bebout

ASSOCIATE CHOREOGRAPHER
John MacInnis

LOGO AND ARTWORK DESIGN
BLT Communications, Inc.

SCOTT RUDIN PRODUCTIONS
Andrew Coles   Peter Cron   Taylor Hess
Robert Hoffman   David Rogers   Jason Sack
Chelsea Salyer   Dan Sarrow   Jason Shrier
Noah Stahl   Christopher Verone

Production Stage Manager .... **Karen Moore**
Stage Manager .... Rachel S. McCutchen

Assistant Stage Manager .... Michael P. Zaleski
Assistant Company Manager .... Brittany Weber
Associate Music Supervisor .... Brian Usifer
Resident Dance Captain .... Graham Bowen
Assistant Dance Captain .... Scott Barnhardt
Associate Scenic Designer .... Frank McCullough
Assistant Scenic Designers ..Lauren Alvarez, Christine Peters
Associate Costume Designers .... Matthew Pachtman,
Michelle Matland
Costume Design Assistant .... Irma Escobar
Associate Lighting Designer .... Benjamin C. Travis
Assistant Lighting Designer .... Carl Faber
Associate Sound Designer .... Ashley Hanson
Production Carpenter .... Mike Martinez
Production Electrician .... Dan Coey
Head Electrician .... Drayton Allison
Production Sound Engineer .... Chris Sloan
Moving Light Programmer .... David John Arch
Lead Front Electrics .... Damian Caza-Cleypool
Sound Engineer .... Jason McKenna
Deck Automation .... Andrew Lanzarotta
Fly Automation .... Scott Dixon
Production Props .... Ken Keneally
Properties Coordinator .... Peter Sarafin
Production Wardrobe Supervisor .... Dolly Williams
Assistant Wardrobe Supervisor .... Fred Castner
Production Hair Supervisor .... Tod L. McKim
Assistant Hair Supervisor .... Matthew Wilson
Dressers .... D'Ambrose Boyd, Michael Harrell,
Melanie McClintock, Virginia Neinenger,
Virginia Ohnesorge, Frank Scaccia,
Elise Tollefsen, Veneda Truesdale
Hair Dresser .... Joel Hawkins
Associate Musical Director .... Adam Ben-David
Electronic Music Programmer .... Randy Cohen
Drum Programmer .... Sean McDaniel
Assistants to the Producers ..... Kurt Nickels, Jack Zegarski
Production Assistants ..Sara Cox Bradley, Derek DiGregorio
Music Department Assistant .... Matthew Aument
Costume Shoppers ..Brenda Abbandandolo, Kate Friedberg
Assistant to Ms. Roth .... Jonathan Schwartz
Research Assistant to Ms. Roth .... Debbe DuPerrieu
Assistants to Mr. MacDevitt .... Ariel Benjamin,
Jonathan Dillard
Prop Shopper .... Buist Bickley
Casting Associate .... Kate S. Boka
Marketing Director .... Steven Cardwell
Assistant Marketing Director .... Chelsea Salyer
Banking .... City National Bank/
Erik Piecuch, Michele Gibbons

Payroll .... Castellana Services, Inc.
Accountant .... Fried & Kowgios CPA's LLP/
Robert Fried, CPA
Controller .... J.S. Kubala
Insurance .... DeWitt Stern Group
Legal Counsel .... Lazarus & Harris LLP/
Scott Lazarus, Esq., Robert C. Harris, Esq.
Advertising .Serino/Coyne, Greg Corradetti, Nancy Coyne,
Carolyn London, Scott Yambor, Doug Murphy
Digital Outreach .... BLT Communications, Inc.
Marketing .... Serino/Coyne, Leslie Barrett,
Mike Rafael, Diana Salameh
Website Design .... BLT Communications, Inc.
Production Photographer .... Joan Marcus
Vocal Consultant .... Liz Caplan
Company Physical Therapists .... PhysioArts
Company Orthopaedist .... David S. Weiss, M.D.
Theatre Displays .... BAM Signs, Inc.
Transportation .... IBA Limousines

CREDITS
Scenery fabrication by PRG-Scenic Technologies, a division of Production Resource Groups, LLC, New Windsor, NY. Lighting equipment provided by PRG Lighting, Secaucus, NJ. Sound equipment provided by Masque Sound. Costumes by Eric Winterling, Inc.; Gilberto Designs, Inc.; Katrina Patterns; Izquierdo Studios, Ltd.; Studio Rouge, Inc. Millinery by Rodney Gordon, Inc. Military clothing provided by Kaufman's Army & Navy. Custom military ammunition by Weapons Specialists, Ltd. Custom fabric printing by First 2 Print LLC. Custom fabric dyeing and painting by Jeff Fender. Eyewear provided by Dr. Wayne Goldberg. Custom footwear by LaDuca Shoes, Inc.; Worldtone Dance. Props executed by Cigar Box Studios, Tom Carroll Scenery, Jerard Studios, Daedalus Design and Production, Joe Cairo, J&M Special Effects, Jeremy Lydic, Josh Yoccom. Wigs made by Hudson Wigs. Makeup provided by M•A•C Cosmetics. Keyboards from Yamaha Corporation of America.

SPECIAL THANKS
John Barlow, Lisa Gajda, Angela Howard, Bruce Howell, Beth Johnson-Nicely, Sarah Kooperkamp, Kristen Anderson-Lopez, Katie Lopez, Annie Lopez, Kathy Lopez, Frank Lopez, Billy Lopez, Brian Shepherd, Eric Stough, Boogie Tillmon, The Vineyard Theatre, Darlene Wilson

Souvenir merchandise designed and created by
The Araca Group.

Rehearsed at the New 42nd Street Studios

The Book of Mormon

BOX OFFICE
(L-R): Thomas Kane, Stanley Shaffer (Treasurer), Keith Stephenson (Assistant Treasurer)

MANAGEMENT
Emily Hare (Theatre Manager),
Michael Composto (Associate Theatre Manager)

MANAGEMENT
(L-R): Rachel S. McCutchen (Stage Manager), Robbie Young,
Sara Cox Bradley (Production Assistant)

MUSICIANS
Front (L-R): Sean McDaniel, Raul Agraz
Back (L-R): Bryan Crook, Dave Phillips, Matt Gallagher

JUJAMCYN THEATERS

JORDAN ROTH
President

ROCCO LANDESMAN
President, Emeritus

PAUL LIBIN
Executive Vice President

JACK VIERTEL
Senior Vice President

MEREDITH VILLATORE
Chief Financial Officer

JENNIFER HERSHEY
Vice President,
Building Operations

MICAH HOLLINGWORTH
Vice President,
Company Operations

HAL GOLDBERG
Vice President,
Theatre Operations

Director of Business Affairs ....Albert T. Kim
Director of Ticketing Services ....Justin Karr
Theatre Operations Managers ....Willa Burke,
　Susan Elrod, Emily Hare, Jeff Hubbard, Albert T. Kim
Theatre Operations Associates ....Carrie Jo Brinker,
　Brian Busby, Michael Composto, Anah Jyoti Klate
Controller ....Tejal Patel
Accounting ....Christina Boursiquot, Cathy Cerge,
　Amy Frank, Alexander Parra
Executive Producer, Red Awning ....Nicole Kastrinos
Director of Sales, Givenik.com ....Karen Freidus

Building Operations Manager ....Erich Bussing
Executive Coordinator ....Ed Lefferson
Executive Assistants ....Hunter Chancellor,
　Danielle DeMatteo, Elisabeth Stern
Receptionist ....Lisa Perchinske
Ticketing and Pricing Associate ....Jonathon Scott
Sales Associate, Givenik.com ....Taylor Kurpiel
Maintenance ....Ralph Santos, Ramon Zapata
Security ....Rasim Hodzic, Terone Richardson
Interns ....Christina Bracco, Drew Factor,
　Morgan Hoit, Henry Tisch

STAFF FOR THE EUGENE O'NEILL THEATRE FOR
THE BOOK OF MORMON

Theatre Manager ....Emily Hare
Associate Theatre Manager ....Michael Composto
Treasurer ....Stanley Shaffer
Head Carpenter ....Donald E. Robinson
Head Propertyman ....Christopher Beck
Head Electrician ....Todd J. D'Aiuto
Flyman ....Kevin Maher
Engineer ....Brian DiNapoli
Assistant Treasurers ....Garry Kenny, Russell P. Owen,
　Keith Stephenson, Sonia Vazquez

Carpenters ....Jake Mooney, Guy Patria
Propertyman ....Gregory Fedigan
Electrician....................................James Gardner
House Sound Engineer ....Mary McGregor
Head Usher ....Saime Hodzic
Ticket-Takers ....Dorothy Lennon, Scott Rippe
Ushers .....Charlotte Brauer, Verna Hobson, Bruce Lucoff,
　Raymond Millan, John Nascenti, Claire Newhouse,
　Sandra Palmer, Irene Vincent, Lorraine Wheeler
Doorman ....Emir Hodzic
Directors ....Pamela F. Martin, Giovanni Monserrate,
　Mili Vela
Head Porter ....Byron Vargas
Porter ....Francisco Lopez
Head Cleaner ....Mara Mijat
Cleaners ....Mujesira Bicic, Maribel Cabrera

Lobby refreshments by Sweet Hospitality Group.

Security provided by GBA Consulting, Inc

BROADWAY green♦alliance　Jujamcyn Theaters is a proud member of the Broadway Green Alliance.

Energy efficient washer/dryer courtesy of LG Electronics.

The Book of Mormon
SCRAPBOOK

Correspondent: Christopher Rice, "Swing"

Milestone Parties, Celebrations and/or Gifts: *The Book of Mormon* celebrated its 1,000th performance on August 17, 2013. Surprise "Man-shower" in February 2013 (Baby Shower) thrown for Graham Bowen to celebrate the upcoming arrival of beautiful baby Bowen. Two-year-celebration Cast Party in April 2013.

Most Exciting Celebrity Visitors: Justin Timberlake, Ben Folds, Seann William Scott (Stifler in *American Pie*), among others.

Original Company Member Who Has the Highest "Attendance"/Performance Record: Tyson Jennette.

Favorite Moment During Each Performance: One of my favorite moments of the show is the opening number because we get to look around and connect with audience members. It is so thrilling to see so many smiling faces and to be reminded how lucky we are to be up on stage sharing this fun material with a new set of people night after night!

Favorite In-Theatre Gathering Place: Cast members continually hang in the stairwells. They have become our greenroom at times because they are the common space between dressing rooms. This is, of course, when we aren't in the actual greenroom that connects with the Stage Managers' office...and who wouldn't want to hang with our great Stage Management team?

Favorite Off-Site Hangout: There is a Scary Movie Club for those in our cast and crew who enjoy horror flicks. They always check out the latest horror films when they

hit theatres. Many cast and crew members also play and hang each week at Broadway Bowling (and Broadway Show League for softball during the summer)!

Favorite Snack Foods: Our fans have brought so many cookies and yummy snacks to the stage door for various events and special days this year. They keep our stomachs happy. We are thankful to all of our fans!!

Mascot: It has got to be the Mormon frog from the Pageant in Act II.

Favorite Therapy: Ricola, Ben Gay, Throat-Coat Tea, Massage, Pilates! All of the above! Many cast members go to the gym regularly, do yoga, get massages, take voice lessons, and take dance classes to stay performance-ready. Also, a HUGE shout-out to our AMAZING team of physical therapists at PhysioArts here in NYC! They work on our bodies here at the theatre as well as at their clinic and really have saved us time and time again. They're the best!

Memorable Ad-Lib: After a slight hold during a performance when the automation needed to be reset to bring on our sets, our Elder McKinley (Matt Loehr) had to lead our Elder Price (Matt Doyle) and Elder Cunningham (Cody Jamison Strand) off stage when he usually leads them into their bedroom on stage. When the set made its way to the stage, we got the "go" to begin the show again. As they returned to the stage, the audience filled the house with supportive applause and cheers. Elder McKinley led them into their bedroom, and, since they had been "walking to their rooms" for several minutes, he ad-libbed "I know, it's a very long hallway, Elders" and the audience went nuts.

Record Number of Cell Phone Rings During a Performance: Too many to count... and always, ALWAYS during quiet moments in the show. (Props to the actors in those scenes for holding the focus of the audience even as those distractions arose!)

1. The cast celebrates its 1,000th performance with cupcakes galore!
2. The company on stage before the show.
3. Portraits of the cast marking the 1,000th performance.

Photos: Courtesy of Christopher Rice

The Book of Mormon
SCRAPBOOK

Memorable Press Encounter: After our 1,000th performance, the entire cast and crew gathered on stage to take pictures with a giant cupcake presentation where all of the cupcakes together created giant numbers "1-0-0-0" (see photo on previous page). It was a blast to gather together and share that moment with the press on our stage.

Memorable Stage Door Fan Encounter: Matthew Marks (Swing) continually was mistaken for Matt Doyle (Elder Price) at the stage door and when Matt would come out to sign, various people would be highly confused after meeting two Matt Doyles back to back. Also, it is fun when people at the stage door would say they came specifically to see a swing go on or a particular understudy jump into a role for the first time. Their support means the world to the cast.

Special Backstage Rituals: During intermission in the Stage Right stairwell, Maia Wilson (Female Ensemble) serenades the cast with original songs she creates on the spot. (See photo at right.) These vary from Gospel tunes to Tribal Chants. Her knack for comedy fuels her outstanding lyrics that bring down the house (or, the dressing rooms), performance after performance. Jason Michael Snow (Ensemble) usually joins in, playing the drum-line on foam rollers while various members of the cast join in, singing these just-learned lyrics in beautiful harmony. The audience for this mid-show entertainment is only the lucky cast and crew at the Eugene O'Neill.

Latest Audience Arrival: During "Man Up" at the end of Act I.

Fastest Costume Change: The Magic Mormon Vest-Change will always remain at the top of this list. With the help of a few claps, we Mormons

Photos: Courtesy of Christopher Rice

"Clap-Off" the lights and moments later as they return, we are wearing something brand new, pink, and maybe a little sparkly. It is extremely fast… for the audience and cast alike!

Who Wore the Heaviest/ Hottest Costume?: The bulkiest costumes have got to be the giant coffee cups several of the Female Ensemble wear during Act II's "Spooky Mormon Hell Dream." Another bulky costume would be the Satan costume worn by original cast member Brian Tyree Henry.

Catchphrases Only the Company Would Recognize: We may not have a catchphrase, but we do play a ton of word games backstage. They usually have to do with rhyming words or phrases. They keep us entertained and keep the energy up backstage between scenes.

Nickname: G-Dawg (our fantastic Dance Captain Graham Bowen).

Embarrassing Moments: Brian Sears flubbed a lyric and referred to the Book of Mormon as a "Nifty, yellow book" while holding a copy for the audience to see… and it was clearly a blue book. Christian Delcroix also flubbed a lyric in the opening number and just began singing "I love it! You should read it. It's great! I really love it, yes I do" to the rhythm of his usual lyric. Everyone backstage thought it was so funny.

Coolest Thing About Being in This Show: Always having a packed house and responsive audience members.

1. (L-R) Yearbook correspondent Christopher Rice with fellow cast mate Tyson Jennette and, from the cast of *Matilda*, Clay Thomson.
2. The *BOM* "intermission Gospel singers" (L-R): Maia Nkenge Wilson, Candice Marie Woods, Anastacia McCleskey, Allison Semmes.
3. "Let's go team!" The *BOM* 2013 Broadway Show League softball team prepares to come out swingin'.

The Bridges of Madison County

First Preview: January 17, 2014. Opened: February 20, 2014.
Closed May 18, 2014 after 37 Previews and 100 Performances.

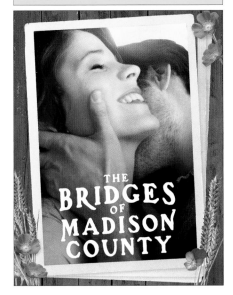

PLAYBILL

The sudden appearance of a studly National Geographic *photographer on her doorstep reawakens the heart of a lonely Iowa farm wife in this new musical romance by Jason Robert Brown and Marsha Norman, based on the 1992 bestseller of the same title. Their passionate affair lasts just a few days but changes both their lives forever.*

CAST
(in order of appearance)

Francesca .... KELLI O'HARA
Carolyn .... CAITLIN KINNUNEN
Michael .... DEREK KLENA
Bud .... HUNTER FOSTER
Marge .... CASS MORGAN
Charlie .... MICHAEL X. MARTIN
Marian/Chiara .... WHITNEY BASHOR
Robert .... STEVEN PASQUALE
State Fair Singer .... KATIE KLAUS
Paolo .... LUKE MARINKOVICH
Ensemble .... EPHIE AARDEMA,
JENNIFER ALLEN, KATIE KLAUS,
LUKE MARINKOVICH, AARON RAMEY,
DAN SHARKEY

SWINGS
CHARLIE FRANKLIN, JESSICA VOSK,
TIM WRIGHT

---

⑤ GERALD SCHOENFELD THEATRE
236 West 45th Street
A Shubert Organization Theatre

Philip J. Smith, *Chairman*   Robert E. Wankel, *President*

Jeffrey Richards   Stacey Mindich   Jerry Frankel

Gutterman Chernoff, Hunter Arnold, Ken Davenport, Carl Daikeler, Michael DeSantis,
Aaron Priest, Libby Adler Mages/Mari Glick Stuart, Scott M. Delman, Independent Presenters Network,
Red Mountain Theatre Company, Caiola Productions, Remmel T. Dickinson, Ken Greiner,
David Lancaster, Bellanca Smigel Rutter, Mark S. Golub & David S. Golub, Will Trice
WITH Warner Bros Theatre Ventures
AND The Shubert Organization
IN ASSOCIATION WITH Williamstown Theatre Festival
PRESENT

Kelli O'Hara   Steven Pasquale
IN

THE
BRIDGES
OF
MADISON COUNTY
A NEW MUSICAL

BOOK BY   MUSIC & LYRICS BY
Marsha Norman   **Jason Robert Brown**

BASED ON THE NOVEL BY **Robert James Waller**

WITH
Hunter Foster

Michael X. Martin   Cass Morgan
Caitlin Kinnunen   Derek Klena   Whitney Bashor

Ephie Aardema Jennifer Allen Charlie Franklin Kevin Kern Katie Klaus Luke Marinkovich
Aaron Ramey Dan Sharkey Jessica Vosk Tim Wright

SCENIC DESIGN	COSTUME DESIGN	LIGHTING DESIGN	SOUND DESIGN
Michael Yeargan	Catherine Zuber	Donald Holder	Jon Weston

HAIR & WIG DESIGN	ORCHESTRATIONS	CASTING	MUSIC COORDINATOR
David Brian Brown	Jason Robert Brown	Telsey + Company Abbie Brady Dalton, CSA	Michael Keller

ADVERTISING	PRESS REPRESENTATIVES	PROPS	ASSOCIATE PRODUCERS
Serino/Coyne	Irene Gandy/Alana Karpoff Thomas Raynor/Christopher Pineda	Kathy Fabian	Steven Strauss Michael Crea PJ Miller

TECHNICAL DIRECTOR	PRODUCTION STAGE MANAGER	COMPANY MANAGER	GENERAL MANAGER
Hudson Theatrical Associates	Jennifer Rae Moore	Katrina Elliott	101 Productions, Ltd.

MOVEMENT
Danny Mefford

MUSIC DIRECTOR
Tom Murray

DIRECTION
Bartlett Sher

World premiere production presented in August 2013 by the Williamstown Theatre Festival
Williamstown, Massachusetts, Jenny Gersten, Artistic Director
Presented with the cooperation of Warner Bros. Theatre Ventures, Inc.
The producers wish to express their appreciation to the Theatre Development Fund for its support of this production.

2/20/14

Steven Pasquale
and Kelli O'Hara

Photo: Joan Marcus

Continued on next page

The Bridges of Madison County

MUSICAL NUMBERS

ACT I

"To Build a Home"	Francesca and Company
"Home Before You Know It"	Bud, Michael, Carolyn and Francesca
"Temporarily Lost"	Robert
"What Do You Call a Man?"	Francesca
"You're Never Alone"	Bud and Company
"Another Life"	Marian
"Wondering"	Robert and Francesca
"Look At Me"	Francesca, Robert, Company
"The World Inside a Frame"	Robert
"Something From a Dream"	Bud
"Get Closer"	Marge and Radio Singers
"Falling Into You"	Robert and Francesca

ACT II

"State Road 21/The Real World"	State Fair Singer, Michael, Carolyn and Company
"Who We Are and Who We Want to Be"	Robert, Francesca, Company
"Almost Real"	Francesca
"Before and After You/One Second & a Million Miles"	Robert and Francesca
"When I'm Gone"	Charlie, Bud, Company
"It All Fades Away"	Robert
"Always Better"	Francesca, Robert, Company

ORCHESTRA

Conductor: TOM MURRAY
Associate Conductor: ANDREW RESNICK
Concertmaster: PAUL WOODIEL
Violin: KATHERINE LIVOLSI-LANDAU
Violin/Viola: ERIN BENIM, KIKU ENOMOTO
Cello: MAIRI DORMAN-PHANEUF

Guitars: JUSTIN GOLDNER, GARY SIEGER
Bass: RANDY LANDAU
Piano: ANDREW RESNICK
Drums/Percussion: BENNY KOONYEVSKY
Music Coordinator: MICHAEL KELLER
Music Preparation: Blane Music Preparation

UNDERSTUDIES

For Francesca: WHITNEY BASHOR
For Robert: KEVIN KERN (Standby),
    AARON RAMEY
For Bud: DAN SHARKEY
For Carolyn: EPHIE AARDEMA, JESSICA VOSK
For Michael: CHARLIE FRANKLIN,
    LUKE MARINKOVICH
For Marge: JENNIFER ALLEN, KATIE KLAUS
For Charlie: DAN SHARKEY, TIM WRIGHT
For Marian/Chiara: JESSICA VOSK,
    KATIE KLAUS

DANCE CAPTAIN

TIM WRIGHT

SETTING

Time: Four days in 1965 and the following years
Place: Winterset, Iowa

Kelli O'Hara

Photo: Joan Marcus

Kelli O'Hara
Francesca

Steven Pasquale
Robert

Hunter Foster
Bud

Michael X. Martin
Charlie

Cass Morgan
Marge

Caitlin Kinnunen
Carolyn

Derek Klena
Michael

Whitney Bashor
Marian/Chiara

Ephie Aardema
Ensemble;
u/s Carolyn

Jennifer Allen
Ensemble; u/s Marge

Charlie Franklin
Swing; u/s Michael

Kevin Kern
Robert Standby

Katie Klaus
Ensemble;
u/s Marge,
Marian/Chiara

Luke Marinkovich
Ensemble;
u/s Michael

The Bridges of Madison County

Aaron Ramey
Ensemble;
u/s Robert

Dan Sharkey
Ensemble;
u/s Charlie, Bud

Jessica Vosk
Swing; u/s Carolyn,
Marian/Chiara

Tim Wright
Dance Captain,
Swing; u/s Charlie

Jason Robert Brown
Music and Lyrics

Marsha Norman
Book

Robert James Waller
Novelist

Bartlett Sher
Director

Michael Yeargan
Scenic Design

Catherine Zuber
Costume Design

Donald Holder
Lighting Design

David Brian Brown
Hair & Wig Design

Tom Murray
Music Director

Danny Mefford
Movement

Bernard Telsey
Telsey + Company
Casting

Michael Keller
Music Coordinator

Kathy Fabian
Prop Supervisor

Neil A. Mazzella
Hudson Theatrical
Associates
Technical Supervisor

Tyne Rafaeli
Associate Director

Wendy Orshan
101 Productions, Ltd.
General Manager

Jeffrey Richards
Producer

Stacey Mindich
Producer

Jerry Frankel
Producer

Jay and Cindy Gutterman
Producers

Cathy Chernoff
Producer

Hunter Arnold
Producer

Ken Davenport
Producer

Michael DeSantis
Producer

Aaron Priest
Producer

Scott M. Delman
Producer

Keith Cromwell
Red Mountain
Theatre Company
Producer

Luigi Caiola & Rose Caiola
Producers

Remmel T. Dickinson
Producer

The Bridges of Madison County

Ken Greiner
Producer

David Lancaster
Producer

Bellanca Smigel
Rutter
Producer

Mark S. Golub
Producer

David S. Golub
Producer

Will Trice
Producer

Mark Kaufman
Warner Bros.
Theatre Ventures
Producer

Raymond Wu
Warner Bros.
Theatre Ventures
Producer

Jenny Gersten
Artistic Director
Williamstown
Theatre Festival
Producer

Steven Strauss
Associate Producer

Michael Crea
Associate Producer

PJ Miller
Associate Producer

Photos: Brian Mapp

BOX OFFICE
(L-R): Brian Goode, Craig Bowley
Not pictured: Allison Holcomb, Tim Moran

WARDROBE
(L-R): Sara Jayne Darneille (Assistant Wardrobe Supervisor), Paul Ludick (Dresser), William Mellette (Dresser), Fran Curry (Ms. O'Hara's Dresser), Cheryl Widner, Molly Jae Chase (Mr. Pasquale's Dresser), Elizabeth Villanova (Stitcher), Pamela Pierzina (Dresser)
Not pictured: Patrick Bevilacqua (Wardrobe Supervisor)

HAIR
(L-R): Ashley Leitzel-Reichenbach
(Hair Supervisor),
Brittnye Batchelor (Hair Assistant)

MANAGEMENT
(L-R): Jennifer Rae Moore (Production Stage Manager), Katie Stevens, Lisa Ann Chernoff (Stage Manager),
B. Bales Karlin (Assistant Stage Manager)
Not pictured: Dane Urban

DOORMAN
Steve Simmons
Not pictured:
Dave McGaughran,
Lype O'Dell

The Bridges of Madison County

Photos: Brian Mapp

FRONT OF HOUSE
Front Row (L-R): Lisa Boyd,
Anthony Martinez, Amber Hill
Second Row (L-R):
Preston Speed, Francine Kramer
Third Row (L-R): Ramona Maben,
Alexandria Williams, Mia Rohrer
Fourth Row (L-R): Edward LaCardo,
Hannah Owens,
Kelsey Campbell,
Jamie Lamchick
Fifth Row (L-R)
David M. Conte (Theatre Manager),
Alexandra Zavilowicz,
Andre Campbell

CARPENTERS
(L-R): Todd Frank (Production Carpenter),
Tim Rossi (Automation Carpenter),
Glenn Ingram, Tim McWilliams

PROPS
Neil Rosenberg (Properties Master), George Meagher,
John Tutalo (Assistant Props), Steve McDonald

ELECTRICIANS
Front (L-R):
Sean Luckey
(Assistant Sound Engineer),
Paul Ker,
Justin Freeman
(Head Electrician),
Leslie Ann Kilian,
Peter Guernsey
(Lead Followspot),
Jason Strangfeld
Back (L-R):
Jillian Walcher
(Followspot),
Daniel Kantor

The Bridges of Madison County

The Bridges of Madison County
SCRAPBOOK

Correspondents: Derek Klena "Michael"; Luke Marinkovich "Paolo"; Caitlin Kinnunen "Carolyn"; Whitney Bashor "Marian/Chiara"

Unique Pre-Show Announcement: When our stage manager Jenn called "Five minutes till the top of Act II" at the top of show. Hunter Foster proceeded to yell down the stairs, "No take-backs."

Opening Night Parties and/or Gifts: Epsom salts from Bartlett Sher. Stevie the steer chocolate poo pops courtesy of Derek. And a kick-ass BBQ from Kelli O'Hara and her family.

Most Exciting Celebrity Visitors: Joel Grey, Henry Winkler, Tony Danza.

Favorite In-Theatre Gathering Place: Stairwell.

Actor Who Performed the Most Roles in This Show: Luke Marinkovich, with five characters.

Special Backstage Rituals: Cast huddle before show led by Steve Pasquale and his inspirational word of the day.

Favorite Backstage Photo: Awkward family photo with Carolyn and Michael.

Most Memorable Audience Reaction: A woman screamed from the audience when Francesca ran to Robert in the rewind.

Memorable Fan Letter: An interesting letter requesting that Stevie the steer be portrayed by cast members dressed in a steer costume. He requested one be the head and one be the butt.

Worst Audience Behavior: Candy unwrapping in the front row while in the conductor's light.

Memorable Ad-Lib: Hunter Foster: "What made you think of the brandy? Did Charge and Marlie come over or Marlie and Charge?"

Memorable Press Encounter: Being asked about our personal experiences/feelings about lust and adultery.

Memorable Stage Door Fan Encounter: A young girl screaming "HOLY SHIT" when Derek Klena came out the stage door. She proceeded to shake uncontrollably for 10 minutes until he signed her program.

Memorable Directorial Note: "Be good, don't fuck it up."

Photos: Joseph Marzullo

Company In-Jokes: Jenn Allen's interpretive dance.

Embarrassing Moments: Caitlin's high-waisted jeans, Derek missing the poop with his shovel so he picked it up with his hand, and Dan Sharkey ripping his pants.

Favorite Moment During Each Performance: Caitlin dancing with her corn dog off right and any encounter with Jeff from Dubuque.

Favorite Off-Site Hangout: Angus or Glass House.

Favorite Snack Foods: Blossom, peanut butter pretzels, chocolate, Schmackary's.

Favorite Therapy: Grethers, Flu Buster juice from Green Symphony, Vick's humidifier.

Pit Stop: Best Story from the Orchestra: When the cart fell onto the cello our first preview.

Public Relations: Best Story from the Ushers and Front-of-House Staff: An usher yelling "This is not an exit" at the tail end of our bows.

Mascot: Stevie the steer.

Catchphrases Only the Company Would Recognize: "So thirsty," "Johnson's," "No toaster ovens please."

Understudy Anecdote: Ephie taking a bite of the corn dog right as she was supposed to sing and having to spit it out in Hunter's hand.

Nicknames: Unicorn (Whitney): Bumblebee (Whitney); Bubba (Steve's nickname for everyone); Sharkey (Dan).

Fastest Costume Change: Any change made in "When I'm Gone" and Kelli's change into "Look at Me."

Who Wore the Heaviest/Hottest Costume: Paolo's Army costume.

Who Wore the Least?: Kelli in the bathtub. She's just wearing bubbles.

What Did You Think of the Web Buzz on Your Show? Positive

Coolest Thing About Being in This Show: To be in an original company of a JRB/Marsha Norman/Bartlett Sher musical!

Who Heads Your Fan Club and What Is Their Website/Newsletter?: Well, this is an invitation for someone to start one!!!

1. Curtain call on opening night with (L-R): songwriter Jason Robert Brown, librettist Marsha Norman and music director Tom Murray. (In back: Steven Pasquale and Hunter Foster.)
2. Director Bartlett Sher (L) with Robert James Waller, author of the book "The Bridges of Madison County."
Recording the cast album:
3. Jason Robert Brown (C) with his stars, Steven Pasquale and Kelli O'Hara.
4. The cast and creatives.

Bronx Bombers

First Preview: January 10, 2014. Opened: February 6, 2014.
Closed March 2, 2014 after 31 Previews and 29 Performances.

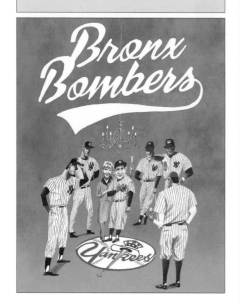

Eric Simonson's new American drama explores the enduring mythos of the New York Yankees baseball team. In 1977 coach Yogi Berra is in a panic that the once-legendary team will not survive a battle of egos between star player Reggie Jackson and manager Billy Martin. In the play's centerpiece, Berra dreams that he and his wife host a dinner party attended by Yankee superstars from the past and future who help him sort out how to handle the crisis.

CAST
(in order of appearance)

Yogi Berra	PETER SCOLARI
Bobby Sturges/	
Derek Jeter	CHRISTOPHER JACKSON
Thurman Munson/Mickey Mantle	BILL DAWES
Billy Martin/Mark	KEITH NOBBS
Reggie Jackson/	
Elston Howard	FRANCOIS BATTISTE
Carmen Berra	TRACY SHAYNE
Babe Ruth	C.J. WILSON
Lou Gehrig	JOHN WERNKE
Joe DiMaggio	CHRIS HENRY COFFEY

The action takes place in a hotel room in the Boston Sheraton in June 1977; the Berra bedroom; the Yankees locker room in September 2008; and in a dining room somewhere in between.

Continued on next page

⬤ CIRCLE IN THE SQUARE

UNDER THE DIRECTION OF
PAUL LIBIN and THEODORE MANN (1924–2012)
SUSAN FRANKEL, General Manager

FRAN KIRMSER   TONY PONTURO
QUINVITA
PRIMARY STAGES
IN ASSOCIATION WITH
THE NEW YORK YANKEES
AND
MAJOR LEAGUE BASEBALL PROPERTIES
PRESENT
PETER SCOLARI
AS YOGI BERRA
IN

Bronx Bombers
A NEW AMERICAN PLAY

WRITTEN AND DIRECTED BY
ERIC SIMONSON

CONCEIVED BY
FRAN KIRMSER

WITH

FRANCOIS BATTISTE   CHRIS HENRY COFFEY   BILL DAWES   CHRISTOPHER JACKSON
KEITH NOBBS   TRACY SHAYNE   JOHN WERNKE   C.J. WILSON
BRANDON DAHLQUIST   CLARK JACKSON   KARYN QUACKENBUSH   JEFF STILL

SCENIC DESIGN	COSTUME DESIGN	LIGHTING DESIGN	ORIGINAL MUSIC AND SOUND DESIGN
BEOWULF BORITT	DAVID C. WOOLARD	JASON LYONS	LINDSAY JONES

WIG AND HAIR DESIGN	CASTING BY	PRODUCTION STAGE MANAGER	MARKETING COORDINATOR
PAUL HUNTLEY	STEPHANIE KLAPPER	ADAM JOHN HUNTER	MARISSA STOLL

PRESS	ADVERTISING & MARKETING	PRODUCTION MANAGER	GENERAL MANAGEMENT
POLK & CO.	SPOTCO	AURORA PRODUCTIONS	RICHARDS/CLIMAN, INC.

THE PRODUCERS WISH TO EXPRESS THEIR APPRECIATION TO THEATRE DEVELOPMENT FUND FOR ITS SUPPORT OF THIS PRODUCTION.
*BRONX BOMBERS RECEIVED ITS WORLD PREMIERE AT PRIMARY STAGES, CASEY CHILDS, EXECUTIVE PRODUCER; ANDREW LEYNSE,
ARTISTIC DIRECTOR; ELLIOT FOX, MANAGING DIRECTOR IN A CO-PRODUCTION WITH FRAN KIRMSER AND TONY PONTURO, OCTOBER 2013,
WITH WORKSHOP DEVELOPMENT AT PERRY MANSFIELD, STEAMBOAT SPRINGS, CO JUNE 2013.
MAJOR LEAGUE BASEBALL TRADEMARKS AND COPYRIGHTS ARE USED WITH PERMISSION OF MAJOR LEAGUE BASEBALL ENTITIES.*

2/6/14

In a dream sequence Peter Scolari (second from L) as Yogi Berra consults Yankee greats.

Photo: Joan Marcus

Bronx Bombers

UNDERSTUDIES

For Yogi Berra, Billy Martin/
Mark, Babe Ruth: JEFF STILL
For Joe DiMaggio, Thurman Munson/
Mickey Mantle, Lou Gehrig,
Billy Martin/Mark: BRANDON DAHLQUIST
For Bobby Sturges/Derek Jeter, Reggie
Jackson/Elston Howard: CLARK JACKSON
For Carmen Berra: KARYN QUACKENBUSH

Peter Scolari
Yogi Berra

Francois Battiste
*Reggie Jackson/
Elston Howard*

Chris Henry Coffey
Joe DiMaggio

Bill Dawes
*Thurman Munson/
Mickey Mantle*

Christopher Jackson
*Bobby Sturges/
Derek Jeter*

Keith Nobbs
Billy Martin/Mark

Tracy Shayne
Carmen Berra

John Wernke
Lou Gehrig

C.J. Wilson
Babe Ruth

Brandon Dahlquist
*u/s Joe DiMaggio,
Thurman Munson/
Mickey Mantle, Lou
Gehrig, Billy Martin/
Mark*

Clark Jackson
*u/s Bobby
Sturges/Derek Jeter,
Reggie Jackson/
Elston Howard*

Karyn Quackenbush
u/s Carmen Berra

Jeff Still
*u/s Yogi Berra,
Billy Martin/Mark,
Babe Ruth*

Eric Simonson
Playwright/Director

Beowulf Boritt
Scenic Design

David C. Woolard
Costume Design

Jason Lyons
Lighting Design

Lindsay Jones
*Original Music &
Sound Design*

Paul Huntley
Wig & Hair Design

Gene O'Donovan
Aurora Productions
*Production
Management*

Ben Heller
Aurora Productions
*Production
Management*

David R. Richards &
Tamar Haimes
Richards/Climan, Inc.
*General
Management*

Stephanie Klapper
Casting

Fran Kirmser
Kirmser Ponturo
Group
*Conceived by,
Producer*

Tony Ponturo
Kirmser Ponturo
Group
Producer

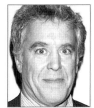

Casey Childs
Executive Producer
Primary Stages
Original Production

Andrew Leynse
Artistic Director
Primary Stages
Original Production

Elliot Fox
Managing Director
Primary Stages
Original Production

Paul Libin
Circle in the Square
Theatre and
Theatre School
President

Theodore Mann
(1924-2012)
Circle in the Square
Theatre and
Theatre School
Artistic Director

Susan Frankel
Circle in the Square
General Manager

Bronx Bombers

BOX OFFICE
(L-R):
Sarah Shutt
(Assistant Treasurer),
Jason C. Hudson
(Box Office Treasurer),
Kathleen Drury
(Assistant Treasurer)

Photos: Brian Mapp

CREW

(L-R): Stephanie Vetter (Production Sound), Stewart Wagner (Head Electrician), Adam John Hunter (Production Stage Manager), Dave Cohen, Anthony Menditto (Head Carpenter), Owen E. Parmele (Prop Master), Kelly Glasow (Stage Manager), AraBella Fischer (Dresser), Emilia Martin (Hair Supervisor), Rob Dagna (Properties Assistant), John Furrow (Wardrobe Supervisor), James Viggiano (Company Manager), John Martinez

FRONT OF HOUSE
Front (L-R): Nina Morozova,
Abbey Watt, Xavier Young
Seated (L-R): Laura Middleton,
Sophie Koufakis (Directress), Rosana Thomatos,
Laurel Brevoort, Barbara Zavilowicz, Mei Kohn
Standing (L-R): Diane Notte, Kelly Varley

STAFF FOR *BRONX BOMBERS*

GENERAL MANAGEMENT
RICHARDS/CLIMAN, INC.
David R. Richards   Tamar Haimes
Michael Sag   Kyle Bonder
Jenny Peek   Rachel Welt

PRODUCTION MANAGEMENT
AURORA PRODUCTIONS
Gene O'Donovan   Ben Heller   Chris Minnick
Anita Shah   Anthony Jusino   Jarid Sumner
Liza Luxenberg   Rachel London
David Cook   Bridget Van Dyke
Melissa Mazdra   Cat Nelson

GENERAL PRESS REPRESENTATIVE
POLK & CO.
Matt Polk
Michelle Bergmann   Jessica Johnson
Layne McNish

CASTING
Stephanie Klapper CSA
Assistants: Lauren O'Connell, Carleen McCarthy

PRODUCTION STAGE MANAGER ..Adam John Hunter

Stage Manager ....Kelly Glasow
Company Manager ....James Viggiano
Assistant Director ....Logan Reed
Properties Supervisor ....Buist Bickley
Associate Scenic Designer ....Jason Lajka
Assistant Scenic Designer ....Alexis Distler
Assistant Costume Designer ....Kim Krumm Sorenson
Assistant Lighting Designers ....Ryan O'Gara,
                                               Grant Wilcoxen
Associate Sound Designer ....Will Pickens
Properties Supervisor Assistant ....Bridget Santaniello
Production Carpenter ....Sazerac
Production Electrician ....Dan Coey
Lighting Programmer ....Timothy Rogers
Properties Assistants ....Michael Bua, Rob Dagna
Automation ....David M. Cohen
Production Sound ....Stephanie Vetter
Wardrobe Supervisor ....John Furrow
Dresser...................................AraBella Fischer
Hair Supervisor ....Emilia Martin
Sound Board Operator ....Stephanie Vetter
Production Assistants ....Erin Gioia Albrecht,
                                               Alexis Schwartz
Prosthetic Designer...............................Lee Ernst
Fight Director ....Joseph Travers
Fight Captain ....John Wernke

Sports Outreach ....Joe Favorito
Advertising ....SpotCo/Drew Hodges, Ilene Rosen,
                  Tom Greenwald, Jim Aquino, Chris Scherer
Marketing and Promotions ....SpotCo/
        Nick Pramik, Kristen Rathbun, Emily Hammerman
Interactive Marketing ....Situation Interactive/
                        Damian Bazadona, Jeremy Kraus,
                           Katie Eskin, Michael Perkins
Publicity Associates .....Tom D'Ambrosio, Colgan McNeil,
             Sasha Pensanti, Frances White, Wayne Wolfe
Production Associate ....Brittany Schmid
Assistant to the Producer ....Rachel Ingram
Banking ....City National Bank/
                        Michele Gibbons, Erik Piecuch
Insurance ....DeWitt Stern Group/
                        Peter Shoemaker, Anthony Pittari
Accountants ....Fried & Kowgios CPAs LLP
Comptroller ....Elliott Aronstam
Legal Counsel ....Loeb & Loeb
Payroll ....Checks and Balances Inc
Production Photographer ....Joan Marcus
Merchandise ....Kirmser Ponturo Group
General Management Interns ....Elliot Miranda,
                        Harriet Taylor, Katie Titley
Opening Night
        Coordination ....The Lawrence Company Events

Bronx Bombers
SCRAPBOOK

Curtain call on opening night at Circle in the Square Theatre

Portrait of Joe DiMaggio in the theatre's lobby

Real-life Carmen and Yogi Berra meet the cast of *Bronx Bombers*

Portrait of Yogi Berra in the theatre's lobby

CREDITS

Scenery built by PRG/Scenic Technologies and Center Line Studios. Automation by PRG/Scenic Technologies. Lighting equipment by Hudson/Christie Lights. Audio equipment by Sound Associates

SPECIAL THANKS

Major League Baseball sponsors and licensees, Steiner Sports, Yogi Berra Museum and Learning Center. Mr. Simonson would like to thank Stuart Spencer, Steven Druckman and Jeffrey Hatcher. The Edgerton Foundation New American Plays Award. The Blanche and Irving Laurie Foundation. Special thanks to all the actors who contributed to the development of *Bronx Bombers*: Richard Topol, Wendy Makkena, Joe Pantoliano, Lee Aaron Rosen, Earl Brown, Maddie Corman, Aaron Clifton Moten, Julie Boyd and Tyler Jacob Rollinson.

Bronx Bombers rehearsed at
Manhattan Theatre Club's Creative Center.

☐ CIRCLE IN THE SQUARE THEATRE

Thespian Theatre, Inc.
Under the direction of Paul Libin
Susan Frankel, *General Manager*

House Manager . . . . .Cheryl Dennis
Head Carpenter . . . . Anthony Menditto
Head Electrician . . . . Stewart Wagner
Prop Master . . . . .Owen E. Parmele
Box Office Treasurer . . . . .Jason C. Hudson
Assistant Treasurers . . . . .Kathleen Drury, Sarah Shutt
Head Usher . . . . .Georgia Keghlian
Ticket Taker . . . . .Patricia Kennedy
Directress . . . . .Sophie Koufakis
Assistant to Susan Frankel . . . . .Tiffany Schleigh

☐ CIRCLE IN THE SQUARE THEATRE SCHOOL

President . . . . .Paul Libin
Theatre School Director . . . . .E. Colin O'Leary
Arts Education/Development . . . . .Jonathan Mann
Administrative Assistant . . . . .David Pleva
Administrative Assistant . . . . Whitney Kaufman
Artistic Director 1961–2012 . . . . Theodore Mann

Government Support

NY State Council on the Arts
NYC Department of Cultural Affairs

Foundation Support

Stephen and Mary Birch Foundation
Akausa Foundation, Blanche and Irving Laurie Foundation, BWF Foundation, C. Daniel Chill Foundation, Frederick Loewe Foundation, Friars Foundation, Geraldine Stutz Foundation, Jerome Robbins Foundation, Kinder Morgan Foundation, Pat & Jay Baker Foundation, Ross Family Foundation, Slovin Foundation, Waldman Foundation, Yudelson Foundation

Patron Support

Anonymous (2), Ira Berkow, Allan Brooks, Robert Cole, Michael and Lauren David, John DiMenna, Frederick & Myrna Gershon, Jessica Jenen, Thomas Kelly, Christine and Alan Kemp, Kirmser Ponturo Group, Elizabeth McCann, Scott Mosberg, Daryl & Steven Roth, Marlene Serby, Joel Singer, Spring Sirkin, Vera Stern, Michael Vitulli, Lester Wohl

Bullets Over Broadway

First Preview: March 11, 2014. Opened: April 10, 2014.
Still running as of May 31, 2014.

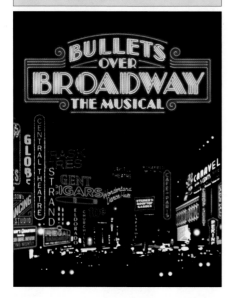

Comedian and film auteur Woody Allen adapts his 1994 film comedy as a stage musical with the help of director/choreographer Susan Stroman, and a score of greater- and lesser-known period songs. A 1920s gangster is saddled with the job of riding herd on his boss' talentless girlfriend who has been cast in a Broadway show undergoing tryouts in Boston. It gradually becomes apparent that the gangster is a better playwright and director than the actual playwright and director and he becomes stagestruck to the point that he is ready to kill to make sure that "his" play is a hit.

CAST

(in order of appearance)

Cheech	NICK CORDERO
Nick Valenti	VINCENT PASTORE
The Atta-Girls	PAIGE FAURE, KELCY GRIFFIN, SARAH LIN JOHNSON, AMANDA KLOOTS-LARSEN, BRITTANY MARCIN, BETH JOHNSON NICELY
Olive Neal	HELÉNE YORKE
Aldo	KEVIN WORLEY
David Shayne	ZACH BRAFF
Ellen	BETSY WOLFE
Sheldon Flender	JAMES MOYE
Kay	JANET DICKINSON
Bohemian Friends	SARAH LIN JOHNSON, ANDY JONES
Julian Marx	LENNY WOLPE
Cotton Club Dancers	PAIGE FAURE, KELCY GRIFFIN
Rocco	PAUL McGILL

Continued on next page

Continued on next page

♦ ST. JAMES THEATRE
A JUJAMCYN THEATRE

JORDAN ROTH, *President*
ROCCO LANDESMAN, *President Emeritus*
PAUL LIBIN, *Executive Vice President* **JACK VIERTEL,** *Senior Vice President*

LETTY ARONSON   JULIAN SCHLOSSBERG
EDWARD WALSON   LEROY SCHECTER   ROY FURMAN   BROADWAY ACROSS AMERICA
JUST FOR LAUGHS THEATRICALS/JACKI BARLIA FLORIN   HAROLD NEWMAN
and
JUJAMCYN THEATERS
Present

BULLETS OVER BROADWAY THE MUSICAL

Written by
WOODY ALLEN

Based on the Screenplay of the Film Bullets Over Broadway by
Woody Allen and **Douglas McGrath**

Starring

**BROOKS ASHMANSKAS   ZACH BRAFF   NICK CORDERO
MARIN MAZZIE   VINCENT PASTORE   BETSY WOLFE
LENNY WOLPE   HELÉNE YORKE   KAREN ZIEMBA**

With

CLYDE ALVES   JIM BORSTELMANN   PRESTON TRUMAN BOYD   JANET DICKINSON
BRYN DOWLING   KIM FAURÉ   PAIGE FAURE   CASEY GARVIN   KELCY GRIFFIN
DAN HORN   SARAH LIN JOHNSON   ANDY JONES   AMANDA KLOOTS-LARSEN
KEVIN LIGON   SYNTHIA LINK   BRITTANY MARCIN   JAMES MOYE
BETH JOHNSON NICELY   ERIC SANTAGATA   KEVIN WORLEY

Scenic Design	Costume Design	Lighting Design	Sound Design
SANTO LOQUASTO	WILLIAM IVEY LONG	DONALD HOLDER	PETER HYLENSKI

Hair & Wig Design	Make-Up Design	Associate Director	Associate Choreographer
PAUL HUNTLEY	ANGELINA AVALLONE	JEFF WHITING	JAMES GRAY

Animal Trainer	Music Supervision	Orchestrations
WILLIAM BERLONI	GLEN KELLY	DOUG BESTERMAN

Music Director/Conductor & Vocal Arrangements	Music Coordinator	Casting
ANDY EINHORN	HOWARD JOINES	TARA RUBIN CASTING

Production Stage Manager	Production Management	Press Representative
ROLT SMITH	AURORA PRODUCTIONS	BONEAU/BRYAN-BROWN

Associate Producer	Company Manager	General Management
DON'T SPEAK, LLC	BRUCE KLINGER	RICHARDS/CLIMAN, INC.

Music Adaptation and Additional Lyrics
GLEN KELLY

Direction and Choreography by
SUSAN STROMAN

4/10/14

"Don't speak!" Zach Braff gets stifled by Marin Mazzie

Photo: Paul Kolnik

Bullets Over Broadway

SCENES AND MUSICAL NUMBERS

Location: New York City, 1929

ACT I

Prologue
Nick's Club:
"Tiger Rag" ....The Atta-Girls, Olive, Nick, Cheech and Gangsters
"Gee Baby, Ain't I Good to You" ....Nick and Olive
David and Ellen's Rooftop:
"Blues My Naughty Sweetie Gives to Me" ....Ellen and David
The Streets of New York:
"'Tain't a Fit Night Out for Man or Beast" ....Valenti Gang, Kustabeck Gang and Flappers
Olive's Apartment:
"The Hot Dog Song" ....Olive
"Gee Baby, Ain't I Good to You" (Reprise) ....Nick
Helen's Penthouse:
"They Go Wild, Simply Wild, Over Me" ....Helen and Julian
The Gowanus Canal:
"Up a Lazy River" ....Cheech
The Belasco Theatre: Onstage Rehearsals
"I'm Sitting on Top of the World" ....David
"Let's Misbehave" ....Warner and Olive
Helen's Terrace Overlooking Times Square:
"There's a Broken Heart for Every Light on Broadway" ....Helen and David
Nick's Club:
"(I'll Be Glad When You're Dead) You Rascal You" ....The Atta-Girls
The Alley Behind the Theatre:
"'Tain't Nobody's Biz-ness If I Do" ....Cheech and the Gangsters
Grand Central Station
"Runnin' Wild" ....Full Company

ACT II

The Wilbur Theatre in Boston: Onstage Rehearsals
"There's a New Day Comin'!" ....Eden and Company
Backstage at the Wilbur Theatre: Opening Night
"There'll Be Some Changes Made" ....Cheech, Warner and the Gangsters
"I Ain't Gonna Play No Second Fiddle" ....Helen and David
Train from Boston to New York:
"Good Old New York" ....The Red Caps
The Gowanus Canal:
"Up a Lazy River" (Reprise) ....Cheech
David and Ellen's Apartment:
"I've Found a New Baby" ....Ellen and David
The Streets of New York:
"The Panic Is On" ....David
The Alley Behind the Theatre:
"'Tain't Nobody's Biz-ness If I Do" (Reprise) ....Cheech
The Belasco Theatre: Opening Night
"Runnin' Wild" (Reprise) ....Company
"Up a Lazy River" (Reprise) ....Cheech
Nick's Club:
"She's Funny That Way" ....David and Ellen
"Finale" ....Company

Cast Continued

Flappers ....PAIGE FAURE, BRITTANY MARCIN, BETH JOHNSON NICELY
Gangsters ....JIM BORSTELMANN, CASEY GARVIN, ANDY JONES, KEVIN LIGON, PAUL McGILL, JAMES MOYE, ERIC SANTAGATA, KEVIN WORLEY
Vendor ....JIM BORSTELMANN
The Four Franks ....CASEY GARVIN, ANDY JONES, PAUL McGILL, ERIC SANTAGATA
Helen Sinclair ....MARIN MAZZIE
Josette ....BETH JOHNSON NICELY
Victim ....JIM BORSTELMANN
Mitchell Sabine ....ERIC SANTAGATA
Lorna ....BRITTANY MARCIN
Warner Purcell ....BROOKS ASHMANSKAS
Eden Brent ....KAREN ZIEMBA
Mr. Woofles..................................TRIXIE
Understudies ....PAIGE FAURE, KEVIN WORLEY
Violet ....KIM FAURÉ
Hilda Marx ....JANET DICKINSON
Train Conductor ....KEVIN LIGON
The Red Caps ....KIM FAURÉ, PAIGE FAURE, KELCY GRIFFIN, SARAH LIN JOHNSON, AMANDA KLOOTS-LARSEN, BRITTANY MARCIN, BETH JOHNSON NICELY

THE ENSEMBLE

JIM BORSTELMANN, JANET DICKINSON, KIM FAURÉ, PAIGE FAURE, CASEY GARVIN, KELCY GRIFFIN, SARAH LIN JOHNSON, ANDY JONES, AMANDA KLOOTS-LARSEN, KEVIN LIGON, BRITTANY MARCIN, PAUL McGILL, JAMES MOYE, BETH JOHNSON NICELY, ERIC SANTAGATA, KEVIN WORLEY

UNDERSTUDIES

For Cheech: JAMES MOYE, PRESTON TRUMAN BOYD
Nick Valenti: JIM BORSTELMANN, KEVIN LIGON
Olive Neal: BRYN DOWLING, KIM FAURÉ
David Shayne: ANDY JONES, KEVIN WORLEY
Ellen: KIM FAURÉ, PAIGE FAURE, SYNTHIA LINK
Julian Marx: PRESTON TRUMAN BOYD, KEVIN LIGON
Helen Sinclair: BRYN DOWLING, JANET DICKINSON
Warner Purcell: PRESTON TRUMAN BOYD, JIM BORSTELMANN, KEVIN LIGON
Eden Brent: JANET DICKINSON, SYNTHIA LINK
Mr. Woofles: ROCCO

Bullets Over Broadway

SWINGS

PRESTON TRUMAN BOYD, BRYN DOWLING,
DAN HORN, SYNTHIA LINK

DANCE CAPTAINS

ERIC SANTAGATA, SYNTHIA LINK

ORCHESTRA

Conductor: ANDY EINHORN
Associate Conductor/Piano/Keyboards:
    GREG ANTHONY RASSEN
Reeds: CHUCK WILSON, DANIEL BLOCK,
    DEBORAH AVERY, ROGER ROSENBERG
Trumpets: KENNY LAVENDER (LEAD),
    TANYA DARBY, RANDY REINHART
Trombones: JOHN ALLRED, HARVEY TIBBS,
    JOE BARATI
French Horn: ADAM KRAUTHAMER
Bass: MARK VANDERPOEL
Guitar/Banjo: SCOTT KUNEY
Drums: BRUCE DOCTOR
Percussion: ANDREW BLANCO
Piano/Keyboards: MARK BERMAN
Violin: ANTOINE SILVERMAN
Music Coordinator: HOWARD JOINES
Music Preparation: Anixter Rice Music Service
Keyboard Programmer: RANDY COHEN

Brooks Ashmanskas
Warner Purcell

Zach Braff
David Shayne

Nick Cordero
Cheech

Marin Mazzie
Helen Sinclair

Vincent Pastore
Nick Valenti

Betsy Wolfe
Ellen

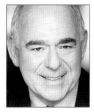
Lenny Wolpe
Julian Marx

Heléne Yorke
Olive Neal

Karen Ziemba
Eden Brent

Jim Borstelmann
*Vendor, Victim,
Ensemble;
u/s Nick, Warner*

Preston Truman Boyd
*Swing; u/s Cheech,
Julian, Warner*

Janet Dickinson
*Kay, Ensemble;
u/s Helen, Eden*

Bryn Dowling
*Swing; u/s Olive,
Helen*

Kim Fauré
*Violet, Ensemble; u/s
Olive, Ellen*

Paige Faure
*Understudy,
Ensemble; u/s Ellen*

Casey Garvin
Ensemble

Kelcy Griffin
Ensemble

Dan Horn
Swing

Sarah Lin Johnson
Ensemble

Andy Jones
Ensemble; u/s David

Amanda Kloots-
Larsen
Ensemble

Kevin Ligon
*Ensemble; u/s Nick,
Julian, Warner*

Synthia Link
*Swing; u/s Ellen,
Eden; Dance Captain*

Brittany Marcin
Lorna, Ensemble

Paul McGill
Rocco, Ensemble

James Moye
*Sheldon Flender,
Ensemble;
u/s Cheech*

Bullets Over Broadway

Beth Johnson Nicely
Josette, Ensemble

Eric Santagata
*Mitchell Sabine,
Ensemble; Dance
Captain*

Kevin Worley
*Aldo, Ensemble;
u/s David*

Woody Allen
Playwright

Susan Stroman
*Director/
Choreographer*

Glen Kelly
*Music Supervision,
Adaptation and
Additional Lyrics*

Santo Loquasto
Scenic Design

William Ivey Long
Costume Design

Donald Holder
Lighting Design

Peter Hylenski
Sound Design

Paul Huntley
Hair & Wig Design

Angelina Avallone
Make-up Design

Jeff Whiting
Associate Director

James Gray
*Associate
Choreographer*

Doug Besterman
Orchestrations

Andy Einhorn
*Music Director/
Conductor and
Vocal Arrangements*

Howard Joines
Music Coordinator

William Berloni
Animal Trainer

Tara Rubin
Tara Rubin Casting
Casting

Douglas McGrath
Original Screenplay

Gene O'Donovan
Aurora Productions
*Production
Management*

Ben Heller
Aurora Productions
*Production
Management*

David R. Richards &
Tamar Haimes
Richards/Climan, Inc.
General Manager

Julian Schlossberg
Producer

Edward Walson
Producer

Roy Furman
Producer

John Gore
Broadway Across
America
Producer

Adam Blanshay
Just For Laughs
Theatricals
Producer

Gilbert Rozon
Just For Laughs
Theatricals
Producer

Jacki Barlia Florin
Producer

Jordan Roth
Jujamcyn Theaters
Producer

Sharon A. Carr
Don't Speak, LLC
Associate Producer

Jed and
Bronna Canaan
Don't Speak, LLC
Associate Producer

Bonnie Osher
Don't Speak, LLC
Associate Producer

Michael Rubenstein
Don't Speak, LLC
Associate Producer

Bullets Over Broadway

Clyde Alves
*Rocco, Gangster,
Frank, Ensemble*

MANAGEMENT
Clockwise from bottom left:
Jennifer Slattery (Assistant Stage Manager),
Rachel Scheer (Assistant Company Manager),
Bruce Klinger (Company Manager),
Rolt Smith (Production Stage Manager),
James Gray (Resident Choreographer/Director),
Stephen R. Gruse (Stage Manager)

FRONT OF HOUSE
Front Row (L-R): Lana Vaca, Kami Martin, Brian Busby (Associate Manager)
Second Row (L-R): Cynthia Lopiano (Head Usher), Leslie Morgenstern, Rochelle Rogers,
Silvia Quizhpi, Julie Wong
Third Row (L-R): Heather Jewels, Jessica Bettini, Peter Hurvitz, Gillian Sheffler
Fourth Row (L-R): Brian Veith, Carla Dawson, Samantha Obreiter, Katia Koziara
Fifth Row (L-R): Jim Barry, Frank Todaro, Chyna Zurich, Leonard Baron
Sixth Row (L-R): Nick Guastella, Jason Barker, Barbara Carroll, Carl Culley
Top Row (L-R): Jeff Hubbard (Manager), James Lynch, Michael Leibring, Benjamin Raffalli

ANIMAL TRAINER/HANDLER
(L-R): William Berloni (Trainer), Trixie, Rocco,
Brian Michael Hoffman (Handler)

BOX OFFICE
(L-R): Vincent Sclafani (Treasurer),
Kathryn Fearon (Assistant Treasurer),
Vincent Siniscalchi (Assistant Treasurer)

WIG DEPARTMENT
(L-R): Jason Joseph (Hair Dresser),
Edward J. Wilson (Associate Hair & Wig
Designer), Thomas Augustine (Hair Dresser)

CONDUCTORS
(L-R): Andy Einhorn (Conductor), Greg Anthony
Rassen (Associate Conductor/Piano/Keyboards)

2013-2014 AWARDS

DRAMA DESK AWARD
Outstanding Costume Design
(William Ivey Long)

THEATRE WORLD AWARD
Outstanding Broadway or Off-Broadway Debut
(Nick Cordero)

OUTER CRITICS CIRCLE AWARDS
Outstanding Featured Actor in a Musical
(Nick Cordero)
Outstanding Featured Actress in a Musical
(Marin Mazzie)
Outstanding Costume Design
(Play or Musical)
(William Ivey Long)

Bullets Over Broadway

Photo: Brian Mapp

WARDROBE
Front (L-R): Maggie Horkey (Dresser),
Raven Jakubowski (Dresser),
Jeannie Naughton (Dresser),
Terry LaVada (Dresser)
Back (L-R): John Rinaldi (Dresser),
Douglas Petitjean (Wardrobe Supervisor),
Ali Maher-Barclay (Dresser),
Roy Seiler (Dresser),
Dede LaBarre (Assistant Wardrobe
Supervisor), Katie Chick (Dresser),
Scotty Cain (Dresser), Amy Nielson (Dresser)
Not pictured: Mark Trezza (Dresser),
Suzanne Delahunt (Dresser)

STAFF FOR *BULLETS OVER BROADWAY*

GENERAL MANAGEMENT
RICHARDS/CLIMAN, INC.
David R. Richards   Tamar Haimes
Michael Sag   Kyle Bonder
Jenny Peek   Rachel Welt

COMPANY MANAGER
Bruce Klinger

GENERAL PRESS REPRESENTATIVE
BONEAU/BRYAN-BROWN
Chris Boneau   Joe Perrotta   Kelly Guiod

PRODUCTION MANAGEMENT
AURORA PRODUCTIONS INC.
Gene O'Donovan   Ben Heller
Chris Minnick   Liza Luxenberg
Anthony Jusino   Jarid Sumner
David Cook   Rachel London   Bridget Van Dyke
Melissa Mazdra   Rob Ward

CASTING
TARA RUBIN CASTING
Tara Rubin CSA, Eric Woodall CSA,
Merri Sugarman CSA, Kaitlin Shaw CSA,
Lindsay Levine CSA, Scott Anderson

LEGAL COUNSEL
LEVINE PLOTKIN & MENIN, LLP
Loren Plotkin, Conrad Rippy, Susan Mindell
Daniel Watkins, Hailey Ferber

PRODUCTION STAGE MANAGER .....ROLT SMITH
Stage Manager ....Stephen R. Gruse
Assistant Stage Manager ....Jennifer Slattery
Assistant Company Manager.................Rachel Scheer
Associate Director/Assistant Choreographer ...Jeff Whiting
Resident Choreographer/Director ....James Gray
Stroman Productions Producer ....Scott Bishop
Dance Captains ....Synthia Link, Eric Santagata
Associate Scenic Designers ....Jason Ardizzone-West,
Jisun Kim
Assistant Scenic Designer ....Antje Ellermann
Production Properties Coordinator ....Peter Sarafin
Model Makers ....Rachel Nemec, Alexander Woodward,
Kina Park, Aram Kim
Associate Costume Designer ....Cathy Parrott
Assistant Costume Designer ....Sarah Cubbage
Costume Assistant ....Isabelle Simone

Costume Shoppers ....Nina Bova, Rebecca Freund
Costume Intern ....Sean Smith
William Ivey Long Studio Director ....Donald Sanders
Associate Lighting Designer ....Carolyn Wong
Assistant Lighting Designer ....Heather Graff
Assistant to the Lighting Designer ....Sarah Bullock
Lighting Design Intern ....Yuki Nakase
Automated Lighting Programmer ....Richard Tyndall
Associate Sound Designer ....Tony Smolenski IV
Associate Hair and Wig
Designers ....Giovanna Calabretta, Edward J. Wilson
Animals ....William Berloni Theatrical Animals, Inc.
Production Assistants ....Erin Gioia Albrecht,
Derric Nolte, Ashley Singh
SDC Observer ....Katherine Pettit
Production Carpenter ....Francis Rapp
Head Carpenter ....Steve Schroettnig
Deck Automation ....Peter Malbuisson
Fly Automation ....David Elmer
Production Electricians .....Randall Zaibek, James Fedigan
Head Electrician ....Stephen Long
Moving Light Technician ....Nicholas Partin
Head Properties ....James Kane
Production Sound Supervisors ....Simon Matthews,
Phil Lojo
Sound Engineer ....Carin Ford
Deck Audio ....Jacob Scudder
Wardrobe Supervisor ....Douglas Petitjean
Assistant Wardrobe Supervisor ....Dede LaBarre
Dressers ....Scotty Cain, Suzanne Delahunt,
Jeannie Naughton, Maggie Horkey, Mark Trezza,
Amy Nielson, Terry LaVada, Roy Seiler, Ali Maher-
Barclay, Katie Chick, Raven Jakubowski, John Rinaldi
Hair Supervisor ....Edward J. Wilson
Hair Dressers ....Thomas Augustine, Jason Joseph
Animal Handler ....Brian Michael Hoffman
Music Rights Consultant ....Jill Meyers
Music Preparation Services .....Anixter Rice Music Service/
Russ Anixter, Don Rice
Music Assistant ....Roberto Sinha
Musical Research ....Michael Lavine
Assistant to Mr. Schlossberg ....Ruth Better
General Management Interns ....Harriet Taylor,
Elliot Miranda, Katie Titley
Advertising ....Serino/Coyne/Nancy Coyne,
Greg Corradetti, Vinny Sainato, Tom Callahan,
Matthew Upshaw, Danielle Boyle,
Erin Daigle, Megan Lacerenza
Marketing and Interactive .....Serino/Coyne/Leslie Barrett,
Jim Glaub, Abby Wolbe, Mark Seeley, Mike Rafael,
Brian DeVito, Catherine Herzog

Press Representative Staff ....Adrian Bryan-Brown,
Jim Byk, Michelle Farabaugh, Jackie Green,
Linnae Hodzic, Kevin Jones, Amy Kass, Holly Kinney,
Emily Meagher, Aaron Meier, Christine Olver,
Amanda Sales, Heath Schwartz, Susanne Tighe
Banking ....City National Bank/Michele Gibbons
Insurance ....DeWitt Stern Group Inc./
Peter Shoemaker, Anthony Pittari
Accountants ....Fried & Kowgios, CPA's LLP
Comptroller ....Elliott Aronstam
Opening Night Coordination ....Suzanne Tobak,
Chrissann Gasparro
Payroll ....CSI/Lance Castellana
Production Photographer ....Paul Kolnik

CREDITS
Scenery built, painted, electrified and automated by Show
Motion, Inc., Milford, Connecticut. Automation and show
control by Show Motion, Inc., Milford, CT, using the AC2
Computerized Motion Control System. 1929 Ford Model A
retrofit into an electric car by Jersey Carts. Mr. Woofles
puppet and basket by Jerard Studio. Warner Purcell's edible
dog biscuits by Just Desserts NYC. Bouncy furniture by
Craig Grigg. Upholstery by R-Ramos Upholstery. Prop
sewing by Anna Light. Prop furniture by Tom Carroll
Scenery, Joseph Cairo and Jeremy Lydic. Custom holsters by
Sherry Accessories. Various prop fabrication by Peter
Sarafin, Jim Cane, Santo Loquasto, Jerard Studios, Tim
McDonough, Eric Dressler and Ray Chan. Lighting
equipment from PRG Lighting. Sound equipment from
Sound Associates. Costumes made by Tricorne Inc., Euroco
Costumes Inc., Jennifer Love Costumes, Katrina Patterns,
Scafati Theatrical Tailors, Giliberto Designs, Jerard Studio.
Millinery by Rodney Gordon, Arnold Levine, Patricia
Underwood, J.J. Hat Center. Custom jewelry by Lawrence
Vrba. Dance shoes by T.O. Dey, LaDuca, World Tone.
Undergarments and hosiery by Bra*tenders. Souvenir
merchandise designed and created by the Araca Group.
Percussion instruments provided by Pearl/Adams and Paiste.

Make-up provided by M•A•C.

Yamaha pianos provided by
Yamaha Artist Services, Nashville.

Rehearsed at the New 42nd Street Studios

MUSIC CREDITS
"Blues My Naughty Sweetie Gives To Me" by McCarron,
Charles; Morgan, Carey; Swanstone, Arthur. Arrangement
and additional lyrics by Glen Kelly. I.D.K. Music LLC

Bullets Over Broadway

Photo: Brian Mapp

CREW

Front (L-R): Peter Malbuisson (Deck Automation), Raymond Chan (Property Man), Steve Schroettnig (Head Carpenter), David Elmer (Fly Automation), Emile LaFargue, Eric Dressler (Property Man), Jason Muldrow (Carpenter)
Back (L-R): Albert Sayers (Head Electrician), Stephen Long (Head Electrician), Justin Borowinski (Carpenter), Jacob Scudder (Deck Audio), Dave Holliman (Electrician), Jacob Greene, Timothy M. McDonough Jr. (Head Propertyman), Ryan McDonough (Flyman), Timothy B. McDonough, Sr. (Head Carpenter), Carin Ford (Sound Engineer), Bill Lewis (Electrician)

(ASCAP). **"Gee Baby, Ain't I Good to You?"** by Razaf, Andy; Redman, Don. Razaf Music (ASCAP), administered by Primary Wave Music Publishing, LLC, administered by Wixen Music Publishing, Inc./Michael H. Goldsen, Inc. (ASCAP). **"Good Old New York"** by Carew, Roy J.; Morton, Ferdinand "Jelly Roll." Tempo-Music Publishing Co. (ASCAP)/Edwin H. Morris & Company, a division of MPL Music Publishing, Inc. (ASCAP). **"Here Comes the Hot Tamale Man"** by Harrison, Charles; Rose, Fred. EMI Feist Catalog Inc. (ASCAP). **"I Ain't Gonna Play No Second Fiddle"** by Bradford, Perry. **"I Want a Hot Dog for My Roll"** by Hammed, Tausha; Williams, Clarence. Universal Music Corp. (ASCAP). **"(I'll Be Glad When You're Dead) You Rascal You"** by Theard, Sam. EMI Mills Music, Inc. (ASCAP). **"I'm Sitting on Top of the World"** by Henderson, Ray; Lewis, Sam M.; Young, Joe. Ray Henderson Music Co., Inc. (ASCAP)/EMI Feist Catalog Inc. (ASCAP)/Warock Corp. (ASCAP). **"I've Found a New Baby"** by Palmer, Jack; Williams, Spencer. Universal Music Corp. (ASCAP). **"Let's Misbehave"** by Porter, Cole. The Cole Porter Musical and Literary Property Trusts (ASCAP)/WB Music Corp. (ASCAP). **"Runnin' Wild"** by Gibbs, A. Harrington; Grey, Joe; Wood, Leo. Arrangement and additional lyrics by Glen Kelly. I.D.K. Music LLC (ASCAP). **"She's Funny That Way"** by Moret, Neil; Whiting, Richard. Chappell & Co., Inc. (ASCAP)/EMI April Music Inc. (ASCAP). **"'Tain't a Fit Night Out for Man or Beast"** by Cahn, Sammy; Chaplin, Saul. Cahn Music Co., administered by Imagem Sounds (ASCAP)/La Salle Music Publishers, Inc. (ASCAP). **"'Tain't Nobody's Biz-ness If I Do"** by Grainger, Porter; Robbins, Everett. Arrangement and additional lyrics by Glen Kelly. I.D.K. Music LLC (ASCAP). **"The Panic Is On"** by Clarke, Burt; Clarke, George; Tharp, Winston. Bourne Co. (ASCAP). **"There'll Be Some Changes Made"** by Higgins, Billy; Overstreet, Benton. Arrangement and additional lyrics by Glen Kelly. I.D.K. Music LLC (ASCAP). **"There's a Broken Heart for Every Light on Broadway"** by Fisher, Fred; Johnson, Howard. Arrangement and additional lyrics by Glen Kelly. I.D.K. Music LLC (ASCAP). **"There's a New Day Comin'"** by Ager, Milton; Young, Joe. WB Music Corp. (ASCAP)/Warock Corp. (ASCAP). **"They Go Wild, Simply Wild, Over Me"** by Fisher, Fred; McCarthy, Joseph. Arrangement and additional lyrics by Glen Kelly. I.D.K. Music LLC (ASCAP). **"Tiger Rag"** by De Costa,

Harry; Edwards, Edwin; LaRocca, James D.; Ragas, W.H.; Sbarbaro, Anthony; Shields, Larry. EMI Feist Catalog Inc. (ASCAP). **"(Up a) Lazy River"** by Arodin, Sidney; Carmichael, Hoagy. Peermusic III, Ltd. (BMI). **"Yes! We Have No Bananas"** by Cohn, Irving; Silver, Frank. Arrangement and additional lyrics by Glen Kelly. I.D.K. Music LLC (ASCAP).

SPECIAL THANKS

Clare Cook, Brittany Marcin Maschmeyer,
Amanda Kloots-Larsen

Trixie, who plays "Mr. Woofles," was adopted from Pet Rescue in Armonk, NY, and her understudy Rocco was adopted from Delaware Humane Association in Wilmington, DE.

---

www.BulletsOverBroadway.com

JORDAN ROTH
President
ROCCO LANDESMAN
President, Emeritus

PAUL LIBIN
Executive Vice President

JACK VIERTEL
Senior Vice President

MEREDITH VILLATORE
Chief Financial Officer

JENNIFER HERSHEY
Vice President,
Building Operations

MICAH HOLLINGWORTH
Vice President,
Company Operations

HAL GOLDBERG
Vice President,
Theatre Operations

Director of Business Affairs ....Albert T. Kim
Director of Ticketing Services ....Justin Karr
Theatre Operations Managers ....Willa Burke, Susan Elrod, Emily Hare, Jeff Hubbard, Albert T. Kim
Theatre Operations Associates ....Carrie Jo Brinker, Brian Busby, Michael Composto, Anah Jyoti Klate
Controller..Tejal Patel
Accounting ....Cathy Cerge, Amy Frank, Tariq Hamami, Alexander Parra
Executive Producer, Red Awning ....Nicole Kastrinos
Director of Sales, Givenik.com ....Karen Freidus
Building Operations Manager ....Erich Bussing
Executive Coordinator ....Ed Lefferson

Executive Assistants ....Hunter Chancellor, Danielle DeMatteo, Elisabeth Stern
Receptionist ....Lisa Perchinske
Ticketing and Pricing Associate ....Jonathon Scott
Sales Associate Givenik.com ....Taylor Kurpiel
Maintenance ....Ralph Santos, Ramon Zapata
Security ....Rasim Hodzic, Terone Richardson
Interns ....Sal Bucci, Ashley Earick, Kathleen Hefferon, Katie Hesketh, Patrick Korkuch, Mollie Thoennes

---

Staff for the St. James Theatre for
Bullets Over Broadway

Manager ....Jeff Hubbard
Associate Manager ....Brian Busby
Treasurer ....Vincent Sclafani
Head Carpenter ....Timothy B. McDonough
Head Propertyman ....Timothy M. McDonough
Head Electrician ....Albert Sayers
Flyman ....Ryan McDonough
Engineer ....Zaim Hodzic
Assistant Treasurers ....Kathryn Fearon, Michael Loiacono, Thomas Motylenski, Vincent Siniscalchi
Carpenters ....Justin Borowinski, Jason Muldrow, Tommy Vercetti
Propertymen ....Raymond Chan, Eric Dressler
Electricians ....Dave Holliman, Bill Lewis, Bob Miller, Susan Pelkofer
Head Usher ....Cynthia Lopiano
Ticket-takers/Directors/Ushers ....Leonard Baron, Jim Barry, Barbara Carroll, Carla Dawson, Paul Fiteni, Heather Jewels, Margaret McElroy, Leslie Morgenstern, Rochelle Rogers, Rebecca Segarra, Jessica Theisen, Donna Vanderlinden, Brian Veith
Doormen ....Russell Buenteo, Adam Hodzic
Head Porter ....Jacobo Medrano
Porters ....Tareq Brown, Francisco Medina, Donnette Niles
Head Cleaner ....Carmela Tenebruso
Cleaners ...Benita Aliberti, Juana Medrano, Antonia Moreno

Lobby refreshments by Sweet Hospitality Group.

Security provided by GBA Consulting, Inc.

 Jujamcyn Theaters is a proud member of the Broadway Green Alliance.

Bullets Over Broadway
Scrapbook

Curtain call on opening night (L-R): *Yearbook* correspondent Nick Cordero, Zach Braff, Marin Mazzie, Heléne Yorke, Vincent Pastore and Karen Ziemba

Correspondent: Nick Cordero, "Cheech"

Memorable Opening Night Speech: Director Susan Stroman sat us down before the opening night performance and gave a little talk about how it was time for the creators to hand over the show to us. She has a great way of naming the significance of each moment. She said, "Take it all in, don't be on your phone at the party, looking at the reviews or other outside stuff. Relish the moment. Be aware of what's going on. This kind of thing doesn't happen all the time." It was an emotional evening for everybody. So much work goes into putting on a show, giving it size and scope. And I made sure to appreciate that moment. It created a bond between all of us that we will never forget.

Opening Night Party and Gifts: We had our opening night party at the Metropolitan Museum, which I heard was the first time the Met had ever done something like that. It was appropriately lavish, grand and spectacular. We received flasks as gifts from the producers. Woody Allen gave me a bullet with my name engraved on it, in a fancy red box with a note said "congratulations and job well done." Susan Stroman gave us a bullet that was a puzzle. It was an amazing evening all around.

Most Exciting Celebrity Visitors: We had Liza Minnelli the other day, and she said the show changed her world. She said she hadn't seen anything that great since *Gypsy* when she was young. Actors from the film stopped by; Dianne Wiest and Jennifer Tilly were really enthusiastic about what they had seen. When Wiest came I wasn't expecting it. She and Woody had seen the show at the matinee and he invited her back. There was a knock on my dressing room door and James Gray, the associate choreographer said, "I have a surprise visitor." I said, "Come on in," and opened the door—and there she was. I've been a fan of hers my entire life and she was so sweet. My voice got soft and our faces were close together and she said she was so happy with what we had done. It was an incredible moment. Wiest has such a great presence.

Special Backstage Rituals: We gather on stage before the show starts, behind our beautiful scrim. The stage is set for the opening club scene and the girls usually run through their dance number. We mingle and hug and say "how was your day?" It's a way of connecting with everybody. And, of course, there's always Brooks Ashmanskas there in his housecoat making everybody laugh.

Memorable Author's Note: At our first notes session, Woody gave me a note that was key to my finding Cheech. I thought to myself, "Wow, I'm getting a note from Woody Allen!" It was a surreal moment. He said something like, "Don't present the punch line so much. Don't hit it on the head too much. If it's funny, then that's great. If it's not, then that will be my fault and not yours. If the situation is funny, then live the truth of the situation rather than trying to sell the joke." I think that was a pretty selfless way of putting it. Sage advice from the master.

Favorite Off-Site Hangout: Angus McIndoe

Favorite In-Theatre Gathering Places: Brooks Ashmanskas' dressing room is done up like a studio apartment. It's like he's running a salon out of the St. James Theatre. He knows so many great people and they all sit in there and have drinks. The girls also run a Thirsty Thursday in the basement: wine and guac, and we have a little drink there before we head out to Angus.

Who Got the Gypsy Robe: Kevin Ligon

Actor Who Performed the Most Roles in This Show: I think it is our swing, Preston Boyd, who covers 11 acting and dance tracks, including all the male dancers. I don't know how swings do it. It's a discipline I don't know if I could achieve.

Memorable Audience Reactions: We usually have the odd person gasp when I get shot at the end. But also the front row usually has enthusiastic fans of the show, or of Marin Mazzie. She inspires incredible loyalty in her fans. We can tell immediately if the Marin fans are in the front row. They are very supportive.

Unique Pre-Show Announcement: Vinny Pastore comes on the house sound system and says "Welcome to da St. James Theatre." His voice is very Bronx, New York, and puts you in the mood right away. He tells people to turn off their cell phones and ends, "Got it?" And the audience always says, "Got it!"

Memorable Stage Door Fan Encounters: Our fans are extraordinarily enthusiastic. We have people who have seen the show six times already [mid May 2014]. These are the kinds of people who will have a big blow-up copy of a 10-year-old headshot mounted on a board the size of your television, and will bring along a pen so you can sign it.

Favorite Snack Food: Betsy Wolfe makes this unbelievable coffee cake. We call it "crack cake" because we can't stop eating it. People gravitate to it like pigeons in the park.

Favorite Therapy: To soothe your throat, Brooks has this Chinese supplement he uses, a syrupy thing that he makes tea out of. He gave me a box of it, and it works like a charm.

Mascots: We have two dogs on stage, Trixie and Rocco. Trixie is a good dog. Rocco is always chewing on something and running someplace.

Catchphrase Only the Company Would Recognize: "Club Angus"

Nicknames: We call Marin "Marin Muh-ZEE." Brooks called her that in rehearsal and it kinda stuck.

Ghostly Encounters Backstage: We sometimes hear a laugh, but usually it's Jim Borstelmann. He changes it up every night.

Embarrassing Moment: The show opens with my "shooting" the title of the show into the scrim with a machine gun. In early previews, when the bells and whistles were still being fine-tuned, the lighting effect did not go off, so all the audience saw was a six-foot-five gangster shooting nothing into the scrim. I tried to save it by turning to the audience and pretending to shoot them, but I've got to tell you, it felt like two hours, even though I was out there for probably ten seconds.

Favorite Moments During Each Performance: When I shoot Olive in the middle of the second act. The audience has been tracking Cheech's journey, and I can see the relief when he bumps off the terrible actress getting in the way between him and greatness. The audience is thrilled for him when he kills someone for his art. It's a sadistic thing between Cheech and the audience. I kill her and she falls into the Gowanus Canal, and the audience applauds! She won't die, so I pump five more bullets into her, and then drive off into the Brooklyn night. I also love the gangster tap number to "'Tain't Nobody's Biz-ness If I Do." It's a very masculine dance, feet pounding into the floor, hands in pockets and fedoras pulled down over the face. The audience always goes wild for Susan's choreography and Don Holder's lighting. It's an amazing moment and I love it.

Cabaret

First Preview: March 21, 2014. Opened: April 24, 2014.
Still running as of May 31, 2014.

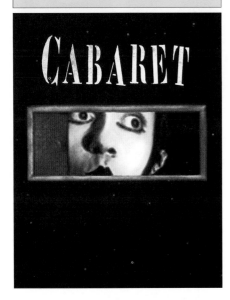

American writer Cliff Bradshaw arrives in Weimar-era Berlin seeking inspiration for a novel. He encounters free-spirited cabaret singer Sally Bowles and a host of her friends and acquaintances—including a growing number of members of the rapidly-strengthening Nazi Party. The conflicts and moral dilemmas raised by these friends, and by Sally's determination to ignore them, are reflected in a series of increasingly sinister floor shows at the Kit Kat Klub—all overseen by a chillingly genial Emcee. This production recreates the Tony-winning 1998 revival that ran at the same theatre with the same director and the same leading man.

CAST

(in order of appearance)

Emcee	ALAN CUMMING

The Kit Kat Girls:

Rosie	JANE PFITSCH
Lulu	KALEIGH CRONIN
Frenchie	ANDREA GOSS
Texas	JESSICA PARISEAU
Fritzie	GAYLE RANKIN
Helga	KRISTIN OLNESS

The Kit Kat Boys:

Bobby	LEEDS HILL
Victor	DYLAN PAUL
Hans	EVAN D. SIEGEL
Herman	BENJAMIN EAKELEY
Sally Bowles	MICHELLE WILLIAMS
Clifford Bradshaw	BILL HECK
Ernst Ludwig	AARON KROHN
Customs Official	BENJAMIN EAKELEY
Fräulein Schneider	LINDA EMOND

Continued on next page

Continued on next page

ROUNDABOUT THEATRE COMPANY

Todd Haimes, Artistic Director
Harold Wolpert, Managing Director
Julia C. Levy, Executive Director
Sydney Beers, General Manager

presents

Alan Cumming   Michelle Williams

in

CABARET

Book by
Joe Masteroff

Music by
John Kander

Lyrics by
Fred Ebb

Based on the play by JOHN VAN DRUTEN and stories by CHRISTOPHER ISHERWOOD

with

Linda Emond   Danny Burstein

Bill Heck

Aaron Krohn   Gayle Rankin

Will Carlyon   Kaleigh Cronin   Caleb Damschroder   Benjamin Eakeley   Andrea Goss
Leeds Hill   Kristin Olness   Kelly Paredes   Jessica Pariseau   Dylan Paul   Jane Pfitsch
Evan D. Siegel   Stacey Sipowicz

Set and Club Design by Robert Brill	Costume Design by William Ivey Long	Lighting Design by Peggy Eisenhauer Mike Baldassari	Sound Design by Brian Ronan
Orchestrations Michael Gibson	Dance & Incidental Music David Krane	Original Musical Coordinator John Monaco	
Hair & Wig Design Paul Huntley	Make-up Design Angelina Avallone	Dialect Coach Deborah Hecht	Production Stage Manager Arthur Gaffin
Casting Jim Carnahan, C.S.A. Jillian Cimini	Associate Choreographer/ Choreography Re-created By Cynthia Onrubia	Associate Director BT McNicholl	Technical Supervisor Steve Beers
Associate Managing Director Greg Backstrom	Director of Marketing & Audience Development Tom O'Connor	Director of Development Lynne Gugenheim Gregory	Press Representative Polk & Co.
Founding Director Gene Feist	Adams Associate Artistic Director* Scott Ellis		

Executive Producer
Sydney Beers

Musical Director/Vocal Arranger
Patrick Vaccariello

Co-Directed & Choreographed by
Rob Marshall

Directed by
Sam Mendes

Proud Sponsor BANK OF AMERICA
Official Airline AMERICAN AIRLINES
Major support for Cabaret provided by The Blanche and Irving Laurie Foundation.
Roundabout Theatre Company is a member of the League of Resident Theatres.   www.roundabouttheatre.org

4/24/14

Alan Cumming as the Emcee introduces Michelle Williams (seated) as Sally Bowles to sing "Don't Tell Mama" with the Kit Kat Girls.

Photo: Joan Marcus

Cabaret

Cast Continued

Fräulein Kost	GAYLE RANKIN
Rudy	EVAN D. SIEGEL
Herr Schultz	DANNY BURSTEIN
Max	BENJAMIN EAKELEY
Gorilla	ANDREA GOSS
Boy Soprano (recording)	ALEX BOWEN

All other parts played by members of the company.

TIME
1929 – 1930
PLACE
Berlin, Germany

STANDBYS AND UNDERSTUDIES

Swings: WILL CARLYON,
  CALEB DAMSCHRODER, KELLY PAREDES,
  STACEY SIPOWICZ
Understudy for Sally Bowles: ANDREA GOSS
For Clifford Bradshaw,
  Ernst Ludwig: BENJAMIN EAKELEY
For Emcee: LEEDS HILL
For Fräulein Kost: KALEIGH CRONIN
Standby for
  Fräulein Schneider: KRISTIE DALE SANDERS
Standby for Herr Schultz: PHILIP HOFFMAN

Inspired by the 1993 production of *Cabaret*
at the Donmar Warehouse, London.
Directed by Sam Mendes.

Dear Audience Member,

Welcome to *Cabaret* at Studio 54. Since the closing of Sam Mendes and Rob Marshall's incredible revival in 2004, I have felt that this landmark production deserves to be seen again. I am happy that a new generation will have the chance to see this incredible piece live on Broadway. *Cabaret* is not only an important part of Roundabout's history, but this show is a true treasure of the American musical theatre canon.

Musicals have the unique ability to present the many sides of complicated characters through the additional expressive avenue of song. Sally Bowles is certainly not a traditional leading lady as established by musicals during the first half of the 20th century, but through the depths of Kander and Ebb's incredible score, we are better able to comprehend her unfamiliar circumstances and be truly captivated by her struggle.

Over at the American Airlines Theatre another unlikely heroine is center stage in *Violet*. Violet, like Sally, knows what it is to be ostracized by the community around her. Both of these women are struggling against a world that sees them as damaged goods, and though the time and place are different, their journeys are equally moving. I am thrilled to have two strong women at the center of both musicals at Roundabout this spring, and I hope you get a chance to catch these contrasting depictions. As always, I welcome you to share your thoughts by emailing me at ArtisticOffice@roundabouttheatre.org. Thank you again for joining us, and I hope that you enjoy *Cabaret*.

Sincerely,
Todd Haimes, Artistic Director

Read interviews with the cast and creative team and learn more about the show at blog.roundabouttheatre.org.
Roundabout Theatre Company also maintains a digital and open access archive,
chronicling the company's half century of theatre history.
Visit archive.roundabouttheatre.org to learn more.

MUSICAL NUMBERS

ACT I

"Willkommen"	Emcee and the Kit Kat Klub
"So What"	Fräulein Schneider
"Don't Tell Mama"	Sally and the Kit Kat Girls
"Mein Herr"	Sally and the Kit Kat Girls
"Perfectly Marvelous"	Sally and Cliff
"Two Ladies"	Emcee, Lulu and Bobby
"It Couldn't Please Me More"	Fräulein Schneider and Herr Schultz
"Tomorrow Belongs to Me"	Emcee
"Maybe This Time"	Sally
"Money"	Emcee and the Kit Kat Girls
"Married"	Herr Schultz, Fräulein Schneider, Fritzie
"Tomorrow Belongs to Me" (Reprise)	Fräulein Kost, Ernst Ludwig and the Company

ACT II

"Entr'Acte"	The Kit Kat Band
"Kick Line"	The Kit Kat Klub
"Married" (Reprise)	Herr Schultz
"If You Could See Her"	Emcee and the Gorilla
"What Would You Do?"	Fräulein Schneider
"I Don't Care Much"	Emcee
"Cabaret"	Sally
"Finale"	The Company

THE KIT KAT BAND

Musical Director and Piano	PATRICK VACCARIELLO
Associate Conductor	MAGGIE TORRE
Drums	ERIC POLAND
Bass	BILLY SLOAT
Trumpet	GARRETT SCHMIDT
Trumpet/Euphonium	STACEY SIPOWICZ
Trombone	DYLAN PAUL
Clarinet/Soprano Sax/Alto Sax	BENJAMIN EAKELEY
Clarinet/Tenor Sax	JESSICA PARISEAU
Clarinet/Tenor Sax	KRISTIN OLNESS
Alto & Tenor Sax	EVAN D. SIEGEL
Alto Sax	KALEIGH CRONIN
Cello	WILL CARLYON
Violin/Piano	ANDREA GOSS
Violin/Clarinet	LEEDS HILL
Violin/French Horn/Trumpet	JANE PFITSCH
Violin/Viola	KELLY PAREDES
Accordion	GAYLE RANKIN
Banjo/Bassoon	CALEB DAMSCHRODER
Banjo	AARON KROHN

Cabaret

Alan Cumming
Emcee

Michelle Williams
Sally Bowles

Linda Emond
Fräulein Schneider

Danny Burstein
Herr Schultz

Bill Heck
Clifford Bradshaw

Aaron Krohn
Ernst Ludwig

Gayle Rankin
Fräulein Kost

Will Carlyon
Swing

Kaleigh Cronin
Lulu, Two Ladies Dance; u/s Fräulein Kost

Caleb Damschroder
Swing

Benjamin Eakeley
Herman, Customs Officer, Max; u/s Clifford Bradshaw, Ernst Ludwig

Andrea Goss
Frenchie, Gorilla; u/s Sally Bowles

Leeds Hill
Bobby, Two Ladies Dancer; u/s Emcee

Kristin Olness
Helga

Kelly Paredes
Swing

Jessica Pariseau
Texas

Dylan Paul
Victor

Jane Pfitsch
Rosie

Evan D. Siegel
Hans, Rudy

Stacey Sipowicz
Swing

Kristie Dale Sanders
Standby for Fräulein Schneider

Philip Hoffman
Standby for Herr Schultz

Joe Masteroff
Book

John Kander (*Music*) & Fred Ebb (*Lyrics*)

Sam Mendes
Director

Rob Marshall
Co-Director, Choreographer

Patrick Vaccariello
Musical Director

Robert Brill
Set & Club Design

William Ivey Long
Costume Design

Peggy Eisenhauer
Lighting Design

Mike Baldassari
Lighting Design

Brian Ronan
Sound Design

Michael Gibson
Orchestrations

David Krane
Dance and Incidental Music

Cynthia Onrubia
Associate Choreographer/ Choreography Re-created By

Cabaret

Paul Huntley
Hair & Wig Design

Angelina Avallone
Make-up Design

Deborah Hecht
Dialect Coach

BT McNicholl
Associate Director

Jim Carnahan, CSA
Casting

Jeff Siebert
*Assistant Stage
Manager/
Dance Captain*

Gene Feist
Roundabout Theatre
Company
Founding Director

Todd Haimes
Roundabout Theatre
Company
Artistic Director

MAKE-UP/HAIR
Robert Amodeo
(Associate Make-up Designer),
Carrie Rohm (Hair & Wig Supervisor)

CREW
Front (L-R): Tom Goehring, Erin Delaney, Erika Warmbrunn, Karissa Riehl, Jessica Morton, Dan Mendeloff
Back (L-R): Steve Jones, Shannon Slaton (Production Sound Engineer), Jim Fossi, Adam Rigby,
Dan Hoffman (Production/House Carpenter), Lawrence Jennino (House Properties),
John Wooding (Production/House Electrician)

FRONT OF HOUSE
Front Row (L-R): Alvin Vega, LaConya Robinson, Samantha Rivera
Second Row (L-R): Raven Riley, Yonathan Vendriger, Dylan Bauer, Linda Gjonbalaj
Third Row (L-R): Andrew Hall, Luis Alvarez Schacht, John Ryan
Fourth Row (L-R): Isaac Hicks, Christopher Morrissey,
Top Row (L-R): Shiomara Diaz, Drew Helton, David Nando

Photos: Brian Mapp

Cabaret

WARDROBE
Front (L-R): Emma Atherton (Dresser), Lacie Pulido (Dresser),
Kimberly Mark (Dresser), Lizet Rubinos (Stitcher)
Back (L-R): Michael D. Hannah (Wardrobe Supervisor),
Phillip Rolfe (Dresser), Christel Murdock (Dresser), Danny Mura (Dresser),
Jackie Gehrt (Dresser), Kelly Saxon (Dresser)

BAR STAFF
Front (L-R): Jackie Freeman, Leah Colhan, Leanne Surace, Ilaria Tarozzi,
Kayla Bryan, Lucienne Spoja, Sean Michael Beck, Debby Ortega
Back (L-R): Brandon Pheltz, Susanna Allen, Beatrice Crosbie,
Andrew Boetcher, Ashley Timm, Anthony Fagon, Blane Pressler,
Blake Smith, Josh Wooster

ROUNDABOUT THEATRE COMPANY STAFF

ARTISTIC DIRECTOR .... TODD HAIMES
MANAGING DIRECTOR .... HAROLD WOLPERT
EXECUTIVE DIRECTOR .... JULIA C. LEVY
ADAMS ASSOCIATE
   ARTISTIC DIRECTOR .... SCOTT ELLIS
DIRECTOR OF ARTISTIC
   DEVELOPMENT .... JIM CARNAHAN
GENERAL MANAGER .... SYDNEY BEERS
ASSOCIATE MANAGING
   DIRECTOR .... GREG BACKSTROM

ARTISTIC STAFF

DIRECTOR OF CASTING .... Jim Carnahan
Artistic Consultant .... Robyn Goodman
Resident Directors .... Doug Hughes, Sam Gold
Associate Artists .... Mark Brokaw, Evan Cabnet,
   Bill Irwin, Pam MacKinnon, Joe Mantello,
   Kathleen Marshall, Theresa Rebeck
Literary Manager .... Jill Rafson
Senior Casting Director .... Carrie Gardner
Casting Director .... Stephen Kopel
Casting Associate .... Jillian Cimini
Casting Assistants .... Lain Kunin, Alexandre Bleau
Artistic Associate .... Amy Ashton
Literary Associate .... Josh Fiedler
Educational Foundation of
   America Commission .... Lydia Diamond
Roundabout Commissions .... Helen Edmundson,
   Adam Gwon & Michael Mitnick, Joshua Harmon,
   Andrew Hinderaker, Stephen Karam, Steven Levenson,
   Matthew Lopez, Kim Rosenstock
Laurents/Hatcher Foundation
   Commission .... Meghan Kennedy
Casting Interns .... Caitlin Morrison, Emma Miller,
   James Scully, Heather Washburn, Claire Yenson
Script Readers .... Shannon Deep, Michael Perlman,
   Alexis Roblan, Nicole Tingir
Artistic Apprentice .... Olivia O'Connor

EDUCATION STAFF

DIRECTOR OF EDUCATION .... Jennifer DiBella
Assistant Director of Education .... Mitch Mattson
Education Program Manager .... Paul Brewster
Education Program Manager .... Kimberley Oria
Education Assistant .... Julia Borowski
Education Dramaturg .... Ted Sod
Teaching Artists .... Cynthia Babak, Victor Barbella,
   LaTonya Borsay, Mark Bruckner, Chloe Chapin,
   Michael Costagliola, Joe Doran, Mathilde Dratwa,
   Elizabeth Dunn-Ruiz, Sarah Ellis, Carrie Ellman-Larsen,
   Theresa Flanagan, Deanna Frieman, Geoffrey Goldberg,
   Sheri Graubert, Adam Gwon, Creighton Irons,
   Devin Haqq, Carrie Heitman, Karla Hendrick,
   Jason Jacobs, Alana Jacoby, Tess James,
   Hannah Johnson-Walsh, Lisa Renee Jordan, Boo Killebrew,
   Anya Klepikov, Sarah Lang, John Lavigne, Erin McCready,
   James Miles, Nick Moore, Meghan O'Neil, Nicole Press,
   Leah Reddy, Amanda Rehbein, Nick Simone,
   Heidi Stallings, Daniel Sullivan, Carl Tallent,
   Vickie Tanner, Laurine Towler, Jennifer Varbalow,
   Kathryn Veillette, Leese Walker, Christopher Weston,
   Gail Winar, Jamie Kalama Wood, Chad Yarborough
Teaching Artist Emeritus .... Reneé Flemings
Education Apprentices ... Rachel Friedman, Rebecca Powell

MANAGEMENT/ADMINISTRATIVE STAFF

ASSOCIATE MANAGING DIRECTOR .. Greg Backstrom
General Manager,
   American Airlines Theatre .... Denise Cooper
General Manager, Steinberg Center ... Nicholas J. Caccavo
Operations Manager .... Valerie D. Simmons
Associate General Manager .... Maggie Cantrick
Assistant Managing Director .... Katharine Croke
Rentals Manager .... Nancy Mulliner
Archivist .... Tiffany Nixon
Assistant to the Executive Director &
   Manager, Government Relations .... Nicole Tingir
Assistant to the
   Managing Director .... Christina Pezzello

Management Apprentice .... Jeesun Choi

FINANCE STAFF

DIRECTOR OF FINANCE .... Susan Neiman
Payroll Director .... John LaBarbera
Accounts Payable Manager .... Frank Surdi
Payroll Benefits Administrator .... Yonit Kafka
Manager Financial Reporting .... Joshua Cohen
Business Office Assistant .... Jackie Verbitski
Lead Receptionist .... Kyle Stockburger
Receptionists .... Jessie Malone, Michael Valentine
Messenger .... Darnell Franklin
Business Office Apprentice .... Gregory Shepard

DEVELOPMENT STAFF

DIRECTOR OF
   DEVELOPMENT .... Lynne Gugenheim Gregory
Assistant to the
   Director of Development .... Jonathan Sokolow
Associate Director of Development .... Christopher Nave
Director, Special Events .... Lane Hosmer
Director, Institutional Giving .... Erica Raven
Associate Director, Individual Giving .... Tyler Ennis
Manager, Special Events .... Natalie Corr
Manager, Membership Programs .... Oliver Pattenden
Manager, Donor Information Systems .... Lise Speidel
Individual Giving Officer, Stewardship ...... Jordan Frausto
Individual Giving Officer, Patron Services .... Maggie Jones
Special Events Assistant .... Genevieve Carroll
Development Assistant .... Martin Giannini
Special Events Apprentice .... Jena Yarley

INFORMATION TECHNOLOGY STAFF

DIRECTOR OF
   INFORMATION TECHNOLOGY .. Daniel V. Gomez
Tessitura & Applications Administrator ..... Yelena Ingberg
Web Administrator .... Robert Parmelee
DBA/Developer .... Ruslan Nikandrov
IT & Help Desk Analyst .... Cary Kim

Cabaret

Photos: Brian Mapp

MANAGEMENT
(L-R): Jeff Siebert (Assistant Stage Manager/Dance Captain), Lee Micklin (Stage Manager), Arthur Gaffin (Production Stage Manager), Roseanna Sharrow (Company Manager)

BOX OFFICE
(L-R): Krystin MacRitchie (Head Treasurer), Laura Marshall (Assistant Treasurer), Kara Harrington (Associate Treasurer)

MARKETING STAFF

DIRECTOR OF MARKETING &
   AUDIENCE DEVELOPMENT ....Tom O'Connor
Senior Marketing Manager ....Rani Haywood
Digital Content Producer ....Mark Cajigao
Graphic Designer ....Darren Melchiorre
Marketing Associate ....Rachel LeFevre-Snee
Digital Marketing Associate ....Alex Barber
Marketing Assistant ....Dayna Johnson
Marketing Apprentices ....Alyssa DeAlesandro,
   Jamie Gottlieb
Digital Marketing Apprentice ....Jennifer Marinelli

AUDIENCE SERVICES STAFF

DIRECTOR OF AUDIENCE
   SERVICES ....Wendy Hutton
Director of Ticketing ....Gabe Johnson
Director of Call Center Operations ....Gavin Brown
Customer Care Manager ....Robert Kane
Call Center Manager ....Patrick Pastor
Box Office Managers ....Edward P. Osborne,
   Jaime Perlman, Krystin MacRitchie, Catherine Fitzpatrick
Assistant Box Office Managers ....Robert Morgan,
   Andrew Clements, Nicki Ishmael, Kara Harrington
Assistant Audience Services Managers .....Lindsay Ericson,
   Vanessa Clark, Jessica Pruett-Barnett,
   Kaia Lay Rafoss, Joe Gallina
Customer Care Associate ....Thomas Walsh
Audience Services ....Jennifer Almgreen, Alexander Barton,
   Solangel Bido, Eric Bridle, Lauren Cartelli, Elizabeth Daly,
   Brittany Duck, Adam Elsberry, Alanna Harms,
   Amy Laisure, Blair Laurie, Rebecca Lewis-Whitson,
   Michelle Maccarone, Mead Margulies, Laura Marshall,
   Chuck Migliaccio, Carlos Morris, Katie Mueller,
   Lauren Murray, Sarah Olsen, Evan Reed, Nikaury Roman,
   Josh Rozett, Heather Seibert, Nalane Singh,
   Ron Tobia, Kate Valiska, Hannah Weitzman
Audience Services Apprentice ....Natalie Donohue

SERVICES

Counsel ....Paul, Weiss,
   Rifkind, Wharton and Garrison LLP/
   Charles H. Googe Jr., Carolyn J. Casselman
Counsel ....Rosenberg & Estis
Counsel ..Andrew Lance/Gibson, Dunn, & Crutcher, LLP
Counsel ...Harry H. Weintraub/Glick and Weintraub, P.C.
Counsel ....Strook & Strook & Lavan LLP
Counsel ....Daniel S. Dokos/Weil, Gotshal & Manges LLP
Counsel ..Claudia Wagner/Manatt, Phelps & Phillips, LLP
Immigration
   Counsel ....Kramer Levin Naftalis & Frankel, LLP/
   Mark D. Koestler, Theodore Ruthizer

House Physicians ....Dr. Theodore Tyberg,
   Dr. Lawrence Katz
House Dentist ....Neil Kanner, D.M.D.
Insurance ....DeWitt Stern Group, Inc.
Accountant ....Lutz & Carr CPAs, LLP
Advertising ....Spotco/Drew Hodges, Tom Greenwald,
   Ilene Rosen, Kara Carothers, Tyler Beddoe, Kyle Carter
Interactive Marketing ....Situation Interactive/
   Damian Bazadona, Eric Bornemann, Elizabeth Kandel
Events Photography ....Anita and Steve Shevett
Production Photographer ....Joan Marcus
Theatre Displays ....King Displays, Wayne Sapper
Lobby Refreshments ....Sweet Hospitality Group
Merchandising ....Marquee Merchandise, LLC/
   Matt Murphy

MANAGING DIRECTOR
   EMERITUS ....Ellen Richard

Roundabout Theatre Company
231 West 39th Street, New York, NY 10018
(212) 719-9393.

GENERAL PRESS REPRESENTATIVE
POLK & CO.
Matt Polk   Jessica Johnson
Michelle Bergmann   Layne McNish

CREDITS FOR *CABARET*

Company Manager ....Roseanna Sharrow
Production Stage Manager ....Arthur Gaffin
Stage Manager ....Lee Micklin
Assistant Stage Manager/Dance Captain ....Jeff Siebert
Assistant Dance Captain ....Stacey Sipowicz
Assistant Musical Director ....Maggie Torre
Associate Director ....BT McNicholl
Assistant Director ....Paul Dobie
Associate Choreographer ....Cynthia Onrubia
Associate Set Designer ....Steven Kemp
Assistant Set Designer ....Julia Lee
Associate Costume Designer ....David Kaley
Assistant Costume Designer ....Tina McCartney
Costume Assistant ....Michelle Ridley
Costume Shopper ....Stephanie Levin
Costume Intern ....Katherine Weeks
Associate Lighting Designer ....Kristina Kloss
Assistant Lighting Designer ....Jonathan Spencer
Associate Sound Designer ....Keith Caggiano
Assistant Sound Designer ....Mike Tracey
Production Sound Engineer ....Shannon Slaton
Associate Makeup Designer ....Robert Amodeo
Assistant Makeup Designer ....Benedetta Celada
Rehearsal Pianist ....Jim Laev

Rehearsal Drummer ....Eric Poland
Keyboard Programmer ....Randy Cohen
Copyist ....Anne Kaye, Doug Houston
Production Carpenter ....Dan Hoffman
Production Electrician ....John Wooding
Moving Light Programmer ....Timothy Rogers
Production Properties Coordinator ....Emiliano Pares
Associate Production Properties ....Tessa Dunning
House Properties ....Lawrence Jennino
Wardrobe Supervisor ....Michael D. Hannah
Hair and Wig Supervisor ....Carrie Rohm
Dressers ....Jackie Gehrt, Kimberly Mark, Danny Mura,
   Christel Murdock, Lacie Pulido, Phillip Rolfe, Kelly Saxon
Stitcher ....Lizet Rubinos, Karl Ruckdeschel
Production Assistants ....Jeff Brancato,
   Mitchell B. Hodges, Andrea Wales

CREDITS

Scenery fabrication by Hudson Scenic Studio Inc. Lighting equipment by PRG Lighting. Audio equipment by PRG Audio. Soft goods by iWeiss Theatrical Solutions. Costumes made by Euroco Costumes Inc., Schneeman Studio Limited, Katrina Patterns, Scafati Theatrical Tailors, Giliberto Designs, Artur & Tailors Ltd., Arnold S. Levine Inc. Knitwear by Mary Pat Klein. Millinery by Rodney Gordon. Dance shoes by T.O. Dey, LaDuca. Fabric painting and dyeing by Jeff Fender Studio, Metro Custom Dyeing. Undergarments and hosiery by Bra*tenders. Hair products provided by Bumble & Bumble.

SPECIAL THANKS

Faust Harrison Pianos
for helping us to acquire our wonderful new
Yamaha Piano,
Nicole Press, Danny Baron,
Tim Monich, Michael Zimmer

MAKE-UP PROVIDED BY M•A•C.

STUDIO 54 THEATRE STAFF

Operations Manager ....Valerie D. Simmons
House Manager ....LaConya Robinson
Associate House Manager ....Jack Watanachaiyot
Head Treasurer ....Krystin MacRitchie
Associate Treasurer ....Kara Harrington
Assistant Treasurers ....Laura Marshall,
   Lindsay Ericson, Blair Laurie
House Carpenter ....Dan Hoffman
House Electrician ....John Wooding
House Properties ....Lawrence Jennino
Security ....Gotham Security
Lobby Refreshments by ....Sweet Hospitality Group

Cabaret
SCRAPBOOK

Correspondent: Kaleigh Cronin, "Lulu"

Memorable Note, Fax or Fan Letter: The stars of our show receive so much fan mail on a daily basis. I think our favorite was when Danny Burstein got a letter from a local playwright asking him to star in his new work "The Man with the Catheter." Hilarious.

Opening Night Parties and/or Gifts: The opening night gifts were overwhelming. The girls' dressing room looked like a floral shop and the boys' more like a well-stocked bar. Out of everything, I think the most sentimental was a beautiful pen case from our composer John Kander with the late Fred Ebb's opening lyrics to "Cabaret" hand-etched into the wood. It was a beautiful and generous gift and will no doubt be displayed in our homes for years to come. Equally as wonderful was Linda Emond making a donation to New York's Holocaust museum in honor of our opening and having tulips planted in Central Park in celebration; appropriate and meaningful.

Most Exciting Celebrity Visitors: We are lucky enough to get to perform onstage with celebrities every night! Alan and Michelle are two of the most humble, wonderful people you could ever work with. We are also visited by many celebrities coming to see the show. Emma Stone was adorable and incredibly sweet, and our personal favorite attendee thus far has been Monica Lewinsky!

Favorite In-Theatre Gathering Place: Alan's dressing room seems to be the hang-out spot of the theatre. He sometimes makes delicious soups in his crock pot between shows and graciously invites us all for a taste! He also kindly has us up for drinks sometimes after the show. I swear this man never gets sick of entertaining!!! His room is amazing and filled with all of his photography and fun gifts from everyone you can imagine. The conversation isn't too shabby either. You could talk to Alan forever and never get bored. SO many stories!

Special Backstage Rituals/Exercises: Since there is not much room backstage at our theatre, the boys began a workout routine on the stage 15 minutes before the house is open for every show. It is lovingly referred to as "Push-Up Palace." The ensemble boys would form a circle and each call out a different exercise for the group to do. We were skeptical at first and called them out for just giving themselves an opportunity to take their shirts off in front of the waitstaff. However, after witnessing the boys' great results, several of the girls and crew members have joined in. Now it's a *Cabaret* family affair! We've expanded our routine to include "Core Castle," our ab exercises, which take place before the evening performance on two-show days.

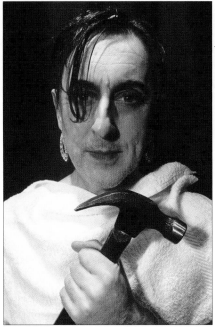

Photo: Danny Burstein

Alan Cumming, dubbed "Emcee Hammer," by fellow cast member Danny Burstein.

Favorite Backstage Photo: My favorite backstage photo was one that Danny Burstein (Herr Schultz) took of Alan during tech. Danny handed Alan a hammer to pose with and snapped a pic—"Emcee Hammer." A clever man that Danny is!

Worst/Best Audience Behavior: We've had some audience members use binoculars from the front row—a bit unnerving when you're dancing in a bra and underwear two feet from their faces. We've had a man bring an enormous hot pretzel on stage to dance with Alan during the audience participation section of the show. There was also an excited fan one night who yelled "Work!" "Fierce!" and "Yaaaasssssss!" during every silence in the show—always at the most inopportune moment.

Unique Pre-Show Announcement: Every now and again our wonderful PSM Artie Gaffin has been known to call an "emergency Equity meeting" before the house opens. This actually means that it's someone's birthday and we get to eat cake and treats! The fact that Artie attempts to disguise it as a meeting always makes us giggle.

Memorable Ad-Lib: Alan usually introduces Sally as "The Toast of Mayfair" and one night slipped and said "The taste of Mayfair." He promptly corrected himself and then added, "but she's tasty too!" There is also a part of the show where Alan brings audience members on stage to dance with him. Each night he has new hilarious material depending on whether or not they're drunk, shy, old, young—he'll find a way to embarrass them!

Memorable Press Encounter: We were the first Broadway show to ever appear on "The Tonight Show Starring Jimmy Fallon!" It was such an exciting experience and he was SO sweet! We all got to meet him and give him a hug after our performance. It is a day we will remember for years to come!

Memorable Stage Door Fan Encounter: I was leaving the theatre to head home after a show when someone in the autograph line yelled to me, "Hey! You with the red hair! You have the best armpit hair I've ever seen on a woman! I'll never forget that image for the rest of my life!" When we were told before rehearsals began that the girls would have to grow their armpit hair, I was absolutely HORRIFIED! Now that I am so comfortable and used to my pit hair, I was thrilled that it got a stage door shout-out! Best and most unique compliment I have ever received!

Memorable Directorial Note: All notes given are probably not appropriate for the *Yearbook*!

Best Story from Rehearsals: The day Michelle's daughter, Matilda, came to visit was one of the most fun days of rehearsal. She is a 30 year old trapped in the body of an eight year old. She desperately wanted to watch one of Michelle's numbers with the girls, but Michelle was nervous about the content, for obvious reasons. After a few lyric and choreo tweaks, we performed a conservative "Don't Tell Mama" for Matilda. She loved it and went on to give us some notes and dancing tips. She hung around the rest of the day and played with us and we had a blast! She also visited our dressing room opening night and gave us paper dolls of our characters that she had made, and left us a pile of jellybeans at each of our

Photo: Courtesy of Kaleigh Cronin

The Kit Kat Girls take a Kit Kat candy bar break (L-R): Jessica Pariseau, Kelly Paredes, *Yearbook* correspondent Kaleigh Cronin, Jane Pfitsch and Andrea Goss.

Cabaret
SCRAPBOOK

stations. She's our best and biggest fan! Adorable!

Company In-Jokes: We were teching the final scene of Act I where the company is onstage and Alan is up on the bandstand mooning the audience with a swastika on his butt cheek. He spent about 10 minutes just trying to position his bare ass in the spotlight and avoid showing his junk while we all watched from below screaming "To the left! No, to the right! No, we can see it!"

Embarrassing Moment: Our first day of tech started with "Willkommen," and it was our first time in costume. I wear a skirt in the show with a tiny, for lack of a better word, crotch strap, underneath. For whatever reason, the skirt had not yet been attached to the under piece, so when I went up into a handstand, the skirt fell out over my body and I was stuck in a handstand with just a small piece of fabric between my butt cheeks. I was yelling, "I'm nude! I'm nude!" upside down as everyone watched and laughed. From then on, Sam Mendes referred to my skirt as my "adult diaper."

Alan Cumming (C) and some of the *Cabaret* cast take a selfie.

Favorite Moment During Each Performance: I think the ensemble can agree that our favorite moment during the show is any time we are sitting up on the bandstand watching. Because the ensemble members all also play instruments, we are able to watch every scene we aren't in from the platform above the stage. It's like having a front row seat to watch and learn from the greatest actors of our generation every night. We are so fortunate.

Favorite Off-Site Hangout: Characters is right across the street from our box office, which makes it an easy hangout spot. We also frequent Sosa Borella, BarBacon, everything in the general vicinity of Studio 54! We have made a couple of family trips to Bathtub Gin, a secret '20s-era speakeasy in Chelsea, to see a sexy burlesque show and hear amazing live jazz.

Favorite Snack Foods: Our stage managers, Artie, Jeff and Lee, keep an entire pantry of snacks fully stocked at all times. We are incredibly spoiled and well fed!! Favorites include Oreos of all flavors, peanut butter-filled pretzels, and every brand of popcorn ever. Artie also goes above and beyond to include gluten- and dairy-free options

The ladies of *Cabaret* offer a toast (L-R): *Yearbook* correspondent Kaleigh Cronin, Andrea Goss, Kristin Olness, Jane Pfitsch, Kelly Paredes, Jessica Pariseau, Stacey Sipowicz. Prosit!

Lso that we can all participate in snacking ourselves to death!

Favorite Therapy: Our bodies take a pretty good beating throughout the course of the show, so we have many methods of therapy! We have rollers and tennis balls all over the place backstage for us to roll out our muscles. Salonpas are used often on our sore muscles and we eat soooo many Grether's Pastilles to soothe our voices. Kristie, in the girls dressing room, is our resident "guru" and has a natural herbal remedy for just about everything you can think of. We come to her with every ache and pain and she always has some trick that works!

Pit Stop: Best Story from the Orchestra: The orchestra is the best! It is comprised of all the ensemble members and our few incredibly talented "ringer musicians"—drums, keys, trumpet, bass. We have such a blast up there on the bandstand with Patrick Vaccariello, our conductor, at the helm. He whacks us on the head with his baton if we play sour notes. We play silent charades when out of sight of the audience, and try to make each other laugh by peeking over our stands. The other day, our drummer was on a train that broke down on its way into the city. He was trapped on board and unable to get to the show in time. After a few minutes of stalling and making some calls to other drummers in the area (all unavailable), our lead trumpet player hopped on the drum kit and said he would play! He was AWESOME! We were all so excited for and proud of him. It ended up being a fantastic show and Garrett Schmidt saved the day!

Mascot: On our first day at the theatre, the girls found a small statue of a gorilla in our dressing room that was left behind by a former occupant. We also somehow acquired a red clown nose and stuck it on the gorilla's head. This has now become the award we present to the girl who was most recently injured during the course of the show. You get a bruise? You get the monkey.

Catchphrases Only the Company Would Recognize: "Das Is Allist"; "CamonOhhvahhh";

"Pit Hair Don't Care"; "The Scottish Step"; "F**k Break"; "Breezy Hoo-has."

Best In-House Parody Lyrics: Caleb and I were chatting after playing "So What" for the millionth time during tech and were inspired to write our own version of the song: "An offer comes…you BAKE! For the yeast will rise and the dough will set…" et cetera. It was a long night. Give us a break. Also, Aaron (Ernst Ludwig), our resident comedian, will often give the girls a new word to chant instead of "money, money, money." We've had "honey, honey, honey"; on Easter it was "bunny, bunny, bunny"; the list goes on.

Tales from the Put-In: What put-in? So far (mid May 2014), we've had four people go on, including two for the leading roles, without a put-in! There was no time! They were all so professional and calm and nailed their performances. We were all incredibly proud.

Understudy Anecdote: In our first copy of the script there was a typo in which the stage direction read as part of the line. Stacey and

Director Sam Mendes (C) with a few of his *Cabaret* cast members.

Kelly (our fantastic female swings) were rehearsing lines with each other and read, "She goes into her room and closes the door" in a German accent as if it were part of the scene. They then realized the mistake, but continued to say the stage direction aloud on the bandstand every night during that scene.

Nicknames: Our youngest Kit Kat Klub member, Will Carlyon, is known to us on the bandstand as "Willaby Gantry Gonzales III." I think we decided he looked like a snobby elitist on the gantry one day and the name took shape. I'm not certain who decided he was also Spanish.

Ghostly Encounters Backstage: We just got here, but we are, after all, at Studio 54. The ghosts will come out eventually. They're probably just still hung over.

Coolest Thing About Being in This Show: The coolest thing about being in this show is getting to work with the most wonderful people in this business. From cast to band to crew to management, everyone at *Cabaret* is so kind and fun and happy to be there. It makes going to work so exciting!

Casa Valentina

First Preview: April 1, 2014. Opened: April 23, 2014.
Still running as of May 31, 2014.

PLAYBILL

CASA VALENTINA

Harvey Fierstein's new play about a 1960s Catskill Mountains retreat where heterosexual men can openly indulge their secret desire to dress and act like women. Trouble starts when one of the group wants to break the wall of secrecy and go public as part of a quest to legalize and normalize their lifestyle. Once the delicate balance is upset, marriages, careers and even lives are on the line.

CAST
(in order of appearance)

Rita .... MARE WINNINGHAM
Jonathon/Miranda .... GABRIEL EBERT
Bessie .... TOM McGOWAN
George/Valentina .... PATRICK PAGE
Charlotte .... REED BIRNEY
Gloria .... NICK WESTRATE
Terry .... JOHN CULLUM
The Judge/Amy .... LARRY PINE
Eleanor .... LISA EMERY

TIME
June, 1962

PLACE
The main house of a run-down bungalow colony in New York State's Catskill Mountains

Stage Manager .... KATHRYN L. McKEE

Continued on next page

Manhattan Theatre Club
Samuel J. Friedman Theatre

ARTISTIC DIRECTOR
Lynne Meadow

EXECUTIVE PRODUCER
Barry Grove

BY SPECIAL ARRANGEMENT WITH
Colin Callender   **Robert Cole**   **Frederick Zollo**   **The Shubert Organization**

PRESENTS

CASA VALENTINA

BY
Harvey Fierstein

WITH

Reed Birney	**John Cullum**	**Gabriel Ebert**
Lisa Emery	**Tom McGowan**	**Patrick Page**
Larry Pine	**Nick Westrate**	**Mare Winningham**

SCENIC DESIGN
Scott Pask

COSTUME DESIGN
Rita Ryack

LIGHTING DESIGN
Justin Townsend

ORIGINAL MUSIC & SOUND DESIGN
Fitz Patton

HAIR, WIG & MAKEUP DESIGN
Jason P. Hayes

CASTING
**Caparelliotis Casting
& Nancy Piccione**

FIGHT DIRECTION
Thomas Schall

PRODUCTION STAGE MANAGER
William Joseph Barnes

ADDITIONAL CASTING
Telsey + Company

DIRECTED BY
Joe Mantello

ARTISTIC PRODUCER
Mandy Greenfield

GENERAL MANAGER
Florie Seery

DIRECTOR OF ARTISTIC DEVELOPMENT
Jerry Patch

DIRECTOR OF MARKETING
Debra Waxman-Pilla

PRESS REPRESENTATIVE
Boneau/Bryan-Brown

PRODUCTION MANAGER
Joshua Helman

ARTISTIC LINE PRODUCER
Lisa McNulty

DIRECTOR OF DEVELOPMENT
Lynne Randall

INSPIRED BY THE BOOK *CASA SUSANNA* BY MICHEL HURST AND ROBERT SWOPE.

LEAD SUPPORT FOR *CASA VALENTINA* IS PROVIDED BY MTC'S PRODUCING FUND PARTNER, **ANDREW MARTIN-WEBER**.
CASA VALENTINA IS A RECIPIENT OF AN EDGERTON FOUNDATION NEW AMERICAN PLAYS AWARD.

MANHATTAN THEATRE CLUB WISHES TO EXPRESS ITS APPRECIATION TO THEATRE DEVELOPMENT FUND FOR ITS SUPPORT OF THIS PRODUCTION.

4/23/14

(L-R) Nick Westrate, Patrick Page and Tom McGowan

Photo: Matthew Murphy

Casa Valentina

John Cullum
as Terry

Reed Birney
as Charlotte

Patrick Page
as Valentina

Tom McGowan
as Bessie

Larry Pine
as Amy

Nick Westrate
as Gloria

Gabriel Ebert
as Miranda

Photos: Matthew Murphy

Cast Continued

UNDERSTUDIES

For Jonathon/Miranda, Gloria:
NICK BAILEY
For George/Valentina, Charlotte:
PETER BRADBURY
For Rita, Eleanor:
JUDITH LIGHTFOOT CLARKE
For Terry, The Judge/Amy:
JACK DAVIDSON
For Bessie:
JOHN TREACY EGAN

AUTHOR AND DIRECTOR'S NOTE

*C*asa Valentina was inspired by events that took place in and around the Chevalier d'Eon Resort in the Catskill Mountains in 1962.

The gentlemen in our play are not drag queens or female impersonators. Although the outward behavior unites them, their need to dress and identify as female is personal and individual to each. For some it's a matter of gender identity. For others the desire is of a sexual nature. But there is nothing frivolous or arbitrary in their behavior.

It might interest you to know that the organization they helped found during the action of this play is still in existence with more than 30 active chapters nationwide.

We would like to thank Katherine Cummings for helping us unlock the gate and slip into this fascinating garden of delights.

And with that, we welcome you to *Casa Valentina*.

Welcome to the world of self-made women.

— Harvey Fierstein and Joe Mantello

Reed Birney
Charlotte

John Cullum
Terry

Gabriel Ebert
Jonathon/Miranda

Lisa Emery
Eleanor

Tom McGowan
Bessie

Patrick Page
George/Valentina

Larry Pine
The Judge/Amy

Nick Westrate
Gloria

Mare Winningham
Rita

Nick Bailey
*u/s Jonathon/
Miranda, Gloria*

Peter Bradbury
*u/s George/
Valentina, Charlotte*

Judith Lightfoot
Clarke
u/s Rita, Eleanor

Jack Davidson
*u/s Terry,
The Judge/Amy*

John Treacy Egan
u/s Bessie

Harvey Fierstein
Playwright

Joe Mantello
Director

Scott Pask
Scenic Design

Rita Ryack
Costume Design

Justin Townsend
Lighting Design

Fitz Patton
*Original Music &
Sound Design*

David Caparelliotis
Caparelliotis Casting
Casting

Casa Valentina

Thomas Schall
Fight Direction

Bernard Telsey
Telsey + Company
Additional Casting

Colin Callender
Producer

Robert Cole
Producer

Frederick Zollo
Producer

Barry Grove
Executive Producer
Manhattan Theatre
Club

Lynne Meadow
Artistic Director
Manhattan Theatre
Club

**Andrew
Martin-Weber**
*Producing Fund
Partner*

BOX OFFICE
David Dillon (Box Office Treasurer), Stephanie Moro

FRONT OF HOUSE
Front (L-R): Patricia Polhill,
Kaitlynn Sepulveda,
Lyanna Alvarado,
Jim Joseph (House Manager),
Richard Ponce
Back (L-R): Wendy Wright,
Vern Lindauer, Rob Abud,
Ed Brashear, Jackson Ero

CREW
Standing (L-R): Louis Shapiro (Sound Engineer), Jeff Dodson (Master Electrician), Timothy Walters (Head Propertyman),
Vaughn Preston (Automation Operator), Andrew Braggs (Apprentice), Matt Abdelnour (Apprentice)
Front (L-R): Sally Hall, Erin Moeller (Company Manager), Erin Kennedy-Lunsford (Hair/Make-Up Supervisor), Tiffany Hicks (Hair/Make-Up Assistant),
William Joseph Barnes (Production Stage Manager), Kathryn L. McKee (Stage Manager)

Casa Valentina

MANHATTAN THEATRE CLUB STAFF

Artistic Director	**Lynne Meadow**
Executive Producer	**Barry Grove**
General Manager	**Florie Seery**
Artistic Producer	**Mandy Greenfield**
Director of Artistic Development	**Jerry Patch**
Director of Artistic Operations	**Amy Gilkes Loe**
Artistic Line Producer	Lisa McNulty

Artistic Associate/
Assistant to the Artistic Director ....Nicki Hunter
Assistant to the Executive Producer ....Melanie Sovern
Assistant to the Artistic Producer ....Ben Ferber
Director of Casting ....**Nancy Piccione**
Associate Casting Director ....Kelly Gillespie
Casting Assistant ....Will DeCamp
Literary Manager/Sloan Project Manager ....Annie MacRae
Associate Director of
Artistic Development ....Elizabeth Rothman
Artistic Development Associate ....Scott Kaplan
Artistic Consultant ....**Daniel Sullivan**
Bank of America/
US Trust Commissions ....Richard Greenberg,
Neil LaBute, Matthew Lopez, John Patrick Shanley
Alfred P. Sloan
Foundation Commissions ....April de Angelis,
Nathan Jackson, Nick Jones,
Juliana Nash & Courtney Baron, Melissa Ross,
Heidi Schreck, Sarah Treem, Bess Wohl
The Writer's Room Commissions ....Adam Bock &
Justin Levine, Rachel Bonds,
Thomas Bradshaw, Frances Ya-Chu Cowhig,
Jackie Sibblies Drury, Samuel D. Hunter,
Sharyn Rothstein, Pig Pen Theatre Company
Mary Mill Commission ....Molly Smith Metzler
Director of Development ....**Lynne Randall**
Director, Individual Giving & Major Gifts ...Emily Fleisher
Director, Institutional Giving ....Patricia Leonard
Director, Special Events ....Stephanie Mercado
Associate Director of
Individual Giving ....Josh Martinez-Nelson
Manager, Individual Giving ....Aubrie Fennecken
Development Associate/Individual Giving ...Jillian Ruben
Development Associate/Special Events ....Molly Clarke
Institutional Giving Manager ....Heather Gallagher
Patrons' Liaison ....Emily Yowell
Database Associate ....Katie Fergerson
Director of Marketing ....**Debra Waxman-Pilla**
Assistant Marketing Director ....Caitlin Baird
Marketing Accounts Manager ....Cody Andrus
Director of Finance ....**Jessica Adler**
Human Resources Director ....**Vincent Losito**
Business Manager ....Ryan Guhde
Business & HR Associate ....Mallory Triest
Business Assistant ....Josiah Grimm
IT Manager ....Mendy Sudranski
Systems Analyst ....Jason Fritzsch
Studio Manager/Receptionist ....Thatcher Stevens
Associate General Manager ....**Lindsey Sag**
Company Manager/
New York City Center ....Samantha Kindler
Director of Subscriber Services ....**Robert Allenberg**
Subscriber Services Manager ....Kevin Sullivan
Subscriber Services Representatives ....Mark Bowers,
Tim Salamandyk, Rosanna Consalvo Sarto

Director of Education ....**David Shookhoff**
Assistant Education Director/Coordinator, Paul A. Kaplan
Theatre Management Program ....Amy Harris
Education Programs Coordinator ....Wade T. Handy
MTC Teaching Artists ....David Auburn, Chris Ceraso,
Charlotte Colavin, Dominic Colon, Allison Daugherty,
Andy Goldberg, Kel Haney, Elise Hernandez,
Jeffrey Joseph, Julie Leedes, Kate Long,
Victor Maog, Andres Munar, Melissa Murray,
Carmen Rivera, Nilaja Sun, Judy Tate,
Candido Tirado, Liam Torres, Joe White
Theatre Management Interns ....Lily Bryant,
Allyson Capetta, Robert Carroll, John Corraro,
Erin Cressy, Emily Hamburger, Samantha Liebman,
Meaghan McLaughlin, Gabriella Napoli,
Susanna Pretzer, Kaitlynn Sepulveda, Lauren Stern

Production Manager	**Joshua Helman**
Associate Production Manager	Bethany Weinstein
Assistant Production Manager	Steven Dalton
Properties Supervisor	**Scott Laule**
Assistant Properties Supervisor	Lily Fairbanks
Props Carpenter	Peter Grimes
Costume Supervisor	**Erin Hennessy Dean**

GENERAL PRESS REPRESENTATION
BONEAU/BRYAN-BROWN

Chris Boneau	Aaron Meier
Emily Meagher	Michelle Farabaugh

Script Readers ....Mirella Cheeseman, Aaron Grunfeld,
Clifford Lee Johnson III, Thomas Park,
Elizabeth Sharpe-Levine

SERVICES

Accountants	Fried & Kowgios CPAs, LLP
Advertising	SpotCo
Website Design	AKA
Legal Counsel	Charles H. Googe, Jr.;
	Caroline Barnard; Carolyn J. Casselman/
	Paul, Weiss, Rifkind, Wharton and Garrison LLP
Real Estate Counsel	Marcus Attorneys
Labor Counsel	Harry H. Weintraub/
	Glick and Weintraub, P.C.
Immigration Counsel	Theodore Ruthizer/
	Kramer, Levin, Naftalis & Frankel, LLP
Media Counsel	Cameron Stracher
Insurance	DeWitt Stern Group, Inc./Anthony Pittari
Maintenance	Reliable Cleaning
Event Photography	Bruce Glikas
Cover Design	SpotCo
Theatre Displays	King Displays

For more information visit
www.ManhattanTheatreClub.com

PRODUCTION STAFF FOR *CASA VALENTINA*

Company Manager	**Erin Moeller**
Production Stage Manager	**William Joseph Barnes**
Stage Manager	Kathryn L. McKee
Assistant Director	David Perlow
Dance Consultant	Christopher Gattelli
Associate Scenic Designer	Orit Jacoby Carroll

Assistant Scenic Designers ....Lauren Alvarez,
Jeff Hinchee, Jerome Martin
Associate Costume Designer ....Richard Schurkamp
Assistant Lighting Designer ....Kirk Fitzgerald
Assistant Sound Designer ....Justin Stasiw
Assistant Hair, Wig & Make-Up Designer ..Davion Edwards
Hair/Make-Up Supervisor ....Davion Edwards
Hair/Make-Up Assistant ....Erin Kennedy-Lunsford
Lighting Programmer ....Marc Polimeni
Flyman ....Richard Klinger
Automation Operator ....Vaughn Preston
Dressers ....Ben Chambliss, David Grevengoed
Production Assistant ....Danny Maly

CREDITS

Scenery fabrication by Showmotion, Inc. Lighting
equipment provided by PRG Lighting. Sound equipment
provided by Masque Sound. Costumes by Eric Winterling,
Inc. Select pieces by Helen Uffner Vintage Clothing LLC.
Makeup provided by M•A•C. Hair care products provided
by Rusk and Davines Hair Care Lines.

SPECIAL THANKS

Richard Eagan, Michael Wartella. The producers wish to
thank the TDF Costume Collection for its assistance in
this production.

MANHATTAN THEATRE CLUB
SAMUEL J. FRIEDMAN THEATRE STAFF

Theatre Manager	**Jim Joseph**
Assistant House Manager	Richard Ponce
Box Office Treasurer	**David Dillon**
Assistant Box Office	
Treasurers	Geoffrey Nixon, Melissa Taustine
Head Carpenter	Chris Wiggins
Head Propertyman	Timothy Walters
Sound Engineer	Louis Shapiro
Master Electrician	Jeff Dodson
Wardrobe Supervisor	Leah Redmond
Apprentices	Matt Abdelnour, Andrew Braggs
Chief Engineer	Deosarran
Maintenance Engineer	Ricky Deosarran
Security	Allied Barton
Lobby Refreshments	Sweet Hospitality Group

2013-2014 AWARDS

DRAMA DESK AWARD
Outstanding Featured Actor in a Play
(Reed Birney)

OUTER CRITICS CIRCLE AWARD
Outstanding Featured Actress in a Play
(Mare Winningham)

RICHARD SEFF AWARD
(Mare Winningham)

Casa Valentina
SCRAPBOOK

Correspondent: Tom McGowan, "Bessie"

Memorable Note: Before joining *Casa Valentina*, I've been playing The Wizard in *Wicked* for the last few years. Both shows are directed by the amazing Joe Mantello. On opening night, Joe wrote me a note saying that he is now considering me for the role of Madame Morrible!

Opening Night Party and Gifts: Our opening night party was held across the street at the Copacabana. It was the first Broadway opening for my daughter, Mary, and I was so happy to have her there with me and my wife, Cathy. For gifts, Patrick Page gave everyone a beautiful engraved compact with our character's name on it.

Most Exciting Celebrity Visitor: There have been so many famous people coming backstage, but since most of them have seen me in my slip and corset, I've tried to block them all out!

Special Backstage Rituals: Before the curtain goes up, we all gather onstage for hugs, but before Act Two, Gabe Ebert goes around and gives all of our fake bosoms a "Good Luck" squeeze.

(L-R): Playwright Harvey Fierstein with *Yearbook* correspondent Tom McGowan, whom he calls "Mary."

Favorite Backstage Photo: After five weeks of rehearsal, plus a week of previews that included daytime rehearsals, when I came into the theatrefor our first two-show day, I saw the legendary John Cullum onstage, by himself, going through his monologues before half hour. I quickly snapped a picture. He has been an inspiration to all of us since the first day of rehearsal. A true professional, hard-working with a terrific sense of humor, John is an actor's actor whose love of performing still shines through, even 50-plus years after his Broadway debut! When I showed this picture to our director, Joe Mantello, he said "Every young actor should be shown this picture and told, 'If you can't do this, get out now!'"

Favorite Moment

During Each Performance: It's hard to pick just a single moment when you get to share so many great moments with this incredible cast, but if I had to choose one, I would say it is the total silence in the theatre after my character asks Rita to marry him late in the play. Staring

Patrick Page displays his two sides as he strikes a pose in heels for the meet-and-greet with the press.

into the great Mare Winningham's eyes, after building this very special relationship throughout the show, it is thrilling to feel the tension in the audience. Joe really wanted that

John Cullum running his monologues, his ritual prior to each show.

moment to linger, and kept asking me to wait longer and longer, which I was afraid to do. But, of course, he was absolutely right and it is now something I look forward to every show. Aside from that moment, I have a whole bunch of classic Harvey Fierstein one-liners that I get to deliver.

Favorite Off-Site Hangout: The Glass House Tavern is directly across the street from the theatre, and they have been so welcoming to us throughout the run. It's a great place to have a drink and they have a nice bar menu. It always seems to be crowded but never too loud.

Favorite Therapy: I'm pretty much a Ricola/Throat Coat Tea kind of guy, but my voice has had no troubles during this run, despite Bessie always having a lot to say!

Nickname: Harvey liked to call me "Mary." He did this so often, that if he called out "Mary!" anywhere in the theatre, I would just go over to him because I knew he had a note for me!

Fastest Costume Change: I have two very fast changes, among the fastest of my career. Both are under a minute before I need to be back onstage! We have great dressers and wig people. I've been doing it so often, that when I get a quick look at myself before jumping back onstage, it doesn't faze me that I'm checking my wig and how my dress is sitting and how my earrings look and whether my slip is showing! I just grab a quick view of Bessie and it's back to work.

Coolest Thing About Being in the Show: Getting to introduce the world to Bessie. This incredible character that Harvey has created has been one of the joys of my career. Also, we are a true ensemble. We worked very closely, supported each other, felt privileged to be together, shared a lot of laughs and we all love this play.

Gabriel Ebert (C) as Miranda gets a makeover from (L-R) Nick Westrate's Gloria, John Cullum's Terry and Tom McGowan's Bessie.

Chicago

First Preview: October 23, 1996. Opened: November 14, 1996.
Still running as of May 31, 2014.

PLAYBILL®

Aspiring vaudeville performer Roxie Hart kills her lover and finds herself plunged into the corrupt legal system of late 1920s Chicago. As fast-talking lawyer Billy Flynn and fellow murderess Velma Kelly teach her that razzle-dazzle outdoes justice, Roxie's whole world starts to look more and more like show business.

THE CAST
(in order of appearance)

Velma Kelly	AMRA-FAYE WRIGHT
Roxie Hart	BIANCA MARROQUIN
Fred Casely	BRIAN O'BRIEN
Sergeant Fogarty	ADAM ZOTOVICH
Amos Hart	PAUL C. VOGT
Liz	NICOLE BRIDGEWATER
Annie	STEPHANIE POPE
June	DONNA MARIE ASBURY
Hunyak	TONYA WATHEN
Mona	ANNE HORAK
Matron "Mama" Morton	ROZ RYAN
Billy Flynn	RYAN SILVERMAN
Mary Sunshine	R. LOWE
Go-To-Hell Kitty	ANGEL REDA
Harry	NATHAN MADDEN
Doctor	JASON PATRICK SANDS
Aaron	DENNY PASCHALL
The Judge	JASON PATRICK SANDS
Bailiff	AMOS WOLFF
Martin Harrison	NATHAN MADDEN
Court Clerk	AMOS WOLFF
The Jury	RYAN WORSING

Continued on next page

The Playbill Broadway Yearbook 2013-2014

⑤ AMBASSADOR THEATRE

A Shubert Organization Theatre

Philip J. Smith, *Chairman*   Robert E. Wankel, *President*

Barry & Fran Weissler
in association with
Kardana/Hart Sharp Entertainment
present

Bianca Marroquin   Amra-Faye Wright
Ryan Silverman
Paul C. Vogt

in

CHICAGO

Lyrics by   Music By   Book by
Fred Ebb   John Kander   Fred Ebb & Bob Fosse

Original Production Directed and Choreographed by **Bob Fosse**

Based on the play by Maurine Dallas Watkins

with

Roz Ryan   R. Lowe

and

Donna Marie Asbury   Nicole Bridgewater   Jennifer Dunne
Anne Horak   David Kent   Nathan Madden   Sharon Moore   C. Newcomer
Brian O'Brien   Denny Paschall   Stephanie Pope   Angel Reda   Jason Patrick Sands
Brian Spitulnik   Tonya Wathen   Amos Wolff   Ryan Worsing   Adam Zotovich

Supervising Music Director	Music Director
Rob Fisher	**Leslie Stifelman**

Scenic Design	Costume Design	Lighting Design
John Lee Beatty	**William Ivey Long**	**Ken Billington**

Sound Design	Orchestrations	Dance Music Arrangements
Scott Lehrer	**Ralph Burns**	**Peter Howard**

Script Adaptation	Musical Coordinator	Hair Design
David Thompson	**Seymour Red Press**	**David Brian Brown**

Casting	Original Casting
Duncan Stewart and Company	**Jay Binder**

Technical Supervisor	Dance Supervisor	Production Stage Manager
Arthur Siccardi	**Gary Chryst**	**David Hyslop**

Executive Producer	Presented in association with
Alecia Parker	**Broadway Across America**

General Manager	Press Representative
B.J. Holt	**Jeremy Shaffer**
	The Publicity Office

Based on the presentation by City Center's Encores!℠

Choreography by
Ann Reinking
in the style of Bob Fosse

Directed by
Walter Bobbie

Cast Recording on RCA Victor

10/1/13

Brian O'Brien (as Billy Flynn) and company in "All I Care About."

Chicago

MUSICAL NUMBERS

ACT I

"All That Jazz"	Velma and Company
"Funny Honey"	Roxie
"Cell Block Tango"	Velma and the Girls
"When You're Good to Mama"	Matron
"Tap Dance"	Roxie, Amos and Boys
"All I Care About"	Billy and Girls
"A Little Bit of Good"	Mary Sunshine
"We Both Reached for the Gun"	Billy, Roxie, Mary Sunshine and Company
"Roxie"	Roxie and Boys
"I Can't Do It Alone"	Velma
"My Own Best Friend"	Roxie and Velma

ACT II

Entr'acte	The Band
"I Know a Girl"	Velma
"Me and My Baby"	Roxie and Boys
"Mister Cellophane"	Amos
"When Velma Takes the Stand"	Velma and Boys
"Razzle Dazzle"	Billy and Company
"Class"	Velma and Matron
"Nowadays"	Roxie and Velma
"Hot Honey Rag"	Roxie and Velma
Finale	Company

Orchestra Conducted by
LESLIE STIFELMAN
Associate Conductor:
SCOTT CADY
Assistant Conductor:
JOHN JOHNSON
Woodwinds: SEYMOUR RED PRESS,
JACK STUCKEY, RICHARD CENTALONZA
Trumpets:
GLENN DREWES, DARRYL SHAW
Trombones:
DAVE BARGERON, BRUCE BONVISSUTO

Piano:
SCOTT CADY
Piano, Accordion:
JOHN JOHNSON
Banjo:
JAY BERLINER
Bass, Tuba:
DAN PECK
Violin:
MARSHALL COID
Drums, Percussion:
RONALD ZITO

Cast Continued

THE SCENE
Chicago, Illinois. The late 1920s.

UNDERSTUDIES
For Roxie Hart: ANNE HORAK,
    TONYA WATHEN
For Velma Kelly: DONNA MARIE ASBURY,
    STEPHANIE POPE, ANGEL REDA
For Billy Flynn: BRIAN O'BRIEN,
    JASON PATRICK SANDS
For Amos Hart: JASON PATRICK SANDS,
    ADAM ZOTOVICH
For Matron "Mama" Morton:
    DONNA MARIE ASBURY,
    NICOLE BRIDGEWATER
For Mary Sunshine: C. NEWCOMER
For Fred Casely: DAVID KENT,
    JASON PATRICK SANDS,
    BRIAN SPITULNIK
For "Me and My Baby": DAVID KENT,
    BRIAN SPITULNIK, AMOS WOLFF.

For all other roles: JENNIFER DUNNE,
    DAVID KENT, SHARON MOORE,
    BRIAN SPITULNIK

Dance Captain: DAVID KENT

"Tap Dance" specialty performed by
DENNY PASCHALL, JASON PATRICK SANDS
& AMOS WOLFF.
"Me and My Baby" specialty performed by
DENNY PASCHALL and RYAN WORSING.
"Nowadays" whistle performed by
JASON PATRICK SANDS.

Original Choreography for "Hot Honey Rag" by
BOB FOSSE

"...if you pop that gum one more time..."

Bianca Marroquin
Roxie Hart

Amra-Faye Wright
Velma Kelly

Ryan Silverman
Billy Flynn

Paul C. Vogt
Amos Hart

Roz Ryan
Matron "Mama"
Morton

R. Lowe
Mary Sunshine

Donna Marie Asbury
June

Chicago

Nicole Bridgewater
Liz

Jennifer Dunne
Swing

Anne Horak
Mona

David Kent
Swing/Dance Captain

Nathan Madden
Harry/Martin Harrison

Sharon Moore
Swing

C. Newcomer
Standby Mary Sunshine

Brian O'Brien
Fred Casely

Denny Paschall
Aaron

Stephanie Pope
Annie

Angel Reda
Go-to-Hell Kitty

Jason Patrick Sands
Doctor/Judge

Brian Spitulnik
Swing

Tonya Wathen
Hunyak

Amos Wolff
Bailiff/Court Clerk

Ryan Worsing
The Jury

Adam Zotovich
Sergeant Fogarty

John Kander & Fred Ebb
Music; Book/Lyrics

Bob Fosse
Book

Walter Bobbie
Director

Ann Reinking
Choreographer

John Lee Beatty
Set Design

William Ivey Long
Costume Designer

Ken Billington
Lighting Designer

Scott Lehrer
Sound Design

David Thompson
Script Adaptation

Rob Fisher
Supervising Music Director

Leslie Stifelman
Musical Director

Seymour Red Press
Music Coordinator

Duncan Stewart
Duncan Stewart
and Company
Casting

Benton Whitley
Duncan Stewart
and Company
Casting

Arthur Siccardi
Theatrical
Services Inc.
Technical Supervisor

Gary Chryst
Dance Supervisor

David Hyslop
Production Stage Manager

Chicago

Alecia Parker
Executive Producer

Fran and Barry Weissler
Producers

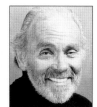

John N. Hart Jr.
Evamere
Entertainment
Producer

Morton Swinsky
Kardana Productions
Producer

John Gore
Broadway Across
America
Producer

Thomas B. McGrath
Broadway Across
America
Producer

Eddie Bennett
Swing

Rachel Bickerton
Annie

Raymond Bokhour
Amos Hart

Cristy Candler
Annie

Michael Cusumano
The Jury

Paige Davis
Roxie Hart

Larisa Dolina
*Matron "Mama"
Morton*

Alexander
Gemignani
Billy Flynn

J. Loeffelholz
*Standby for
Mary Sunshine*

Terra C. MacLeod
Velma Kelly

Adam Pascal
Billy Flynn

Christine Pedi
*Matron "Mama"
Morton*

Amy Spanger
Roxie Hart

Wendy Williams
*Matron "Mama"
Morton*

Carol Woods
*Matron "Mama"
Morton*

Brent Barrett
Billy Flynn

Eddie Bennett
Swing

David Bushman
*Swing, Dance
Captain*

Dylis Croman
Mona

Christopher
Fitzgerald
Amos Hart

Adam Jepsen
Bailiff, Court Clerk

J. Loeffelholz
*Standby for
Mary Sunshine*

Melissa Rae Mahon
Go-To-Hell Kitty

Bebe Neuwirth
*Matron "Mama"
Morton*

Dani Spieler
Mona

Chicago

Elvis Stojko
Billy Flynn

Carol Woods
Matron "Mama" Morton

The ladies of *Chicago* as of June 2013.

ORCHESTRA
Front Row (L-R): Marshall Coid, Bruce Williamson
Middle Row (L-R): Jack Stuckey, Glenn Drewes, Dave Bargeron, Darryl Shaw, Bruce Bonvissuto, Leslie Stifelman (Musical Director), Eddie Salkin
Back Row (L-R): Jay Berliner, Rick Centalonza, Ronald Zito, Dan Peck, John Johnson
Not pictured: Scott Cady (Associate Conductor)

Chicago

MANAGEMENT
Front (L-R): Rina L. Saltzman (Company Manager), Mindy Farbrother (Stage Manager)
Back (L-R): Terrence J. Witter (Stage Manager),
David Hyslop (Production Stage Manager), Mahlon Kruse (Stage Manager)

Photos: Jeremy Daniel

WARDROBE/HAIR
Front (L-R): Jenna Brauer (Hair Supervisor), Cleopatra Matheos (Dresser),
Jo-Ann Bethell (Dresser)
Back (L-R): Rick Meadows (Dresser), Kathy Dacey (Dresser),
Kevin Woodworth (Wardrobe Supervisor), Patrick Rinn (Dresser)

FRONT OF HOUSE
First Row (L-R): Jack Donaghy, Tyrone Hendrix, Sue Roberts, Timothy Newsome
Second Row: Arlene Peters
Third Row (L-R): Beatrice Carney, Tasha Allen, Dottie Bentley
Top Row: (L-R): Jonathan Rodriguez, Belen Bekker, Ellen Cogan

CREW
Front Row (L-R):
Michael Phillips (Production Carpenter),
Ronald Jacobson (Head Electrician)
Kevin Fedigan (Front Lite Operator)
Middle Row (L-R):
Michael Guggino (Front Lite Operator),
Eileen Macdonald LaSpina (Deck Sound),
John Montgomery
(Production Sound Engineer)
Back Row (L-R):
Lee Iwanski (House Electrician),
Dennis Smalls (House Props),
James Werner (Front Lite Operator),
Fred Phelan (Production Props),
Ken Anderson (Flyman)
Not pictured:
Luciana Fusco (Head Electrician)

Chicago
SCRAPBOOK

Correspondent: Brian O'Brien, "Fred Casely"; u/s "Billy Flynn"

Milestones, Parties, Celebrations, Gifts: Milestones: After playing our 7,000th performance on September 24, *Chicago* went on to celebrate 17 years on Broadway in November. **Parties:** The annual summer picnic at the spectacular Westchester home of Barry and Fran Weissler was held in mid July. It was a beautiful day made even more beautiful with the attendance of the cast of *Pippin*, also produced by the Weisslers. **Gifts:** This year's holiday gift was the hot-off-the-presses new biography of Bob Fosse, "Fosse" by Sam Wasson. And we're always presented with an incredible selection of pies from Fran Weissler every Thanksgiving. Ann Reinking sent everyone champagne in honor of our 17th anniversary, in addition to her annual holiday gift of roses.

Most Exciting Celebrity Visitor and What They Did/Said: Kardashian matriarch Kris Jenner came to the show—with her camera crew of course—to have her visit documented for an episode of "Keeping Up with the

(L-R) Jason Patrick Sands, Amra-Faye Wright, Roz Ryan, Bianca Marroquin, Ryan Silverman cut the cake to celebrate *Chicago*'s 17th anniversary.

Kardashians." During the photo op the boys went to sweep her off her feet for the traditional *Chicago* lift pose. However, she warned us that she wasn't wearing any underwear.

Which Actor Performed the Most Roles in This Show?: We have extraordinary swings that cover a multitude of individual performances. But Jason Patrick Sands, in addition to his dual ensemble roles as the Doctor and the Judge, also understudies Fred Casely, Amos Hart and Billy Flynn, showing great versatility.

Who Has Done the Most Shows?: Donna Marie Asbury and Sharon Moore have been a part of the *Chicago* family for over 15 years! And this past October, Roz Ryan, as Matron "Mama" Morton, broke the record for having played more performances than any other female principal in *Chicago*'s 17-year history on Broadway—224 weeks.

Special Backstage Rituals: Every holiday throughout the year is celebrated by decorating the common areas, whether it's Christmas, Valentine's or Spring. For Halloween, we have The Haunted Wall of Shame in which company members have their publicity photos posted to be defaced (in good taste) with clip art and markers.

STAFF FOR CHICAGO

GENERAL MANAGEMENT
B.J. Holt, General Manager
Nina Skriloff, International Manager

PRESS REPRESENTATIVE
THE PUBLICITY OFFICE
Jeremy Shaffer   Marc Thibodeau   Michael Borowski

CASTING
DUNCAN STEWART AND COMPANY
Duncan Stewart, C.S.A.; Benton Whitley, C.S.A.;
Andrea Zee

COMPANY MANAGER
Rina L. Saltzman

Production Stage Manager	**David Hyslop**

Stage Managers ....Terrence J. Witter, Mahlon Kruse, Mindy Farbrother
General Management Associate ....Stephen Spadaro
Assistant Director ....Jonathan Bernstein
Associate Lighting Designer ....John McKernon
Assistant Choreographer ....Debra McWaters
Assistant Set Designers ......Eric Renschler, Shelley Barclay
Wardrobe Supervisor ....Kevin Woodworth
Hair Supervisor ....Jenna Brauer
Costume Assistant ....Donald Sanders
Personal Asst to Mr. Billington ....Jon Kusner
Assistant to Mr. Lehrer ....Thom Mohrman
Production Carpenter ....Michael Phillips
Production Electrician ....James Fedigan
Head Electrician ....Luciana Fusco
Front Lite Operator ....Michael Guggino
Production Sound Engineer ....John Montgomery
Production Props ....Fred Phelan
Dressers ....Jo-Ann Bethell, Kathy Dacey, Cleopatra Matheos, Rick Meadows, Patrick Rinn

Banking ....City National Bank, Stephanie Dalton, Michele Gibbons
Music Prep ....Chelsea Music Services, Inc.
Payroll ....Castellana Services, Inc.
Accountants ....Rosenberg, Neuwirth & Kuchner Mark A. D'Ambrosi, Marina Flom
Insurance ....Industrial Risk Specialists
Counsel ....Seth Gelblum/Loeb & Loeb
Art Design ....Spot Design
Advertising ....SpotCo/Drew Hodges, Ilene Rosen, Tom Greenwald, Stephen Sosnowski, Juliana Hannett, Chris Scherer, Kyle Young, Kristen Bardwil
Merchandising ....Creative Goods, Inc.
Displays...King Display

NATIONAL ARTISTS MANAGEMENT CO.
Head of Business Affairs/
     Associate Producer ....Daniel M. Posener
Chief Financial Officer ....Bob Williams
Head of Marketing Strategy ....Clint Bond Jr.
Manager of Accounting/Admin ....Marian Albarracin
Associate to the Weisslers ....Brett England
Assistant to Mrs. Weissler ....Nikki Pelazza
Executive Assistant ....Cristina Boccitto
Director of Marketing ....Ken Sperr

SPECIAL THANKS
Additional legal services provided by Jay Goldberg, Esq. and Michael Berger, Esq. Tuxedos by Brioni.

CREDITS
Lighting equipment by PRG Lighting. Scenery built and painted by Hudson Scenic Studios. Specialty Rigging by United Staging & Rigging. Sound equipment by PRG Audio. Shoulder holster courtesy of DeSantis Holster and Leather Goods Co. Period cameras and flash units by George Fenmore, Inc. Colibri lighters used. Bible courtesy of Chiarelli's Religious Goods, Inc. Black pencils by

Dixon-Ticonderoga. Gavel courtesy of The Gavel Co. Zippo lighters used. Garcia y Vega cigars used. Shoes by T.O. Dey. Orthopaedic Consultant, David S. Weiss, M.D.

Energy-efficient washer/dryer courtesy of
LG Electronics.

 THE SHUBERT ORGANIZATION, INC.
Board of Directors

Philip J. Smith	**Robert E. Wankel**
Chairman	President
Wyche Fowler, Jr.	**Diana Phillips**
Lee J. Seidler	**Michael I. Sovern**
Stuart Subotnick	

Chief Financial Officer ....Elliot Greene
Sr. Vice President, Ticketing ....David Andrews
Vice President, Finance ....Juan Calvo
Vice President, Human Resources ....Cathy Cozens
Vice President, Facilities ....John Darby
Vice President, Theatre Operations ....Peter Entin
Vice President, Marketing ....Charles Flateman
Vice President, Audit ....Anthony LaMattina
Vice President, Ticket Sales ....Brian Mahoney
Vice President, Creative Projects ............D.S. Moynihan
Vice President, Real Estate ....Julio Peterson

Theatre Manager ....Manuel Levine

BROADWAY green alliance   The Shubert Organization is a proud member of the Broadway Green Alliance.

Chicago
SCRAPBOOK

Favorite Moment During the Show: This is a backstage moment, but it's anytime Amra-Faye Wright regales us with a character from her overflowing bag of costumes and wigs. "Cyril" is a favorite.

Favorite In-Theatre Gathering Place: The basement of The Ambassador serves as the wardrobe department and, when not being used for its official purposes, it becomes the "kitchen table" for the *Chicago* family to share our ups and downs and many, many laughs.

Favorite Off-Site Hangout: E&E Grillhouse, our neighbor on 49th Street, has welcomed the *Chicago* company with open arms. It's a great, elegant, yet informal, gathering spot to meet up for dinner between shows or cocktails post show. Bar manager Tom, and GM David know many of us by name (and beverage).

Favorite Snack Food: Pringles had become the snack of choice with company members bringing in the various and mildly absurd new flavors like "pecan pie" and "chicken" flavors, yet, when the press started referring to them as "cancer in a can," we decided to move on to Pepperidge Farm Goldfish.

Company Mascot: Jack Raymond Stifelman, born March 12, 2013 to longtime company member Melissa Rae Mahon and her wife, *Chicago* musical director Leslie Stifelman. Mamma Melissa was back in "*Chicago* shape" baring her legendary abs within seven months.

Memorable Ad-Lib: The talented and dashing Ryan Silverman often had a way with words, but always remained as cool as a cucumber. During "Razzle" he once changed "...Razzle Dazzle 'em and they'll never catch wise" to "Razzle Dazzle 'em...and you got..(pause)..surprise!"

What Do We Think of the Web Buzz on Our Show?: Popular opinion might suggest that a show that is currently in its 18th year on Broadway might suffer from fatigue, yet, by all accounts, be it the press, fans or industry insiders, *Chicago* has stood the test of time and is a fresh as ever!

Busiest Day at the Box Office: During the 2013 Christmas/New Year week *Chicago* broke a box office record at the Ambassador by taking in over $1,059,000.00 in ticket sales.

Who Wore the Heaviest Costume?: R. Lowe sports the "Layered Look" as Mary Sunshine.

Who Wore the Least?: We're talking about *Chicago* here!

Orchestra Member that Played the Most Instruments: Reed and woodwind master Rick Centalonza.

Photos: Jeremy Daniel

Company Legends: #BebesBack!!! The one and only Bebe Neuwirth rejoined the company as Matron "Mama" Morton, having previously performed the role of Roxie Hart in 2007, and her Tony Award winning original portrayal of Velma Kelly in 1996.

Understudy Anecdote: Jason Patrick Sands and Brian O'Brien collaborated on the semi-autobiographical comedy web series about the competitive world of understudies in a long running show. Keep an eye out for "Covers."

Embarrassing Moment: Company member Ryan Worsing gives the "thumbs up" to a celebrity guest.

"Carols for a Cure": "Jolly Old St. Nicholas" Arranged by Richard Rockage and performed by Anne Horak and Paul Vogt as a send-up

of the traditional "Night before Christmas" with Santa visiting Roxie and Amos.

Gypsy of the Year: "Good Comrades Go to Heaven" was an intricately original dance/movement piece created by company member Nathan Madden featuring nine cast members in a mostly seated formation.

Easter Bonnet: Christine Pedi and company performed a comic scenario sketch of what goes through an actor's mind during the split second in which they have forgotten a line. It was conceived by Chris Sieber and directed and choreographed by Nathan Madden.

Coolest Thing About Being in This Show: *Chicago* has become an internationally-recognized brand, and to be a part of its Broadway legacy and working so closely with those who created this phenomenon is extraordinary. Additionally, there is a comfort in having the good fortune of being in such a long-running show. Lasting friendships and a sense of family, with all that that implies, are omnipresent at the Ambassador Theatre.

Other Stories and Memories: We were joined by talkshow host Wendy Williams as Matron "Mama" Morton for seven weeks over the summer and were treated to many "shout outs" during her live broadcasts of "The Wendy Williams Show." A documentary chronicling her experience on the Great White Way was made for TVGuide Network titled "How You Doin' Broadway?" Russian recording legend Larisa Dolina joined the company as Matron "Mama" Morton for a week in preparation for her Moscow production of *Chicago*. Her sultry voice and effusive charms were quite popular both on and off stage. Following the return of the great Christopher Sieber as Billy Flynn, *Rent* and *Aida* star Adam Pascal joined the company, giving our classic score just the right amount of his distinctive vocal edge.

1. Jason Patrick Sands as Billy Flynn, one of the many roles he covers.
2. Bebe Neuwirth as Matron "Mama" Morton, the *third* role she's played in *Chicago*.
3. R. Lowe as Mary Sunshine wins for the heaviest costume in the show. Not too difficult to do in *Chicago*, where few are fully clothed!
4. As of October 2013, Roz Ryan, as Matron "Mama" Morton, broke the record for having played more performances than any other female principal.
5. (L-R): Donna Marie Asbury, Stephanie Pope and Tonya Wathen toast the 7,000th performance.

The Cripple of Inishmaan

First Preview: April 12, 2014. Opened: April 20, 2014.
Still running as of May 31, 2014.

PLAYBILL®

THE CRIPPLE OF INISHMAAN

Broadway debut of Martin McDonagh's comedy about an Irish village turned upside down by the arrival of an American film company hiring locals for a feature being shot on location nearby. Billy, a physically handicapped youth, believes he has as much a chance of landing a role as anyone else, including Helen, the flame-haired beauty he loves from afar. Daniel Radcliffe, star of the Harry Potter films and two previous Broadway shows, plays the Cinderella-like Billy in this production, which transferred from a hit London engagement.

CAST
(in order of appearance)

Eileen Osbourne	GILLIAN HANNA
Kate Osbourne	INGRID CRAIGIE
Johnnypateenmike	PAT SHORTT
Billy	DANIEL RADCLIFFE
Bartley McCormick	CONOR MacNEILL
Helen McCormick	SARAH GREENE
Babbybobby	PÁDRAIC DELANEY
Doctor	GARY LILBURN
Mammy	JUNE WATSON

The play is set on the island of Inishmaan in 1934.

UNDERSTUDIES
For Billy, Bartley: JOSH SALT
For Kate Osbourne, Eileen Osbourne, Mammy:
LESLIE LYLES
For Helen: HELEN CESPEDES
For Johnnypateenmike, Babbybobby, Doctor:
AIDAN REDMOND

The actors in *The Cripple of Inishmaan* are appearing with the permission of Actors' Equity Association.

⑥ CORT THEATRE
138 West 48th Street
A Shubert Organization Theatre

Philip J. Smith, *Chairman*   **Robert E. Wankel,** *President*

Michael Grandage Company   Arielle Tepper Madover   L.T.D. Productions
Stacey Mindich   Starry Night Entertainment   Scott M. Delman
Martin McCallum   Stephanie P. McClelland   Zeilinger Productions

and

The Shubert Organization

present

Michael **GRANDAGE** *Company*

Daniel Radcliffe

in

THE CRIPPLE OF INISHMAAN

by

Martin McDonagh

with

Ingrid Craigie   Pádraic Delaney   Sarah Greene   Gillian Hanna
Gary Lilburn   Conor MacNeill   Pat Shortt   June Watson
Helen Cespedes   Leslie Lyles   Aidan Redmond   Josh Salt

Set and Costume Designer	**Lighting Designer**	**Composer and Sound Designer**
Christopher Oram	Paule Constable	Alex Baranowski
Hair Designer	**Press Representative**	**Advertising/Marketing**
Campbell Young	Boneau/Bryan Brown	Serino/Coyne
U.K. Casting	**Company Manager**	**Associate Director**
Anne McNulty, CDG	Thom Clay	Timothy Koch

Production Stage Manager	**Production Management**	**Associate Producer**	**General Management**
Peter Wolf	Aurora Productions	Just For Laughs	101 Productions, Ltd.

Directed by

Michael Grandage

4/20/14

Photo: Johan Persson

(L-R): Daniel Radcliffe, Ingrid Craigie, Gillian Hanna, Pat Shortt

The Cripple of Inishmaan

DIRECTOR'S NOTE

Welcome to the Broadway premiere of *The Cripple of Inishmaan* by Martin McDonagh.

Inishmaan is one of the three Aran Islands off the western coast of Ireland. The fictionalized action of the play is based on the real-life occasion of director Robert J. Flaherty coming to the neighboring island of Inishmore to make his 1934 documentary, *The Man of Aran*. McDonagh's comedy continues his long-standing relationship with Broadway. The play examines an ordinary coming-of-age in extraordinary circumstances and confirms his position as one of the most original Irish voices to emerge in the second half of the twentieth century.

This production also marks the New York debut of the Michael Grandage Company following its critically acclaimed launch in London last year. The company's central role is to engage with the next generation of theatre makers through access and training (www.mgcfutures.com). It is also dedicated to bringing quality theatre to all audiences, and we are delighted to continue the lower-priced ticket policy started in our London season two years ago by offering 10,000 tickets at $27 as part of our commitment to engage with as many young people as possible for our run at the Cort Theatre.

On behalf of the entire company, led by the inspirational Daniel Radcliffe, I would like to say how honored we are to bring this play to New York and be part of this great Broadway community.

Michael Grandage

Daniel Radcliffe
Billy

Ingrid Craigie
Kate Osbourne

Pádraic Delaney
Babbybobby

Sarah Greene
Helen McCormick

Gillian Hanna
Eileen Osbourne

Gary Lilburn
Doctor

Conor MacNeill
Bartley McCormick

Pat Shortt
Johnnypateenmike

June Watson
Mammy

Helen Cespedes
u/s Helen McCormick

Leslie Lyles
u/s Kate Osbourne, Eileen Osbourne, Mammy

Aidan Redmond
u/s Johnnypateenmike, Babbybobby, Doctor

Josh Salt
u/s Billy, Bartley McCormick

Martin McDonagh
Playwright

Michael Grandage
Director and Producer

Christopher Oram
Scenic and Costume Design

Paule Constable
Lighting Design

Alex Baranowski
Composer and Sound Design

Campbell Young
Campbell Young Associates
Hair and Make-up Design

Luc Verschueren
Campbell Young Associates
Hair and Make-up Design

Gene O'Donovan
Aurora Productions
Production *Management*

Ben Heller
Aurora Productions
Production *Management*

Wendy Orshan
101 Productions, Ltd.
General Manager

James Bierman
Michael Grandage Company
Producer

Arielle Tepper
Madover
Producer

Roger Thompson
L.T.D. Productions Inc.
Producer

Nancy Thompson
L.T.D. Productions Inc.
Producer

Stacey Mindich
Producer

The Cripple of Inishmaan

Michael Shulman
Starry Night
Entertainment
Producer

Scott M. Delman
Producer

Stephanie P.
McClelland
Producer

Scott Zeilinger
Producer

Brian Zeilinger
Producer

Philip J. Smith
The Shubert
Organization
Producer

Robert E. Wankel
The Shubert
Organization
Producer

Adam Blanshay
Just for Laughs
Theatricals
Associate Producer

Gilbert Rozon
Just for Laughs
Theatricals
Associate Producer

Photos: Brian Mapp

FRONT OF HOUSE
Front: Robert Evans
Middle (L-R): Mario Carillo, Robert DeJesus, William Denson, Kathryn Schwartz
Back (L-R): Michael Lonergan, Luis Molina, Brian Gold

BOX OFFICE
(L-R): Tom Morgan, Greer Bond (Head Treasurer), Joseph Kane

2013-2014 AWARD

THEATRE WORLD AWARD
(Sarah Greene)

MANAGEMENT
Front:
Peter Wolf
(Production Stage Manager)
Back:
Thom Clay
(Company Manager),
Lisa Buxbaum
(Stage Manager)

The Cripple of Inishmaan

Photo: Brian Mapp

STAFF FOR *THE CRIPPLE OF INISHMAAN*

GENERAL MANAGEMENT
101 PRODUCTIONS, LTD.
Wendy Orshan   Jeffrey M. Wilson
Elie Landau
Ron Gubin
Chris Morey

COMPANY MANAGER
Thom Clay

GENERAL PRESS REPRESENTATIVE
BONEAU/BRYAN-BROWN
Adrian Bryan-Brown
Jim Byk   Christine Olver

MICHAEL GRANDAGE COMPANY
Michael Grandage   James Bierman

ATM PRODUCTIONS
Arielle Tepper Madover   Holly Ferguson
Sam Levy   Allie Keller

U.S. CASTING CONSULTANT
TELSEY + COMPANY
Bernard Telsey CSA, Will Cantler CSA, David Vaccari CSA,
Bethany Knox CSA, Craig Burns CSA,
Tiffany Little Canfield CSA, Rachel Hoffman CSA,
Justin Huff CSA, Patrick Goodwin CSA,
Abbie Brady-Dalton CSA,
David Morris, Cesar A. Rocha CSA,
Andrew Femenella CSA, Karyn Casl CSA,
Kristina Bramhall, Conrad Woolfe, Rachel Nadler,
Rachel Minow, Sean Gannon

PRODUCTION MANAGEMENT
AURORA PRODUCTIONS
Gene O'Donovan   Ben Heller
Chris Minnick   Liza Luxenberg   Jarid Sumner
Anthony Jusino   Rachel London   David Cook
Bridget Van Dyke   Melissa Mazdra   Rob Ward

Production Stage Manager ....Peter Wolf
Stage Manager ....Lisa Buxbaum
Associate Director ....Timothy Koch
Associate Scenic Designer ....Tim Mackabee
Associate Costume Designer ....Amanda Seymour
Associate Lighting Designer ....Gina Scherr

Associate Sound Designer ....Chris Cronin
UK Associate Set &
    Costume Designers.......Lee Newby, David Woodhead
Head Carpenter ....Eric Stewart
House Carpenter ....Eddie Diaz
Flyman ....Jennifer Diaz
Production Electrician ....Jon Lawson
Head Props ....Robert Presley
House Props ....Lonnie Gaddy
Production Sound ....Brad Gyorgak
Lighting Programmer ....Michael Hill
UK Technical Director ....Paul Handley
Wardrobe Supervisor ....Eileen Miller
Mr. Radcliffe's Dresser ....Sandy Binion
Dresser ....Kevin O'Brien
Hair & Wig Supervisor ....Ruth Carsch
Dialect/Vocal Coach ....Penny Dyer
Production Assistants .....Patricia L. Grabb, Brae Singleton
Assistant to the General Managers ....Michael Rudd
101 Productions, Ltd. Staff ....Beth Blitzer,
        Caitlin Clements, Mark Gagliardi, Richard Jones,
            Kathy Kim, Steve Supeck, Andrew White
101 Productions, Ltd. Interns ....Justin Coffman,
                                        Eric Vigdorov
Legal Counsel ..Lazarus and Harris LLP/Scott Lazarus, Esq.
Immigration Attorney ....David King/
                Entertainment Visa Consultants LLC
UK Visa Consultant ....Lisa Carr
Accountant ....Fried & Kowgios CPA's LLP
Controller ....Galbraith & Co./Sarah Galbraith
Advertising ....Serino/Coyne/Angelo Desimini,
        Vinny Sainato, Matthew Upshaw, Danielle Boyle,
            Erin Daigle, Megan Lacerenza, Aaron Coleman
Marketing and Interactive ....Serino/Coyne/
            Leslie Barrett, Kevin Keating, Jim Glaub,
            Abby Wolbe, Mark Seeley, Mike Rafael,
                Brian DeVito, Catherine Herzog
Banking ....Signature Bank
Insurance ....Robertson Taylor Worldwide
Opening Night Coordinator ....Serino/Coyne Events/
                                    Suzanne Tobak
Merchandising ....Creative Goods Merchandising LLC
Production Photographer ....Hugo Glendinning
Payroll Services ....Castellana Services Inc.
Theatre Displays ....Fine Art Imaging
Production Photography ....Johan Persson,
                                    Hugo Glendinning

To learn more about the production, please visit
www.crippleofinishmaan.com

Please follow us on Twitter, Facebook & Instagram:
@InishmaanBway

CREDITS
Scenery modification by Showmotion. Lighting by PRG
Lighting. Sound by Sound Associates. Eggs provided by
FreshDirect. Cloth by Promptside. Set built and painted by
Bay. Costumes by Angels.

Footage of *Man of Aran*
with kind permission from ITN Source.

SPECIAL THANKS
Frankie Bridges, Richard Clark, Rhiannon Harper, Barbara
Houseman, Janis Price, Jonathan Lyle, Fiona McCallum,
Kate Mitchell, Kate Morley, Anna Roberto, Whitelight,
Beverly Edwards

This production was rehearsed at
The Pershing Square Signature Center

 The Shubert Organization is a proud
member of the Broadway Green Alliance.

The Cripple of Inishmaan
SCRAPBOOK

Correspondent: Pat Shortt, "Johnnypateenmike"

Memorable Note, Fax or Fan Letter: I would have to say the fan mail that Sarah Greene received from a keen leg watcher and sensual Aries gave us all a laugh.

Most Exciting Celebrity Visitor: We had Seth Meyers in and a host of others but Jessica Lange was a lady and called on all the cast. Everyone was blown away with her.

Favorite In-Theatre Gathering Place: On the fire escape.

Special Backstage Rituals: The first call actors, which is half the cast, gather on the stage before the show starts. We get into the excitement of the show laughing and joking behind the black less than a foot from the front row.

Most Memorable Audience Reaction: At the end of scene four with the mother and Johnnypateenmike a man shouted, "Is that you, Jack?" I think he just woke up.

Worst Audience Behavior: It had no effect on the cast, but a family had brought buckets of KFC into the theatre and passed them between each other. The problem was they were not all seated together so they were up and down throughout the first act swapping napkins and drinks.

Memorable Ad-Lib: In one of the first shows we did, on Johnnypateen's entrance, the door didn't open. Johnnypateen had to knock and the Aunties had to open the door to let him in.

There was a lot of lock action and we weren't sure if it was ever going to open.

Favorite Off-Site Hangouts: Every bar in the theatre district and a few downtown.

Favorite Snack Food: The cupcakes that the producers send over. Please stop. We are all putting on so much weight. They are divine.

Favorite Therapy: A cup of Barry's Gold Blend Irish Tea. It would set you up for any audience.

Public Relations: Best Story From the Ushers and Front-of-House Staff: Robert at front of house is a trained pastry chef and makes us a beautiful cake every Sunday. It's amazing.

Mascot: Conor MacNeill. They say if you catch him you can make a wish.

Catchphrases Only the Company Would Recognize: "Up the yard with ya." "There's a smell of Benji off ya."

Fastest Costume Change: This would have to be Bartley (Conor MacNeill) after Helen breaks four eggs over his head. He washes his hair, dries it and changes into a new costume in less than six minutes.

Who Wore the Heaviest/Hottest Costume?: June Watson who plays Mammy. She is not just in costume, but also wrapped in bed sheets or in the wheelchair wrapped in blankets.

Who Wore the Least?: It would have to be Bartley showing leg with those gorgeous Daisy Dukes short pants.

Web Buzz on the Show: It beats Johnnypateen's three pieces of news.

Ghostly Encounters Backstage: After our director Michael Grandage had returned to London, we could still feel his presence in the theatre.

Coolest Thing About Being in This Show: Working with Conor MacNeill—the smallest, but coolest, actor we have worked with.

1. *Yearbook* correspondent Pat Shortt as Johnnypateenmike with June Watson (Mammy), who wears the heaviest costumes, in a scene from *The Cripple of Inishmaan* at the Cort Theatre.
2. At the after-party with (L-R): producer James Bierman, playwright Martin McDonagh, Daniel Radcliffe, producer Arielle Tepper Madover and director Michael Grandage.
3. At the curtain call (L-R): Gary Lilburn, Conor MacNeill (the company's mascot), Ingrid Craigie and Sarah Greene.

First Date

First Preview: July 9, 2013. Opened: August 8, 2013.
Closed January 5, 2014 after 34 Previews and 174 Performances.

Nerdy Aaron and boho goddess Casey have been set up on a blind date by well-meaning friends in this new musical by Broadway first-timers. Things seem to be going disastrously for the mismatched couple at first, but gradually they begin to see how their differences kind of mesh. But will it be enough to lead to a second date? A notable aspect of the production is the way the various friends, family and former significant others keep popping up from Aaron and Casey's imagination to nag, prod, comment and sometimes just sing along.

CAST

Aaron ....ZACHARY LEVI
Casey ....KRYSTA RODRIGUEZ
Man #1 (Gabe/Young Aaron/
    Edgy British Guy) ....BRYCE RYNESS
Man #2 (Reggie/Aaron's Future Son/
    Edgy Rocker Guy) ....KRISTOFFER CUSICK
Man #3 (Waiter/Casey's Father/
    Friendly Therapist) ....BLAKE HAMMOND
Woman #1 (Grandma Ida/Lauren/
    Aaron's Mother) ....SARA CHASE
Woman #2 (Allison/
    Young Casey) ....KATE LOPREST

STANDBYS

For Aaron, Man #1, Man #2, Man #3:
ERIC ANKRIM, KEVIN KERN
For Casey, Woman #1, Woman #2:
VICKI NOON, SYDNEY SHEPHERD
Dance Captain: KEVIN KERN

Continued on next page

⊛ LONGACRE THEATRE
220 West 48th Street
A Shubert Organization Theatre

Philip J. Smith, *Chairman*   **Robert E. Wankel,** *President*

Junkyard Dog Productions
Stem Productions Altar Identity Studios Alex and Katya Lukianov
Susan and Jim Blair Linda and Bill Potter

in association with

Yasuhiro Kawana Vijay and Sita Vashee Kevin and Lynn Foley Jeff and Julie Goldstein
Edward and Mimi Kirsch Frank and Denise Phillips Steve Reynolds and Paula Rosput Reynolds Land Line Productions
Alhadeff Family Productions/Sheri and Les Biller Pat Halloran/Laura Little Theatrical Productions
Tony Meola/Remmel T. Dickinson and John Yonover ShadowCatcher Entertainment/Tom and Connie Walsh

present

ZACHARY LEVI   KRYSTA RODRIGUEZ

in

FIRST DATE

Book by
AUSTIN WINSBERG

Music and Lyrics by
ALAN ZACHARY & MICHAEL WEINER

featuring

SARA CHASE	KRISTOFFER CUSICK	BLAKE HAMMOND	KATE LOPREST	BRYCE RYNESS

with

ERIC ANKRIM   KEVIN KERN   VICKI NOON   SYDNEY SHEPHERD

Scenic and Media Design	Costume Design	Lighting Design	Sound Design
DAVID GALLO	DAVID C. WOOLARD	MIKE BALDASSARI	KAI HARADA

Hair Design	Casting by	Assistant Director	Associate Choreographer
JOSH MARQUETTE	TELSEY + COMPANY RACHEL HOFFMAN CSA	BRANDON IVIE	LEE WILKINS

Orchestrations	Conductor	Music Coordinator
AUGUST ERIKSMOEN	DOMINICK AMENDUM	MICHAEL KELLER

General Manager	Production Stage Manager	Production Management	Press Agent	Advertising and Marketing
ALCHEMY PRODUCTION GROUP CARL PASBJERG & FRANK SCARDINO	ARTURO E. PORAZZI	JUNIPER STREET PRODUCTIONS, INC.	THE HARTMAN GROUP	AKA

Music Supervision, Vocal and Incidental Music Arrangements by
DOMINICK AMENDUM

Musical Staging by
JOSH RHODES

Directed by
BILL BERRY

Originally co-produced by The 5th Avenue Theatre
David Armstrong, Executive Producer and Artistic Director; Bernadine Griffin, Managing Director; Bill Berry, Producing Director
and
A Contemporary Theatre, Seattle, WA
Kurt Beattie, Artistic Director and Carlo Scandiuzzi, Executive Director
The producers wish to express their appreciation to Theatre Development Fund for its support of this production.

8/8/13

Zachary Levi and Krysta Rodriguez meet for their first date.

Photo: Joan Marcus

First Date

MUSICAL NUMBERS

"The One"	Company
"First Impressions"	Aaron and Casey
"Bailout Song #1"	Reggie
"The Girl for You"	Company
"The Awkward Pause"	Company
"Allison's Theme #1"	Allison
*"Forever Online"	Young Aaron, Young Casey, Aaron and Casey
"That's Why You Love Me"	Bad Boys
"Bailout Song #2"	Reggie
"Safer"	Casey
"I'd Order Love"	Waiter
"Allison's Theme #2"	Aaron, Allison, Gabe
"The Things I Never Said"	Aaron and Aaron's Mother
"Bailout Song #3"	Reggie
"In Love With You"	Aaron
"The Check!"	Company
"Something That Will Last"	Casey, Aaron and Company

* Note: Two characters (Young Aaron and Young Casey) and their song "Forever Online" were cut soon after the opening night PLAYBILL was printed.

Cast Continued

SETTING
New York City. The present.

BAND
Conductor: DOMINICK AMENDUM
Associate Conductor: MATT HINKLEY

Keyboard 1: DOMINICK AMENDUM
Keyboard 2/Guitars: MATT HINKLEY
Reeds/Keyboard 3: CHARLES PILLOW
Guitars: J.J. McGEEHAN
Bass: RANDY LANDAU
Drums: STEVE BARTOSIK

Music Preparation:
ZACH REDLER and RYAN DRISCOLL
Music Coordinator: MICHAEL KELLER
Keyboard/Drum Programmer: BRYAN CROOK

Zachary Levi
Aaron

Krysta Rodriguez
Casey

Sara Chase
Woman #1

Kristoffer Cusick
Man #2

Blake Hammond
Man #3

Kate Loprest
Woman #2

Bryce Ryness
Man #1

Eric Ankrim
Standby

Kevin Kern
Standby

Vicki Noon
Standby

Sydney Shepherd
Standby

Austin Winsberg
Book

Alan Zachary
Music and Lyrics

Michael Weiner
Music and Lyrics

Bill Berry
Director

Josh Rhodes
Musical Staging

David Gallo
Scenic and Media Design

David C. Woolard
Costume Design

Mike Baldassari
Lighting Design

Kai Harada
Sound Design

Josh Marquette
Hair Design

First Date

Bernard Telsey
Telsey + Company
Casting

Brandon Ivie
Assistant Director

Lee Wilkins
*Associate
Choreographer*

August Eriksmoen
Orchestrations

Dominick Amendum
*Music Director/
Conductor/
Music Supervisor/
Arrangements*

Michael Keller
Music Coordinator

Carl Pasbjerg
Alchemy Production
Group LLC
*General
Management*

Ana Rose Greene, Guy Kwan,
Joseph DeLuise, Hillary Blanken
Juniper Street Productions
Production Manager

Randy Adams
Junkyard Dog
Productions
Producer

Marleen Alhadeff
Junkyard Dog
Productions
Producer

Kenny Alhadeff
Junkyard Dog
Productions
Producer

Sue Frost
Junkyard Dog
Productions
Producer

Joseph Craig
Stem Productions
Producer

Wade Bradley
Altar Identity Studios
Producer

Helen Rosenberg
Altar Identity Studios
Producer

Alex Lukianov
Producer

Katya Lukianov
Producer

Susan Blair
Producer

Jim Blair
Producer

Linda Potter
Producer

Bill Potter
Producer

Yasuhiro Kawana
Producer

Sita Vashee
Producer

Vijay Vashee
Producer

Lynn and Kevin Foley
Producers

Jeff Goldstein
Producer

Julie Goldstein
Producer

Edward Kirsch
Producer

Mimi Kirsch
Producer

Frank Phillips
Producer

Denise Phillips
Producer

Steve Reynolds and
Paula Rosput
Reynolds
Producers

Sheri Biller
Producer

First Date

Les Biller
Producer

Pat Halloran
Producer

Laura Little
Laura Little Theatrical
Productions
Producer

Tony Meola
Producer

Remmel T. Dickinson
Producer

John B. Yonover
Producer

Tom Walsh
Producer

Connie Walsh
Producer

David Armstrong
Executive Producer
& Artistic Director
5th Avenue Theatre
Originating Theatre

Bernadine C. Griffin
Managing Director
5th Avenue Theatre
Originating Theatre

Kurt Beattie
Artistic Director
A Contemporary
Theatre
*Co-Originating
Theatre*

Carlo Scandiuzzi
Executive Director
A Contemporary
Theatre
*Co-Originating
Theatre*

Photos: Brian Mapp

DOORMAN
Enrico "Rick" Bozzacco

> **2013-2014 AWARD**
> THEATRE WORLD AWARD
> (Zachary Levi)

FRONT OF HOUSE
Front Row (L-R): John Barbaretti,
Monica Ramirez, Joseph Spezzano
Middle Row (L-R): Patricia Roehrich,
Nancy Reyes, Mary Sheehan,
Janice Jenkins, Shirley Wagner, Elsie Grosvenor
Back Row (L-R): Danielle Banyai, Rosetta Jlelaty,
Bob Reilly, Kathleen Reiter, Carla Dawson

MANAGEMENT
(L-R): Gary Mickelson (Stage Manager), Laura Wilson (Assistant Stage
Manager), Arturo E. Porazzi (Production Stage Manager),
Andrea Wales (Production Assistant)

CREW
Front Row (L-R): Ric Rogers, Timothy Greer (Dresser),
Sarah Levine (Hair Supervisor),
Elizabeth Coleman (Assistant Audio), André Gray
Middle Row (L-R): Scott Butler (Lead Followspot),
Scott Mendelsohn, Paul Wimmer
Back Row (L-R): John Lofgren, Wilbur Graham,
Jamie Englehart, Jessica Dermody (Wardrobe Supervisor),
Christopher Robinson (Head Electrician),
Chad Woerner (Head Carpenter)

First Date

(L-R): Bryce Ryness, Kristoffer Cusick, Zachary Levi, Krysta Rodriguez, Kate Loprest, Sara Chase

STAFF FOR *FIRST DATE*

GENERAL MANAGEMENT
ALCHEMY PRODUCTION GROUP
Carl Pasbjerg   Frank P. Scardino

COMPANY MANAGER
Jim Brandeberry

PRODUCTION MANAGEMENT
JUNIPER STREET PRODUCTIONS
Hillary Blanken   Joseph DeLuise
Ana Rose Greene   Guy Kwan

GENERAL PRESS REPRESENTATIVE
THE HARTMAN GROUP
Michael Hartman
Wayne Wolfe   Emily McGill

CASTING
TELSEY + COMPANY
Bernard Telsey, CSA, Will Cantler CSA,
David Vaccari CSA, Bethany Knox CSA,
Craig Burns CSA, Tiffany Little Canfield CSA,
Rachel Hoffman CSA, Justin Huff CSA,
Patrick Goodwin CSA, Abbie Brady-Dalton CSA,
David Morris, Cesar A. Rocha CSA,
Andrew Femenella CSA, Karyn Casl CSA,
Kristina Bramhall, Conrad Woolfe, Amelia Nadler

Production Stage Manager ....Arturo E. Porazzi
Stage Manager ....Gary Mickelson
Assistant Stage Manager ....Laura Wilson
Assistant Company Manager ....Amanda S. Coleman
General Management Associate ....Anthony McDonald
Dance Captain ....Kevin Kern
Associate Scenic Designer ....Steven Kemp
Associate Video Designer ....Brad Peterson
Assistant Scenic and Video Design ....Hana Kim
Associate Sound Designer ....Jana Hoglund
Assistant Lighting Designer ....Karen Spahn
Assistant Costume Designer ....Justin Hall
Assistant to the Costume Designer ....Kara Harmon
Lighting Draftsman ....Kristina Kloss
Moving Light Programmer ....Jason Marin
Projections Programmer ....Paul Vershbow
Production Carpenter ....Erik E. Hansen
Head Carpenter ....Chad Woerner

Production Flyman/Automation ....Scott "Gus" Poitras
Production Electricians .....James Fedigan, Randall Zaibek
Head Electrician ....Christopher Robinson
Lead Followspot ....Scott Butler
Production Video Technician ....Eric Norris
Production Property Master ....Mike Pilipski
Head Property Master ....John Paull
Production Sound Engineer ....Patrick Pummill
Advance Sound Engineer ....Michael "Fodder" Carrico
Assistant Audio ....Elizabeth Coleman
Wardrobe Supervisor ....Jessica Dermody
Dressers ....Jamie Englehart, Timothy Greer
Hair Supervisor ....Sarah Levine
Music Copying ....Ryan Driscoll
Keyboard and
    Electronic Drum Programming ....Bryan Crook
Music Looping ....Derik Lee, August Eriksmoen
Music Department Assistants ....Aaron Jodoin,
                                             Rachel Ziering
Production Assistants ....Lori Amondson, Sophie Quist,
                                             Andrea Wales
Technical Production Assistants ....Jeremy McComish,
                                             Johnny Kruger
Design Studio Managers ....Sarah Zeitler, Maggie Baker
Design Studio Interns .....Samantha Schaffer, Paula Dixon
Advertising/Marketing/Digital ....AKA/
           Elizabeth Furze, Scott Moore, Bashan Aquart,
           Elizabeth Findlay, Kyle Hall, Janette Roush, Erik Alden,
           Danielle Barcheto, Sarah Borenstein, Tomris Laffly,
                            Emily Yarbrough, Flora Pei
Web Design/Maintenance ....AKA
JYD Associate Producer ....Carolyn D. Miller
JYD Associate...............................Sarah Nashman
JYD Interns ....Andi Alhadeff, Lauren Fischetti,
                                             Daria Maurer
Accountant ....Fried & Kowgios LLC
Controller...................................Sarah Galbraith
Legal Counsel ....Franklin, Weinrib, Rudell, & Vassallo
Payroll Services ....Castellana Services, Inc.
Banking ....Signature Bank
Insurance................................Dewitt Stern Group
Opening Night Coordination .....The Lawrence Company
Merchandising ....The Araca Group
Theatre Displays..........................King Displays Inc.

CREDITS
Scenery fabrication by Scenic Technologies, a division of
Production Resource Group, LLC, New Windsor, NY.

Show control and scenic motion control featuring stage
command systems® by Scenic Technologies, a division of
Production Resource Group, LLC, New Windsor, NY.
Additional scenery and scenic effects built, painted and
electrified by ShowMotion Inc., Norwalk, CT. Scenic
painting by Scenic Arts Studios, Newburgh, NY. Lighting
equipment provided by PRG Lighting. Sound equipment
provided by PRG Audio. Video and projection equipment
provided by Scharff Weisberg/WorldStage – East Coast.
Props provided by Prop N Spoon, LLC, Rahway NJ.
Costume shops: Tricorne Inc., John Kristiansen New
York Inc. Millinery by Arnold S. Levine Inc. Custom
fabric printing by Gene Mignola. Screen printing by
Jeff Fender Studio. Wigs by Hudson Wigs. Special thanks to
Ellen Pilipski.

Rehearsed at the New 42nd Street Studios.

 **THE SHUBERT ORGANIZATION, INC.**
Board of Directors

Philip J. Smith	**Robert E. Wankel**
Chairman	President
Wyche Fowler, Jr.	**Diana Phillips**
Lee J. Seidler	**Michael I. Sovern**

Stuart Subotnick

Chief Financial Officer ....Elliot Greene
Sr. Vice President, Ticketing ....David Andrews
Vice President, Finance ....Juan Calvo
Vice President, Human Resources ....Cathy Cozens
Vice President, Facilities ....John Darby
Vice President, Theatre Operations ....Peter Entin
Vice President, Marketing ....Charles Flateman
Vice President, Audit ....Anthony LaMattina
Vice President, Ticket Sales ....Brian Mahoney
Vice President, Creative Projects ...........D.S. Moynihan
Vice President, Real Estate ....Julio Peterson

House Manager ....Bob Reilly

 The Shubert Organization is a proud
member of the Broadway Green Alliance.

First Date
SCRAPBOOK

Correspondent: Sara Chase, "Woman #1"
Opening Night Parties and/or Gifts: Our choreographer Josh Rhodes and associate Lee Wilkins gave us tote bags with Zac's line printed on the side: "We 'totes' got through it." Very funny and appropriate.
Most Exciting Celebrity Visitor: Giuliana and Bill Rancic! Nice, good looking, and charming.
Favorite In-Theatre Gathering Place: Wardrobe. They have candy, a cute dog, and hot water for tea.
Actor Who Performed the Most Roles in This Show: Sara Chase's track does five different characters.
Special Backstage Ritual: At "places" the cast circles up stage right and checks in with each other.
Most Memorable Audience Reaction: When Aaron calls Casey a "Blind Date Slut" sometimes the audience goes "Ooooooh."
Worst Audience Behavior: Tie: A woman in the front row in bright white jeans was smacking her gum, legs up on stage, and reading her program the entire time. Another time a young couple in the front row kept taking photos on their phone with the flash. One actor mouthed "You can't do that!" but they kept on the entire show.
Memorable Ad-Lib: Zac's mic went out on stage (he now wears two!) and he had to leave the stage right away, leaving the rest of us in limbo for three minutes, and Krysta stag on her date. When he came back, he said "Sorry. Sometimes I get diarrhea and I just have to go."
Memorable Fan Encounter: One time during bows, a guy jumped up on stage and tried to dance with us. Security promptly escorted him out, but he showed up at the stage door anyway expecting autographs.
Company In-Joke: We can't believe there are only seven actors on stage. We always say, "Is this really all of us?" So one day someone joked "Wait, where's Heather?!" and fictional Heather has been a part of our cast ever since. Sometimes she signs up her backstage guests, sometimes we hold the curtain for her. She is a consummate unprofessional and probably a drunk.
"Carols for a Cure" Carol: "Go Tell It on the Mountain."
Favorite Off-Site Hangout: Hurley's. We are always at Hurley's.
Favorite Therapy: We love Throat Coat Tea. Secret: Zac isn't drinking beer the whole time on stage, he's drinking Throat Coat that's been thrown in a blender to create the foam on top!
Pit Stop: Best Story from the Orchestra: The band likes to call Matt Hinkley, our guitarist, "Matalie Hinklestein."
Public Relations: Best Story from Ushers and Front-of-House Staff: A woman once left her husband passed out on the sidewalk to ask the box office for a refund instead of only focusing on him. A few minutes later, another man asked the box office if he could have their seats, since he assisted them and knew they were not going to be sitting there. How very New York!
Mascot: Truffles the dog! He is a bichon poodle

1. The cast and creators recording the original cast album (L-R): Kristoffer Cusick, Kate Loprest, Blake Hammond, Austin Winsberg, Bill Berry, Krysta Rodriguez, Zachary Levi, Michael Weiner, *Yearbook* correspondent Sara Chase, Alan Zachary and Bryce Ryness.
2. Krysta Rodriguez at the recording session.
3. Creative team at the Longacre Theatre (L-R): librettist Austin Winsberg, songwriters Alan Zachary and Michael Weiner.

rescue dog of Jessica Dermody, our wardrobe supervisor. We compete for his affection. Every night on stage, Zac's character orders "the burger" and Truffles gets to eat whatever Zac doesn't finish. A tail has never wagged faster!
Catchphrases Only the Company Would Recognize: Blake Hammond is the master of all catchphrases. He introduces catchphrases left and right. His most popular one, however, is: "I wanna live...!" It can be used in any context. If you're tired, if you hear a loud noise, if you're happy. You can respond with "I wanna live!"
Understudy Anecdote: The swings watched all of tech from the mezzanine where they had all the best candy. They deemed it "Halloween in the Mezzanine."
Nickname: Sydney Shepherd, one of our female swings, is right out of college, so Kevin Kern nicknamed her "Syd the Kid." It's stuck. We love it.
Fastest Costume Change: Sara Chase changes into Grandma Ida on stage in three bars

of music.
Heaviest/Hottest Costume: Blake Hammond wears two vests as the waiter, one over the other, because one miraculously changes into an entire preacher's robe on stage.
Actor Who Wore the Least: Krysta has the least amount to wear. She's basically wearing a short slip on stage.
Web Buzz: People on social media are the best. The demographic of our show really lends itself to reaching out to fans via the internet.
Coolest Thing About Being in This Show: It's 90 minutes!!
Also: Because there is no ensemble in this show, no one was eligible for the Gypsy Robe. We suspected Blake Hammond might be disappointed, as this would have been his first time. The cast and wardrobe got together and created his very own Gypsy Robe. On opening night, we all gathered on stage and presented him with our very own Gypsy Robe. There was not a dry eye on stage. It was very moving.

A Gentleman's Guide to Love & Murder

First Preview: October 22, 2013. Opened: November 17, 2013.
Still running as of May 31, 2014.

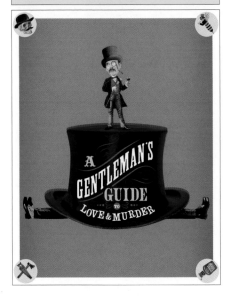

PLAYBILL

A new musical comedy presented in the style of 19th century melodrama. Down-at-heels Monty Navarro discovers that his late mother was disowned and mistreated by her family, the wealthy D'Ysquith clan, and that he actually is ninth in line to inherit an earldom. So Monty sets out to get revenge (and a fortune) by murdering those in line ahead of him, finding love in the process. This production is notable for the fact that all the murder victims were played by a single actor, Jefferson Mays.

CAST

Monty Navarro	BRYCE PINKHAM
Miss Shingle	JANE CARR
Sibella Hallward	LISA O'HARE
Asquith D'Ysquith, Jr.	JEFFERSON MAYS
Tour Guide	JENNIFER SMITH
Lord Adalbert D'Ysquith	JEFFERSON MAYS
Reverend Lord Ezekial D'Ysquith	JEFFERSON MAYS
Miss Barley	CATHERINE WALKER
Lord Asquith D'Ysquith, Sr.	JEFFERSON MAYS
Henry D'Ysquith	JEFFERSON MAYS
Tom Copley	JEFF KREADY
Phoebe D'Ysquith	LAUREN WORSHAM
Lady Hyacinth D'Ysquith	JEFFERSON MAYS
Newsboys	JEFF KREADY, PRICE WALDMAN, JOANNA GLUSHAK, JENNIFER SMITH
Major Lord Bartholomew D'Ysquith	JEFFERSON MAYS
Lady Salome D'Ysquith Pumphrey	JEFFERSON MAYS

Continued on next page

Continued on next page

♀ WALTER KERR THEATRE
A JUJAMCYN THEATRE

JORDAN ROTH, *President*

ROCCO LANDESMAN, *President Emeritus*

PAUL LIBIN, *Executive Vice President*   **JACK VIERTEL,** *Senior Vice President*

JOEY PARNES   S.D. WAGNER   JOHN JOHNSON

50 CHURCH STREET PRODUCTIONS   JOAN RAFFE & JHETT TOLENTINO   JAY ALIX & UNA JACKMAN
CATHERINE & FRED ADLER   RHODA HERRICK   KATHLEEN K. JOHNSON   MEGAN SAVAGE
SHADOWCATCHER ENTERTAINMENT   RON SIMONS   TRUE LOVE PRODUCTIONS   JAMIE deROY
FOUR LADIES & ONE GENT   JOHN ARTHUR PINCKARD   GREG NOBILE   STEWART LANE & BONNIE COMLEY
EXETER CAPITAL/TED SNOWDON   RYAN HUGH MACKEY   CRICKET-CTM MEDIA/MANO-HORN PRODUCTIONS
DENNIS GRIMALDI/MARGOT ASTRACHAN   HELLO ENTERTAINMENT/JAMIE BENDELL
MICHAEL T. COHEN/JOE SIROLA   JOSEPH & CARSON GLEBERMAN/WILLIAM MEGEVICK

AND

GREEN STATE PRODUCTIONS

IN ASSOCIATION WITH

THE HARTFORD STAGE AND THE OLD GLOBE

PRESENT

JEFFERSON MAYS   BRYCE PINKHAM

A GENTLEMAN'S GUIDE
TO LOVE & MURDER

BASED ON A NOVEL BY ROY HORNIMAN

BOOK AND LYRICS BY   MUSIC AND LYRICS BY
ROBERT L. FREEDMAN   STEVEN LUTVAK

WITH

LISA O'HARE   LAUREN WORSHAM

PAMELA BOB   JOANNA GLUSHAK   EDDIE KORBICH   JEFF KREADY
MARK LEDBETTER   JENNIFER SMITH   PRICE WALDMAN   CATHERINE WALKER

AND

JANE CARR

SCENIC DESIGN	COSTUME DESIGN	LIGHTING DESIGN	SOUND DESIGN
ALEXANDER DODGE	LINDA CHO	PHILIP S. ROSENBERG	DAN MOSES SCHREIER

PROJECTION DESIGN	HAIR & WIG DESIGN	CASTING
AARON RHYNE	CHARLES LaPOINTE	BINDER CASTING JAY BINDER/JASON STYRES

ORCHESTRATIONS	MUSIC DIRECTOR	VOCAL ARRANGEMENTS	MUSIC COORDINATOR
JONATHAN TUNICK	PAUL STAROBA	DIANNE ADAMS McDOWELL & STEVEN LUTVAK	SEYMOUR RED PRESS

PRODUCTION STAGE MANAGER	ADVERTISING & MARKETING	PRESS REPRESENTATIVE
SUSIE CORDON	SPOTCO	O&M CO

CHOREOGRAPHY
PEGGY HICKEY

DIRECTED BY
DARKO TRESNJAK

WORLD PREMIERE PRESENTED BY THE HARTFORD STAGE: DARKO TRESNJAK, ARTISTIC DIRECTOR, MICHAEL STOTTS, MANAGING DIRECTOR AND
THE OLD GLOBE: BARRY EDELSTEIN, ARTISTIC DIRECTOR, MICHAEL MURPHY, MANAGING DIRECTOR.

A GENTLEMAN'S GUIDE TO LOVE & MURDER WAS DEVELOPED, IN PART, AT THE 2009 SUNDANCE INSTITUTE THEATRE LAB AT THE SUNDANCE RESORT
WITH ADDITIONAL POST-LAB SUPPORT THROUGH ITS INITIATIVE WITH THE ANDREW W. MELLON FOUNDATION.

THE PRODUCERS WISH TO EXPRESS THEIR APPRECIATION TO THEATRE DEVELOPMENT FUND FOR ITS SUPPORT OF THIS PRODUCTION.

11/17/13

Jefferson Mays (L) as Henry D'Ysquith and Bryce Pinkham (R) as Monty Navarro, sing "It's Better With a Man"

Photo: Joan Marcus

A Gentleman's Guide to Love & Murder

MUSICAL NUMBERS

ACT I

"A Warning to the Audience" ....Ensemble
"You're a D'Ysquith" ....Miss Shingle, Monty
"I Don't Know What I'd Do" ....Sibella
"Foolish to Think" ....Monty
"A Warning to Monty" ....Ensemble
"I Don't Understand the Poor" ....Lord Adalbert, Ensemble
"Foolish to Think" (Reprise) ....Monty
"Poison in My Pocket" ....Monty, Asquith Jr., Miss Barley
"Poor Monty" ....Sibella, Company
"Better With a Man" ....Henry, Monty
"Inside Out" ....Phoebe, Monty
"Lady Hyacinth Abroad" ....Lady Hyacinth, Ensemble
"The Last One You'd Expect" ....Company

ACT II

"Why Are All the D'Ysquiths Dying" ....Mourners, Lord Adalbert
"Sibella" ....Monty
"I've Decided to Marry You" ....Phoebe, Sibella, Monty
"Final Warning" ....Ensemble
"Poison in My Pocket" (Reprise) ....Monty
"Looking Down the Barrel of a Gun" ....Lord Adalbert
"Stop! Wait! What?!" ....Monty
"That Horrible Woman" ....Sibella, Phoebe, Detective, Magistrate, Guard
"Finale" ....Company

Cast Continued

Actors ....PRICE WALDMAN,
EDDIE KORBICH, JEFF KREADY
Lady Eugenia ....JOANNA GLUSHAK
Mr. Gorby ....EDDIE KORBICH
Chief Inspector Pinckney ......PRICE WALDMAN
Guard ....JEFF KREADY
Magistrate ....EDDIE KORBICH
Chauncey ....ROGER PURNELL
Ensemble....................JOANNA GLUSHAK,
EDDIE KORBICH, JEFF KREADY,
JENNIFER SMITH, PRICE WALDMAN,
CATHERINE WALKER

UNDERSTUDIES

For The D'Ysquith Family: PRICE WALDMAN
For Monty Navarro: JEFF KREADY,
    MARK LEDBETTER
For Sibella Hallward: CATHERINE WALKER,
    PAMELA BOB
For Phoebe D'Ysquith: CATHERINE WALKER,
    PAMELA BOB
For Miss Shingle: JENNIFER SMITH,
    PAMELA BOB

SWINGS

MARK LEDBETTER, PAMELA BOB

DANCE CAPTAIN

MARK LEDBETTER

TIME AND PLACE

London, 1909

ORCHESTRA

Music Director.......................PAUL STAROBA
Associate Music Director ....MIKE RUCKLES

Clarinet: LES SCOTT
Oboe/English Horn: KEVE WILSON
Bassoon: TOM SEFCOVIC
French Horn: PATRICK PRIDEMORE
Trumpet: DANIEL URNESS
Concert Mistress: SUZANNE ORNSTEIN
Violin: KRISTINA MUSSER
Viola: DAVID BLINN
Cello: MAIRI DORMAN
Bass: DICK SARPOLA
Drums/Percussion: ERIK CHARLSTON

Contractor ....SEYMOUR RED PRESS
Music Copying ..Emily Grishman Music Preparation/
KATHARINE EDMONDS,
EMILY GRISHMAN

Jefferson Mays (C) as
Lord Adalbert D'Ysquith,
Bryce Pinkham (behind him)
as Monty Navarro,
Jane Carr (R) as Miss Shingle
and the cast.

Photo: Joan Marcus

Jefferson Mays
The D'Ysquith Family

Bryce Pinkham
Monty Navarro

Lisa O'Hare
Sibella Hallward

Lauren Worsham
Phoebe D'Ysquith

A Gentleman's Guide to Love & Murder

Jane Carr
Miss Shingle

Pamela Bob
Swing

Joanna Glushak
Lady Eugenia

Eddie Korbich
Magistrate

Jeff Kready
Tom Copley

Mark Ledbetter
Swing

Jennifer Smith
Tour Guide

Price Waldman
Detective

Catherine Walker
Miss Barley

Robert L. Freedman
Book and Lyrics

Steven Lutvak
Music and Lyrics

Darko Tresnjak
*Director and
Hartford Stage
Artistic Director*

Alexander Dodge
Scenic Design

Linda Cho
Costume Design

Dan Moses Schreier
Sound Design

Aaron Rhyne
Projection Design

Charles G. LaPointe
Hair and Wig Design

Jay Binder
*Binder Casting
Casting*

Jonathan Tunick
Orchestrations

Paul Staroba
Music Director

Seymour Red Press
Music Coordinator

Susie Cordon
*Production Stage
Manager*

Joey Parnes
Producer

S.D. Wagner
Producer

John Johnson
Producer

Rick Costello
*50 Church Street
Productions
Producer*

Joan Raffe
Producer

Jhett Tolentino
Producer

Catherine Adler
Producer

Kathleen K. Johnson
Producer

Megan Savage
Producer

Ron Simons
Producer

Jeanne Donovan
Fisher
True Love
Productions
Producer

Laurie Gilmore
True Love
Productions
Producer

Jamie deRoy
Producer

A Gentleman's Guide to Love & Murder

Louise H. Beard
Four Ladies and
One Gent
Producer

Barbara Freitag
Four Ladies and
One Gent
Producer

Ruth Hendel
Four Ladies and
One Gent
Producer

Heni Koenigsberg
Four Ladies and
One Gent
Producer

Michael Filerman
Four Ladies and
One Gent
Producer

John Arthur Pinckard
Producer

Stewart F. Lane & Bonnie Comley
Producer

Ted Snowdon
Producer

Cricket Jiranek/
CTM Media Group
Producer

Barbara
Manocherian
Mano-Horn
Productions
Producer

Larry Hirschhorn
Mano-Horn
Productions
Producer

Dennis Grimaldi
Producer

Margot Astrachan
Producer

David Garfinkle
Hello Entertainment
Producer

Joe Sirola
Producer

Michael Stotts
Hartford Stage
Managing Director

Barry Edelstein
The Old Globe
Artistic Director

Greg Jackson
*Standby for
D'Ysquith Family*

CREW
Front Row (L-R): Vincent J. Valvo (Head Electrician), Timothy Bennet (Head Propertyman), George E. Fullum, Julian Andres Arango (Dresser),
Chris Doornbos (Head Electrician), Tree Lonon (Dresser), Trevor Ricci (Assistant Props), David Gotwald (Production Sound Engineer),
Dillon Cody (Assistant Sound Engineer)
Back Row (L-R): Sean Breault, Dylan Foley (Head Props), Sam Patt, Peter J. Iacoviello, Paul Valvo (Follow Spot Operator), Bill Craven (Head Carpenter),
Moose Johnson (Propertyman)

Photo: Brian Mapp

A Gentleman's Guide to Love & Murder

STAGE MANAGEMENT
(L-R): Jason Hindelang, Tripp Phillips

ORIGINAL STAGE MANAGEMENT
(L-R): Brian Rardin (Stage Manager),
Rachel Zack (Assistant Stage Manager),
Alex Mark (Substitute Stage Manager)

BOX OFFICE
(L-R): Gail Yerkovich (Assistant Treasurer), Harry Jaffie (Treasurer),
Robert Ricchiuti (Assistant Treasurer)

FRONT OF HOUSE
Front Row (L-R): Juliett Cipriati, T.J. D'Angelo (Head Usher),
Alison Traynor (Ticket Taker)
Middle Row (L-R): Mallory Sims, Shelby Wong, Jared Pike, Heather Jewels
Back Row (L-R): Manuel Sandridge, Rochelle Rogers, Leslie Morgenstern

Photos: Brian Mapp

STAFF FOR
A GENTLEMAN'S GUIDE TO LOVE AND MURDER

GENERAL MANAGEMENT
JOEY PARNES PRODUCTIONS
Joey Parnes
S.D. Wagner   John Johnson
Jillian Robbins

COMPANY MANAGERS
Kit Ingui & Cathy Kwon

CASTING
JAY BINDER CASTING
Jay Binder, CSA
Jack Bowdan, CSA   Mark Brandon, CSA
Jason Styres

PRESS REPRESENTATIVE
O&M CO.
Rick Miramontez   Andy Snyder
Scott Braun

MAKEUP DESIGNER
Brian Strumwasser

Production Stage Manager ....Susie Cordon
Stage Manager ....Brian Rardin
Assistant Stage Manager ....Rachel Zack

Associate Company Manager	Kim Sellon
Management Associate	Jillian Robbins
Dialect Coach	Gillian Lane-Plescia
Fight Director	Jeff Barry
Fight Captain	Mark Ledbetter
Assistant Director	Christina Pellegrini
Assistant Choreographer	Adam Cates
Associate Scenic Designer	Colin McGurk
Assistant Scenic Designers	Kevin Judge, Evan Adamson, Steven Kemp
Associate Costume Designer	Nancy A. Palmatier
Assistant Costume Designer	Sarah Smith
Associate Lighting Designer	Craig Stelzenmuller
Associate Sound Designer	Nicholas Pope
Associate Projection Designer	Bart Cortright
Projection Design Assistant	Dylan James Amick
Assistant Hair & Wig Designer	Brittany Hartman
Production Carpenter	Larry Morley
Head Carpenter	Bill Craven
Production Properties	Mike Smanko
Head Props	Dylan Foley
Assistant Props	Trevor Ricci
Prop Artisan	Sydney Schatz
Outside Props	James Keane
Production Electrician	Dan Coey
Head Electrician	Chris Doornbos
Moving Lights Programmer	Alex Fogel
Projection Programmer	Matthew Mellinger

Production Sound Engineer	David Gotwald
Assistant Sound Engineer	Dillon Cody
Wardrobe Supervisor	Roberto Bevenger Gonzales
Dressers	Julian Andres Arango, Cat Dee, Amy Kaskeski, Tree Lonon
Hair/Wig Supervisor	Monica Costea
Hair/Wig Assistant	Jennifer Pendergraft
Production Assistant	Alex Mark
Management Assistant	Jesse Rothschild
Casting Assistant	Joanna Levinger
Casting Intern	Stephanie McGillen
Press Associates	Sarah Babin, Molly Barnett, Philip Carrubba, Jon Dimond, Joyce Friedmann, Michael Jorgensen, Yufen Kung, Chelsea Nachman, Marie Pace, Ryan Ratelle, Pete Sanders
Press Interns	Nancy Alligood, Patrick Lazour
Advertising/Marketing/Interactive	SpotCo/Drew Hodges, Tom Greenwald, Nick Pramik, Stephen Sosnowski, Stacey Lieberman Prince, Stephen Santore, Ryan Zatcoff, Kristen Rathbun, Julie Wechsler, Kyle Young, Steven Tartick, Callie Goff
Merchandise	Creative Goods Merchandise LLC/ Pete Milano
Legal Counsel	Lazarus & Harris LLP/ Scott Lazarus, Esq., Robert C. Harris, Esq.
Accountants	Marks Paneth & Shron/Mark A. D'Ambrosi, Patricia M. Pedersen, Petrina Moritz

A Gentleman's Guide to Love & Murder

Banking ....City National Bank/
  Stephanie Dalton, Michelle Gibbons
Insurance ....AON/Albert G. Ruben/
  George Walden, Claudia B. Kaufman
Payroll ....Castellana Services Inc./
  Lance Castellana, James Castellana, Norman Sewell
Physical Therapy ....Encore Physical Therapy/
  Mark Hunter-Hall
Orthopedist............................David S. Weiss, MD/
  NYU Langone Medical Center
Production Photographer ....Joan Marcus
Opening Night Coordination ....The Lawrence Company/
  Michael Lawrence
Housing Coordination ....Road Concierge/Lisa Morris

FOR HARTFORD STAGE

Artistic Director ....Darko Tresnjak
Managing Director ....Michael Stotts
Associate Artistic Director ....Maxwell Williams
Senior Dramaturg ....Elizabeth Williamson
General Manager ....Emily Van Scoy
Production Manager ....Bryan Holcombe
Director of Education ....Jennifer Roberts
Director of Development ....John Bourdeaux
Director of Marketing ....David Henderson
Director of Finance ....Michael Sandner

FOR THE OLD GLOBE

Artistic Director ....Barry Edelstein
Managing Director ....Michael G. Murphy
General Manager ....Amy Allison
Director of Marketing ....Dave Henson
Director of Development ....Todd Schultz
Director of Finance ....Mark Somers
Director of Production ....Robert Drake
Director of Education ....Roberta Wells-Famula

FOR THE SUNDANCE INSTITUTE

Artistic Director ....Philip Himberg
Producing Director ....Christopher Hibma
Executive Director ....Keri Putnam
Co-Managing Director ....Laurie Hopkins
Co-Managing Director ....Sarah Pearce

CREDITS

Scenery and scenic effects built, painted and automated by Show Motion, Inc., Milford, Connecticut. Automation and show control by Show Motion, Inc., Milford, CT, using the AC2 Computerized Motion Control System. Lighting equipment by PRG Lighting. Sound equipment by Sound Associates. Video/projection equipment by WorldStage Inc. Costumes executed by John Kristiansen New York Inc.;

Lisa O'Hare as Sibella Hallward and Bryce Pinkham as Monty Navarro

Photo: Joan Marcus

Eric Winterling, Inc.; Jennifer Love Costumes; Carmen Gee. Millinery by Lynne Mackey Studio, Rodney Gordon and Arnold Levine. Tailoring by Scafati, Giliberto Designs and Cego Shirt Maker. Shoes by Gino at T.O. Dey. False teeth by Dr. Marc Beshar.

Makeup provided by INGLOT.

Rehearsed at the Manhattan Movement & Arts Center.

SPECIAL THANKS

Rodgers and Hammerstein Foundation, Ucross Foundation, Brush Creek Foundation, New York Theatre Barn and Other Voices (Jeff Oppenheim, Artistic Director), Julian Christenberry, Jane Pfeffer, Louise Foisy, Barry Rosenberg, Stuart Levy, John Cowlese, Jean Feng, Rosey Gonzolas, Mitch at Madison Ave. Furs, Kathy at Tricorne, Carolyn at Carelli, David at Menkes, Hartford Stage Costume Shop, Harriette Holmes and Aaron Porter.

JUJAMCYN THEATERS

JORDAN ROTH
President
ROCCO LANDESMAN
President, Emeritus

PAUL LIBIN	**JACK VIERTEL**
Executive Vice President	Senior Vice President
MEREDITH VILLATORE	**JENNIFER HERSHEY**
Chief Financial Officer	Vice President,
	Building Operations
MICAH HOLLINGWORTH	**HAL GOLDBERG**
Vice President,	Vice President,
Company Operations	Theatre Operations

Director of Business Affairs ....Albert T. Kim
Director of Ticketing Services ....Justin Karr
Theatre Operations Managers ...Willa Burke, Susan Elrod,
  Emily Hare, Jeff Hubbard, Albert T. Kim
Theatre Operations Associates ....Carrie Jo Brinker,
  Brian Busby, Michael Composto, Anah Jyoti Klate

Controller ....Tejal Patel
Human Resources Coordinator ....Mimi Feng
Accounting ....Christina Boursiquot, Cathy Cerge,
  Amy Frank, Tariq Hamami, Alexander Parra
Executive Producer, Red Awning ....Nicole Kastrinos
Director of Sales, Givenik.com ....Karen Freidus
Building Operations Manager ....Erich Bussing
Executive Coordinator ....Ed Lefferson
Executive Assistants ....Hunter Chancellor,
  Danielle DeMatteo, Elisabeth Stern
Receptionist ....Lisa Perchinske
Ticketing and Pricing Associate ....Jonathon Scott
Sales Associate, Givenik.com ....Taylor Kurpiel
Maintenance ....Ralph Santos, Ramon Zapata
Security ....Rasim Hodzic, Terone Richardson
Interns ....Christina Bracco, Drew Factor,
  Patrick Korkuch, Simone Scully, Mollie Thoennes

STAFF FOR THE WALTER KERR THEATRE FOR *A GENTLEMAN'S GUIDE TO LOVE AND MURDER*

Theatre Manager ....Susan Elrod
Associate Theatre Manager ....Brian Busby
Treasurer ....Harry Jaffie
Head Carpenter ....George E. Fullum
Head Propertyman ....Timothy Bennet
Head Electrician ....Vincent J. Valvo
Flyman ....Richard M. Fullum
Follow Spot Operators ....Greg Peeler, Paul Valvo
Propertyman ....Moose Johnson
Engineer ....Zaim Hodzic
Assistant Treasurers ....Tracie Giebler,
  Robert Ricchiuti, Gail Yerkovich
Head Usher ...................................T.J. D'Angelo
Director ....Michelle Fleury
Ticket Takers ....Alison Traynor, Robert Zwaschka
Ushers .....Kaiser Akram, Florence Arcaro, Juliett Cipriati,
  Tatiana Gomberg, Aaron Kendall, Rochelle Rogers,
  Manuel Sandridge, Ilir Velovich
Doormen ....Brandon Houghton, Kevin Wallace
Head Porter ....Marcio Martinez
Porter ....Rudy Martinez
Head Cleaner ....Sevdija Pasukanovic
Cleaner ....Lourdes Perez

Lobby refreshments by Sweet Hospitality Group.

Ice machines provided by Scotsman Ice Systems.

Security provided by GBA Consulting, Inc.

 Jujamcyn Theaters is a proud member of the Broadway Green Alliance.

2013-2014 AWARDS

TONY AWARDS
Best Musical
Best Direction of a Musical
(Darko Tresnjak)
Best Book of a Musical
(Robert L. Freedman)
Best Costume Design of a Musical
(Linda Cho)
DRAMA DESK AWARDS
Outstanding Musical
Outstanding Actor in a Musical
(Jefferson Mays)

Outstanding Featured Actress in a Musical
(Lauren Worsham)
Outstanding Director of a Musical
(Darko Tresnjak)
Outstanding Lyrics
(Robert L. Freedman and Steven Lutvak)
Outstanding Book of a Musical
(Robert L. Freedman)
Outstanding Projection Design
(Aaron Rhyne)
DRAMA LEAGUE AWARD
Outstanding Production of a Musical

OUTER CRITICS CIRCLE AWARDS
Outstanding New Broadway Musical
Outstanding Book of a Musical
(Broadway or Off Broadway)
(Robert L. Freedman)
Outstanding Director of a Musical
(Darko Tresnjak)
Outstanding Actor in a Musical
(Jefferson Mays)

THEATRE WORLD AWARD
(Lauren Worsham)

A Gentleman's Guide to Love & Murder
SCRAPBOOK

Correspondents: The Company of *A Gentleman's Guide to Love & Murder*

Opening Night Party: *GGLAM*'s opening night party was the swankiest, most amazing NYC experience! It was held at the Pierre Hotel, and it was like stepping back into old New York society—the kind you only have imagined and didn't think existed anymore. But the best part about it was, it was fun, too!!!

Memorable Opening Night Gift: Print of cartoon featuring all of the characters in the show. The original was drawn for Jefferson Mays by a friend of his.

Favorite In-Theatre Gathering Place: There is not a lot of space at the Walter Kerr. We have a greenroom set up in the basement. It is really just a table with a coffee set-up and every other Sunday we have a pot luck brunch. Everyone crams downstairs and makes a plate of food and then finds places to eat throughout the building. The table is right by where the hair department is set up. I'm always afraid someone is going to spill coffee on a show wig!

Special Backstage Rituals: Jeff Kready and our prop guy, Moose, have a bromance. Every day before the Lady Salome scene, Moose hides the wreath Jeff uses in the scene. It is a game of hot and cold until he finds it. Lauren Worsham does a bump and grind dance with her dresser Tree and anyone else that will join in towards the end of Act I during a section of "The Last One You'd Expect." It is hysterical to see her in her period costume dancing in a very modern way. On my way across the stage (behind the curtain) for my first scene, I do a little dance move for Jane Carr and it has become part of my show. The other night it got so BIG that I actually knocked over a table...oops! Since we have different opening lyrics for the different curtain times, as a reminder, we ask Joanna Glushak "What time is it?" She tells everyone today's lyrics: 8 p.m.—"It's only just past eight, it's not too late."; 7 p.m.—"You'd be a fool to wait, it's not too late."; 3 p.m.—"It's only just past three, while you're still free."; 2 p.m.—"It's only just past two, so here's your cue." "For God's sake, go!"

Company In-Joke: When in doubt... BHANG!

Most Memorable Audience Reaction: In one of our surprise twists at the end of the show, a woman literally sang "Oh, nooooooo" like an opera singer. The whole cast nearly lost it!

Worst Audience Behavior: Sleeping in the front row.

Memorable Directorial Note: Darko's two favorites: "Does that make sense?" and "Little big note."

Embarrassing Moments: Every time the Austrian curtain failed to work during previews. But the worst was when it didn't come in at the end of a number where we were supposed to be frozen. That night, we all very awkwardly un-froze and just walked off stage. It was the worst!

Pit Stop: Best Story from the Orchestra: The barrage of things they've had thrown or dropped on them from the passerelle.

Catchphrase Only the Company Would Recognize: "Yes I am, I AM talking to you!!"

Best In-House Parody Lyrics: To the tune of "Sibella": "I've got your nose, and look, here's a coin. And now a hat with a rabbit inside! And here are two doves that will fly, if I'll let them try, or perhaps I'll make them hide."

Photo: Courtesy of the production

What Did You Think of the Web Buzz on Your Show?: Fortunately for us, the buzz has been great! It's so wonderful to know that the critics and audiences think that our show is as wonderful as we do!

Which Actor Performed the Most Roles in This Show?: JEFFERSON!!! No one on Broadway beats Jefferson Mays. Eight roles and the quickest costumes changes in history!

Favorite Backstage Photo: This pic (left) of Jefferson was taken during our holiday/Christmas schedule when we had 12 shows in a row and we were all pretty tired. So Jefferson hopped into the toy donation box in an act of sheer exhaustion and going slightly crazy. ;) We all had a very much needed laugh.

Most Memorable Audience Reaction: One performance, after the opening song, a man in the front row said, "Did he just spit on me???" Unfortunately for him, yes, he was unintentionally spat on. Those are the risks you take when you sit in the front row!

Favorite Off-Site Hangout: Hurley's.

Fastest Costume Change: ALL of Jefferson's changes!

Coolest Thing About Being in This Show: Being in a true ensemble with the most gifted and unique actors, all of whom are very giving, grounded and loving! Seeing Jefferson give 200 percent every single performance, and being in a piece that is truly a perfect gem to be proud of!

Favorite Moment During Each Performance: The Highhurst dinner scene. It is never the same twice and the audience just eats it up. It is so absurd and over the top.

Most Exciting Celebrity Visitor: Daniel Radcliffe—"I want the music to 'Poison in My Pocket' immediately. I have to memorize it because it's brilliant!"

Memorable YouTube Clip: Jefferson Mays posted an hilarious YouTube clip acceptance speech for his Lead Actor in a Musical award from the San Diego Theatre Critics Circle, in character as Lord Adalbert D'Ysquith: www.facebook.com/photo.php?v= 650044521703244.

Photo: Monica Simoes

1. Jefferson Mays, in a moment of pure exhaustion after 12 straight shows, jumps into the Toys for Tots donation bin.

2. Curtain call on opening night at the Walter Kerr Theatre (L-R): Jane Carr, Lisa O'Hare, Bryce Pinkham, Jefferson Mays, Lauren Worsham.

The Glass Menagerie

First Preview: September 5, 2013. Opened: September 26, 2013.
Limited Engagement. Closed February 23, 2014 after 24 Previews and 173 Performances.

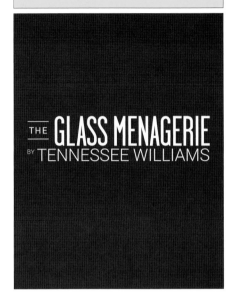

A revival of Tennessee Williams' classic "memory play" about a slowly-crumbling Southern family and their increasingly desperate and inept attempts to grapple with an excessively harsh world. Tom, a clerk in a shoe factory, is bullied by his mother into bringing home a "gentleman caller" to woo his painfully shy sister Laura.

CAST
(in order of appearance)

Tom ....ZACHARY QUINTO
Laura ....CELIA KEENAN-BOLGER
Amanda ....CHERRY JONES
The Gentleman Caller..............BRIAN J. SMITH

UNDERSTUDIES

For Tom, The Gentleman Caller: NICK REHBERGER
For Amanda: KAREN MacDONALD
For Laura: KATHLEEN LITTLEFIELD

ⓢ BOOTH THEATRE
222 West 45th Street
A Shubert Organization Theatre

Philip J. Smith, *Chairman*   **Robert E. Wankel,** *President*

JEFFREY RICHARDS   JOHN N. HART JR.   JERRY FRANKEL

LOU SPISTO / LUCKY VIII   INFINITY STAGES   SCOTT M. DELMAN   JAM THEATRICALS
MAURO TAYLOR   REBECCA GOLD   MICHAEL PALITZ
CHARLES E. STONE   WILL TRICE   GFOUR PRODUCTIONS

PRESENT

CHERRY JONES   ZACHARY QUINTO
CELIA KEENAN-BOLGER   BRIAN J. SMITH

IN THE AMERICAN REPERTORY THEATER PRODUCTION OF

THE GLASS MENAGERIE
BY TENNESSEE WILLIAMS

SCENIC & COSTUME DESIGN
BOB CROWLEY

LIGHTING DESIGN
NATASHA KATZ

SOUND DESIGN
CLIVE GOODWIN

MUSIC
NICO MUHLY

PRODUCTION STAGE MANAGER
STEVEN ZWEIGBAUM

CASTING
JIM CARNAHAN, CSA
STEPHEN KOPEL, CSA

TECHNICAL SUPERVISION
HUDSON THEATRICAL ASSOCIATES

PRESS REPRESENTATIVE
IRENE GANDY/ALANA KARPOFF

ADVERTISING
AKA

GENERAL MANAGEMENT
RICHARDS/CLIMAN, INC.

ASSOCIATE PRODUCERS
GOLDEN · GOLD, YOHEI DARIUS SUYAMA, GREENLEAF PRODUCTIONS
MAXIMILIAN TRABER, CHARLES REETZ, MICHAEL CREA, PJ MILLER

MOVEMENT
STEVEN HOGGETT

DIRECTOR
JOHN TIFFANY

THE GLASS MENAGERIE is presented by special arrangement with The University of the South, Sewanee, Tennessee.

First performed at the American Repertory Theater at Harvard University 2 February 2013
Diane Paulus, Artistic Director, Diane Borger, Producer

The Producers wish to express their appreciation to the Theatre Development Fund for its support of this production.

9/26/13

The Gentleman Caller comes to visit. (L-R): Zachary Quinto, Cherry Jones, Brian J. Smith, Celia Keenan-Bolger

Photo: Michael J. Lutch

The Glass Menagerie

Cherry Jones
Amanda

Zachary Quinto
Tom

Celia Keenan-Bolger
Laura

Brian J. Smith
The Gentleman Caller

Kathleen Littlefield
u/s Laura

Karen MacDonald
u/s Amanda

Nick Rehberger
u/s Tom, The Gentleman Caller

Tennessee Williams
Author

John Tiffany
Director

Bob Crowley
Scenic/Costume Design

Natasha Katz
Lighting Design

Clive Goodwin
Sound Design

Steven Hoggett
Movement

Nico Muhly
Music

Benjamin Shaw
Associate Director

Diane Paulus
American Repertory Theater (A.R.T.)

Jim Carnahan, C.S.A.
Casting

Neil A. Mazzella
Hudson Theatrical Associates
Technical Supervisor

David R. Richards
and Tamar Haimes
Richards/Climan, Inc.
General Manager

Jeffrey Richards
Producer

John N. Hart Jr.
Producer

Jerry Frankel
Producer

Lou Spisto
Producer

Mary Beth O'Connor/
Lucky VIII
Producer

Scott M. Delman
Producer

Arny Granat
Jam Theatricals
Producer

Steve Traxler
Jam Theatricals
Producer

Scott Mauro
Producer

Deborah Taylor
Producer

Rebecca Gold
Producer

Michael Palitz
Producer

Charles E. Stone
Producer

Will Trice
Producer

Kenneth Greenblatt
GFour Productions
Producer

Seth Greenleaf
GFour Productions
Producer

The Glass Menagerie

David Beckerman
GFour Productions
Producer

Alan Glist
GFour Productions
Producer

Marc Goldman
GFour Productions
Producer

Peg McFeeley
Golden
Associate Producer

Candy Gold
Associate Producer

Yohei Darius Suyama
Associate Producer

Michael Crea
Associate Producer

PJ Miller
Associate Producer

A reflective moment with Tom (Zachary Quinto) and Amanda (Cherry Jones) on Bob Crowley's set

FRONT OF HOUSE
Front Row (L-R):
Timothy Wilhelm (Chief Usher),
Marjorie Glover (Usher),
Dorothy Battaia (Porter)
Back Row (L-R):
Andrew Mackay,
Reginald Browne,
Nadine Space,
Daniel Rosario (Ushers)

CREW
Front Row (L-R): James Keane (House Props),
Susan Bennett-Goulet (House Electrician),
Kelly Reed (Hair Supervisor),
Beth Berkeley (Sound Operator),
Chris Smith (House Carpenter)
Back Row (L-R):
Chris De Camillis (Stage Manager),
Steven Zweigbaum
(Production Stage Manager),
Kimberly Prentice (Dresser)

The Glass Menagerie

Photos: Michael J. Lutch

Laura (Celia Keenan-Bolger) shows
The Gentleman Caller (Brian J. Smith)
her prized unicorn.

2013-2014 AWARDS

TONY AWARD
Best Lighting Design of a Play
(Natasha Katz)

DRAMA DESK AWARD
Outstanding Featured Actress in a Play
(Celia Keenan-Bolger)
Outstanding Music in a Play
(Nico Muhly)

OUTER CRITICS CIRCLE AWARD
Outstanding Revival of a Play
(Broadway or Off Broadway)
Outstanding Actress in a Play
(Cherry Jones)
Outstanding Featured Actor in a Play
(Brian J. Smith)

DRAMA LEAGUE AWARD
Outstanding Revival of a Play
Founders Award for Ecellence in Directing
(John Tiffany)

THEATRE WORLD AWARD
Dorothy Loudon Award for Excellence in the Theatre
(Celia Keenan-Bolger)

Hedwig and the Angry Inch

First Preview: March 29, 2014. Opened: April 22, 2014.
Still running as of May 31, 2014.

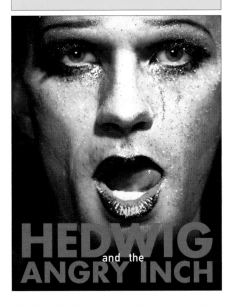

PLAYBILL®

Neil Patrick Harris stars in the Broadway debut of this 1998 musical about an East German punk rocker who uses a concert stage as a confessional to tell his story about a loveless childhood and a botched sex-change operation that lead him on a transcontinental search for his sexual identity—and self-acceptance.

CAST

Hedwig......................NEIL PATRICK HARRIS
Yitzhak ....LENA HALL

THE ANGRY INCH

Skszp (Music Director, Guitar,
    Keyboards, Vocals)................JUSTIN CRAIG
Jacek (Bass, Guitar,
    Keyboards, Vocals) ....MATT DUNCAN
Krzyzhtoff (Guitar, Vocals) ....TIM MISLOCK
Schlatko (Drums, Vocals) ......PETER YANOWITZ

UNDERSTUDIES

For Lena Hall: SHANNON CONLEY

⑤ BELASCO THEATRE
111 West 44th Street
A Shubert Organization Theatre

Philip J. Smith, *Chairman*   Robert E. Wankel, *President*

DAVID BINDER
JAYNE BARON SHERMAN   BARBARA WHITMAN
LATITUDE LINK   PATRICK CATULLO   RAISE THE ROOF   PAULA MARIE BLACK   COLIN CALLENDER
RUTH HENDEL   SHARON KARMAZIN   MARTIAN ENTERTAINMENT   STACEY MINDICH   ERIC SCHNALL
and
THE SHUBERT ORGANIZATION

present

NEIL PATRICK HARRIS
in

HEDWIG
and the
ANGRY INCH

book by
JOHN CAMERON MITCHELL

music and lyrics by
STEPHEN TRASK

with
LENA HALL

JUSTIN CRAIG   MATT DUNCAN   TIM MISLOCK   PETER YANOWITZ   SHANNON CONLEY

scenic designer JULIAN CROUCH	costume designer ARIANNE PHILLIPS	lighting designer KEVIN ADAMS	wigs & make-up designer MIKE POTTER

sound designer TIM O'HEIR	projection designer BENJAMIN PEARCY FOR 59 PRODUCTIONS	casting CALLERI CASTING	dialect coach STEPHEN GABIS

music supervisor & coordinator ETHAN POPP	music director JUSTIN CRAIG	vocal supervisor LIZ CAPLAN

press representative BONEAU/BRYAN-BROWN	advertising SERINO/COYNE	marketing director ERIC SCHNALL	company manager BARBARA CROMPTON

production management AURORA PRODUCTIONS	production stage manager LISA IACUCCI	associate producer MARK BERGER	executive producer 101 PRODUCTIONS, LTD.

musical staging
SPENCER LIFF

directed by
MICHAEL MAYER

Originally produced in New York City by David Binder
Produced off-Broadway by Peter Askin, Susann Brinkley and James B. Freydberg

4/22/14

Neil Patrick Harris
as Hedwig

Photo: Joan Marcus

Hedwig and the Angry Inch

MUSICAL NUMBERS

"Tear Me Down"
"The Origin of Love"
"Sugar Daddy"
"Angry Inch"
"Wig in a Box"
"Wicked Little Town"
"The Long Grift"
"Hedwig's Lament"
"Exquisite Corpse"
"Wicked Little Town" (Reprise)
"Midnight Radio"

Orchestrations by Stephen Trask
Arrangement for "Sugar Daddy"
by Justin Craig and Stephen Trask

HEDWIG AND THE ANGRY INCH is happy to
support Hetrick-Martin Institute.
For more information visit www.hmi.org

Lena Hall and
Neil Patrick Harris

Photo: Joan Marcus

Neil Patrick Harris
Hedwig

Lena Hall
Yitzhak

Shannon Conley
Understudy Yitzhak

Justin Craig
Skszp,
Music Director

Matt Duncan
Jacek

Tim Mislock
Krzyzhtoff

Peter Yanowitz
Schlatko

John Cameron
Mitchell
Book

Stephen Trask
Music and Lyrics

Michael Mayer
Director

Spencer Liff
Musical Staging

Julian Crouch
Scenic Design

Arianne Phillips
Costume Design

Kevin Adams
Lighting Design

Mike Potter
Wigs and
Makeup Design

Tim O'Heir
Sound Design

Benjamin Pearcy
for 59 Productions
Projection Design

James Calleri
Calleri Casting
Casting

Paul Davis
Calleri Casting
Casting

Erica Jensen
Calleri Casting
Casting

Ethan Popp
Music Supervisor
& Coordinator

Hedwig and the Angry Inch

Liz Caplan
Liz Caplan Vocal
Studios, LLC
Vocal Supervisor

Stephen Gabis
Dialect Coach

Johanna McKeon
Associate Director

Gene O'Donovan
Aurora Productions
*Production
Management*

Ben Heller
Aurora Productions
*Production
Management*

Mark Berger
Associate Producer

Wendy Orshan
101 Productions, Ltd.
*Executive Producer,
General Manager*

David Binder
Producer

Jayne Baron
Sherman
Producer

Barbara Whitman
Producer

Ralph Bryan
Latitude Link
Producer

Patrick Catullo
Producer

Harriet Newman Leve
Raise the Roof
Producer

Jennifer Isaacson
Raise the Roof
Producer

Paula Marie Black
Producer

Colin Callender
Producer

Ruth Hendel
Producer

Sharon Karmazin
Producer

Carl D. White
Martian
Entertainment
Producer

Gregory Rae
Martian
Entertainment
Producer

Stacey Mindich
Producer

Eric Schnall
*Producer/
Marketing Director*

Philip J. Smith
The Shubert
Organization
Producer

Robert E. Wankel
The Shubert
Organization
Producer

Photo: Brian Mapp

COMPANY MANAGEMENT
Barbara Crompton (Company Manager), Richard Jones

2013-2014 AWARDS

TONY AWARDS
Best Revival of a Musical
Best Performance by an Actor in a Leading Role in a Musical
(Neil Patrick Harris)
Best Performance by an Actress in a Featured Role in a Musical
(Lena Hall)
Best Lighting Design of a Musical
(Kevin Adams)

DRAMA DESK AWARDS
Outstanding Revival of a Musical
Outstanding Actor in a Musical
(Neil Patrick Harris)

DRAMA LEAGUE AWARDS
Outstanding Revival of a Musical
Distinguished Performance Award
(Neil Patrick Harris)

OUTER CRITICS CIRCLE AWARDS
Outstanding Revival of a Musical (Broadway or Off-Broadway)
Outstanding Lighting Design (Play or Musical)
(Kevin Adams)

Hedwig and the Angry Inch

Photos: Brian Mapp

FRONT OF HOUSE
Front (L-R): Maria Lugo, Eugenia Raines, Raya Konyk (Head Usher), Stephanie Wallis (Theatre Manager)
Second Row (L-R): Kate Reiter, Pamela Loetterle
Third Row (L-R): Jennifer Stock, Michele Moyna, Philip Escobedo
Fourth Row (L-R): Kathy Dunn, Joseph Pittman (Ticket Taker), Laura Kaye
Back Row (L-R): David Josephson, Shuwanda Nzikou-Ilagou

MANAGEMENT/HAIR/WARDROBE
Lower Left: Steven "Perfidia" Kirkham (Hair Supervisor)
First Row (L-R): George Dummitt, Brian Munroe (Production Carpenter), Antoinette T. Martinez (Dresser), Rachel A. Wolff (Stage Manager),
John Sibley (Assistant Production Sound Engineer), Lisa Iacucci (Production Stage Manager)
Second Row (L-R): Daniel Paul (Mr. Harris's Dresser), Katie Campbell, Carlos Jaramillo, Rob Ward (Production Props), Mike Potter (Make-up Supervisor),
Nicole Bridgeford (Assistant Hair & Make-up Designer)
Back Row (L-R): Scott Westervelt (Wardrobe Supervisor), Bob Etter (Production Sound Engineer), "Mystery Woman"

Hedwig and the Angry Inch

To learn more about the production, please visit
www.HedwigBroadway.com

Please follow us on Twitter, Facebook & Instagram:
@HedwigOnBway

CREDITS
Scenery constructed by PRG Scenic Technologies, a division of Production Resource Group, LLC. Lighting and sound equipment provided by PRG. Projection equipment provided by Sound Associates. Flying by Foy. Costumes by Eric Winterling Costumes, Tricorne Costumes, Desi Santiago, Michael Velasquez, Bill Hargate Costumes, Michael Schmidt Studios, Nano Hernandez. Shoes by Andre No. 1 Shoe Design, Gio Diev. Crystals by Swarovski. Military supplies by Jim Korn and Kaufman's Army & Navy, NYC. Screen printing by Pete's Print Shop. Fabric painting by Jeff Fender. Select props by Tom Carroll Scenery. "Hurt Locker: The Musical" Playbill® created by Mike Albo and Amanda Duarte and designed by Stuart Rogers/RED.

PRE- AND POST-SHOW MUSIC CREDITS
"Success" by David Bowie, Ricky Gardiner and Iggy Pop, used by permission of BMG, EMI and RZO. "Marquee Moon" by Tom Verlaine, used by permission of Verlaine Music. "Editions of You" by Bryan Ferry, used by permission of BMG. "Jesse" and "Wasted" performed by The Deafening, used by permission. "The Keys," "Rube Goldberg Machine" and "Idle Hands" performed by Matt Duncan, used by permission. "A-OK" and "Walking in Soho" performed by Peter Yanowitz, used by permission.

SPECIAL PROMOTIONAL CONSIDERATION FURNISHED BY
Blackstar Amplification, Ltd., Dunlop Manufacturing, Inc., Gibson Guitars, G&L Guitars, Hoshino USA - Tama, M•A•C Cosmetics, Korg U.S.A., Inc., Marshall Electronics/Mogami Cable, The Music Zoo, Paiste America, Inc., Q Drum Co., Remo Inc., Strymon, Swarovski Crystals,

Sweetwater Sound, Inc., Tour Supply, Vic Firth Company, Vox Amplification, Ltd.

SPECIAL THANKS
Peter Askin, Jerry Mitchell, Daria Musk, Philip S. Birsh/Playbill, Lee Zalben/Peanut Butter & Co., Alison Roehs, Cassandra Simon, Deanna Weiner, Geoff Barone, Jeremy Berman, Mike Bigel, Jim Felber, Michael Keller, John Miller, Jace McDonald, Phil Tennison, Joe Testa, Scott Uchida, Priscilla Vega, Aaron Vishria, Matt Wood/ Kenny Bergle.

This production was rehearsed at
New York Theatre Workshop and
The New 42nd Street Studios

BROADWAY green alliance   The Shubert Organization is a proud member of the Broadway Green Alliance.

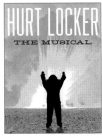 

A running gag in this production is that it is taking place on the set of another play, *Hurt Locker: The Musical,* which supposedly closed the previous night after a single performance. As the audience enters, the floor of the Belasco is littered with fake PLAYBILLS for the closed show. Written by Amanda Duarte and Mike Albo, the contents parody the style and features of a real PLAYBILL. The cover and billboard page are reproduced above. The entire faux PLAYBILL can be read under the *Hedwig and the Angry Inch* listing at www.PlaybillVault.com, in the "Inside the Playbill" section.

Hedwig and the Angry Inch
SCRAPBOOK

Correspondent: Lena Hall, "Yitzhak"

Memorable Opening Night Notes: Most of the other shows sent us opening night wishes, saying things like, "Have a great show" and "NPH we love you!" But my favorite was from my family back at *Kinky Boots*, saying, "Lena, we're so proud of you," which we posted on the door. They were so supportive of me.

Opening Night Gift: I'm going to boast here and say my gift to everyone was by far the coolest. I commissioned an artist to do a large, comic book-style drawing of the cast with Neil as Hedwig on a motorcycle jumping over the band, and on the other side is me tied down to a platform he is no doubt going to land on. Everybody got a copy. It's frameable.

Most Exciting Celebrity Visitors: Our visitors are amazing but usually they never recognize me because I look so different offstage. Either I have to introduce myself or Neil will tell them. Bryan Cranston came backstage and he was so complimentary to me on my acting and my body language. That's something I've held on to! Annie Leibovitz came with Calvin Klein and Donna Karan. Annie Leibovitz said, "You're so pretty when you come out of your shell." Oh God, I'm locking that in my memory! Sam Rockwell, who has always been a heartthrob of mine, said he was blown away by the show and said, "Your voice is incredible." Here's one that not too many people will know: I'm a total stupid fangirl of the HGTV show "Property Brothers," and one night I spotted them in the audience. (They are huge men.) And I ran around backstage saying "Oh God, the Property Brothers are here!" I was totally fangirling out.

Favorite In-Theatre Gathering Place: Our theatre has a giant basement. There is a three-story drop beneath the stage, supposedly built for Houdini's disappearing elephant act. We've installed couches, a ping-pong table, a foosball table and other fun stuff. It's now total hangout land.

Unique Pre-Show Announcement: I shuffle to the microphone in character as Yitzhak. I tap the mike and read from a paper. "Oprecite. (That's "excuse me" in Croatian.) Welcome to Belasco Theatre. Dis show have no intermission. Plizz, absolutely, to turn off all cellular phones. Dis show is loud but there are quiet parts and, trust me, you don't want to be That Person with this bitch!" (Meaning Hedwig, of course.)

Special Backstage Rituals: I write Hedwig a card every night in character as Yitzhak and I hand-give it to her. It describes Yitzhak's day and includes drawings of her in wedding attire or jokes that have to do with the show. And it always ends with "I love you" in Croatian. Like the day the *New Yorker* published drawings of the show. I wrote, "Today I

submeet a drawink of us to magazine *New Yorkers*. Dey say dey will get back to me." Every once in a while I will get a letter back from Hedwig—usually horribly insulting, and containing a used Q-tip or a wad of chewed gum. It's a great little ritual that I started on our first preview. It's extra work, but it's fun.

Memorable Audience Reaction: This past Saturday I walked out on stage for the 10 p.m. show and I saw down front an entire group of big burly men—not your average theatregoers—dudes you would find at a heavy metal show by the bar. And there was a ton of them. When they saw me they screamed, "Yitzhak!" I didn't know what to do. I didn't want to egg on that kind of response. But I thought, "They love me! They love me!" Then again, they were probably soused.

Worst Audience Behavior: Any time someone tries to be cheeky and replies to "Phyllis Stein, are you in the house?" There also was the infamous time someone shouted, "I love you, Neil!" and Neil cursed at them—in character, of course. You see, it's one thing for someone to shout, "I love you, Hedwig," because it's supposed to be a Hedwig concert. But to use our real names and say "I love you, Neil" takes the audience out of the story. I feel Neil handled it really well.

Memorable Ad-Lib: I'm in charge of all Hedwig's cords and microphones, and I have to make sure everything happens right when he moves around the stage with them. Usually, if he gets caught in something, I will wait until after a punchline and then clear the cord, or unhook something. One night, when he was behind the car, the cord got stuck. He kept futzing with the cord and I was waiting for a punchline, but finally he ad-libbed to me, "Why don't you get over here and do something about this? All you ever do is mope around. Why don't you put this cord around your neck and do something with your life?" The audience just died, and I had a hard time keeping a straight face.

Memorable Directorial Note: You have to know that I am horrible at spitting. I don't know how to spit right. But in the show I have to spit right in Neil's face at one point. So one night I managed to get a huge amount of spit on Neil's face. It was in his eyes and running down his cheek. It was horrible. The next day I get this note, "Wow, that was the best spit ever!" The director loved it.

Favorite Moment During Each Performance: For me it's the moment where I come down the aisle, transformed, in the butterfly dress with my arms in the air. (See

Hugs and kisses for Neil Patrick Harris on opening night at the Belasco Theatre:
1. Co-star and *Yearbook* correspondent Lena Hall.
2. Director Michael Mayer.
3. Songwriter Stephen Trask.
4. Librettist and original Hedwig, John Cameron Mitchell.

Hedwig and the Angry Inch
SCRAPBOOK

Favorite Cast Snack Food: Gummi bears.
Mascot: Neil Patrick Harris.
Who Wore the Least: Neil Patrick Harris.
Heaviest/Hottest Costume: Neil again. In one scene I have to pick up his clothes and throw them in the car. They are SO heavy. His costume at the beginning of the show weighs a ton and is magnetized so it sticks to the car. It's SO hard getting it off the car. It's like wrestling a bear.
April Fools' Prank: We were rehearsing, and just screwing around. I mentioned to someone that it was April Fools' Day and Neil must have heard me. You have to know that he's a really good pratfaller. So not five minutes later he suddenly falls on his face and just lies there. Everyone is running around saying, "We should go help him." "Is he really hurt?" And I was thinking to myself, "I don't think he really is." But now he's moaning and saying, "I think I heard something snap." But then, when everyone was gathered around

prank on [producer] David Binder. We called him and said, "We don't know what happened. We're taking Neil to the emergency room." So now David's in a panic. Neil is on

photo, top right.) It feels really good. I helped develop that dress. When they first put out the idea it was more like an evening gown with a high slit. They were, like,

"We've got to see as much of your body as possible." I suggested that we have the front open and the back more like a train. I just love that moment.
Memorable Stage Door Fan Encounter: Our fans are pretty awesome. They can get a little crazy, but they're always nice and generous. There was one thing that sucked. One day after the show I was just mindlessly saying "thanks so much" to people and signing autographs. One lady was standing there holding her Playbill over the barricade and I thought she wanted it signed, so I reached for it. But she yanked it back out of my hand super hard. God! Then I heard her say, "Is it rude of me to say I only want Neil to sign?" Yes, it was totally rude. I only just worked my ass off for you onstage. But, hey, it's cool. I get it.
Favorite Off-Site Hangout: Café Un Deux Trois is the place.

him, he got up and said "April Fool!" And everyone was, like, "You bitch!" So now, of course, Michael wanted to pull the same

the phone saying, "I *think* I'll be all right." But then he came clean, and that was the best. We were dying.
Ghostly Encounters Backstage: None yet. Maybe David Belasco thinks I'm a dude.
Coolest Thing About Being in This Show: Being in this show. It's the coolest show ever.

(Editor's note: Yearbook *Correspondent Lena Hall won the 2014 Tony Award as Best Featured Actress in a Musical.)*

More curtain call photos:
1. Neil Patrick Harris strikes a pose.
2. Lena Hall (*Yearbook* correspondent) works the butterfly dress (Matt Duncan in the background).
3. The cast and band of *Hedwig and the Angry Inch* (L-R): Tim Mislock, Peter Yanowitz, Lena Hall, Neil Patrick Harris, Matt Duncan, Justin Craig.
4. At the after-party, Neil Patrick Harris and his partner David Burtka.

If/Then

First Preview: March 5, 2014. Opened: March 30, 2014.
Still running as of May 31, 2014.

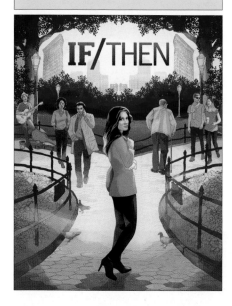

An original new musical with a sci-fi premise. A divorced thirtysomething woman returns to New York hoping to pick up the pieces of her life. From there, the story splits into two overlapping narratives, showing two ways her life might play out, depending on how she reacts to people she meets in a park one seemingly trivial afternoon. In one life she becomes a successful urban planner, in the other she marries an Army doctor and becomes a mother. The only constant is the good friends who help and support her along the various paths her life takes.

CAST

Elizabeth	IDINA MENZEL
Kate	LaCHANZE
Lucas	ANTHONY RAPP
Josh	JAMES SNYDER
Stephen	JERRY DIXON
Anne	JENN COLELLA
David	JASON TAM
Elena	TAMIKA LAWRENCE
Deputy Mayor and others	JOE CASSIDY
A Bartender and others	MIGUEL CERVANTES
A Soldier and others	CURTIS HOLBROOK
A Flight Attendant and others	STEPHANIE KLEMONS
A Street Musician and others	TYLER McGEE
Paulette and others	RYANN REDMOND
An Architect and others	JOE AARON REID
Cathy and others	ANN SANDERS

Continued on next page

140

RICHARD RODGERS THEATRE
UNDER THE DIRECTION OF JAMES M. NEDERLANDER AND JAMES L. NEDERLANDER

DAVID STONE
JAMES L. NEDERLANDER   BARBARA WHITMAN   PATRICK CATULLO
NANCY NAGEL GIBBS   FOX THEATRICALS
MARC PLATT

present

IDINA MENZEL

IF/THEN

Music	Book & Lyrics
TOM KITT	BRIAN YORKEY

Starring

LaCHANZE	ANTHONY RAPP

JERRY DIXON

JENN COLELLA   JASON TAM
TAMIKA LAWRENCE   JACKIE BURNS

JAMES SNYDER

JOE CASSIDY   MIGUEL CERVANTES   CURTIS HOLBROOK   STEPHANIE KLEMONS
TYLER McGEE   RYANN REDMOND   JOE AARON REID   ANN SANDERS
MARC DELACRUZ   CHARLES HAGERTY   JANET KRUPIN   PEARL SUN

Set Design	Costume Design	Lighting Design	Sound Design
MARK WENDLAND	EMILY REBHOLZ	KENNETH POSNER	BRIAN RONAN

Wig & Hair Design	Vocal Arrangements	Music Coordinator
DAVID BRIAN BROWN	ANNMARIE MILAZZO	MICHAEL KELLER

Casting	Technical Supervision	Production Stage Manager
TELSEY + COMPANY	JAKE BELL & LILY TWINING	JUDITH SCHOENFELD

General Management	Press Representation
321 THEATRICAL MANAGEMENT	POLK & Co.

Orchestrations
MICHAEL STAROBIN

Music Director
CARMEL DEAN

Choreographer
LARRY KEIGWIN

Director
MICHAEL GREIF

3/30/14

(L-R): Tamika Lawrence, Jenn Colella, LaChanze and Idina Menzel

Photo: Joan Marcus

If/Then

SWINGS
MARC delaCRUZ, CHARLES HAGERTY,
JANET KRUPIN, PEARL SUN

UNDERSTUDIES & STANDBYS
Standby for Elizabeth: JACKIE BURNS
Understudies for Kate: PEARL SUN,
TAMIKA LAWRENCE
For Lucas: CURTIS HOLBROOK, JOE CASSIDY
For Josh: CHARLES HAGERTY, TYLER McGEE
For Stephen: JOE AARON REID, JOE CASSIDY
For Anne: STEPHANIE KLEMONS,
ANN SANDERS
For David: MARC delaCRUZ,
MIGUEL CERVANTES
For Elena: STEPHANIE KLEMONS,
JANET KRUPIN

DANCE CAPTAIN
STEPHANIE KLEMONS

TIME
The recent past

PLACE
Madison Square Park and all around New York City

ORCHESTRA
Conductor: CARMEL DEAN
Associate Conductor: MARCO PAGUIA
Assistant Conductor: RANDY COHEN
Concertmaster: SYLVIA D'AVANZO
Violin: MATTHEW LEHMANN
Viola: ALISSA SMITH
Cello: ALISA HORN
Reeds: DAVID NOLAND, RICK HECKMAN
Trumpet: BUD BURRIDGE
Guitars: ALEC BERLIN, JIM HERSHMAN
Bass: BRIAN HAMM
Keyboards: MARCO PAGUIA, RANDY COHEN
Drums: DAMIEN BASSMAN

Music Coordinator: MICHAEL KELLER
Music Copying: EMILY GRISHMAN
Music Preparation: EMILY GRISHMAN,
KATHARINE EDMONDS
Keyboard Programming: RANDY COHEN

Idina Menzel
Elizabeth

LaChanze
Kate

Anthony Rapp
Lucas

James Snyder
Josh

Jerry Dixon
Stephen

Jenn Colella
Anne

Jason Tam
David

Tamika Lawrence
Elena; u/s Kate

Jackie Burns
Standby for Elizabeth

Joe Cassidy
Ensemble; u/s Lucas, Stephen

Miguel Cervantes
Ensemble; u/s David

Curtis Holbrook
Ensemble; u/s Lucas

Stephanie Klemons
Ensemble; u/s Anne, Elena

Tyler McGee
Ensemble; u/s Josh

Ryann Redmond
Ensemble

Joe Aaron Reid
Ensemble; u/s Stephen

Ann Sanders
Ensemble; u/s Anne

Marc delaCruz
Swing; u/s David

Charles Hagerty
Swing; u/s Josh

Janet Krupin
Swing; u/s Elena

Pearl Sun
u/s Kate

Tom Kitt
Music

Brian Yorkey
Book and Lyrics

If/Then

Michael Greif
Director

Larry Keigwin
Choreographer

Idina Menzel and James Snyder

Photo: Joan Marcus

Mark Wendland
Set Design

Emily Rebholz
Costume Design

Kenneth Posner
Lighting Design

Brian Ronan
Sound Design

David Brian Brown
Wig/Hair Design

Michael Starobin
Orchestrations

Carmel Dean
Music Director

AnnMarie Milazzo
Vocal Arrangements

Michael Keller
Music Coordinator

Kathy Fabian
Prop Supervisor

Bernard Telsey
Telsey + Company
Casting

Jake Bell
Technical Supervisor

Marcia Goldberg, Nancy Nagel Gibbs
and Nina Essman
321 Theatrical Management
General Management

Judith Schoenfeld
Production Stage Manager

Paul J. Smith
Stage Manager

Monica A. Cuoco
Assistant Stage Manager

David Alpert
Associate Director

Nicole Wolcott
Associate Choreographer

Mark Myars
Associate Choreographer

David Stone
Producer

James L.
Nederlander
Producer

Barbara Whitman
Producer

Patrick Catullo
Producer

Nancy Nagel Gibbs
Producer

Kristin Caskey
Fox Theatricals
Producer

Mike Isaacson
Fox Theatricals
Producer

Marc Platt
Producer

If/Then
Scrapbook

Correspondent: Ryann Redmond "Ensemble"
Memorable Fan Gifts: We get tons of gifts delivered to our stage door. Some favorites include hand-painted cookies, cupcakes, and pretty much anything sweet!
Opening Night Party: Our opening night party was at the Edison Ballroom. It was a beautiful evening filled with great friends and great vibes. It was truly an amazing celebration of the hard work we put into creating a brand new musical!
Most Exciting Celebrity Visitor: The coolest celebrity experience so far was when Phil Collins came to a show a few weeks ago. After the show, we were doing an auction for Broadway Cares and he ended up being one of the bidders

that won! I thought that was super sweet of him to donate to BC/EFA.
Favorite In-Theatre Gathering Place: LaChanze's dressing room is off stage right and my castmates and I go in there frequently when we are not on stage. She has tons of snacks (including my favorite: Goldfish). Her room is so beautifully decorated, it makes it easy to hang out and chat with her.
Which Actor Performed the Most Roles in This Show?: The ensemble plays tons of different parts, so I'd say we all tie for that title.
Special Backstage Rituals/Exercises: We have a game that we play at places called Mediocre Rhymes. Our own Tamika Lawrence (who plays Elena) came up with this. Basically, everyone

claps to a beat and we go around the circle and someone does a freestyle rap. They turn out pretty funny when people are spitting out stream-of-consciousness rhymes.
Favorite Backstage Photo: I love this photo of Ann, Stephanie, Idina and I! Idina took it after a LONG day of rehearsal in D.C. (where we did our out-of-town tryout). I think it perfectly sums up all of our personalities.
Most Memorable Audience Reaction: Well, since we have the amazing Idina Menzel in our show, we expect raucous applause when the audience first sees her. So, aside from the usual "We love you, Idina!," I'd have to say the most memorable reaction came in one of the quieter scenes where Joe Aaron is chatting

---

STAFF FOR IF/THEN

GENERAL MANAGEMENT
321 THEATRICAL MANAGEMENT
Marcia Goldberg
Nina Essman   Nancy Nagel Gibbs

GENERAL PRESS REPRESENTATIVE
POLK & CO.
Matt Polk   Tom D'Ambrosio
Frances White   Sasha Pensanti

CASTING
TELSEY + COMPANY
Bernard Telsey CSA   Craig Burns CSA

MARKETING SERVICES
bdb MARKETING
Betsy Bernstein   Julie Kruger   Ashley Warmack

TECHNICAL SUPERVISOR
Jake Bell   Lily Twining

COMPANY MANAGER
Tracy Geltman

PRODUCTION STAGE MANAGER ...Judith Schoenfeld
Stage Manager ....Paul J. Smith
Assistant Stage Manager ....Monica A. Cuoco
Makeup Design ....Joseph Dulude II
Props................................Kathy Fabian/Propstar
Assistant Company Manager ....Brent McCreary
Associate Director ....David Alpert
Associate Choreographer ......Nicole Wolcott, Mark Myars
Associate General Manager ....Ken Silverman
Associate Scenic Designer ....Brett Banakis
Assistant Scenic Designer ....Jason Ardizzone-West
Assistant Scenic Designer ....Rachel Nemec
Associate Costume Designer ....Sarah Laux
Assistant Costumer Designer ....Ren LaDassor
Associate Lighting Designer ....Joel Shier
Assistant Lighting Designer ....Nick Solyom
Associate Sound Designer ....Cody Spencer
Production Carpenter ....Rick Howard
Head Carpenter ....Sean Collins
Automation Carpenter ....David Campbell
Advance Rigger ....Matt Levy
Production Electrician ....Gregory Husinko
Head Electrician ....Evan Vorono

Follow Spot Operator ....Brian Messina
Moving Light Technician ....Derek Healy
Sound Engineer ....David Dignazio
Assistant Sound Engineer ....Jim Wilkinson
Advance Sound ....Brett Bingman
Vari Light Programmer ....David Arch
Associate Props ....Carrie Mossman, John Estep
Property Master ....Jill Johnson
Assistant Property Master ....Andrew Miller
Wardrobe Supervisor ....Linda Lee
Associate Wardrobe Supervisor ....Andrea Gonzalez
Dressers ....Betty Gillespie, Joe Hickey, Joby Horrigan,
    Mark Jones, Ronald Tagert, Lolly Totero, Shonte Walker
Hair Supervisor ....JT Franchuk
Production Photographer ....Joan Marcus
Associate to Mr. Stone ....Aaron Glick
Assistant to Brian Yorkey ....Kat Ramsburg
Production Assistants ...Katie Barnhard, Heather Englander
Assistant to the Technical Supervisors ......Hannah Shafran
Costume Shoppers ....Kalere Payton, Michelle Ridley
Costume Intern ....Celina Lam
Casting ....Telsey + Company/Will Cantler CSA,
    David Vaccari CSA, Bethany Knox CSA,
    Tiffany Little Canfield CSA, Rachel Hoffman CSA,
    Justin Huff CSA, Patrick Goodwin CSA,
    Abbie Brady-Dalton CSA, David Morris,
    Cesar A. Rocha CSA, Andrew Femenella CSA,
    Karyn Casl CSA, Kristina Bramhall, Conrad Woolfe,
    Amelia Nader, Rachel Nadler, Rachel Minow,
    Sean Gannon, Scott Galina
Advertising ....Serino/Coyne, Inc./Nancy Coyne,
    Greg Corradetti, Robert Jones, Drew Nebrig,
    Ben Skinner, David Barrineau, Vinny Sainato
Digital Marketing ....Situation Interactive/
    Damian Bazadona, Adam Beal, Jessica Friedman,
    Jeremy Kraus, Elizabeth Kandel, Michael Perkins
Souvenir Merchandise ....The Araca Group
Group Sales ....Broadway.com/Groups
Banking ....JP Morgan Chase Bank/Christina Ciniglio
Payroll ....Checks and Balances
Accountant ....Fried & Kowgios Partners CPAs
Insurance ....AON/Albert G. Ruben Insurance
Legal Counsel ....Schreck, Rose and Dapello/
    Nancy Rose, David Berlin

321 THEATRICAL MANAGEMENT
Bob Brinkerhoff, Amy Merlino Coey, Mattea Cogliano-
Benedict, Kirk Curtis, Veronica Decker, Tara Geesaman,

Andrew Hartman, Susan Keappock, Alex Owen, Rebecca
Peterson, Susan Sampliner, Spencer Smith, Haley Ward

www.ifthenthemusical.com

Rehearsed at New 42nd Street Studios

If/Then was first performed at the National Theatre in
Washington D.C., November 2013.

CREDITS
Show control and scenic motion control featuring Stage
Command Systems® by PRG-Scenic Technologies, a
division of Production Resource Group, LLC, New
Windsor, NY. Lighting by PRG Lighting. Sound by Masque
Sound. Products furnished by Apple, Inc. (Suzanne
Lindergh and George Pulios). Prop artisans are Mary
Wilson, Daniel Moss. Specialty props by Tom Carroll
Scenery Inc., Aardvark Interiors, Costume Armour,
Izquierdo Studio, Alexandra Geiger. Distressing by Jeff
Fender. Built costumes by Marc Happel. Hair products by
L'Oreal Professional. Special thanks to the New York
Yankees, Derek Jeter and the family of Bob Sheppard.

Chairman	**James M. Nederlander**
President	**James L. Nederlander**

Executive Vice President
Nick Scandalios

Vice President	Senior Vice President
Corporate Development	Labor Relations
Charlene S. Nederlander	**Herschel Waxman**

Chief Financial Officer
Freida Sawyer Belviso

HOUSE STAFF FOR
THE RICHARD RODGERS THEATRE
House Manager ....Timothy Pettolina
Box Office Treasurer ....Fred Santore Jr.
Assistant Treasurer ....Corinne Russ
Electrician ....Steve Carver
Carpenter ....Kevin Camus
Propertymaster ....Stephen F. DeVerna
Engineer ....Sean Quinn

If/Then
Scrapbook

The mascots

Curtis Holbrook makes the rounds in his Gypsy Robe.

with Beth on the airplane. He mentions the Burnham Award (an award given for excellence in Planning) and a particular man in the audience let out an extremely loud scream. It was pretty startling in the quiet moment, but a good story nonetheless! But we may never know why he screamed. We can only assume that he had some sort of affiliation with the award.

Worst Audience Behavior: Nothing too crazy has happened. I would just say people being late or illegally recording the show are among the worst things we've seen. Be on time to the theatre, people!

Who Wrote the Easter Bonnet Sketch and What It Was About: Unfortunately, our show opened right around the same time as the Easter Bonnet Competition! But we have been collecting for BC/EFA for the past few weeks and we raised about $120,000! Idina and Anthony have even dusted off some *Rent* songs to auction for the cause.

Unique Pre-Show Announcement: On the weekends, Curtis goes around to all of the dressing rooms and plays a song called "Best Day Ever." It was originally sung by SpongeBob SquarePants. It's hilarious.

Memorable Press Encounter: When we were in D.C., Nancy Pelosi came to the show and loved it.

Memorable Stage Door Fan Encounter: Our fans are amazing! It is so amazing to leave the stage door each night to tons of adoring audience members. Their love for the show truly shows and it fuels our performances each night. Not to mention, Idina has a humongous *Frozen* following, so it is always amusing to see little girls dressed as Elsa at the stage door.

Memorable Directorial Note: Michael has a saying when something goes well in the show, which is, "That was a triumph!" We always love to hear that.

Company In-Jokes: Joe Aaron has taken a liking to scaring people lately, so we all have to keep an eye out backstage. He pops out of nowhere!

Embarrassing Moments: The other night, Miguel was about to enter the stage for one of his

solo lines, but he grabbed a quick sip of water beforehand. Apparently, it went down the wrong pipe and resulted in him choking onstage and not being able to get his line out. Needless to say, hilarity ensued for the rest of the number.

Favorite Moments During Each Performance: I love performing the song "Ain't No Man Manhattan." It's so high energy and catchy, so we are humming it long after we leave the stage. And I also love playing the Intern that has an odd speech pattern.

Favorite Off-Site Hangout: LaChanze has a friend that owns a hangout called Convo Bar. We have gone to this place frequently. It has a great vibe, great food, and great drinks! But we also frequent the usuals: Angus, Glass House, etc.

Favorite Snack Foods: We love all sweets at the show, so some favorites are Schmackary's, Baked by Melissa Cupcakes, and candy. Lots and LOTS of candy. Our amazing Prop Mistress, Jill Johnson, always supplies us with a bottomless candy stash.

Favorite Therapy: We are big fans of Ricola and Altoids here at the show.

Pit Stop: Best story from the Orchestra: Our wonderful Music Director, Carmel Dean, has a series of HILARIOUS tweets from things she overhears in the pit or things people tell her from surrounding audience members. A favorite of mine is when a man leaned over to her and said, "I'd help you out [with conducting], but I have trouble counting to four."

Mascots: We have three alpacas that our amazing costume designers, Emily and Sarah, bought Stephanie, Ann and I during our run in Washington, D.C. Their names are Juan Valdez, Stüvensen, and Stephen (she's a girl). Anyone who enters our dressing room has to touch them.

Catchphrase Only the Company Would Recognize: Dey's at da doe'!

A long day in Washington, D.C. (clockwise from top) Ann Sanders, Idina Menzel, *Yearbook* correspondent Ryann Redmond and Stephanie Klemons.

Best In-House Parody Lyrics: James sings a line in "Hey, Kid," a song sung to his unborn child that reads, "I've wanted you forever, and I'll never do you wrong." But sometimes Curtis will be backstage and sing, "I've wanted you forever, and I'll let you wear my thong!" Ha!

Nicknames: I have several nicknames in *If/Then*! One day, Michael Greif, our director, combined both of my names and called me Raymond, and it stuck like glue. Another favorite is "Young Lungs" (coined by Idina since I am the baby of the cast). Other castmates have some good ones, too: Joe Aaron is JAR; Joe Cassidy is Cha-Cha; Curtis is Cweetuth (said with a lisp)... and the list goes on!

Fastest Costume Change: Pretty much any change that Idina has is the fastest!

Who Wore the Heaviest/Hottest Costume?: We all wear modern street clothes in the show, so nothing is too heavy. But I would probably say James Snyder in his army fatigues and large duffel bag probably takes the cake.

Who Wore the Least?: Probably Idina because she changes on stage in the bedroom scene.

What Did You Think of the Web Buzz on Your Show?: The web buzz on our show was amazing! Since it is Idina's big return to Broadway, everyone was highly anticipating the run. And the buzz continues. Follow us on twitter @ifthenmusical.

Ghostly Encounters Backstage: Tamika says her lights flicker and LaChanze's shelf fell during tech when no one was in the room. That's about as ghostly as it gets!

Coolest Thing About Being in This Show: The coolest thing about being in this show is that these superstars have now become my family. It is such an all-star cast and creative team and the fact that I get to call these people my friends is the greatest gift I could receive. We are all so close and I wouldn't trade it for the world!

Who Heads Your Fan Club and What Is Their Website/Newsletter?: We have several fans clubs on Twitter. There are too many to name! Pretty much anyone with *If/Then* in their handle is a part of the fan club!

Il Divo—A Musical Affair

Opened: November 7, 2013.
Limited Engagement. Closed November 13, 2013 after 6 Performances.

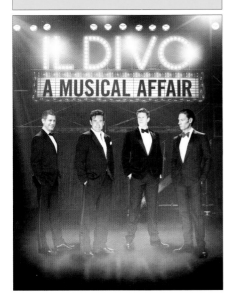

Four international vocalists—French pop singer Sébastien Izambard, Spanish baritone Carlos Marin, American tenor David Miller, and Swiss tenor Urs Bühler—assembled into a quartet by "American Idol" judge Simon Cowell, perform a concert of showtunes and pop, accompanied by Broadway diva Heather Headley.

CAST
IL DIVO

URS BÜHLER

SÉBASTIEN IZAMBARD

CARLOS MARIN

DAVID MILLER

GUEST ARTIST
HEATHER HEADLEY

ORCHESTRA
Arranged by AWR Music:
ARNOLD ROTH and FRITZ HOCKING

✹N✹ MARQUIS THEATRE
UNDER THE DIRECTION OF JAMES M. NEDERLANDER AND JAMES L. NEDERLANDER

PRESENTED BY LIVE NATION, JAMES L. NEDERLANDER, AND PROPER ARTIST MANAGEMENT

MARQUIS THEATRE

A MUSICAL AFFAIR

THE GREATEST SONGS FROM THE WORLD'S FAVORITE MUSICALS

PERFORMED BY
IL DIVO

CARLOS MARIN
SEBASTIEN IZAMBARD
URS BÜHLER
DAVID MILLER

FEATURING SPECIAL GUEST STAR **HEATHER HEADLEY**

Directed by
BRIAN BURKE

Musical and Vocal Arrangements	Additional Show Orchestrations	Show Musical Director
ALBERTO QUINTERO	**STEVE SIDWELL**	**ANDREW SMALL**

Musical Staging	Associate Director / Production Stage Manager	Visual Design
KIM CRAVEN	**JUSTIN MABARDI**	**ALEX DOSS**
Lighting Designer	Scenic Designer	Assistant Director
JOSHUA HUTCHINGS	**BRIAN BURKE**	**RICHARD J HINDS**
Video Designer	Speechwriter	Show Stylist
MATT MCADAM	**MALCOLM WILLIAMSON**	**ROBERT MORRISON**

11/7/13

Il Divo (L-R): Sébastien Izambard, Carlos Marin, David Miller, Urs Bühler

Photo: Max Dodson

Il Divo–A Musical Affair

MUSICAL NUMBERS

Overture

"Tonight"

"Some Enchanted Evening"

"If Ever I Would Leave You"

"Who Can I Turn To?"

"Don't Cry for Me Argentina"

"Can You Feel the Love Tonight" — Duet with Heather

"Home" — Heather

"Run to You" — Heather

"Memory" — Duet with Heather

"Unchained Melody"

"Impossible Dream"

Entr'acte

"Who Wants to Live Forever"

"Love Changes Everything"

"The Winner Takes It All"

"Bring Him Home"

"Music of the Night" — Duet with Heather

"Somewhere Over the Rainbow"

"I Will Always Love You"

"Somewhere"

"My Way"

Encore

Urs Bühler
Tenor, Switzerland

Sébastien Izambard
Pop Singer, France

Carlos Marin
Baritone, Spain

David Miller
Tenor, U.S.A.

Heather Headley
Guest Artist

Brian Burke
Director, Scenic Designer

Steve Sidwell
Additional Orchestrations

Andrew Small
Musical Director

Kim Craven
Musical Staging

Justin Mabardi
Associate Director and Production Stage Manager

Alex Doss
Visual Design

Richard J. Hinds
Assistant Director

David Zedeck/
Live Nation
Promoter

James L.
Nederlander
Promoter

STAFF FOR IL DIVO: A MUSICAL AFFAIR

WORLDWIDE MANAGEMENT
PROPER ARTIST MANAGEMENT
Peter Rudge   Meredith Plant
Alistair Norbury   Kat Fisher   Vicky Potts

FOR HEATHER HEADLEY
ARTIST NATION
John Baruck   Cerisa Roulston

BOOKING AGENT
CAA
(The Americas, Asia, Australia & New Zealand)
Rob Light

Mario Tirado
Marlene Tsuchii
Alli McGregor
SOLO (ROW)
John Giddings

PROMOTERS
LIVE NATION
David Zedeck   Jason Miller   Randy Henner
Scott Holtz   Jennifer Divietri
Donna Eichmeyer   Gaby Pino

NEDERLANDER
James L. Nederlander   Nick Scandalios
David Perry   Sean Free

Show Director ....Brian Burke
Associate Director/
    Production Stage Manager ....Justin Mabardi
Lighting Design and
    Programming ....Joshua Hutchings
Assistant Director ....Richard J Hinds
Musical Staging ....Kim Craven
Speechwriter ....Malcolm Williamson
Concept/Visual Design ....Brian Burke, Alex Doss
Content Design & Production ....Matt McAdam
Production Assistant ....Benjamin Rush
Musical and Vocal Arrangements.........Alberto Quintero
Additional Show Orchestrations ....Steve Sidwell
Show Musical Director ....Andrew Small

Il Divo—A Musical Affair

IL DIVO'S MUSICAL AFFAIR WITH
BROADWAY AND BEYOND

This year marks the tenth anniversary of the formation of Il Divo, the genre-busting singing troupe that straddles the worlds of pop and classical music to make something new with expert and effortless ease. They were created by producer Simon Cowell from four different nationalities, training and sensibilities too, and quickly became an international brand—and sensation.

Now they're stepping out of the box and onto Broadway, the world home of musical theatre, to do something new yet again, and it promises to stretch them—and Broadway itself—in different and challenging directions.

"There is nothing like Broadway," comments Urs Bühler, the Swiss-born tenor. "Around the world, when you say the word 'Broadway,' everyone knows what you're talking about! And it feels like we're going to dive into a completely different world of music. Getting in touch with this whole world of music is out of my comfort zone, so it is exciting and challenging."

For David Miller, the American tenor, New York is now his adopted home city, though he grew up in Colorado. "I've been living in New York for the last six years, so it'll be good to be staying at home for a while!" But it's also a welcome return to Broadway for him, too: "This will be the second time I've appeared on Broadway, but for the second time I'm not doing a musical as such—the first time I did Broadway it was in *La Bohème,* the opera that was directed by Baz Luhrmann, and now I'm appearing as part of this musical revue."

But then Il Divo has constantly broken the mold of what's expected. As David goes on to say, "The thing that Il Divo brings to music in general is being outside the box and revamping something that people are already very familiar with."

Now they're doing so with the classic repertoire of Broadway, giving it the classic Il Divo treatment, but also challenging them once again to look at things in a different way. "It has created a sense of focus in all four of us," says David.

Sébastien Izambard, who came to Il Divo in the midst of a successful pop career in his native France, had some experience of musical theatre in Paris, when he appeared in a French musical version of *The Little Prince* there. "Not only was it an opportunity to sing in a different way, as a bridge between opera and a pop musical, but also there was a lot of acting to do."

So he is looking forward to embracing the world of Broadway now. "It's a completely different world again. I remember when I first joined Il Divo. Going into the studio and hearing the huge vibratos, I wondered what I was doing there—when you sing pop, you usually sing in straight tones. But when we did 'Unbreak My Heart' all four of us realized that we had something that could open the door to people who'd never heard opera—which included me—to appreciate it."

"This is going to be a fantastic surprise," says Carlos Marin, the Spanish baritone. "The audience is going to be really, really pleased, I think—we've got well-known songs here, but we have a new sound and concept for them, and being on Broadway will also be a chance to try something really new and theatrical for us."

Of course, this isn't the first time Il Divo has sung Broadway songs. As David points out, "We've been doing selections here and there—'Somewhere' from *West Side Story* was on one of our earlier albums, we did 'Music of the Night' from *The Phantom of the Opera* with Barbra Streisand when we were on tour with her and we once put together our own version of 'The Impossible Dream' from *Man of La Mancha* as an encore on one of our tours."

Coming to the Great White Way now is an opportunity to connect Il Divo to Broadway's audiences and repertoire like nothing else. They also, of course, bring their distinctive signature to the songs, too. As Urs says, "We give a different twist to all these songs, just purely from the fact that songs that were written as solo numbers are sung by the four of us. We've managed to create versions of these songs that are different than anything else out there. All these musicals have played throughout the world, and been interpreted by lots of different people. But our goal is always to take the musical material and do something with it that has not been heard before."

— Mark Shenton, UK and international theatre critic

Tour and Production Manager ....Andy Proudfoot
FOH Engineer ....Joseph Pearce
Monitor Engineer ....Phil Down
Associate Lighting Designer ....Dan Reed
Lighting Programming and
 Operation ....Gregory Bloxham
Backline Tech ....Marcus Lindsay
Video Crew Chief ....Stuart Merser
Kynesis Operator ....Jeffrey Sharratt
Show Stylist ....Robert Morrison
Fashion Coordinator ....Sumaira Lateef
Orchestra Arranged by ....AWR Music/
 Arnold Roth, Fritz Hocking
Drums ....Andrew Small
Sound ....Clair Audio/Robert Kosloskie, ML Procise III
Lighting ....PRG/Tim Murch
Video ....XL Video/Paul McCauley
Staging ....All Access/Robert Achimbari, Jennifer Davies
Freight ....Rock It Cargo/Matt Wright
Truck Transportation ....Upstaging/Jennifer Clark
Travel Management ....Music By Appointment
Tour Insurance
 Brokers ....Robertson Taylor Insurance Brokers

MERCHANDISE
Live Nation/De-lux Merchandise Co. Ltd.
Mark Stredwick Ben Rawling Emily Theobald

SYCO ENTERTAINMENT
Sonny Takhar Laurence Boakes

COLUMBIA RECORDS
Rob Stringer John Doelp Sofia Abbasi
Dariel Abramowitz

TOUR PR
On behalf of IL DIVO
The Door
Lois Najarian, Sophie Latapie, Nadia Ali
Fran DeFeo Public Relations
Fran DeFeo
On behalf of the Nederlander Organization
Sunshine Sachs
Ken Sunshine, Tiffany Shipp

BUSINESS MANAGEMENT
PS BUSINESS MANAGEMENT, LLC INT'L
Phil Sarna Jody Giberti Dil Ahmed (International)
OJK LTD.
Pat Savage Julie Symes (UK)

LEGAL REPRESENTATION
MICHAEL SIMKINS LLP
Paddy Grafton Green
SHERIDANS
James Sully

PRODUCED BY ARRANGEMENT WITH
LIVE NATION, JAMES L. NEDERLANDER
AND PROPER ARTIST MANAGEMENT.

www.ildivo.com

NEDERLANDER

Chairman ....**James M. Nederlander**
President ....**James L. Nederlander**

Executive Vice President
Nick Scandalios

Vice President   Senior Vice President
Corporate Development Labor Relations
Charlene S. Nederlander **Herschel Waxman**

Chief Financial Officer
Freida Sawyer Belviso

STAFF FOR THE MARQUIS THEATRE
Manager ....David Calhoun
Assistant Managers ....Sean Coughlin, Carolann Falasca
Treasurer ....Rick Waxman
Assistant Treasurer ....John Rooney
Carpenter ....Joseph P. Valentino
Electrician ....James Mayo
Property Man ....Scott Mecionis

Jersey Boys

First Preview: October 4, 2005. Opened: November 6, 2005.
Still running as of May 31, 2014.

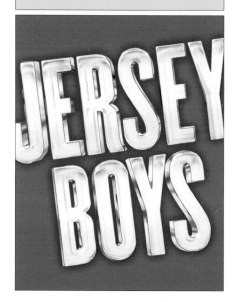

PLAYBILL

A musical based on the lives and careers of the close-harmony pop group The Four Seasons. We meet founder Tommy DeVito, a bad boy who is constantly in trouble with the law, supportive Nick Massi, songwriter Bob Gaudio, and finally lead singer Frankie Valli, whose soulful falsetto helps loft the foursome to international success. That success, along with DeVito's troubles with the mob and changes in the public's musical taste, helps splinter the original group. But the indefatigable Valli and the prolific Gaudio help make sure that the music lives on.

CAST
(in alphabetical order)

Nick DeVito, Stosh, Billy Dixon, Norman Waxman,
    Charlie Calello (and others) .....MILES AUBREY
Officer Petrillo, Hank Majewski, Crewe's PA,
    Joe Long (and others) ....ERIK BATES
Nick Massi...........................MATT BOGART
Frankie Valli
    (Wed. & Sat. Matinees) ..JOSEPH LEO BWARIE
French Rap Star, Detective One, Hal Miller,
    Barry Belson, Police Officer,
    Davis (and others) ....JOHN EDWARDS
Joey, Recording Studio Engineer
    (and others) ....RUSSELL FISCHER
Mary Delgado, Angel
    (and others) ....NATALIE GALLO
Bob Gaudio ....DREW GEHLING
Bob Crewe (and others) ....PETER GREGUS
Tommy DeVito ....ANDY KARL
Gyp DeCarlo (and others) ....MARK LOTITO

Continued on next page

148

9 AUGUST WILSON THEATRE
A JUJAMCYN THEATRE

JORDAN ROTH, *President*
ROCCO LANDESMAN, *President Emeritus*
PAUL LIBIN, *Executive Vice President* JACK VIERTEL, *Senior Vice President*

Dodger Theatricals   Joseph J. Grano   Tamara and Kevin Kinsella   Pelican Group
in association with Latitude Link   Rick Steiner/Osher/Staton/Bell/Mayerson Group

present

JERSEY BOYS

The Story of Frankie Valli & The Four Seasons

Book by
Marshall Brickman & Rick Elice

Music by
Bob Gaudio

Lyrics by
Bob Crewe

with

Matt Bogart   Drew Gehling   Andy Karl   Dominic Scaglione Jr.

Miles Aubrey   Erik Bates   Candi Boyd   Jared Bradshaw   Joseph Leo Bwarie
Ken Dow   John Edwards   Russell Fischer   Natalie Gallo   Katie O'Toole   Joe Payne
Jessica Rush   Nathan Scherich   Sara Schmidt   Taylor Sternberg
with Peter Gregus and Mark Lotito

Scenic Design	Costume Design	Lighting Design	Sound Design
Klara Zieglerova	Jess Goldstein	Howell Binkley	Steve Canyon Kennedy
Projection Design	Wig and Hair Design	Fight Director	Production Supervisor
Michael Clark	Charles LaPointe	Steve Rankin	Richard Hester
Orchestrations	Music Coordinator	Conductor	Production Stage Manager
Steve Orich	John Miller	Andrew Wilder	Michelle Bosch
Technical Supervisor	East Coast Casting	West Coast Casting	Company Manager
Peter Fulbright	Tara Rubin Casting	Sharon Bialy C.S.A. Sherry Thomas C.S.A.	Sandra Carlson
Associate Producers	Executive Producer	Promotions	Press Representative
Lauren Mitchell Rhoda Mayerson Stage Entertainment	Sally Campbell Morse	Red Rising Marketing	Boneau/Bryan-Brown

Music Direction, Vocal Arrangements & Incidental Music
Ron Melrose

Choreography
Sergio Trujillo

Directed by
Des McAnuff

World Premiere Produced by La Jolla Playhouse, La Jolla, CA
Christopher Ashley, Artistic Director & Michael S. Rosenberg, Managing Director

The producers wish to thank Theatre Development Fund for its support of this production.

10/1/13

(L-R) Matt Bogart, Dominic Scaglione, Jr.,
Drew Gehling, Andy Karl

Photo: Joan Marcus

Jersey Boys

MUSICAL NUMBERS

ACT I

"Ces Soirées-La (Oh What a Night)" – Paris, 2000 .... French Rap Star, Backup Group
"Silhouettes" .... Tommy DeVito, Nick Massi, Nick DeVito, Frankie Castelluccio
"You're the Apple of My Eye" .... Tommy DeVito, Nick Massi, Nick DeVito
"I Can't Give You Anything But Love" .... Frankie Castelluccio
"Earth Angel" .... Tommy DeVito, Full Company
"Sunday Kind of Love" .... Frankie Valli, Tommy DeVito, Nick Massi, Nick's Date
"My Mother's Eyes" .... Frankie Valli
"I Go Ape" .... The Four Lovers
"(Who Wears) Short Shorts" .... The Royal Teens
"I'm in the Mood for Love/Moody's Mood for Love" .... Frankie Valli
"Cry for Me" .... Bob Gaudio, Frankie Valli, Tommy DeVito, Nick Massi
"An Angel Cried" .... Hal Miller and The Rays
"I Still Care" .... Miss Frankie Nolan and The Romans
"Trance" .... Billy Dixon and The Topix
"Sherry" .... The Four Seasons
"Big Girls Don't Cry" .... The Four Seasons
"Walk Like a Man" .... The Four Seasons
"December, 1963 (Oh What a Night)" .... Bob Gaudio, Full Company
"My Boyfriend's Back" .... The Angels
"My Eyes Adored You" .... Frankie Valli, Mary Delgado, The Four Seasons
"Dawn (Go Away)" .... The Four Seasons
"Walk Like a Man" (reprise) .... Full Company

ACT II

"Big Man in Town" .... The Four Seasons
"Beggin'" .... The Four Seasons
"Stay" .... Bob Gaudio, Frankie Valli, Nick Massi
"Let's Hang On (To What We've Got)" .... Bob Gaudio, Frankie Valli
"Opus 17 (Don't You Worry 'Bout Me)" .... Bob Gaudio, Frankie Valli and The New Seasons
"Bye Bye Baby" .... Frankie Valli and The Four Seasons
"C'mon Marianne" .... Frankie Valli and The Four Seasons
"Can't Take My Eyes Off You" .... Frankie Valli
"Working My Way Back to You" .... Frankie Valli and The Four Seasons
"Fallen Angel" .... Frankie Valli
"Rag Doll" .... The Four Seasons
"Who Loves You" .... The Four Seasons, Full Company

Cast Continued

Church Lady, Miss Frankie Nolan, Bob's Party Girl,
    Angel, Lorraine (and others) ...... JESSICA RUSH
Frankie Valli .... DOMINIC SCAGLIONE JR.
Frankie's Mother, Nick's Date, Angel, Francine
    (and others) .... SARA SCHMIDT
Thugs .... KEN DOW, JOE PAYNE

SWINGS
CANDI BOYD, JARED BRADSHAW,
KATIE O'TOOLE, NATHAN SCHERICH,
TAYLOR STERNBERG

Dance Captain: KATIE O'TOOLE
Assistant Dance Captain: JARED BRADSHAW

UNDERSTUDIES
For Tommy DeVito:
ERIK BATES, JARED BRADSHAW
For Nick Massi:
MILES AUBREY, NATHAN SCHERICH
For Frankie Valli:
JOSEPH LEO BWARIE, RUSSELL FISCHER,
TAYLOR STERNBERG
For Bob Gaudio:
JARED BRADSHAW, NATHAN SCHERICH
For Gyp DeCarlo:
MILES AUBREY, NATHAN SCHERICH
For Bob Crewe:
ERIK BATES, JARED BRADSHAW,
NATHAN SCHERICH

ORCHESTRA
Conductor: ANDREW WILDER
Associate Conductor: DEBRA BARSHA
Keyboards: DEBRA BARSHA,
    STEPHEN "HOOPS" SNYDER
Guitars: JOE PAYNE, STEVE GIBB
Bass: KEN DOW
Drums: KEVIN DOW
Reeds: MATT HONG, BEN KONO
Trumpet: DAVID SPIER
Music Coordinator: JOHN MILLER

Matt Bogart
Nick Massi

Drew Gehling
Bob Gaudio

Andy Karl
Tommy DeVito

Dominic Scaglione
Jr.
Frankie Valli

Peter Gregus
*Bob Crewe and
others*

Mark Lotito
*Gyp DeCarlo
and others*

Miles Aubrey
*Norm Waxman
and others*

Jersey Boys

Erik Bates
Hank Majewski and others

Candi Boyd
Swing

Jared Bradshaw
Swing

Joseph Leo Bwarie
Frankie Valli on Wed. & Sat. matinees

Ken Dow
Thug, Bass

John Edwards
Hal Miller and others

Russell Fischer
Joey, Recording Studio Engineer and others

Natalie Gallo
Mary Delgado and others

Katie O'Toole
Swing, Dance Captain

Joe Payne
Thug, Guitars

Jessica Rush
Lorraine and others

Nathan Scherich
Swing

Sara Schmidt
Francine and others

Taylor Sternberg
Swing

Marshall Brickman
Book

Rick Elice
Book

Bob Gaudio
Composer

Bob Crewe
Lyricist

Des McAnuff
Director

Sergio Trujillo
Choreographer

Ron Melrose
Music Direction, Vocal Arrangements and Incidental Music

Klara Zieglerova
Scenic Design

Jess Goldstein
Costume Design

Howell Binkley
Lighting Design

Steve Canyon Kennedy
Sound Design

Michael Clark
Projection Design

Charles G. LaPointe
Wig/Hair Design

Steve Rankin
Fight Director

Richard Hester
Production Supervisor

Steve Orich
Orchestrations

John Miller
Music Coordinator

Andrew Wilder
Conductor

Jeff Siebert
Assistant Stage Manager

Peter Fulbright/Tech Production Services
Technical Supervisor

Tara Rubin
Tara Rubin Casting Casting

Jersey Boys

(L-R): Candi Boyd, Katie Webber, Sara Schmidt, Cara Cooper, Katie O'Toole sing "I Still Care."

Photo: Joan Marcus

Sharon Bialy
West Coast Casting

Sherry Thomas
West Coast Casting

Stephen Gabis
Dialect Coach

Michael David
Dodger Theatricals
Producer

Edward Strong
Dodger Theatricals
Producer

Rocco Landesman
Dodger Theatricals
Producer

Joseph J. Grano
Producer

Kevin Kinsella
Producer

Tamara Kinsella
Producer

Ivor Royston
The Pelican Group
Producer

Rick Steiner
Producer

John and Bonnie
Osher
Producer

Dan Staton
Producer

Marc Bell
Producer

Frederic H.
Mayerson
Producer

Lauren Mitchell
Associate Producer

Rhoda Mayerson
Associate Producer

Joop van den Ende
Stage Entertainment
Associate Producer

Christopher Ashley
Artistic Director
La Jolla Playhouse
Original Producer

Michael S.
Rosenberg
Managing Director
La Jolla Playhouse
Original Producer

Jersey Boys

Renée Marino
*Mary Delgado,
Angel and others*

Colin Trahan
*Gyp DeCarlo
and others*

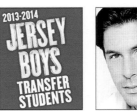

John Lloyd Young
Frankie Valli

Richard H. Blake
Tommy DeVito

Cara Cooper
*Mary Delgado,
Angel and others*

Nick Cosgrove
*Frankie Valli
alternate*

John Gardiner
Tommy DeVito

Mauricio Pérez
Swing

Kyli Rae
*Church Lady, Miss
Frankie Nolan, Bob's
Party Girl, Angel,
Lorraine*

Kirsten Scott
*Church Lady, Miss
Frankie Nolan, Bob's
Party Girl, Angel,
Lorraine*

Katie Webber
*Church Lady, Miss
Frankie Nolan, Bob's
Party Girl, Angel,
Lorraine*

MANAGEMENT
(L-R): Pam Remler (Assistant Stage Manager),
Michelle Bosch (Production Stage Manager),
Brendan M. Fay (Stage Manager)

BOX OFFICE
(L-R): Tara Giebler, Nick Russo, Jeanne Halal

Photos: Brian Mapp

FRONT OF HOUSE
Bottom Left: Ralph Santos (Engineer)
Sitting on stairs Row 1 (L-R): Rose Balsamo (Head Usher), Carmella Galante, Anah Klate (Manager)
Sitting on stairs Row 2 (L-R): Murray Bradley, Barbara Hill, Farah Guzman
Standing on stairs from top (L-R): Lenny Baron, Henry Hernandez, Robert Fowler, J. Ariel Martinez,
Seth Tucker, Amy Marquez, Fatima Eljaouhari, Patrick Korkuch, Samantha Obreiter

Jersey Boys

USHER
Raymond Polanco

CREW
(L-R): Peter Wright (Flyman), Michael W. Kelly (Production Carpenter), Ron Fucarino (Fly Automation), Dan Dour (Head Carpenter), Greg Burton (Deck Automation)

HAIR
Tim Miller, Hazel Higgins

Photos: Brian Mapp

SOUND AND ELECTRONICS
Front (L-R): Jan Nebozenko (with guitar) and David Shepherd (House Sound Engineers)
Back (L-R): Steve Pugliese, Brian Aman (Head Electrician),
Rick Baxter (Head Electrician), Kevin Fedigan, Sean Fedigan (Follow Spot Operator)

PROPS
Front: Ken Harris
Back (L-R): Noah Pilipski, Scott Mulrain (Head Propertyman), Kevin Dyal

WARDROBE
(Clockwise from top)
Lee J. Austin (Production
Wardrobe Supervisor),
Mary Rutherford,
Ben Chambliss,
Julie Tobia,
Michelle Sesco
(Assistant Wardobe Supervisor),
Nick Staub,
Davis Duffield,
Shaun Ozminski

Jersey Boys

STAFF FOR *JERSEY BOYS*

GENERAL PRESS REPRESENTATION
BONEAU/BRYAN-BROWN
Adrian Bryan-Brown   Susanne Tighe
Heath Schwartz

COMPANY MANAGER
Sandra Carlson

PRODUCTION
    STAGE MANAGER ....MICHELLE BOSCH
Stage Manager ....Brendan M. Fay
Assistant Stage Manager ....Jeff Siebert
Senior Associate General Manager ......Jennifer F. Vaughan
Associate General Manager ....Flora Johnstone
General Management Assistant ....Lauren Freed
Production Manager ....Jeff Parvin
Production Management Assistant ....Lyndsey Goode
Associate Company Manager ....Tim Sulka
Technical Supervision ....Tech Production Services/
    Peter Fulbright, Mary Duffe
Music Technical Design ....Deborah N. Hurwitz
Musician Swing ....Steve Gibb
Associate Director ....West Hyler
Assistant Director ....Holly-Anne Ruggiero
Second Assistant Director ....Alex Timbers
Associate Choreographers .....Danny Austin, Kelly Devine
Dialect Coach ....Stephen Gabis
Fight Captain ....Erik Bates
Associate Scenic Designers ....Nancy Thun, Todd Ivins
Assistant Scenic Designers ....Sonoka Gozelski,
    Matthew Myhrum
Associate Costume Designer ....Alejo Vietti
Assistant Costume Designers ....China Lee,
    Elizabeth Flauto
Associate Lighting Designer ....Patricia Nichols
Assistant Lighting Designer ....Sarah E. C. Maines
Associate Sound Designer ....Andrew Keister
Associate Projection Designer ....Jason Thompson
Assistant Projection Designer ....Chris Kateff
Story Board Artist ....Don Hudson
Casting Directors .Tara Rubin, CSA; Merri Sugarman, CSA
Casting Associates ....Eric Woodall, CSA;
    Laura Schutzel, CSA; Dale Brown, CSA
Casting Assistants ....Kaitlin Shaw, Lindsay Levine
Automated Lighting Programmer ....Hillary Knox
Projection Programming ....Paul Vershbow
Set Model Builder ....Anne Goelz
Production Carpenter ....Michael W. Kelly
Deck Automation ....Greg Burton
Production Electrician ....James Fedigan
Head Electrician ....Brian Aman
Assistant Electrician ....Gary L. Marlin
Production Sound Engineer ....Andrew Keister
Head Sound Engineer ....Julie M. Randolph
Production Props ....Emiliano Pares
Assistant Props ....Kenneth Harris Jr.
Production Wardrobe Supervisor ....Lee J. Austin
Assistant Wardobe Supervisor ....Michelle Sesco
Wardrobe Department ....Davis Duffield,
    Kristen Gardner, Kelly Kinsella,
    Shaun Ozminski, Nicholas Staub, Ricky Yates
Hair Supervisor ....Amy Neswald
Hair Department ....Hazel Higgins, Tim Miller
Assistant to John Miller ....Charles Butler

Synthesizer Programming ....Deborah N. Hurwitz,
    Steve Orich
Music Copying ....Anixter Rice Music Service
Music Production Assistant ....Alexandra Melrose
Dramaturg ....Allison Horsley
Associate to Messrs. Michael David
    and Ed Strong ....Pamela Lloyd
Advertising ....Serino Coyne, Inc./Scott Johnson,
    Marci Kaufman, Tom Callahan, Sarah Marcus
Marketing ....Dodger Marketing/Jessica Ludwig,
    Jessica Morris, Ann E. Van Nostrand,
    Tony Lance, Priya Iyer
Promotions ....Red Rising Marketing/
    Michael Redman, Nicole Pando
Banking ....Signature Bank/Barbara von Borstel
Payroll ....Castellana Services Inc./
    Lance Castellana, Norman Sewell, James Castellana
Accountants ....Schall and Ashenfarb, C.P.A.
Finance Director ....Paula Maldonado
Insurance ......AON/Albert G. Rubin Insurance Services/
    George Walden, Claudia Kaufman
Counsel ....Nan Bases, Esq.
Special Events ....John L. Haber
Travel Arrangements ....The "A" Team at Tzell Travel/
    Andi Henig
Information Technology Management ....ITelagen, Inc.
Web Design ....Curious Minds Media, Inc.
Production Photographer ....Joan Marcus
Theatre Displays ....King Displays

DODGERS
DODGER THEATRICALS
Christina Aguilar, Michael Altbaum, Mark Andrews, Michael Camp, Sandra Carlson, Ben Cohen, Dhyana Colony, Michael David, Anne Ezell, Lauren Freed, Mariann Fresiello, John Gendron, Lyndsey Goode, John L. Haber, Richard Hester, West Hyler, Priya Iyer, Flora Johnstone, Kimberly Kelley, Deana Marie Kirsch, Daniel Kogan, Abigail Kornet, Tony Lance, Pamela Lloyd, James Elliot Love, Jessica Ludwig, Paula Maldonado, Lauren Mitchell, Jessica Morris, Sally Campbell Morse, Jeff Parvin, Jason Pelusio, Samuel Rivera, Maureen Rooney, Andrew Serna, Dana Sherman, Edward Strong, Tim Sulka, Ashley Tracey, Ann E. Van Nostrand, Jennifer F. Vaughan, Laurinda Wilson, Claire Yenson

Dodger Group Sales 1-877-5DODGER
Exclusive Tour Direction ....Steven Schnepp/
    Broadway Booking Office NYC

CREDITS
Scenery, show control and automation by ShowMotion, Inc., Norwalk, CT. Lighting equipment from PRG Lighting. Sound equipment by Masque Sound. Projection equipment by Sound Associates. Selected men's clothing custom made by Saint Laurie Merchant Tailors, New York City. Costumes executed by Carelli Costumes, Studio Rouge, Carmen Gee, John Kristiansen New York, Inc. Selected menswear by Carlos Campos. Props provided by The Spoon Group, Downtime Productions, Tessa Dunning. Select guitars provided by Gibson Guitars. Laundry services provided by Ernest Winzer Theatrical Cleaners. Additional set and hand props courtesy of George Fenmore, Inc. Rosebud matches by Diamond Brands, Inc., Zippo lighters used. Rehearsed at the New 42nd Street Studios. Emergen-C by Alacer Corporation. PLAYBILL® cover photo by Chris Callis.

Grammy Award-winning cast album now available on Rhino Records.

www.jerseyboysinfo.com

Scenic drops adapted from *George Tice: Urban Landscapes*/W.W. Norton. Other photographs featured are from *George Tice: Selected Photographs 1953–1999*/David R. Godine. (Photographs courtesy of the Peter Fetterman Gallery/Santa Monica.)

SONG CREDITS
"Ces Soirees-La ("Oh What a Night")" (Bob Gaudio, Judy Parker, Yannick Zolo, Edmond David Bacri). Jobete Music Company Inc., Seasons Music Company (ASCAP). **"Silhouettes"** (Bob Crewe, Frank Slay, Jr.), Regent Music Corporation (BMI). **"You're the Apple of My Eye"** (Otis Blackwell), EMI Unart Catalog Inc. (BMI). **"I Can't Give You Anything But Love"** (Dorothy Fields, Jimmy McHugh), EMI April Music Inc., Aldi Music Company, Cotton Club Publishing (ASCAP). **"Earth Angel"** (Jesse Belvin, Curtis Williams, Gaynel Hodge), Embassy Music Corporation (BMI). **"Sunday Kind of Love"** (Barbara Belle, Anita Leanord Nye, Stan Rhodes, Louis Prima), LGL Music Inc./Larry Spier, Inc. (ASCAP). **"My Mother's Eyes"** (Abel Baer, L. Wolfe Gilbert), Abel Baer Music Company, EMI Feist Catalog Inc. (ASCAP). **"I Go Ape"** (Bob Crewe, Frank Slay, Jr.), MPL Music Publishing Inc. (ASCAP). **"(Who Wears) Short Shorts"** (Bob Gaudio, Bill Crandall, Tom Austin, Bill Dalton), EMI Longitude Music, Admiration Music Inc., Third Story Music Inc., and New Seasons Music (BMI). **"I'm in the Mood for Love"** (Dorothy Fields, Jimmy McHugh), Famous Music Corporation (ASCAP). **"Moody's Mood for Love"** (James Moody, Dorothy Fields, Jimmy McHugh), Famous Music Corporation (ASCAP). **"Cry for Me"** (Bob Gaudio), EMI Longitude Music, Seasons Four Music (BMI). **"An Angel Cried"** (Bob Gaudio), EMI Longitude Music (BMI). **"I Still Care"** (Bob Gaudio), Hearts Delight Music, Seasons Four Music (BMI). **"Trance"** (Bob Gaudio), Hearts Delight Music, Seasons Four Music (BMI). **"Sherry"** (Bob Gaudio), MPL Music Publishing Inc. (ASCAP). **"Big Girls Don't Cry"** (Bob Gaudio, Bob Crewe), MPL Music Publishing Inc. (ASCAP). **"Walk Like a Man"** (Bob Crewe, Bob Gaudio), Gavadima Music, MPL Communications Inc. (ASCAP). **"December, 1963 (Oh What a Night)"** (Bob Gaudio, Judy Parker), Jobete Music Company Inc, Seasons Music Company (ASCAP). **"My Boyfriend's Back"** (Robert Feldman, Gerald Goldstein, Richard Gottehrer), EMI Blackwood Music Inc. (BMI). **"My Eyes Adored You"** (Bob Crewe, Kenny Nolan), Jobete Music Company Inc, Kenny Nolan Publishing (ASCAP), Stone Diamond Music Corporation, Tannyboy Music (BMI). **"Dawn, Go Away"** (Bob Gaudio, Sandy Linzer), EMI Full Keel Music, Gavadima Music, Stebojen Music Company (ASCAP). **"Big Man in Town"** (Bob Gaudio), EMI Longitude Music (BMI), Gavadima Music (ASCAP). **"Beggin'"** (Bob Gaudio, Peggy Farina), EMI Longitude Music, Seasons Four Music (BMI). **"Stay"** (Maurice Williams), Cherio Corporation (BMI). **"Let's Hang On (To What We've Got)"** (Bob Crewe, Denny Randell, Sandy Linzer), EMI Longitude Music, Screen Gems-EMI Music Inc., Seasons Four Music (BMI). **"Opus 17 (Don't You Worry 'Bout Me)"** (Denny Randell, Sandy Linzer) Screen Gems-EMI Music Inc, Seasons Four Music (BMI). **"Everybody Knows My Name"** (Bob Gaudio, Bob Crewe), EMI Longitude Music, Seasons Four Music (BMI). **"Bye Bye Baby"** (Bob

Jersey Boys
SCRAPBOOK

Correspondent: Russell Fischer, "Joey," "Recording Studio Engineer" and others
Memorable Note, Fax, or Fan Letter: Yayoi, who writes to us from Japan and brings us treats from there.
Memorable Gift: Rubber duckies fashioned after The Four Seasons.
Most Exciting Celebrity Visitor: Clint Eastwood.
Which Actor Performed the Most Roles in This Show?: Either Nathan Scherich or Jared Bradshaw.
Who Has Done the Most Shows?: Richard Blake—15.
"Carols for a Cure" Carol: "Bad Girls Need Christmas Too."
Special Backstage Ritual: "Saturday Night Scream."
Favorite Moment During Each Performance: Post-"Rag Doll" Stage Right Comedy Hour, dance parties, "assume the position."
Favorite In-Theatre Gathering Place: "NUNYA Lounge" (Drew's dressing room)

The cast of *Jersey Boys*, including the ladies with the heavy beaded dresses, for the Finale.

Photo: Joan Marcus

Favorite Off-Site Hangouts: Brickyard, Ivy, Sosa Borella, Skylark, Toloache.
Favorite Snack Foods: Anything in the stage management office or wardrobe department, Rick Baxter's candy basket, Joe Leo Bwarie's baked treats.
Favorite Therapies: Steaming, acupuncture, massages and...Bourbon (hehe).
Latest Audience Arrival: Usually in the pizza scene, or the first studio scene (a quarter of the way into the show).

Fastest Costume Change: The "Mary Delgado" track.
Who Wore the Heaviest/Hottest Costume?: The girls in "My Boyfriend's Back" wear beaded dresses that are pretty heavy.
Who Wore the Least?: Any of the girls in our show.
Catchphrase Only the Company Would Recognize: "Ride the Snake."
Sweethearts Within the Company: Miles Aubrey and Donuts
Which Band Member Played the Most Instruments?: Steve Gibb, our sub-musician, but the winds section picks up several different types of instruments every night.
Which Band Member Played the Most Consecutive Performances Without a Sub?: Stephen "Hoops" Snyder.
Company Legends: Peter Gregus, Mark Lotito and Sara Schmidt.
Nicknames: Any and all of the names given to us by Dominic Scaglione Jr.

Crewe, Bob Gaudio), EMI Longitude Music, Seasons Four Music (BMI). **"C'mon Marianne"** (L. Russell Brown, Ray Bloodworth), EMI Longitude Music and Seasons Four Music (BMI). **"Can't Take My Eyes Off You"** (Bob Gaudio, Bob Crewe), EMI Longitude Music, Seasons Four Music (BMI). **"Working My Way Back to You"** (Denny Randell, Sandy Linzer), Screen Gems–EMI Music Inc, Seasons Four Music (BMI). **"Fallen Angel"** (Guy Fletcher, Doug Flett), Chrysalis Music (ASCAP). **"Rag Doll"** (Bob Crewe, Bob Gaudio), EMI Longitude Music (BMI), Gavadima Music (ASCAP). **"Who Loves You?"** (Bob Gaudio, Judy Parker), Jobete Music Company Inc, Seasons Music Company (ASCAP).

SPECIAL THANKS

Peter Bennett, Elliot Groffman, Karen Pals, Janine Smalls, Chad Woerner, Dan Whitten. The authors, director, cast and company of *Jersey Boys* would like to express their love and thanks to Jordan Ressler.

IN MEMORY

It is difficult to imagine producing anything without the presence of beloved Dodger producing associate James Elliot Love. Friend to everyone he met, James stood at the heart of all that is good about the theatrical community. He will be missed, but his spirit abides.

The producers would like to use this space to remember Mark Fearon, and in the spirit of this production, to contemplate the abiding joy of youth.

In memory of Jairo "Jay" Santos

JORDAN ROTH
President

ROCCO LANDESMAN
President, Emeritus

PAUL LIBIN	**JACK VIERTEL**
Executive Vice President	Senior Vice President
MEREDITH VILLATORE	**JENNIFER HERSHEY**
Chief Financial Officer	Vice President, Building Operations
MICAH HOLLINGWORTH	**HAL GOLDBERG**
Vice President, Company Operations	Vice President, Theatre Operations

Director of Business Affairs ....Albert T. Kim
Director of Ticketing Services ....Justin Karr
Theatre Operations Managers ....Willa Burke, Susan Elrod, Emily Hare, Jeff Hubbard, Albert T. Kim
Theatre Operations Associates ....Carrie Jo Brinker, Brian Busby, Michael Composto, Anah Jyoti Klate
Controller ....Tejal Patel
Accounting ....Christina Boursiquot, Cathy Cerge, Amy Frank, Alexander Parra
Executive Producer, Red Awning ....Nicole Kastrinos
Director of Sales, Givenik.com ....Karen Freidus
Building Operations Manager ....Erich Bussing
Executive Coordinator ....Ed Lefferson
Executive Assistants ....Hunter Chancellor, Danielle DeMatteo, Elisabeth Stern
Receptionist ....Lisa Perchinske
Ticketing and Pricing Associate ....Jonathon Scott
Sales Associate, Givenik.com ....Taylor Kurpiel
Maintenance ....Ralph Santos, Ramon Zapata
Security ....Rasim Hodzic, Terone Richardson
Interns ....Christina Bracco, Drew Factor, Morgan Hoit, Henry Tisch

STAFF FOR THE AUGUST WILSON THEATRE

Theatre Manager ....Willa Burke
Associate Theatre Manager ....Anah Jyoti Klate
Treasurer ....Nick Russo

Head Carpenter ....Dan Dour
Head Propertyman ....Scott Mulrain
Head Electrician ....Rick Baxter
Flyman ....Peter Wright
Engineer ....Ralph Santos
Assistant Treasurers ......Kevin Dublynn, Matthew Fearon, Tara Giebler, Jeanne Halal, George Licata, John Tobin
Fly Automation ....Ron Fucarino
Carpenter ....Alex Gutierrez
Propertyman ....John Thomson
Follow Spot Operators ....Andrew Dean, Sean Fedigan, Michael Lyons
House Sound Engineers ..Jan Nebozenko, David Shepherd
Head Usher ....Rose Balsamo
Ticket-Takers/Directors/Ushers ....Fatima Eljaouhari, Helen Flaherty, Robert Fowler, Carmella Galante, Bree Geiggars, Joan Gilmore, Farah Guzman, Barbara Hill, Sally Lettieri, Amy Marquez, J. Ariel Martinez, Raymond Polanco, Katie Schmidt
Doorpersons ....Gustavo Catuy, Christine Snyder
Line Control ....Nancy Rutter
Head Porter ....Natividad Nery
Porters ....Pedro Martinez, Lourdes Moreno
Head Cleaner ....Maria Giria
Cleaners ....Antonia Duran, Lorraine Feeks

Lobby refreshments by Sweet Hospitality Group.

Security provided by GBA Consulting, Inc.

BROADWAY
green◆alliance

Jujamcyn Theaters is a proud member of the Broadway Green Alliance.

Energy efficient washer/dryer courtesy of LG Electronics.

Kinky Boots

First Preview: March 3, 2013. Opened: April 4, 2013.
Still running as of May 31, 2014.

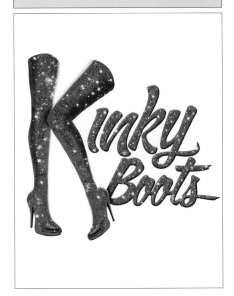

PLAYBILL®

The heir to a failing north England shoe factory revitalizes his business (and his life) when he teams up with a kick line of drag queens to manufacture a fabulous line of sexy women's boots...designed for men. He finds an unexpected soul mate in one of the dragsters, and they both work out their daddy issues as they collaborate to change their respective worlds.

CAST

(in order of appearance)

Mr. Price	STEPHEN BERGER
Young Charlie	JONAH HALPERIN
Young Lola	JADEN JORDAN
Simon Sr.	EUGENE BARRY-HILL
Nicola	LENA HALL
Charlie Price	STARK SANDS
George	MARCUS NEVILLE
Don	DANIEL STEWART SHERMAN
Lauren	ANNALEIGH ASHFORD
Pat	TORY ROSS
Harry	ANDY KELSO
Lola	BILLY PORTER
Angels	PAUL CANAAN,

KEVIN SMITH KIRKWOOD,
KYLE TAYLOR PARKER, KYLE POST,
CHARLIE SUTTON, JOEY TARANTO

Trish	JENNIFER PERRY
Richard Bailey	JOHN JEFFREY MARTIN
Milan Stage Manager	ADINAH ALEXANDER
Ensemble	ADINAH ALEXANDER,

EUGENE BARRY-HILL, STEPHEN BERGER,
ANDY KELSO, ERIC LEVITON,

Continued on next page

♥ AL HIRSCHFELD THEATRE
A JUJAMCYN THEATRE

JORDAN ROTH, *President*
ROCCO LANDESMAN, *President Emeritus*
PAUL LIBIN, *Executive Vice President* JACK VIERTEL, *Senior Vice President*

DARYL ROTH HAL LUFTIG

JAMES L. NEDERLANDER TERRY ALLEN KRAMER INDEPENDENT PRESENTERS NETWORK
CJ E&M JAYNE BARON SHERMAN JUST FOR LAUGHS THEATRICALS/JUDITH ANN ABRAMS
YASUHIRO KAWANA JANE BERGÈRE ALLAN S. GORDON & ADAM S. GORDON
KEN DAVENPORT HUNTER ARNOLD LUCY & PHIL SUAREZ BRYAN BANTRY
RON FIERSTEIN & DORSEY REGAL JIM KIERSTEAD/GREGORY RAE
BB GROUP/CHRISTINA PAPAGJIKA MICHAEL DeSANTIS/PATRICK BAUGH
BRIAN SMITH/TOM & CONNIE WALSH WARREN TREPP and JUJAMCYN THEATERS

present

Kinky Boots

Book by
HARVEY FIERSTEIN

Music & Lyrics by
CYNDI LAUPER

Based on the Miramax motion picture *Kinky Boots*
Written by Geoff Deane and Tim Firth

starring

STARK SANDS

ANNALEIGH ASHFORD
DANIEL STEWART SHERMAN

BILLY PORTER

LENA HALL
MARCUS NEVILLE

PAUL CANAAN KEVIN SMITH KIRKWOOD KYLE TAYLOR PARKER KYLE POST CHARLIE SUTTON JOEY TARANTO
ANDY KELSO TORY ROSS JENNIFER PERRY JONAH HALPERIN JADEN JORDAN
ADINAH ALEXANDER DOUGLAS BALDEO EUGENE BARRY-HILL STEPHEN BERGER STEPHEN CARRASCO
CAMERON COLLEY SANDRA DeNISE ERIC LEVITON ELLYN MARIE MARSH JOHN JEFFREY MARTIN NATHAN PECK
ROBERT PENDILLA LUCIA SPINA STEPHEN TEWKSBURY TIMOTHY WARE CORTNEY WOLFSON

Scenic Design DAVID ROCKWELL	*Costume Design* GREGG BARNES	*Lighting Design* KENNETH POSNER	*Associate Director* D.B. BONDS	*Sound Design* JOHN SHIVERS
Hair Design JOSH MARQUETTE	*Make-up Design* RANDY HOUSTON MERCER	*Associate Choreographer* RUSTY MOWERY		*Casting* TELSEY + COMPANY JUSTIN HUFF, CSA
Music Director BRIAN USIFER	*Music Coordinator* MICHAEL KELLER	*Technical Supervisor* CHRISTOPHER C. SMITH		*Production Stage Manager* LOIS L. GRIFFING
Associate Producer AMUSE INC.	*Advertising* SPOTCO	*Marketing* TYPE A MARKETING	*Press Representative* O&M CO.	*General Management* FORESIGHT THEATRICAL AARON LUSTBADER

Music Supervision, Arrangements & Orchestrations by
STEPHEN OREMUS

Directed and Choreographed by
JERRY MITCHELL

10/1/13

Stark Sands and Billy Porter (C) and company in "Sex Is in the Heel."

Photo: Matthew Murphy

Kinky Boots

MUSICAL NUMBERS

ACT I

"Price & Son Theme"	Full Company
"The Most Beautiful Thing in the World"	Full Company
"Take What You Got"	Harry, Charlie, Ensemble
"Land of Lola"	Lola, Angels
"Land of Lola (Reprise)"	Lola, Angels
"Step One"	Charlie
"Sex Is in the Heel"	Lola, Pat, George, Angels, Ensemble
"The History of Wrong Guys"	Lauren
"Not My Father's Son"	Lola, Charlie
"Everybody Say Yeah"	Charlie, Lola, Angels, Ensemble

ACT II

"Entr'acte/Price & Son Theme - Reprise"	Full Company
"What a Woman Wants"	Lola, Pat, Don, Ensemble
"In This Corner"	Lola, Don, Pat, Trish, Angels, Ensemble
"Soul of a Man"	Charlie
"Hold Me in Your Heart"	Lola
"Raise You Up/Just Be"	Full Company

ORCHESTRA

Conductor/Keyboard 1: BRIAN USIFER
Associate Conductor/Keyboard 2:
WILL VAN DYKE
Drums: SAMMY MERENDINO
Bass: MICHAEL VISCEGLIA
Guitars: MICHAEL AARONS, JOHN PUTNAM
Trumpet: JAMES DE LA GARZA
Trombone: KEITH O'QUINN
Reeds: DAN WILLIS

Concertmaster: HIROKO TAGUCHI
Violin: PHILIP PAYTON
Violin/Viola: DENISE STILLWELL
Cello: ALLISON SEIDNER

Synthesizer Programmer: RANDY COHEN
Music Coordination: MICHAEL KELLER
Music Copying: Emily Grishman Music Preparation
EMILY GRISHMAN/KATHARINE EDMONDS

Stark Sands
Charlie

Billy Porter
Lola

Annaleigh Ashford
Lauren

Lena Hall
Nicola

Cast Continued

ELLYN MARIE MARSH,
JOHN JEFFREY MARTIN, JENNIFER PERRY,
TORY ROSS, STEPHEN TEWKSBURY,
CORTNEY WOLFSON

STANDBYS AND UNDERSTUDIES

Standby for Young Charlie: CAMERON COLLEY
Standby for Young Lola: DOUGLAS BALDEO

Understudy for Lola: TIMOTHY WARE,
KEVIN SMITH KIRKWOOD,
KYLE TAYLOR PARKER
Charlie: ANDY KELSO,
JOHN JEFFREY MARTIN
Lauren: SANDRA DeNISE,
ELLYN MARIE MARSH
Nicola: SANDRA DeNISE,
CORTNEY WOLFSON
Don: ERIC LEVITON, STEPHEN TEWKSBURY
George: ERIC LEVITON,
STEPHEN TEWKSBURY
Mr. Price: ERIC LEVITON,
STEPHEN TEWKSBURY
Simon Sr.: KEVIN SMITH KIRKWOOD,
TIMOTHY WARE
Trish: ADINAH ALEXANDER, LUCIA SPINA
Pat: ADINAH ALEXANDER,
ELLYN MARIE MARSH, LUCIA SPINA
Harry: JOHN JEFFREY MARTIN, KYLE POST
Richard Bailey: ROBERT PENDILLA,
KYLE POST, CHARLIE SUTTON,
TIMOTHY WARE
Milan Stage Manager: SANDRA DeNISE,
LUCIA SPINA
Angels: STEPHEN CARRASCO,
NATHAN PECK, ROBERT PENDILLA,
TIMOTHY WARE

Dance Captain: NATHAN PECK
Assistant Dance Captain: PAUL CANAAN

SWINGS

STEPHEN CARRASCO, SANDRA DeNISE,
NATHAN PECK, ROBERT PENDILLA,
LUCIA SPINA, TIMOTHY WARE

Daniel Stewart Sherman
Don

Marcus Neville
George

Adinah Alexander
Milan Stage Manager/Ensemble

Douglas Baldeo
Young Lola Standby

Eugene Barry-Hill
Simon Sr./Ensemble

Stephen Berger
Mr. Price/Ensemble

Paul Canaan
Angel/Asst. Dance Captain/Ensemble

Kinky Boots

Stephen Carrasco
Swing

Cameron Colley
Young Charlie Standby

Sandra DeNise
Swing

Jonah Halperin
Young Charlie

Jaden Jordan
Young Lola

Andy Kelso
Harry/Ensemble

Kevin Smith Kirkwood
Angel/Ensemble

Eric Leviton
Ensemble

Ellyn Marie Marsh
Ensemble

John Jeffrey Martin
Richard Bailey/ Ensemble

Kyle Taylor Parker
Angel/Ensemble

Nathan Peck
Dance Captain/ Swing

Robert Pendilla
Swing

Jennifer Perry
Trish/Ensemble

Kyle Post
Angel/Ensemble

Tory Ross
Pat/Ensemble

Lucia Spina
Swing

Charlie Sutton
Angel/Ensemble

Joey Taranto
Angel/Ensemble

Stephen Tewksbury
Ensemble

Timothy Ware
Lola Standby/Swing

Cortney Wolfson
Ensemble

Harvey Fierstein
Playwright

Cyndi Lauper
Composer and Lyricist

Jerry Mitchell
Director/ Choreographer

Stephen Oremus
Music Supervisor/ Arranger/ Orchestrator

David Rockwell
Scenic Design

Gregg Barnes
Costume Design

Kenneth Posner
Lighting Design

John Shivers
Sound Design

Josh Marquette
Hair Design

Randy Houston Mercer
Make-up Design

Kathy Fabian Propstar
Properties Coordinator

Brian Usifer
Music Director

Michael Keller
Music Coordinator

Kinky Boots

Rusty Mowery
*Associate
Choreographer*

D.B. Bonds.
Associate Director

Amy Jo Jackson
Dialect Coach

Bernard Telsey
Telsey + Company
Casting

Christopher C. Smith
Smitty/
Theatersmith, Inc.
Technical Supervisor

Aaron Lustbader
Foresight Theatrical
General Manager

Daryl Roth
Producer

Hal Luftig
Producer

James L.
Nederlander
Producer

Terry Allen Kramer
Producer

Byeong Seok Kim
CJ E&M Live
Entertainment
Producer

Jayne Baron
Sherman
Producer

Adam Blanshay
Just for Laughs
Theatricals
Producer

Gilbert Rozon
Just for Laughs
Theatricals
Producer

Judith Ann Abrams
Producer

Yasuhiro Kawana
Producer

Jane Bergère
Producer

Allan S. Gordon
Producer

Adam S. Gordon
Producer

Ken Davenport
Producer

Hunter Arnold
Producer

(L-R): Billy Porter, Jeanna de Waal,
Andy Kelso, Marcus Neville and
Natalie Joy Johnson

Photo: Matthew Murphy

Kinky Boots

Phil and Lucy Suarez
Producer

Bryan Bantry
Producer

Ron Fierstein
Producer

Dorsey Regal
Producer

Jim Kierstead
Producer

Gregory Rae
Producer

Christina Papagjika
Producer

Michael DeSantis
Producer

Patrick Baugh
Producer

Brian Smith
Producer

Connie and Tom Walsh
Producer

Warren Trepp
Producer

Jordan Roth
Jujamcyn Theaters
Producer

Eric Anderson
Ensemble

Caroline Bowman
Ensemble

Cole Bullock
Standby for Young Lola

Colin Critchley
Standby for Young Charlie

Marquise Neal
Young Lola

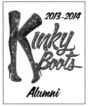

Sebastian Hedges
Thomas
Young Charlie

Lauren Nicole
Chapman
Ensemble

Jeanna de Waal
Lauren

Anna Eilinsfeld
Ensemble

Christy Faber
Swing

Natalie Joy Johnson
Pat, Ensemble

D'Andre Lee
Standby for Young Lola

Abby Mueller
Swing

Jake Odmark
Harry/Ensemble

Sebastian Hedges
Thomas
Young Charlie

Nicky Torchia
Standby for Young Charlie

Kinky Boots

MANAGEMENT
Front: Kenneth J. McGee (Assistant Stage Manager)
Back (L-R): Ashley Berman (Associate Company Manager),
Thomas Recktenwald (Stage Manager), Lois L. Griffing (Production
Stage Manager), Marc Borsak (Company Manager)

BOX OFFICE
Julie Lui

HAIR/MAKE-UP
(L-R): Guy Smith (Make-up Artist),
Sabana Majeed (Hair and Wig Stylist), Joshua First
(Asst. Hair Supervisor)

WARDROBE
(L-R): Ginny Hounsel, Jason Blair, Kim Kaldenberg, Joshua Burns, Susan Kroeter

FRONT OF HOUSE
First Row (L-R): John Barker, Lorraine Feeks, Hollis Miller, Theresa Lopez
Second Row (L-R): Lisé Greaves, Heather Gilles, Mark Maciejewski, Janice Rodriguez
Third Row (L-R): Kevin Shinnick, William Meyers, Donald Royal
Top Row (L-R): Albert Kim, Carrie Jo Brinker (Associate Theatre Manger), Lawrence Levins

Kinky Boots

ORCHESTRA
(L-R): Michael Aarons, Mike Visceglia, Will Van Dyke, Brian Usifer (Conductor), John Putnam, Denise Stillwell, Sammy Merendino, Allison Seidner, Keith O'Quinn

CREW
Front (L-R): Mike Reininger (Automation Carpenter), Gabe Harris (Flyman), Tom Burke (Electrician), Dan Tramontozzi, John Blixt (Electrician),
Pitsch Karrer (Head Sound Engineer), Patrick Shea (Production/Head Carpenter), Richard Anderson (Head Property Person),
Joseph J. Maher, Jr. (Head Carpenter), Bradley Brown (Assistant Electrician), Joe Mooneyham (Carpenter)
Stairs (Top to Bottom): Jake White, Jessica Provenzale, Raymond Ranellone (Property Person), Chris Conrad, Ralph Samford,
Michele Gutierrez (Head Electrician)

STAFF FOR *KINKY BOOTS*	**MARKETING**	Production Stage Manager ....Lois L. Griffing
	TYPE A MARKETING	Stage Manager.........................Thomas Recktenwald
GENERAL MANAGEMENT	Elyce Henkin John McCoy Andrew Cole	Assistant Stage Manager ....Kenneth J. McGee
FORESIGHT THEATRICAL		Associate Company Manager ....Ashley Berman
Alan Wasser Allan Williams	**CASTING**	Dialect Coach ....Amy Jo Jackson
Aaron Lustbader Mark Shacket	TELSEY + COMPANY	Dance Captain ....Nathan Peck
Mark Barna	Bernard Telsey CSA, Will Cantler CSA,	Assistant Dance Captain ....Paul Canaan
	David Vaccari CSA,	Associate Scenic Designer ....Dick Jaris
COMPANY MANAGER	Bethany Knox CSA, Craig Burns CSA,	Assistant Scenic Designers ..................T.J. Greenway,
Marc Borsak	Tiffany Little Canfield CSA, Rachel Hoffman CSA,	Jerome Martin, Michael Carnahan, Gaetane Bertol
	Justin Huff CSA, Patrick Goodwin CSA,	Associate Costume
GENERAL PRESS REPRESENTATIVE	Abbie Brady-Dalton CSA,	Designers ....Thomas Charles LeGalley,
O&M CO.	David Morris, Cesar A. Rocha CSA,	Matthew Pachtman
Rick Miramontez	Andrew Femenella, Karyn Casl CSA,	Assistant Costume Designers ....Rachel Attridge,
Molly Barnett Chelsea Nachman	Kristina Bramhall, Jessie Malone, Conrad Woolfe	Dana Burkart
		Associate Lighting Designer ....Anthony Pearson
		Assistant Lighting Designers ....Jeremy Cunningham,
		Keri Thibodeau

Kinky Boots

Associate Sound Designer ....David Patridge
Additional Arrangements ....Brian Usifer
Associate Synthesizer Programmer ....Tim Crook
Music Track Editor ....Derik Lee
Electronic Drum Programmer ....Sammy Merendino
Music Department Assistant ....Aaron Jodoin
Moving Lighting Programmer ....Aland Henderson
Production/Head Carpenter ....Patrick Shea
Automation Carpenter ....Mike Reininger
Production Flyman ....Gabe Harris
Production Electricians ...... James Fedigan, Randy Zaibek
Head Electrician ....Michael Brown
Assistant Electrician ....Bradley Brown
Moving Light Technician ....Rocco Williams
Properties Coordinator ....Kathy Fabian/Propstar
Head Properties Supervisor ....Andrew Meeker
Assistant Properties Supervisor ....Jacob White
Production Sound Engineer ....David Patridge
Head Sound Engineer ....Pitsch Karrer
Deck Audio ....Karen Zabinski
Advance Production Audio ....Kevin Kennedy
Wardrobe Supervisor ....James Hall
Dressers ....Jason Blair, Megan Bowers, Joshua Burns,
          Dan Foss, Ginny Hounsel, Susan Kroeter
Hair Supervisor ....Richard Orton
Assistant Hair Supervisor ....Mitchell Beck
Hair and Wig Stylist ....Sabana Majeed
Makeup Artist ....Guy Smith
Advertising ....SpotCo/Drew Hodges, Jim Edwards,
          Tom Greenwald, Stephen Sosnowski,
          Michael Crowley, Tim Falotico
Website & Interactive Marketing ......SpotCo/Kyle Young,
          Callie Goff, Marisa Reo Delmore
Legal Counsel ....Lazarus & Harris LLP/
          Scott Lazarus, Esq., Robert Harris, Esq.
Accounting ....Marks Paneth & Shron/
          Christopher Cacace, Ruthie Skochil
General Management Associates ...Jake Hirzel, Lane Marsh
General Management Office ....Kaitlin Boland,
          Lauren Friedlander, Nina Lutwick,
      Mary Catharine McDonald, Jennifer O'Connor
Assistants to Daryl Roth ....Greg Raby, Megan Smith
Assistant to Hal Luftig ....Scott Sinclair
Production Photographer ....Matthew Murphy
Production Assistants ....Derek Michael DiGregorio,
          Mitchell Anderson, Shannon Hammonds
Child Guardian ....Bridget Mills
Associate Props Coordinators ....Cassie Dorland,
          Carrie Mossman/Propstar
Props Artisans and Shoppers ..Mary Wilson, Becca Wright,
          Daniel Moss, Joshua Hackett, J. Michael Stafford,
          Will Barrios, Jasmine Roberts, John Estep
Assistant to Technical Director ....Rhiannon Hansen
Tutoring ....On Location Education
Press Associates ....Sarah Babin, Scott Braun,
          Philip Carrubba, Jon Dimond, Joyce Friedmann,
          Michael Jorgensen, Yufen Kung, Marie Pace, Pete Sanders,
          Andy Snyder, Sean Kincaid, Farnaz Mansouri,
          Clio McConnell, Kevin O'Malley
Physical Therapy ....Performing Arts Physical Therapy/
          Sean Gallagher, PT
Insurance ....Ventura Insurance Brokerage/Jessica Brown
Banking ....City National Bank/Erik Piecuch,
          Anne McSweeney, Michael Tynan
Payroll ....Checks and Balances Payroll Inc./
          Sarah Galbraith, Anthony Walker

Merchandising ....Broadway Merchandising LLC/
          Adam S. Gordon, David Eck
Opening Night Coordination ....Serino/Coyne Events/
          Suzanne Tobak, Chrissann Gasparro
Shoe Industry Consultant ....Larry Waller,
          Walrus Shoe and Leather Co, LLC
Travel ....Road Rebel Travel and Touring Inc.
Theatre Displays ....King Displays

CREDITS AND ACKNOWLEDGEMENTS

Scenery and scenic effects built, painted, electrified and automated by Showmotion, Inc., Milford, CT. Lighting equipment from PRG Lighting. Sound equipment by Masque Sound. Specialty props by Daedalus Design and Production, Tom Carroll Scenery and MINE metal art. Costumes by Eric Winterling Inc., Lynne Baccus, Donna Langman Costumes LLC, Tricorne Inc., Giliberto Inc., Pete's Print Shop, Polly Isham Kinney, By Barak LLC. Millinery by Rodney Gordon, Inc. Custom fabric painting and printing by Jeff Fender Studios and Gene Mignola, Inc. Custom shoes and boots by LaDuca and T.O. Dey. Onstage guitars courtesy of Taylor Guitars. Soft goods by iWeiss Theatrical Solutions. Scenic painting by Scenic Art Studios. Trucking by Anthony Augliera, Inc.

SPECIAL THANKS

Lisa Barbaris, Sonor Drums, Paiste Cymbals and Roland USA, Matthew Taylor, Mark Koss, Jessica Colley-Mitchell, Roselaine Fox, Kate Nowacki, Lindsay McWilliams, Jennifer Chapman, John Dunnett, Michael Harrell, BraTenders, Maria Ficalora, Katrina Patterns, Michael Piscitelli, On Stage Dancewear, Peanut Butter & Co., Mike Dereskewicz, Morgan Moore, Joanie Schlafer, Jim Waterhouse, Marina Pulliam. Promotional consideration furnished by Apple, George Poulios and Suzanne Lindbergh. Custom red pump courtesy of Kenneth Cole.

Cyndi Lauper wishes to thank her collaborators:
Sammy James Jr., Steve Gaboury,
Rich Morel and Tom Hammer, Stephen Oremus

Makeup provided by
M•A•C Cosmetics

New York Group Sales
Group Sales Box Office/Stephanie Lee
1-800-Broadway ext. 2

Rehearsed at the New 42nd Street Studios

www.KinkyBootsthemusical.com

JUJAMCYN THEATERS

JORDAN ROTH
President
ROCCO LANDESMAN
President, Emeritus

PAUL LIBIN	**JACK VIERTEL**
Executive Vice President	Senior Vice President
MEREDITH VILLATORE	**JENNIFER HERSHEY**
Chief Financial Officer	Vice President,
	Building Operations
MICAH HOLLINGWORTH	**HAL GOLDBERG**
Vice President,	Vice President,
Company Operations	Theatre Operations

Director of Business Affairs ....Albert T. Kim
Director of Ticketing Services ....Justin Karr
Theatre Operations Managers ...Willa Burke, Susan Elrod,
          Emily Hare, Jeff Hubbard, Albert T. Kim
Theatre Operations Associates ....Carrie Jo Brinker,
          Brian Busby, Michael Composto, Anah Jyoti Klate
Controller ....Tejal Patel
Accounting ....Christina Boursiquot, Cathy Cerge,
          Amy Frank, Alexander Parra
Executive Producer, Red Awning ....Nicole Kastrinos
Director of Sales, Givenik.com ....Karen Freidus
Building Operations Manager ....Erich Bussing
Executive Coordinator ....Ed Lefferson
Executive Assistants ....Hunter Chancellor,
          Danielle DeMatteo, Elisabeth Stern
Receptionist ....Lisa Perchinske
Ticketing and Pricing Associate ....Jonathon Scott
Sales Associate, Givenik.com ....Taylor Kurpiel
Maintenance ....Ralph Santos, Ramon Zapata
Security ....Rasim Hodzic, Terone Richardson
Interns ....Christina Bracco, Drew Factor,
          Morgan Hoit, Henry Tisch

Staff for the Al Hirschfeld Theatre for
Kinky Boots

Theatre Manager ....Albert T. Kim
Associate Theatre Manager ....Carrie Jo Brinker
Treasurer ....Carmine LaMendola
Head Carpenter ....Joseph J. Maher, Jr.
Head Propertyperson ....Richard Anderson
Head Electrician ....Michele Gutierrez
Flyman ....Gabe Harris
Engineer ....David Neville
Assistant Treasurers ....Jeffrey Nevin, Julie Lui,
          Brendan McCaffrey, Vicci Stanton, Janette Wernegreen
Carpenters ....Joe Mooneyham, Hank Hale
Propertyperson ....Raymond Ranellone
Electricians ....John Blixt, Tom Burke, Rocco Williams
Head Usher ....Janice Rodriguez
Ticket-Takers ....Tristan Blacer, Lorraine Feeks
Doormen ....Henry E. Menendez, Neil Perez
Front of House Directors ....Julie Burnham,
          Heather Gilles, Lawrence Levens, William Meyers
Head Porter ....Jose Nunez
Head Cleaner ....Bethania Alvarez
Ushers ......John Barker, Clifford Ray Berry, Peter Davino,
          Lisé Greaves, Theresa Lopez, Mark Maciejewski,
          Mary Marzan, Hollis Miller, Donald Royal,
          Christina Ruiz, Bart Ryan
Porters ....Roberto Ellington, Alex Nunez
Cleaners ....Michelina Annarumma, Mirjan Aquino

Lobby refreshments by Sweet Hospitality Group.

Security provided by GBA Consulting, Inc.

 Jujamcyn Theaters is a proud member of the Broadway Green Alliance.

2013-2014 AWARD

GRAMMY AWARD
Best Musical Theater Album

Kinky Boots
SCRAPBOOK

Correspondent: Ellyn Marie Marsh, "Ensemble" Hello everyone reading the *Playbill Broadway Yearbook*! It's Ellyn Marie Marsh, self-appointed social media president. It's been quite a season for us here at *Kinky Boots*. After winning the Tony and the Grammy, we've been on cloud nine. It's a wild ride every day over at the Hirschfeld. It's not perfect, we have our ups and downs, but mostly we do a lot of laughing. At each other.

Memorable Note, Fax or Fan Letter from the Past Season: We are very fond of letters attached to baked goods. Whoopi Goldberg sent some amazing cookies that we love. Hollis Stern sent us brownies with…WAIT FOR IT… Heath Bars in them! Elaine Berger sent cookies with Kinky K's on it. Jessica Zellermayer, Kim Fountain and Rachel Tuckerman are always filling our bellies with deliciousness! All of these things had crack in them. Which we also enjoy.

Milestone Parties, Celebrations and/or Gifts: We've had two weddings: Annaleigh and our SM Ken McGee married their loves. Five engagements: Andy and Tory. Not to each other… To their significant others. Our amazing vacation swing Stephen Carrasco; our Musical Director Brian Usifer proposed to his girlfriend Carrie in Itlay (fancy!). And our PSM proposed to her long time partner Mindy in the kitchen on Thanksgiving by saying, "Hey, do you wanna get married?" Two babies: Our house props Ray had a granddaughter and our deck elec Rocco had a baby boy. Our Christmas party thrown by our loving producers Daryl Roth and Hal Luftig was super fun with food and dancing. We use pretty much any excuse to celebrate.

Most Exciting Celebrity Visitors: We've had some sensational guests backstage at the Hirschfeld. Some would say Tina Fey was a highlight; others Sara Bareilles, Mike Myers, Michael J. Fox and his family were lovely. Diana Ross was a huge highlight. We've all been excited by one person or another: Goldie Hawn, Robert De Niro. BUT, if you ask the crew who their favorite was, chances are they'll all give the same answer: Pamela Anderson. Needless to say, we've been lucky to have so many people come and enjoy the show!

Most Memorable Special Guests: There was a 7-year-old boy who identifies as female who came backstage to our show. He was enthralled by the costumes and the Angels. It was so special to make this little special person feel amazing and accepted. He touched our hearts. Then there was the kindergarten class whose teach taught them "Raise You Up" and "Just Be" for their spring concert and they came and performed on our stage. They were incredible. There wasn't a dry eye among us.

Actor Who Performed the Most Roles in This Show: Robert Pendilla. Our swings are all incredible, but Robert has played almost all the Angels (there are six of them) and all the factory workers as well. Go Robert!

Who Has Done the Most Broadway Shows in Their Career: Ken McGee (SM)—17; Lois Griffing (PSM)—10; Charlie Sutton (cast)—9.

Special Backstage Rituals: So the factory workers (as said last year) have an all hands in chant "Oi oi oi shoes" in Act I and "Oi oi oi boots" in Act II. What we DIDN'T mention is before "Land of Lola," the Angels have a similar circle up and say "Lady! Lady! Lady! Steal the show." Many of us also take a moment—a hug, a fist bump to our crew—we would be nothing without them. We all have several times to take a moment or a chat, catch up with people backstage. It's all timed out perfectly so as not to miss any cues.

Favorite Moments During Each Performance: Well, MY favorite moment (since I'm writing this, I get to hog the answers, I suppose) was the quitting scene. (Oops! Is that a spoiler? Ah well, you should have see the show by now) when Trish (our amazing Jen Perry) says, "What's say we clear out." The look on Starks' face, with those piercing blue eyes, broke my heart every night. But most people would say the finale. Our finale is so gorgeous and fun and epic, seeing the audiences' faces every night is worth every sore muscle, every tired bone. It's a fantastic feeling. No one leaves our theater NOT smiling.

Favorite In-Theatre Gathering Places: Stage management has the candy, pretzels and coffee. Everyone makes a pit stop there. Angels host SNOB (Saturday Night on Broadway) parties and the character ladies' floor does it up right. Listen, I'm not gonna lie. We've had some awesome parties complete with a stripper for someone's pajama jammy jam bachelorette party.

I'm not gonna say who, but her name begins with a T and ends with ory Ross.

Favorite Off-Site Hangouts: Bocca di Bacco on Ninth is very nice to us, as is Iron Bar, Beer Culture, Harley's, Lillie's. Places with food. And drinks. Wine. Sometimes beer. You know, we like to eat when we're hungry and drink when we're thirsty.

Favorite Snack Foods: That depends on who you ask. Angels: air; Character/factory workers: Schmackary's.

Mascot: Widdie Bantour.

Favorite Therapies: Throat Coat, Emergen-C and sucking it up.

Memorable Ad-Libs: The line (for Billy Porter) is, "As Oscar Wilde says, 'Be yourself, everyone else is already taken.'" What Billy said: "As Oscar Wilde said, be happy, and you'll be all right." The other one also involved Billy. In the song "The Sex Is in the Heel," he broke…his heel. Just…star of the show hobbling around, looking for a heel. The audience got a good laugh that night.

Record Number of Cell Phone Rings or Texting Incidents During a Performance: I think people forget that we can see them sometimes? We see people texting ALL the time, and we usually give them a look from stage. MAAAAYBE once or twice people have said something, but I'm not naming names…. :-/

1. From the Football Hall of Fame to the Footwear Hall of Fame? Michael Strahan dons a pair of the famous *Kinky Boots* boots for a walk-on.
2. What time is it? Time to greet one of the many celebrity visitors backstage at the Hirschfeld Theatre. Michael J. Fox flanked by last year's *Yearbook* correspondent Tory Ross (L) and this year's correspondent Ellyn Marie Marsh.
3. (L-R): Andy Kelso, Sky (winner of the 2014 Westminster Dog Show), Billy Porter, Annaleigh Ashford.

Kinky Boots
SCRAPBOOK

Memorable Press Encounter: Probably the most fun and most hands-on was Michael Strahan, the Football Hall-of-Famer turned co-host of "Live with Kelly and Michael." He was a celebrity walk-on, but he had lines and choreography and wore…KINKY BOOTS (see photo). He was such a fun guy and a good sport. He had a factory name and was totally a welcomed cast member for the day.

Memorable Stage Door Fan Encounters: We have a few people with various *Kinky* tattoos, whether it's the symbol, lyrics from the show and EVEN some cast members' signatures. That's pretty wild, but spectacular that our show touched someone enough to put ink in their skin! I love it!

Web Buzz: Our "Girls Just Wanna Have Fun" video (a tribute to Cyndi and 30 years of "Girls…") went viral. That was shot by Ray Lee and was so fun to make! https://www.youtube.com/watch?v=0_TmLhtKZ6I

Who Wore the Least?: That answer will always and forever be Charlie Sutton's boxing scene outfit.

Catchphrases Only the Company Would Recognize: "You need to think about your life and think about your choices" and "TRANNY SMACK DOWN." If you haven't seen our videos, check Paul Canaan's Facebook page. You won't regret it.

Which Orchestra Member Played the Most Consecutive Performances Without a Sub?: Sammy Merendino. Our LEGENDARY drummer. Sammy was Cyndi's drummer for years on tour. Always wears a tie and is just a rock star. He played every rehearsal with us and every show in Chicago. He was the last person to get a sub. We love you, Sammy!

Cast Turnover: Our beautiful Caroline Bowman left us to go play Eva on the *Evita* tour. Our spirited Eric Anderson went to bring Broadway its medicine in *Soul Doctor*. Our sweet Marquise Neal, our original young Lola, left us in September. Our cruise director Tory Ross left to move to California to get MARRIED. Lucia Spina, our original female swing, departed with Tory. Jonah Halperin (young Charlie standby) left us to go revolt at the Shubert with the *Matilda* kids and the captain of our ship, Stark Sands, left his teary cast in January.

Company In-Joke: "That apple fritter f$&?!d me up."

Company Legend: Legend has it that Jerry Mitchell has secretly hidden cameras in all parts of the theatre to pinpoint those not going FULL OUT at all times.

Tales from the Put-In: Andy Kelso, who was taking over for Stark Sands, missed his own put-in. LUCKILY he'd done it once or twice.

Understudy Anecdote: So Eugene Barry-Hill and Tim Ware are a lovely couple that live in Jersey. They were stuck in traffic one day and Tim is Eugene's understudy. Sooooo, to be Billy Porter's father…one should…be of the same race? Maybe? Color-blind casting? So we went to the next best thing…Robert Pendilla, our Asian brother in boots. He faced slightly upstage of his young black son.

Shortest Contract: Colin Critchley. Came in as vacation young Charlie standby. He was here a WEEK(!), then booked another Broadway show. Get those credits, kiddo!

Embarrassing Moment: This is hilarious. At the top of the show, I take 13 pairs of shoes off a conveyor belt and place them on a shoe rack. Okay. So one day. Said shoe rack? Not there. But that conveyor belt was flying. So I start grabbing them, trying to manage. 13 pairs of shoes… that's TWENTY-SIX shoes. Imagine "I Love Lucy" with men's shoes. I was trying to stop them with my body, all the while actually crying with tears of laughter. But the awesome thing is? I have a rock-solid company that I can always turn to in times of need. Oh, no, wait. They were all pissing themselves laughing. Finally, I chuck a handful to Andy Kelso then run stage left and load them off with Rich, our props master. It was not only my funniest moment, it was the world's. The world's funniest moment on stage.

"Carols for a Cure" Carol: Our song this year was written by Jen Perry and Tory Ross, arranged by Brian Usifer. It was called "Carol of the Boots" (to "Carol of the Bells") with lyrics for our show: "We make the shoes for Price and Son/but we went bust, our jobs are done/Chambers sent back all of our shoes/this is bad news…." We have some guest appearances in the song…take a listen.

Cyndi-isms (Sh*t Cyndi Lauper says): "Ya gotta find the pocket." "I gotta go look famous."

"Gypsy of the Year" Skit and Who Wrote It: So, let's talk about "Gypsy of the Year." WE WON! fundraising. We not only won, we kiiiinda wiped the floor with everyone. We raised $377, 301 in SIX WEEKS. I mean, it's for charity, it's not a competition, but it is. So. We won. But seriously, our cast and crew worked TIRELESSLY, stayed late, shipped out special gifts. A lot of work goes into those fundraising weeks for BC/EFA and we could not have been prouder of the work we did. GO Team *Kinky*. Our skit, because of the time of year it ran, featured Eric Leviton, Douglas Baldeo and Ellyn Marie Marsh (me), and Eric and I wrote it.

Ghostly Encounters Backstage: The Angels as boys. We forget what they look like.

Coolest Memento: So, they call the Tonys the Super Bowl of musical theatre aaaaand we WON the Tony for best musical. Andy Kelso headed up the first official Tony ring. Complete with best musical, our signature "K," the year on one side and a Tony on the other. These are the coolest mementos in the history of Broadway mementos.

Superlatives*: Most likely to fall in the finale dressed as a nine-foot-tall Union Jack: Kyle Post. Most likely to regret eating actual food: Angels. Most likely to direct *Kinky Boots* at Gateway: Paul Canaan. Most likely to accidentally lock themselves INSIDE their apartment, missing a show: Kyle Taylor Parker. Most likely to cook in between shows: Adinah Alexander. Most likely to drop a boot into the pit: Ellyn Marie Marsh. Most likely to lose their company Christmas present only to find it after a panicked search: Jen Perry. Most likely to leave the show to shoot a movie with Cameron Diaz: Sebastian Thomas. Most likely to throw a purse into the audience: Charlie Sutton. Best dressed: Dougie Baldeo. Best hair: Joey Taranto. Best dancer: Stephen Berger. Most improved Tweeter: Daryl Roth.

*These superlatives brought to you by actual events!

Coolest Thing About Being in This Show: I sound like a cheeseball, but there are so many things. We are truly a family. The good and the bad parts of a family. When I say that, I don't mean just everyone on stage. I mean our associates, our crew, our PR team, producers… everyone. We have been such a huge part of each other's lives through this roller coaster of a year. From weddings to births, to deaths, awards, Twitter outrages over our parade performance. But, in the end? All the long hours, all the crazy call times and put-in rehearsals, broken heels and hurt muscles…we get to tell an awesome story every night, bring a theatre to its feet cheering and smiling through tears. We are truly a lucky bunch of so and so's. And though at times we can forget that, it is never for long. As Jerry Mitchell would say, "THIS IS BROADWAY, PEOPLE," and that's freakin' awesome.

1. *Kinky Boots* wins the top prize at "Gypsy of the Year" by taking in a record-breaking $377,301. (L-R): *Yearbook* correspondent Ellyn Marie Marsh, Douglas Baldeo and Eric Leviton.
2. The first-ever Tony Ring!
3. The cast backstage at the 2013 Tony Awards at Radio City Music Hall.

Lady Day at Emerson's Bar & Grill

First Preview: March 25, 2014. Opened: April 13, 2014.
Limited engagement. Still running as of May 31, 2014.

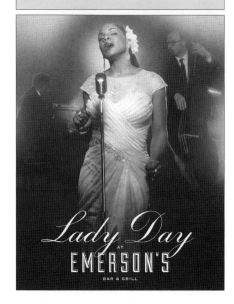

PLAYBILL®

The Circle in the Square Theatre is converted into an intimate South Philadelphia nightclub where jazz singer Billie "Lady Day" Holiday, nearing the end of her life, looks back with anger, pride, bitterness, fondness and more forgiveness than some people deserve as she rouses herself to sing a few of her greatest hits despite advanced drug and alcohol addiction. Notable about this production is star Audra McDonald's Tony-winning dead-on impersonation of Holiday.

CAST

Billie Holiday	AUDRA McDONALD
Jimmy Powers	SHELTON BECTON
Pepi	ROXIE

MUSICAL NUMBERS

"I Wonder Where Our Love Has Gone"
"When a Woman Loves a Man"
"What a Little Moonlight Can Do"
"Crazy He Calls Me"
"Pig Foot (And a Bottle of Beer)"
"Baby Doll"
"God Bless the Child"
"Foolin' Myself"
"Somebody's on My Mind"
"Easy Livin'"
"Strange Fruit"
"Blues Break"
"T'ain't Nobody's Business If I Do"
"Don't Explain"/
"What a Little Moonlight Can Do" (Reprise)
"Deep Song"

○ CIRCLE IN THE SQUARE

UNDER THE DIRECTION OF
PAUL LIBIN and THEODORE MANN (1924–2012)
SUSAN FRANKEL, General Manager

Jeffrey Richards   Jerry Frankel   Jessica Genick   Will Trice
Ronald Frankel   Rebecca Gold   Roger Berlind   Ken Greiner
Gabrielle Palitz   Irene Gandy   GFour Productions

PRESENT

AUDRA McDONALD

Lady Day
AT
EMERSON'S
BAR & GRILL

BY

LANIE ROBERTSON

SCENIC DESIGN	COSTUME DESIGN	LIGHTING DESIGN	SOUND DESIGN
JAMES NOONE	ESOSA	ROBERT WIERZEL	STEVE CANYON KENNEDY

ANIMAL TRAINER	TECHNICAL SUPERVISOR	MUSICAL ARRANGEMENTS/ ORCHESTRATIONS	CONDUCTOR/PIANIST
WILLIAM BERLONI	HUDSON THEATRICAL ASSOCIATES	TIM WEIL	SHELTON BECTON

PRODUCTION STAGE MANAGER	ASSOCIATE DIRECTOR	ADVERTISING
TIMOTHY R. SEMON	MATT COWART	SERINO/COYNE

PRESS REPRESENTATIVE	ASSOCIATE PRODUCERS	COMPANY MANAGER	GENERAL MANAGER
JEFFREY RICHARDS ASSOCIATES	GREENLEAF PRODUCTIONS MICHAEL CREA, PJ MILLER	DANIEL HOYOS	RICHARDS/CLIMAN, INC.

DIRECTED BY

LONNY PRICE

New York City premiere production was first produced in June 1986 at the Vineyard Theatre.
Douglas Aibel, Artistic Director

4/13/14

Audra McDonald
with Shelton Becton
at the piano

Photo: Evgenia Eliseeva

Lady Day at Emerson's Bar & Grill

Audra McDonald and Shelton Becton

Photo: Evgenia Eliseeva

Audra McDonald
Billie Holiday

Shelton Becton
Jimmy Powers

Roxie
Pepi

Lanie Robertson
Playwright

Lonny Price
Director

James Noone
Scenic Designer

ESosa
Costume Designer

Robert Wierzel
Lighting Designer

Steve Canyon Kennedy
Sound Designer

William Berloni
Animal Trainer

Tim Weil
Musical Arrangements/ Orchestrations

Matt Cowart
Associate Director

Neil A. Mazzella
Hudson Theatrical Associates
Technical Supervisor

David R. Richards and Tamar Haimes
Richards/Climan, Inc.
General Management

Jeffrey Richards
Producer

Jerry Frankel
Producer

Jessica Genick
Producer

Will Trice
Producer

Rebecca Gold
Producer

Roger Berlind
Producer

Ken Greiner
Producer

Lady Day at Emerson's Bar & Grill

Gabrielle Palitz
Producer

Irene Gandy
Producer

Kenneth Greenblatt
GFour Productions
Producer

Seth Greenleaf
GFour Productions
Producer

David Beckerman
GFour Productions
Producer

Alan Glist
GFour Productions
Producer

Marc Goldman
GFour Productions
Producer

Michael Crea
Associate Producer

PJ Miller
Associate Producer

Paul Libin
Circle in the Square
Theatre and Theatre
School
President

Theodore Mann
(1924-2012)
Circle in the Square
Theatre and
Theatre School
Artistic Director

Susan Frankel
Circle in the Square
General Manager

MUSICIANS
(L-R): Shelton Becton, Clayton Craddock, George Farmer

Photos: Brian Mapp

BOX OFFICE
(L-R): Sarah Shutt (Assistant Treasurer),
Jason C. Hudson (Box Office Treasurer),
Kathleen Drury (Assistant Treasurer)

2013-2014 AWARDS

TONY AWARDS
Best Performance by an Actress
in a Leading Role in a Play
(Audra McDonald)
Best Sound Design of a Play
(Steve Canyon Kennedy)

DRAMA DESK AWARD
Outstanding Actress in a Play
(Audra McDonald)

OUTER CRITICS CIRCLE AWARD
Outstanding Actress in a Musical
(Audra McDonald)

CREW
(L-R): Rob Dagna, Stephanie Vetter (Audio Engineer), Anthony Menditto (Head Carpenter),
Owen E. Parmele (Prop Master), Stewart Wagner (Head Electrician), Steve Hills

Lady Day at Emerson's Bar & Grill

Photos: Brian Mapp

WARDROBE/HAIR/MAKE-UP
Brendan O'Neal (Hair and Make-up Supervisor),
Katherine Sorg (Wardrobe Supervisor)

MANAGEMENT
(L-R): Timothy R. Semon (Production Stage Manager),
Lara Hayhurst (Assistant Stage Manager), Daniel Hoyos (Company Manager)

STAFF FOR
LADY DAY AT EMERSON'S BAR & GRILL

GENERAL MANAGEMENT
RICHARDS/CLIMAN, INC.
David R. Richards   Tamar Haimes
Michael Sag   Kyle Bonder
Rachel Welt   Jenny Peek

COMPANY MANAGER
Daniel Hoyos

PRODUCTION MANAGEMENT
HUDSON THEATRICAL ASSOCIATES
Neil A. Mazzella   Sam Ellis
Alexis Prussack   Irene Wang

GENERAL PRESS REPRESENTATIVE
JEFFREY RICHARDS ASSOCIATES
Irene Gandy   Alana Karpoff
Thomas Raynor   Christopher Pineda

Production Stage Manager ....Timothy R. Semon
Assistant Stage Manager ....Lara Hayhurst
Dialect Coach ....Deborah Hecht
Makeup Designer ....Jill Oshry
Wig Design & Special Makeup Effects ....J. Jared Janas
& Rob Greene
Assistant Scenic Designer ....Paul DePoo
Assistant to Mr. Noone ....William Moser
Assistant Costume Designer ....Dede Ayite
Costume Intern ....Rita Wu
Associate Lighting Designer ....Paul Hackenmueller
Assistant Lighting Designer ....Jeff Harris
Associate Sound Designer/
Production Sound ....Walter Trarbach
Production Electrician ....James Maloney
Associate Production Electrician ....Jeff Koger
Light Programmer ....Hillary Knox
Follow Spot Operator ....Steve Hills
Audio Engineer ....Stephanie Vetter
Production Props Supervisor ....Emiliano Pares
Wardrobe Supervisor ....Katherine Sorg
Hair and Makeup Supervisor.............Brendan O'Neal
Fight Consultant ....Rick Sordelet
Press Assistant ....Steven Strauss
Production Assistant ....Ali Keller
Music Coordinator ....Michael Keller
Music Copyist ....Kaye-Houston Music/
Anne Kaye, Doug Houston

Advertising ....Serino/Coyne/Greg Corradetti,
Tom Callahan, Vinny Sainato, Robert Jones,
Drew Nebrig, Ben Skinner
Interactive/Marketing.............Serino/Coyne/Jim Glaub,
Kevin Keating, Erin Daigle, Mark Seeley
Interactive Marketing Service ......Broadway's Best Shows/
Andy Drachenberg, Lindsay Hoffman
Banking ....Signature Bank/Thomas Kasulka,
Mary Ann Fanelli, Margaret Monigan
Insurance ....DeWitt Stern Group/
Peter K. Shoemaker, Anthony Pittari
Accountants ....Fried & Kowgios CPAs LLP
Comptroller ....Elliott Aronstam
Production Legal Counsel ....Lazarus Harris/
Scott Lazarus, Robert Harris
Payroll ....Castellana Services
Merchandise ....Max Merchandise
Production Photographer ....Joan Marcus
Company Mascots ....Skye, Franco, Butler

CREDITS

Scenery built by Hudson Scenic Studio. Lighting provided by Hudson Sound & Light. Costumes built by Tricorne and Gilberto Design. Sound equipment from Sound Associates.

SPECIAL THANKS

Bra*Tenders, Raynelle Wright, Steve Roath,
Arnold S. Levine, Hochi Asiatico

MUSIC CREDITS

"Foolin' Myself" written by Jack Lawrence and Peter Tinturin. Used by permission of Range Road Music, Inc. "God Bless the Child" and "Somebody's on My Mind" written by Billie Holiday, Arthur Herzog, Jr. Used by permission of Edward B. Marks Music Company. "Deep Song" words and music by George Cory, Douglas Cross. All rights owned or administered by ©Universal Music Corp. (ASCAP). Used by permission. "Don't Explain" words and music by Arthur Herzog, Jr., Billie Holiday. All rights owned or administered by ©Songs of Universal, Inc. (BMI) Used by permission. "Gimme a Pigfoot and a Bottle of Beer" words and music by Wesley A. Wilson. All rights owned or administered by ©Universal Music Corp. (ASCAP). Used by permission. "T'ain't Nobody's Bizness" words and music by Porter Grainger, Everett Robbins. All rights owned or administered by ©Universal Music Corp. (ASCAP) Used by permission.

Lady Day at Emerson's Bar & Grill
rehearsed at Pearl Studios, NYC.

❑ **CIRCLE IN THE SQUARE THEATRE**
Thespian Theatre, Inc.
Under the direction of Paul Libin
Susan Frankel, *General Manager*
House Manager ....Cheryl Dennis
Head Carpenter ....Anthony Menditto
Head Electrician ....Stewart Wagner
Prop Master ....Owen E. Parmele
Box Office Treasurer ....Jason C. Hudson
Assistant Treasurers ....Kathleen Drury, Sarah Shutt
Head Usher ....Georgia Keghlian
Ticket Taker ....Patricia Kennedy
Directress ....Sophie Koufakis
Assistant to Susan Frankel ....Tiffany Schleigh

❑ **CIRCLE IN THE SQUARE THEATRE SCHOOL**
President ....Paul Libin
Theatre School Director ....E. Colin O'Leary
Arts Education/Development ....Jonathan Mann
Assistant to the Director ....David Pleva
Student Affairs Coordinator ....Whitney Kaufman
Artistic Director 1961–2012 ....*Theodore Mann*

Government Support
New York State Council on the Arts
New York City Department of Cultural Affairs
New York State Office of Parks, Recreation
and Historic Preservation

Foundation Support
Stephen and Mary Birch Foundation
Akausa Foundation, Blanche and Irving Laurie Foundation, BWF Foundation, C. Daniel Chill Foundation, Frederick Loewe Foundation, Friars Foundation, Geraldine Stutz Foundation, Jerome Robbins Foundation, Kinder Morgan Foundation, Pat & Jay Baker Foundation, Ross Family Foundation, Slovin Foundation, Waldman Foundation, Yudelson Foundation

Patron Support
Ira Berkow, Allan Brooks, Robert Cole, Michael and Lauren David, John DiMenna, Frederick & Myrna Gershon, Jessica Jenen, Thomas Kelly, Christine and Alan Kemp, Kirmser Ponturo Group, Elizabeth McCann, Scott Mosberg, Daryl & Steven Roth, Marlene Serby, Joel Singer, Spring Sirkin, Vera Stern, Michael Vitulli, Lester Wohl, Anonymous (2)

Les Misérables

First Preview: March 1, 2014. Opened: March 23, 2014.
Still running as of May 31, 2014.

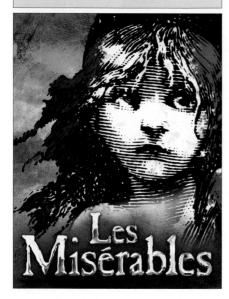

Revival of the 1987 Tony-winning musical based on Victor Hugo's epic novel about a fanatical police inspector who chases a runaway convict for decades through the underworld of 19th century France. Along the way the convict (Jean Valjean) pledges to protect and raise a motherless child. But the inspector (Javert) seems always to be waiting around the corner for him, even when Paris is plunged into revolution. They both learn lessons about humanity, mercy, forgiveness, sacrifice, and the realization that "To love another person is to see the face of God."

CAST

(in order of appearance)

Jean Valjean	RAMIN KARIMLOO
Javert	WILL SWENSON
Farmer	DENNIS MOENCH
Laborer	CHRIS McCARRELL
Innkeeper's Wife	CHRISTIANNE TISDALE
Innkeeper	ANDREW KOBER
The Bishop of Digne	ADAM MONLEY
Constables	NATHANIEL HACKMANN, ARBENDER J. ROBINSON
Factory Foreman	NATHANIEL HACKMANN
Fantine	CAISSIE LEVY
Factory Girl	BETSY MORGAN
Old Woman	EMILY CRAMER
Wigmaker	NATALIE CHARLE ELLIS
Bamatabois	JOHN RAPSON
Fauchelevent	CHRIS McCARRELL
Champmathieu	AARON WALPOLE

Continued on next page

Continued on next page

CAMERON MACKINTOSH
presents
THE NEW PRODUCTION OF BOUBLIL & SCHÖNBERG'S

A musical based on the novel by VICTOR HUGO

Music by CLAUDE-MICHEL SCHÖNBERG
Lyrics by HERBERT KRETZMER
Original French text by ALAIN BOUBLIL and JEAN-MARC NATEL

Additional material by JAMES FENTON
Adaptation by TREVOR NUNN and JOHN CAIRD

Original Orchestrations by JOHN CAMERON
New Orchestrations by CHRISTOPHER JAHNKE
STEPHEN METCALFE and STEPHEN BROOKER

Musical Supervisor	Associate Director	Musical Director
STEPHEN BROOKER	ANTHONY LYN	JAMES LOWE
Executive Producers	Casting by	General Management
NICHOLAS ALLOTT	TARA RUBIN CASTING, CSA	AARON LUSTBADER for
SETH SKLAR-HEYN		FORESIGHT THEATRICAL

Musical Staging by MICHAEL ASHCROFT and GEOFFREY GARRATT
Projections realized by FIFTY-NINE PRODUCTIONS
Sound by MICK POTTER

Lighting by PAULE CONSTABLE
Costume design by ANDREANE NEOFITOU and CHRISTINE ROWLAND
Set and Image Design by MATT KINLEY
inspired by the paintings of VICTOR HUGO

Directed by
LAURENCE CONNOR
and
JAMES POWELL

3/23/14

The cast of *Les Misérables* in the Act I closer, "One Day More."

Photo: Matthew Murphy

Les Misérables

SCENES AND MUSICAL NUMBERS

PROLOGUE: 1815, DIGNE

Prologue	The Company
"Soliloquy"	Valjean

1823, MONTREUIL-SUR-MER

"At the End of the Day"	Unemployed and Factory Workers
"I Dreamed a Dream"	Fantine
"Lovely Ladies"	Clients
"Who Am I?"	Valjean
"Fantine's Death"	Fantine and Valjean
"Castle on a Cloud"	Cosette

1823, MONTFERMEIL

"Master of the House"	Thénardier, his Wife and Customers
"The Bargain"	M. and Mme. Thénardier and Valjean

1832, PARIS

"Paris"	Gavroche and the Beggars
"Stars"	Javert
"ABC Café"	Enjolras, Marius and the Students
"The People's Song"	Enjolras, the Students and the Citizens
"In My Life"	Cosette, Valjean, Marius and Éponine
"A Heart Full of Love"	Cosette, Marius and Éponine
"One Day More"	The Company

INTERMISSION

"On My Own"	Éponine
"A Little Fall of Rain"	Éponine and Marius
"Drink With Me to Days Gone By"	Feuilly, Grantaire, Students and "Women"
"Bring Him Home"	Valjean
"Dog Eats Dog"	Thénardier
"Soliloquy"	Javert
"Turning"	Women
"Empty Chairs at Empty Tables"	Marius
"Wedding Chorale"	Guests
"Beggars at the Feast"	M. and Mme. Thénardier
Finale	The Company

Cast Continued

Little Cosette (Tues. Eve., Wed. Mat.,
Fri. Eve, Sat. Mat.) .... ANGELI NEGRON
(Wed., Thurs., Sat.,
Sun. Eves.) .... MCKAYLA TWIGGS
Madame Thénardier .... KEALA SETTLE
Young Éponine (Wed., Thurs., Sat.,
Sun. Eves.) .... ANGELI NEGRON
(Tues. Eve., Wed. Mat.,
Fri. Eve, Sat. Mat.) .... MCKAYLA TWIGGS
Thénardier .... CLIFF SAUNDERS
Gavroche (Tues. Eve., Wed. Mat.,
Fri. Eve, Sat. Mat.) .... JOSHUA COLLEY
(Wed., Thurs., Sat.,
Sun. Eves.) .... GATEN MATARAZZO
Éponine .... NIKKI M. JAMES
Cosette .... SAMANTHA HILL

Thénardier's Gang

Montparnasse .... ARBENDER J. ROBINSON
Babet .... ANDREW KOBER
Brujon .... AARON WALPOLE
Claquesous .... DENNIS MOENCH

Students

Enjolras .... KYLE SCATLIFFE
Marius .... ANDY MIENTUS
Combeferre .... ADAM MONLEY
Feuilly .... JASON FORBACH
Courfeyrac .... NATHANIEL HACKMANN
Joly .... CHRIS McCARRELL
Grantaire .... JOHN RAPSON
Lesgles .... TERANCE CEDRIC REDDICK
Jean Prouvaire .... MAX QUINLAN
Loud Hailer .... AARON WALPOLE
Major Domo .... JOHN RAPSON
Ensemble .... ERIN CLEMONS, EMILY CRAMER,
NATALIE CHARLE ELLIS, HEIDI GIBERSON,
MIA SINCLAIR JENNESS,
MELISSA MITCHELL, BETSY MORGAN,
MELISSA O'NEIL, CHRISTIANNE TISDALE

SWINGS

CATHRYN BASILE, JOHN BRINK,
BEN GUNDERSON,

WESTON WELLS OLSON,
RACHEL RINCIONE

DANCE CAPTAIN/FIGHT CAPTAIN

BEN GUNDERSON

UNDERSTUDIES

For Jean Valjean: NATHANIEL HACKMANN,
AARON WALPOLE
For Javert: NATHANIEL HACKMANN,
ADAM MONLEY
For Cosette: HEIDI GIBERSON,
MELISSA MITCHELL
For Fantine: BETSY MORGAN,
MELISSA O'NEIL
For Thénardier: DENNIS MOENCH,
JOHN RAPSON
For Madame Thénardier: EMILY CRAMER,
CHRISTIANNE TISDALE
For Éponine: ERIN CLEMONS,
MELISSA O'NEIL
For Marius: CHRIS McCARRELL,
ARBENDER J. ROBINSON
For Enjolras: JASON FORBACH,
MAX QUINLAN
For Little Cosette/Young Éponine:
MIA SINCLAIR JENNESS
For The Bishop of Digne: JOHN RAPSON,
TERANCE CEDRIC REDDICK
For Factory Foreman: ANDREW KOBER,
TERANCE CEDRIC REDDICK
For Factory Girl: NATALIE CHARLE ELLIS,
RACHEL RINCIONE
For Bamatabois: BEN GUNDERSON,
ANDREW KOBER
For Grantaire: BEN GUNDERSON,
DENNIS MOENCH

ORCHESTRA

Conductor: JAMES LOWE
Associate Conductor: MARK C. MITCHELL
Assistant Conductor: DANNY PERCEFULL
Reeds: KEITH BONNER, LYNNE COHEN,
PAVEL VINNITSKY
Trumpet/Flugelhorn: DAN URNESS
French Horns: CHRIS KOMER,
PATRICK PRIDEMORE
Bass Trombone/Tuba: JEFF NELSON
Violins: BELINDA WHITNEY (Concert Master),
KARL KAWAHARA
Violas: DAVID CRESWELL, WILL CURRY
Cello: LAURA BONTRAGER,
SUMMER BOGGESS
Bass: JEFFREY CARNEY
Percussion/Drums: WILSON TORRES
Keyboards: MARK C. MITCHELL,
DANNY PERCEFULL
Music Coordinator: JOHN MILLER

Les Misérables

Cathryn Basile
Swing

John Brink
Swing

Erin Clemons
Ensemble;
u/s Éponine

Joshua Colley
Gavroche

Emily Cramer
Old Woman; u/s
Madame Thénardier

Natalie Charle Ellis
Wigmaker;
u/s Factory Girl

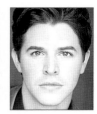
Jason Forbach
Feuilly; u/s Enjolras

Heidi Giberson
Ensemble;
u/s Cosette

Ben Gunderson
Swing, Dance
Captain, Fight
Captain;
u/s Bamatabois,
Grantaire

Nathaniel Hackmann
Constable, Foreman,
Courfeyrac; u/s Jean
Valjean, Javert

Samantha Hill
Cosette

Nikki M. James
Éponine

Mia Sinclair Jenness
Ensemble;
u/s Little Cosette,
Young Éponine

Ramin Karimloo
Jean Valjean

Andrew Kober
Innkeeper, Babet;
u/s Factory Foreman,
Bamatabois

Caissie Levy
Fantine

Gaten Matarazzo
Gavroche

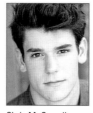
Chris McCarrell
Laborer,
Fauchelevent, Joly;
u/s Marius

Andy Mientus
Marius

Melissa Mitchell
Ensemble;
u/s Cosette

Dennis Moench
Farmer, Claquesous;
u/s Thénardier,
Grantaire

Adam Monley
Bishop of Digne,
Combeferre;
u/s Javert

Betsy Morgan
Factory Girl;
u/s Fantine

Angeli Negron
Little Cosette/
Young Éponine

Weston Wells Olson
Swing

Melissa O'Neil
Ensemble;
u/s Fantine, Éponine

Max Quinlan
Jean Prouvaire;
u/s Enjolras

John Rapson
Bamatabois,
Grantaire,
Major Domo;
u/s Thénardier,
Bishop of Digne

Terance Cedric
Reddick
Lesgles;
u/s Bishop of Digne,
Factory Foreman

Rachel Rincione
Swing;
u/s Factory Girl

Arbender J.
Robinson
Constable,
Montparnasse;
u/s Marius

Cliff Saunders
Thénardier

Kyle Scatliffe
Enjolras

Keala Settle
Madame Thénardier

Will Swenson
Javert

Les Misérables

Photo: Matthew Murphy

Ramin Karimloo
as Jean Valjean

Christianne Tisdale
Innkeeper's Wife; u/s Madame Thénardier

Mckayla Twiggs
Little Cosette/ Young Éponine

Aaron Walpole
Champmathieu, Brujon, Loud Hailer; u/s Jean Valjean

Alain Boublil
Book & Original French Text

James Fenton
Additional Material

Trevor Nunn
Adaptor

John Caird
Adaptor

Laurence Connor
Director

James Powell
Director

Matt Kinley
Set & Image Designer

Andreane Neofitou
Costume Designer

Paule Constabile
Lighting Designer

Mick Potter
Sound Designer

Michael Ashcroft
Musical Staging

Geoffrey Garratt
Musical Staging

James Lowe
Musical Director

Stephen Brooker
Musical Supervision, New Orchestrations

John Cameron
Original Orchestrations

Christopher Jahnke
New Orchestrations

Stephen Metcalfe
New Orchestrations

Jean-Marc Natel
Original French Text

Anthony Lyn
Associate Director

Campbell Young
Campbell Young Associates
Hair & Wig Designer

Luc Verschueren
Campbell Young Associates
Hair & Wig Designer

Tara Rubin
Tara Rubin Casting
Casting

Claude-Michel Schönberg
Book & Music

Cameron Mackintosh
Producer

Herbert Kretzmer
Lyrics

John Miller
Musical Coordinator

Alan Wasser
Foresight Theatrical
General Manager

Les Misérables

Allan Williams
Foresight Theatrical
General Manager

Aaron Lustbader
Foresight Theatrical
General Manager

Nicholas Allott
Executive Producer

Seth Sklar-Heyn
Executive Producer

Julie Benko
*Ensemble;
u/s Cosette*

Photos: Jeremy Daniel

HAIR
Front (L-R): Amber Morrow (Assistant Hair Supervisor),
Susan Corrado (Hair Supervisor)
Back (L-R): Sarah Levine, Troy Beard

STAGE MANAGEMENT
(L-R): Mary Kathryn Flynt (Stage Manager), Trinity Wheeler (Production Stage Manager),
Davin De Santis (Assistant Stage Manager)

COMPANY MANAGEMENT
Laura Eichholz (Associate Company Manager) Cosette LeBoeuf (Intern),
Dave Ehle (Company Manager)

BOX OFFICE
Jennifer Holze

WARDROBE
Front (L-R): Libby "Cookiepuss" Villanova,
Helen Toth (Associate Costume Designer/
Wardrobe Supervisor),
Steve Epstein (Dresser)
Back (L-R): Heather Conlin Torres,
Kim Kaldenberg,
Steve Chazaro Medina (Dresser),
Marisa Tchornobai,
Sandy Wilding (Dresser)

Les Misérables

Photo: Jeremy Daniel

CREW
Front (L-R): Dominick Intagliato, Heidi Brown (House Properties), Patrick Johnston (Head Electrician)
Middle (L-R): Kevin Clifford, Keala Settle (actor), Dave Fulton, Edward De Jesus (Assistant Properties), Jane Masterson, Justin Sanok, Tim Altman, Chad Woerner (Head Carpenter), Anthony Ferrer, Max Mooney
Back (L-R): Daniel Mueller (Assistant Electrician), Alex Brandwine (Assistant Carpenter), Walter Bullard (House Carpenter), Scott Butler (Assistant Electrician), Mike Hermges

STAFF FOR *LES MISÉRABLES*

GENERAL MANAGER
FORESIGHT THEATRICAL
Aaron Lustbader Alan Wasser
Allan Williams Mark Shacket
Mark Barna

COMPANY MANAGER
Dave Ehle
Associate Company Manager
Laura Eichholz

GENERAL PRESS REPRESENTATIVE
THE PUBLICITY OFFICE
Marc Thibodeau Michael S. Borowski
Jeremy Shaffer

MARKETING
TYPE A MARKETING
Elyce Henkin John McCoy Erica Jacobson

CASTING
TARA RUBIN CASTING
Tara Rubin CSA, Eric Woodall CSA
Merri Sugarman CSA, Kaitlin Shaw CSA
Lindsay Levine CSA, Scott Anderson

PRODUCTION MANAGER
Kevin Broomell

Production Stage Manager ....TRINITY WHEELER
Stage Manager ....Mary Kathryn Flynt
Assistant Stage Manager ....Davin De Santis
Fight Director ....Joe Bostick
Dance Captain/Fight Captain ....Ben Gunderson
Hair & Wig Designer..........Campbell Young Associates/
                                                    Luc Verschueren
Associate Scenic Designer ....Christine Peters
Associate Costume Designer ....Helen Toth
UK Associate Costume Designer.......Roxanne Armstrong
UK Costume Coordinator ....Nicole Smith
Assistant Costume Designer ....Travis Chinick
Associate Lighting Designer ....Karen Spahn
Associate Sound Designer ....Adam Fisher
Associate Hair & Wig Designer ....Susan Corrado
Associate Production Manager ....Ana Rose Greene
Lighting Programmer ....Tommy Hague
Keyboard Programmer ....Stuart Andrews
Projection Programmer ....Jonathan Lyle
UK Production Manager ....Chris Boone
Production Carpenter ....Jack Anderson
Head Carpenter ....Chad Woerner
Assistant Carpenter ....Alex Brandwine
Advance Carpenters ...Scott "Gus" Poitras, Matthew Lynch

House Carpenter ....Walter Bullard
Production Electricians .....James Fedigan, Randall Zaibek
Head Electrician ....Patrick Johnston
Assistant Electricians ....Scott Butler, Daniel Mueller
House Electrician ....Manny Diaz
Production Properties Supervisors ....Meghan Abel,
                                                    Timothy M. Abel
Head Properties ....Jerry Marshall
Assistant Properties ....Edward De Jesus
House Properties ....Heidi Brown
Production Sound Engineer ....Colle T. Bustin
Head Sound Engineer ....George Huckins
Assistant Sound Engineer ....Scott Anderson
Wardrobe Supervisor ....Helen Toth
Assistant Wardrobe Supervisor ......Abbey Rayburn Hirons
Dressers ....Steve Epstein, Maya Hardin, Carly Hirschberg,
        Lyle Jones, Steve Chazaro Medina, Jen Molloy,
                        Tom Reiter, Sandra Wilding
Hair Supervisor ....Susan Corrado
Assistant Hair Supervisor ....Amber Morrow
Hairstylists........................Troy Beard, Sarah Levine
General Management Associates ...Steve Greer, Lane Marsh
General Management Office ....Rob Abud, Kaitlin Boland,
        Stefano Fuchs, Nina Greene, Jennifer O'Connor
Production Assistants ....Michael Ulreich,
        Tom Kordenbrock, Sean Devine, Michael Tosto

Les Misérables

ORCHESTRA

Front (L-R): Wilson Torres (Percussion), David Creswell (Viola), Pavel Vinnitsky (Clarinet/Bass Clarinet/Recorder), Chris Komer (French Horn), James Lowe (Musical Director/Conductor), Karl Kawahara (Violin), Jeff Nelson (Bass Trombone/Tuba)
Back (L-R): Stuart Andrews (Keyboard Programmer), Jeffrey Carney (Bass), Lynne Cohen (Oboe/English Horn), Keith Bonner (Flute/Piccolo/Recorder), Will Curry (Viola), Belinda Whitney (Violin/Concertmaster), John Miller (Music Coordinator), Stephen Brooker (Musical Supervision/New Orchestrations), Laura Bontrager (Cello), Patrick Pridemore (French Horn), Summer Boggess (Cello), Stephen Metcalfe (New Orchestrations), Dan Urness (Trumpet/Flugelhorn), Mark C. Mitchell (Associate Conductor/Keyboard), Danny Percefull (Assistant Conductor/Keyboard)

Child Guardian .... Jill A. Valentine
Music Coordinator .... John Miller
Assistant to John Miller .... Nichole Jennino
Rehearsal Pianist .... Eric Ebbenga
Advertising .... Serino/Coyne/Nancy Coyne,
  Greg Corradetti, Tom Callahan, Vinny Sainato,
  Marci Kaufman Meyers, Sarah Marcus,
  Bobby Lima, Doug Ensign, Adina Levin
Website & Interactive Marketing .... Serino/Coyne/
  Jim Glaub, Whitney Creighton,
  Crystal Chase, Brian DeVito, Kevin Keating
Canadian Casting .... Stephanie Gorin
Legal Counsel .... F. Richard Pappas
Accounting .... Marks Paneth & Shron/
  Christopher Cacace, Ruthie Skochil
Tutoring .... On Location Education
Insurance .... DeWitt Stern/
  Peter K. Shoemaker, Cathy Dumancela
Banking .... Signature Banking/Barbara von Borstel,
  Margaret Monigan, Mary Ann Fanelli
Payroll .... Checks and Balances Payroll, Inc./
  Sarah Galbraith, Anthony Walker
Merchandising .... Platypus Productions, LLC
Opening Night Coordination .... Jhada Productions
Travel .... Road Rebel Travel and Touring
Housing .... ABA/IDEAL/Elizabeth Helke
Theatre Displays .... King Displays
Production Photographers .... Michael Le Poer Trench,
  Matthew Murphy

Town at Dusk, Landscape with Three Trees, Planets and *My Destiny* by Victor Hugo courtesy of the Maison de Victor Hugo, Paris, and the Bridgeman Art Library.

Graphics designed by Dewynters Plc, London.

CREDITS AND ACKNOWLEDGEMENTS

Scenery fabrication and automation by Scenic Technologies, a division of Production Resource Group, LLC, New Windsor, NY, and F&D Scene Changes, Calgary, Alberta,
Canada. Additional scenic painting by Scenic Arts Studios, Newburgh, NY. Lighting equipment provided by PRG, Secaucus, NJ. Sound equipment provided by Sound Associates, Yonkers, NY. Video projection system engineered and provided by WorldStage, New York, NY. Softgoods provided by I. Weiss and Sons Inc., Fairview, NJ. Hauling by Clark Transfer, Inc., Harrisburg, PA. Costume construction by Seamless Costumes, Emma Jealouse, Kate Allen, Keith Watson, Phil Reynolds, David Plunkett, Demitakus Shirtmakers, Jenny Aidey, Sean Barett, Gamba, Nicola Kleen, Jeff Fender and Claudia Diaz. Undergarments and hosiery by Bra*Tenders. Shoes by T.O. Dey. Wigs made by Campbell Young Associates.

SPECIAL THANKS

Bumble and Bumble, William Dailey,
Juniper Street Productions, Ricola and John Ward.

The producers wish to thank Fred Hanson for his contribution to the development of this new 25th anniversary production.

FOR CAMERON MACKINTOSH, LTD.

Directors .... Cameron Mackintosh (Chairman)
  Nicholas Allott (Chief Executive)
  Richard Johnston
Deputy Managing Director .... Robert Noble
Financial Controller .... Richard Knibb
Executive Producer and Casting Director ... Trevor Jackson
Executive Producer .... Thomas Schönberg
Technical Director .... Jerry Donaldson
Production Manager .... Chris Boone
Head of Marketing .... David Dolman
Assistant to Cameron Mackintosh .... Jane Austin
Assistant to Nicholas Allott .... Claire Mistry
Assistant to Robert Noble .... Helen Lloyd

FOR CAMERON MACKINTOSH, INC.

Managing Director .... Nicholas Allott
Executive Producer .... Seth Sklar-Heyn

Production Associate .... Shidan Majidi

STOCK AND AMATEUR RIGHTS

exclusively represented by Music Theatre International, NY

Rehearsed at Gibney Dance Studios/890 Broadway

www.LesMiz.com
Facebook, Twitter, YouTube, Instagram: LesMizBway

THE SHUBERT ORGANIZATION, INC.
Board of Directors

Chief Financial Officer .... Elliot Greene
Sr. Vice President, Ticketing .... David Andrews
Vice President, Finance .... Juan Calvo
Vice President, Human Resources .... Cathy Cozens
Vice President, Facilities .... John Darby
Vice President, Theatre Operations .... Peter Entin
Vice President, Marketing .... Charles Flateman
Vice President, General Counsel .... Gilbert Hoover
Vice President, Audit .... Anthony LaMattina
Vice President, Ticket Sales .... Brian Mahoney
Vice President, Creative Projects .... D.S. Moynihan
Vice President, Real Estate .... Julio Peterson

House Manager .... Joann Swanson

 The Shubert Organization is a proud member of the Broadway Green Alliance.

Let It Be: A Celebration of the Music of the Beatles

First Preview: July 16, 2013. Opened: July 24, 2013.
Limited Engagement. Closed September 1, 2013 after 10 Previews and 46 Performances.

More of a concert than a revue, this show uses a rotating roster of performers to recreate the sound and look of the rock group the Beatles. Backed by projections and film clips from the 1960s, the band plays several dozen of the Beatles' greatest hits, arranged to sound as exactly like the original recordings as possible.

MUSICIANS

GRAHAM ALEXANDER
JOHN BROSNAN
RYAN COATH
JAMES FOX
REUVEN GERSHON
CHRIS McBURNEY
LUKE ROBERTS
RYAN ALEX FARMERY
JOHN KORBA
DANIEL A. WEISS

ST. JAMES THEATRE
A JUJAMCYN THEATRE

JORDAN ROTH, *President*
ROCCO LANDESMAN, *President Emeritus*
PAUL LIBIN, *Executive Vice President* JACK VIERTEL, *Senior Vice President*

Annerin Productions   Yasuhiro Kawana   BB Promotion   Rubin Fogel

AND

Jujamcyn Theaters

PRESENT

LET IT BE

A CELEBRATION *OF THE* MUSIC *OF* THE BEATLES

Graham Alexander   John Brosnan   Ryan Coath   James Fox
Reuven Gershon   Chris McBurney   Luke Roberts

Ryan Alex Farmery   John Korba   Daniel A. Weiss

SET DESIGNER Tim McQuillen-Wright	US LIGHTING DESIGNER Jason Lyons	SOUND DESIGNER Gareth Owen
VIDEO DESIGNER Duncan McLean	ORIGINAL VIDEO DESIGNS Darren McCaulley & Mathieu St. Arnaud	COSTUME SUPERVISOR Jack Galloway
PRODUCTION & CREATIVE DIRECTOR Scott Christensen	TECHNICAL SUPERVISORS Arthur Siccardi Pat Sullivan	PRODUCTION STAGE MANAGER Bonnie L. Becker
PRESS & PR The Hartman Group	ADVERTISING & MARKETING AKA GENERAL MANAGEMENT Bespoke Theatricals	UK GENERAL MANAGEMENT Jamie Hendry Productions

MUSICAL SUPERVISOR & US DIRECTOR
John Maher

THIS PRODUCTION IS NOT ENDORSED BY APPLE CORPS LIMITED, OR THE BEATLES.

7/24/13

Meet the Beatles (L-R): James Fox, John Brosnan, Luke Roberts, Reuven Gershon

Photo: Chad Batka

Let It Be: A Celebration of the Music of the Beatles

Graham Alexander
Musician

John Brosnan
Musician

Ryan Coath
Musician

James Fox
Musician

Reuven Gershon
Musician

Chris McBurney
Musician

Luke Roberts
Musician

Ryan Alex Farmery
Musician

John Korba
Musician

Daniel A. Weiss
Musician

John Maher
Musical Supervisor & U.S. Director

Tom McQuillen-Wright
Scenic Designer

Jason Lyons
Lighting Designer

Gareth Owen
Sound Designer

Duncan McLean
Video Designer

Arthur Siccardi
Arthur Siccardi Theatrical Services
Production Supervision

Maggie Brohn
Bespoke Theatricals
General Management

Amy Jacobs
Bespoke Theatricals
General Management

Devin Keudell
Bespoke Theatricals
General Management

Nina Lannan
Bespoke Theatricals
General Management

Jamie Hendry
Jamie Hendry Productions
U.K. General Management

Jeff Parry
Annerin Productions
Producer

Yasuhiro Kawana
Producer

Rubin Fogel
Producer

Jordan Roth
Jujamcyn Theaters
Producer

TRANSFER STUDENTS 2013-2014

Roberto Angelelli
Musician

Jimmy Coburn
Musician

Tony Coburn
Musician

JT Curtis
Musician

Tyson Kelly
Musician

BOX OFFICE
(L-R): Vincent Siniscalchi,
Kate Fearon,
Vincent Sclafani

Let It Be: A Celebration of the Music of the Beatles

Photos: Courtesy of the production

FRONT OF HOUSE
Front Row (L-R):
Kris Kaye, Tegan McDuffie,
Andrew Mackay,
Donna Vanderlinden,
Francisco Medina (Porter)
Back Row (L-R):
Ryan Turner, Barbara Kagan,
Leslie Morgenstern,
Lenny Baron,
Cynthia Lopiano (Head Usher),
Rochelle Rogers, Heather Jewels,
Brian Veith, Jim Barry,
Kaiser Akram, Brian Pelaccio,
Donnette Niles (Porter)

CREW
Front Row (L-R): Susan Pelkofer (Electrician), Bob Miller (Electrician), Emile LaFargue (Electrician), Steve Gough, Bonnie L. Becker (Production Stage Manager), Dawn Marcoccia (Wardrobe Supervisor)
Back Row (L-R): Nick Keslake, JD Frizsell, Mark Kane, Ryan McDonough (Flyman), Jason Muldrow, Timothy M. McDonough (Head Propertyman), Kevin Hurdman, Timothy B. McDonough (Head Carpenter), Mike Wojchik, Carol M. Oune, Richard Fabris (Hair Supervisor)

STAFF FOR *LET IT BE*

ANNERIN PRODUCTIONS

Producer ....Jeff Parry
Chief Operating Officer ....Ralph Schmidtke
Chief Financial Officer ....Stuart Peterson
Production & Creative Director ....Scott Christensen
Assistant Financial Controller ....Candace Fairbairn
Technical Production Coordinator ....Dwayne Olde
Production Assistant ....Steve Wirzba
Marketing ....Laura Hristow

GENERAL MANAGEMENT
BESPOKE THEATRICALS
Amy Jacobs   Nina Lannan
Maggie Brohn   Devin Keudell

COMPANY MANAGER
Carol M. Oune

GENERAL PRESS REPRESENTATIVE
THE HARTMAN GROUP
Michael Hartman   Matt Ross
Nicole Capatasto

Production Stage Manager ....Bonnie L. Becker
US Associate Sound Designer ....Joanna Lynne Staub
UK Sound Engineer ....Olly Steel
Moving Light Programmer ....Tim Rogers
Video Programmer ....Christopher Herman
Production Electricians......................James Fedigan,
                                              Michael Brown
Head Electrician ....Alan Shuster
Video Operator ....Brandon Epperson
US Sound Engineers ....Craig Van Tassel,
                                              Michael Wojchik
Backline Tech ....Kevin Hurdman,
                                           Eric Kaczmarczyk
Wardrobe Supervisor ....Dawn Marcoccia
Dresser ....Renee Borys
Hair Supervisor ....Richard Fabris
Advertising/Marketing/Digital ....AKA/Scott A. Moore,
      Elizabeth Furze, Bashan Aquart, Joshua Lee Poole,
      Erik Alden, Pippa Bexon, Adam Jay, Tomris Laffly,
          Jacob Matsumiya, Flora Pei, Janette Roush
Web Design/Maintenance ....AKA
Press Associates .Tom D'Ambrosio, Whitney Holden Gore,
      Bethany Larsen, Emily McGill, Colgan McNeil,
        Leslie Papa, Frances White, Wayne Wolfe

Legal Counsel ....Davis Wright Tremain LLP/
                      M. Graham Coleman, Andrew Owens
Immigration Legal
    Counsel ....Entertainment Visa Consultants LLC
Accountant ....FK Partners/Robert Fried
Controller ....Galbraith & Co./Kenneth Noth
Banking ....City National Bank/Michele Gibbons
Insurance ... Aon/Albert G. Ruben Insurance Services, Inc.
Payroll Services ......Checks and Balances/Anthony Walker
Travel Agent.....................Tzell Travel/The "A" Team
Housing Services ....Road Concierge,
                  An ALTOUR Company/Lisa Morris
Merchandising ....Encore Merchandising/Joey Boyles
Associate General Managers ....Steve Dow,
                      David Roth, Danielle Saks
General Management Office Manager ....Jimmy Wilson
General Management Interns ...Alex Hajjar, Reeve Pierson

CREDITS
Scenery built by Great Lakes Scenic Studios. Lighting by Christie Lighting. Sound and video equipment by Sound Associates. Special thanks to Gibson brands.

Let It Be: A Celebration of the Music of the Beatles
SCRAPBOOK

Curtain call at the premiere (L-R): Reuven Gershon, James Fox, John Brosnan, Luke Roberts and Ryan Alex Farmery. This was the opening night cast; twelve performers rotated in and out of the four main roles at different performances.

Correspondent: Chris McBurney, "Ringo"

Opening Night Party: We had a blast partying at the Glass House Tavern on opening night. I got there late and was immediately shoved into the press line before I could catch my breath. It was a bit of a whirlwind, but we all had so much fun with the press and drank into the wee hours of the night.

Special Backstage Rituals: Fist-bumps on stage before the curtain rises.

Favorite Moment During Each Performance: Playing the encore. Everyone in the house is on their feet, waving their arms and singing at the top of their lungs: Nah Nah Nah Nah-Nah-Nah-Nah!!! "Hey Jude" is such an iconic and anthemic song. It moves so many people. It's pretty powerful stuff.

Favorite In-Theatre Gathering Place: No one really hangs in the greenroom too much. I'd say either the quick-change room or my dressing room.

Most Memorable Audience Reaction: Two ladies in the box seats screaming, "We love Ringo!"

Favorite Off-Site Hangout: O'Flaherty's Ale House and the Market Diner.

Favorite Snack Foods: Twizzlers and Zone Bars.

Favorite Therapy: Acupuncture and Icy Hot.

Memorable Ad-Lib: JT throwing in George's line from *A Hard Day's Night,* "I'd be quite prepared for that eventuality."

Memorable Press Encounter: Entertainment Tonight stopped by to do a piece on their OMG! segment. We did a lot of horsing around, of which most was wisely edited out.

Memorable Stage Door Fan Encounter: A group of young teens all obsessed by the Beatles. One girl couldn't stop crying because she was so moved. I think she actually thought we were the Beatles. It was a tad creepy.

Fastest Costume Change: Getting out of the Shea Stadium costume and into the Sgt. Pepper costume, changing my hairstyle, gluing on sideburns and moustache and penciling in a soul patch.

Sweethearts Within the Company: Bonnie Becker... best Production Stage Manager in the biz.

Embarrassing Moment: My moustache starting to fall off while singing "With a Little Help From My Friends."

Best In-House Parody Lyric: "My independence seems to vanish Isaac Hayes," from the song "Help."

Coolest Thing About Being in This Show: Getting to play some of the best music in the world for many different generations of Beatles fans.

JUJAMCYN THEATERS

JORDAN ROTH
President

ROCCO LANDESMAN
President Emeritus

PAUL LIBIN
Executive Vice President

JACK VIERTEL
Senior Vice President

MEREDITH VILLATORE
Chief Financial Officer

JENNIFER HERSHEY
Vice President,
Building Operations

MICAH HOLLINGWORTH
Vice President,
Company Operations

HAL GOLDBERG
Vice President,
Theatre Operations

Director of Business Affairs . . . . Albert T. Kim
Director of Ticketing Services . . . . Justin Karr
Theatre Operations Managers . . . . Willa Burke, Susan Elrod, Emily Hare, Jeff Hubbard, Albert T. Kim
Theatre Operations Associates . . . . Carrie Jo Brinker, Brian Busby, Michael Composto, Anah Jyoti Klate
Controller . . . . Tejal Patel
Accounting . . . . Cathy Cerge, Amy Frank, Tariq Hamami, Alexander Parra

Executive Producer, Red Awning . . . . Nicole Kastrinos
Director of Sales, Givenik.com . . . . Karen Freidus
Building Operations Associate . . . . Erich Bussing
Executive Coordinator . . . . Ed Lefferson
Executive Assistants . . . . Hunter Chancellor, Beth Given
Receptionist . . . . Lisa Perchinske
Ticketing and Pricing Associate . . . . Jonathon Scott
Sales Associate Givenik.com . . . . Taylor Kurpiel
Maintenance . . . . Ralph Santos, Ramon Zapata
Security . . . . Rasim Hodzic, Terone Richardson
Interns . . . . Christina Boursiquot, Brittany Clark, Pierre Crosby, Morgan Hoit, Kristen Morale, Danielle DeMatteo, Henry Tisch

---

Staff for the St. James Theatre for
Let It Be

Manager . . . . Jeff Hubbard
Associate Manager . . . . Brian Busby
Treasurer . . . . Vincent Sclafani
Head Carpenter . . . . Timothy B. McDonough
Head Propertyman . . . . Timothy M. McDonough
Head Electrician . . . . Albert Sayers
Flyman . . . . Ryan McDonough
Engineer . . . . Zaim Hodzic

Assistant Treasurers . . . . Michael Loiacono, Vincent Siniscalchi
Electricians . . . . Paul Coltoff, Emile LaFargue, Bob Miller, Susan Pelkofer
Head Usher . . . . Cynthia Lopiano
Ticket-takers/Directors/Ushers . . . . Leonard Baron, Jim Barry, Murray Bradley, Barbara Carroll, Caroline Choi, Heather Jewels, Barbara Kagan, Andrew Mackay, Margaret McElroy, Leslie Morgenstern, Rochelle Rogers, Rebecca Segarra, Jessica Theisen, Donna Vanderlinden
Doormen . . . . Russell Buenteo, Adam Hodzic
Head Porter . . . . Jacobo Medrano
Porters . . . . Tareq Brown, Francisco Medina, Donnette Niles
Head Cleaner . . . . Carmela Tenebruso
Cleaners . . . . Benita Aliberti, Juana Medrano, Antonia Moreno

Lobby refreshments by Sweet Hospitality Group.

Security provided by GBA Consulting, Inc.

 BROADWAY green alliance · Jujamcyn Theaters is a proud member of the Broadway Green Alliance.

The Lion King

First Preview: October 15, 1997. Opened: November 13, 1997.
Still running as of May 31, 2014.

PLAYBILL®

THE LION KING

When the evil lion Scar kills his brother, King Mufasa, and seizes the throne of the African Pridelands, young Prince Simba flees into the wilderness. There he is transformed by some new friends and finally returns to reclaim his crown. Performed by actors in puppetlike costumes designed by director Julie Taymor.

CAST
(in order of appearance)

Rafiki .... TSHIDI MANYE
Mufasa .... ALTON FITZGERALD WHITE
Sarabi .... CHONDRA LA-TEASE PROFIT
Zazu .... JEFFREY KUHN
Scar .... GARETH SAXE
Young Simba (Tues., Fri.,
   Sat. Eve., Sun. Eve.) .... DEREK JOHNSON
   (Wed., Thurs., Sat.
   Mat., Sun. Mat.) .... CALEB McLAUGHLIN
Young Nala
   (Tues., Fri., Sat.
   Mat., Sun. Mat.) .... BOBBI BORDLEY
   (Wed., Thurs., Sat.
   Eve., Sun. Eve.) .... TESHI THOMAS
Shenzi .... BONITA J. HAMILTON
Banzai .... JAMES BROWN-ORLEANS
Ed .... ENRIQUE SEGURA
Timon .... FRED BERMAN
Pumbaa .... BEN JEFFREY
Simba .... AARON NELSON
Nala .... CHANTEL RILEY
Ensemble Singers .... DERRICK DAVIS,
    LINDIWE DLAMINI, BONGI DUMA,

Continued on next page

MINSKOFF THEATRE
UNDER THE DIRECTION OF
JAMES M. NEDERLANDER, JAMES L. NEDERLANDER,
SARA MINSKOFF ALLAN AND THE MINSKOFF FAMILY

Disney
PRESENTS

THE LION KING

Music & Lyrics by
ELTON JOHN & TIM RICE

Additional Music & Lyrics by
LEBO M, MARK MANCINA, JAY RIFKIN, JULIE TAYMOR, HANS ZIMMER

Book by
ROGER ALLERS & IRENE MECCHI

Starring

GARETH SAXE   ALTON FITZGERALD WHITE   TSHIDI MANYE
JEFFREY KUHN   BEN JEFFREY   FRED BERMAN
AARON NELSON   CHANTEL RILEY
JAMES BROWN-ORLEANS   BONITA J. HAMILTON   ENRIQUE SEGURA
BOBBI BORDLEY   DEREK JOHNSON   CALEB McLAUGHLIN   TESHI THOMAS

LAWRENCE ALEXANDER LaMAR BAYLOR ELISHAH BOWMAN DERRICK DAVIS LINDIWE DLAMINI
BONGI DUMA ANGELICA EDWARDS JIM FERRIS CHRISTOPHER FREEMAN MUKELISIWE GOBA DEIDREA HALLEY
PIA HAMILTON JAMAL LEE HARRIS LINDSEY HOLMES KENNY INGRAM JOEL KARIE RON KUNENE
LISA LEWIS MDUDUZI MADELA JAYSIN McCOLLUM RAY MERCER KYLE LAMAR MITCHELL
WILLIA-NOEL MONTAGUE S'BU NGEMA SINDISIWE NXUMALO CHONDRA La-TEASE PROFIT JACQUELINE RENÉ
KELLEN STANCIL JEREMIAH TATUM THULISILE THUSI TORYA DONNA MICHELLE VAUGHN
THOM CHRISTOPHER WARREN REMA WEBB ALAN WIGGINS CAMILLE WORKMAN

Adapted from the screenplay by
IRENE MECCHI & JONATHAN ROBERTS & LINDA WOOLVERTON

Produced by
PETER SCHNEIDER & THOMAS SCHUMACHER

Scenic Design	*Costume Design*	*Lighting Design*	*Mask & Puppet Design*
RICHARD HUDSON	JULIE TAYMOR	DONALD HOLDER	JULIE TAYMOR & MICHAEL CURRY

Sound Design	*Hair & Makeup Design*	*Associate Director*	*Associate Choreographer*
STEVE CANYON KENNEDY	MICHAEL WARD	JOHN STEFANIUK	MAREY GRIFFITH

Associate Producer	*Technical Director*	*Production Stage Manager*	*Production Supervisor*
ANNE QUART	DAVID BENKEN	RON VODICKA	DOC ZORTHIAN

Music Supervisor	*Music Director*	*Associate Music Producer*	*Music Coordinator*	*Orchestrators*
CLEMENT ISHMAEL	KARL JURMAN	ROBERT ELHAI	MICHAEL KELLER	ROBERT ELHAI DAVID METZGER BRUCE FOWLER

Music Produced for the Stage & Additional Score by	*Additional Vocal Score, Vocal Arrangements & Choral Director*	*Casting*	*Fight Director*
MARK MANCINA	LEBO M	BINDER CASTING/ MARK BRANDON, C.S.A.	RICK SORDELET

Choreography by
GARTH FAGAN

Directed by
JULIE TAYMOR

Disney ON BROADWAY

©Disney

10/1/13

Photo: Joan Marcus

The animals gather at Pride Rock for "The Circle of Life."

The Lion King

SCENES AND MUSICAL NUMBERS

ACT I

Scene 1	Pride Rock	
	"Circle of Life" with "Nants' Ingonyama" …………………………Rafiki, Ensemble	
Scene 2	Scar's Cave	
Scene 3	Rafiki's Tree	
Scene 4	The Pridelands	
Scene 5	Scar's Cave	
Scene 6	The Pridelands	
	"I Just Can't Wait to Be King" ……………Young Simba, Young Nala, Zazu, Ensemble	
Scene 7	Elephant Graveyard	
	"Chow Down" ………………………………………………Shenzi, Banzai, Ed	
Scene 8	Under the Stars	
	"They Live in You" ………………………………………………Mufasa, Ensemble	
Scene 9	Elephant Graveyard	
	"Be Prepared" ………………………………Scar, Shenzi, Banzai, Ed, Ensemble	
Scene 10	The Gorge	
Scene 11	Pride Rock	
	"Be Prepared" (Reprise) ………………………………………Scar, Ensemble	
	"Nao Tse Tsa" ………………………………Rafiki, Sarabi, Young Nala	
Scene 12	Rafiki's Tree	
Scene 13	The Desert/The Jungle	
	"Hakuna Matata"………………Timon, Pumbaa, Young Simba, Simba, Ensemble	

ACT II

Entr'acte	"One by One" ………………………………………………………Ensemble	
Scene 1	Scar's Cave	
	"The Madness of King Scar" …………………Scar, Zazu, Banzai, Shenzi, Ed, Nala	
Scene 2	The Pridelands	
	"Shadowland" ………………………………………Nala, Rafiki, Ensemble	
Scene 3	The Jungle	
Scene 4	Under the Stars	
	"Endless Night" ………………………………………………Simba, Ensemble	
Scene 5	Rafiki's Tree	
Scene 6	The Jungle	
	"Can You Feel the Love Tonight" ………………Timon, Pumbaa, Simba, Nala, Ensemble	
	"He Lives in You" (Reprise) …………………………………Rafiki, Simba, Ensemble	
Scene 7	Pride Rock	
	"King of Pride Rock"/"Circle of Life" (Reprise) …………………………Ensemble	

SONG CREDITS

All songs by Elton John (music) and Tim Rice (lyrics) except as follows:

"Circle of Life" by Elton John (music) and Tim Rice (lyrics)
with "Nants' Ingonyama" by Hans Zimmer and Lebo M
"He Lives in You" ("They Live in You"): Music and lyrics by Mark Mancina, Jay Rifkin, and Lebo M
"Nao Tse Tsa": Music and lyrics by Jacques Loubelo
"One by One": Music and lyrics by Lebo M
"Shadowland": Music by Lebo M and Hans Zimmer, lyrics by Mark Mancina and Lebo M
"Endless Night": Music by Lebo M, Hans Zimmer, and Jay Rifkin, lyrics by Julie Taymor
"King of Pride Rock": Music by Hans Zimmer, lyrics by Lebo M.

ADDITIONAL SCORE

Grasslands chant and Lioness chant by Lebo M
Rafiki's chants by Tsidii Le Loka

Cast Continued

MUKELISIWE GOBA, JAMAL LEE HARRIS,
JOEL KARIE, RON KUNENE,
MDUDUZI MADELA, S'BU NGEMA,
SINDISIWE NXUMALO,
CHONDRA LA-TEASE PROFIT,
THULISILE THUSI, REMA WEBB
Ensemble Dancers ….LAWRENCE ALEXANDER,
LaMAR BAYLOR, ELISHAH BOWMAN,
CHRISTOPHER FREEMAN, PIA HAMILTON,
LINDSEY HOLMES, LISA LEWIS,
JAYSIN McCOLLUM, RAY MERCER, TORYA,
DONNA MICHELLE VAUGHN,
CAMILLE WORKMAN

UNDERSTUDIES

Rafiki: ANGELICA EDWARDS,
  MUKELISIWE GOBA, THULISILE THUSI,
  REMA WEBB
Mufasa: DERRICK DAVIS, JAMAL LEE HARRIS
Sarabi: SINDISIWE NXUMALO,
  JACQUELINE RENÉ, REMA WEBB
Zazu: JIM FERRIS, ENRIQUE SEGURA,
  THOM CHRISTOPHER WARREN
Scar: DERRICK DAVIS,
  THOM CHRISTOPHER WARREN
Shenzi: ANGELICA EDWARDS
Banzai: KENNY INGRAM, JOEL KARIE,
  MDUDUZI MADELA
Ed: KENNY INGRAM, JAYSIN McCOLLUM
Timon: JIM FERRIS, ENRIQUE SEGURA
Pumbaa: JIM FERRIS,
  THOM CHRISTOPHER WARREN
Simba: JOEL KARIE, MDUDUZI MADELA,
  ALAN WIGGINS
Nala: SINDISIWE NXUMALO,
  CHONDRA LA-TEASE PROFIT,
  JACQUELINE RENÉ, REMA WEBB

SWINGS

ANGELICA EDWARDS, DEIDREA HALLEY,
KENNY INGRAM, KYLE LAMAR MITCHELL,
WILLIA-NOEL MONTAGUE,
JACQUELINE RENÉ, KELLEN STANCIL,
JEREMIAH TATUM, ALAN WIGGINS

DANCE CAPTAINS

WILLIA-NOEL MONTAGUE,
  KELLEN STANCIL

SPECIALTIES

Circle of Life Vocals: MDUDUZI MADELA,
  S'BU NGEMA
Mouse Shadow Puppet: JOEL KARIE
Ant Hill Lady: DONNA MICHELLE VAUGHN
Guinea Fowl: LAWRENCE ALEXANDER
Buzzard Pole: CHRISTOPHER FREEMAN
Gazelle Wheel: PIA HAMILTON

The Lion King

Gazelle: JAYSIN McCOLLUM
Lioness Chant Vocal: S'BU NGEMA
Acrobatic Trickster: RAY MERCER
Stilt Giraffe Cross: ELISHAH BOWMAN
Giraffe Shadow Puppets: MDUDUZI MADELA,
    JAYSIN McCOLLUM
Cheetah: LISA LEWIS
Scar Shadow Puppets: LAWRENCE ALEXANDER,
    MDUDUZI MADELA, JAYSIN McCOLLUM
Simba Shadow Puppets: LaMAR BAYLOR,
    CHRISTOPHER FREEMAN, RAY MERCER
One by One Vocal: BONGI DUMA,
    SINDISIWE NXUMALO
One by One Dance: BONGI DUMA,
    RON KUNENE, S'BU NGEMA
Fireflies: LINDSEY HOLMES
Pumbaa Pole Puppet: MDUDUZI MADELA
Nala Pole Puppet: LISA LEWIS
Lioness/Hyena Shadow Puppets:
    LINDIWE DLAMINI, MUKELISIWE GOBA,
    RON KUNENE, SINDISIWE NXUMALO,
    THULISILE THUSI

Mukelisiwe Goba, Mduduzi Madela, Sindisiwe Nxumalo and Thulisile Thusi are appearing with the permission of Actors' Equity Association.

ORCHESTRA
Conductor: KARL JURMAN
Keyboard Synthesizer/
    Associate Conductor: CHERIE ROSEN
Synthesizers: TED BAKER, PAUL ASCENZO
Wood Flute Soloist/Flute/Piccolo: DAVID WEISS
Concertmaster: FRANCISCA MENDOZA
Violins: KRYSTOF WITEK, AVRIL BROWN
Violin/Viola: RALPH FARRIS
Cellos: ELIANA MENDOZA, DIANE BARERE
Flute/Clarinet/Bass Clarinet: ROBERT DeBELLIS
French Horns: PATRICK MILANDO,
    ALEXANDRA COOK, GREG SMITH
Trombone: ROCK CICCARONE
Bass Trombone/Tuba: MORRIS KAINUMA
Upright and Electric Basses: TOM BARNEY
Drums: CARTER McLEAN
Guitar: KEVIN KUHN
Percussion/Assistant Conductor:
    ROLANDO MORALES-MATOS
Mallets/Percussion: VALERIE DEE NARANJO,
    TOM BRETT
Percussion: JUNIOR "GABU" WEDDERBURN
Music Coordinator: MICHAEL KELLER

Based on the Disney Film *The Lion King*
Directed by ROGER ALLERS and ROB MINKOFF
Produced by DON HAHN
Special thanks to all the artists and staff of
Walt Disney Feature Animation

Gareth Saxe
Scar

Alton Fitzgerald
White
Mufasa

Tshidi Manye
Rafiki

Jeffrey Kuhn
Zazu

Ben Jeffrey
Pumbaa

Fred Berman
Timon

Aaron Nelson
Simba

Chantel Riley
Nala

James
Brown-Orleans
Banzai

Bonita J. Hamilton
Shenzi

Enrique Segura
Ed

Bobbi Bordley
Young Nala
at certain
performances

Derek Johnson
Young Simba
at certain
performances

Caleb McLaughlin
Young Simba
at certain
performances

Teshi Thomas
Young Nala
at certain
performances

Lawrence Alexander
Ensemble

LaMar Baylor
Ensemble

Elishah Bowman
Ensemble

Derrick Davis
Ensemble

Lindiwe Dlamini
Ensemble

The Lion King

Bongi Duma
Ensemble

Angelica Edwards
Swing

Jim Ferris
Standby Zazu, Timon, Pumbaa

Christopher Freeman
Ensemble

Mukelisiwe Goba
Ensemble

Deidrea Halley
Swing

Pia Hamilton
Ensemble

Jamal Lee Harris
Ensemble

Lindsey Holmes
Ensemble

Kenny Ingram
Swing

Joel Karie
Ensemble

Ron Kunene
Ensemble

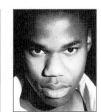
Lisa Lewis
Ensemble

Mduduzi Madela
Ensemble

Jaysin McCollum
Ensemble

Ray Mercer
Ensemble

Kyle Lamar Mitchell
Swing

Willia-Noel Montague
Swing, Dance Captain

S'bu Ngema
Ensemble

Sindisiwe Nxumalo
Ensemble

Chondra La-Tease Profit
Sarabi/Ensemble

Jacqueline René
Swing

Kellen Stancil
Swing, Dance Captain

Jeremiah Tatum
Swing

Thulisile Thusi
Ensemble

Torya
Ensemble

Donna Michelle Vaughn
Ensemble

Thom Christopher Warren
Standby Scar, Pumbaa, Zazu

Rema Webb
Ensemble

Alan Wiggins
Swing

Camille Workman
Ensemble

Elton John
Music

Tim Rice
Lyrics

Roger Allers
Book

Irene Mecchi
Book

The Lion King

Julie Taymor
Director, Costume Design, Mask/Puppet Co-Design, Additional Lyrics

Garth Fagan
Choreographer

Lebo M
Additional Music & Lyrics, Additional Vocal Score, Vocal Arrangements, Choral Director

Mark Mancina
Additional Music & Lyrics, Music Produced for the Stage, Additional Score

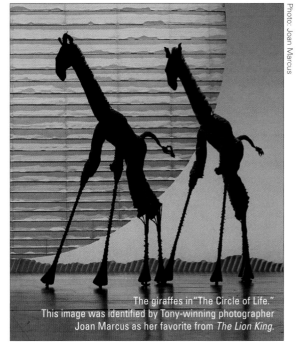

The giraffes in "The Circle of Life." This image was identified by Tony-winning photographer Joan Marcus as her favorite from *The Lion King*.

Photo: Joan Marcus

Hans Zimmer
Additional Music & Lyrics

Jay Rifkin
Additional Music & Lyrics

Richard Hudson
Scenic Design

Donald Holder
Lighting Designer

Michael Curry
Mask & Puppet Co-Design

Steve Canyon Kennedy
Sound Design

Michael Ward
Hair & Make-up Design

Mark Brandon, CSA Binder Casting
Casting

David Benken
Technical Director

John Stefaniuk
Associate Director

Karl Jurman
Music Director/Conductor

Darren Katz
Resident Director

Ruthlyn Salomons
Resident Dance Supervisor

Robert Elhai
Associate Music Producer, Orchestrator

David Metzger
Orchestrator

Bruce Fowler
Orchestrator

Michael Keller
Music Coordinator

Chris Montan
Executive Music Producer

Thomas Schumacher
Disney Theatrical Productions

ALUMNI
2013-2014

Jeff Binder
Zazu

Izell O. Blunt
Swing

Camille M. Brown
Ensemble Dancer

Gabriel Croom
Ensemble Dancer

Charity de Loera
Ensemble Dancer

The Lion King

Andile Gumbi
Simba

Michael Alexander
Henry
Ensemble Singer

Derek Johnson
Young Simba

Nicole Adell Johnson
Zazu

Jaden Jordan
Young Simba

Sheryl McCallum
Ensemble Singer

Nteliseng Nkhela
Ensemble Singer

Cameron Pow
Zazu

LaShonda Reese
Ensemble Singer

Arbender J. Robinson
Swing

Derek Smith
Scar

Vusi Sondiyazi
Ensemble Singer

Sophia Stephens
Ensemble Singer

L. Steven Taylor
Ensemble Singer

Bravita Threatt
Dancer

Natalie Turner
Swing

Buyi Zama
Rafiki

India Bolds
Ensemble Dancer

Cole Bullock
Young Simba

Gabriel Croom
Ensemble Dancer

André Jackson
u/s Ed; Swing

Nokubonga
Khuzwayo
Ensemble Singer

Ben Lipitz
Pumbaa

Kimberly Marable
Ensemble Singer

Nteliseng Nkhela
Rafiki

Esteban Oliver
Zazu

James A. Pierce III
Swing

Devin L. Roberts
Swing

Thandazile A. Soni
Ensemble Singer

Sophia Stephens
Swing

Robbie Swift
*Standby Zazu, Timon,
Pumbaa*

Natalie Turner
Swing

Kaci Walfall
Young Nala

Kyle Wrentz
Swing

The Lion King

Photo: Joan Marcus

Tshidi Manye as Rafiki, singing "The Circle of Life."

Photo: Brian Mapp

FRONT OF HOUSE
Front Row (L-R): Meryl A. Rosner,
David Eschinger,
David R. Calhoun (House Manager)
Second Row (L-R): Magdalena Clavano,
Joanne Shannon, Carolann Falasca, Stephen A. Feiler
Third Row (L-R): Joseph V. Melchiorre, Elaine R. Healey
Fourth Row (L-R): Cheryl A. Budd,
Louis Musano, Marion L. Mooney
Fifth Row (L-R): Vicky Thompson, Rose Ann Corrigan,
Anthony F. Ventura, Rose Zingale
Back Row (L-R): Miriam Santaliz,
Ada Ocasio, Judith Pirouz, Maria Compton

Photo: Brian Mapp

CREW/MUSICIANS
Front Row (L-R): Paul Ascenzo (Synthesizers), Alan Farnham, Aldo "Butch" Servilio (Automation Carpenter), James Hodges, Ilya Vett (Puppet Dayworker)
Second Row (L-R): Karl Jurman (Music Director/Conductor), Ralph Farris (Violin/Viola), Rick Plaugher (Child Wrangler), Courtney R. Alfrey (Dresser), Elizabeth Cohen (Production Make-up Supervisor), Brenda O'Brien (Make-up Artist)
Third Row (L-R): Patrick Milando (French Horn), Alain Van Achte (Head Sound), Donald McKennan (Sound Assistant), Scott Scheidt (Sound Assistant), Brian Strumwasser, Paula Schaffer
Back Row (L-R): John Benthal, Sean Farrugia (Carpenter), Pixie Esmonde (Dresser), Frank Illo (House Propman), Doug Graf (Key Spot Operator), Herman Rivera

The Lion King

Staff for *THE LION KING* Worldwide

Associate Producer ....Anne Quart
Production Supervisor ....Doc Zorthian
Senior Production Manager ....Myriah Perkins
Production Manager ....Thomas Schlenk
Production Manager.......................Michael Height
Associate Director ....John Stefaniuk
Associate Choreographer ....Marey Griffith
Music Supervisor ....Clement Ishmael
Dance Supervisor ....Celise Hicks
Supervising Resident Director ....Anthony Lyn
Associate Music Supervisor ....David Kreppel
Associate Scenic Designer ....Peter Eastman
Associate Costume Designer ......Mary Nemecek Peterson
Associate Mask & Puppet Designer ....Louis Troisi
Associate Sound Designer ....John Shivers
Associate Hair & Makeup Designer........Carole Hancock
Associate Lighting Designer ....Jeanne Koenig
Assistant Lighting Designer ....Marty Vreeland
Assistant Sound Designer ....Shane Cook
Automated Lighting Designer ....Aland Henderson
Production Coordinator ....Kelly Archer
Management Assistant ....Zachary Baer

DISNEY ON BROADWAY PUBLICITY
Senior Publicist.............................Dennis Crowley
Associate Publicist ....Michael Strassheim

CASTING
BINDER CASTING
Jay Binder, CSA
Jack Bowdan, CSA, Mark Brandon, CSA
Jason Styres

Staff for *THE LION KING* New York

Company Manager ....THOMAS SCHLENK
Associate Company Manager ....Christopher A. Recker
Production Stage Manager ....Ron Vodicka
Resident Director ....Darren Katz
Resident Dance Supervisor ....Ruthlyn Salomons
Musical Director/Conductor ....Karl Jurman

Stage Managers ....Antonia Gianino, Amy McCraney,
  Arabella Powell, Tom Reynolds
Dance Captains ......Willia-Noel Montague, Kellen Stancil
Fight Captain ....Ray Mercer
Assistant Choreographers ....Norwood J. Pennewell,
  Natalie Rogers
South African Dialect Coach ....Ron Kunene
Casting Associates ....Jack Bowdan, C.S.A.;
  Mark Brandon, C.S.A.
Casting Assistant ....Jason Styres
Corporate Counsel ....Michael Rosenfeld
Physical Therapy.............Neuro Tour Physical Therapy/
  Tarra Taylor
Consulting Orthopedist ....Neil Roth, M.D.
Child Wrangler ....Rick Plaugher
Executive Travel ....Robert Arnao, Patt McRory
Production Travel ....Jill L. Citron
Web Design Consultant ....Joshua Noah
Advertising ....Serino/Coyne Inc.
Interactive Marketing..................Situation Marketing
Production Carpenter ....Drew Siccardi
Head Carpenter ....Michael Trotto
House Carpenter ....Patrick Sullivan
Assistant Carpenters.........Kirk Bender, Michael Phillips

Automation Carpenters ....Aldo "Butch" Servilio,
  George Zegarsky
Carpenters ....Sean Farrugia, Daniel Macormack,
  Duane Mirro
Flying Supervision ....Dave Hearn
Production Flymen ....Kraig Bender, Dylan Trotto
House Flyman ....Richard McQuail
Production Electrician ....James Maloney
House Electrician ....Michael Lynch
Board Operator ....Edward Greenberg
House Assistant Electrician ....Stephen Speer
Automated Lighting Technician ....Sean Strohmeyer
Key Spot Operator................................Doug Graf
Assistant Electricians ....William Brennan,
  David Holliman, David Lynch, Joseph P. Lynch
Production Propman ....Victor Amerling
House Propman ....Frank Illo
Props ..Matthew Lavaia, Michael Lavaia, Robert McCauley
Head Sound ....Alain Van Achte
Sound Assistants ....Donald McKennan, Scott Scheidt
Production Wardrobe Supervisor ....Kjeld Andersen
Assistant Wardrobe Supervisor ....Cynthia Boardman
Puppet Supervisor ....Anne Salt
Puppet Dayworkers...........Islah Abdul-Rahiim, Ilya Vett
Mask/Puppet Studio ....Jeff Curry
Dressers ....Courtney R. Alfrey, Meredith Chase-Boyd,
  Andy Cook, Tom Daniel, Theresa DiStasi, Donna Doiron,
  Pixie Esmonde, Hilda Garcia-Suli,
  Michelle Gore-Butterfield, Douglas Hamilton,
  Mark Houston, Matthew Keating, Mark Lauer,
  Kathryn Rohe, Rita Santi, Sheila Terrell, Dave Tisue
Stitcher ....Janeth Iverson
Production Hair Supervisor ....Jon Jordan
Assistant Hair Supervisor ....Adenike Wright
Production Makeup Supervisor ....Elizabeth Cohen
Assistant Makeup Supervisor ....Christina Grant
Makeup Artist ....Brenda O'Brien

Music Development ....Nick Glennie-Smith
Music Preparation ....Donald Oliver and Evan Morris/
  Chelsea Music Service, Inc.
Synthesizer Programmer ....Ted Baker
Orchestral Synthesizer Programmer ......Christopher Ward
Electronic Drum Programmer ....Tommy Igoe
Addt'l Percussion Arrangements ....Valerie Dee Naranjo
Music Assistant ....Elizabeth J. Falcone
Personal Assistant to Elton John ....Bob Halley
Assistant to Tim Rice ....Eileen Heinink
Assistant to Mark Mancina ....Chuck Choi

Associate Scenic Designer ....Jonathan Fensom
Assistant Scenic Designer ....Michael Fagin
Lighting Design Assistant ....Karen Spahn
Automated Lighting Tracker ....Lara Bohon
Projection Designer ....Geoff Puckett
Projection Art ....Caterina Bertolotto
Assistant Sound Designer ....Kai Harada
Assistant Costume Designer ....Tracy Dorman
Stunt Consultant ....Peter Moore
Children's Tutoring ....On Location Education
Production Photography ..Joan Marcus, Marc Bryan-Brown
Associate Producer 1996–1998 ....Donald Frantz
Associate Producer 1997–2011 ....Michele Steckler
Project Manager 1996–1998 ....Nina Essman
Associate Producer 1998–2002 ....Ken Denison
Associate Producer 2000-2003 ....Pam Young
Associate Producer 2002-2007 ....Todd Lacy
Associate Producer 2003-2008 ....Aubrey Lynch

Original Music Director ....Joseph Church

 The Lion King is a proud member of the Broadway Green Alliance.

Disney's *The Lion King* is a registered trademark owned by The Walt Disney Company and used under special license by Disney Theatrical Productions.

HOUSE STAFF FOR THE MINSKOFF THEATRE
House Manager ....David Calhoun
Treasurer ....Nicholas Loiacono
Assistant Treasurer ....Richard Loiacono

CREDITS
Scenery built and mechanized by Hudson Scenic Studio, Inc. Additional scenery by Chicago Scenic Studios, Inc.; Edge & Co., Inc.; Michael Hagen, Inc.; Piper Productions, Inc.; Scenic Technologies, Inc.; I. Weiss & Sons, Inc. Lighting by Westsun, vari*lite® automated lighting provided by Vari-Lite, Inc. Props by John Creech Design & Production. Sound equipment by Pro-Mix, Inc. Additional sound equipment by Walt Disney Imagineering. Rehearsal Scenery by Brooklyn Scenic & Theatrical. Costumes executed by Parsons-Meares Ltd., Donna Langman, Eric Winterling, Danielle Gisiger, Suzie Elder. Millinery by Rodney Gordon, Janet Linville, Arnold Levine. Ricola provided by Ricola, Inc. Shibori dyeing by Joan Morris. Custom dyeing and painting by Joni Johns, Mary Macy, Parsons-Meares Ltd., Gene Mignola. Additional Painting by J. Michelle Hill. Knitwear by Maria Ficalora. Footwear by Sharlot Battin, Robert W. Jones, Capezio, Vasilli Shoes. Costume development by Constance Hoffman. Special Projects by Angela M. Kahler. Custom fabrics developed by Gary Graham and Helen Quinn. Puppet Construction by Michael Curry Design, Inc. and Vee Corporation. Shadow puppetry by Steven Kaplan. Pumbaa Puppet Construction by Andrew Benepe. Flying by Foy. Trucking by Clark Transfer. Wigs made at The Wigworkshop by Sam Fletcher. Specialist brushes made by Joseph Begley. Cheetah skins and make-up stamps made by Mike Defeo in the USA. Dry cleaning by Ernest Winzer Cleaners. Marimbas by De Morrow Instruments, Ltd. Latin Percussion by LP Music Group. Drumset by DrumWorkshop. Cymbals by Zildjian. Bass equipment by Eden Electronics. Paper products supplied by Green Forest.

Song excerpts (used by permission): "Supercalifragilisticexpialidocious" written by Richard M. Sherman and Robert B. Sherman; "Five Foot Two, Eyes of Blue" written by Sam Lewis, Joe Young, and Ray Henderson; "The Lion Sleeps Tonight" written by Hugo Peretti, George David Weiss, Luigi Creatore and Solomon Linda.

Chairman ....**James M. Nederlander**
President ....**James L. Nederlander**

Executive Vice President
Nick Scandalios

Vice President
Corporate Development
Charlene S. Nederlander

Senior Vice President
Labor Relations
Herschel Waxman

Chief Financial Officer
Freida Sawyer Belviso

The Lion King
SCRAPBOOK

Correspondents: James Brown-Orleans, Bonita J. Hamilton and Enrique Sequra, "Hyenas"

Milestone Parties, Celebrations and/or Gifts: We had a fantastic 15th anniversary party at Gotham Hall!

Most Exciting Celebrity Visitor and What They Did/Said: Michael Jackson is still the most exciting celebrity visitor that we have ever had. Matthew McConaughey was exciting, and so was Julia Roberts. They all thought that our show was awe-inspiring!

Actor Who Performed the Most Roles in This Show: Angelica Edwards and Kenny Ingram each perform nine roles.

Who Has Done the Most Shows: James Brown-Orleans has done well over 3,500 performances.

Special Backstage Rituals: We have many. Just before the Mufasa apparition, the dancer ensemble hold the Mufasa mask pieces and gather in the corner in a circle and say "Kumbayah Forever." Before the "Chow Down" scene, during the last note of "I Just Can't Wait to Be King," the three hyenas get in a circle, link legs and say, "Chow Down."

Favorite Moment During Each Performance: A favorite moment backstage among ensemble members is a special slow dance during Simba's song, "Endless Night," on the last show of the week.

Favorite In-Theatre Gathering Place: The lobby of the Minskoff Theatre. With its glass facade it gives a perfect birdseye view of Times Square, the crossroads of the world!!

Favorite Off-Site Hangout: One of our favorites is Ça Va in the lobby of the InterContinental Hotel.

Favorite Therapy: Emergen-C, coffee, Ricola and lots of Pilates!

Memorable Ad-Lib: During the confrontation scene, instead of saying, "Give me one good reason why I shouldn't rip you apart," one of our Simbas said to Scar, "Give me one good reason why I shouldn't rip your clothes off."

Memorable Stage Door Fan Encounter: There was a young man we met at our stage door, and the next day, we saw him sitting front row center, really enjoying the show and at certain points becoming quite overwhelmed. After the show, we invited him for a backstage tour, and we learned that he worked in a grocery store in Massachusetts. He had just moved there from Brazil, where he had seen the show, and came to New York specifically to see *The Lion King*. He bought a bus ticket, a hotel room in Times Square, and a ticket to the show. We really appreciated meeting him.

Latest Audience Arrival: Someone came in at intermission thinking the show started an hour later!

Fastest Costume Change: Simba's change into his flying harness.

Who Wore the Least: Young Nala and Young Simba have the lightest costumes.

Catchphrases Only the Company Would Recognize: "Holla Ladies and Germs!"

Sweethearts Within the Company: Bongi Duma and Lindiwe Dlamini.

Best In-House Parody Lyrics: The lyrics, "Ingonyama nengw' enamabala" from "The Circle of Life," are often thought to be "pink pajamas penguins on the bottom."

Memorable Directorial Note: "Faster, Louder, Funnier...does that make sense?"

Company Legends: Rema Webb is the first and only woman to cover all three principal roles and be legendary while playing them.

"Gypsy of the Year" Skit and Who Wrote It: "Bound to the Playground," choreographed and directed by Ray Mercer. We won!!!!

Coolest Thing About Being in This Show: I think the coolest thing about being in *The Lion King* is that this show knows no boundaries. It transcends age, culture, and race barriers and tells one universal story.

DISNEY THEATRICAL PRODUCTIONS

President ....Thomas Schumacher
EVP & Managing Director ....David Schrader
Senior Vice President, International ....Ron Kollen
Vice President, International, Europe ....Fiona Thomas
Vice President, International, Australia ....James Thane
Vice President, Operations ....Dana Amendola
Vice President, Domestic ....Jack Eldon
Director, Human Resources ....Marie-Pierre Varin
Director, Domestic Touring ....Michael Buchanan
Director, Worldwide Publicity ....Michael Cohen
Director, Regional Engagements ....Scott A. Hemerling
Director, Regional Engagements ....Kelli Palan
Manager, Domestic Touring & Planning ....Liz Botros
Manager, Human Resources ....Jewel Neal
Manager, Human Resources &
    Labor Relations ....Valerie Hart
Manager, Publicity ....Lindsay Braverman
Project Manager ....Ryan Pears
Manager, Technical Services & Support ....Michael Figliulo
Senior Computer Support Analyst ....Kevin A. McGuire

Creative & Production

Executive Music Producer ....Chris Montan
VP, Creative Development ....Ben Famiglietti
VP, Production ....Anne Quart
Director, International Production ....Felipe Gamba
Director, Production ....Mimi Intagliata
Director, Labor Relations ....Edward Lieber
Associate Director ....Jeff Lee
Production Supervisor ....Clifford Schwartz
Senior Production Manager ....Myriah Perkins
Production Manager ....Eduardo Castro
Production Manager ....Thomas Schlenk
Production Manager ....Michael Height

Associate Production Manager ....Kerry McGrath
Production Coordinator ....Kelly Archer
Manager, Labor Relations ....Stephanie Cheek
Manager, Physical Production ....Karl Chmielewski
Sr. Manager, Creative Development ....Jane Abramson
Sr. Manager, Education & Outreach ....Lisa Mitchell
Manager, Theatrical Licensing ....David R. Scott
Dramaturg & Literary Manager ....Ken Cerniglia

Marketing and Sales

Senior Vice President, Marketing & Sales ....Andrew Flatt
Vice President, Sales, CRM & Partnerships ..Bryan Dockett
Director, Marketing ....Robin Wyatt
Director, Creative Resources ....Victor Adams
Director, Synergy & Partnership ....Kevin Banks
Director, Sales & Ticketing ....Nick Falzon
Director, Licensed Brands ....Gary Kane
National Sales Manager ....Victoria Cairl
Sr. Manager, Data Modeling &
    Consumer Insights ....Craig Trachtenberg
Marketing Manager, *The Lion King* ....Jared Comess
Marketing Manager, *Newsies* ....Lauren Daghini
Marketing Manager ....Jason Zammit
Manager, Sales & Ticketing ....Erin Dooley
Manager, Sales & Ticketing ....Jenifer Thomas
Manager, Digital Marketing ....Peter Tulba
Manager, Digital Marketing & Social Media ...Greg Josken
Design Manager ....James Anderer
Assistant Manager, Synergy & Partnerships ...Cara Epstein

Business and Legal Affairs

Senior Vice President ....Jonathan Olson
Director ....Seth Stuhl
Counsel ....Naila McKenzie
Sr. Paralegal ....Jessica White
Paralegal ....Michael DiFonzo

Finance

VP, Finance/Business Development ....Mario Iannetta
Director, Finance ....Joe McClafferty
Director, Accounting ....Leena Mathew
Manager, Finance ....Liz Jurist Schwarzwalder
Manager, Accounting ....Adrineh Ghoukassian
Manager, Production Accounting ....Arlene Smith
Senior Financial Analyst ....Mikhail Medvedev
Senior Business Planner ....Jennifer August
Production Accountant ....Angela DiSanti
Production Accountant ....Jessica Bochman
Assistant Production Accountant ....Isander Rojas

Administrative Staff

Zachary Baer, Elizabeth Boulger, Jonelle Brown, Preston Copley, Jubie Deane, Michael Dei Cas, Leah Diaz, Adam Dworkin, Nicholas Faranda, Sarah Funk, Phil Grippe, Frankie Harvey, Andrew Hollenbeck, Christina Huschle, Julie Lavin, Sarah Malone, Colleen McCormack, Will Murdock, Misael Nunez, Brendan Padgett, Marisa Perry, Jessica Petschauer, Matt Quinones, Meaghan Shea, Suzanne Sheptock, Bri Silva, Lee Taglin, Anji Taylor

---

DISNEY THEATRICAL MERCHANDISE

Vice President ....Steven Downing
Merchandise Manager ....Neil Markman
Sr. District Manager, Retail Strategy & Ops ..Alyssa Somers
Associate Buyer ....Violet Burlaza
On-Site Retail Manager ....Jeff Knizer
On-Site Assistant Retail Manager ....Jana Cristiano
Corp. Sales &
    Product Development Manager ....Ellete Poulin

Disney Theatrical Productions
dtg.guestservices@disney.com

Luis Bravo's Forever Tango

First Preview: July 9, 2013. Opened: July 14, 2013.
Limited Engagement. Closed September 15, 2013 after 7 Previews and 73 Performances.

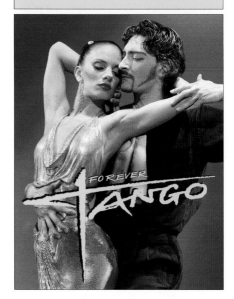

PLAYBILL®

An encore engagement for this revue of Argentinian tango dancing. The production showcases eight couples and a singer, backed by a live orchestra including four players of the distinctive tango instrument, the bandoneón, plus producer/director Luis Bravo himself on cello. Guest-starring dancers and singers joined the company for a few weeks at a time.

MUSICAL NUMBERS

ACT I

Preludio del Bandoneón y la Noche
Performed by Victoria Galoto & Juan Paulo Horvath

Overture
Orchestra

El Suburbio
Company
Victoria Galoto & Gilberto Santa Rosa
Natalia Turelli & Ariel Manzanares
"Zumo" Leguizamón & Belén Bartolomé
Mariana Bojanich & Juan Paulo Horvath
Hernán Lazart & Florencia Blanco
Aldana Silveyra & Diego Ortega

A Los Amigos
Orchestra

Derecho Viejo
Performed by "Zumo" Leguizamón
& Belén Bartolomé

Garúa
Performed by Gilberto Santa Rosa

La Mariposa
Performed by Sebastián Ripoll
& Mariana Bojanich

Continued on next page

WALTER KERR THEATRE
A JUJAMCYN THEATRE

JORDAN ROTH, *President*
ROCCO LANDESMAN, *President Emeritus*
PAUL LIBIN, *Executive Vice President*   **JACK VIERTEL**, *Senior Vice President*

LUIS BRAVO PRODUCTIONS AND JUJAMCYN THEATERS
PRESENT

Luis Bravo's
FOREVER TANGO

WITH SPECIAL GUEST STARS
GILBERTO SANTA ROSA
AND
KARINA SMIRNOFF & MAKSIM CHMERKOVSKIY

ORCHESTRA DIRECTOR   ARRANGEMENTS & ORCHESTRATIONS
VÍCTOR LAVALLÉN   **LISANDRO ADROVER**

DANCERS
VICTORIA GALOTO & JUAN PAULO HORVATH
MARCELA DURAN & GASPAR GODOY   "ZUMO" LEGUIZAMÓN & BELÉN BARTOLOMÉ
FLORENCIA BLANCO & HERNÁN LAZART   NATALIA TURELLI & ARIEL MANZANARES
DIEGO ORTEGA & ALDANA SILVEYRA   SEBASTIÁN RIPOLL & MARIANA BOJANICH
SOLEDAD BUSS & CÉSAR PERAL

ORCHESTRA
BANDONEONS: **VÍCTOR LAVALLÉN   CARLOS NIESI   JORGE TRIVISONNO   EDUARDO MICELI**
VIOLINS: **LEONARDO FERREYRA   JOSÉ LUIS MARINA**   VIOLA: **WASHINGTON WILLIMAN**
CELLO: **LUIS BRAVO**   BASS: **HÉCTOR PINEDA**
KEYBOARD: **MAURIZIO NAJT**   PIANO: **JORGE VERNIERI**

COSTUME DESIGN   SOUND DESIGN   MAKE UP DESIGN
ARGEMIRA AFFONSO   **ROLANDO OBREGÓN**   **JEAN LUC DON VITO**

ASSISTANT DIRECTOR   TECHNICAL SUPERVISION   PRODUCTION MANAGER
MARCELA DURAN   **HUDSON THEATRICAL ASSOCIATES**   **CARLOS DÍAZ**
NEIL MAZZELLA

ADVERTISING & MARKETING   HISPANIC MARKETING & PRESS CONSULTANT   PRESS REPRESENTATIVE
SERINO/COYNE   **PUBLI-CITY**   **O&M CO.**

ASSOCIATE PRODUCER   GENERAL MANAGEMENT   EXECUTIVE PRODUCER
CHRISTINE L. BARKLEY/CBA   **FRANKEL GREEN THEATRICAL MANAGEMENT**   **RED AWNING**
JOE WATSON

CHOREOGRAPHY BY
THE DANCERS

CREATED AND DIRECTED BY
LUIS BRAVO

PIANO BY STEINWAY & SONS

7/14/13

Maksim Chmerkovskiy and Karina Smirnoff tango to "Comme I'll Faut"

Photo: Walter McBride

Luis Bravo's Forever Tango

Musical Numbers Continued

Comme I'll Faut
*Performed by Karina Smirnoff
& Maksim Chmerkovskiy
Choreography by Juan Paulo Horvath
& Victoria Galoto*

La Beba
*Performed by Hernán Lazart
& Florencia Blanco*

Zum
Performed by Diego Ortega & Aldana Silveyra

La Tablada
*Performed by Natalia Turelli
& Ariel Manzanares*

Si Te Dijeron
Performed by Gilberto Santa Rosa

Responso
Orchestra

Oro y Plata
*Candombe
Performed by Gilberto Santa Rosa,
Karina Smirnoff & Maksim Chmerkovskiy
Natalia Turelli & Ariel Manzanares
"Zumo" Leguizamón & Belén Bartolomé
Mariana Bojanich & Juan Paulo Horvath
Aldana Silveyra & Diego Ortega*

INTERMISSION

ACT II

Que Alguien Me Diga
*Performed by Gilberto Santa Rosa & Company
Choreography by Juan Paulo Horvath
& Victoria Galoto
"Zumo" Leguizamón & Belén Bartolomé*

Tanguera
Performed by Soledad Buss & César Peral

Quejas de Bandoneón
*Performed by Sebastián Ripoll
& Mariana Bojanich*

El Día Que Me Quieras
Performed by Gilberto Santa Rosa

La Cumparsita
*Performed by Hernán Lazart
& Florencia Blanco
"Zumo" Leguizamón & Belén Bartolomé
Sebastián Ripoll & Mariana Bojanich*

Romance Entre el Dolor y Mi Alma
*(2nd Mov Concerto for Cello, Bandoneon
& Orchestra by Lisandro Adrover)
Performed by Karina Smirnoff
& Maksim Chmerkovskiy
Choreography by Juan Paulo Horvath
& Victoria Galoto*

Jealousy
*Orchestra
Soloist: Leonardo Ferreyra*

Prepárense
Performed by Diego Ortega & Aldana Silveyra

Felicia
Performed by Natalia Turelli & Ariel Manzanares

La Conciencia
Performed by Gilberto Santa Rosa

Preludio a Mi Viejo
Orchestra

A Mis Viejos
Performed by Gaspar Godoy & Marcela Duran

Soledad
Performed by Soledad Buss & César Peral

Vampitango
*Performed by "Zumo" Leguizamón
& Belén Bartolomé*

Romance del Bandoneón y la Noche
*Performed by Victoria Galoto
& Juan Paulo Horvath*

Finale
Company

Encore
*Performed by Gilberto Santa Rosa
& Karina Smirnoff & Maksim Chmerkovskiy
& Company*

Gilberto Santa Rosa
Guest Star

Karina Smirnoff
Guest Star

Maksim Chmerkovskiy
Guest Star

Juan Paulo Horvath
Dance Captain

Victoria Galoto
Dancer

Marcela Duran
Dancer

Gaspar Godoy
Dancer

Mariana Bojanich &
Sebastián Ripoll
Dancers

Soledad Buss &
César Peral
Dancers

Natalia Turelli &
Ariel Manzanares
Dancers

Aldana Silveyra &
Diego Ortega
Dancers

Belén Bartolomé &
"Zumo" Leguizamón
Dancers

Florencia Blanco
Dancer

Hernán Lazart
Dancer

Luis Bravo
Director/Creator

Richard Frankel
Frankel Green
Theatrical
Management
General Manager

Laura Green
Frankel Green
Theatrical
Management
General Manager

Neil A. Mazzella
Hudson Theatrical
Associates
Technical Supervisor

Luis Bravo's Forever Tango

Jordan Roth
Jujamcyn Theaters
Producer

Nicole Kastrinos
Red Awning
Executive Producer

Martín de León
Singer

Luis Enrique
Guest Star

Luis Fonsi
Guest Star

STAFF FOR *LUIS BRAVO'S FOREVER TANGO*

GENERAL MANAGEMENT
FRANKEL GREEN THEATRICAL MANAGEMENT
Richard Frankel   Laura Green
Joe Watson   Joshua A. Saletnik

COMPANY MANAGER
Oscar Leguizamón

NEW YORK COMPANY MANAGER
Sammy Ledbetter

GENERAL PRESS REPRESENTATIVES
O&M CO.
Rick Miramontez
Ryan Ratelle   Michael Jorgensen

HISPANIC MARKETING CONSULTANTS/ PRESS & GUEST STAR CASTING
PUBLI-CITY
Carmen Sepulveda   Cova Najera-Aleson

PRODUCTION MANAGEMENT
HUDSON THEATRICAL ASSOCIATES
Neil A. Mazzella
Sam Ellis   Irene Wang

Dance Captain... ....Juan Paulo Horvath
Advance Electrician ....James Maloney
Lighting Engineer.......................Alexander Kordics
Wardrobe Supervisor ....Argemira Affonso
Assistant Wardrobe Supervisor ....Alicia Aballi

Advertising ..Serino/Coyne/Greg Corradetti, Tom Callahan,
       Danielle Boyle, Drew Nebrig, Doug Ensign
Digital Outreach & Website ....Serino/Coyne/
       Jim Glaub, Chip Meyrelles, Laurie Connor,
       Kevin Keating, Mark Seeley, Brian DeVito
Marketing ....Serino/Coyne/
       Leslie Barrett, Diana Salameh, Catherine Herzog
Press Associates ...Sarah Babin, Molly Barnett, Scott Braun,
       Philip Carrubba, Jon Dimond, Joyce Friedman,
       Yufen Kung, Chelsea Nachman, Pete Sanders, Marie Pace
Press Interns ....Brian Falduto, Kevin O'Malley
Theatre Displays ....King Displays

FRANKEL GREEN THEATRICAL MANAGEMENT
Finance Director ....Sue Bartelt
Assistant to Richard Frankel ....Heidi Libby
Assistant to Steven Baruch & Tom Viertel ....Liz Krane
Assistant to Joe Watson ....Jaime Totti
Associate Finance Manager ....Amanda Hayek
Information Technology Manager ....Ben Bigby
Office Manager ....Emily Wright

Receptionists ....Rebekah Hughston, Christina Lowe
Interns ....Jenna Lloyd, Hayley Barnes, Amanda Harper,
       Sarah Linn Reedy, Hayley Reynolds, Dylan Bustamante

CREDITS AND ACKNOWLEDGEMENTS
Scenery provided by Hudson Scenic Studio, Inc. Lighting equipment provided by Hudson Sound & Light, LLC. Sound equipment provided by Sound Associates. Special thanks to Debra Chou and Vivian Chiu from Steinway & Sons. Company housing provided with gracious help from Frank Laufer and Elizabeth Helke at ABA/Ideal, Tayler Barry at Road Rebel and Lisa Morris at Road Concierge.

SPECIAL THANKS
Luis Bravo would like to extend very special thanks to his former producers and partners: Richard Frankel, Tom Viertel, Steven Baruch and Marc Routh.

JUJAMCYN THEATERS

JORDAN ROTH
President
ROCCO LANDESMAN
President, Emeritus

PAUL LIBIN	**JACK VIERTEL**
Executive Vice President	Senior Vice President
MEREDITH VILLATORE	**JENNIFER HERSHEY**
Chief Financial Officer	Vice President,
	Building Operations
MICAH HOLLINGWORTH	**HAL GOLDBERG**
Vice President,	Vice President,
Company Operations	Theatre Operations

Director of Business Affairs ....Albert T. Kim
Director of Ticketing Services ....Justin Karr

Gilberto Santa Rosa

Photo: Walter McBride

Theatre Operations Managers ...Willa Burke, Susan Elrod,
       Emily Hare, Jeff Hubbard, Albert T. Kim
Theatre Operations Associates ....Carrie Jo Brinker,
       Brian Busby, Michael Composto, Anah Jyoti Klate
Controller ....Tejal Patel
Accounting ....Cathy Cerge, Amy Frank,
       Tariq Hamami, Alexander Parra
Executive Producer, Red Awning ....Nicole Kastrinos
Director of Sales, Givenik.com ....Karen Freidus
Building Operations Associate ....Erich Bussing
Executive Coordinator ....Ed Lefferson
Executive Assistants ....Hunter Chancellor, Beth Given
Receptionist ....Lisa Perchinske
Ticketing and Pricing Associate ....Jonathon Scott
Sales Associate Givenik.com ....Taylor Kurpiel
Maintenance ....Ralph Santos, Ramon Zapata
Security ....Rasim Hodzic, Terone Richardson
Interns ....Christina Boursiquot, Brittany Clark,
       Pierre Crosby, Morgan Hoit, Kristen Morale,
       Danielle DeMatteo, Henry Tisch

STAFF FOR THE WALTER KERR THEATRE FOR *FOREVER TANGO*
Theatre Manager ....Susan Elrod
Treasurer ....Harry Jaffie
Head Carpenter ....George E. Fullum
Head Propertyman ....Timothy Bennet
Head Electrician ....Vincent J. Valvo
Flyman ....Richard M. Fullum
Follow Spot Operator ....Paul Valvo
Deck Electrician ....Peter Donovan
Sound Engineer ....Wallace Flores
Engineer ....Zaim Hodzic
Assistant Treasurers ....Tracie Giebler,
       Robert Ricchiuti, Gail Yerkovich
Head Usher .....................................T.J. D'Angelo
Director ....Michelle Fleury
Ticket Takers ....Alison Traynor, Robert Zwaschka
Ushers ..Florence Arcaro, Juliett Cipriati, Tatiana Gomberg,
       Aaron Kendall, Manuel Sandridge, Mallory Simms,
       Phillip Taratula, Ilir Velovich, Shelby Wong
Doormen ....Brandon Houghton, Kevin Wallace
Head Porter ....Marcio Martinez
Porter ....Rudy Martinez
Head Cleaner ....Sevdija Pasukanovic
Cleaner ....Lourdes Perez

Lobby refreshments by Sweet Hospitality Group.

Security provided by GBA Consulting, Inc.

Jujamcyn Theaters is a proud member of the Broadway Green Alliance.

Luis Bravo's Forever Tango

SCRAPBOOK

Photos: Joseph Marzullo

1. Juan Paulo Horvath (kneeling) and partner Victoria Galoto lead the cast in curtain calls on opening night.
2. Guest stars Karina Smirnoff (also *Yearbook* correspondent) and Maksim Chmerkovskiy strike a pose backstage at the Kerr.

Correspondent: Karina Smirnoff, Guest Star

Memorable Fan: We had a girl come to the show once who melted our hearts. Her name is Christina. She's about 13 years old and was a dancer her whole life until she contracted a bacteria that temporarily paralyzed her legs. When we met Christina she was already in a wheelchair for over half a year and was about to start her treatment. We brought her back to see another show and took her backstage. She brought us sweet cards and pictures we took the first time we met and she made us beautiful bracelets.

Opening Night Gifts and Notes: For the opening night, I was given a lot of flowers, champagne and sweet notes. The notes that I still have pinned up on the wall are from my godson Royce and Phyllis Macchio (Ralph's wife).

Most Exciting Backstage Visitors: My parents. The look on my mom's and dad's faces after they had just watched the show was priceless.

Coolest Thing About Being in This Show: Every night we dance to a live 11-piece orchestra. It's breathtaking. And some shows Luis Bravo plays cello, which is always a special treat for the whole cast.

Superstition That Turned Out to Be True: The two rules that the whole cast follows are that we never whistle inside the theatre and we never say "Macbeth." One of our dancers didn't know of the superstition and was whistling before the show. In that show he pulled a muscle.

Favorite Moment During Each Performance: My favorite moment is when we get into the position for our second solo, and I know the audience is there, but as the music starts, we forget that we are on stage and just dance as if no one is watching.

Favorite In-Theatre Gathering Place: It's def the make-up room! Something crazy and fun always happens there!

Most Memorable Audience Reaction: In the middle of one of the bows, a little girl jumped onto the stage and brought me flowers. At first I was a little shocked because I've never seen anything like that on a Broadway stage, but it was so sweet, that I couldn't stop smiling.

Favorite Off-Site Hangout: The Gansevoort Park Hotel—from hanging out by the pool, or in the sports bar Windsor to catch a game or enjoying a delicious dinner at Asellina, this place has truly become my home away from home.

Favorite Snack Foods: Silk almond milk, kale and ginger smoothie or dark chocolate!

Mascot: My godson Royce! Everyone loves having Royce at the theatre.

Favorite Therapy: Massage, Bengay patches and a spa mani/pedi.

Memorable Ad-Lib: We all sing along with Luis Enrique. (Even though it's in Spanish, it doesn't stop me.)

Cell Phones and Other Technological Issues: I'm always in the moment and don't notice those things while I'm dancing, but I've heard about some people getting in trouble.

Memorable Press Encounter: When we were doing a press conference for Spanish-speaking TV and radio outlets with Luis Bravo and Luis Enrique, most of the questions and answers were in Spanish. So Maks and I just tried to look like we understood what was happening.

Memorable Stage Door Fan Encounter: Every night I get to meet the most incredible fans. Their excitement makes me feel so much joy. I look forward to meeting everyone after each show.

What Did You Think of the Web Buzz on Your Show: It's incredible! And very humbling!

Fastest Costume Change: My changes are not crazy fast, but we have a couple of costume changes where the girls have to be ready in 60 seconds!

Who Wore the Heaviest/Hottest Costume: I think Maks for sure. He has to wear a tail suit for one of the dances and he always says that he's sweating just by putting it on.

Who Wore the Least: Soledad. One of our amazing dancers wears a see-through lace bodysuit and is very popular amongst my male friends.

Catchphrases Only the Company Would Recognize: "Yo No Se Mañana." "Pare le Bronco Compadritto." "Per ditto peddito." "This is where we are gonna draw the line."

Sweethearts Within the Company: Victoria and Paloma—Luis Bravo's and Marcella's daughters.

Pit Stop—Best Story from the Orchestra: When Luis Bravo was directing the music and light cues while playing cello live.

Memorable Directorial Note: Luis Bravo said to me: "Dance for yourself, and the others will join you."

Embarrassing Moments: I lost my shoe in the middle of one of the dances and had to finish a dance with only one shoe on.

Ghostly Encounters Backstage: We have a friendly theatre and no ghosts, lol.

Fan Club and Website: My website is www.KarinaSmirnoff.com. A great guy Tim updates it regularly and always has the latest about my projects up there. Also, I'm always sharing moments from the show via my Twitter and Instagram, which are @Karina_Smirnoff / Karina_Smirnoff.

Macbeth

First Preview: October 25, 2013. Opened: November 21, 2013.
Limited Engagement. Closed January 12, 2014 after 30 Previews and 60 Performances.

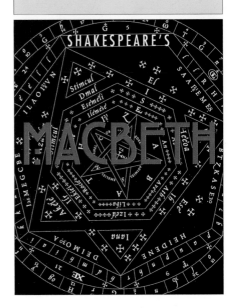

Shakespeare's four hundred-year-old "tale of sound and fury" gets its forty-eighth recorded Broadway production. A kind of Elizabethan horror movie, the "Scottish Play" charts military general Macbeth's plot to murder his way to the Scottish throne, only to see it all fall apart as his marriage, his friendships, his good name, his crown and finally his life are fed into the fire of his—and his wife's—unholy ambition.

CAST

(in order of appearance)

Hecate	FRANCESCA FARIDANY
Witch (Bloody Sergeant/A Lord)	BYRON JENNINGS
Witch (A Porter/Murderer 3)	JOHN GLOVER
Witch (Angus)	MALCOLM GETS
Graymalkin	PATRICK VAILL
Paddock	PAUL KITE
Harpier	STEPHANIE FIEGER
Duncan, King of Scotland	RICHARD EASTON
Malcolm, his son	JONNY ORSINI
Donalbain, his son	RUY ISKANDAR
Macduff	DANIEL SUNJATA
Lennox	DEREK WILSON
Rosse	AARON KROHN
Menteth	TRINEY SANDOVAL
Cathness	JOHN PATRICK DOHERTY
Macbeth	ETHAN HAWKE
Banquo	BRIAN d'ARCY JAMES
Lady Macbeth	ANNE-MARIE DUFF

Continued on next page

André Bishop
Producing Artistic Director

Adam Siegel
Managing Director

Hattie K. Jutagir
Executive Director of
Development & Planning

presents

SHAKESPEARE'S
MACBETH

with (in alphabetical order)

Bianca Amato   Shirine Babb   John Patrick Doherty   Anne-Marie Duff
Austin Durant   Richard Easton   Francesca Faridany   Stephanie Fieger
Malcolm Gets   John Glover   Ethan Hawke   Ben Horner   Ruy Iskandar
Brian d'Arcy James   Byron Jennings   Paul Kite   Aaron Krohn
Jeremiah Maestas   Christopher McHale   Jonny Orsini   Sam Poon
Triney Sandoval   Nathan Stark   Daniel Sunjata
Patrick Vaill   Tyler Lansing Weaks   Derek Wilson

Scott Pask Sets	**Catherine Zuber** Costumes	**Japhy Weideman** Lighting	**Mark Bennett** Original Music and Sound
Jeff Sugg Projections	**Steve Rankin** Fight Director	**David Brian Brown** Hair/Wigs	**Angelina Avallone** Make-up
Tripp Phillips Stage Manager	**Daniel Swee** Casting	**Linda Mason Ross** Director of Marketing	**Philip Rinaldi** General Press Agent
	Jessica Niebanck General Manager	**Jeff Hamlin** Production Manager	

Directed by
Jack O'Brien

Leadership support is provided by the Bernard Gersten LCT Productions Fund.

Major support is provided by The Peter Jay Sharp Foundation's Special Fund for LCT.
Additional support is provided by the Henry Nias Foundation courtesy of Dr. Stanley Edelman.
American Airlines is the Official Airline of Lincoln Center Theater.
LCT wishes to express its appreciation to Theatre Development Fund for its support of this production.

11/21/13

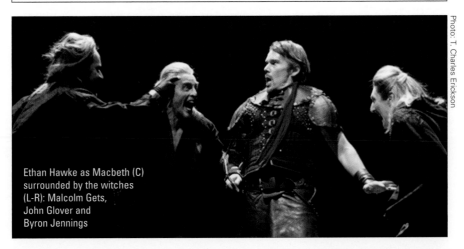

Ethan Hawke as Macbeth (C)
surrounded by the witches
(L-R): Malcolm Gets,
John Glover and
Byron Jennings

Photo: T. Charles Erickson

Macbeth

Seyton ....JEREMIAH MAESTAS
Fleance, son to Banquo ....NATHAN STARK
An Old Man ....CHRISTOPHER McHALE
Murderer 1 ....BEN HORNER
Murderer 2 ....AUSTIN DURANT
Lady Macduff ....BIANCA AMATO
Macduff Boy ....SAM POON
A Messenger ....CHRISTOPHER McHALE
An English Doctor ......CHRISTOPHER McHALE
Siward, Earl
   of Northumberland ....AUSTIN DURANT
Young Siward, his son ..TYLER LANSING WEAKS
Attendants, Soldiers, Servants,
   Thanes, Lords ....SHIRINE BABB,
     JOHN PATRICK DOHERTY,
    AUSTIN DURANT, STEPHANIE FIEGER,
     BEN HORNER, RUY ISKANDAR,
    PAUL KITE, JEREMIAH MAESTAS,
     CHRISTOPHER McHALE,
      TRINEY SANDOVAL,
    NATHAN STARK, PATRICK VAILL,
  TYLER LANSING WEAKS, DEREK WILSON

Assistant Stage Manager ......JASON HINDELANG

UNDERSTUDIES

For Hecate, Lady Macduff: STEPHANIE FIEGER
For Witch (Bloody Sergeant/
  A Lord): JOHN PATRICK DOHERTY
For Witch (A Porter/
  Murderer 3): JOHN PATRICK DOHERTY,
  PATRICK VAILL
For Witch (Angus), Murderer 1: PATRICK VAILL
For Graymalkin, Donalbain,
  Fleance: TYLER LANSING WEAKS
For Paddock, Lady Macbeth: SHIRINE BABB
For Harpier: SHIRINE BABB,
  JEREMIAH MAESTAS
For Duncan, Banquo: AUSTIN DURANT
For Malcolm, Young Siward: RUY ISKANDAR
For Macduff, Lennox: BEN HORNER
For Rosse, An Old Man, A Messenger,
  An English Doctor: TRINEY SANDOVAL
For Menteth: NATHAN STARK
For Cathness, Seyton: PAUL KITE
For Macbeth: DEREK WILSON
For Murderer 2,
  Siward: CHRISTOPHER McHALE
For Macduff Boy: ZANE KING BEERS

Bianca Amato
Lady Macduff

Shirine Babb
*Macbeth Attendant,
Ensemble*

John Patrick Doherty
Cathness, Ensemble

Anne-Marie Duff
Lady Macbeth

Austin Durant
*Murderer 2, Siward,
Ensemble*

Richard Easton
Duncan

Francesca Faridany
Hecate

Stephanie Fieger
Harpier, Ensemble

Malcolm Gets
Witch, Angus

John Glover
*Witch, A Porter/
Murderer 3*

"The Seal of God's Truth," the late Middle Age mandala pictured center, is the inspiration for a major element in the set design, and also serves as the artwork for this production of *Macbeth*. This magical design is composed of two circles, a pentagram and three heptagons, labeled with the name of God and his angels. Its origin dates back to the 13th century and is believed to be a complete system of planetary magic based on the Hebrew Kabala. Adorning amulets and talismans, the symbol empowered the practiced magician who utilized it to control the lives of all creatures — with the exception of archangels.

This version of "The Seal of God's Truth" was created in 1582 by Dr. John Dee (1527-1608 or '09), a mathematician, astronomer and scholar who was a member of the court of Queen Elizabeth I.

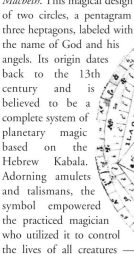

Believed to be Shakespeare's inspiration for the character Prospero in *The Tempest*, Dr. Dee was also an occultist who devoted much of his life to alchemy, divination and Hermetic philosophy. He created "The Seal of God's Truth" by communication with angels through Edward Kelly, the go-to medium of the day.

The stage design for this production of *Macbeth*, clearly, is more an impression by designer Scott Pask than an actual replica of this symbol of power, magic and even spiritualism. This use of the Dee "Seal of God's Truth" might not only serve well as a magical space for acting, but also serve as a "safe talisman" for anyone still slightly suspicious of the reputation of this haunting, and haunted, play. A company of actors standing on a conversation with angels, whether we believe it or not, can be as mysterious as it is beautiful.

Macbeth

Ethan Hawke
Macbeth

Ben Horner
Murderer 1, Ensemble

Ruy Iskandar
Donalbain, Ensemble

Brian d'Arcy James
Banquo

Byron Jennings
Witch, Bloody Sergeant/ A Lord

Anne-Marie Duff as Lady Macbeth and Ethan Hawke as Macbeth

Photo: T. Charles Erickson

Paul Kite
Paddock, Ensemble

Aaron Krohn
Rosse

Jeremiah Maestas
Seyton, Ensemble

Christopher McHale
An Old Man, A Messenger, An English Doctor, Ensemble

Jonny Orsini
Malcolm

Sam Poon
Macduff Boy

Triney Sandoval
Menteth, Ensemble

Nathan Stark
Fleance, Ensemble

Daniel Sunjata
Macduff

Patrick Vaill
Graymalkin, Ensemble

Tyler Lansing Weaks
Young Siward, Ensemble

Derek Wilson
Lennox, Ensemble

Zane King Beers
Understudy

Jack O'Brien
Director

Scott Pask
Sets

Catherine Zuber
Costumes

Japhy Weideman
Lighting

Mark Bennett
Original Music and Sound

Jeff Sugg
Projections

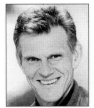
Steve Rankin
Fight Director

David Brian Brown
Hair/Wigs

Angelina Avallone
Make-up

Benjamin Endsley Klein
Associate Director

Elizabeth Smith
Voice and Speech Consultant

André Bishop
Lincoln Center Theater
Producing Artistic Director

Macbeth

BOX OFFICE
(L-R): Robert A. Belkin (Assistant Treasurer),
Geoffrey Bonis
Not Pictured: Fred Bonis, Milton Wright,
Mark Friedenreich

MANAGEMENT
Sitting (L-R): Matthew Markoff (Company Manager),
Tripp Phillips (Stage Manager)
Standing (L-R): Jessica Fried (Assistant Company
Manager), Robbie Peters,
Jason Hindelang (Assistant Stage Manager)
Not Pictured: Matt Dickson

HAIR
(L-R): Cindy Demand (Hair Supervisor),
Christen Edwards (Hair Assistant)

FRONT OF HOUSE
First Row (L-R): Eleanor Rooks, Paula Gallo-Kcira, Barbara Hart, Susan Lehman
Second Row (L-R): Joie Jacobsen, Diana Lounsbury, Amy Yedowitz,
Jeff Goldstein, Donna Zurich
Third Row (L-R): Margie Blair, Catherine Thorpe, Candice Burridge,
Farida Asencio, Denise Bergen
Back Row (L-R): Officer Douglas Charles, Mike Murray, Nick Andors, Steve Bratton,
Rheba Flegelman (House Manager), Larry Hincher

WARDROBE
Front: Actor John Glover (honorary wardrobe dresser)
Sitting (L-R): Dressers Kimberly Mark, Pamela Pierzina,
Emily Merriweather, Claire Verlaet-Manzano
Standing (L-R): Dressers Geoffrey Polischuk, John Hardy,
Adele Miskie, William Mellette, David Grevengoed

CREW
Front Row (L-R): Gerard Fortunato, Jeff Ward, John Weingart (Production Flyman), Adam Smolenski, Matt Henderson, Brant Underwood, Fred Bredenbeck,
Kyle Barrineau, Karl Rausenberger (Production Propertyman), Joe Pizzuto, Chris Noke
Back Row (L-R): Ray Skillin, Bruce Rubin, Andrew Belits, Sean Jones, Greg Cushna, William Nagle (Production Carpenter),
Patrick Merryman (Production Electrician), Kevin McNeill, John Ross, Rudy Wood, Marc Salzberg (Production Soundman), Dan Rich, Frank Linn

Macbeth

LINCOLN CENTER THEATER

ANDRÉ BISHOP
Producing Artistic Director

ADAM SIEGEL
Managing Director

HATTIE K. JUTAGIR
Executive Director of Development & Planning

ADMINISTRATIVE STAFF

GENERAL MANAGER .... JESSICA NIEBANCK
Associate General Manager .... Meghan Lantzy
General Management Assistant .... Laura Stuart
Facilities Manager .... Alex Mustelier
Associate Facilities Manager .... Michael Assalone
GENERAL PRESS AGENT .... PHILIP RINALDI
Press Associate .... Amanda Dekker Kaus
Press Assistant .... Elena Box
PRODUCTION MANAGER .... JEFF HAMLIN
Associate Production Manager .... Paul Smithyman

(L-R): Brian d'Arcy James (Banquo) and Ethan Hawke (Macbeth)

DEVELOPMENT

Associate Director of Development ...... Rachel Norton
Manager of Special Events and Advisor,
 LCT Young Angels .... Karin Schall
Grants Writer .... Neal Brilliant
Manager, Patron Program .... Sheilaja Rao
Assistant to the Executive Director of
 Development & Planning .... Raelyn R. Lagerstrom
Development Associate/
 LCT Young Angels &
 Special Events .... Jenny Rosenbluth-Stoll
Development Assistant/
 Patron Program &
 LCT Young Angels .... Sydney Rais-Sherman
DIRECTOR OF FINANCE .... DAVID S. BROWN
Controller .... Susan Knox
Finance Assistant .... Kristen Parker
Systems Manager .... Stacy Valentine
IT Support Assistant .... Allotey Peacock
DIRECTOR OF MARKETING .. LINDA MASON ROSS
Associate Director of Marketing .... Ashley Dunn
Digital Marketing Associate .... Rebecca Leshin
Marketing Assistant .... David Cannon
DIRECTOR OF EDUCATION .... KATI KOERNER
Associate Director of Education .... Alexandra Lopez
Education Projects Manager .... Jennifer Wintzer
Executive Assistant .... Barbara Hourigan
Office Manager .... Mike Adank
Messenger .... Esau Burgess
Reception .... Kira Rice, Michelle Metcalf

ARTISTIC STAFF

ASSOCIATE DIRECTORS ...... GRACIELA DANIELE,
 NICHOLAS HYTNER, JACK O'BRIEN,
 SUSAN STROMAN, DANIEL SULLIVAN
RESIDENT DIRECTOR .... BARTLETT SHER
DRAMATURG and DIRECTOR,
 LCT DIRECTORS LAB .... ANNE CATTANEO
CASTING DIRECTOR .... DANIEL SWEE, CSA
MUSICAL THEATER ASSOCIATE
 PRODUCER .... IRA WEITZMAN
ARTISTIC DIRECTOR/LCT3 .... PAIGE EVANS
Artistic Administrator .... Julia Judge
Casting Associate .... Camille Hickman
LCT3 Associate .... Natasha Sinha
Lab Assistant .... Alice Pencavel

HOUSE STAFF

HOUSE MANAGER .... RHEBA FLEGELMAN
Production Carpenter .... William Nagle
Production Electrician .... Patrick Merryman
Production Soundman .... Marc Salzberg
Production Propertyman .... Karl Rausenberger

Ethan Hawke and Anne-Marie Duff (Lady Macbeth)

Production Flyman .... John Weingart
House Technician .... Linda Heard
Chief Usher .... M.L. Pollock
Box Office Treasurer .... Fred Bonis
Assistant Treasurer .... Robert A. Belkin

SPECIAL SERVICES

Advertising .... Serino/Coyne/Jim Russek,
 Stephen O'Connor, Nick Nolte, Ryan Murphy
Marketing Promotion .... Serino/Coyne/
 Leslie Barrett, Diana Salameh
Digital Outreach ...... Serino/Coyne/Jim Glaub, Ian Weiss,
 Whitney Creighton, Crystal Chase, Isabel Hittleman
Principal Poster Artist .... James McMullan
Counsel .... Charles H. Googe, Esq.;
 Carolyn J. Casselman, Esq.; and Caroline Barnard, Esq.
 of Paul, Weiss, Rifkind, Wharton & Garrison
Immigration Counsel .... Theodore Ruthizer, Esq.;
 Mark D. Koestler, Esq.
 of Kramer, Levin, Naftalis & Frankel, LLP
Labor Counsel .... Michael F. McGahan, Esq.
 of Epstein, Becker & Green, P.C.
Auditor .... Frederick Martens, C.P.A., Lutz & Carr, L.L.P.
Insurance .... Jennifer Brown of DeWitt Stern Group
Production Photographer .... T. Charles Erickson
Video Services .... Fresh Produce Productions/Frank Basile
Blogger-in-Residence .... Brendan Lemon
Consulting Architect .... Hugh Hardy,
 H3 Hardy Collaboration Architecture
Construction Manager .... Yorke Construction
Payroll Service .... Castellana Services, Inc.

Merchandising .... Marquee Merchandise, LLC/
 Matt Murphy
Lobby Refreshments .... Sweet Hospitality Group
Database Consulting .... SGP International

STAFF FOR *MACBETH*

COMPANY MANAGER .... MATTHEW MARKOFF
Assistant Company Manager .... Jessica Fried
Dramaturg .... Dakin Matthews
Associate Set Designers .. Jeff Hinchee, Frank McCullough
Associate Costume Designer .... Ryan Park
Associate Lighting Designer .... Gary Slootskiy
Lighting Programmer .... Colin Scott
Associate Sound Designer .... Charles Coes
Associate Composer .... Curtis Moore
Lead Projections Animator .... Gabriel Aronson
Associate Projections Designer .... Dan Vatsky
Projections Programmer .... Adam Farquharson
Assistant Fight Director .... Shad Ramsey
Props Supervisor .... Faye Armon-Troncoso
Props Assistants .... John Michael Creenan,
 Alison Mantilla, Polina Minchuk

(L-R): Daniel Sunjata (Macduff) and Ethan Hawke

Assistant Hair/
 Wigs Designers .... Mitchell Beck, JT Franchuk
Hair Supervisor .... Cindy Demand
Hair Assistant .... Christen Edwards
Assistant Make-up Designer .... Robert Amodeo
Make-up Supervisor .... Benedetta Celada
Wardrobe Supervisor .... Patrick Bevilacqua
Dressers .... John Hardy, Claire Verlaet Manzano,
 Kimberly Mark, William Mellette, Emily Merriweather,
 Adele Miskie, Pamela Pierzina, Geoffrey Polischuk
Production Assistants .... Robbie Peters, Matt Dickson
Fight Captain .... Derek Wilson
Children's Guardian .... Jean Marie Hufford
Children's Tutoring .... On Location Education

Associate Director .... Benjamin Endsley Klein

Voice and Speech Consultant .... Elizabeth Smith

CREDITS

Scenery by Hudson Scenic Studio, PRG/Scenic Technologies and Show Motion, Inc. Costumes by Euroco, Angels the Costumiers, Brian Hemesath, John Cowles, Arel Studio, Bra*Tenders. Lighting equipment from PRG Lighting. Sound equipment by Masque Sound. Video equipment from PRG Video. Special Thanks: 8DIO (Troels Folmann, Tawnia Knox).

Visit www.lct.org

Photos: T. Charles Erickson

Macbeth
SCRAPBOOK

Aaron and Derek's tribute diorama. (And yes, that's Brian d'Arcy James in the cauldron.)

Correspondents: Stephanie Fieger "Harpier" and Shirine Babb "Macbeth Attendant," a.k.a. the "Familiars."

The *Macbeth* Curse: We have John Dee's mandala on the program cover, on our posters and painted onto our stage. It has an amazing history. The designer was known to communicate with angels and he created an image that has blessed the show and has given us the protection of the angels. So now we never have to worry about the so-called *Macbeth* Curse! We can say the title all the time backstage and we don't ever encounter any of those things people talk about (and we've had shows on Halloween, Friday the 13th, and the Solstice)! Director Jack O'Brien's reaction? "I don't believe in those things, but I don't *not* believe in those things."

Opening Night Parties and Gifts: We had a big, beautiful opening night party at Avery Fisher Hall, right across the plaza here at Lincoln Center. But the real party that will be remembered was the after-party at the Players Club down on Gramercy Park. There was a lot of pool playing and tall drinks and celebrities from the international and Broadway scene. Our favorite gifts were Tiffany key chains from Lincoln Center Theater, and t-shirts from Ethan with a picture of Hecate on the front and quotes and prints of the Familiars on the back. It's an original. One I'll really treasure is a photoshopped image of J Glo (John Glover) in his Weird Sister costume, blowing bubbles that turn into planets. And it bears a wonderful quote by John Wooden, "Things turn out best for the people who make the best of the way things turn out." Completely ethereal.

Most Exciting Celebrity Visitor: Our most exciting visitor was actually made up. One night, on the callboard, someone wrote that Ryan Gosling was coming to see Brian d'Arcy James. Of course we were all like "Is this real?!" There was such a stir backstage because everyone thought he was coming. Everyone was excited to

meet him...especially the ladies. A total prank by one of our boys. Hilarious.

Favorite In-Theatre Gathering Place: The greenroom, for sure. The dressing rooms are arranged along two very distant hallways and the people from one side never get to see the ones from the other side unless they meet halfway in the greenroom. The left side hallway—our hallway—is definitely the livelier hallway. The right side is much quieter. The greenroom brings both worlds together. And the constant flow of baked goods don't hurt :)

Special Backstage Rituals: When we're all about to enter for the coronation scene, we four attendants have to assist both Lady M and Mac. It's become part of our ritual to all line up by the back part of the stage until they enter from quick-change, like when they pass into the manor, and Lady M gestures for us to take our places. Another ritual comes after that scene when we exit into the vom. We then have about ten minutes before we have to enter again, and Mo, our awesome sound guy, sets up a video on his computer. Every day it's different and a surprise. Sometimes it's puppies, sometimes Looney Tunes, Charlie Chaplin, or Buster Keaton. Also, every day when we make our final exit we find waiting for us one of the child understudy covers, Zane King Beers, waiting for us offstage right to slap everybody's hand as they walk offstage. We have to mention the Crossword, KenKen, and Angel Cards with Cindy and Christen in the wig room. Everyone participates at one point or another, and we all are uplifted by the positive guidance from the cards.

Company In-Jokes: Cracker-eating contest at the cocktail party. Aaron: 15. Austin: 14.

Mascot: The Familiars are all animals, so we feel like we're the mascots. Backstage, we have Stephanie's dog Charlie, a poodle mix. He's a very soulful, peaceful pup, and everyone drops what they're doing to cuddle with him.

The Mascots check each other out.

Us! Stephanie & Shirine...Lady M Attendants (and *Yearbook* Correspondents) joined at the hip.

Memorable Audience Reactions: Our show begins with seven really loud beats. Jack O'Brien calls them "Hecate's footsteps." The fifth one is the loudest and that takes all the lights out. It certainly puts everyone at attention. We are in the vom before the show begins, and we can hear the audience reaction. Once, early in the run, we heard someone say, "Ooh! I'm so excited!" All of us in the vom heard it and almost lost it. We do student matinees and we've had some great student audiences. During the Banquo murder scene everything is done pretty much in the dark. Austin does a scream-out as Fleance is leaving him. One matinee the kids were really into it, so he did an extra scream. This takes place very close to the stage-left area. The kids in that part of the house just let out a great yelp of their own. It was like they were screaming along with a horror movie. It was insane.

Memorable Fan Mail: Anne-Marie received a care package from someone who came to see the show. Her initial comments about the performance were not very positive, and yet the package was full of goodies. You would have thought she was her biggest fan. I've gotten two Playbills sent directly to me by a fan who asked me to pass them around for the whole cast to sign.

Worst Audience Behavior: People like to take photos during the cauldron scene and during curtain call. Also, during one of the student matinees, a kid near Ethan just as he was about to make his entrance, asked if he could touch him. Ethan just looked at him and shook his head "no."

Unique Pre-Show Announcement: Our King Duncan, Richard Easton, made the pre-show recording, telling people to unwrap their candies, which always gets a nice chuckle. On the night before Thanksgiving during the scene when we enter with the vase of flowers, the table that is supposed to rise up automatically...didn't. We had no place to put the vase. We lingered a moment or two, then exited. Our stage manager

Macbeth
SCRAPBOOK

Madame Hecate (Francesca Faridany) with the "mini-me" winning cookie!

Tripp Phillips had to make the announcement, "Pardon me, ladies and gentlemen, but we are having technical difficulties..." The hydraulics had failed with no explanation, which had never happened to us before, and we had to cancel the show. In that moment Ethan, who had previously mentioned that he had his guitar, decided to go out and play for the audience. He sang "You Belong to Me," but he could only remember a verse, not the chorus. It was a beautiful, heartfelt moment and he got a big hand for it. Everyone was sad not to do the show, but it was a beautiful send-off for the night before Thanksgiving.

Memorable Ad-Lib: Shirine had two great lines in the boudoir scene when we are undressing Lady M. On this particular day, as she was stepping out of her dress, the heel of her shoe got caught in the under part of her dress, and she didn't realize it. She had already started her lines and Shirine kept saying "Pardon, pardon," under her breath. Eventually Lady M realized and stepped away from the dress enough for it to be freed.

Memorable Directorial Notes: There are countless inspiring quotes from Mr. Jack O'Brien. When he speaks, it is incredibly poetic, reflecting his life experience. Here are two that have stuck with us: "Prose enters the air and goes to the mind, but poetry enters the air and goes to your soul." "Life is a series of exercises in letting go."

Embarrassing Moments: Tripping on our costumes going up or down the vom stairs. It's happened to nearly everyone.

Favorite Moments During Each Performance: Two big ones. Every day after our first scene together with the vase of flowers, Ethan is always there to greet us as we walk offstage into the vom. Sometimes we get an embrace. One day he kneeled. Yesterday we got a back massage. It's

very fun and silly. It's the first time we see him throughout the night, and so our moment to check in. Our second favorite moment, takes place onstage in the coronation scene. The Beaumont stage is like an airplane hangar and looking out and seeing that sea of people in front of you is so empowering. To have that huge audience in the palm of our hands is very satisfying.

Catchphrase Only the Company Would Recognize: "His knoll is knelled."

Quick Bite Before Shows: Indie Food and Wine right next door, Gourmet Garage, or PJ Clarke's. We had our awesome holiday party at the Players' Club, also hosted by Ethan.

Favorite Snack Foods: We personally have a snack corner in our dressing room, always stocked with everything from peanut butter pretzels to pomegranates. Exotic fruits are Shirine's specialty :) Mo, our sound guy, is an avid baker, and constantly has cookies and banana bread and pretzels and you-name-it down there. He even made maple-bacon cookies once. There's also a big jar of candy in the wig room—it's like Halloween every day. Brian d'Arcy James always goes through and selects his favorites. There's also a steady flow of dark chocolate wherever you go.

Favorite Therapies: Tiger Balm. I'm always very physical, and fell in love with it. I brought some to the theatre and now it has become quite the antidote for sore muscles. The foam roller is incredibly popular and floats from dressing room to dressing room every night. We also have PT every week, primarily for the witches and the familiars. Everyone has these crazy asymmetrical choices they've made with their bodies, and feels it in their muscles. Stage manager Tripp Phillips is also very big on Altoids and brings in many different flavors: ginger, spearmint, cinnamon—they're everywhere.

Fastest Costume Change: Probably Mackers or Lady M, but nothing crazy. Maybe thirty seconds.

A tribute to Geoffrey, one of our wonderful dressers, and his "favorite" National Geographic cover.

J Glo being Jane.

Heaviest/Hottest Costume: Hecate probably wins, not so much because the costume itself is hot or heavy but because her headdress is challenging to maneuver. Lady M's dresses are gorgeous, so hers is definitely hot—as in "smoking hot."

Who Wore the Least: We [The Familiars] wear these tiny body stockings...and then are covered in feathers.

Coolest Thing About Being in This Show: In spite of the impressive credentials of the majority of the cast members, we can honestly say that this is an ensemble show through and through. Everyone is incredibly generous, happy to be here, to support Jack's vision. It's a joy to come to work every night in such a supportive and selfless environment.

Holiday Stories: The holidays were particularly special at LCT, with everyone getting into the spirit from Thanksgiving onward: Hallway and door decorating headed up by our stellar dressers and wardrobe team, a very successful toy drive, canned food drive, and Stockings with Care event where company members each provided gifts for a specific child in need. At one point, nearly every actor at LCT paid a visit to the wrapping station down in one of the rehearsal rooms; it was a sight to behold. And of course, there was a lot of Secret Santa sneaking around, culminating in a pre-show Christmas Eve gathering with cookies, singing around the piano (accompanied by our own Malcolm Gets), and the S.S. reveal. If that weren't enough holiday cheer, my husband (associate director Benjamin Klein) and I hosted a cookie-decorating party for the cast in between shows one Saturday, which acted as our opening night gift to the company. Six dozen allergen-friendly cookies and countless decorations were set up for everyone to create whatever their heart desired. A top-cookie contest ensued, voting took place throughout our Act I, and the winner announced at intermission. Naturally, *Macbeth*-themed cookies won out...and rightfully so (see photo, upper left, this page).

Machinal

First Preview: December 20, 2013. Opened: January 16, 2014.
Limited Engagement. Closed March 2, 2014 after 28 Previews and 52 Performances.

A revival of Sophie Treadwell's stylized, ahead-of-its-time 1928 drama about a woman trapped and stifled by her own life. Every bold step she takes to free herself—getting a job to escape her nagging mother, marrying to escape the grind of work, having an affair to escape her boorish husband—only makes her sink deeper into the quicksand. Her existence becomes a nightmare in which every traditionally comforting human institution from religion to parenthood turns on her and smothers her further, until even the ultimate escape of death threatens further enslavement.

CAST

(in alphabetical order)

Husband in Tenement/Second Man/
  Bailiff/Barber ....DAMIAN BALDET
Telephone Girl/
  Young Girl in Tenement ....ASHLEY BELL
Mother ....SUZANNE BERTISH
Doctor/Judge ....JEFF BIEHL
Man in Bar/Defense Lawyer......ARNIE BURTON
Husband ....MICHAEL CUMPSTY
Filing Clerk/Boy in Bar/
  Second Reporter ....RYAN DINNING
First Reporter/
  Second Guard...........SCOTT DRUMMOND
Man in Tenement /Man in Bar/
  First Guard ....DION GRAHAM
Young Woman ....REBECCA HALL
Adding Clerk/Priest ...EDWARD JAMES HYLAND

Continued on next page

AMERICAN AIRLINES THEATRE

ROUNDABOUT THEATRE COMPANY

Todd Haimes, Artistic Director
Harold Wolpert, Managing Director
Julia C. Levy, Executive Director
Sydney Beers, General Manager

presents

Rebecca Hall

in

MACHINAL

By
Sophie Treadwell

with

Suzanne Bertish   Morgan Spector   *and* Michael Cumpsty

Damian Baldet   Ashley Bell   Jeff Biehl   Arnie Burton
Ryan Dinning   Scott Drummond   Dion Graham
Edward James Hyland   Jason Loughlin   Maria-Christina Oliveras
Daniel Pearce   Henny Russell   Karen Walsh   Michael Warner

Set Design	*Costume Design*	*Lighting Design*	*Sound Design*
Es Devlin	Michael Krass	Jane Cox	Matt Tierney
Original Music	*Hair & Wig Design*	*Choreography*	*Dialect Coach*
Matthew Herbert	Paul Huntley	Sam Pinkleton	Kate Wilson
Production Stage Manager	*Production Management*		
Beverly Jenkins	Aurora Productions		
Casting	*Machinal General Manager*	*Press Representative*	
Jim Carnahan, C.S.A.	Denise Cooper	Polk & Co.	
Carrie Gardner, C.S.A.			
Associate Managing Director	*Director of Marketing & Audience Development*	*Director of Development*	
Greg Backstrom	Tom O'Connor	Lynne Gugenheim Gregory	
Founding Director	*Adams Associate Artistic Director**		
Gene Feist	Scott Ellis		

Directed by
Lyndsey Turner

*Generously underwritten by Margot Adams, in memory of Mason Adams.

Roundabout Theatre Company is a member of the League of Resident Theatres.
www.roundabouttheatre.org

1/16/14

(Foreground L-R): Ashley Bell, Rebecca Hall,
Morgan Spector, Damian Baldet
(Background L-R): Daniel Pearce, Scott Drummond

Photo: Joan Marcus

201

Machinal

Cast Continued

Bellboy/Barber .... JASON LOUGHLIN

Woman in Tenement/Woman in Bar/Nurse/
    Court Reporter .... MARIA-CHRISTINA
                                                    OLIVERAS

Jailer .... DANIEL PEARCE

Stenographer/Mother in Tenement/
    Matron .... HENNY RUSSELL

Lover .... MORGAN SPECTOR

Wife in Tenement/
    Woman in Bar .... KAREN WALSH

Man in Bar/
    Prosecution Lawyer .... MICHAEL WARNER

Other roles played by members of the company.

TIME

1922-1928

PLACE

New York City

Episode 1: To Business
Episode 2: Home
Episode 3: Honeymoon
Episode 4: Maternal
Episode 5: Prohibited
Episode 6: Intimate
Episode 7: Domestic
Episode 8: The Law
Episode 9: A Machine

UNDERSTUDIES

For Young Woman: ASHLEY BELL

For Man in Tenement/Man in Bar/First Guard,
    Doctor/Judge, Man in Bar/
    Prosecution Lawyer: SCOTT DRUMMOND

For Lover, Filing Clerk/Boy in Bar/Second Reporter,
    Husband in Tenement/Second Man/
    Bailiff/Barber: JASON LOUGHLIN

For Stenographer/Mother in Tenement/Matron,
    Wife in Tenement/Woman
    in Bar: MARIA-CHRISTINA OLIVERAS

For Man in Bar/Defense Lawyer,
    Adding Clerk/Priest: DANIEL PEARCE

For Husband: MICHAEL WARNER

Production Stage Manager: BEVERLY JENKINS
Stage Manager: MARK DOBROW

Michael Cumpsty and Rebecca Hall

Dear Audience Member,

Welcome to Sophie Treadwell's *Machinal* at the American Airlines Theatre. This is the play's first production on Broadway since its debut in 1928; far too long, in my opinion. Treadwell's expressionistic, "ripped from the headlines" masterpiece has always intrigued me. Her writing is incredibly evocative, and her ability to draw us so deeply into the tumultuous psyche of her central character is truly unique.

Stylistically, we are running the gamut at Roundabout this season. Over at the Laura Pels Theatre, Donald Margulies presents a contemporary take on modern love and marriage in his Pulitzer Prize-winning play, *Dinner With Friends*. Where *Machinal* tells its story through soundscape and stylized language, *Dinner With Friends* holds a mirror up to a world that should look and sound very familiar to the sensibilities of today. Both plays offer great emotional insight, but their methods of sharing that with the audience couldn't be more different.

The rest of our season continues this wide variety of styles, with the return of Kander, Ebb and Masteroff's dark musical classic *Cabaret* and the first-ever Broadway production of the segregation-set musical *Violet*. I am very pleased to have such a breadth of work represented on our stages, and I am eager to hear how you respond to it. Please share your thoughts by emailing me at ArtisticOffice@roundabouttheatre.org. Thank you again for joining us, and I hope that you enjoy *Machinal*.

Sincerely,
Todd Haimes, Artistic Director

Rebecca Hall and Morgan Spector

Rebecca Hall
Young Woman

Suzanne Bertish
Mother

Morgan Spector
Lover

Michael Cumpsty
Husband

Damian Baldet
Husband in Tenement/Second Man/Bailiff/Barber

Ashley Bell
Telephone Girl/Young Girl in Tenement; u/s Young Woman

Jeff Biehl
Doctor/Judge

Machinal

Foreground: Rebecca Hall
Background: Ryan Dinning

Arnie Burton
*Man in Bar/
Defense Lawyer*

Ryan Dinning
*Filing Clerk/Boy
in Bar/Second
Reporter*

Scott Drummond
*First Reporter/
Second Guard; u/s
Man in Tenement/
Man in Bar/First
Guard; Doctor/Judge*

Dion Graham
*Man in Tenement/
Man in Bar/
First Guard*

**Edward James
Hyland**
Adding Clerk/Priest

Jason Loughlin
*Bellboy/Barber; u/s
Lover; Filing Clerk/
Boy in Bar/Second
Reporter; Husband
in Tenement*

**Maria-Christina
Oliveras**
*Woman in
Tenement/Woman in
Bar/Nurse/Court
Reporter*

Daniel Pearce
*Jailer; u/s Man in
Bar/Defense
Lawyer; Adding
Clerk/Priest*

Henny Russell
*Stenographer/
Mother in
Tenement/Matron*

Karen Walsh
*Wife in Tenement/
Woman in Bar*

Michael Warner
*Man in Bar/
Prosecution Lawyer;
u/s Husband*

Sophie Treadwell
Playwright

Es Devlin
Set Design

Jane Cox
Lighting Design

Matt Tierney
Sound Design

Matthew Herbert
Original Music

Paul Huntley
Wig and Hair Design

Kate Wilson
Dialect Coach

Sam Pinkleton
Choreography

Jim Carnahan
Casting

Carrie Gardner
Casting

Gene O'Donovan
*Aurora Productions
Production
Management*

Ben Heller
*Aurora Productions
Production
Management*

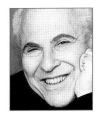

Gene Feist
*Roundabout Theatre
Company
Founding Director*

Todd Haimes
*Roundabout Theatre
Company
Artistic Director*

2013-2014 AWARDS

DRAMA DESK AWARD
Outstanding Sound Design of a Play
(Matt Tierney)

THEATRE WORLD AWARD
(Rebecca Hall)

Machinal

SECURITY
Carl Meade

FRONT OF HOUSE
(L-R): Celia Torres, Zipporah Aguasvivas, Sheila Portorreal,
Crystal Suarez, Oscar Castillo

Photos: Brian Mapp

BOX OFFICE
Front (L-R): Solangel Bido, Mead Margulies
Back (L-R): Robert Morgan (Assistant Box Office Manager),
Ted Osborne (Box Office Manager)

CREW
Front (L-R): Brian Carfi (Automation), Michael Day (Deck), Glenn Merwede (Production/House Carpenter), Dale Carman (Dresser), Hannah Overton (Sound Operator), Dara Fargotstein (Wardrobe Dayworker), Emile Metcalf (IA Apprentice), Carly DiFulvio Allen (Company Manager), Julia Sandy
Back (L-R): Susan J. Fallon (Wardrobe Supervisor), Nellie LaPorte (Wig/Hair Supervisor), Ksusha Vanyan, Sarah Conyers (Deck), Brendan O'Neal, Beverly Jenkins (Production Stage Manager), Adam Adelman (Dresser), Robert W. Dowling II (House Properties), Jennifer Fisher (Dresser), Beth DuBon (Dresser), Barb Bartel (Deck), Brian Maiuri (Production/House Electrician), Mark Dobrow (Stage Manager)

ROUNDABOUT THEATRE COMPANY STAFF
ARTISTIC DIRECTOR ....TODD HAIMES
MANAGING DIRECTOR ....HAROLD WOLPERT
EXECUTIVE DIRECTOR ....JULIA C. LEVY
ADAMS ASSOCIATE
   ARTISTIC DIRECTOR ....SCOTT ELLIS
GENERAL MANAGER ....SYDNEY BEERS

ARTISTIC STAFF
DIRECTOR OF ARTISTIC DEVELOPMENT/
   DIRECTOR OF CASTING ....Jim Carnahan
Artistic Consultant ....Robyn Goodman
Resident Directors ....Doug Hughes, Sam Gold
Associate Artists ....Mark Brokaw, Evan Cabnet,
   Scott Elliott, Bill Irwin, Pam MacKinnon, Joe Mantello,
     Kathleen Marshall, Theresa Rebeck
Literary Manager ....Jill Rafson
Senior Casting Director ....Carrie Gardner
Casting Director ....Stephen Kopel
Casting Associate ....Jillian Cimini
Casting Assistants ....Lain Kunin, Logan Reid
Artistic Associate ....Amy Ashton

Literary Associate ....Josh Fiedler
Educational Foundation of
   America Commission ....Lydia Diamond
Laurents/Hatcher Foundation
   Commission ....Meghan Kennedy
Roundabout Commissions.............Helen Edmundson,
   Adam Gwon & Michael Mitnick,
   Joshua Harmon, Andrew Hinderaker,
   Stephen Karam, Matthew Lopez, Kim Rosenstock
Casting Interns ....Joyah Spangler, Steven Laing,
   Ragan Rhodes
Script Readers ....Shannon Deep, Michael Perlman,
   Alexis Roblan, Nicole Tingir
Artistic Apprentice ....Olivia O'Connor

EDUCATION STAFF
DIRECTOR OF EDUCATION ....Jennifer DiBella
Assistant Director of Education ....Mitch Mattson
Education Program Manager ....Paul Brewster
Education Program Manager ....Kimberley Oria
Education Assistant ....Julia Borowski
Education Dramaturg ....Ted Sod

Teaching Artists ....Cynthia Babak, Victor Barbella,
   LaTonya Borsay, Mark Bruckner, Chloe Chapin,
   Michael Costagliola, Joe Doran, Mathilde Dratwa,
   Elizabeth Dunn-Ruiz, Sarah Ellis, Carrie Ellman-Larsen,
   Theresa Flanagan, Deanna Frieman, Geoffrey Goldberg,
   Sheri Graubert, Adam Gwon, Creighton Irons,
   Devin Haqq, Carrie Heitman, Karla Hendrick,
   Jason Jacobs, Alana Jacoby, Tess James,
   Hannah Johnson-Walsh, Lisa Renee Jordan, Boo Killebrew,
   Anya Klepikov, Sarah Lang, John Lavigne, Erin McCready,
   James Miles, Nick Moore, Meghan O'Neil, Nicole Press,
   Leah Reddy, Amanda Rehbein, Nick Simone,
   Heidi Stallings, Daniel Sullivan, Carl Tallent,
   Vickie Tanner, Laurine Towler, Jennifer Varbalow,
   Kathryn Veillette, Leese Walker, Christopher Weston,
   Gail Winar, Jamie Kalama Wood, Chad Yarborough
Teaching Artist Emeritus ....Reneé Flemings
Education Apprentices ...Rachel Friedman, Rebecca Powell

MANAGEMENT/ADMINISTRATIVE STAFF
ASSOCIATE MANAGING
   DIRECTOR ....Greg Backstrom

Machinal

General Manager,
American Airlines Theatre ....Denise Cooper
General Manager, Steinberg Center ....Nicholas J. Caccavo
Operations Manager ....Valerie D. Simmons
Associate General Manager ....Maggie Cantrick
Assistant Managing Director ....Katharine Croke
Rentals Manager ....Nancy Mulliner
Archivist ....Tiffany Nixon
Assistant to the Executive Director ....Nicole Tingir
Assistant to the Managing Director ....Christina Pezzello
Management Apprentice ....Jeesun Choi

FINANCE STAFF
DIRECTOR OF FINANCE ....Susan Neiman
Payroll Director ....John LaBarbera
Accounts Payable Manager ....Frank Surdi
Payroll Benefits Administrator ....Yonit Kafka
Manager Financial Reporting ....Joshua Cohen
Business Office Assistant ....Jackie Verbitski
Receptionists ....Dee Beider, Elisa Papa, Allison Patrick
Messenger ....Darnell Franklin
Business Office Apprentice ....Gregory Shepard

DEVELOPMENT STAFF
DIRECTOR OF
DEVELOPMENT ....Lynne Gugenheim Gregory
Assistant to the
Director of Development ....Jonathan Sokolow
Associate Director of Development ....Christopher Nave
Director, Special Events.......................Lane Hosmer
Director, Institutional Giving ....Erica Raven
Associate Director, Individual Giving ....Tyler Ennis
Manager, Telefundraising ....Gavin Brown
Manager, Special Events......................Natalie Corr
Manager, Membership Programs ....Oliver Pattenden
Manager, Donor Information Systems ....Lise Speidel
Individual Giving Officer, Stewardship .....Jordan Frausto
Special Events Assistant ....Genevieve Carroll
Development Assistant ....Martin Giannini
Special Events Apprentice ....Jena Yarley

INFORMATION TECHNOLOGY STAFF
DIRECTOR OF
INFORMATION TECHNOLOGY ...Daniel V. Gomez
Systems Administrator ....Jim Roma
Tessitura & Applications Administrator .....Yelena Ingberg
Web Administrator ....Robert Parmelee
DBA/Developer ....Ruslan Nikandrov
IT Associate ....Cary Kim

MARKETING STAFF
DIRECTOR OF MARKETING &
AUDIENCE DEVELOPMENT ....Tom O'Connor
Senior Marketing Manager ....Rani Haywood
Digital Content Producer ....Mark Cajigao
Marketing Associate ....Rachel LeFevre-Snee
Digital Marketing Associate ....Alex Barber
Marketing Assistant ....Dayna Johnson
Telesales Manager ....Patrick Pastor
Telesales Office Coordinator ....Adam Unze
Marketing Apprentices ....Alyssa DeAlesandro,
Jamie Gottlieb
Digital Marketing Apprentice ....Jennifer Marinelli

AUDIENCE SERVICES STAFF
DIRECTOR OF AUDIENCE
SERVICES ....Wendy Hutton

Customer Care Manager ....Robert Kane
Box Office Managers ....Edward P. Osborne,
Jaime Perlman, Krystin MacRitchie, Catherine Fitzpatrick
Assistant Box Office Managers ....Robert Morgan,
Andrew Clements, Nicki Ishmael
Assistant Audience Services Managers .....Lindsay Ericson,
Jessica Pruett-Barnett, Kaia Lay Rafoss, Joe Gallina
Customer Care Associate ....Thomas Walsh
Audience Services ....Jennifer Almgreen, Solangel Bido,
Josh Boscarino, Eric Bridle, Lauren Cartelli,
Adam Elsberry, Alanna Harms, Kara Harrington,
Blair Laurie, Rebecca Lewis-Whitson, Michelle Maccarone,
Mead Margulies, Laura Marshall, Chuck Migliaccio,
Carlos Morris, Katie Mueller, Sarah Olsen, Josh Rozett,
Austin Ruffer, Heather Seibert, Nalane Singh,
Ron Tobia, Hannah Weitzman
Audience Services Apprentice ....Natalie Donohue

SERVICES
Counsel ..Paul, Weiss, Rifkind, Wharton and Garrison LLP,
Charles H. Googe Jr., Carol M. Kaplan
Counsel ....Rosenberg & Estis
Counsel ..Andrew Lance/Gibson, Dunn, & Crutcher, LLP
Counsel ..Harry H. Weintraub/Glick and Weintraub, P.C.
Counsel ....Stroock & Stroock & Lavan LLP
Counsel ....Daniel S. Dokos/Weil, Gotshal & Manges LLP
Counsel ..Claudia Wagner/Manatt, Phelps & Phillips, LLP
Immigration Counsel ....Mark D. Koestler and
Theodore Ruthizer
House Physicians ....Dr. Theodore Tyberg,
Dr. Lawrence Katz
House Dentist ....Neil Kanner, D.M.D.
Insurance ....DeWitt Stern Group, Inc.
Accountant ....Lutz & Carr CPAs, LLP
Advertising ....Spotco/Drew Hodges, Tom Greenwald,
Ilene Rosen, Josh Fraenkel, Kara Carothers, Kyle Carter
Interactive Marketing ....Situation Interactive/
Damian Bazadona, Eric Bornemann,
Elizabeth Kandel, Danielle Migliaccio
Events Photography ....Anita and Steve Shevett
Production Photographer ....Joan Marcus
Theatre Displays ....King Displays, Wayne Sapper
Lobby Refreshments ....Sweet Hospitality Group
Merchandising ..Marquee Merchandise LLC/Matt Murphy

MANAGING DIRECTOR
EMERITUS ....Ellen Richard

Roundabout Theatre Company
231 West 39th Street, New York, NY 10018
(212) 719-9393.

GENERAL PRESS REPRESENTATIVE
POLK & CO.
Matt Polk
Jessica Johnson   Michelle Bergmann   Layne McNish

STAFF FOR MACHINAL
Company Manager ....Carly DiFulvio Allen
Production Stage Manager ....Beverly Jenkins
Assistant Stage Manager ....Mark Dobrow
Production Management ....Aurora Productions Inc./
Gene O'Donovan and Ben Heller with Chris Minnick,
Jarid Sumner, Anthony Jusino, Anita Shah,
Liza Luxenberg, Rachel London, David Cook,
Bridget Van Dyke, Melissa Mazdra
Assistant Director ....Osheen Jones

Makeup Designer ....Tiffany Hicks
Associate Set Designer ....Evan Adamson
Associate Costume Designer ....Tracy Christensen
Assistants to the Costume Designer ....Isabelle Coler,
Robert Croghan, Lillian Kingery
Associate Lighting Designer ....Tess James
Assistant to the Lighting Designer ....Alex Mannix
Associate Sound Designer ....Alex Neumann
Production Properties Supervisor ....Buist Bickley
Production Properties Assistant ....Polina Minchuk
Assistant to the Choreographer ....Amanda Chambers
Production Carpenter ....Glenn Merwede
Production Electrician ....Brian Maiuri
Running Properties ....Robert W. Dowling II
Sound Operator ....Hannah Overton
Automation ....Brian Carfi
Deck ....Barb Bartel, Michael Day, Sarah Conyers
Wardrobe Supervisor ....Susan J. Fallon
Dressers ......Adam Adelman, Dale Carman, Beth DuBon,
Jennifer Fisher, Ksenia Vanyan
Wardrobe Dayworker ....Dara Fargotstein
Hair and Wig Supervisor ....Nellie LaPorte
IA Apprentice ....Emile Metcalf
Production Assistant ....Joseph Heaton

CREDITS
Scenery fabrication by Scenic Technologies, a division of
Production Resource Group, LLC, New Windsor, NY.
Show control and scenic motion control featuring Stage
Command Systems® by Scenic Technologies, a division of
Production Resource Group, LLC, New Windsor, NY.
Lighting equipment by PRG. Sound equipment by PRG
Audio. Costumes constructed by Cygnet Studios, Claudia
Diaz Costumes, Paul Chang Custom Tailors and Scafati
Theatrical Tailors. Additional costumes by Western
Costume Co.; Helen Uffner Vintage Clothing, LLC; and
Early Halloween. Alterations by Timberlake Studios.
Additional prop construction by Daddy-O Productions,
Inc. and Center Line Studios. Special thanks to Lincoln
Center Theater, Manhattan Theatre Club, and to
Bra*Tenders for hosiery and undergarments.

Machinal is presented through special arrangement with
the Roman Catholic Diocese of Tucson.

AMERICAN AIRLINES THEATRE STAFF
Company Manager ....Carly DiFulvio Allen
House Carpenter ....Glenn Merwede
House Electrician ....Brian Maiuri
House Properties ....Robert W. Dowling II
House Sound ....Hannah Overton
IA Apprentice ....Emile Metcalf
Wardrobe Supervisor ....Susan J. Fallon
Box Office Manager ....Ted Osborne
Assistant Box Office Manager ....Robert Morgan
House Manager ....Stephen Ryan
Associate House Manager ....Zipporah Aguasvivas
Head Usher ....Crystal Suarez
House Staff ....Oscar Castillo, Shaquanna Cole,
Saira Flores, Ashley Flowers, Anne Ezell, Rebecca Knell,
Jim Lynch, Enrika Nicholas, Martin Ortiz,
Sheila Portorreal, Celia Torres, Dominga Veloz
Security ....Julious Russell
Additional Security ....Gotham Security
Maintenance .... Jason Battle, Jerry Hobbs

Mamma Mia!

First Preview: October 5, 2001. Opened: October 18, 2001.
Still running as of May 31, 2014.

PLAYBILL

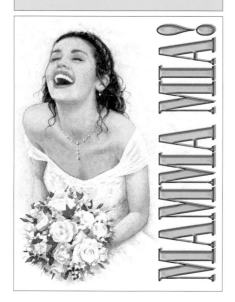

As her wedding approaches, Sophie decides to figure out which among three of her free-spirited mother's ex-lovers is her actual father. So she invites all three men to the wedding without telling mom. Set to the hits of the music group ABBA.

CAST

(in order of speaking)

Sophie Sheridan	LAURIE VELDHEER
Ali	TRACI VICTORIA
Lisa	THOMASINA E. GROSS
Tanya	FELICIA FINLEY
Rosie	LAUREN COHN
Donna Sheridan	JUDY McLANE
Sky	ZAK RESNICK
Pepper	JACOB PINION
Eddie	ALBERT GUERZON
Harry Bright	GRAHAM ROWAT
Bill Austin	DANIEL COONEY
Sam Carmichael	AARON LAZAR
Father Alexandrios	JOHN HEMPHILL

THE ENSEMBLE

DEANNA AGUINAGA, SYDNI BEAUDOIN,
BRENT BLACK, NATALIE BRADSHAW,
ALLYSON CARR, FELICITY CLAIRE,
MARK DANCEWICZ, STACIA FERNANDEZ,
JOHN HEMPHILL, CORINNE MELANÇON,
PAUL HEESANG MILLER, JENNIFER NOTH,
ELENA RICARDO, GERARD SALVADOR,
VICTOR WALLACE, BLAKE WHYTE

Continued on next page

 BROADHURST THEATRE

235 West 44th Street
A Shubert Organization Theatre

Philip J. Smith, *Chairman*   **Robert E. Wankel,** *President*

JUDY CRAYMER, RICHARD EAST AND BJÖRN ULVAEUS
FOR LITTLESTAR IN ASSOCIATION WITH UNIVERSAL

PRESENT

MAMMA MIA!

MUSIC AND LYRICS BY

BENNY ANDERSSON
BJÖRN ULVAEUS

AND SOME SONGS WITH STIG ANDERSON

BOOK BY CATHERINE JOHNSON

PRODUCTION DESIGNED BY
MARK THOMPSON

LIGHTING DESIGNED BY
HOWARD HARRISON

SOUND DESIGNED BY
**ANDREW BRUCE &
BOBBY AITKEN**

MUSICAL SUPERVISOR, ADDITIONAL MATERIAL
& ARRANGEMENTS
MARTIN KOCH

CHOREOGRAPHY
ANTHONY VAN LAAST

DIRECTED BY
PHYLLIDA LLOYD

10/28/13

The men of *Mamma Mia!* (L-R): Aaron Lazar, Graham Rowat, Daniel Cooney

Photo: Joan Marcus

Mamma Mia!

MUSICAL NUMBERS

(in alphabetical order)

CHIQUITITA
DANCING QUEEN
DOES YOUR MOTHER KNOW
GIMME! GIMME! GIMME!
HONEY, HONEY
I DO, I DO, I DO, I DO, I DO
I HAVE A DREAM
KNOWING ME, KNOWING YOU
LAY ALL YOUR LOVE ON ME
MAMMA MIA
MONEY, MONEY, MONEY
ONE OF US
OUR LAST SUMMER
SLIPPING THROUGH MY FINGERS
S.O.S.
SUPER TROUPER
TAKE A CHANCE ON ME
THANK YOU FOR THE MUSIC
THE NAME OF THE GAME
THE WINNER TAKES IT ALL
UNDER ATTACK
VOULEZ-VOUS

Cast Continued

UNDERSTUDIES

For Sophie Sheridan: NATALIE BRADSHAW, FELICITY CLAIRE
For Ali: NATALIE BRADSHAW, ELENA RICARDO
For Lisa: SYDNI BEAUDOIN, FELICITY CLAIRE
For Tanya: STACIA FERNANDEZ, CORINNE MELANÇON, JENNIFER NOTH
For Rosie: STACIA FERNANDEZ, JENNIFER NOTH
For Donna Sheridan: CORINNE MELANÇON, JENNIFER NOTH
For Sky: TONY GONZALEZ, BLAKE WHYTE
For Pepper: MARK DANCEWICZ, GERARD SALVADOR
For Eddie: JON-ERIK GOLDBERG, TONY GONZALEZ, PAUL HEESANG MILLER
For Harry Bright: JOHN HEMPHILL, VICTOR WALLACE
For Bill Austin: BRENT BLACK, JOHN HEMPHILL
For Sam Carmichael: BRENT BLACK, JOHN HEMPHILL, VICTOR WALLACE

For Father Alexandrios: BRENT BLACK, TONY GONZALEZ, VICTOR WALLACE

SWINGS

AJ FISHER, JON-ERIK GOLDBERG, TONY GONZALEZ, CHRISTOPHER HUDSON MYERS, LAUREN SAMBATARO, LEAH ZEPEL

DANCE CAPTAIN

TONY GONZALEZ

SETTING

On a Greek Island, a wedding is about to take place...

PROLOGUE

Three months before the wedding

ACT ONE

The day before the wedding

ACT TWO

The day of the wedding

THE BAND

Music Director/Conductor/Keyboard 1:
WENDY BOBBITT CAVETT
Associate Music Director/Keyboard 2:
ROB PREUSS
Keyboard 3:
STEVE MARZULLO
Keyboard 4:
MYLES CHASE
Guitar 1:
DOUG QUINN
Guitar 2:
JEFF CAMPBELL
Bass:
PAUL ADAMY
Drums:
RAY MARCHICA
Percussion:
DAVID NYBERG
Music Coordinator:
MICHAEL KELLER
Synthesizer Programmer:
NICHOLAS GILPIN

Photo: Joan Marcus

The women of *Mamma Mia!* (put on their dancing shoes (L-R): Felicia Finley, Judy McLane, Lauren Cohn

Judy McLane
Donna Sheridan

Laurie Veldheer
Sophie Sheridan

Lauren Cohn
Rosie

Felicia Finley
Tanya

Aaron Lazar
Sam Carmichael

Daniel Cooney
Bill Austin

Graham Rowat
Harry Bright

Mamma Mia!

Zak Resnick
Sky

Traci Victoria
Ali

Thomasina E. Gross
Lisa

Jacob Pinion
Pepper

Albert Guerzon
Eddie

Deanna Aguinaga
Ensemble

Sydni Beaudoin
Ensemble; u/s Lisa

Brent Black
Ensemble; u/s Bill, Sam, Father Alexandrios

Natalie Bradshaw
Ensemble; u/s Sophie, Ali

Allyson Carr
Ensemble

Felicity Claire
Ensemble; u/s Sophie, Lisa

Mark Dancewicz
Ensemble; u/s Pepper

Stacia Fernandez
Ensemble; u/s Tanya, Rosie

AJ Fisher
Swing

Jon-Erik Goldberg
Swing; u/s Eddie

Tony Gonzalez
Swing, Dance Captain; u/s Sky, Eddie, Father Alexandrios

John Hemphill
Father Alexandrios, Ensemble; u/s Sam, Bill, Harry

Corinne Melançon
Ensemble; u/s Donna, Tanya

Paul Heesang Miller
Ensemble; u/s Eddie

Christopher Hudson Myers
Swing

Jennifer Noth
Ensemble; u/s Donna, Tanya, Rosie

Elena Ricardo
Ensemble; u/s Ali

Gerard Salvador
Ensemble; u/s Pepper

Lauren Sambataro
Swing

Victor Wallace
Ensemble; u/s Sam, Harry, Father Alexandrios

Blake Whyte
Ensemble; u/s Sky

Leah Zepel
Swing

Björn Ulvaeus
Music & Lyrics

Benny Andersson
Music & Lyrics

Catherine Johnson
Book

Phyllida Lloyd
Director

Anthony Van Laast, MBE
Choreographer

Mark Thompson
Production Designer

Howard Harrison
Lighting Designer

Andrew Bruce
Sound Designer

Mamma Mia!

Bobby Aitken
Sound Designer

Martin Koch
*Musical Supervisor;
Additional Material;
Arrangements
Musical Supervisor*

David Holcenberg
*Associate Music
Supervisor*

Wendy Bobbitt
Cavett
*Musical Director/
Conductor*

Nichola Treherne
*Associate
Choreographer*

Martha Banta
Resident Director

Janet Rothermel
*Associate
Choreographer*

Tara Rubin
Tara Rubin Casting
Casting

David Grindrod
Casting Consultants

Arthur Siccardi
Arthur Siccardi
Theatrical
Services, Inc.
Production Manager

Judy Craymer
Producer

Richard East
Producer

Maggie Brohn
Bespoke Theatricals
*General
Management*

Amy Jacobs
Bespoke Theatricals
*General
Management*

Devin Keudell
Bespoke Theatricals
*General
Management*

Nina Lannan
Bespoke Theatricals
*General
Management*

Andrew Treagus
*International
Executive Producer*

ALUMNI
2013-2014

Christy Altomare
Sophie

Bryan Scott Johnson
*Father Alexandrios,
Ensemble;
u/s Bill, Harry*

Monica Kapoor
Lisa

Michael Pemberton
Bill Austin

TRANSFER
STUDENTS
2013-2014

Alan Campbell
Sam Carmichael

Tony Clements
*Ensemble;
u/s Sam, Bill,
Father Alexandrios*

Paul DeBoy
Harry Bright

Natalie Gallo
Ensemble; u/s Ali

Corey Greenan
*Swing; u/s Sky,
Eddie*

Adam Michael Hart
Swing

Bryan Scott Johnson
*Father Alexandrios,
Ensemble;
u/s Bill, Harry*

Jon Jorgenson
Sky

Ashley Park
Ensemble; u/s Ali

Neil Starkenberg
Pepper

Jennifer Swiderski
*Ensemble; u/s
Donna, Tanya, Rosie*

Troy Woodcroft
Ensemble

Mamma Mia!

FRONT OF HOUSE
Front: Bob Reilly (House Manager)
(L-R): Michael Gilbert, Dieuna Sinca, Nancy Reyes, Hugh Lynch, Seymone Cummings, Aishah Kelly, Janise Beckwith, Chris Caiol

CREW
Seated (L-R): Carlos Parra, Charlene Speyerer, photo of Sherry Cohen (Stage Manager), Irene L. Bunis (Wardrobe Supervisor), Carey Bertini (Dresser), Andrew Fenton (Production Stage Manager)
Standing (L-R): Chris Whyte, David Karlson, Rodd Sovar (Dresser), Don Lawrence (Head Electrician), Brian Strumwasser, Aaron Kinchen (Assistant Hair Supervisor), Stephen Burns (Assistant Carpenter), Dean R. Greer (Stage Manager), Charles DeVerna

BAND
(L-R): Paul Adamy, David Nyberg, Wendy Bobbitt Cavett, Jeff Campbell, Doug Quinn

Mamma Mia!

Photo: Brian Mapp

CAST AND BAND

Front (L-R): Natalie Bradshaw, Thomasina E. Gross, Ashley Park, Sydni Beaudoin, Leah Zepel
Middle (L-R): Gerard Salvador, John Hemphill, Judy McLane, David Nyberg, Traci Victoria, Christopher Hudson Myers, Jon-Erik Goldberg,
Paul HeeSang Miller, Allyson Carr, Deanna Aguinaga, Felicity Claire, Paul DeBoy, Elena Ricardo, Adam Michael Hart
Back (L-R): Doug Quinn, Jeff Campbell, Paul Adamy, Victor Wallace, Neil Starkenberg, Wendy Bobbitt Cavett, Mark Dancewicz, Corinne Melançon,
Lauren "Coco" Cohn, Alan Campbell, AJ Fisher, Tony Clements, Jennifer Noth, Albert Guerzon, Felicia Finley

LITTLESTAR SERVICES LIMITED

Directors ....Judy Craymer, Benny Andersson, Björn Ulvaeus
International Executive Producer ....Andrew Treagus
Business & Finance Director ....Ashley Grisdale
Administrator....................................Peter Austin
PA to Judy Craymer ....Katie Wolfryd
Marketing & Communications Manager ....Claire Teare
Marketing & Communications Assistant ...Alice Woodhall
Head of Accounts ....Jo Reedman
Accountant ....Sheila Egbujie
Assistant Accountant..........................Ricky Whitaites
Administrative Assistant ....Matthew Willis
Receptionist ....Kimberley Wallwork
Legal Services ......Barry Shaw, Howard Jones at Sheridans
Production Insurance Services ....W & P Longreach
Business Manager for Benny Andersson and Björn Ulvaeus
   & Scandinavian Press ....Görel Hanser

ANDREW TREAGUS ASSOCIATES LIMITED

General Manager ....Philip Effemey
International Manager ....Mark Whittemore
Production Coordinator ....Felicity White
International Travel Manager ....Lindsay Jones

EXECUTIVE PRODUCER ....NINA LANNAN

GENERAL MANAGEMENT
BESPOKE THEATRICALS
Devin Keudell
Maggie Brohn   Amy Jacobs   Nina Lannan

COMPANY MANAGER.......J. ANTHONY MAGNER
Assistant Company Manager ....Margaret Skoglund

PRODUCTION TEAM

ASSOCIATE
   CHOREOGRAPHER ....NICHOLA TREHERNE
ASSOCIATE
   CHOREOGRAPHER ....JANET ROTHERMEL
RESIDENT DIRECTOR ....MARTHA BANTA
ASSOCIATE
   MUSIC SUPERVISOR ......DAVID HOLCENBERG
ASSOCIATE
   SCENIC DESIGNER (US) ....NANCY THUN
ASSOCIATE
   SCENIC DESIGNER (UK) .....JONATHAN ALLEN
ASSOCIATE COSTUME DESIGNERS...LUCY GAIGER
                              SCOTT TRAUGOTT
ASSOCIATE HAIR DESIGNER ....JOSH MARQUETTE
ASSOCIATE
   LIGHTING DESIGNERS ....DAVID HOLMES
             ED MCCARTHY, ANDREW VOLLER
ASSOCIATE SOUND
   DESIGNERS ....BRIAN BUCHANAN
                              DAVID PATRIDGE
MUSICAL TRANSCRIPTION .....ANDERS NEGLIN
CASTING CONSULTANT ....DAVID GRINDROD

CASTING
TARA RUBIN CASTING
Tara Rubin CSA, Eric Woodall CSA,
Laura Schutzel CSA, Merri Sugarman CSA,
Dale Brown CSA,
Kaitlin Shaw, Lindsay Levine

PRESS REPRESENTATIVE
BONEAU/BRYAN-BROWN
Adrian Bryan-Brown   Joe Perrotta
Kelly Guiod

ADVERTISING AND MARKETING
SERINO COYNE INC.
Nancy Coyne   Greg Corradetti
Advertising ....Drew Nebrig, Danielle Boyle
Marketing ....Leslie Barrett, Uma McCrosson,
                         Diana Salameh, Mike Rafael

MUSIC PUBLISHED BY EMI GROVE PARK MUSIC,
INC. AND EMI WATERFORD MUSIC, INC.

STAFF FOR *MAMMA MIA!*
PRODUCTION
STAGE MANAGER................ANDREW FENTON
Stage Managers ....Sherry Cohen, Dean R. Greer

PRODUCTION MANAGER......ARTHUR SICCARDI

Head Carpenter ....Chris Nass
Assistant Carpenters ......Stephen Burns, Clark Middleton
Production Electrician ....Rick Baxter
Head Electrician ....Don Lawrence
Assistant Electrician ....Andy Sather
Vari*Lite Programmer ....Andrew Voller
Production Sound ....David Patridge
Head Sound ....Craig Cassidy
Assistant Sound ....Colin Ahearn
Production Properties ....Simon E.R. Evans
Head Properties...............................Gregory Martin
Wardrobe Supervisor ....Irene L. Bunis
Assistant Wardrobe Supervisor ....Ron Glow
Dressers ....Dani Berger, Carey Bertini, Jim Collum,
   Phillip Heckman, Lauren Kievit, Christine Richmond,
                              Rodd Sovar, I Wang
Hair Supervisor ....Sandy Schlender
Assistant Hair Supervisor ....Aaron Kinchen

Mamma Mia!
Scrapbook

Photo: Joseph Marzullo

Photo: Courtesy of Lauren Cohn

Photo: Courtesy of Lauren Cohn

Correspondent: Lauren Cohn, "Rosie"
Memorable Milestone Party: We had a wonderful 5,000th performance celebration at Sardi's just after making the move from the Winter Garden to the Broadhurst Theatre in November 2013. Part of the celebration included the unveiling of our wonderful producer Judy Craymer's caricature. It was a truly special time.

1. (L-R) *Yearbook* correspondent Lauren Cohn with Judy McLane and Felicia Finley at Sardi's celebrating the 5,000th performance, Nov. 9, 2013.
2. Lauren Cohn and *Mamma Mia*'s director Phyllida Lloyd.
3. Daniel Cooney and Lauren Cohn at the last "Mega Mix" at the Winter Garden.

Most Exciting Celebrity Visitor: We haven't had too many celebrity visitors in recent days,

but we sometimes play a game (which I suspect was developed by Albert Guerzon) where a rumor gets around how some celebrity is out there who actually is not. I think "Martha Stewart" celebrated Labor Day with us.
Actor Who Performed the Most Roles in This Show: Hmmm. I think John Hemphill may hold this title. Before I arrived on the island, he spent a year playing the role of Sam.

Assistant Lighting Designer ....Jeffrey Lowney
Assistant Costume Designer ....Angela Kahler
House Crew ....Richard Carney, Reginald Carter, Holly Hanson, Mai-Linh Lofgren, Meredith Kievit, Aarne Lofgren, Francis Lofgren, John Maloney, Michael Maloney, Glenn Russo, Dennis Wiener
Rehearsal Pianists ....Robert Bray, Sinai Tabak
Box Office ....Mary Cleary, Steve Cobb, James Drury, Sue Giebler, Michael O'Neill, Ron Schroeder
Associates to Casting Consultant ....Stephen Crockett, Will Burton
Legal Counsel (U.S.) ....Lazarus & Harris LLP Scott Lazarus, Esq., Robert Harris, Esq.
Immigration Counsel ....Mark D. Koestler/ Kramer Levin Naftalis & Frankel LLP
Accounting ....Marks Paneth & Shron LLP/ Christopher Cacace, In Woo
Interactive Marketing ....Situation Interactive/ Damian Bazadona, John Lanasa, Maris Smith, Michael Perkins
Press Office Staff ....Chris Boneau, Jim Byk, Michelle Farabaugh, Jackie Green, Linnae Hodzic, Amy Kass, Holly Kinney, Kevin Jones, Emily Meagher, Aaron Meier, Christine Olver, Heath Schwartz, Susanne Tighe
Production Photographer ....Joan Marcus
Merchandising ....Max Merchandise, LLC/ Randi Grossman, Meridith Maskara Merchandising Manager: Marc Bonanni
Theater Displays................................King Display
Insurance ....Dewitt, Stern/Walton & Parkinson Ltd.
Orthopedic Consultant ....Dr. Phillip A. Bauman
Banking................................City National Bank
Travel Agent ....Tzell Travel

Original Logo Design ....© Littlestar Services Limited

PLAYBILL Edition # 620

CREDITS AND ACKNOWLEDGMENTS

Scenery constructed and painted by Hudson Scenic Studio, Inc. and Hamilton Scenic Specialty. Computer motion control and automation by Feller Precision, Inc. SHOWTRAK computer motion control for scenery and rigging. Sound equipment supplied by Masque Sound. Lighting equipment supplied by Fourth Phase and Vari*Lite, Inc. Soft goods by I. Weiss and Sons. Costumes by Barbara Matera, Ltd., Tricorne New York City and Carelli Costumes, Inc. Additional costume work by Allan Alberts Productions. Millinery by Lynne Mackey. Wet suits by Aquatic Fabricators of South Florida. Custom men's shirts by Cego. Custom knitting by C.C. Wei. Custom fabric printing and dyeing by Dye-namix and Gene Mignola. Shoes by Native Leather, Rilleau Leather and T. O. Dey. Gloves by Cornelia James - London. Hair color by Redken. Properties by Paragon Theme and Prop Fabrication. Cough drops provided by Ricola U.S.A. Physical therapy provided by Sean Gallagher. Drums provided by Pearl. Cymbals provided by Zildjian. Drumsticks provided by Vic Firth. Drum heads provided by Remo.

Mamma Mia! was originally produced in London by LITTLESTAR SERVICES LIMITED on April 6, 1999.

Experience *Mamma Mia!* around the world:
London/Novello Theatre/mamma-mia.com
Broadway/Broadhurst Theatre/telecharge.com
International Tour/mamma-mia.com
For more information on all our
global productions visit: www.mamma-mia.com

Energy-efficient washer/dryer courtesy of
LG Electronics.

 THE SHUBERT ORGANIZATION, INC.
Board of Directors

Philip J. Smith	**Robert E. Wankel**
Chairman	President
Wyche Fowler, Jr.	**Diana Phillips**
Lee J. Seidler	**Michael I. Sovern**

Stuart Subotnick

Chief Financial Officer.........................Elliot Greene
Sr. Vice President, Ticketing ....David Andrews
Vice President, Finance ....Juan Calvo
Vice President, Human Resources ....Cathy Cozens
Vice President, Facilities ....John Darby
Vice President, Theatre Operations.............Peter Entin
Vice President, Marketing ....Charles Flateman
Vice President, General Counsel ....Gilbert Hoover
Vice President, Audit ....Anthony LaMattina
Vice President, Ticket Sales ....Brian Mahoney
Vice President, Creative Projects ...........D.S. Moynihan
Vice President, Real Estate ....Julio Peterson

---

House Manager ....Bob Reilly

BROADWAY green✚alliance   The Shubert Organization is a proud member of the Broadway Green Alliance.

Mamma Mia!
Scrapbook

A while later, he joined us in the ensemble as a triple cover, adding Harry and Bill to his arsenal. Now he is going to spend the next year officially playing Bill.

Who Has Done the Most Shows: Brent Black stayed in his track for the full run of the show from opening night to February 4, 2014. He spent thirteen years as part of the *Mamma Mia!* family. Benny and Björn even gave him a video shout-out during the 5,000th performance celebration! But I may hold the attendance

But I am happy to report that we have had VERY few cellphone incidents of any kind since I joined the cast in June of 2012.

Actor Who Wore the Heaviest/Hottest Costume: We have it pretty easy in this department. There is a lot of linen in our show...it's a Greek Island...but in the summer months, poor Graham's weirdly tweedy wedding suit overheats and he feels like he's "wearing a sofa."

Catchphrases Only the Company Would Recognize: "Conka-chonk!" "I do what I want!" "Punky!" (All

record for this year.

Special Backstage Rituals: I have a series of quirky routines, but I don't know if they have reached ritual status yet. But Judy comes around with Angel Cards each night during the overture. Our favorite word is "abundance."

Favorite Moment During Each Performance: Sadly, my favorite moment got lost in the move from the Winter Garden to the Broadhurst. I savored every last hydraulic lift in full Spandex glory for the Dynamos finale. It was a rock star moment each show! Gonna have to find a new favorite moment this year.

Cell Phone Rings, Cell Phone Photos or Texting Incidents During a Performance: A performance does not pass without a zillion people blatantly filming the MegaMix. I mean with full-sized iPads. I think the ushers no longer even try to keep that from happening.

1. Where's Lauren Cohn? Looks like she's been defaced/refaced on a subway poster.
2. Curtain call at the 5,000th performance, November 9, 2013.
3. The cast celebrating the 11th Anniversary Party on October 18, 2012.

thanks to Judy McLane).

Sweethearts Within the Company: Too many to list. *Mamma Mia!* is better than Match.com!

Orchestra Member Who Played the Most Consecutive Performances Without a Sub: I don't have an exact number, but word is that the answer is guitarist Doug Quinn without a doubt.

Favorite Therapy: FOAM ROLLERS!!!

"Carols for a Cure" Carol: Last season we did a fantastic arrangement of "Soul Cake" (and some of the gang did an exceptional reprise of it for "Gypsy of the Year"). This season we "Rejoice"d. Thank you Wendy Bobbitt Cavett.

Coolest Thing About Being in This Show: The faces of the fans that hang out after. There's a lot of JOY around the house!

Matilda the Musical

First Preview: March 4, 2013. Opened: April 11, 2013.
Still running as of May 31, 2014.

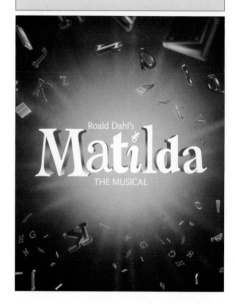

PLAYBILL

Based on Roald Dahl's novelette, this musical tells the story of a little girl genius who refuses to be ground down by parents who despise her or by a cartoonishly evil school headmistress named Miss Trunchbull who is determined to break her spirit. With the help of her kindly schoolteacher Miss Honey, Matilda uses her intelligence, her love of books and a mysterious secret super power to prevail over those who would repress her—and to turn Miss Honey's life around too.

CAST

Party Entertainer .... SEAN MONTGOMERY
Doctor .... JOHN ARTHUR GREENE
Mrs. Wormwood .... LESLI MARGHERITA
Mr. Wormwood .... MATT HARRINGTON
Matilda ..PAIGE BRADY, GABRIELLA PIZZOLO,
         RIPLEY SOBO, AVA ULLOA
Michael Wormwood .... TAYLOR TRENSCH
Mrs. Phelps .... KAREN ALDRIDGE
Miss Honey .... JILL PAICE
The Escape Artist .... BEN THOMPSON
The Acrobat .... JENNIFER BOWLES
Miss Trunchbull .... CHRISTOPHER SIEBER
Rudolpho .... PHILLIP SPAETH
Sergei .... SEAN MONTGOMERY
Other Parts Played By .... GARETT HAWE,
     MARISA KENNEDY, BETSY STRUXNESS,
               TRAVIS WALDSCHMIDT
Bruce .... MITCHELL SINK
  And on Occasion .... SAWYER NUNES,
                    CHRIS SUMPTER

Continued on next page

⑯ **SAM S. SHUBERT THEATRE**
225 West 44th Street
A Shubert Organization Theatre
Philip J. Smith, *Chairman*   **Robert E. Wankel,** *President*

Royal Shakespeare Company and the Dodgers
present
Roald Dahl's
Matilda
THE MUSICAL

BOOK
Dennis Kelly

MUSIC & LYRICS
Tim Minchin

with

Paige Brady   Gabriella Pizzolo   Ripley Sobo   Ava Ulloa

Matt Harrington   Lesli Margherita   Jill Paice   Christopher Sieber

Karen Aldridge, Jennifer Bowles, Scott Difford, John Arthur Greene, Garett Hawe,
Nadine Isenegger, Colin Israel, Marisa Kennedy, Sean Montgomery, Celia Mei Rubin,
Phillip Spaeth, Betsy Struxness, Heather Tepe, Ben Thompson, Taylor Trensch, Travis Waldschmidt

Grace Capeless, Marcus D'Angelo, Ava DeMary, Jonah Halperin, Alexa Shae Niziak, Sawyer Nunes,
Sofia Roma Rubino, Analise Scarpaci, Mitchell Sink, Chris Sumpter, Beatrice Tulchin, Ted Wilson

ASSOCIATE CHOREOGRAPHERS	ASSOCIATE DIRECTORS
Ellen Kane Kate Dunn	Thomas Caruso Luke Sheppard Lotte Wakeham

RSC COMMISSIONING DRAMATURG	CASTING	VOICE DIRECTOR
Jeanie O'Hare	Jim Carnahan C.S.A. Nora Brennan C.S.A.	Andrew Wade

MUSICAL DIRECTOR	MUSIC COORDINATOR	PRODUCTION STAGE MANAGER	COMPANY MANAGER
David Holcenberg	Howard Joines	Kelly A. Martindale	Kimberly Kelley

ADVERTISING/MARKETING	PRESS REPRESENTATIVES	PRODUCTION MANAGEMENT
AKA	Boneau/Bryan-Brown	Aurora Productions

EXECUTIVE PRODUCER	EXECUTIVE PRODUCER	GENERAL MANAGER
Denise Wood	André Ptaszynski	Dodger Management Group

SOUND DESIGN	LIGHTING DESIGN	ILLUSION
Simon Baker	Hugh Vanstone	Paul Kieve

ORCHESTRATIONS & ADDITIONAL MUSIC
Chris Nightingale

SET & COSTUME DESIGN
Rob Howell

CHOREOGRAPHY
Peter Darling

DIRECTOR
Matthew Warchus

Matilda The Musical is profoundly grateful for the support of Patty Baker, Melissa & Daniel Berger, Adam Blanshay, The Broadway Consortium/Stephanie Rosenberg, Gail and Ralph Bryan, Jed & Bronna Canaan, Scott M. Delman, Jerry Frankel, Ronald Frankel, Greenleaf Productions, Dede Harris, Independent Presenters Network, Indigo Arts & Entertainment, Elizabeth McCann, Des McAnuff, Mighty Chippewa Partnership, National Artists Mgt. Co., Michael & Gabrielle Palitz, Pittsburgh CLO, Remarkable Partners, Parag & Usha Saxena, Terry Schnuck, Tom Smedes & Peter Stern, TheatreDreams North America, Elizabeth Williams, Archana Vats & David Gartside.

Matilda The Musical is a Royal Shakespeare Company Commission. First performed in Stratford-upon-Avon on 9 November 2010.
RSC Artistic Director Gregory Doran, RSC Executive Director Catherine Mallyon
Support for the work of the Royal Shakespeare Company in the United States is led by Royal Shakespeare Company America, Inc.

4/14/14

Phillip Spaeth (Rudolpho),
Jill Paice (Miss Honey) and
Lesli Margherita (Mrs. Wormwood)

Photo: Joan Marcus

Matilda the Musical

MUSICAL NUMBERS

ACT I

"Miracle"	Company
"Naughty"	Matilda
"School Song"	Company
"Pathetic"	Miss Honey
"The Hammer"	Miss Trunchbull, Miss Honey and Children
"The Chokey Chant"	Company
"Loud"	Mrs. Wormwood and Rudolpho
"This Little Girl"	Miss Honey
"Bruce"	Children

ACT II

"Telly"	Mr. Wormwood and Michael Wormwood
"When I Grow Up"	Company
"I'm Here"	Matilda and The Escape Artist
"The Smell of Rebellion"	Miss Trunchbull, Miss Honey and Children
"Quiet"	Matilda
"My House"	Miss Honey
"Revolting Children"	Company

ORCHESTRA

Music Supervisor/Orchestrator:
CHRIS NIGHTINGALE
Music Director/Conductor:
DAVID HOLCENBERG
Associate Conductor/Keyboard 1:
MICHAEL GACETTA
Children's Music Director/Assistant Conductor:
DEBORAH ABRAMSON
Associate Conductor/Keyboard 2:
SUE ANSCHUTZ
Flute, Clarinet, Alto Sax: STEVE KENYON
Clarinet, Bass Clarinet, Tenor Sax:
HIDEAKI AOMORI
Trumpet 1: MATTHEW PETERSON

Trumpet 2: CJ CAMERIERI
Trombone/Bass Trombone: MIKE BOSCHEN
Drums/Percussion: HOWARD JOINES
Bass: MAT FIELDES
Guitars: ERIC B. DAVIS
Violin/Concertmaster: JONATHAN DINKLAGE
Violin: ELIZABETH LIM-DUTTON
Viola/Violin: WHITNEY LaGRANGE
Cello: JEANNE LeBLANC
Music Technology: PHIJ ADAMS
London Music Preparation: LAURIE PERKINS
New York Music Copyist: Emily Grishman Music
   Preparation/EMILY GRISHMAN and
   KATHARINE EDMONDS
Music Coordinator: HOWARD JOINES

Cast Continued

Lavender	GRACE CAPELESS
And on Occasion	AVA DeMARY, SOFIA ROMA RUBINO, HEATHER TEPE
Nigel	JONAH HALPERIN
And on Occasion	MARCUS D'ANGELO, SAWYER NUNES, HEATHER TEPE, TED WILSON
Amanda	BEATRICE TULCHIN
And on Occasion	AVA DeMARY, SOFIA ROMA RUBINO, HEATHER TEPE
Eric	TED WILSON
And on Occasion	MARCUS D'ANGELO, SAWYER NUNES, HEATHER TEPE
Alice	ALEXA SHAE NIZIAK
And on Occasion	CELIA MEI RUBIN, ANALISE SCARPACI, HEATHER TEPE
Hortensia	AVA DeMARY
And on Occasion	CELIA MEI RUBIN, ANALISE SCARPACI, HEATHER TEPE
Tommy	CHRIS SUMPTER
And on Occasion	CELIA MEI RUBIN, SAWYER NUNES, HEATHER TEPE

UNDERSTUDIES

For Miss Trunchbull: SEAN MONTGOMERY,
   BEN THOMPSON
For Mrs. Wormwood: MARISA KENNEDY,
   BETSY STRUXNESS
For Mr. Wormwood: JOHN ARTHUR GREENE,
   SEAN MONTGOMERY, BEN THOMPSON
For Mrs. Phelps: JENNIFER BOWLES,
   MARISA KENNEDY, CELIA MEI RUBIN
For Miss Honey: JENNIFER BOWLES,
   NADINE ISENEGGER

SWINGS

MARCUS D'ANGELO, SCOTT DIFFORD,
NADINE ISENEGGER, COLIN ISRAEL,
SAWYER NUNES, CELIA MEI RUBIN,
SOFIA ROMA RUBINO, ANALISE SCARPACI,
HEATHER TEPE

DANCE CAPTAIN

NADINE ISENEGGER

ASSISTANT/CHILDREN'S DANCE CAPTAIN

CELIA MEI RUBIN

GYM CAPTAIN

SCOTT DIFFORD

Ted Wilson is appearing with the permission of
Actors' Equity Association.

Photos: Joan Marcus

Christopher Sieber
as Miss Trunchbull

Jill Paice as
Miss Honey

Matilda the Musical

Paige Brady
Matilda

Gabriella Pizzolo
Matilda

Ripley Sobo
Matilda

Ava Ulloa
Matilda

Matt Harrington
Mr. Wormwood

Lesli Margherita
Mrs. Wormwood

Jill Paice
Miss Honey

Christopher Sieber
Miss Trunchbull

Karen Aldridge
Mrs. Phelps

Jennifer Bowles
*The Acrobat;
u/s Mrs. Phelps,
Miss Honey*

Scott Difford
Swing

John Arthur Greene
*Doctor;
u/s Mr. Wormwood*

Garett Hawe
Ensemble

Nadine Isenegger
*Swing; u/s Miss
Honey, Dance
Captain*

Colin Israel
Swing

Marisa Kennedy
*Ensemble; u/s
Mrs. Wormwood/
Mrs. Phelps*

Sean Montgomery
*Party Entertainer/
Sergei; u/s Miss
Trunchbull, Mr.
Wormwood*

Celia Mei Rubin
*Swing; u/s Mrs.
Phelps; Assistant/
Children's Dance
Captain*

Phillip Spaeth
Rudolpho

Betsy Struxness
*Ensemble;
u/s Mrs. Wormwood*

Heather Tepe
Swing

Ben Thompson
*The Escape Artist;
u/s Miss Trunchbull,
Mr. Wormwood*

Taylor Trensch
Michael Wormwood

Travis Waldschmidt
Ensemble

Grace Capeless
Lavender

Marcus D'Angelo
Swing

Ava DeMary
Hortensia

Jonah Halperin
Nigel

Alexa Shae Niziak
Alice

Sawyer Nunes
Swing

Sofia Roma Rubino
Swing

Analise Scarpaci
Swing

Mitchell Sink
Bruce

Chris Sumpter
Tommy

Beatrice Tulchin
Amanda

Matilda the Musical

Ted Wilson
Eric

Roald Dahl
Writer

Dennis Kelly
Book

Tim Minchin
Music and Lyrics

Matthew Warchus
Director

Peter Darling
Choreography

Rob Howell
Set and Costume Design

Chris Nightingale
Orchestrations, Additional Music and Music Supervision

Simon Baker
Sound Design

Hugh Vanstone
Lighting Design

Paul Kieve
Illusion

Kate Dunn
Associate Choreographer

Thomas Caruso
Associate Director

Lotte Wakeham
Associate Director

Paul Weimer
Associate Set Designer

Daryl A. Stone
Associate Costume Designer

Joel Shier
Associate Lighting Designer

Jim Carnahan C.S.A.
Casting Director

Nora Brennan C.S.A.
Casting Director

Andrew Wade
Voice Director

David Holcenberg
Musical Director

Howard Joines
Music Coordinator

Deborah Abramson
Children's Music Director

Gene O'Donovan
Aurora Productions
Production Management

Ben Heller
Aurora Productions
Production Management

Kelly A. Martindale
Production Stage Manager

Gregory Doran
Artistic Director
Royal Shakespeare Company
Producer

Catherine Mallyon
Executive Director
Royal Shakespeare Company
Producer

Michael David
The Dodgers
Producer

Edward Strong
The Dodgers
Producer

Frenie Acoba
Lavender

Erica Simone Barnett
Swing

Natalie Venetia Belcon
Mrs. Phelps

Judah Bellamy
Tommy

Matilda the Musical

Richard H. Blake
The Escapologist

Jack Broderick
Bruce

Bertie Carvel
Miss Trunchbull

Gabriel Ebert
Mr. Wormwood

Yurel Echezarreta
Swing

Sophia Gennusa
Matilda

Chris Hoch
*Miss Trunchbull,
Party Entertainer/
Sergei;
u/s Mr. Wormwood*

Emma Howard
Hortensia

Thayne Jasperson
Ensemble

Oona Laurence
Matilda

Tamika Sonja
Lawrence
*Ensemble;
u/s Mrs. Phelps.
Mrs. Wormwood*

Luke Kolbe Mannikus
Swing

Madilyn Jaz Morrow
Swing

Jared Parker
Nigel

Bailey Ryon
Matilda

John Sanders
*Party Entertainer,
Sergei;
u/s Miss Trunchbull,
Mr. Wormwood*

Milly Shapiro
Matilda

Ryan Steele
Ensemble

Samantha Sturm
*The Acrobat;
u/s Mrs. Phelps,
Miss Honey*

Clay Thomson
Swing, Gym Captain

Lauren Ward
Miss Honey

Geoff Packard
*The Escape Artist;
u/s Miss Trunchbull,
Mr. Wormwood*

MUSICIANS
Front (L-R): Deborah Abramson (Children's Music Director),
Eric B. Davis (Guitars), David Holcenberg (Music Director),
Howard Joines (Music Coordinator, Drums, Percussion),
Hideaki Aomori (Woodwinds), John Replogle (Trumpet)
Back (L-R): Chris Haberl (Keyboards),
T.O. Sterrett (Keyboards), Mike Boschen (Trombone)

MANAGEMENT
Front (L-R): KimberlyKelley (Company Management),
Michael Altbaum (Company Management), David Lober (Stage Management),
Amy Marsico (Stage Management)
Back (L-R): Andrew C. Gottlieb (Stage Management), Samantha Preiss (Stage Management)

Matilda the Musical

PRESS OFFICE
(L-R): Kelly Guiod,
Jackie Green

BOX OFFICE
Front: Rodney Giebler
Back (L-R): Mike Russo, Willow Norton,
Pat Kenary

CHILD GUARDIANS
(L-R): Alissa Zulvergold, Robert Wilson, John Mara, Jr., Krystal Rowley

Photos: Brian Mapp

STAGE DOOR
Rose Alaio

FRONT OF HOUSE
Front (L-R): Dhiandra Romero, Maura Gaynor, Erin O'Donnell, Joanne Blessington, Delia Pozo, Janet Kay
Back (L-R): Martin Cooper, Paul Rodriguez, Kathryn Tavares, Stephen Ivelja, Elvis Caban, Jim Wooley, Leo Ruiz

CREW
Front (L-R): Shazia J. Saleem, Isabelle Decauwert (Assistant Hair Supervisor), Pam Kurz (Dresser; on swing), Jenna Barrios (Hair & Make-up Supervisor), Janet Smith (on swing), Michael Maher, Jr., Michael Cornell (Head Electrician), Marcia McIntosh (Dresser; on swing), Russell Easley, Jessica Scoblick (Dresser; on swing)
Back (L-R): Jesse Hancox, Hank Hale, Jake Hall (Sound Deck), Gary Fernandez, Joseph Bradford (Lead Frontlight Operator), David L. Bornstein (Head Props), Jonathan Cohen, Ronnie Vitelli, Jr., Joel DeRuyter (Deck Automation Carpenter), Jesse Vitelli, Kyp Seiferth (Assistant Props), David Lee Earl, Peggy Kazdan (Dresser), John Funk (Dresser), Terri Purcell (Wardrobe Supervisor), Dann Wojnar, Peggie Kurz (Assistant Wardrobe Supervisor)

Matilda the Musical

Matilda the Musical
SCRAPBOOK

Correspondent: Lesli Margherita, "Mrs. Wormwood"

Milestone Party: When the original Matildas were getting their portrait at Sardi's, the company arranged an "Autumn Party." That is what they told the girls was happening. We were all in on it. Keeping our collective mouths shut was HUGE. It was such a great surprise for them.

Also, for Halloween, the kids dressed up as the adults' characters. Adorable.

Who Has Done the Most Shows: ME!!!! I'm very proud of it. I've only missed 12 shows out of 440 so far. That's a lot of jump splits.

Special Backstage Rituals: The kids have a special "pump it up!" routine they do before each show, but they seriously never need pumping up! We all have so many rituals, we are a superstitious cast. Handshakes, hugs, looks—all of it must be done each show.

Favorite Moments During Each Performance: Onstage, it's being whirled around on a hospital gurney by the gorgeous Phillip Spaeth. Disco Ball lighting while in a hospital gown? Come on! Offstage, it's watching "Revolting Children" from the back of the house. Those kids never cease to amaze.

Favorite In-Theatre Gathering Place: The Men's Ensemble room is the place. They have all the junk food. And the gossip.

Favorite Snack Foods: We (gladly) get a lot of Schmackary's cookies delivered. There is always something in the entryway that one of the kids' parents has brought in. Horrible place for a diet. Horrible.

"Carols for a Cure" Carol: "Bring a Little Joy Into the World."

Mascot: Maggot!

Favorite Therapies: We have a colony of foam rollers. Every color, every size. The theatre has an amazing Tiger Balm aroma as well.

Memorable Ad-Lib: A Matilda forgot to say some dialogue with the very important plot line of the Acrobat being pregnant. Samantha Sturm was playing the Acrobat, and very

Above: *Yearbook* Correspondent Lesli Margherita (top) with fellow cast members at the first anniversary party.
Below: The huge anniversary cake.

casually during a scene had to tell Ben Thompson, "Oh by the way, I'm pregnant."

Memorable Stage Door Fan Encounter: We have had quite a few former Newsies in our show, so the amount of screaming/crying teens is large. Someone brought me ears of corn. I still haven't figured that one out.

Web Buzz on the Show: It was impressive yet

scary. The expectation of this show was unlike anything I had ever encountered. We knew we had a lot to prove. I think we did.

Fastest Costume Change: ME! Into a raincoat. Eight seconds.

Heaviest/Hottest Costume: It has to be The Trunchbull. Her boobs alone are about 50 pounds.

Who Wore the Least: The salsa dancers in "Loud."

Memorable Directorial Note: My very first note ever from tech is still hung up in my dressing room. It says: "Seeing up skirt on hospital gurney. Miracle."

Nicknames: The theatre is "The Shubes," and the alligator floatie that Rudolpho carries is nicknamed "Shubert Alley-gator."

Embarrassing Moments: Between blocks, gates, vaults and scooters...there is a fair amount of falling that happens.

Coolest Thing About Being in This Show: That we are in this show.

Matilda London production departments who have generously shared their knowledge and experience with the Broadway team. We are especially grateful for the continuing support of the RSC Board, including the generosity of those Board members who supported the development of the show and underwrote the London run. And we thank our senior advisor for America, Ric Wanetik, who also serves as the Executive President of RSC America, for his invaluable counsel on *Matilda*, as well as his ongoing work connecting the RSC to the U.S. Our sincere thanks also to Ronald Daitz, Kimberly Blanchard and Mark Schwed of Weil, Gotshal & Manges LLP for all their pro bono support for the RSC.

RSC, ROYAL SHAKESPEARE COMPANY and the RSC logo are registered trademarks of the Royal Shakespeare Company.

Photos: Courtesy Lesli Margherita

Mothers and Sons

First Preview: February 23, 2014. Opened: March 24, 2014.
Still running as of May 31, 2014.

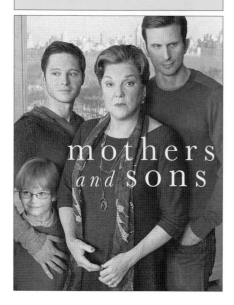

A Texas matron, still grieving the son who died of AIDS in 1994. makes a surprise visit to Cal, the man who was her son's lover. After his own long grief, Cal is now happily, legally married and raising a young son, a lifestyle inconceivable during the worst of the plague years. This enrages the mother, who doesn't understand gay life, doesn't understand why her wonderful son is being forgotten by the world, and ultimately doesn't understand the point of her own life. The show claims to be the first on Broadway to present a married gay couple.

CAST
(in order of appearance)

Katharine Gerard .... TYNE DALY
Cal Porter .... FREDERICK WELLER
Bud Ogden-Porter .... GRAYSON TAYLOR
Will Ogden .... BOBBY STEGGERT

UNDERSTUDIES AND STANDBYS
Standby for Katharine Gerard:
CAITLIN O'CONNELL
For Cal Porter/Will Ogden:
DAVID CHRISTOPHER WELLS
For Bud Ogden-Porter:
ALEX AMMERMAN

⊛ GOLDEN THEATRE
A Shubert Organization Theatre
Philip J. Smith, *Chairman* Robert E. Wankel, *President*

TOM KIRDAHY ROY FURMAN PAULA WAGNER & DEBBIE BISNO BARBARA FREITAG & LORAINE ALTERMAN BOYLE
HUNTER ARNOLD PAUL BOSKIND KEN DAVENPORT LAMS PRODUCTIONS MARK LEE & ED FILIPOWSKI
ROBERTA PEREIRA/BRUNISH-TRINCHERO SANFORD ROBERTSON TOM SMEDES & PETER STERN JACK THOMAS/SUSAN DIETZ

PRESENT

mothers
and sons

A PLAY BY

TERRENCE McNALLY

STARRING

TYNE DALY

FREDERICK WELLER BOBBY STEGGERT
GRAYSON TAYLOR

| SCENIC DESIGN | COSTUME DESIGN | LIGHTING DESIGN | SOUND DESIGN |
| JOHN LEE BEATTY | JESS GOLDSTEIN | JEFF CROITER | NEVIN STEINBERG |

| PRODUCTION STAGE MANAGER | CASTING BY | TECHNICAL SUPERVISION |
| JAMES HARKER | TARA RUBIN CASTING | HUDSON THEATRICAL ASSOCIATES |

| PRESS REPRESENTATIVE | ADVERTISING | COMPANY MANAGER | GENERAL MANAGEMENT |
| O&M CO. | SPOTCO | EDWARD NELSON | RICHARDS/CLIMAN, INC. |

DIRECTED BY

SHERYL KALLER

WORLD PREMIERE ORIGINALLY PRODUCED AT THE BUCKS COUNTY PLAYHOUSE, JUNE 2013
JED BERNSTEIN, PRODUCING DIRECTOR (2011-2013)
THE PRODUCERS WISH TO EXPRESS THEIR APPRECIATION TO THE
THEATRE DEVELOPMENT FUND FOR ITS SUPPORT OF THIS PRODUCTION

3/24/14

(L-R): Bobby Steggert, Frederick Weller, Grayson Taylor and Tyne Daly

Photo: Joan Marcus

Mothers and Sons

Tyne Daly
Katharine Gerard

Frederick Weller
Cal Porter

Bobby Steggert
Will Ogden

Grayson Taylor
Bud Ogden-Porter

Alex Ammerman
u/s Bud Ogden-Porter

Caitlin O'Connell
u/s Katharine Gerard

...

David Christopher
Wells
*u/s Cal Porter,
Will Ogden*

Terrence McNally
Playwright

Sheryl Kaller
Director

John Lee Beatty
Scenic Design

Jess Goldstein
Costume Design

Jeff Croiter
Lighting Design

Nevin Steinberg
Sound Design

Tara Rubin
Tara Rubin Casting
Casting

Neil A. Mazzella
Hudson Theatrical
Associates
Technical Supervisor

David R. Richards
and Tamar Haimes
Richards/Climan, Inc.
General Manager

Tom Kirdahy
Producer

Roy Furman
Producer

Paula Wagner
Producer

Debbie Bisno
Producer

Barbara Freitag
Producer

Photo: Joan Marcus

(L-R): Bobby Steggert
and Frederick Weller

Loraine Alterman
Boyle
Producer

Hunter Arnold
Producer

Paul Boskind
Producer

David Siesko...
Ken Davenport
Producer

Bradley Reynolds
LAMS Productions
Producer

David Siesko
LAMS Productions
Producer

Roberta Pereira
Producer

Corey Brunish
Brunish & Trinchero
Producer

Mothers and Sons

Brisa Trinchero
Brunish & Trinchero
Producer

Sanford Robertson
Producer

Tom Smedes
Producer

Peter Stern
Producer

Jack Thomas
Producer

Susan Dietz
Producer

Jed Bernstein
Bucks County
Playhouse
Originating Theatre

Photos: Brian Mapp

BOX OFFICE
(L-R): Theresa Hoffmann-Rizzo, Vigi Cadunz, Melissa Jorgensen

CREW
(L-R): Shanna Allison (Child Guardian), Gayle Palmieri (Wardrobe Supervisor), Valerie Gladstone (Dresser)

FRONT OF HOUSE
Front (L-R): Sheila Staffney, Camille Vasquez, Julia Gonzalez, Cookie Harlin
Back (L-R): Mae Smith, Andrew MacKay, Helen Bentley, Patricia Byrne

DOORMAN
John Green

STAGE MANAGEMENT/CREW
(L-R): James Harker (Production Stage Manager), Bethany Russell (Stage Manager), Sylvia Yoshioka, Scott Sanders (Production Sound Engineer), Tom Mitchell, Terry McGarty

Mothers and Sons
SCRAPBOOK

Correspondent: Bobby Steggert, "Will Ogden"
Opening Night Party: Sardi's was packed with every actor to ever do a McNally play.
Special Backstage Ritual: Tyne walked up five flights of stairs before EVERY show to hug me.
Memorable Celebrity Guests: So many Momma Roses...Tyne, Patti, Bernadette, the ghost of Ethel.
Favorite Off-Site Hangout: We tend to go old school with Joe Allen's.
Favorite Snack Food: Oreos, of course.
Favorite Therapy: Naps on the set's incredibly comfy couch.

Photos: Joseph Marzullo

Playwright Terrence McNally takes a bow on opening night at the Golden Theatre as Frederick Weller looks on.

Mascot: Grayson Taylor and/or Terrence McNally's socks.
Catchphrase Only the Company Would Recognize: Separate Realities.
Who Wore the Heaviest/Hottest Costume?: Tyne's fur coat was the play's fifth character.
What Did You Think of the Web Buzz on Your Show? I'm completely in the dark when it comes to internets.
Coolest Thing About Being in This Show: Getting to square off with one of our best actresses and having to pretend to dislike someone so likable.

(L-R): Bobby Steggert, Tyne Daly, Terrence McNally, Frederick Weller, director Sheryl Kaller, producer Tom Kirdahy and (front) Grayson Taylor.

Taking their bows on opening night (L-R): Grayson Taylor, Frederick Weller, Tyne Daly and *Yearbook* correspondent Bobby Steggert.

STAFF FOR *MOTHERS AND SONS*

GENERAL MANAGEMENT
RICHARDS/CLIMAN, INC.
David R. Richards   Tamar Haimes
Michael Sag   Jenny Peek
Kyle Bonder   Rachel Welt

COMPANY MANAGER
Edward Nelson

PRODUCTION MANAGEMENT
HUDSON THEATRICAL ASSOCIATES
Neil A. Mazzella   Sam Ellis
Caitlin McInerney   Irene Wang

GENERAL PRESS REPRESENTATIVE
O&M CO.
Rick Miramontez   Andy Snyder
Scott Braun   Michael Jorgensen

CASTING
TARA RUBIN CASTING
Tara Rubin CSA, Eric Woodall CSA
Merri Sugarman CSA, Kaitlin Shaw CSA
Lindsay Levine CSA, Scott Anderson

PRODUCTION STAGE MANAGER ......James Harker
Stage Manager ....Bethany Russell
Assistant Director ....Srda Vasiljevic
Associate Scenic Designer ....Kacie Hultgren
Associate Costume Designer ....China Lee
Associate Lighting Designer.......................Rob Ross
Associate Sound Designer ....Jason Crystal
Assistant Sound Designer ....Palmer Hefferen
Advance Production Carpenter ....Andrew Sullivan
Production Electrician ....James Maloney, Jr.

Moving Light Programmer ....Alex Fogel
Production Sound Engineer ....Scott Sanders
Properties Supervisor ....Buist C. Bickley
Wardrobe Supervisor ....Jessica Worsnop
Hair Supervisor ....Geordie Sheffer
Dresser ....Valerie Gladstone
Child Guardian ....Lisa Susanne Schwartz
Assistant to Terrence McNally ....Logan Reed
Advertising, Marketing, Interactive ....SpotCo
Assistant to Ms. Daly ....John V. Fahey
General Management Interns ....Harriet Taylor,
       Elliot Miranda, Katie Titley
Casting Associate ....Kaitlin Shaw, CSA
Casting Assistant ....Scott Anderson
Press Associates ....Sarah Babin, Molly Barnett,
       Philip Carrubba, Jon Dimond, Andrew Esposito,
       Joyce Friedmann, Yufen Kung, Patrick Lazour,
       Chelsea Nachman, Marie Pace, Ryan Ratelle,
       Pete Sanders, Andy Snyder
Press Interns ....Nancy Alligood, Louise de Silva
Banking ....Signature Bank/Mary Ann Fanelli
Insurance ....DeWitt Stern Group Inc./Anthony Pittari
Accountants ....Fried & Kowgios CPAs LLP
Comptroller ....Elliott Aronstam
Production Legal
    Counsel ...Levine Plotkin & Menin LLP/Loren Plotkin
Payroll ....Castellana Services
Merchandise ....Max Merchandise
Production Photographer ....Joan Marcus
Opening Night Coordination ....Serino/Coyne Events/
       Suzanne Tobak, Chrissann Gasparro

CREDITS
Scenery built by Hudson Scenic. Lighting provided by PRG Lighting. Sound equipment from Masque Sound. Ms. Daly's fur provided by Steven Corn Furs. Ms. Daly's wig by Paul Huntley.

SPECIAL THANKS
Manhattan Theatre Club, Lincoln Center Theater, Rosi Zingales, Studio Rouge, Alex Ringler, Polina Minchuk, Naomi O'Connell

---

 THE SHUBERT ORGANIZATION, INC.
Board of Directors

Philip J. Smith   **Robert E. Wankel**
Chairman   President

Wyche Fowler, Jr.   **Diana Phillips**

Lee J. Seidler   **Michael I. Sovern**

Stuart Subotnick

Chief Financial Officer..........................Elliot Greene
Sr. Vice President, Ticketing ....David Andrews
Vice President, Finance ....Juan Calvo
Vice President, Human Resources ....Cathy Cozens
Vice President, Facilities ....John Darby
Vice President, Theatre Operations.............Peter Entin
Vice President, Marketing ....Charles Flateman
Vice President, General Counsel ....Gilbert Hoover
Vice President, Audit ....Anthony LaMattina
Vice President, Ticket Sales ....Brian Mahoney
Vice President, Creative Projects ............D.S. Moynihan
Vice President, Real Estate ....Julio Peterson

---

House Manager ....Carolyne A. Jones-Barnes

 BROADWAY green♦alliance   The Shubert Organization is a proud member of the Broadway Green Alliance.

Motown: The Musical

First Preview: March 11, 2013. Opened: April 14, 2013.
Still running as of May 31, 2014.

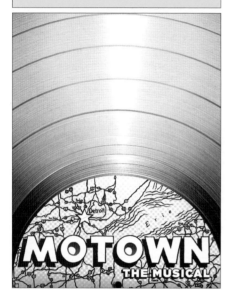

PLAYBILL

This autobiographical jukebox musical traces the turbulent life and career of Berry Gordy, early 1960s founder of Motown Records, which provided an artistic home to two generations of mainly African-American soul, r&b and pop stars including Diana Ross, Marvin Gaye, Smokey Robinson, Gladys Knight, Stevie Wonder and Michael Jackson. The production features faithful recreations of these and many other acts by young performers, many of them chosen by Gordy himself.

CAST

BRANDON VICTOR DIXON ....Berry Gordy
VALISIA LeKAE ....Diana Ross
CHARL BROWN ....Smokey Robinson
BRYAN TERRELL CLARK ....Marvin Gaye
DARIUS KALEB ....Young Berry/Stevie/Michael
RAYMOND LUKE, JR...................Young Berry/
Stevie/Michael

ENSEMBLE

TIMOTHY J. ALEX ....Roger Campbell,
Tom Clay, Pirate DJ
MICHAEL ARNOLD ......Jackie Wilson Manager,
Harold Noveck, Studio Head
NICHOLAS CHRISTOPHER ....Four Top,
Norman Whitfield
REBECCA E. COVINGTON ....Gwen Gordy,
Vandella, Gladys Horton, Cindy Birdsong
ARIANA DeBOSE ....Mary Wilson
ANDREA DORA ....Suzanne de Passe
WILKIE FERGUSON III ....Jr. Walker All Star

Continued on next page

&N& **LUNT-FONTANNE THEATRE**
UNDER THE DIRECTION OF
JAMES M. NEDERLANDER AND JAMES L. NEDERLANDER

KEVIN McCOLLUM DOUG MORRIS AND BERRY GORDY
Present

MOTOWN
THE MUSICAL

Book by
BERRY GORDY

Music and Lyrics from
THE LEGENDARY MOTOWN CATALOG

BASED UPON THE BOOK *TO BE LOVED:
THE MUSIC, THE MAGIC, THE MEMORIES
OF MOTOWN* BY BERRY GORDY

MUSIC BY ARRANGEMENT WITH
SONY/ATV MUSIC PUBLISHING

MOTOWN® IS USED UNDER LICENSE FROM UMG RECORDINGS, INC.

Starring
BRANDON VICTOR DIXON
VALISIA LeKAE

CHARL BROWN   **BRYAN TERRELL CLARK**

TIMOTHY J. ALEX   MICHAEL ARNOLD   NICHOLAS CHRISTOPHER   REBECCA E. COVINGTON   ARIANA DeBOSE
ANDREA DORA   PRESTON W. DUGGER III   WILKIE FERGUSON III   DIONNE FIGGINS   MARVA HICKS   TIFFANY JANENE HOWARD
SASHA HUTCHINGS   LAUREN LIM JACKSON   JAWAN M. JACKSON   MORGAN JAMES   JOHN JELLISON
CRYSTAL JOY   DARIUS KALEB   GRASAN KINGSBERRY   JAMIE LaVERDIERE   RAYMOND LUKE, JR.   KRISHA MARCANO   MARIELYS MOLINA
SYDNEY MORTON   MAURICE MURPHY   JARRAN MUSE   JESSE NAGER   MILTON CRAIG NEALY   N'KENGE   DOMINIC NOLFI
SAYCON SENGBLOH   RYAN SHAW   JAMAL STORY   ERIC LaJUAN SUMMERS   EPHRAIM M. SYKES
JULIUS THOMAS III   DANIEL J. WATTS   DONALD WEBBER, JR.

Scenic Design	Costume Design	Lighting Design	Sound Design	Projection Design
DAVID KORINS	ESOSA	NATASHA KATZ	PETER HYLENSKI	DANIEL BRODIE

Casting	Hair & Wig Design	Associate Director	Assistant Choreographer
TELSEY + COMPANY BETHANY KNOX, CSA	CHARLES G. LaPOINTE	SCHELE WILLIAMS	BRIAN H. BROOKS

Production Stage Manager	Technical Supervisor	General Management	Executive Producer
JULIA P. JONES	DAVID BENKEN	BESPOKE THEATRICALS	NINA LANNAN

Advertising & Marketing	Marketing Outreach	Press Representative	Music Coordinator
SpotCo	MARCIA PENDELTON	BONEAU/BRYAN-BROWN	MICHAEL KELLER

Orchestrations	Music Director/Conductor	Dance Music Arrangements	Additional Arrangements
ETHAN POPP & BRYAN CROOK	JOSEPH JOUBERT	ZANE MARK	BRYAN CROOK

Script Consultants
DAVID GOLDSMITH & DICK SCANLAN

Creative Consultant
CHRISTIE BURTON

Music Supervision & Arrangements by
ETHAN POPP

Choreographed by
PATRICIA WILCOX & WARREN ADAMS

Directed by
CHARLES RANDOLPH-WRIGHT

10/1/13

The Temptations (L-R): Jesse Nager, Donald Webber, Jr., Julius Thomas III, Ephraim M. Sykes, Jawan M. Jackson

Photo: Joan Marcus

Motown: The Musical

MUSICAL NUMBERS

Motown music courtesy of Sony/ATV Music Publishing.

"ABC"
"A Breathtaking Guy"
"Ain't No Mountain High Enough"
"Ain't Too Proud to Beg"
"Baby I Need Your Lovin'"
"Baby Love"
"Ball of Confusion"
"Brick House"
"Buttered Popcorn"
"Bye Bye Baby/Two Lovers"
"Can I Close the Door" *
"Cruisin'"
"Dancing in the Street"
"Do You Love Me"
"Get Ready"
"Give It to Me, Baby"
"Good Morning, Heartache"
"Got a Job"
"Happy Birthday"
"Hey Joe (Black Like Me)" *
"I Can't Get Next to You"
"I Can't Help Myself (Sugar Pie, Honey Bunch)"
"I Got the Feelin' "
"I Hear a Symphony"
"I Heard It Through the Grapevine"
"(I Know) I'm Losing You"
"I'll Be There"
"It's What's in the Grooves That Counts" *
"I Want You Back"

"Lonely Teardrops"
"Love Is Here and Now You're Gone"
"Mercy, Mercy Me (The Ecology)"
"Money (That's What I Want)"
"My Girl"
"My Guy"
"My Mama Done Told Me"
"Please, Mr. Postman"
"Reach Out (I'll Be There)"
"Reach Out and Touch"
"Reet Petite"
"Remember Me"
"Shop Around"
"Shotgun"
"Signed, Sealed, Delivered I'm Yours"
"Square Biz"
"Stop in the Name of Love"
"Stubborn Kind of Fellow"
"Super Freak"
"The Happening"
"The Love You Save"
"To Be Loved"
"Two Lovers"
"War"
"What's Going On"
"Where Did Our Love Go"
"Who's Loving You"
"You're All I Need to Get By"
"You're Nobody 'Til Somebody Loves You"
"You've Really Got a Hold on Me"

* Songs written for this production by Berry Gordy and Michael Lovesmith

ORCHESTRA

Conductor: JOSEPH JOUBERT
Associate Conductor: JASON MICHAEL WEBB
Reeds: TODD GROVES,
JACK BASHKOW, ALDEN BANTA
Trumpets: JOHN CHUDOBA,
BRIAN PARESCHI
Trombones: BRUCE EIDEM, JASON JACKSON
Violin: SEAN CARNEY
Violin/Viola: ORLANDO WELLS
Cello: AMY RALSKE

Keyboard 1: JASON MICHAEL WEBB
Keyboard 2: ALVIN HOUGH
Guitars: KENNY BRESCIA, BOBBY BAXMEYER
Bass: LUICO HOPPER
Drums: BUDDY WILLIAMS
Percussion: GARY SELIGSON,
ROGER SQUITERO

Music Coordinator: MICHAEL KELLER
Keyboard Programmer: RANDY COHEN
Music Preparation:
Emily Grishman Music Preparation

Cast Continued

MARVA HICKS ......Esther Gordy, Lula Hardaway, Gladys Knight
TIFFANY JANENE HOWARD ....Anna Gordy, Marvelette
SASHA HUTCHINGS ....Claudette Robinson, Billie Jean Brown, Marvelette
JAWAN M. JACKSON ....Melvin Franklin, Miracle, Commodore
MORGAN JAMES ....Landlady, Teena Marie
JOHN JELLISON ....Ed Sullivan, Shelly Berger, Dudley Buell
GRASAN KINGSBERRY ....Four Top, Contour, Jackson 5, Georgie Woods
MARIELYS MOLINA ....Marvelette, French Announcer
SYDNEY MORTON ....Florence Ballard
MAURICE MURPHY ....Dennis Edwards, Miracle, Jr.Walker, Commodore
JESSE NAGER ....Temptation, Magnificent Montague, Commodore
MILTON CRAIG NEALY ....Pop Gordy, Commodore, Pip
N'KENGE ....Mary Wells, Mother Gordy, Vandella
DOMINIC NOLFI ....Barney Ales
SAYCON SENGBLOH ....Edna Anderson, Martha Reeves, Chattie Hattie
RYAN SHAW ....Stevie Wonder, Levi Stubbs, Miracle, Pip
JAMAL STORY ....Contour, Hitsville Employee
ERIC LaJUAN SUMMERS ....Jackie Wilson, Four Top, Contour, Brian Holland, Jackson 5, Rick James
EPHRAIM M. SYKES ...Temptation, Robert Gordy, Contour, Jackson 5
JULIUS THOMAS III ....Lamont Dozier, David Ruffin, Jackson 5, Jermaine Jackson, Miller London, Pip
DANIEL J. WATTS ....Contour, Eddie Holland
DONALD WEBBER, JR. ....Temptation, Mickey Stevenson, Martin Luther King Jr., Commodore

SWINGS

PRESTON W. DUGGER III,
WILKIE FERGUSON III,
DIONNE FIGGINS, CRYSTAL JOY,
JAMIE LaVERDIERE,
KRISHA MARCANO, JARRAN MUSE

DANCE CAPTAINS

DIONNE FIGGINS, JAMAL STORY

UNDERSTUDIES

For Berry Gordy:
JULIUS THOMAS III, DONALD WEBBER, JR.

Photo: Joan Marcus

Raymond Luke, Jr. (C)
as Michael Jackson
with the Jackson 5

Continued on next page

Motown: The Musical

Cast Continued

For Diana Ross:
ARIANA DeBOSE, DIONNE FIGGINS
For Smokey Robinson:
NICHOLAS CHRISTOPHER, JARRAN MUSE
For Marvin Gaye:
MAURICE MURPHY, JARRAN MUSE

SCENES

ACT 1

1983: Pasadena Civic Auditorium,
Berry Gordy's House – Los Angeles

1938: The Gordy Family Home –
Detroit, Urban Street

1957: Flame Show Bar, Gwen's House,
Jackie Wilson's Manager's Office,
Gordy Home

1959: Hitsville House, WJBK Radio

1962: Motortown Revue, Hitsville Office/
A Payphone in Birmingham

1963: Hitsville Studio A

1964: Caravan Of Stars, Ed Sullivan Theatre Stage

1965: Theater – Manchester, England – Backstage
& Onstage, Paris Hotel, The Copacabana

1968: In and Around Hitsville

ACT 2

1968: Performance Stage

1968: In And Around Hitsville

1969: Hollywood Palace

1970: Frontier Hotel - Outer Lobby & Stage

1971: L.A. Recording Studios, A Resort in the
Bahamas, Smokey's Hotel Room -
Los Angeles, Berry's Office, Sales Dept./
Southern Distributor's Office

1972: Diana's Dressing Room,
Hollywood Movie Set

1975: Motown L.A. Offices

1981: Diana's Dressing Room, Onstage

1983: Berry Gordy's House,
Pasadena Civic Auditorium

A NOTE FROM BERRY GORDY

At Motown, we called ourselves a family and we were – a big family. While it is impossible to list here the many people who helped create Motown with their love and passion, I personally want to thank them all. Their dedication and talent contributed to our success, as well as helped to inspire me to bring our story to Broadway.

Motown was a dream that happened to come true, and it's because of all of you. Thank you.

Berry Gordy
Founder, Motown

Brandon Victor Dixon
Berry Gordy

Valisia LeKae
Diana Ross

Charl Brown
Smokey Robinson

Bryan Terrell Clark
Marvin Gaye

Timothy J. Alex
Ensemble

Michael Arnold
Ensemble

Nicholas Christopher
Ensemble

Rebecca E.
Covington
Ensemble

Ariana DeBose
Ensemble

Andrea Dora
Ensemble

Preston W.
Dugger III
Swing

Wilkie Ferguson III
*Ensemble, Partial
Swing*

Dionne Figgins
*Swing, Dance
Captain*

Marva Hicks
Ensemble

Tiffany Janene
Howard
Ensemble

Sasha Hutchings
Ensemble

Lauren Lim Jackson
Ensemble

Jawan M. Jackson
Ensemble

Morgan James
Ensemble

John Jellison
Ensemble

Motown: The Musical

Crystal Joy
Swing

Darius Kaleb
*Young Berry Gordy,
Michael Jackson,
Stevie Wonder*

Grasan Kingsberry
Ensemble

Jamie LaVerdiere
Swing

Raymond Luke, Jr.
*Young Berry Gordy,
Michael Jackson,
Stevie Wonder*

Krisha Marcano
Swing

Marielys Molina
Ensemble

Sydney Morton
Ensemble

Maurice Murphy
Ensemble

Jarran Muse
Swing

Jesse Nager
Ensemble

Milton Craig Nealy
Ensemble

N'Kenge
Ensemble

Dominic Nolfi
Ensemble

Saycon Sengbloh
Ensemble

Ryan Shaw
Ensemble

Jamal Story
*Ensemble,
Dance Captain*

Eric LaJuan
Summers
Ensemble

Ephraim M. Sykes
Ensemble

Julius Thomas III
Ensemble

Daniel J. Watts
Ensemble

Donald Webber, Jr.
Ensemble

Berry Gordy
Book, Producer

Charles
Randolph-Wright
Director

Patricia Wilcox
Choreographer

Warren Adams
Choreographer

David Korins
Scenic Design

ESosa
Costume Design

Natasha Katz
Lighting Design

Peter Hylenski
Sound Design

Daniel Brodie
Projection Design

Ethan Popp
*Music Supervision,
Orchestrations,
Arrangements*

Bryan Crook
*Orchestrations,
Additional
Arrangements*

Zane Mark
*Dance Music
Arrangements*

Joseph Joubert
*Music Director,
Conductor*

Motown: The Musical

Michael Keller
Music Coordinator

Bernard Telsey
Telsey + Company
Casting

Charles G. LaPointe
Hair & Wig Design

J. Jared Janas
Make-up Design

David Goldsmith
Script Consultant

Dick Scanlan
Script Consultant

David Benken
Technical Supervisor

Rod Lemmond
Associate Scenic Designer

Marcia Pendelton
Walk Tall Girl Productions
Marketing Outreach

Maggie Brohn
Bespoke Theatricals
General Management

Amy Jacobs
Bespoke Theatricals
General Management

Devin Keudell
Bespoke Theatricals
General Management

Nina Lannan
Executive Producer
Bespoke Theatricals
General Management

Kevin McCollum
Producer

Doug Morris
Producer

Felicia Boswell
Diana Ross

Rickey Tripp
Contour, Eddie Holland

Nik Walker
Swing

TRANSFER STUDENTS

Gerald Avery
Contour, Hitsville Employee

Felicia Boswell
Diana Ross

Krystal Joy Brown
Diana Ross

Dwayne Cooper
Melvin Franklin, Miracle, Commodore

Darius Crenshaw
Temptation, Robert Gordy, Contour, Jackson 5

Rod Harrelson
Swing

Afra Hines
Claudette Robinson, Billie Jean Brown, Marvelette

Dana Marie Ingraham
Swing

Marcus Paul James
Swing

David Josefsberg
Swing

Aaron Kaburick
Jackie Wilson Manager, Harold Noveck, Studio Head

Mykal Kilgore
Dennis Edwards, Miracle, Jr. Walker, Commodore; u/s Marvin Gaye

Prince George Maynard
Young Berry/Stevie/Michael

Motown: The Musical

(L-R): Marva Hicks (Esther Gordy), Brandon Victor Dixon (Berry Gordy) and cast

Tracy McDowell
Landlady, Teena Marie

Jevon McFerrin
Four Top, Norman Whitfield; u/s Smokey Robinson

Moeisha McGill
Swing

Angela Wildflower Polk
Mary Wells, Mother Gordy, Vandella

Allison Semmes
Florence Ballard; u/s Diana Ross

Jaquez André Sims
Swing

Sabrina Sloan
Florence Ballard

Nik Walker
Swing

Lisa Nicole Wilkerson
Anna Gordy, Marvelette

Syndee Winters
Mary Wells, Mother Gordy, Vandella

Dashaun Young
Temptation, Mickey Stevenson, Martin Luther King, Jr., Commodore; u/s Berry Gordy

CREW
Front Row (L-R): Kat Martin (Dresser), Erik Bergrin, Sherry Wong (Dresser), Mikey Goodmark, Christina M. Ainge (Wardrobe Supervisor), Sally Dennison, Heather Wright (Hair/Wig Supervisor), Michael Ferguson, Samantha Wiener, Jeff Blackwood, Pinky Pusillo (Dresser), Ron Fleming (Dresser)
Back Row (L-R): Lauren Hirsch, Melissa Joy Crawford (Assistant Wardrobe Supervisor), Michael Hyman (Head Electrician), Brendan Lynch, David Brickman, Jeff Zink (Head Carpenter), Michael L. Shepp Jr. (Deck Automation), Vanessa Anderson (Hair Assistant), Gabby Vincent (Hair Assistant), Eric Speed Smith (Head Props), Adele Miskie (Dresser), Patti Luther (Dresser), Denise Martin

Motown: The Musical

MANAGEMENT
(L-R): Julia P. Jones (Production Stage Manager), Matthew Lacey (Stage Manager),
Mary MacLeod (Assistant Stage Manager), Amber Dickerson (Assistant Stage Manager)

BOX OFFICE
(L-R): Joe Olcese (Head Treasurer), Lynne Olcese, John Rooney

STAGE DOOR
(L-R): Joey Cintron, Ray Guerrera

FRONT OF HOUSE
First Row (L-R): Tracey Malinowski (House Manager), Raymond LukeJr. (Actor), Jessica Gonzalez (Chief Usher), Evelyn Fernandez, Maxi Abdallah,
Madeline Flores, Raymond Luke Sr.
Second Row (L-R): Lauren Banyai, Stephanie Martinez, Kirstin DeCicco, Philip Zhang, Melissa Ocasio, Charles Thompson, Roberto Calderon
Third Row (L-R): Virginia Goebel, Diane Mashburn, Richard Darbasie, Marienell Clavano, Sheron James-Richardson, Sharon Grant, Gina Sanabria,
Carmela Cambio, Stephanie Colon
Back Row (L-R): Anthony Marcello, Jason Fonseca, Guest Visitor, Paul Perez, Spencer Cordeiro, Tracy Moss, Megan Mulligan

Motown: The Musical

Motown: The Musical

Brandon Victor Dixon as Berry Gordy (C) and the cast of *Motown*.

Whitfield, Norman J./Strong, Barrett Stone Agate Music (BMI) **"Brick House"** by Richie, Lionel/Lapread, Ronald/Orange, Walter/Williams, Milan/McClary, Thomas/ King, William Jobete Music Co. Inc. OBO itself and Cambrae Music/Hanna Music/Libren Music/ Macawrite Music/Old Fashion Publishing/Walter Orange Music (ASCAP) **"Buttered Popcorn"** by Gordy, Berry Jr./Ales, Barney Jobete Music Co. Inc. (ASCAP)/ Stone Agate Music (BMI) **"Bye Bye Baby"** by Wells, Mary Stone Agate Music (BMI) **"Can I Close the Door"** Written by Berry Gordy and Michael Lovesmith **"Cruisin'"** by Robinson, Smokey/Tarplin, Marvin Jobete Music Co. Inc. OBO Bertam Music Company (ASCAP) **"Dancing in the Street"** by Gaye, Marvin P/Hunter, Ivy Jo/Stevenson, William Stone Agate Music (BMI)/Jobete Music Co. Inc. OBO itself and MGIII Music, NMG Music and FCG Music (ASCAP) **"Do You Love Me"** by Gordy, Berry Jr. Jobete Music Co. Inc. (ASCAP) **"Get Ready"** by Robinson, Smokey Jobete Music Co. Inc. (ASCAP) **"Give It to Me Baby"** by James, Rick Jobete Music Co. Inc. (ASCAP) **"Good Morning Heartache"** by Drake, Ervin M./Fisher, Dan/Higginbotham, Irene Lindabet Music Corporation, Microhits Music Corp., Sony/ATV Tunes, LLC. (ASCAP) **"Got a Job"** by Robinson, Smokey/Gordy, Berry Jr./Carlo, Tyran Jobete Music Co. Inc. obo itself and Taj Mahal Music/ Third Above Music Inc. (ASCAP) **"Happy Birthday"** by Wonder, Stevie Jobete Music Co. Inc. and Black Bull Music c/o EMI April Music Inc. (ASCAP) **"Hey Joe (Black Like Me)"** Written by Berry Gordy and Michael Lovesmith **"I Can't Get Next to You"** by Whitfield, Norman J./Strong, Barrett Stone Agate Music (BMI) **"I Can't Help Myself (Sugar Pie Honey Bunch)"** by Holland, Brian/Dozier, Lamont Herbert/Holland, Edward, Jr. Stone Agate Music (BMI) **"I Got the Feelin'"** by James Brown Bro N Sis Music, Inc. (BMI) **"I Hear a Symphony"** by Holland, Brian/Dozier, Lamont Herbert/Holland, Edward, Jr. Stone Agate Music (BMI) **"I Heard It Through the Grapevine"** by Whitfield, Norman J./Strong, Barrett Stone Agate Music (BMI) **"(I Know) I'm Losing You"** by Whitfield, Norman J./Holland, Edward, Jr./Grant, Cornelius Stone Agate Music (BMI) **"I'll Be There"** by Davis, Hal/Gordy, Berry Jr./West, Bob/Hutch, Willie Jobete Music Co. Inc. (ASCAP) **"Inner City Blues (Make Me Wanna Holler)"** by Gaye, Marvin P./Nyx, James Jobete Music Co. Inc. obo itself and MGIII Music, NMG Music and FCG Music (ASCAP) **"It's What's in the Grooves That Counts"** Written by Berry Gordy and Michael Lovesmith **"Itsy Bitsy Teeny Weeny Yellow Polka Dot Bikini"** by Pockriss, Lee J./Vance, Paul Emily Music Corp, Music Sales Corp (ASCAP) **"I Want You Back"** by Perren, Freddie/Mizell, Alphonso J./Gordy, Berry Jr./Richards, Deke Jobete Music Co. Inc. (ASCAP) **"Lonely Teardrops"** by Gordy, Berry

Jr./Fuqua, Gwendolyn Gordy/ Carlo, Tyran Jobete Music Co. Inc. obo Old Brompton Road Music. (ASCAP)/Third Above Music Inc. (ASCAP) **"Love Is Here and Now You're Gone"** by Holland, Brian/Dozier, Lamont Herbert/ Holland, Edward, Jr. Stone Agate Music (BMI) **"Mama Done Told Me (My)"** by Robinson, Smokey/Gordy, Berry Jr./Carlo, Tyran Jobete Music Co. Inc. (ASCAP) **"Mercy Mercy Me (The Ecology)"** by Gaye, Marvin P. Jobete Music Co. Inc. obo itself and MGIII Music, NMG Music and FCG Music (ASCAP) **"Money (That's What I Want)"** by Gordy, Berry Jr./Bradford, Janie Jobete Music Co. Inc. (ASCAP)/Stone Agate Music (BMI) **"My Girl"** by White, Ronald/Robinson, Smokey Jobete Music Co. Inc. (ASCAP) **"My Guy"** by Robinson, Smokey Jobete Music Co. Inc. (ASCAP) **"My World Is Empty Without You"** by Brian Holland, Lamont Dozier, Edward Holland Jr Stone Agate Music (BMI) **"Papa Was a Rollin' Stone"** by Whitfield, Norman J./Strong, Barrett Stone Diamond Music Corp. (BMI) **"Please, Mr. Postman"** by Garrett, William/ Dobbins, Georgia/Holland, Brian/ Gorman, Freddie/ Bateman, Robert Jobete Music Co. Inc. (ASCAP)/Stone Diamond Music Corp. (BMI)/EMI Blackwood Music Inc. (BMI) **"Reach Out and Touch (Somebody's Hand)"** by Ashford, Nickolas/Simpson, Valerie Jobete Music Co. Inc. (ASCAP) **"Reach Out I'll Be There"** by Holland, Brian/Dozier, Lamont Herbert/ Holland, Edward, Jr. Stone Agate Music (BMI) **"Reet Petite (The Sweetest Girl in Town)"** by Gordy, Berry Jr./Carlo, Tyran Jobete Music Co. Inc. (ASCAP)/Third Above Music Inc. (ASCAP) **"Remember Me"** by Ashford, Nickolas/ Simpson, Valerie Jobete Music Co. Inc. (ASCAP) **"Shop Around"** by Robinson, Smokey/Gordy, Berry Jr Jobete Music Co. Inc. (ASCAP) **"Shotgun"** by Dewalt, Autry Stone Agate Music (BMI) **"Signed, Sealed, Delivered I'm Yours"** by Wonder, Stevie/Wright, Syreeta/Garrett, Lee/ Hardaway, Lula Mae Jobete Music Co. Inc. and Black Bull Music c/o EMI April Music Inc. (ASCAP)/Swandi Music (BMI) c/o EMI Blackwood Music Inc. (BMI) **"Square Biz"** by Brockert, Mary C./MC Grier, Allen Henry Jobete Music Co. Inc. obo itself and McNella Music (ASCAP) **"Stop in the Name of Love"** by Holland, Brian/Dozier, Lamont Herbert/Holland, Edward, Jr. Stone Agate Music (BMI) **"Stubborn Kind of Fellow"** by Gaye, Marvin P./Gordy, George/Stevenson, William Stone Agate Music (BMI)/ Jobete Music Co. Inc. obo itself aAnd MGIII Music, NMG Music and FCG Music (ASCAP) **"Super Freak"** by James, Rick/Miller, Alonzo Jobete Music Co. Inc. (ASCAP)/Stone Diamond Music Corp. (BMI) **"The Happening"** by Dozier, Lamont Herbert/Holland, Edward, Jr./Holland, Brian/De Vol, Frank Jobete Music Co. Inc. (ASCAP)/Stone Agate Music (BMI) **"The Love You Save"** by Perren, Freddie/Mizell, Alphonso J/Gordy, Berry Jr./Richards, Deke Jobete Music

Co. Inc. (ASCAP) **"Theme From Mahogany 'Do You Know Where You're Going To'"** by Goffin, Gerry/Masser, Michael Jobete Music Co. Inc. (ASCAP)/ Screen Gems-EMI Music Inc. (BMI) **"To Be Loved"** by Gordy, Berry Jr./Fuqua, Gwendolyn Gordy/Carlo, Tyran Jobete Music Co. Inc. obo Old Brompton Road Music. (ASCAP)/Third Above Music Inc. (ASCAP) **"Two Lovers"** by Robinson, Smokey Jobete Music Co. Inc. (ASCAP) **"Up the Ladder to the Roof"** by Vincent DiMirco and Frank Edward Wilson Stone Agate Music (BMI) **"War"** by Whitfield, Norman J./Strong, Barrett Stone Agate Music (BMI) **"What's Going On"** by Benson, Renaldo/Cleveland, Alfred W/Gaye, Marvin P. Stone Agate Music (BMI)/Jobete Music Co. Inc. obo itself and MGIII Music, NMG Music and FCG Music (ASCAP) **"Where Did Our Love Go"** by Holland, Edward, Jr./Holland, Brian/ Dozier, Lamont Herbert Stone Agate Music (BMI) **"Who's Lovin' You"** by Robinson, Smokey Jobete Music Co. Inc. (ASCAP) **"You Can't Hurry Love"** by Holland, Edward, Jr./Holland, Brian/Dozier, Lamont Herbert Stone Agate Music (BMI) **"You're All I Need to Get By"** by Ashford, Nickolas/ Simpson, Valerie Jobete Music Co. Inc. (ASCAP) **"You're Nobody 'Til Somebody Loves You"** by Cavanaugh, James/Morgan, Russ/Stock, Larry Larry Stock Music Co.; Shapiro Bernstein & Co., Inc.; Southern Music Publishing Co., Inc. (ASCAP) **"You've Really Got a Hold on Me"** by Robinson, Smokey Jobete Music Co. Inc. (ASCAP)

NEDERLANDER

Chairman . . . . .James M. Nederlander
President . . . . .James L. Nederlander

Executive Vice President
Nick Scandalios

Vice President
Corporate Development
Charlene S. Nederlander

Senior Vice President
Labor Relations
Herschel Waxman

Chief Financial Officer
Freida Sawyer Belviso

STAFF FOR THE LUNT-FONTANNE

House Manager . . . .**Tracey Malinowski**
Treasurer . . . . .Joe Olcese
Assistant Treasurer . . . . .Kevin Lynch
House Carpenter . . . . .Terry Taylor
House Electrician . . . . .Dennis Boyle
House Propertyman . . . . .Andrew Bentz
House Flyman . . . . .Matt Walters
House Engineers . . . . .Robert MacMahon, Joseph Riccio III

Motown: The Musical
SCRAPBOOK

Correspondent: Charl Brown, "Smokey Robinson"

Milestone Gifts: Beats By Dre Studio headphones from our producers. Best opening night present ever!

Most Exciting Celebrity Visitors: Having Diana Ross, Stevie Wonder, Gladys Knight, Mary Wilson and, of course, Smokey Robinson all at opening night and come out on stage with us at the end of the show was a thrill and a memory none of us will ever forget. And the best part is whenever Smokey sees me now, he says, "Hey, Me!" I am overwhelmed still every time.

Actor Who Performed the Most Roles in This Show: Our tireless and multi-talented swing Jarran Muse covers 11 tracks in the show, including two principals. In one performance, not only was he on for Marvin Gaye, which is a principal track, but he also had to play a Temptation, Junior Walker and a Miracle, all in the same show.

Who Has Done the Most Performances: Eric LaJuan Summers has done the most performances, over 350. He was the last person to miss a show so he was the last man standing (I came in third) and, as of February 2014, Eric is the only original cast member not to have taken a week's vacation.

Special Backstage Ritual: There is a cast prayer on deck every night at places.

Favorite Moment During Each Performance: When I sing "You've Really Got a Hold on Me."

Valisia LeKae ("Diana Ross") and Brandon Victor Dixon ("Berry Gordy") perform at the signing event for the release of the *Motown* cast recording.

Favorite Snack Foods: I LOVE CHEEZ-ITS and Vita Coco coconut water.

Favorite Therapy: I have a Grether's Pastille every show before I go on.

Memorable Press Encounter: The best press moment of my life was being interviewed on the Red Carpet at my first Tony Awards at which I was also a nominee, by my good friend Frank DiLella for NY1.

"Carols for a Cure" Carol: I had the pleasure of singing lead vocals along with the marvelous Marva Hicks on the *Motown* "Carols for a Cure" song "Deck the Halls (It's Christmas)/Come on Home," which was written by our assistant conductor Jason Michael Webb.

Coolest Thing About Being in This Show: The coolest thing about being in this show is being an official part of the historic Motown legacy.

Web Buzz: The best web buzz was a video that went viral of a mother sobbing after receiving tickets to our show for Christmas. It was the most touching thing ever! (See photo below.)

Latest Audience Arrival: During "What's Going On" at the end of Act I. (What was really going on?)

Fastest Costume Change: Brandon Victor Dixon has a full shirt, tie, pants, shoe and wig change in 30 seconds.

Busiest Day at the Box Office: We sold $700,000 in one day at the box office after one of our television appearances.

Who Wore the Least?: Eric LaJuan Summers has his entire chest and abs exposed as Rick James (and the crowd goes wild).

Catchphrase Only the Company Would Recognize: "This is *Motown*. This is what we do."

Sweethearts Within the Company: *Motown* never kisses and tells.

Company In-Jokes: "As Cast."

Understudy Anecdote: "As Cast."

Fan Club Information: For all info about me and upcoming appearances, check my website: www.charlbrown.com or follow me on twitter: @thecharlbrown

Also!: My favorite memory was performing with my cast at the Macy's Thanksgiving Day Parade.

Cast members (in blue jackets) welcome "Motown Mom" Lysanias Taylor (with flowers) whose video clip sobbing with delight at getting a ticket to *Motown* from her daughters for Christmas went viral on YouTube in early 2014. (L-R): Eric LaJuan Summers, daughter Afftene Taylor, Berry Gordy, Taylor, Darius Crenshaw, Rod Harrelson, daughter Kwanfari Herndon, Grasan Kingsberry, and Rickey Tripp. View the clip at www.youtube.com/watch?v=m3415ZNTC1k.

Newsies

First Preview: March 15, 2012. Opened: March 29, 2012.
Still running as of May 31, 2014.

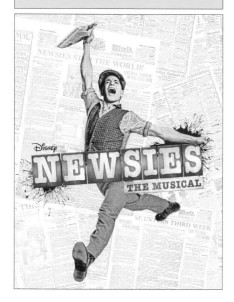

A musical based on the cult 1992 Disney film about the real-life 1899 New York City newsboy strike. Street-wise "newsie" Jack Kelly reaches his limit when wealthy publisher Joseph Pulitzer tries to squeeze a few more precious pennies out of the hardworking street-hawkers. With help from a crusading journalist, the plucky Jack organizes the newsboys of all the papers in all the boroughs into a union, and manages—despite a series of setbacks—to push the city's publishers into an unexpected corner. But what about Jack's dream to chuck it all and move to a better life in Santa Fe?

CAST

(in order of appearance)

Jack Kelly	COREY COTT
Crutchie	ANDY RICHARDSON
Race	RYAN BRESLIN
Albert	DANIEL QUADRINO
Specs	JOHN MICHAEL FIUMARA
Henry	IAIN YOUNG
Finch	AARON J. ALBANO
Elmer	EVAN KASPRZAK
Romeo	TOMMY MARTINEZ
Mush	DAVID GUZMAN
Katherine	KARA LINDSAY
Darcy	HOGAN FULTON
Nuns	LaVON FISHER-WILSON, JULIE FOLDESI, LIANA HUNT
Morris Delancey	ADAM KAPLAN
Oscar Delancey	BRENDON STIMSON
Wiesel	JOHN E. BRADY
Davey	BEN FANKHAUSER

Continued on next page

⟩N⟨ NEDERLANDER THEATRE

UNDER THE DIRECTION OF
JAMES M. NEDERLANDER AND JAMES L. NEDERLANDER

Disney Theatrical Productions
under the direction of
Thomas Schumacher

Presents

ᴅɪsɴᴇʏ NEWSIES
THE MUSICAL

Music by	Lyrics by	Book by
ALAN MENKEN	**JACK FELDMAN**	**HARVEY FIERSTEIN**

Based on the Disney film written by BOB TZUDIKER and NONI WHITE

Starring
COREY COTT

JOHN DOSSETT   KARA LINDSAY   LaVON FISHER-WILSON   BEN FANKHAUSER
ANDY RICHARDSON   JOSHUA COLLEY   LUCA PADOVAN

AARON J. ALBANO   MARK ALDRICH   TOMMY BRACCO   JOHN E. BRADY   RYAN BRESLIN
CAITLYN CAUGHELL   JULIAN DeGUZMAN   MICHAEL FATICA   JP FERRERI   JOHN MICHAEL FIUMARA   JULIE FOLDESI
HOGAN FULTON   DAVID GUZMAN   JACOB GUZMAN   LIANA HUNT   ADAM KAPLAN   EVAN KASPRZAK
JESS LePROTTO   STUART MARLAND   TOMMY MARTINEZ   DANIEL QUADRINO   TOM ALAN ROBBINS
JACK SCOTT   BRENDON STIMSON   NICK SULLIVAN   IAIN YOUNG   STUART ZAGNIT

Scenic Design	Costume Design	Lighting Design	Sound Design
TOBIN OST	**JESS GOLDSTEIN**	**JEFF CROITER**	**KEN TRAVIS**

Projection Design	Hair & Wig Design	Fight Direction	Casting
SVEN ORTEL	**CHARLES G. LAPOINTE**	**J. ALLEN SUDDETH**	**TELSEY + COMPANY JUSTIN HUFF, CSA**

Associate Producer	Technical Supervision	Production Manager	Production Stage Manager
ANNE QUART	**NEIL MAZZELLA & GEOFFREY QUART**	**EDUARDO CASTRO**	**THOMAS J. GATES**

Music Director/ Dance Music Arrangements	Music Coordinator	Associate Director	Associate Choreographer
MARK HUMMEL	**JOHN MILLER**	**RICHARD J. HINDS**	**LOU CASTRO**

Orchestrations by
DANNY TROOB

Music Supervision
Incidental Music &
Vocal Arrangements by
MICHAEL KOSARIN

Choreographed by
CHRISTOPHER GATTELLI

Directed by
JEFF CALHOUN

World Premiere, Paper Mill Playhouse, in Millburn, New Jersey on September 25, 2011.   Mark S. Hoebee, Producing Artistic Director, Todd Schmidt, Managing Director

10/1/13

Newsboys (L-R): Aaron J. Albano and Jess LeProtto in "Seize the Day."

Photo: Deen van Meer

Newsies

MUSICAL NUMBERS

ACT I

Prologue: Rooftop, Dawn
"Santa Fe" (Prologue) .... Jack, Crutchie
Scene 1: Newsie Square
"Carrying the Banner" .... Jack, Newsies
Scene 2: Pulitzer's Office, Afternoon
"The Bottom Line" .... Pulitzer, Seitz, Bunsen, Hannah
Scene 3: A Street Corner
Scene 4: Medda's Theater
"That's Rich" .... Medda
"I Never Planned on You/Don't Come a-Knocking" .... Jack, Bowery Beauties
Scene 5: Newsie Square, Next Morning
"The World Will Know" .... Jack, Davey, Les, Newsies
Scene 6: Jacobi's Deli and Street, Afternoon
"The World Will Know" (Reprise) .... Newsies
Scene 7: Katherine's Office
"Watch What Happens" .... Katherine
Scene 8: Newsie Square, Next Morning
"Seize the Day" .... Davey, Jack, Newsies
Scene 9: Rooftop
"Santa Fe" .... Jack

ACT II

Entr'acte
Scene 1: Jacobi's Deli, Next Morning
"King of New York" .... Davey, Katherine, Les, Newsies
Scene 2: Medda's Theater
"Watch What Happens" (Reprise) .... Davey, Jack, Katherine, Les
Scene 3: Pulitzer's Office and Cellar, Afternoon
"The Bottom Line" (Reprise) .... Pulitzer, Seitz, Mayor
Scene 4: Brooklyn Bridge and Medda's Theater
"Brooklyn's Here" .... Spot Conlon, Newsies
Scene 5: Rooftop
"Something to Believe In" .... Katherine, Jack
Scene 6: Pulitzer's Cellar
"Seize the Day" (Reprise) .... Newsies
"Once and for All" .... Jack, Davey, Katherine, Newsies
Scene 7: Pulitzer's Office, Next Morning
"Seize the Day" (Reprise) .... Newsies
Scene 8: Newsie Square
"Finale" .... Jack, Newsies

Cast Continued

Les (Tues., Wed. Eve.,
   Sat. Eve., Sun.) .... JOSHUA COLLEY
   (Mon., Wed. Mat.,
   Fri., Sat. Mat.) .... LUCA PADOVAN
Joseph Pulitzer .... JOHN DOSSETT
Seitz .... MARK ALDRICH
Bunsen .... NICK SULLIVAN
Hannah .... LIANA HUNT
Snyder .... STUART MARLAND
Medda Larkin .... LaVON FISHER-WILSON
Stage Manager .... JOHN E. BRADY
Mr. Jacobi .... JOHN E. BRADY
Scabs .... TOMMY BRACCO,
   JACOB GUZMAN, JESS LePROTTO
Mayor .... JOHN E. BRADY
Spot Conlon .... TOMMY BRACCO
Bill .... DANIEL QUADRINO
Governor Roosevelt .... TOM ALAN ROBBINS
Citizens of New York .... AARON J. ALBANO,
   MARK ALDRICH, TOMMY BRACCO,
   JOHN E. BRADY, RYAN BRESLIN,
   JOHN MICHAEL FIUMARA, JULIE FOLDESI,
   HOGAN FULTON, DAVID GUZMAN,
   JACOB GUZMAN, LIANA HUNT,
   ADAM KAPLAN, EVAN KASPRZAK,
   JESS LePROTTO, STUART MARLAND,
   TOMMY MARTINEZ, DANIEL QUADRINO,
   TOM ALAN ROBBINS, BRENDON STIMSON,
   NICK SULLIVAN, IAIN YOUNG

SWINGS
CAITLYN CAUGHELL, JULIAN DeGUZMAN,
MICHAEL FATICA, JP FERRERI,
JACK SCOTT, STUART ZAGNIT

UNDERSTUDIES
For Jack Kelly: ADAM KAPLAN,
BRENDON STIMSON
Katherine: CAITLYN CAUGHELL,
LIANA HUNT
Davey: RYAN BRESLIN, DANIEL QUADRINO
Crutchie: TOMMY MARTINEZ,
DANIEL QUADRINO
Medda: CAITLYN CAUGHELL, JULIE FOLDESI
Pulitzer: JOHN E. BRADY, STUART MARLAND
Roosevelt: MARK ALDRICH, STUART ZAGNIT
Seitz/Bunsen: AARON J. ALBANO,
EVAN KASPRZAK, STUART ZAGNIT
Snyder: NICK SULLIVAN, STUART ZAGNIT
Wiesel/Stage Manager/Jacobi/Mayor:
NICK SULLIVAN, STUART ZAGNIT
Hannah: CAITLYN CAUGHELL,
JULIE FOLDESI

DANCE CAPTAIN
MICHAEL FATICA

Corey Cott
Jack Kelly

John Dossett
Joseph Pulitzer

Kara Lindsay
Katherine

LaVon Fisher-Wilson
Medda

Newsies

ASSISTANT DANCE CAPTAIN
JULIAN DeGUZMAN

FIGHT CAPTAIN
MARK ALDRICH

PLACE
Lower Manhattan

TIME
Summer, 1899

ORCHESTRA
Conductor:
MARK HUMMEL
Associate Conductor:
STEVEN MALONE
Assistant Conductor:
MAT EISENSTEIN
Woodwinds:
TOM MURRAY, MARK THRASHER
Trumpet/Flugel:
JEREMY MILOSZEWICZ
Trombone:
DAN LEVINE
Guitar:
BRIAN KOONIN
Bass:
RAY KILDAY
Drums:
PAUL DAVIS
Percussion:
ED SHEA
Keyboards:
MAT EISENSTEIN, STEVEN MALONE
Violin:
MARY ROWELL
Cello:
DEBORAH ASSAEL-MIGLIORE
Electronic Music Programmer:
JEFF MARDER
Music Coordinator:
JOHN MILLER

Newsies was inspired by the book
Children of the City by DAVID NASAW

Ben Fankhauser
Davey

Andy Richardson
Crutchie

Joshua Colley
Les

Luca Padovan
Les

Aaron J. Albano
Finch, Ensemble

Mark Aldrich
Seitz, Ensemble

Tommy Bracco
Spot Conlon, Scab, Ensemble

John E. Brady
Wiesel, Stage Manager, Mr. Jacobi, Mayor, Ensemble

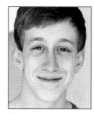
Ryan Breslin
Race, Ensemble

Caitlyn Caughell
Swing

Julian DeGuzman
Swing, Assistant Dance Captain

Michael Fatica
Swing, Dance Captain

JP Ferreri
Swing

John Michael Fiumara
Specs, Ensemble

Julie Foldesi
Ensemble

Hogan Fulton
Darcy, Ensemble

David Guzman
Mush, Ensemble

Jacob Guzman
Sniper, Scab, Ensemble

Liana Hunt
Hannah, Ensemble

Adam Kaplan
Morris Delancey, Ensemble

Evan Kasprzak
Elmer, Ensemble

Jess LeProtto
Buttons, Scab, Ensemble

Stuart Marland
Snyder, Ensemble

Newsies

Tommy Martinez
Romeo, Ensemble

Daniel Quadrino
Albert, Bill, Ensemble

Tom Alan Robbins
Roosevelt, Ensemble

Jack Scott
Swing

Brendon Stimson
Oscar Delancey, Ensemble

Nick Sullivan
Bunsen, Ensemble

Iain Young
Henry, Ensemble

Stuart Zagnit
Swing

Alan Menken
Composer

Jack Feldman
Lyrics

Harvey Fierstein
Book

Bob Tzudiker
Original Screenplay

Noni White
Original Screenplay

Jeff Calhoun
Director

Christopher Gattelli
Choreographer

Tobin Ost
Scenic Design

Jess Goldstein
Costume Design

Jeff Croiter
Lighting Design

Ken Travis
Sound Design

Sven Ortel
Projection Design

Michael Kosarin
Music Supervisor, Vocal and Incidental Music Arrangements

Danny Troob
Orchestrations

Mark Hummel
Music Director, Dance Music Arrangements

John Miller
Music Coordinator

Charles G. Lapointe
Hair & Wig Design

J. Allen Suddeth
Fight Director

Bernard Telsey
Telsey + Company
Casting

Richard J. Hinds
Associate Director

Lou Castro
Associate Choreographer

Neil A. Mazzella
Technical Supervisor

Geoffrey Quart
Technical Supervisor

Thomas Schumacher
Disney Theatrical Productions
Producer

Garett Hawe
Albert, Bill, Ensemble

Nicholas Lampiasi
Les

Newsies

Giuseppe Bausilio
Race, Ensemble

Jeremy Greenbaum
Davey

STAGE MANAGEMENT
Front: Becky Fleming
(Assistant Stage Manager),
Timothy Eaker (Stage Manager)
Back: Thomas J. Gates
(Production Stage Manager)

Photos: Brian Mapp

Molly Jobe
Hannah, Ensemble

Clay Thomson
*Spot Conlon, Scab,
Ensemble*

Zachary Unger
Les

COMPANY MANAGEMENT
(L-R): Brendan Beggs
(Assistant Company Manager),
Eduardo Castro
(Company Manager)

ORCHESTRA
Front (L-R): Ray Kilday, Deborah Assael-Migliore, Jeremy Miloszewicz, Dan Levine, Mary Rowell
Back (L-R): Brian Koonin, Dan Berkery, Tom Murray, Paul Davis, Matt Gallagher, Mark Hummel, Steven Malone

FRONT OF HOUSE
(L-R): Iris Cortes, Joseph Candelaria, Jesse White (House Manager), Gusti Bogok, Jeremy Wein, Amy Carcaterra, Marlon Pichardo, Angel Serrano

Newsies

NIGHTTIME DOORMAN
Joaquin Quintana

CHILDREN'S GUARDIAN
Vanessa Brown (C) with
(L-R) Luca Padovan, Zachary Unger

MERCHANDISE
(L-R): Jessica Buckridge, Scott Koonce, Lauren McQuillan, Jeremy Wein

Photos: Brian Mapp

WARDROBE
(L-R): Jack Scott, Bill Hubner, Joelyn Wilkosz, Susan Checklick, Brian Moreland, Franc Weinperl

BOX OFFICE
(L-R): John Stange, Samantha Seijas, Spencer Taustine

STAFF FOR NEWSIES

COMPANY MANAGER ....EDUARDO CASTRO
Production Stage Manager ....Thomas J. Gates
Assistant Company Manager ....Brendan Beggs
Stage Manager ....Timothy Eaker
Assistant Stage Manager ....Becky Fleming
Production Coordinator ....Kerry McGrath
Dance Captain ....Michael Fatica
Assistant Dance Captain ....Julian DeGuzman
Fight Captain ....Mark Aldrich
Production Assistants ....Bryan Bradford, Patrick Egan,
        Aaron Elgart, Mark A. Stys, Amanda Tamny

DISNEY ON BROADWAY PUBLICITY

Senior Publicist ....Dennis Crowley
Associate Publicist ....Michael Strassheim

Associate Scenic Designer ....Christine Peters
Assistant Scenic Designer ....Jerome Martin
Assistant Set Designer ....John Raley
Associate Costume Designer ....Mike Floyd
Associate Costume Designer ....China Lee
Associate Lighting Designer ....Cory Pattak
Assistant Lighting Designer ....Wilburn Bonnell
Associate Sound Designer ....Alex Hawthorn
Moving Light Programmer ....Victor Seastone
Assistant Projection Designer ....Lucy Mackinnon
Assistant to the
        Projection Designer ....Gabe Rives-Corbett
Projection Programmer ....Florian Mosleh
Assistant Hair and Wig Designer ....Leah J. Loukas
Assistant Fight Director ....Ted Sharon
Technical Supervision ....Neil A. Mazzella
Technical Supervision ....Troika Entertainment
Technical Associates ....Irene Wang, Sam Ellis
Technical Production Assistant ....Canara Price

Advance Carpenter ....Sam Mahan
Head Carpenter ....Eddie Bash
Automation ....Karl Schuberth
Carpenter ....Michael Allen
Production Electrician ....James Maloney
Associate Production Electrician ....John Wooding
Production Properties ....Emiliano Pares
Head Properties ....Brian Schweppe
Assistant Properties.......................Michael Critchlow
Production Sound ....Phil Lojo, Paul DelCioppo
Head Sound ....John M. Dory
Sound Assistant ....Jana Hoglund
Wardrobe Supervisor ....Rick Kelly
Dressers ....Jenny Barnes, Gary Biangone,
        Franklin Hollenbeck, Phillip Rolfe,
        Keith Shaw, Franc Weinperl
Hair Supervisor ....Frederick Waggoner
Hairdresser ....Isaac Grnya
Associate Music Director ....Steven Malone
Additional Orchestrations ....Steve Margoshes, Dave Siegel
Music Preparation ....Anixter Rice Music Services
Electronic Music Programming ....Jeff Marder
Associate to Mr. Menken ....Rick Kunis
Assistant to John Miller ....Jennifer Coolbaugh
Rehearsal Musicians ....Paul Davis, Mat Eisenstein
Music Production Assistant ....Brendan Whiting
Dialect & Vocal Coach ....Shane Ann Younts
Assistant to Mr. Calhoun ....Derek Hersey
Children's Guardian ....Vanessa Brown
Children's Tutoring ....On Location Education/
        Nancy Van Ness, Beverly Brennan
Physical Therapy ....PhysioArts

CASTING

TELSEY + COMPANY
Bernard Telsey CSA, Will Cantler CSA,
David Vaccari CSA, Bethany Knox CSA,
Craig Burns CSA, Tiffany Little Canfield CSA,
Rachel Hoffman CSA, Justin Huff CSA,
Patrick Goodwin CSA, Abbie Brady-Dalton CSA,
David Morris, Cesar A. Rocha CSA,
Andrew Femenella CSA, Karyn Casl CSA,
Kristina Bramhall, Conrad Woolfe, Amelia Nadler

Advertising ....Serino Coyne, Inc.
Production Photography ....Deen Van Meer
Production Travel ....Jill L. Citron
Payroll Managers ....Anthony DeLuca, Cathy Guerra
Counsel–Immigration ....Michael Rosenfeld

CREDITS

Custom scenery and automation by Hudson Scenic Studio,
Inc. Lighting equipment by Production Resource Group,
LLC. Sound equipment by Masque Sound. Video
projection system provided by Scharff Weisberg, Inc. Soft
goods by iWeiss. Costumes by Carelli Costumes, Jennifer
Love Studios, Claudia Diaz Costumes. Millinery by Rodney
Gordon. Shoes by JC Theatrical & Custom Footwear Inc.;
T.O. Dey; Capezio. Rehearsal sets by Proof Productions,
Inc. Smoke effect by Jauchem & Meeh, NYC. Dry cleaning
by Ernest Winzer Cleaners. Special thanks to Bra*Tenders
for undergarments and hosiery. Ricola cough drops courtesy
of Ricola USA, Inc. Fabric painting and distressing by Jeff
Fender Studios.

NEWSIES rehearsed at the
New 42nd Street Studios & Ripley Grier Studios

THANKS

Thanks to the TDF Costume Collection; Paper Mill
Playhouse; Prop N Spoon; Jake Zerrer

Newsies

CREW

(L-R): Aaron Strauss, Chris Robinson, Cassy Givens, Rick Poulin (House Electrician), Gerald Urciuoli, Leah Schneider, Joseph Ferreri Jr. (Flyman), Brian Schweppe (Head Properties), Danny Braddish, Jason LaPenna, Billy Wright Jr., Eddie Bash (Head Carpenter), Chris Riggins, Michael Critchlow (Assistant Properties), Andy Trotto, Michael Allen (Carpenter), Mark Davidson, John M. Dory (Head Sound)

NEDERLANDER

Chairman	**James M. Nederlander**
President	**James L. Nederlander**

Executive Vice President
Nick Scandalios

Vice President	Senior Vice President
Corporate Development	Labor Relations
Charlene S. Nederlander	**Herschel Waxman**

Chief Financial Officer
Freida Sawyer Belviso

STAFF FOR THE NEDERLANDER THEATRE

House Manager	Jesse White
Treasurer	Anthony Giannone
Assistant Treasurer	Bob Wilamowski
House Carpenter	Joseph Ferreri Sr.
Flyman	Joseph Ferreri Jr.
House Electrician	Rick Poulin
House Properties	William Wright
Head Usher	Trish Ryan

DISNEY THEATRICAL PRODUCTIONS

President	Thomas Schumacher
EVP & Managing Director	David Schrader
Senior Vice President, International	Ron Kollen
Vice President, International, Europe	Fiona Thomas
Vice President, International, Australia	James Thane
Vice President, Operations	Dana Amendola
Vice President, Domestic	Jack Eldon
Director, Human Resources	Marie-Pierre Varin
Director, Domestic Touring	Michael Buchanan
Director, Worldwide Publicity	Michael Cohen
Director, Regional Engagements	Scott A. Hemerling
Director, Regional Engagements	Kelli Palan
Manager, Domestic Touring & Planning	Liz Botros
Manager, Human Resources	Jewel Neal
Manager, Human Resources & Labor Relations	Valerie Hart
Manager, Publicity	Lindsay Braverman
Project Manager	Ryan Pears

Manager, Technical Services & Support	Michael Figliulo
Senior Computer Support Analyst	Kevin A. McGuire

Creative and Production

Executive Music Producer	Chris Montan
VP, Creative Development	Ben Famiglietti
VP, Production	Anne Quart
Director, International Production	Felipe Gamba
Director, Production	Mimi Intagliata
Director, Labor Relations	Edward Lieber
Associate Director	Jeff Lee
Production Supervisor	Clifford Schwartz
Senior Production Manager	Myriah Perkins
Production Manager	Eduardo Castro
Production Manager	Thomas Schlenk
Production Manager	Michael Height
Associate Production Manager	Kerry McGrath
Production Coordinator	Kelly Archer
Manager, Labor Relations	Stephanie Cheek
Manager, Physical Production	Karl Chmielewski
Sr. Manager, Creative Development	Jane Abramson
Sr. Manager, Education & Outreach	Lisa Mitchell
Manager, Theatrical Licensing	David R. Scott
Dramaturg & Literary Manager	Ken Cerniglia

Marketing and Sales

Senior Vice President, Marketing & Sales	Andrew Flatt
Vice President, Sales, CRM & Partnerships	Bryan Dockett
Director, Marketing	Robin Wyatt
Director, Creative Resources	Victor Adams
Director, Synergy & Partnership	Kevin Banks
Director, Sales & Ticketing	Nick Falzon
Director, Licensed Brands	Gary Kane
National Sales Manager	Victoria Cairl
Sr. Manager, Data Modeling & Consumer Insights	Craig Trachtenberg
Marketing Manager, *The Lion King*	Jared Comess
Marketing Manager, *Newsies*	Lauren Daghini
Marketing Manager	Jason Zammit
Manager, Sales & Ticketing	Erin Dooley
Manager, Sales & Ticketing	Jenifer Thomas
Manager, Digital Marketing	Peter Tulba
Manager, Digital Marketing & Social Media	Greg Josken
Design Manager	James Anderer

Assistant Manager, Synergy & Partnerships	Cara Epstein

Business and Legal Affairs

Senior Vice President	Jonathan Olson
Director	Seth Stuhl
Counsel	Naila McKenzie
Sr. Paralegal	Jessica White
Paralegal	Michael DiFonzo

Finance

VP, Finance/Business Development	Mario Iannetta
Director, Finance	Joe McClafferty
Director, Accounting	Leena Mathew
Manager, Finance	Liz Jurist Schwarzwalder
Manager, Accounting	Adrineh Ghoukassian
Manager, Production Accounting	Arlene Smith
Senior Financial Analyst	Mikhail Medvedev
Senior Business Planner	Jennifer August
Production Accountant	Angela DiSanti
Production Accountant	Jessica Bochman
Assistant Production Accountant	Isander Rojas

Administrative Staff

Kelly Archer, Zachary Baer, Elizabeth Boulger, Jonelle Brown, Preston Copley, Jubie Deane, Michael DeiCas, Leah Diaz, Adam Dworkin, Nicholas Faranda, Sarah Funk, Phil Grippe, Frankie Harvey, Andrew Hollenbeck, Christina Huschle, Julie Lavin, Sarah Malone, Colleen McCormack, Kerry McGrath, Will Murdock, Misael Nunez, Brendan Padgett, Marisa Perry, Jessica Petschauer, Matt Quinones, Meaghan Shea, Suzanne Sheptock, Bri Silva, Lee Taglin, Anji Taylor

DISNEY THEATRICAL MERCHANDISE

Vice President	Steven Downing
Sr. District Manager, Retail Strategy & Ops	Alyssa Somers
Merchandise Manager	Neil Markman
Associate Buyer	Violet Burlaza
On-Site Retail Manager	Scott Koonce
Senior Lead Sales Associates	Luke Camp, Lauren McQuillan
Corp. Sales & Product Development Manager	Ellete Poulin

Disney Theatrical Productions
dtg.guestservices@disney.com

Newsies
SCRAPBOOK

Liana Hunt and company

Photo: Matthew Murphy

Correspondents: The "Newsies" (compiled by Michael Fatica, Swing/Dance Captain)

Memorable Note, Fax or Fan Letter: We get a lot of amazing feedback and love from our "fansies" (an affectionate nickname for our fans). Adam Kaplan ("Morris Delancey") remembers someone sharing their college application essay with him, which was inspired by the Newsies' perseverance and drive to better their world. The fansies also did a "Newsies Secret Santa," where we all received thoughtful goodies through the mail during the holidays. Jacob Guzman ("Sniper") earned his nickname from a fan who mistakenly left the "C" out of his name in a drawing. He'll be "Jaob" to us forever.

Milestone Party: The Newsies celebrated our one-year anniversary last year, and took this time to really celebrate a year of hard work! Disney threw us an awesome party with a perfect view of Times Square, where the night was capped off with a rap battle between our own Ryan Breslin and Liana Hunt, as well as a memorable fashion show by Associate Choreographer Lou Castro.

Most Exciting Celebrity Visitors: It's always a treat when actors we respect come! Some of the year's favorites include Robert De Niro, Whoopi Goldberg, Michael Douglas, Catherine Zeta-Jones and Sting. For many of the Newsies, Olympic Gold Medalist Gabby Douglas's visit was a memorable one. She took so much time after to meet the cast, even indulging in a handstand contest with five of the Newsies. Obviously, she won by a long shot. Many of the Newsies are also huge fans of "The Office," and geeked out over Jenna Fischer's (a.k.a. "Pam") visit. She was, of course, sweet as can be.

Actor Who Performed the Most Roles: The Newsie swings for the show, Michael Fatica, Julian DeGuzman and Jack Scott, have each performed 14 tracks.

Who Has Done the Most Performances: Mark Aldrich, who plays "Seitz," has NEVER missed a show, aside from one week of vacation. He has, at this moment, performed in 742 shows.

Special Backstage Rituals: The cast has a number of rituals, some to prepare for the show and some that just keep on happening! Every day before places, there is a prayer/focus circle offstage right, which is a perfect way for the cast to get centered and connected before the show. Tommy Bracco regularly leads a dance party upstairs in the Newsie dressing room.

Favorite Moment During Each Performance: The Newsies voted "King of New York." A close second is watching Liana Hunt do her PT exercises offstage right before entering for "Seize the Day."

Favorite In-Theatre Gathering Place: Due to a lack of a greenroom, the women's ensemble dressing room on the third floor has been adopted as a common space. The cast can squeeze up to ten boys in there at a time. Sorry, Girlsies!

Favorite Off-Site Hangout: During the spring, Central Park for *Newsies* softball in the Broadway Show League!

Favorite Snack Foods: John Dossett, who plays Pulitzer, hands out mints to the whole cast before the show. Also, we were lucky enough to have a COOKIE named after the show by Schmackary's Cookies. They concocted a chocolate and pretzel cookie, affectionately dubbed the "King of New York" cookie.

Mascot: Tommy Bracco

Favorite Therapy: Physical therapy is the *Newsies* cast's saving grace. There is a plethora of foam rollers, tennis balls and TheraBands strewn around the theatre. Also seen everywhere around the theatre are Throat Coat tea, various forms of ginger, and apple cider vinegar.

Memorable Ad-Lib: "Pulitzer's OURS!," as ad-libbed by Ben Fankhauser very audibly during our performance on "Dancing with the Stars."

Memorable Stage Door Fan Encounters: This year, we had someone bring a cardboard cutout of Ryan Breslin to the stage door for people to sign. Also, Corey Cott got an actual smooch on the lips while signing autographs!

Web Buzz: We're so lucky to have such an active following on Twitter, Facebook, Instagram, and plenty of blogs/Tumblrs. It's a great way to get the word out about our show. It also keeps our moms happy...plenty of material for the Christmas Card!

Latest Audience Arrivals: The head of our sound department, Cassy Givens, reports that we get people arriving up to an hour after curtain.

Fastest Costume Change: The Delancey Brothers in "Carrying the Banner"...they even underdress protective gear.

Heaviest/Hottest Costume: Our guess is LaVon Fisher-Wilson, as Medda Larkin. There are a lot of bangles and flowers on that dress!

Who Wore the Least: John Michael Fiumara, Iain Young and David Guzman are shirtless at points in the show.

Catchphrases Only the Company Would Recognize: "YOYOYO," "Chimes," "yea FOLDY," "oknnjjaaaypeeee," "ee-ai-ee-ai-en."

Sweethearts Within the Company: JP Ferreri

and BuzzFeed.

Orchestra Member Who Played the Most Instruments: Ed Shea, our percussionist, takes the cake. When asked this question, he replied, "Oh...10 and some toys."

Best In-House Parody Lyrics: The song "Once and for All" has been aptly renamed "Bunsen for All," after Nick Sullivan's character "Bunsen." Also, the Newsies performed a version of "That's Rich" before Kara Lindsay's wedding week, called "Kara's Getting Hitched."

Company In-Jokes: Luca and Josh's mint stash, Hangela, Meatpacking (#beef), Guibamanation.

Company Legends: When asked this question, Ryan Breslin said simply, "Jeremy Jordan."

Tales from the Put-In: It's always a treat to watch the new actors playing Les take their first ride on the towers.

Understudy Anecdote: The swings have many code words and shorthand about what to do if they're on in a pinch. If you hear someone backstage saying, "In CTB, you get the goods first from Nun 1 and clump by 3," they aren't crazy. Probably.

Nicknames: There are too many to document. Some favorites include: Iain Young (Bambi, E-I-E-I-EN), Jacob Guzman (Jaob, based on a misprinted fan letter), Michael Fatica (Farticus).

Embarrassing Moment: David Guzman forgetting his line "Not so fast, Boss. Harlem wants to know what Brooklyn's gonna do," instead saying, "Woah Woah Woah....Harlem's coming if...Brooklyn's... comin'."

"Carols for a Cure" Carol: Our resident composing genius, Julie Foldesi, wrote an original song for us this year. She was approached by Steven Malone, our Associate Music Director, about writing a song about Christmas in NYC. After a few that ended up in the "corny" bin, she ended up with a charming piece we all loved, called "Take Me to Manhattan in December."

"Gypsy of the Year" Skit and Who Wrote It: The Newsies wanted to stretch our dancin' bones and do something a little different than what we do in the show. Jacob, David, Jess, Evan and Julian spearheaded a contemporary piece to "Cosmic Love" by Florence and the Machine, which placed second in the competition!

Ghostly Encounters Backstage: Besides some living people who like to hide in other people's dressing rooms for a scare, there is no cosmic activity that we know about!

Coolest Thing About Being in This Show: Being onstage with this cast every day.

Fan Club Website/Newsletter: As far as we know, there isn't a specific fan website. *Newsies* fans, nicknamed "fansies," are so supportive all across the different social media. Keep an eye out for Twitter Fan Accounts, *Newsies*-themed Tumblrs, and blogs devoted to *Newsie* lovin'!

A Night With Janis Joplin

First Preview: September 20, 2013. Opened: October 10, 2013.
Closed February 9, 2014 after 22 Previews and 140 Performances.

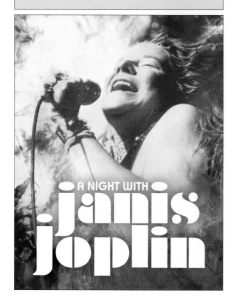

Soulful and doomed 1960s pop icon Janis Joplin, who had a voice like a raw wound, chats with the audience about her roots and influences, and tries to define the meaning of the word "Blues" in between performances of her hits. The concert-style show features a supporting cast that offers impressions of Joplin's beloved blues singers Bessie Smith, Odetta, Nina Simone, et al. The production is notable for the title performance by Mary Bridget Davies (evenings only), whose singing voice sounds uncannily similar to Joplin's.

CAST

Janis Joplin ....MARY BRIDGET DAVIES
Janis Joplin
   (at certain performances) ....KACEE CLANTON
The Joplinaires
   featured as Chantel, Bessie Smith,
   Blues Singer ....TAPRENA MICHELLE
                      AUGUSTINE
   featured as Chantel, Nina Simone,
   Odetta ....De'ADRE AZIZA
   featured as Blues Woman,
   Aretha Franklin ....ALLISON BLACKWELL
   featured as Etta James,
   Chantel ....NIKKI KIMBROUGH

UNDERSTUDIES

For Janis Joplin:
KACEE CLANTON, ALISON CUSANO
For Joplinaires:
ALLISON BLACKWELL

Continued on next page

Continued on next page

⊛ LYCEUM THEATRE
149 West 45th Street
A Shubert Organization Theatre
Philip J. Smith, *Chairman*   **Robert E. Wankel,** *President*

Daniel Chilewich   Todd Gershwin   Michael Cohl
Jeffrey Jampol   TCG Entertainment   Stephen Tenenbaum   Richard Winkler
Michael J. Moritz Jr./Brunish & Trinchero   Ginger Productions   Claudio Loureiro   Keith Mardak
Ragovoy Entertainment   Bob and Laurie Wolfe/Neil Kahanovitz   Mike Stoller & Corky Hale Stoller
Darren P. DeVerna   Susan DuBow   Tanya Grubich   Jeremiah H. Harris   Jerry Rosenberg/AJ Michaels

PRESENT

A NIGHT WITH janis joplin

Presented in association with The Estate of Janis Joplin and Jeffrey Jampol for JAM, Inc.

STARRING

Mary Bridget Davies

Taprena Michelle Augustine   De'Adre Aziza   Allison Blackwell   Nikki Kimbrough
Alison Cusano
AND
Kacee Clanton

SCENIC & LIGHTING DESIGN	COSTUME DESIGN	SOUND DESIGN	PROJECTION DESIGN
Justin Townsend	Amy Clark	Carl Casella	Darrel Maloney

HAIR & MAKE-UP DESIGN	CREATIVE CONSULTANT	CASTING
Leah J. Loukas	Red Awning/Jack Viertel	Laura Stanczyk Casting

PRODUCTION MANAGER	PRESS REPRESENTATIVE	ADVERTISING & MARKETING
Hudson Theatrical Associates	Boneau Bryan-Brown	Serino/Coyne

GENERAL MANAGER	PRODUCTION STAGE MANAGER	EXECUTIVE PRODUCER
Bespoke Theatricals	J. Philip Bassett	Red Awning

MUSIC DIRECTOR & CONDUCTOR	ORIGINAL MUSIC ARRANGER & DIRECTOR	MUSIC COORDINATOR
Ross Seligman	Len Rhodes	Howard Joines

CHOREOGRAPHY BY
Patricia Wilcox

WRITTEN AND DIRECTED BY
Randy Johnson

Produced in 2012 by Arena Stage
Molly Smith, Artistic Director   Edgar Dobie, Executive Director

Produced in 2012 by Cleveland Play House
Michael Bloom, Artistic Director   Kevin Moore, Managing Director

The Producers wish to express their appreciation to Theatre Development Fund for its support of this production.

10/10/13

Mary Bridget Davies
as Janis Joplin

Photo: Joan Marcus

A Night With Janis Joplin

MUSICAL NUMBERS

ACT I

"Combination of the Two" .... Joplinaires and the Band
"Tell Mama" .... Janis Joplin, Etta James and the Joplinaires
"My Baby" .... Janis Joplin and the Band
"Maybe" .... The Chantels
"Summertime" .... Blues Woman
"Summertime" .... Janis Joplin
"Turtle Blues" .... Janis Joplin
"Down on Me" .... Odetta
"Down on Me" .... Janis Joplin
"Piece of My Heart" .... Janis Joplin and Joplinaires
"Today I Sing the Blues" .... Blues Singer
"Nobody Knows You When You're Down and Out" .... Bessie Smith
"A Woman Left Lonely" .... Janis Joplin
"Spirit in the Dark" .... Aretha Franklin, Janis Joplin and Joplinaires

ACT II

"Try (Just a Little Bit Harder)" .... Janis Joplin and the Band
"Maybe" .... Janis Joplin and the Band
"Little Girl Blue" .... Janis Joplin and Nina Simone
"Cry Baby" .... Janis Joplin
"Kozmic Blues/I Shall Be Released Medley" .... Blues Woman, Nina Simone,
Bessie Smith and Etta James
"Me and Bobby McGee" .... Janis Joplin
"I'm Gonna Rock My Way to Heaven" .... Janis Joplin and the Band
"Ball and Chain" .... Janis Joplin
"Kozmic Blues" .... Janis Joplin
"Stay With Me" .... Janis Joplin and Joplinaires
"I'm Gonna Rock My Way to Heaven" .... Janis Joplin, Joplinaires and the Band
"Mercedes Benz" .... Janis Joplin

SWING
ALISON CUSANO

DANCE CAPTAIN
TAPRENA MICHELLE AUGUSTINE

ORCHESTRA
Music Director/Guitar:
ROSS SELIGMAN
Guitar:
STEPHEN FLAKUS
Bass:
PATRICK HARRY
Associate Music Director/Keyboard:
TYLER EVANS
Drums:
MITCH WILSON
Saxophone:
JOHN SCARPULLA
Trumpet:
CRAIG TAYLOR
Trombone:
MICHAEL BOSCARINO

Original Music Director and Arranger:
LEN RHODES
Music Contractor:
HOWARD JOINES

2013-2014 AWARD
THEATRE WORLD AWARD
(Mary Bridget Davies)

Mary Bridget Davies
Janis Joplin

Kacee Clanton
Janis Joplin Alternate

Taprena Michelle Augustine
Joplinaire, Chantel, Bessie Smith, Blues Singer, Dance Captain

De'Adre Aziza
Joplinaire, Chantel, Nina Simone, Odetta

Allison Blackwell
Joplinaire, Blues Woman, Aretha Franklin; u/s Joplinaire

Nikki Kimbrough
Joplinaire, Etta James, Chantel

Alison Cusano
u/s Janis Joplin, Joplinaire Swing

Randy Johnson
Writer/Director

Patricia Wilcox
Choreography

Justin Townsend
Scenic and Lighting Design

Amy Clark
Costume Design

Carl Casella
Sound Design

Darrel Maloney
Projection Design

Len Rhodes
Original Music Director and Arranger

A Night With Janis Joplin

Ross Seligman
Musical Director

Howard Joines
Music Coordinator

Jack Viertel
Creative Consultant

Leah J. Loukas
Hair and Make-Up Design

J. Philip Bassett
Production Stage Manager

Laura Stanczyk
Laura Stanczyk Casting
Casting

Neil A. Mazzella
Hudson Theatrical Associates
Production Management

Maggie Brohn
Bespoke Theatricals
General Management

Amy Jacobs
Bespoke Theatricals
General Management

Devin Keudell
Bespoke Theatricals
General Management

Nina Lannan
Bespoke Theatricals
General Management

Daniel Chilewich
Producer

Todd Gershwin
Producer

Michael Cohl
Producer

Jeffrey Jampol
Producer

Richard Winkler
Producer

Michael J. Moritz Jr.
Producer

Corey Brunish
Brunish & Trinchero
Producer

Brisa Trinchero
Brunish & Trinchero
Producer

Mike Stoller & Corky Hale Stoller
Producers

Susan DuBow
Producer

Jere Harris
Producer

Nicole Kastrinos
Red Awning
Executive Producer

Michael Bloom
Artistic Director
Cleveland Playhouse
Originating Theatre

Kevin Moore
Managing Director
Cleveland Playhouse
Originating Theatre

Molly Smith
Artistic Director
Arena Stage
Originating Theatre

Edgar Dobie
Executive Producer
Arena Stage
Originating Theatre

Janis Joplin

NaTasha Yvette Williams
Blues Woman, Aretha Franklin, Joplinaire

Emmy Raver-Lampman
Swing; u/s Joplinaire

NaTasha Yvette Williams
Blues Woman, Aretha Franklin, Joplinaire

A Night With Janis Joplin

Photos: Brian Mapp

CREW

Front Row (L-R): Stephen Epstein, Ray Chan, Leah Nelson, Jens McVoy, Gayle Palmieri (Dresser), Karen L. Eifert (Wardrobe Supervisor), Jennifer Hohn (Dresser) Back Row (L-R): Jamie Greathouse (Stage Manager), Mark Diaz, Brad Gyorgak, Michael Pitzer (Production Properties), Dominick Intagliato, Paul Brydon (Flyman), Robert Miller, Adam Rigby (Head Sound)

BOX OFFICE
Michael Taustine
(Head Treasurer)

FRONT OF HOUSE
Front Row (L-R): Debbie Vogel, Gerry Belitsis, Robert Lugo, Dolores Danska
Back Row (L-R): Alex, Jack Donaghy, Kevin Keenan, Danielle Banyai, Carmen Sanchez, Chris Santiago, Thia Calloway (House Manager)

MUSICIANS
(L-R): Mitch Wilson (Drums), Patrick Harry (Bass), Tyler Evans (Associate Music Director/Keyboard)

STAFF FOR *A NIGHT WITH JANIS JOPLIN*

GENERAL MANAGEMENT
BESPOKE THEATRICALS
Maggie Brohn
Amy Jacobs   Devin Keudell   Nina Lannan
Associate General Manager ....Steve Dow

COMPANY MANAGER
Roseanna Sharrow

EXECUTIVE PRODUCER
RED AWNING
Nicole Kastrinos

PRODUCTION MANAGEMENT
HUDSON THEATRICAL ASSOCIATES
Neil A. Mazzella, Sam Ellis, Geoff Quart, Irene Wang

GENERAL PRESS REPRESENTATIVE
BONEAU/BRYAN-BROWN
Chris Boneau
Aaron Meier   Amy Kass   Michelle Farabaugh

CASTING
LAURA STANCZYK CASTING
Laura Stanczyk, CSA
Nicholas Petrovich, Ilana Bolotsky, Carrie Watt,
Chrystal Vassilyadi

PRODUCTION STAGE MANAGER ... J. Philip Bassett
Stage Manager ....Jamie Greathouse
Associate Director ....Tyler Rhodes

Dance Captain ....Taprena Michelle Augustine
Vocal Coach ....Deborah Hecht
Associate Scenic Designer ....Caleb Levengood
Associate Costume Designer ....Justin Hall
Costume Assistant ....Chloe Paisley
Associate Lighting Designer ....Dan Ozminkowski
Moving Light Programmer ....Alex Fogel
Projection Programmers ....Benjamin Keightley,
                                            Asher Robinson
Assistant Projection Designer ....David Bengali
Assistant Projection Designer ....Lucy Mackinnon
Associate Sound Designer/Advance Sound .....Josh Liebert
Assistant to the Hair/
    Wig Designer ....Jessica Ray Harrison
Advance Carpenter ....Ed Diaz
Flyman ....Paul Brydon
Production Electrician ....Michael Pitzer
Head Sound ....Adam Rigby
Advance Video ....Greg Peeler
Production Properties ....Rob Presley
Wardrobe Supervisor ....Karen L. Eifert
Dressers ....Gayle Palmieri, Jennifer Hohn
Hair/Wig Supervisor ....Shari Besanceney
Production Assistant ....Zach Kaufer
SDCF Choreographer Observer ....Kelly Shook
Production Photographer ....Joan Marcus
Executive Producer Assistant ....Danielle DeMatteo
Advertising ..Serino Coyne/Greg Corradetti, Tom Callahan,
                Robert Jones, Vanessa Javier, Ben Skinner
Digital Outreach/Website/Video ....Serino Coyne/
    Jim Glaub, Chip Meyrelles, Laurie Connor,
    Kevin Keating, Whitney Creighton, Jenna Lauren Freed,
                        Andrea Cuevas, Ian Weiss

Marketing ....Serino Coyne/Leslie Barrett, Diana Salameh,
                    Mike Rafael, Catherine Herzog
Press Representatives ....Adrian Bryan-Brown, Jim Byk,
    Jackie Green, Kelly Guiod, Linnae Hodzic,
    Kevin Jones, Holly Kinney, Emily Meagher,
    Christine Olver, Joe Perrotta, Amanda Sales,
                    Heath Schwartz, Susanne Tighe
Accountant ....Marks Paneth & Shron LLP/
                            Christopher Cacace
Comptroller ...Marks Paneth & Shron LLP/Petrina Moritz
General Management Associates ....Lisa Jaeger,
                                        Jimmy Wilson
General Management Interns ...Alex Hajjar, Reeve Pierson
Insurance ....AON Albert G. Ruben
                Insurance Services, Inc./Claudia Kaufman
Banking ....City National Bank/Michele Gibbons
Payroll ....Checks and Balances Payroll Inc.
Travel Agent ....Tzell Travel/The "A" Team, Andi Henig
Housing Services ....ABA IDEAL/Elizabeth Helke
Legal Counsel ....Sendroff & Baruch, LLP/Jason Baruch
Music Clearances ....Sendoff & Baruch, LLP/
                                Carter Anne McGowan
Merchandising ....Perryscope Productions, LLC

www.anightwithjanisjoplin.com

CREDITS

Scenery constructed by Hudson Scenic Studios. Costumes by John Kristiansen New York Inc., Michael Velasquez, Jennifer Love Costumes. Millinery by Arnold Levine. Lighting equipment by Hudson Sound & Light, LLC. Sound equipment by Sound Associates. Video projection system is provided by World Stage, Inc.

A Night With Janis Joplin
SCRAPBOOK

Photo: courtesy Nikki Kimbrough

Joplin's shoulder-panel addition to the Gypsy Robe.

Correspondent: Nikki Kimbrough, "Etta James."

Opening Night Gifts: Opening night was so memorable for all of us!!! The love and support from everyone was just amazing. Some memorable gifts include:
a) A Tiffany silver heart necklace from our producers Dan, Todd and Michael. You always feel loved when you walk into your dressing room to a signature blue Tiffany box!!
b) Mary Bridget Davies (Janis) gave us all beautiful individual gifts from Henri Bendel. So thoughtful!
c) One of the best gifts was from our castmate Taprena Michelle Augustine. She gave us all huge album covers with our faces on it as our characters.

Most Exciting Celebrity Visitors: We've had so many great visitors! A few favorites:
a) Joan Rivers!! She was so wonderful! She said, "I loved the show!" in her Joan Rivers voice.
b) Olivia Newton John!! We all love her! To all of us, it was like the legendary "Sandy" from *Grease* came to see us!!
c) Freddie Jackson! "I'm coming back! I'm going to tell everyone and bring them to this show! Wonderful!"

Favorite In-Theatre Gathering Place: We're all so excited to have our own dressing rooms that we dressing room-hop to see each other. Or we yell down the hall. :)

Actor Who Performed the Most Roles in This Show: De'Adre Aziza, with four: Odetta, Nina Simone, Joplinaire, Chantel.

Memorable Audience Reaction: The invited dress was so amazing! It was the first time we performed in front of an audience. We had nine standing ovations during the show. We had no idea that the audience would respond with so much love. They loved the show! It was such a rush!! It took all of us hours to come down that night!

Unique Pre-Show Announcement: One night an audience member in the mezzanine had a little too much to drink and got so excited he threw a glass over the mezzanine and it hit another audience member. Eeek! The ushers wanted stage management to announce, "Please do not throw your glasses over the mezzanine." Stage management thought it was an odd request since it was an isolated situation. So it was a unique announcement that never happened.

Embarrassing Moment: Maybe not an embarrassing moment, but an odd moment.

SPECIAL THANKS/SPONSORS
Bra*Tenders. Gibson Guitars.
Makeup provided by M•A•C.

Special thanks to Janis's original band, Big Brother and the Holding Company (James Gurley, Sam Andrew, Peter Albin and Dave Getz) for their contributions to Janis Joplin, to rock and roll history, and their continuing support of *A Night With Janis Joplin*.

A Night With Janis Joplin rehearsed at Pearl Studios

MUSIC CREDITS

"Ball and Chain" written by Willie Mae Thornton. Published by Bro 'n Sis Music, Inc. (ASCAP) c/o Carlin America, Inc. Used with permission. "Today I Sing the Blues" written by Curtis Reginald Lewis. Published by Bess Music (ASCAP). Used with permission. "Combination of the Two" written by Sam Andrew. Published by Cheap Thrills Music (ASCAP). Used by permission. "I Shall Be Released" written by Bob Dylan. Published by Dwarf Music (ASCAP). Used by permission. "Tell Mama" by Clarence George Carter, Marcus Lewis Daniel and Wilbur Terrell. Published by EMI-Screen Gems Music (BMI). Used by permission. "Maybe" by Richard Barrett. Published by EMI Longitude Music (BMI). Used with permission. "Me and Bobby McGee" written by Fred L. Foster and Kris Kristofferson. Published by Combine Music Corp (BMI) administered by EMI Music Publishers. Used by permission. "Little Girl Blue," music by Richard Rodgers, lyrics by Lorenz Hart. This selection is used by special arrangement with Rodgers & Hammerstein: an Imagem Company, www.rnh.com. All rights reserved. "Kozmic Blues" written by Janis Joplin and Gabriel Mekler. Published by Strong Arm Music (ASCAP) and Universal Music Publishers (ASCAP). Used by permission. All rights reserved. "Turtle Blues" written by Janis Joplin. Published by Strong Arm Music (ASCAP). Used by permission. All rights reserved. "Down on Me" written by Janis Joplin. Published by Strong Arm Music (ASCAP). Used by permission. All rights reserved. "Mercedes Benz" written by Janis Joplin, Michael McClure and Robert Neuwirth. Published by Strong Arm Music (ASCAP). Used by permission. All rights reserved. "Summertime" from Porgy and Bess, words and music by George Gershwin, DuBose and Dorothy Heyward and Ira Gershwin. Copyright ©1935 (renewed), Nokawi Music (ASCAP)/George Gershwin Music (ASCAP)/Ira Gershwin Music (ASCAP)/DuBose and Dorothy Heyward Memorial Fund (ASCAP). Nokawi Music administered in the United States by Imagem Music, LLC. George Gershwin Music, Ira Gershwin Music and DuBose and Dorothy Heyward Memorial Fund administered by WB Music Corp. Used by permission. International copyright secured. All rights reserved. "I'm Gonna Rock My Way to Heaven" written by Jerry Ragovoy and Jenny Dean. Published by the Tune Room (ASCAP). Used with permission. "Nobody Knows You When You're Down and Out" by James Cox. Published by Universal Music Publishers (ASCAP). Used with permission. "Raise Your Hand" written by Stephen Lee Cropper, Eddie Floyd and Alvertis Isbell. Published by Cotillion Music Inc. (BMI) and Irving Music (BMI). Used with permission. "Try Just a Little Bit Harder" written by Jerry Ragovoy and Chip Taylor. Published by Unichappell Inc. (BMI). Used with permission. "Stay With Me" written by Jerry Ragovoy and George David Weiss. Published by Chappell & Co (ASCAP). Used with permission. "A Woman Left Lonely" written by Spooner Oldham and Dan Penn. Published by Embassy Music Corp. (BMI) and Dan Penn Music (BMI). "Cry Baby" written by Jerry Ragovoy (aka Norman Meade) and Bert Berns. Published by Sloopy II Inc. (ASCAP), EMI Music Publishers (ASCAP) and Sony/ATV Music Publishers (ASCAP). Used by permission. "Piece of My Heart" written by Bert Berns and Jerry Ragovoy, published by Sloopy II Inc. (ASCAP), Sony/ATV Music Publishers (ASCAP) and Warner/Chappell Music Publishers (ASCAP). "Spirit in the Dark" by Aretha Franklin. Published by Springtime Music (ASCAP). Used with permission. "Bye Bye Baby" written by Powell St. John.

Published by Mainspring Watchworks Music (ASCAP), administered by Bicycle Music. Used with permission.

The 2011 world premiere of
One Night With Janis Joplin
was produced by and performed at
Portland Center Stage, Portland, OR
Chris Coleman, Artistic Director

THE SHUBERT ORGANIZATION, INC.
Board of Directors

A Night With Janis Joplin
SCRAPBOOK

Allison Blackwell's (Aretha Franklin) mic was not on in the beginning of "Spirit in the Dark." We kept thinking it was going to come on, but it didn't. So once she came down the steps off the cat walk, De'Adre gave AB her mic with such ease and coolness. The crowd went crazy!!!

Company In-Joke: "Uh-huh, yeah girl, uh-huh...Snap!" Ha ha!! Inside joke between our director, Randy, and the Joplinaires.

Favorite Moment During Each Performance: The crowd's response to Mary singing "Ball and Chain." I also love when she throws the mic stand down. That song! She's so into it! It gives you chills. My other favorite moment is the end, singing "Rock My Way to Heaven!" I always get a little emotional because we are all on stage together singing and living our lives! And of course "Spirit in the Dark!" I love when the audience gets up and "moves with the spirit," with us!! It give me chills and the excitement just keeps growing!

Favorite Off-Site Hangout: We haven't established one yet, but we will soon. The show is so demanding vocally, we go home to rest, but now we're getting the hang of things, so we'll find our spot soon! Right now we just laugh in our dressing rooms.

Favorite Snack Foods: Allison Blackwell loves her pretzels and going next door to "the ole deli!" De'Adre loves her Nutri Bullet. Nikki loves her protein shakes. Taprena doesn't really snack during the show. Mary doesn't snack during the show...because she's on stage the entire time! Whew! She's amazing!

Favorite Therapies: We are always popping those Grether's Pastilles. Also: Ricolas (herbal), Throat Coat and ginger tea, Entertainer's Secret Spray and water, water, and more water!

Pit Stop: Best Story From the Orchestra: We don't have an orchestra, we have a freaking rocking band clad in wigs and hippie clothes. These guys rock it out every night! I love when Ross Seligman, our MD and guitarist, has his guitar solo on "Ball and Chain." Ross is living with the lights flickering back and forth. Then he finishes with a satisfied purpose and a grin on his face. I love it, and so does the crowd. Go Ross!

Public Relations: Best Story from the Ushers and Front-of-House Staff: We have a great staff led by Ms. Thia. They love being part of a show where they can be part of the audience participation too. I love watching the ushers encourage the audience members not to be afraid to respond and get up and enjoy themselves. Just don't hurt anyone or take photos. Ha!

Who Got the Gypsy Robe: Taprena Augustine. She read a sketch about the history of the gypsy robe, how it's supposed to bless the theatre and the show. She passed the robe on at the *After Midnight* opening night.

Nicknames: Allison Blackwell: "A.B." Alison Cusano: "Ali." Taprena Michelle Augustine: "Prena." De'Adre Aziza: "Dee." Nikki Kimbrough: "the little one." (An audience member called Nikki this.)

Catchphrases Only the Company Would

Mary Bridget Davies and Joplinaires at curtain call on opening night.

Cast at the opening night party including (third from right) *Yearbook* correspondent Nikki Kimbrough.

Recognize: "She's not well!" (AB always says this!) "Ahhh Snap" (Randy Johnson). "Baby!" in Taprena Michelle Augustine's New Orleans accent.

Understudy Anecdote: Unfortunately, NaTasha Williams broke her foot during our put-in, two days before the invited dress. We were so upset for so many reasons. 1) She was our fierce leader 2) She's amazing and it was right before we started previews. What do we do? Well, Allison Blackwell, affectionately known as "AB," our super swing, stepped in like a true professional and champion as Aretha Franklin! She has done an amazing job. She is definitely an example of how you should always be prepared because you never know when it's going to be your turn to step in, save the day and shine!

Fastest Costume Change: Without a doubt Taprena! She leaves "Piece of My Heart," changes immediately into The Blues Woman, then goes off, changes into Bessie Smith, comes right back on, then goes off stage right, comes to stage left

and changes for Aretha Franklin's background singer!! Whew!!

Heaviest/Hottest Costume: Allison Blackwell/ NaTasha Williams' outfit as Aretha Franklin. The heavy sequined dress and coat with feathers.

Web Buzz: We're so excited about the buzz! It's amazing! People love the show!

Coolest Thing About Being in This Show: Being in a show with such powerful, amazing women. And we all play iconic, inspiring women. It gives you chills!

Also: We have the best dressers and wardrobe and hair and make-up staff. They rock! Not only do they get us ready, they are like our moms, sisters and great friend rolled up into one. We're so blessed. We also have the best PSM and SM and company manager. And just a rocking crew. It's the best!

One More Thing: It's a pleasure to watch Mary Bridget Davies perform every night. She really embodies the spirit of Janis Joplin. Come see our show! You will have "a rockin' good time!"

Photo: Joseph Marzullo
Photo courtesy Nikki Kimbrough

No Man's Land/Waiting for Godot

First Preview: October 26, 2013. Opened: November 24, 2013. Closed March 30, 2014. Limited Engagement.

No Man's Land played 15 Previews and 68 Performances in repertory with *Waiting for Godot*, which played 16 Previews and 77 Performances.

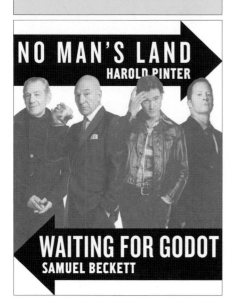

Film stars McKellen and Stewart return to their stage roots with this pair of modern classics. Waiting for Godot is Beckett's Absurdist masterpiece about two tramps attempting to amuse themselves as they anticipate the arrival of a mysterious individual for reasons that are never fully disclosed. Equally enigmatic and pregnant with possibilities is Pinter's No Man's Land, about a writer and his manservant who bring home a down-at-heels poet who may or may not be an old acquaintance of his host.

NO MAN'S LAND

Hampstead Heath. London. Summer 1975.

CAST

(in order of speaking)

Hirst .... PATRICK STEWART
Spooner .... IAN McKELLEN
Foster .... BILLY CRUDUP
Briggs .... SHULER HENSLEY

WAITING FOR GODOT

CAST

(in order of appearance)

Estragon .... IAN McKELLEN
Vladimir .... PATRICK STEWART
Lucky .... BILLY CRUDUP
Pozzo .... SHULER HENSLEY
Boy .... COLIN CRITCHLEY, AIDAN GEMME

Continued on next page

⑤CORT THEATRE
138 West 48th Street
A Shubert Organization Theatre

Philip J. Smith, *Chairman* **Robert E. Wankel**, *President*

STUART THOMPSON NOMANGO PRODUCTIONS
JON B. PLATT ELIZABETH WILLIAMS / JACK M. DALGLEISH

present

BILLY CRUDUP **SHULER HENSLEY**
IAN McKELLEN **PATRICK STEWART**

in

SCENIC DESIGN & COSTUME DESIGN	LIGHTING DESIGN	ORIGINAL MUSIC & SOUND DESIGN	PROJECTION DESIGN
STEPHEN BRIMSON LEWIS	PETER KACZOROWSKI	ROB MILBURN & MICHAEL BODEEN	ZACHARY BOROVAY

HAIR & MAKE-UP DESIGN	CASTING	DIALECT CONSULTANT	ACTION COORDINATOR
TOM WATSON	ILENE STARGER, C.S.A. ZOE E. ROTTER, C.S.A.	ELIZABETH SMITH	CHRISTIAN KELLY-SORDELET

PRODUCTION STAGE MANAGER	PRODUCTION MANAGEMENT	PRESS REPRESENTATIVE
WILLIAM JOSEPH BARNES	AURORA PRODUCTIONS	BONEAU/ BRYAN-BROWN

ASSOCIATE PRODUCER	GENERAL MANAGEMENT
KEVIN EMRICK	STP/MARSHALL B. PURDY

DIRECTED BY
SEAN MATHIAS

NO MAN'S LAND WAS ORIGINALLY PRODUCED BY BERKELEY REPERTORY THEATRE, AUGUST, 2013.
TONY TACCONE, ARTISTIC DIRECTOR; SUSAN MEDAK, MANAGING DIRECTOR.

THE PRODUCERS WISH TO EXPRESS THEIR APPRECIATION TO THEATRE DEVELOPMENT FUND FOR ITS SUPPORT OF THIS PRODUCTION.

11/24/13

Photo: Joan Marcus

(L-R): Ian McKellen and Patrick Stewart in Harold Pinter's *No Man's Land*.

No Man's Land/Waiting for Godot

UNDERSTUDIES

For Hirst, Spooner, Estragon, Vladimir:
JOEL LEFFERT
For Foster, Briggs, Lucky, Pozzo:
COLIN RYAN

Ian McKellen is appearing with the permission
of Actors' Equity Association.

Billy Crudup
Foster/Lucky

Shuler Hensley
Briggs/Pozzo

Ian McKellen
Spooner/Estragon

Patrick Stewart
Hirst/Vladimir

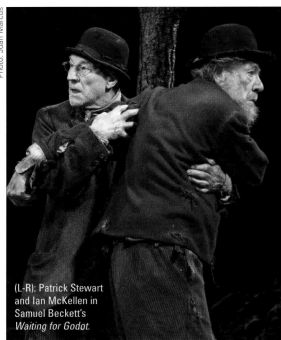

Photo: Joan Marcus

(L-R): Patrick Stewart and Ian McKellen in Samuel Beckett's *Waiting for Godot*.

Colin Critchley
Boy

Aidan Gemme
Boy

Joel Leffert
*u/s Spooner,
Estragon, Hirst,
Vladimir*

Colin Ryan
*u/s Foster, Lucky,
Briggs, Pozzo*

Harold Pinter
*Playwright:
No Man's Land*

Samuel Beckett
*Playwright:
Waiting for Godot*

Sean Mathias
Director

Stephen
Brimson Lewis
*Scenic and
Costume Design*

Peter Kaczorowski
Lighting Design

Rob Milburn and Michael Bodeen
Original Music and Sound Design

Zachary Borovay
Projection Design

Tom Watson
*Hair and
Make-up Design*

Elizabeth Smith
Dialect Consultant

Christian
Kelly-Sordelet
Action Coordinator

Ilene Starger
Casting

Zoe E. Rotter
Casting

Andrew Britt
Assistant Director

Gene O'Donovan
Aurora Productions
*Production
Management*

Ben Heller
Aurora Productions
*Production
Management*

Marshall B. Purdy
General Manager

Stuart Thompson
Producer

No Man's Land/Waiting for Godot

Jon B. Platt
Producer

Elizabeth Williams
Producer

Jack M. Dalgleish
Producer

Kevin Emrick
Associate Producer

Tony Taccone
Berkeley Repertory
Theatre
Artistic Director

Susan Medak
Berkeley Repertory
Theatre
Managing Director

Photos: Brian Mapp

BOX OFFICE
(L-R): Michael Kolbrenner,
Alexis Greer Bond (Head Treasurer),
Joseph Kane

CREW
Center: Natasha Harper (Child Guardian)
(L-R): Fraser Weir (Production Electrician), William Joseph Barnes (Production Stage Manager),
Laurie Goldfeder (Stage Manager), Renee Borys (Dresser), Kyle Skillin (Hair/Make-up Supervisor),
Lonnie Gaddy, Wayne Smith (Head Sound Engineer)
Back (L-R): Jennifer Diaz, Rob Brenner (Head Properties Supervisor)

FRONT OF HOUSE
Front Row (L-R):
Adolpho Blaire,
Alicia Kee,
William Denson
Middle Row (L-R):
Michael Rhodus,
Danielle Smith,
Robert Evans,
Lynette Myers
Back Row (L-R):
Andre Campbell,
Robert DeJesus,
Mario Carillo

No Man's Land/Waiting for Godot

(L-R): Shuler Hensley, Patrick Stewart, Billy Crudup and Ian McKellen in *Waiting for Godot.*

STAFF FOR
NO MAN'S LAND AND *WAITING FOR GODOT*

GENERAL MANAGEMENT
STUART THOMPSON PRODUCTIONS
Stuart Thompson   Marshall B. Purdy   David Turner
Lily Alia   Gregg Arst   Kevin Emrick   James Lawson
Michele Haberman   Nick Lugo   Adam Miller
Shaun Moorman   Julie Schneider   Zachary Spitzer
Caitlyn Thomson   Brittany Weber   Matthew L. Wright

COMPANY MANAGER
Megan Curren

PRODUCTION MANAGEMENT
AURORA PRODUCTIONS
Gene O'Donovan   Ben Heller
Chris Minnick   Liza Luxenberg   Anita Shah
Anthony Jusino   Jarid Sumner
Rachel London   David Cook   Bridget Van Dyke
Melissa Mazdra   Cat Nelson

PRESS REPRESENTATIVE
BONEAU/BRYAN-BROWN
Adrian Bryan-Brown   Susanne Tighe   Christine Olver

Production Stage Manager ....William Joseph Barnes
Stage Manager ....Laurie Goldfeder
Assistant Director ....Andrew Britt
Choreographic Movement ....Lorin Latarro
Production Assistant ....Michelle Heller
Associate Scenic Designer ....Paul Weimer
Associate Costume Designer ....China Lee
Associate Lighting Designer ....Gina Scherr
Associate Sound Designer ....Chris Cronin
Associate Projection Designer ....Caite Hevner Kemp
Production Carpenter ....Edward Diaz
Production Properties ....Buist Bickley
Head Properties Supervisor ....Rob Brenner
Production Electrician ....Fraser Weir
Moving Light Programmer ....Jay Penfield
Head Sound Engineer ....Wayne Smith
Wardrobe Supervisor ....Kay Grunder
Dresser ....Renee Borys
Hair & Makeup Supervisor ....Kyle Skillin
Child Guardian ....Natasha Harper
Tutoring Services ....On Location Education
General Management Intern ....Jillian Ruben
SDC Foundation Director
    Observer ....Paula D'Alessandris

Press Representatives ....Boneau/Bryan-Brown/
    Chris Boneau, Adrian Bryan-Brown, Jim Byk,
    Michelle Farabaugh, Jackie Green, Kelly Guiod,
    Linnae Hodzic, Kevin Jones, Amy Kass, Holly Kinney,
    Emily Meagher, Aaron Meier, Christine Olver, Joe
    Perrotta, Amanda Sales, Heath Schwartz, Susanne Tighe
Advertising ....SpotCo/Drew Hodges, Ilene Rosen Flowers,
    Tom Greenwald, Nick Pramik,
    Juliana Hannett, Cletus McKeown
Marketing ....Kristen Rathbun, Julie Wechsler
Digital Outreach & Website ....Kyle Yong,
    Steven Tartick, Alex Lalak
Production Photographer ....Joan Marcus
Accountant ....Fried & Kowgios CPA's LLP/
    Robert Fried, CPA
Controller ....Joseph S. Kubala
Insurance ....DeWitt Stern Group
Legal Counsel ....Davis Wright Tremaine LLP/
    M. Graham Coleman, Robert J. Driscoll
Music Rights ....Suzanne Coffman, Yolanda Ferraloro/
    Music Rightz
Banking ....City National Bank/Michele Gibbons
Payroll ....Castellana Services, Inc.
Theatre Displays ....BAM Signs/Adam Miller
Transportation ....R & R Road Limousine
Travel ....Tzell Travel/Andi Henig
Housing ....ABA-IDEAL National Corporate Housing

PRODUCTION CREDITS
Scenery constructed and automated by Showman Fabricators Inc., Long Island City, NY, and the Berkeley Repertory Theatre Scene Shop, Berkeley, CA. Lighting equipment from PRG Lighting, a division of Production Resource Group, LLC, New Windsor, NY. Sound equipment by Sound Associates. Projection equipment provided by WorldStage/Scharff Weisberg. Props built or supplied by SFDS Fabrication and Design Shop, Brooklyn, NY; Hickory Hollow Nursery and Garden Center, Tuxedo Park, NY; Jeremy Lydic; Joseph Cairo; Emily Walsh; Faye Armon; Bridget Santaniello. Costumes provided by Berkeley Repertory Theatre Costume Shop, Claudia Diaz, Morgenthal Frederics, David Samuel Menkes.

SPECIAL THANKS
Tony Taccone, Susie Medak, Tom Pearl, Jean-Paul Gressieux, and the staff at Berkeley Repertory Theatre.

Waiting for Godot by Samuel Beckett presented through special arrangement with Georges Borchardt, Inc. on behalf of The Estate of Samuel Beckett. All rights reserved.

MUSIC CREDITS
"Underneath the Arches" performed by Flanagan & Allen. By Bud Flanagan, Reg Connelly and Joseph McCarthy Jr. ©1932 Sony/ATV Music Publishing LLC, EMI Robbins Catalog Inc., Campbell Connelly Inc. All rights on behalf of Sony/ATV Music Publishing LLC and EMI Robbins Catalog Inc. administered by Sony/ATV Music Publishing LLC. Courtesy of Parlophone Records Ltd. By arrangement with Warner Music Group Film & TV Licensing. All rights reserved. Used by permission.

Souvenir merchandise designed and created by
The Araca Group

Rehearsed at the New 42nd Street Studios

www.twoplaysinrep.com

CORT THEATRE
House Manager ....Joseph Traina

 The Shubert Organization is a proud member of the Broadway Green Alliance.

No Man's Land/Waiting for Godot
SCRAPBOOK

Correspondent: Colin Ryan, u/s "Foster," "Lucky," "Briggs," "Pozzo"

Opening Night Parties and/or Gifts: Among the many thoughtful and lovely gifts from opening night, one that stands out: Colin Critchley, one of the young actors playing The Boy in *Waiting for Godot*, gave the ladies bracelets with two arrows, inspired by the production logo, and the men cufflinks featuring the tree from the *Godot* set, one without and one with leaves.

Most Exciting Celebrity Visitor and What They Did/Said: Consensus seems to be Hugh Jackman, who came to visit three of his past costars and charmed many backstage.

Favorite In-Theatre Gathering Place: The sumptuous "lower lobby" a.k.a. the lounge of the ladies' restroom. (See photo above.)

Most Memorable Audience Reaction: A graceful underhand toss from the front row to return a wayward turnip to the waiting hands of Sir Patrick, in *Waiting for Godot*.

Memorable Ad-Lib: The other time that a turnip made its way to the front row, the audience member, sensing that he had acquired an unique souvenir, didn't toss it back. Sir Patrick, having dived to his stomach trying to catch it, simply turned to Sir Ian and shrugged, "It's gone now."

Favorite Off-Site Hangout: In the first week of previews, Num Pang, a Cambodian sandwich shop, opened just up the street and there was much rejoicing. It's not uncommon to run into cast, staff or crew in line.

Favorite Snack Foods: Homemade cookies and cakes abound, as the company is full of bakers, but special mention must be made of the two daily gifts from the props department: leftover roast chicken at each *Godot*, and the leftover toast points from Spooner's breakfast in each *No Man's Land*.

Mascot: A pair of battered old bowler hats.

Catchphrase Only the Company Would Recognize: C**t (blame Harold Pinter).

Understudy Anecdote: As we have only two understudies, and each show has four roles, some parts need filling for each understudy rehearsal. Our stage management team usually steps in, and ably so, but, one afternoon, Estragon was portrayed by none other than Sir Ian himself.

Who Wore the Heaviest/Hottest Costume?: Shuler Hensley as Pozzo in *Waiting for Godot*, though Billy Crudup's Lucky takes first prize for overall weight carried, albeit in prop form.

Who Wore the Least: Sir Ian's feet.

What Did You Think of the Web Buzz on Your Show?: Everyone was thrilled with the warm and expectant web chatter, especially the enthusiastic embrace of the #gogodididonyc Twitter series.

Coolest Thing About Being in This Show: Not only is this a wonderful company to which every member brings good humor, warmth and a consistent level of excellence eight times a week, but everyone takes a special pleasure in knowing they are working on a production that people will tell their grandchildren about.

Other Stories or Memories: For several weeks after opening, both of the young actors, Aidan Gemme and Colin Critchley, were a two-man prank squad, deploying snapping gum, a snake in a can, and a pencil on a retracting string. True responsibility for the reign of mischief lay with Sir Patrick, who gave them a box full of these tricks.

Photo: Courtesy of the production

Photo: Joseph Marzullo

1. The last notes session in the cast's favorite place, the ladies' room in the Cort Theatre!
2. (L-R): Sirs Ian McKellen and Patrick Stewart do a little dance at the curtain call on the opening night of *Waiting for Godot*.
3. (L-R): Shuler Hensley, Patrick Stewart, Ian McKellen and Billy Crudup take a bow on opening night of *No Man's Land*.

Photo: Joseph Marzullo

Of Mice and Men

First Preview: March 19, 2014. Opened: April 16, 2014.
Still running as of May 31, 2014.

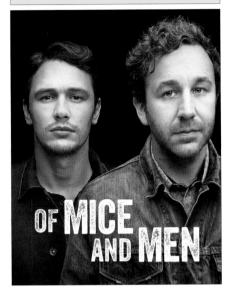

Revival of John Steinbeck's 1937 classic about a pair of migrant farm workers who sustain themselves with their castle-on-a-cloud dream of someday owning their own little farm. Chris O'Dowd plays the retarded but powerful Lennie. James Franco plays his friend and partner George who watches over Lennie and helps him out of the scrapes his simplemindedness sometimes gets him into. But just as their dream comes within reach, Lennie makes one fatal mistake.

CAST

George	JAMES FRANCO
Lennie	CHRIS O'DOWD
Curley's Wife	LEIGHTON MEESTER
Candy	JIM NORTON
Crooks	RON CEPHAS JONES
Curley	ALEX MORF
The Boss	JIM ORTLIEB
Slim	JIM PARRACK
Carlson	JOEL MARSH GARLAND
Whit	JAMES McMENAMIN

TIME

The 1930s

PLACE

The Salinas Valley of California

UNDERSTUDIES

For George, Whit, Slim, Curley:
MICHAEL DEMPSEY

Continued on next page

ⓢ LONGACRE THEATRE

220 West 48th Street
A Shubert Organization Theatre

Philip J. Smith, *Chairman*   **Robert E. Wankel,** *President*

DAVID BINDER

KATE LEAR   DARREN BAGERT   ADAM ZOTOVICH

LATITUDE LINK/PIEDMONT PRODUCTIONS   RAISE THE ROOF   PAULA MARIE BLACK   MARC TURTLETAUB

RUTH HENDEL/ BARBARA WHITMAN   MARIANNE MILLS/JAYNE BARON SHERMAN

MARTIN MASSMAN   JUDY KENT/WENDY KNUDSEN   KEVIN NIU   MICHAEL WATT

AND

THE SHUBERT ORGANIZATION

PRESENT

JAMES FRANCO   CHRIS O'DOWD

OF MICE AND MEN

BY

JOHN STEINBECK

STARRING

LEIGHTON MEESTER

WITH

RON CEPHAS JONES   ALEX MORF

JOEL MARSH GARLAND   JAMES MCMENAMIN   JIM ORTLIEB   JIM PARRACK

MICHAEL DEMPSEY   KEVIN JACKSON   ERICA LUTZ   STEPHEN PAYNE

AND

JIM NORTON

SCENIC DESIGN	COSTUME DESIGN	LIGHTING DESIGN	SOUND DESIGN
TODD ROSENTHAL	SUTTIRAT LARLARB	JAPHY WEIDEMAN	ROB MILBURN & MICHAEL BODEEN

ORIGINAL MUSIC	FIGHT DIRECTION	HAIR & WIG DESIGN	CASTING	TECHNICAL SUPERVISOR
DAVID SINGER	THOMAS SCHALL	CHARLES G. LAPOINTE	CALLERI CASTING	HUDSON THEATRICAL ASSOCIATES

PRESS REPRESENTATIVE	ADVERTISING	MARKETING DIRECTOR/ ASSOCIATE PRODUCER	ASSOCIATE PRODUCERS
POLK & CO.	SERINO/COYNE	ERIC SCHNALL	MARK BERGER MATTHEW MASTEN

PRODUCTION STAGE MANAGER	COMPANY MANAGER	EXECUTIVE PRODUCER
JANE GREY	BOBBY DRIGGERS	101 PRODUCTIONS, LTD.

DIRECTED BY

ANNA D. SHAPIRO

4/16/14

Photo: Richard Phibbs

James Franco (L) as George
and Chris O'Dowd as Lennie

Of Mice and Men

James Franco
George

Chris O'Dowd
Lennie

Leighton Meester
Curley's Wife

Jim Norton
Candy

Ron Cephas Jones
Crooks

Alex Morf
Curley

Joel Marsh Garland
Carlson

James McMenamin
Whit

Jim Ortlieb
The Boss

Jim Parrack
Slim

Michael Dempsey
*u/s George, Slim,
Whit, Curley*

Kevin Jackson
u/s Crooks

Erica Lutz
u/s Curley's Wife

Stephen Payne
*u/s Carlson, The
Boss, Candy*

John Steinbeck
Playwright

Anna D. Shapiro
Director

Todd Rosenthal
Scenic Design

Suttirat Larlarb
Costume Design

Japhy Weideman
Lighting Design

David Singer
Original Music

Rob Milburn & Michael Bodeen
Sound Design

Thomas Schall
Fight Director

Charles G. LaPointe
Hair and Wig Design

James Calleri
Calleri Casting
Casting

Paul Davis
Calleri Casting
Casting

Erica Jensen
Calleri Casting
Casting

Neil A. Mazzella
Hudson Theatrical
Associates
Technical Supervisor

Cambra Overend
Stage Manager

Wendy Orshan
101 Productions
*General Manager/
Executive Producer*

David Binder
Producer

Kate Lear
Co-Producer

Of Mice and Men

Darren Bagert
Co-Producer

Adam Zotovich
Co-Producer

Ralph Bryan
Latitude Link
Co-Producer

Bruce D. Long
Piedmont
Productions
Co-Producer

Morgan Sills
Piedmont
Productions
Co-Producer

Harriet Leve
Raise the Roof
Co-Producer

Jennifer Isaacson
Raise the Roof
Co-Producer

Paula Marie Black
Co-Producer

Ruth Hendel
Co-Producer

Barbara Whitman
Co-Producer

Jayne Baron
Sherman
Co-Producer

Martin Massman
Co-Producer

Michael Watt
Co-Producer

Philip J. Smith
The Shubert
Organization
Co-Producer

Robert E. Wankel
The Shubert
Organization
Co-Producer

Eric Schnall
Marketing Director/
Associate Producer

Matthew Masten
Associate Producer

Photos: Brian Mapp

STAGE MANAGEMENT
(L-R): Sara J. Grady (Assistant Stage Manager), Howard Tilkin,
Jane Grey (Production Stage Manager)

WARDROBE/HAIR/MAKE-UP
Front: Robert Guy (Wardrobe Supervisor)
Middle (L-R): Alex Rozansky (Stitcher), Susan Cook (Dresser), Michael Louis (Dresser)
Top (L-R): John McNulty (Hair & Wig Supervisor), David Page (Mr. Franco's Dresser)

ASST. COMPANY MANAGER
Katie Pope

DOORMAN
Regan Kimmel

2013-2014 AWARD

THEATRE WORLD AWARD
For Outstanding Broadway
or Off-Broadway Debut
(Chris O'Dowd)

Of Mice and Men

CREW
Front (L-R): Ric Rogers, Jane Grey (Production Stage Manager), John Lofgren, Ray King, Wayne Smith (Advance Production Sound)
Back (L-R): Paul Wimmer (Production Carpenter), André Gray, Vince Goga (Associate Production Electrician),
Chris Pantuso (Production Props), Wilbur Graham

FRONT OF HOUSE
Front (L-R): Keith Gartner, Nina Morozova, Elsie Grosvenor, Judi Wilfore (House Manager)
Back (L-R): Erich Loetterle, David Chiu, Jessica Carollo, Daniel Rosario

---

STAFF FOR *OF MICE AND MEN*

GENERAL MANAGEMENT
101 PRODUCTIONS, LTD.
Wendy Orshan   Jeffrey M. Wilson
Elie Landau
Ron Gubin
Chris Morey

COMPANY MANAGER
Bobby Driggers

ASSISTANT COMPANY MANAGER
Katie Pope

GENERAL PRESS REPRESENTATIVE
POLK & CO.
Matt Polk   Wayne Wolfe   Colgan McNeil
Sasha Pensanti

CASTING
CALLERI CASTING
James Calleri, CSA
Erica Jensen, CSA   Paul Davis, CSA

TECHNICAL SUPERVISOR
HUDSON THEATRICAL ASSOCIATES
Neil A. Mazzella   Sam Ellis
Caitlin McInerney   Irene Wang

Production Stage Manager ....Jane Grey
Stage Manager ....Cambra Overend
Assistant Stage Manager ....Sara J. Grady
Assistant Directors ....Jonathan Berry, Cat Miller
Fight Captain ....James McMenamin
Associate Scenic Designer ....Kevin Depinet
Associate Costume Designer ....Moria Sine Clinton
Associate Lighting Designer ....Gary Slootskiy

Associate Sound Designer ....Chris Cronin
Assistant Scenic Designer ....Courtney O'Neill
Assistant Lighting Designer ....Jax Messenger
Make-up Designer ....John McNulty
Production Carpenter ....Paul Wimmer
Production Electrician ....James Maloney
Associate Production Electrician ....Vince Goga
Production Properties Supervisor ....Faye Armon-Troncoso
Production Props ....Chris Pantuso
Advance Production Sound ....Wayne Smith
Moving Light Programmer ....Colin Scott
Wardrobe Supervisor ....Robert Guy
Mr. Franco's Dresser ....David Page
Dressers ....Susan Cook, Michael Louis
Stitcher ....Alex Rozansky
Hair & Wig Supervisor ....John McNulty
Dialect/Vocal Coach ....Cecilie O'Reilly
Fight Director ....Thomas Schall

Photos: Brian Mapp

Of Mice and Men
SCRAPBOOK

Correspondent: Alex Morf, "Curley"

Opening Night Parties and/or Gifts: We received the most delicious cookies from our #1 fan, Whoopi Goldberg.

Most Exciting Celebrity Visitor: Lady Gaga came to the show on her birthday dressed in a pink Little Bo Peep costume. She offered James Franco a Butterfinger for his moving performance.

Favorite In-Theatre Gathering Place: Every Saturday, the greenroom transforms into Susy's

place (the Brothel in *OMAM*) and we sip whiskey, eat corn nuts, and cast and crew members bring instruments and jam out in a late night Hootenanny.

Special Backstage Rituals: We always dance a jig backstage to the music before the start of scene three.

Most Memorable Audience Reaction: Nightly sobs at the final moment of our show.

Memorable Press Encounter: Basically anything that James posts on Instagram.

Memorable Stage Door Fan Encounter: James regularly gets beautiful paintings of himself from his adoring fans.

Memorable Directorial Note: "The most important person in the room is the person across from you on that stage."

Favorite Off-Site Hangout: Hurley's.

Favorite Snack Food: Corn Nuts.

Favorite Therapy: Our hair and make-up artist John McNulty is everyone's therapist.

Mascot: Our two beautiful show dogs, Blue and Violet.

1. The always social media-connected James Franco in his dressing room.
2. Show mascots and cast members, Blue and Violet.
3. Whoopi Goldberg and *Yearbook* correspondent Alex Morf get photobombed by Chris O'Dowd.
4. Backstage at the Longacre Theatre with (L-R): Taylor Kinney, James Franco, Lady Gaga, Jim Parrack.

Catchphrase Only the Company Would Recognize: "By God, let's do her."

Nicknames: Five out of 10 cast members are named Jim or James. So they go by Franco, McMenamin, Ortlieb, Jim (Norton), and Jimmy (Parrack).

Coolest Thing About Being in This Show: Sharing Steinbeck with young people who have never experienced his simple genius.

Animal Trainer for "Violet"
and "Blue" ......Lydia DesRoche/Sit Stay Dog Training
Costume Assistant ....Martin Schnellinger
Assistant Properties ....Alison Mantilla
Assistant to Mr. Binder ....Mark Berger
Assistant to the General Managers ....Michael Rudd
101 Productions, Ltd. Staff ....Beth Blitzer,
    Caitlin Clements, Mark Gagliardi, Richard Jones,
    Kathy Kim, Steve Supeck, Andrew J. White
101 Productions, Ltd. Interns ....Justin Coffman,
    Eric Vigdorov
Legal Counsel ....Loeb & Loeb/Seth Gelblum, Esq.
Immigration Lawyer ....David King/
    Entertainment Visa Consultants LLC
Accountant ....Fried & Kowgios CPA's LLP
Controller ....Galbraith & Co./Tabitha Falcone
Marketing Director ....Eric Schnall
Advertising ....Serino/Coyne/Greg Corradetti,
    Vinny Sainato, Marci Kaufman Meyers, Vanessa Javier
Social Media ....ESP
Interactive Marketing...................Situation Interactive/
    Damian Bazadona, Jeremy Kraus,
    Mollie Shapiro, Sarah Sheppard, Ryan Muth
Banking......................................City National Bank
Insurance ....DeWitt Stern
Opening Night Event Coordinator ...Serino/Coyne Events/
    Suzanne Tobak, Chrissann Gasparro
101 Opening Night Coordinators ....Maria Di Dia,
    Andrew J. White

Merchandising ....Creative Goods NYC
Production Photographer ....Richard Phibbs
Payroll Services ....Castellana Services Inc.
Theatre Displays ....King Displays
Group Sales ....Telecharge.com Group Sales

To learn more about the production, please visit
www.ofmiceandmenonbroadway.com
Please follow us on Twitter, Facebook and Instagram:
@MiceAndMenBway

CREDITS

Scenery constructed by Hudson Scenic Studio and PRG. Automation by PRG Scenic Technologies. Lighting by Hudson Sound and Light. Sound by Sound Associates. Ladies wear by John Kristiansen. Men's tailoring by Daniel Weger and Brian Turpin. Aging and distressing by Jeff Fender Studio. Makeup provided by M•A•C.

SPECIAL THANKS

Penguin Books, The National Steinbeck Center, Lisa Morris, Tzell Travel, Lookingglass Theatre Company, Aaron Snook, Nick Heggestad, Joel Hobson, Amalgamated Classic Clothing and Dry Goods, Shelly White, Gene Elm, Bobby From Boston, Luke Brown, Tom McAlister, Linda Wingerter, Matt Chapman, Christine McManemin, Polina Minchuk, Karla Braunesreither, the Public Theater, Lizzie Donelan, Michael Keller, RRL, Stuart Levy.

This production was rehearsed at
The Pershing Square Signature Center.

Once

First Preview: February 28, 2012. Opened: March 18, 2012.
Still running as of May 31, 2014.

A bittersweet romantic musical based on the 2006 Oscar-winning film of the same title, about an Irish street musician who gains new inspiration when he meets a Czech piano player. She reawakens his musical muse—and his heart. Staged with a company of actors who also function as the onstage orchestra.

CAST

(in alphabetical order)

Eamon .... ADAM WESLEY BROWN
    Guitar, Piano, Melodica, Harmonica, Percussion
Girl .... JOANNA CHRISTIE
    Piano
Guy .... ARTHUR DARVILL
    Guitar
* Ivanka .... LAUREL GRIGGS
Da .... DAVID PATRICK KELLY
    Mandolin
* Ivanka .... JILLIAN LEBLING
Réza .... KATRINA LENK
    Violin
Baruška .... ANNE L. NATHAN
    Piano, Accordion, Percussion, Melodica, Concertina
Švec .... LUCAS PAPAELIAS
    Banjo, Guitar, Mandolin, Drum Set
Bank Manager .... ANDY TAYLOR
    Violin, Accordion, Cello, Guitar, Mandolin
Andrej .... CARLOS VALDES
    Electric Bass, Ukulele, Percussion, Guitar, Piano
Ex-Girlfriend .... ERIKKA WALSH
    Violin, Percussion

Continued on next page

⑤ BERNARD B. JACOBS THEATRE

242 West 45th Street
A Shubert Organization Theatre

Philip J. Smith, *Chairman*   **Robert E. Wankel,** *President*

BARBARA BROCCOLI   JOHN N. HART JR.   PATRICK MILLING SMITH   FREDERICK ZOLLO
BRIAN CARMODY   MICHAEL G. WILSON   ORIN WOLF PRODUCTIONS   THE SHUBERT ORGANIZATION
ROBERT COLE, EXECUTIVE PRODUCER

in association with

NEW YORK THEATRE WORKSHOP

present

Once

book
ENDA WALSH

music and lyrics
GLEN HANSARD & MARKÉTA IRGLOVÁ

based on the motion picture written and directed by
JOHN CARNEY

starring

ARTHUR DARVILL   **JOANNA CHRISTIE**

ADAM WESLEY BROWN   LAUREL GRIGGS   DAVID PATRICK KELLY   JILLIAN LEBLING
KATRINA LENK   ANNE L. NATHAN   LUCAS PAPAELIAS   ANDY TAYLOR
CARLOS VALDES   ERIKKA WALSH   PAUL WHITTY   J. MICHAEL ZYGO

scenic and costume design
BOB CROWLEY

lighting design
NATASHA KATZ

sound design
CLIVE GOODWIN

dialect coach
STEPHEN GABIS

casting
JIM CARNAHAN, CSA/STEPHEN KOPEL

production stage manager
BESS MARIE GLORIOSO

production manager
AURORA PRODUCTIONS

press representative
BONEAU/BRYAN-BROWN

company manager
LISA M. POYER

music supervisor and orchestrations
MARTIN LOWE

movement by
STEVEN HOGGETT

directed by
JOHN TIFFANY

Once was originally developed at the American Repertory Theater, Cambridge, Massachusetts, in April 2011,
Diane Paulus, Artistic Director, Diane Borger, Producer
The producers wish to express their appreciation to Theatre Development Fund for its support of this production.

10/1/13

Guy and Girl make music:
Arthur Darvill and
Joanna Christie

Photo: Joan Marcus

Once

MUSICAL NUMBERS

ACT I

"Leave"	Guy
"Falling Slowly"	Guy & Girl
"North Strand"	Ensemble
"The Moon"	Andrej (as Ensemble)
"Ej, Pada, Pada, Rosicka"	Ensemble
"If You Want Me"	Guy, Girl, Ensemble
"Broken Hearted Hoover Fixer Sucker Guy"	Guy
"Say It to Me Now"	Guy
"Abandoned in Bandon"	Bank Manager
"Gold"	Guy & Ensemble

ACT II

"Sleeping"	Guy
"When Your Mind's Made Up"	Guy, Girl, Ensemble
"The Hill"	Girl
"Gold" (A capella)	Company
"The Moon"	Company
"Falling Slowly" (Reprise)	Guy, Girl, Ensemble

Cast Continued

Billy ....PAUL WHITTY
    Guitar, Ukulele, Percussion, Mandolin
Emcee ....J. MICHAEL ZYGO
    Guitar, Percussion

* Laurel Griggs and Jillian Lebling alternate in the role of Ivanka.

DANCE CAPTAIN
J. MICHAEL ZYGO

MUSIC CAPTAIN
ANDY TAYLOR

Arthur Darvill and Joanna Christie are appearing with the support of Actors' Equity Association pursuant to an exchange program between American Equity and UK Equity.

UNDERSTUDIES

For Eamon: BRANDON ELLIS, DON NOBLE,
   ARI McKAY WILFORD
For Andrej: BRANDON ELLIS,
   ARI McKAY WILFORD
For Réza: ANDREA GOSS, ERIKKA WALSH
For Guy: J. MICHAEL ZYGO
For Da: DON NOBLE
For Girl: ANDREA GOSS, ERIKKA WALSH
For Baruška: JOANNE BORTS
For Švec: BRANDON ELLIS,
   ARI McKAY WILFORD
For Bank Manager: BRANDON ELLIS
For Ex-Girlfriend: ANDREA GOSS
For Billy: BRANDON ELLIS, J. MICHAEL ZYGO
For Emcee: DON NOBLE,
   ARI McKAY WILFORD

STANDBYS
For Girl: LAURA DREYFUSS
For Guy: BEN HOPE

Arthur Darvill
Guy

Joanna Christie
Girl

Adam Wesley Brown
Eamon

Laurel Griggs
Ivanka

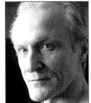

David Patrick Kelly
Da

Jillian Lebling
Ivanka

Katrina Lenk
Réza

Anne L. Nathan
Baruška

Lucas Papaelias
Švec

Andy Taylor
*Bank Manager,
Music Captain*

Carlos Valdes
Andrej

Erikka Walsh
*Ex-Girlfriend;
u/s Girl, Réza*

Paul Whitty
Billy

J. Michael Zygo
*Emcee; u/s Guy,
Billy; Dance Captain*

Joanne Borts
u/s Baruška

Once

Laura Dreyfuss
Standby

Brandon Ellis
u/s Bank Manager, Billy, Andrej, Svec, Eamon

Andrea Goss
u/s Girl, Réza, Ex-Girlfriend

Ben Hope
Standby

Don Noble
u/s Da, Eamon, Emcee

Ari McKay Wilford
u/s Eamon, Andrej, Svec, Emcee

Enda Walsh
Playwright

Glen Hansard
Music and Lyrics

Markéta Irglová
Music and Lyrics

John Carney
Writer and Director of the Film, Once

John Tiffany
Director

Steven Hoggett
Movement

Martin Lowe
Musical Supervisor, Orchestrations, and Additional Material

Bob Crowley
Scenic and Costume Design

Natasha Katz
Lighting Design

Clive Goodwin
Sound Design

Stephen Gabis
Dialect Coach

Liz Caplan
Liz Caplan Vocal Studios, LLC
Vocal Supervisor

Jim Carnahan
Casting

Gene O'Donovan
Aurora Productions
Production Management

Ben Heller
Aurora Productions
Production Management

Barbara Broccoli
Producer

John N. Hart Jr.
Producer

Patrick Milling Smith
Producer

Frederick Zollo
Producer

Brian Carmody
Producer

Michael G. Wilson
Producer

Orin Wolf
Orin Wolf Productions
Producer

Philip J. Smith
The Shubert Organization
Producer

Robert E. Wankel
The Shubert Organization
Producer

Robert Cole
Executive Producer

James C. Nicola
Artistic Director NYTW
Producer

Diane Paulus
Artistic Director A.R.T.
Workshop Producer

Charles Stone
Associate Producer

Once

David Abeles
Eamon, Music Captain

Joe Carroll
u/s Eamon, Andrej, Svec, Emcee

Eliza Holland Madore
Ivanka

Erica Swindell
u/s Girl, Réza, Ex-Girlfriend

Charleene Closshey
u/s Réza, Ex-Girlfriend

Elisabeth Evans
u/s Girl, Réza, Ex-Girlfirend

Jessie Fisher
Standby Girl

Brandon McGibbon
Svec

Paul Alexander Nolan
Guy

Madeleine Pace
Ivanka

Ryan Vona
Andrej

Photos: Brian Mapp

BOX OFFICE
(L-R): Marshall Kolbrenner, Karen Coscia, Michael Kolbrenner

STAGE MANAGEMENT
(L-R): Ana M. Garcia (Stage Manager), Bess Marie Glorioso (Production Stage Manager), Katherine Shea (Assistant Stage Manager)

WARDROBE
(L-R): Cailin Anderson, Katie Chihaby, Kathleen Gallagher (Wardrobe Supervisor)

Once

CREW
(L-R): Fred Ricci, Reid Hall, Reg Vessey (Production Props), Jason Choquette (Sound Engineer, sitting), Jonathan Cohen, Wally Flores, Martin Perrin

FRONT OF HOUSE
Standing: William Mitchell (House Manager)
Front: Kair Martin
Second Row (L-R): Eva Frances Laskow (Head Usher), Holly Madison, Joy Mayweather
Third Row: Rosa Pesante
Fourth Row (L-R): Gerry Bellitus, John Seid, Leo Ruiz
Top: Sean Cutler (Ticket Taker)

Once

Company Manager ....Lisa M. Poyer
Associate Company Manager ....Susan Keappock
Assistant Company Manager ....Megan Ringeling

Production Stage Manager ....Bess Marie Glorioso
Stage Manager ....Ana M. Garcia
Assistant Stage Manager ....Katherine Shea

Associate Producer ....Charles Stone
Associate Producer ....Ben Limberg
Associate Director ....Shaun Peknic
Associate Movement Director ....Yasmine Lee
Resident Music Supervisor ....Jason DeBord
Associate Music Supervisor ....Rob Preuss
Vocal Supervisor ....Liz Caplan Vocal Studios, LLC
Associate Scenic Designer ....Frank McCullough
Assistant Lighting Designers ....Peter Hoerburger,
Yael Lubetzky
Sound Design Associate ....Alex Hawthorn
Assistant Sound Designer/
Advance Audio ....Brian Walters
Czech Diction and Translation ....Suzanna Halsey

Assistant to John N. Hart Jr ....Maximillian Traber
Assistant to Patrick Milling Smith ....Catherine Waage
Assistant to Robert Cole &
Frederick Zollo ....Molly Clifford

Production Carpenter......................Rebecca O'Neill
Production Electrician ....Michael Pitzer
Production Props ....Reg Vessey
Production Sound Engineer ...Phillip Lojo/Paul Delcioppo
Head Electrician ....Eric Norris
Sound Engineer ....Jason Choquette
Instrument Technician ....Luca Bartoccioli
Props Supervisor ....Matt Hodges
UK Props ....Lisa Buckley
Moving Light Programmer ....Sean Beach
Advance Production Sound ....Jason Choquette
NYTW Costume Liaison ....Jeffery Wallach
Wardrobe Supervisor ....Kathleen Gallagher
Dressers ....Cailin Anderson, Katie Chihaby
Child Actor Guardian ....Jillian Zygo
Tutoring ....On Location Education/Muriel Kester
Production Assistants ....Kyle Beckley,
William Bernstein, Will Dietzler, Dale Ducko,

The new Guy in town: Paul Alexander Nolan

Olivia Gunderson, Jerron Herman, Patrick Kanaley,
Ryan McCurdy, Miguel Mendiola, Katie Summerfield,
Raleigh Tyler, Haley Ward, Katie Young

Advertising ....SpotCo/Drew Hodges, Tom Greenwald,
Nick Pramik, Caraline Sogliuzzo, Mikel Lynn Pihakis
Website and Online Marketing ....SpotCo/Kyle Young,
Marisa Delmore, Callie Goff
Marketing and Promotions ....SpotCo/
Kristen Rathbun, Sara Barton
Legal
Counsel ....Franklin, Weinrib, Rudell & Vassallo, P.C./
Jonathan Lonner, Heather Reid
Additional Legal
Counsel ....Frankfurt, Kurnit, Klein & Selz, P.C./
Mark A. Merriman
Immigration Counsel ....Shannon K. Such
Immigration
Counsel ....Kramer Levin Naftalis & Frankel LLP/
Mark D. Koestler
Accountant ....Fried & Kowgios CPAs LLP/
Robert Fried, CPA
Comptroller ....Anne Stewart FitzRoy, CPA
Orthopaedist ....David S. Weiss, M.D.
Banking ....City National Bank/
Anne McSweeney, Michael Tynan
Insurance ....Dewitt Stern Group/
Peter K. Shoemaker, Rebecca LaFazia
Payroll Service ....Castellana Payroll Services, Inc./
Lance Castellana, James Castellana, Norman Sewell
Travel ....Gregory Stillwell/Road Rebel Entertainment
Production Photographer ....Joan Marcus
Opening Night
Coordination ....The Lawrence Company Events, Inc./
Michael P. Lawrence
Theatre Displays ....King Displays, Inc.
Group Sales ....Telecharge.com Group Sales/
212-239-6262, 1-800-432-7780,
www.telecharge.com/groups

International Booking
Inquiries ......National Artists Management Company/
Alecia Parker

NEW YORK THEATRE WORKSHOP STAFF
Artistic Director ....JAMES C. NICOLA
Managing Director ....WILLIAM RUSSO
Associate Artistic Director ....LINDA S. CHAPMAN
General Manager ....BARRACK EVANS
Director of Development ....ALISA SCHIERMAN
Director of Education ....BRYN THORSSON
Director of Finance ....RACHEL McBETH
Marketing Director ....REBEKAH PAINE
Casting Director ....JACK DOULIN

Photo: Joan Marcus

Technical Director ....PAUL BRADLEY

CREDITS
Scenery and scenic effects built, painted, electrified and
automated by Show Motion, Inc., Milford, CT. Automation
and show control by Show Motion, Inc., Milford, CT, using
the AC2 Computerized Motion Control System. Lighting
equipment from PRG Lighting. Video equipment from
PRG Video. Sound equipment by Masque Sound™.
Banjo built by Nechville Musical Products. Mandolins
supplied by Sound to Earth, Ltd. Drum kit supplied by
Carroll Musical Instrument Rentals, LLC. Violins and cellos
provided by Samuel Kolstein & Son Violinmakers. Hosiery
and undergarments supplied by Bra*Tenders.

MUSIC CREDITS
"On Raglan Road" by Patrick Kavanagh is performed by
kind permission of the Trustees of the Estate of the late
Katherine B. Kavanagh, through the Jonathan Williams
Literary Agency. "Gold" composed by Fergus O'Farrell,
published by Yell Music Ltd. "Abandoned in Bandon"
composed by Martin Lowe, Andy Taylor and Enda Walsh.

Souvenir merchandise designed and created by
The Araca Group

Original Broadway cast recording
available on Sony Masterworks

Thanks to Claire Candela
for being a part of the Once family.

SPECIAL THANKS
C.F. Martin and Company is the official guitar of the
Broadway musical Once. American Airlines.

www.oncemusical.com

BROADWAY green♦alliance   The Shubert Organization is a proud
member of the Broadway Green Alliance.

Once
SCRAPBOOK

Correspondent: Paul Whitty, "Billy." Plays guitar, mandolin, ukulele, cajon, miscellaneous percussion

Memorable Stage Door Fan Encounters: I had no idea how big of a thing "Dr. Who" was. I am amazed that it spanned so much time, and yet escaped me. And that's why, when Arthur Darvill joined our cast, I was blown away to see all these people at the stage door with their "Dr. Who" memorabilia.

I got a fan—like, a Japanese-type fan—from a fan. When I came out of the stage door he handed it to me without saying anything. He was just grateful for the performance. It's interesting how people decide to express themselves. We had a guy who got a tattoo of the *Once* logo on his arm, with the date he first saw the show. I am just amazed by that. He said the show changed his life. It's extremely humbling to think something you're involved with has had such an effect on someone's life.

Memorable Parties: Oh man! We've had a lot of really cool celebrations. I was in the original cast, so obviously the Tony Awards and everything that went along with that. There was one really great party they threw at Sardi's after the nominations came out. Composer Glen Hansard [also the model for the main character, Guy] was there. He and I had become friends since the beginning of the process of creating the show. We connected. He came up to me and said, "Hey, man, if you aren't doing anything later, I'm going to Bono's birthday party. You should come." So, a few of us went down to a bar in the Village and hung out with Bono and Sean Penn and sang with them. I kept thinking to myself, "The only way I could ever get to do anything like this in my life is by being involved in this show." Glen is extremely humble and very generous to us all. This show was his baby and he gave it to us and said, "OK, you guys play with it now."

Most Exciting Celebrity Visitors: When Liza Minnelli came to see the show she came up to me and said, "You were so good, it was stupid." I called my mother afterward and

told her. Vice President Joe Biden came and it was cool because it was very top-secret. The Secret Service had to check everything before he got here. They snuck us back into a corner backstage so we could meet him. He is a really funny guy. He enjoyed the show, and said he was there because of his wife. A real charmer, that guy. Big smile. Real good at making the ladies laugh.

Actor Who Plays the Most Roles in This Show: The person who has the most to do is our swing, Brandon Ellis. He has to cover five tracks, so he has to play 15 instruments: all four of mine, plus banjo, drums, bass guitar, piano, melodica, tambourine and a lot of little percussive things.

Special Backstage Rituals: David Patrick Kelly is a machine. He's very strict with his routine. His ritual is coming to the theatre

and doing voice warmups. He's also very diligent about what he eats. He's a real pro. My rituals change over time. But in the beginning, I used to go around and take an inventory of all the instruments on stage, to make sure they were all in their place. After a while I decided to name them. They all have female names. The piano is Rosie. She's probably the most important instrument. Although I don't play her in the show, she is the instrument I touch the most because I'm

1. *Yearbook* correspondent Paul Whitty and Rosie the piano.
2. Ripley Sobo (an original "Ivanka") stopped by the Jacobs to give Paul Whitty a hug.
3. (L-R): Paul Whitty, Ben Hope, J. Michael Zygo, and Carlos Valdes having a little off-campus jam session.

responsible for rolling her around the stage. The character of Guy has a bunch of different guitars, all with different tunings for different songs. His main guitar for "Falling Slowly" I named Regina, queen of all the guitars. My guitar is Ophelia and my cajon is named Bonnie.

We give a pre-show concert every day. That I would say is our shared ritual. The last three songs are always the same, but the first three always change. We try to mix it up a little bit so we don't get bored. It serves as a buffer between the rest of our lives and doing the show. Jamming like that every night, we get to blow off steam and focus on what's ahead.

Who Has Done the Most Shows: Anne L. Nathan has done the most performances of *Once*, but I'm not sure if it's her or David Patrick Kelly who has been in the most shows on Broadway. Anne is someone whose guidance I count on regularly. If I have an issue, whether it be personal or professional, I can always trust that I will get sound advice from Anne because she knows from experience.

Favorite Moment During Each Performance: It's a delicate show and I'm onstage for most of it. I love and am terrified by a moment I have at the end of the show, on the beach, right after the end of the recording session. I have a moment with the banker where we make amends. He says, "You can't have"—I'm going to start crying here as I think of it—"You can't have a city without music, Billy, Dublin needs you." So much vitriol has been going back and forth between me and the banker. It's interesting to be able to admit when you're wrong, that you've become something you're not proud of. And that person can still forgive you and be your friend. That moment is all you ever wanted to hear. I love playing it especially opposite Andy Taylor. He keeps it so simple and genuine. My character has been hurtling through space, and finally someone catches him and says, "You're here." That little bit of dialogue

Once

SCRAPBOOK

Entertaining the lunchtime crowds at "Broadway in Bryant Park": Arthur Darvill (Guy), also known to fans as Rory on "Dr. Who."

was added for our move up to Broadway. I think it really ties together and finishes the story of Billy and the Banker.

Favorite In-Theatre Gathering Place: The trap under the stage at the Jacobs. Our show is not heavy on sets and trap doors, so there is not a lot of machinery down there. It's our greenroom. We do our birthday gatherings there, cake at "half-hour," that sort of thing. I actually spend a lot of time down there. I have to eat before a show. Some can't eat before a performance, but I have to. So I go to the Starlite Deli on 44th Street, get a sandwich, then go straight to the trap and eat and read the newspaper until 7:15. Our stage is off limits until about then because the crew has to tune all instruments.

Favorite Off-Site Hangout: We tend to go to St. Andrews because they have a really great Irish traditional band that plays there. You'd think we would have had enough of that by doing the show, but they have a trio there, Mary, Patrick and Doney, and they are just unreal. So we go there to have beers and watch them shred. It's very fun. Sometimes, after a couple of drinks, they invite us to get up there and play a song or two with them.

Favorite Snack Food: Schmackary's cookies seem to end up constantly at our stage door and I am easily ten pounds heavier because of that. Also, it doesn't help that Stephanie Warren from New York Theatre Workshop is always coming to visit us at the Jacobs with homemade decadent treats such as peanut butter snicker brownies. Me and Stephanie both came to New York from Myrtle Beach, South Carolina, and I love that she always brings a little slice of home. It's one that threatens the waistline, but so be it.

Special Attitude: When we started we felt like the outsider kids on Broadway.

Everything about our show was so different from other shows. So we decided that our approach to everything would be a little different too; a little off center. So, when someone would suggest something that wasn't quite right, we'd say, "That's not what *Once* does."

Catchphrases Only the Company Would Recognize: "What's the Bullshit?" At some point early in the process, the pre-show list went up one night and someone jokingly said, "Ugh, that's Bullshit!" and it stuck. Now, we lovingly refer to the pre-show list as the "Bullshit."

Best In-House Parody Music and Lyrics: Lucas Papaelias does "Major-Minor." He takes songs in a major key and plays them in a minor key and vice versa. He has crafted this into an incredible medley of songs from

the show. He also sometimes changes the lyrics. On "Falling Slowly," instead of singing "I don't know you/But I want to," he sings "I don't know you/I don't care to."

Memorable Stage Manager Notes: We get a lot of different kinds of notes because we are playing and singing and doing choreography and acting. Bess, Ana, Katherine and Mel are amazing. They run a tight ship, keep the show in top form, and do their absolute best to keep all of us complicated actor/musician types happy. Just make sure you wash your hands after using the bathroom or there will be hell to pay!

"Carols for a Cure" Carol: "Coventry Carol."

"Gypsy of the Year" Skit: Two of our PAs, Ryan and Eric, who normally wrangle our pre-show stage visitors, did a mashup of the Mendelssohn piece that Girl plays, and Miley Cyrus's "Wrecking Ball."

Superstitions: Our director, John Tiffany, is very anti-superstition. He was also directing *Macbeth* on Broadway and would get annoyed when people were afraid to say the title backstage. He would tell them, "Oh go ahead and say it." So far so good!

Coolest Thing About Being in This Show: I'm in the fucking coolest band ever. I get to play in this really cool band every night and I get to do all the things I've always loved to do. I had a moment a few years ago when I called my mother and said, "Mom, I don't think I'm going to do acting any more. I'm just going to play music." Usually you have a parent who says, "Be a lawyer." But my mom said, "No you have to still be an actor because you're a good actor." I said, "But I'm really happy playing music." And she said, "Find a way to do both." I thank my lucky stars that I get to do both. That's pretty cool to me.

Joanna Christie (Girl) plays in Bryant Park.

Outside Mullingar

First Preview: January 3, 2014. Opened: January 23, 2014.
Limited Engagement. Closed March 16, 2014 after 22 Previews and 61 Performances.

PLAYBILL

A new American play by the author of Doubt *and* Moonstruck, *about long-frustrated passion between two neighbors in rural Ireland. At first it seems to be a drama about who will inherit two adjacent farms, but then it turns into a comedic romance. Many long-buried secrets rise to the surface as Anthony Reilly and Rosemary Muldoon discover that what appeared to be a family feud actually hid various kinds of love.*

CAST

(in order of appearance)

Anthony Reilly ....BRÍAN F. O'BYRNE
Tony Reilly ....PETER MALONEY
Aoife Muldoon ....DEARBHLA MOLLOY
Rosemary Muldoon ....DEBRA MESSING

TIME

Recently

PLACE

The Midlands of Ireland

Stage Manager ....CARLOS MAISONET

UNDERSTUDIES

For Tony Reilly:
RON CRAWFORD
For Aoife Muldoon:
KIT FLANAGAN
For Anthony Reilly:
KEVIN KELLY

Manhattan Theatre Club
Samuel J. Friedman Theatre

ARTISTIC DIRECTOR
Lynne Meadow

EXECUTIVE PRODUCER
Barry Grove

PRESENTS

Outside Mullingar

BY

John Patrick Shanley

WITH

Brían F. O'Byrne   **Debra Messing**
Peter Maloney   **Dearbhla Molloy**

SCENIC DESIGN	COSTUME DESIGN	LIGHTING DESIGN	ORIGINAL MUSIC & SOUND DESIGN
John Lee Beatty	Catherine Zuber	Mark McCullough	Fitz Patton

HAIR & WIG DESIGN	DIALECT COACH	PRODUCTION STAGE MANAGER	CASTING
Tom Watson	Stephen Gabis	Winnie Y. Lok	Nancy Piccione

DIRECTED BY
Doug Hughes

ARTISTIC PRODUCER
Mandy Greenfield

GENERAL MANAGER
Florie Seery

DIRECTOR OF ARTISTIC DEVELOPMENT	DIRECTOR OF MARKETING	PRESS REPRESENTATIVE
Jerry Patch	Debra Waxman-Pilla	Boneau/Bryan-Brown

PRODUCTION MANAGER	ARTISTIC LINE PRODUCER	DIRECTOR OF DEVELOPMENT
Joshua Helman	Lisa McNulty	Lynne Randall

OUTSIDE MULLINGAR WAS COMMISSIONED BY MTC THROUGH THE U.S. TRUST NEW AMERICAN PLAY COMMISSIONING PROGRAM.
OUTSIDE MULLINGAR IS A RECIPIENT OF AN EDGERTON FOUNDATION NEW AMERICAN PLAYS AWARD. MANHATTAN THEATRE CLUB WISHES TO EXPRESS ITS APPRECIATION TO THEATRE DEVELOPMENT FUND FOR ITS SUPPORT OF THIS PRODUCTION.

1/23/14

Photo: Joan Marcus

Brian F. O'Byrne and Debra Messing

Outside Mullingar

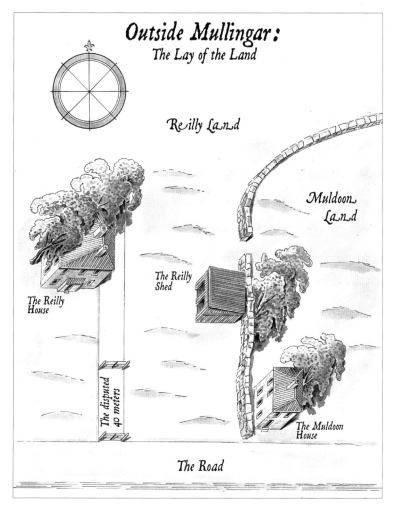

Outside Mullingar:
The Lay of the Land

Reilly Land

Muldoon Land

The Reilly House

The Reilly Shed

The Muldoon House

The disputed 40 meters

The Road

Brían F. O'Byrne
Anthony Reilly

Debra Messing
Rosemary Muldoon

Peter Maloney
Tony Reilly

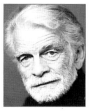

Dearbhla Molloy
Aoife Muldoon

Ron Crawford
u/s Tony Reilly

Kit Flanagan
u/s Aoife Muldoon

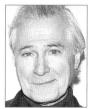

Kevin Kelly
u/s Anthony Reilly

John Patrick Shanley
Playwright

Doug Hughes
Director

John Lee Beatty
Scenic Design

Catherine Zuber
Costume Design

Mark McCullough
Lighting Design

Fitz Patton
Original Music & Sound Design

Tom Watson
Hair & Wig Design

Stephen Gabis
Dialect Coach

Lynne Meadow
Manhattan Theatre Club
Artistic Director

Barry Grove
Manhattan Theatre Club
Executive Producer

BOX OFFICE
David Dillon and Melissa Taustine

Photo: Brian Mapp

Outside Mullingar

Photos: Brian Mapp

CREW
Sitting (L-R): Matt McDonough (Flyman), Erin Moeller (Company Manager), Winnie Y. Lok (Production Stage Manager), Natasha Steinhagen (Hair/Make-Up Supervisor), Carlos Maisonet (Stage Manager), Leah Redmond (Wardrobe Supervisor), Skye Bennett (Dresser)
Standing (L-R): Lou Shapiro (House Sound), Andrew Braggs (Apprentice), Tim Walters (House Props), Matthew Abdelnour (Apprentice), Jeff Dodson (House Electrician, in photo), John Wilson (House Electrician sub. holding photo), Andrew Sliwinski (Sound Department), Vaughn Preston (Automation Operator)

FRONT OF HOUSE
Front (L-R): Sarah Crounse, Cindy Lopiano, Lily Bryant, Lyanna Alvarado, Katelynne Sepulveda
Back (L-R): Patricia Polhill, Vern Lindauer, Jim Joseph, Ed Brashear, Richard Ponce, Jackson Ero

Outside Mullingar

(L-R): Peter Maloney and Brian F. O'Byrne

MANHATTAN THEATRE CLUB STAFF

Artistic Director ....**Lynne Meadow**
Executive Producer ....**Barry Grove**
General Manager ....**Florie Seery**
Artistic Producer ....**Mandy Greenfield**
Director of Artistic Development ....**Jerry Patch**
Director of Artistic Operations ....**Amy Gilkes Loe**
Artistic Line Producer ....Lisa McNulty
Artistic Associate/
    Assistant to the Artistic Director ....Nicki Hunter
Assistant to the Executive Producer ....Melanie Sovern
Assistant to the Artistic Producer ....Abby Lee
Director of Casting ....**Nancy Piccione**
Associate Casting Director ....Kelly Gillespie
Casting Assistant ....Darragh Garvey
Literary Manager/
    Sloan Project Manager ....Annie MacRae
Associate Director of
    Artistic Development ....Elizabeth Rothman
Artistic Development Associate ....Scott Kaplan
Artistic Consultant ....**Daniel Sullivan**
Bank of America/
    US Trust Commissions ....Richard Greenberg,
        Neil LaBute, Matthew Lopez, Richard Nelson,
            Richard Pevear and Larissa Volokhonsky
Alfred P. Sloan
    Foundation Commissions ....April de Angelis,
        Madeleine George, Nathan Jackson, Nick Jones,
        Juliana Nash & Courtney Baron, Greg Pierce,
           Heidi Schreck, Sarah Treem, Bess Wohl
The Writer's Room
    Commissions ....Adam Bock & Justin Levine,
        Rachel Bonds, Thomas Bradshaw,
      Frances Ya-Chu Cowhig, Jackie Sibblies Drury,
    Samuel D. Hunter, Pig Pen Theatre Co., Sharyn Rothstein
Mary Mill Commission ....Molly Smith Metzler
Kenyon College Commission ....Halley Feiffer
Director of Development ....**Lynne Randall**
Director, Individual Giving &
    Major Gifts ....Emily Fleisher
Director, Institutional Giving ....Patricia Leonard
Director, Special Events ....Stephanie Mercado
Associate Director of
    Individual Giving ....Josh Martinez-Nelson
Manager, Individual Giving ....Aubrie Fennecken
Development Associate/Individual Giving ...Laura Petrucci
Development Associate/Special Events ....Molly Clarke
Institutional Giving Manager ....Heather Gallagher
Patrons' Liaison ....Emily Yowell
Database Associate ....Katie Fergerson
Director of Marketing ....**Debra Waxman-Pilla**
Assistant Marketing Director ....Caitlin Baird
Marketing Accounts Manager ....Cody Andrus
Director of Finance ....**Jessica Adler**
Director of Human Resources ....**Stephanie Dolce**

Business Manager ....Ryan Guhde
Business & HR Associate ....Mallory Triest
Business Assistant ....Josiah Grimm
IT Manager ....Mendy Sudranski
Systems Analyst ....Jason Fritzsch
Studio Manager/Receptionist ....Thatcher Stevens
Associate General Manager ....**Lindsey Sag**
Company Manager/
    NY City Center Theatre ....Samantha Kindler
General Management Assistant ....Derrick Olson
Director of Subscriber Services ....**Robert Allenberg**
Subscriber Services Manager ....Kevin Sullivan
Subscriber Services Representatives ....Mark Bowers,
    Tim Salamandyk, Rosanna Consalvo Sarto, Paul Winkler
Director of Education ....**David Shookhoff**
Assistant Education Director/Coordinator, Paul A. Kaplan
    Theatre Management Program ....Amy Harris
Education Programs Coordinator ....Wade T. Handy
MTC Teaching Artists ...Stephanie Alston, David Auburn,
    Chris Ceraso, Charlotte Colavin, Dominic Colon,
    Allison Daugherty, Stephen DiMenna, Andy Goldberg,
    Kel Haney, Elise Hernandez, Jeffrey Joseph, Julie Leedes,
    Kate Long, Victor Maog, Andres Munar, Melissa Murray,
    Angela Pietropinto, Carmen Rivera, Judy Tate,
    Candido Tirado, Liam Torres, Joe White
Theatre Management Interns ....Lily Bryant,
    Allyson Capetta, John Carraro, Robert Carroll,
    Erin Cressy, Emily Hamburger, Samantha Liebman,
    Meghan McLaughlin, Gabriella Napoli, Susanna Pretzer,
    Katelynn Sepulveda, Lauren Stern

Production Manager ....**Joshua Helman**
Associate Production Manager ....Bethany Weinstein
Assistant Production Manager ....Steven Dalton
Properties Supervisor ....**Scott Laule**
Assistant Properties Supervisor ....Lily Fairbanks
Props Carpenter ....Peter Grimes
Costume Supervisor ....**Erin Hennessy Dean**

GENERAL PRESS REPRESENTATION
BONEAU/BRYAN-BROWN

Chris Boneau   Aaron Meier
Emily Meagher   Michelle Farabaugh

Script Readers ....Mirella Cheeseman, Aaron Grunfeld,
    Clifford Lee Johnson III, Thomas Park,
    Elizabeth Sharpe-Levine

SERVICES

Accountants ....Fried & Kowgios CPAs, LLP

Advertising ....SpotCo/Drew Hodges, Tom Greenwald,
    Ilene Rosen, Tim Falotico, Laura Fraenkel
Web Design ....SpotCo Interactive
Legal Counsel ....Charles H. Googe, Jr.;

Caroline Barnard; Carolyn J. Casselman/
    Paul, Weiss, Rifkind, Wharton and Garrison LLP
Real Estate Counsel ....Marcus Attorneys
Labor Counsel ....Harry H. Weintraub/
    Glick and Weintraub, P.C.
Immigration Counsel ....Theodore Ruthizer/
    Kramer, Levin, Naftalis & Frankel, LLP
Media Counsel ....Cameron Stracher
Insurance ....DeWitt Stern Group, Inc./Anthony Pittari
Maintenance ....Reliable Cleaning
Production Photographer ....Joan Marcus
Event Photography ....Bruce Glikas
Cover Design ....SpotCo
Cover Photograph ....Andrew Eccles
Theatre Displays ....King Displays
Merchandise .....Creative Goods Merchandise/Pete Milano

For more information visit
www.ManhattanTheatreClub.com

PRODUCTION STAFF FOR
OUTSIDE MULLINGAR

Company Manager ....**Erin Moeller**
Production Stage Manager ....**Winnie Y. Lok**
Stage Manager ....Carlos Maisonet
Associate Director ....Alexander Greenfield
Associate Scenic Designer ....Kacie Hultgren
Associate Costume Designers ....Patrick Bevilacqua,
    Shawn McCulloch
Associate Lighting Designer ....Kenneth Wills
Assistant Sound Designer ....Justin Stasiw
Hair/Make-Up Supervisor ....Natasha Steinhagen
Lighting Programmer ....John Wilson
Automation Operator ....Vaughn Preston
Flyman ....Richard Klinger
Dresser ....Skye Bennett
Production Assistant ....Ashley K. Singh

CREDITS

Scenery fabrication by Great Lakes Scenic Studios and PRG
Scenic Technologies. Rain effects by J&M Special Effects.
Lighting equipment provided by PRG Lighting. Sound
equipment provided by Masque Sound. Makeup provided
by M•A•C.

MANHATTAN THEATRE CLUB
SAMUEL J. FRIEDMAN THEATRE STAFF

Theatre Manager ....**Jim Joseph**
Assistant House Manager ....Richard Ponce
Box Office Treasurer ....**David Dillon**
Assistant Box Office Treasurers ....Geoffrey Nixon,
    Melissa Taustine
Head Carpenter ....Chris Wiggins
Head Propertyman ....Timothy Walters
Sound Engineer ....Louis Shapiro
Master Electrician ....Jeff Dodson
Wardrobe Supervisor ....Leah Redmond
Apprentices ....Andrew Braggs, Matthew Abdelnour
Chief Engineer ....Deosarran
Maintenance Engineer ....Ricky Deosarran
Security ....Allied Barton
Lobby Refreshments ....Sweet Concessions

Outside Mullingar
SCRAPBOOK

Correspondent: Winnie Y. Lok, Stage Manager

Memorable Note, Fax or Fan Letter: We received so much love from family, friends and colleagues on a daily basis here, but we were especially grateful on opening night to get all the greetings from the Broadway community!

Opening Night Parties and/or Gifts: We celebrated our opening night across the street at the lovely Copacabana! Manhattan Theatre Club provided the company with the apropos gift of *Outside Mullingar* Guinness glasses!

Most Exciting Celebrity Visitor and What They Did/Said: Two of the celebrities that we were most excited to have backstage to visit were Meryl Streep and Joan Rivers. They were lovely!

Favorite In-Theatre Gathering Place: We have a small cast so everyone likes to prepare for the show in their own spaces. However, Dearbhla Molloy likes to keep her door open most of the time so you can find her in conversation with various people as you travel up or down the tower.

Special Backstage Rituals: Because it is raining outside at the top of show, Brían F. O'Byrne and Peter Maloney have to be wetted down before their entrance. It's always fun to watch.

Favorite Backstage Photo (and the Story That Goes with It): My favorite backstage photo is one I took from where I call the show. The calling station is on a jump that's about 18 feet up in the air. I took a picture during preview rehearsals of Carlos Maisonet, my Assistant Stage Manager, on stage through the yoke of a lighting instrument. Debra Messing also liked to take pictures of the rain effect and the lighting while we were in tech for the show. There's a great picture that Debra took of Carlos through the rain. (See photo above.)

Most Memorable Audience Reaction: At the end of the play, Anthony (played by Brían F. O'Byrne) and Rosemary (played by Debra Messing) share a long-awaited kiss. On some nights we've received applause and cheers, but on one night in particular, an overexcited patron exclaimed, "Yeah, Tony!!!"

Memorable Ad-Lib: In the first scene of the play, Tony (played by Peter Maloney) walks over to the lamp on top of the washing machine to turn it on. One night, he accidentally knocked the lampshade off the

on. He was struggling with it while still performing the dialogue with his son Anthony (Brían F. O'Byrne). Now, Tony is the kind of father that lets his son do everything for him. So Brían at one point said, "Da, let me take care of that," and Peter let him.

Favorite Moment During Each Performance: One of my favorite moments is watching everyone get ready for the show to start on my

backstage infrared camera. Once places is called, I see our three actors gather, greet one another and take a peek out at the audience through a gap we have in the set. It tickles me to watch them do this every night. A close second would be during Scene 1 when I watch Carlos, the ASM, head backstage to charge the glo-tape on the X that Rosemary (played by Debra Messing) has to stand on in the transition. It's a fun moment to watch him do that.

Favorite Off-Site Hangout: This is not necessarily the company for the hanging out, but the Glass House Tavern is across the street from the theatre and folks will go there more often then not. They treat us like family there and the food is wonderful!

Favorite Therapy: We use the regular Ricola as well as the Sugar Free Lemon Mint ones. Throat Coat tea with honey is used and we are definitely a company of coffee drinkers. Some of the company even have their own French Presses in their dressing rooms!

Fastest Costume Change: Brían has two quick changes in the show and Debra has one. They are both quick, but comparable.

Who Wore the Heaviest/Hottest Costume?: Luckily, our show takes place in the present day in rural Ireland so there isn't anything too heavy. It does rain during the show so we have our fair share of raincoats and wellies. Brían gets to wear a work coverall in one scene that looked so comfortable and nice that Debra inquired about getting one for herself to have offstage.

Who Wore the Least?: At one point, Peter Maloney's character is getting ready for bed so he wears just a pair of long johns.

Coolest Thing About Being in This Show: Working with a great playwright like John Patrick Shanley. The play is a departure for John and it's so wonderful because it covers the gamut: life, death, love, religion, the land, everything! And it does so in such a beautiful, natural and lovely way. Plus, it doesn't hurt that it has such an uplifting ending that people can't help but cheer at the end!

1. Assistant Stage Manager Carlos Maisonet as seen through the rain by Debra Messing.
2. At the opening night party (L-R): playwright John Patrick Shanley, Dearbhla Molloy, Brían F. O'Byrne, Debra Messing, Peter Maloney and director Doug Hughes.
3. Winnie Lok's view of ASM Carlos Maisonet.

The Phantom of the Opera

First Preview: January 9, 1988. Opened: January 26, 1988.
Still running as of May 31, 2014.

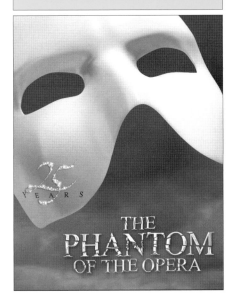

PLAYBILL

THE PHANTOM OF THE OPERA

The dashing Raoul is in love with Christine Daaé, a pretty soprano in the chorus of the Paris Opera. But Raoul discovers that she is under the spell of the legendary Phantom of the Opera, a disfigured musical genius who haunts the endless grottos beneath the ancient opera house. The obsessed Phantom demands that Christine be elevated to star and that the company produce an unplayable opera he has written. When his commands are not obeyed the Phantom becomes violent, even murderous. Raoul strives ever more desperately to free Christine from his clutches. As a torch-wielding mob closes in on his lair, the Phantom makes one last bid for Christine's love.

CAST

The Phantom of the Opera .... NORM LEWIS
Christine Daaé .... SIERRA BOGGESS
Christine Daaé (Thurs. & Sat. Mat.
    Performances) .... SARA JEAN FORD
Raoul, Vicomte de Chagny .... JEREMY HAYS
Carlotta Giudicelli .... MICHELE McCONNELL
Carlotta Giudicelli
    (Sat. Performances) .... HEATHER HILL
Monsieur André .... LAIRD MACKINTOSH
Monsieur Firmin .... TIM JEROME
Madame Giry .... ELLEN HARVEY
Ubaldo Piangi .... CHRISTIAN ŠEBEK
Meg Giry .... DEANNA DOYLE
Auctioneer/Don Attilio
    ("Il Muto") .... CARRINGTON VILMONT
Monsieur Reyer/Hairdresser
    ("Il Muto") .... JIM WEITZER

Continued on next page

CAMERON MACKINTOSH
and
THE REALLY USEFUL
THEATRE COMPANY, INC.

present

THE PHANTOM OF THE OPERA®

Starring
NORM LEWIS
SIERRA BOGGESS
JEREMY HAYS

LAIRD MACKINTOSH   TIM JEROME   MICHELE McCONNELL
ELLEN HARVEY   CHRISTIAN ŠEBEK   DEANNA DOYLE

At certain performances
SARA JEAN FORD
plays the role of "Christine"

Music by
ANDREW LLOYD WEBBER
Lyrics by **CHARLES HART**
Additional Lyrics by RICHARD STILGOE
Book by RICHARD STILGOE & ANDREW LLOYD WEBBER
Based on the novel "Le Fantôme de L'Opéra" by **GASTON LEROUX**
Production Design by MARIA BJÖRNSON   Lighting by ANDREW BRIDGE
Sound Design by MICK POTTER   Original Sound Design by MARTIN LEVAN
Musical Supervision & Direction DAVID CADDICK   Musical Director KRISTEN BLODGETTE
Production Supervisor SETH SKLAR-HEYN   Associate Choreographer DENNY BERRY
Orchestrations by DAVID CULLEN & ANDREW LLOYD WEBBER

Casting by TARA RUBIN CASTING   Original Casting by JOHNSON-LIFF ASSOCIATES

General Management ALAN WASSER ASSOCIATES

Musical Staging & Choreography by GILLIAN LYNNE
Directed by **HAROLD PRINCE**

5/12/14

Sierra Boggess and Norm Lewis in "The Music of the Night."

Photo: Matthew Murphy

273

The Phantom of the Opera

MUSICAL NUMBERS

PROLOGUE
The stage of the Paris Opéra House, 1911

OVERTURE

ACT I—PARIS, LATE NINETEENTH CENTURY

Scene 1—The dress rehearsal of "Hannibal"
"Think of Me" .... Carlotta, Christine, Raoul
Scene 2—After the Gala
"Angel of Music" .... Christine and Meg
Scene 3—Christine's dressing room
"Little Lotte/The Mirror" (Angel of Music) .... Raoul, Christine, Phantom
Scene 4—The Labyrinth underground
"The Phantom of the Opera" .... Phantom and Christine
Scene 5—Beyond the lake
"The Music of the Night" .... Phantom
Scene 6—Beyond the lake, the next morning
"I Remember/Stranger Than You Dreamt It" .... Christine and Phantom
Scene 7—Backstage
"Magical Lasso" .... Buquet, Meg, Madame Giry and Ballet Girls
Scene 8—The Managers' office
"Notes/Prima Donna" .... Firmin, André, Raoul, Carlotta, Giry, Meg,
Piangi and Phantom
Scene 9—A performance of "Il Muto"
"Poor Fool, He Makes Me Laugh" .... Carlotta and Company
Scene 10—The roof of the Opéra House
"Why Have You Brought Me Here/Raoul, I've Been There" ...... Raoul and Christine
"All I Ask of You" .... Raoul and Christine
"All I Ask of You" (Reprise) .... Phantom

ENTR'ACTE

ACT II—SIX MONTHS LATER

Scene 1—The staircase of the Opéra House, New Year's Eve
"Masquerade/Why So Silent" .... Full Company
Scene 2—Backstage
Scene 3—The Managers' office
"Notes/Twisted Every Way" .... André, Firmin, Carlotta, Piangi, Raoul,
Christine, Giry and Phantom
Scene 4—A rehearsal for "Don Juan Triumphant"
Scene 5—A graveyard in Perros
"Wishing You Were Somehow Here Again" .... Christine
"Wandering Child/Bravo, Bravo" .... Phantom, Christine and Raoul
Scene 6—The Opéra House stage before the Premiere
Scene 7—"Don Juan Triumphant"
"The Point of No Return" .... Phantom and Christine
Scene 8—The Labyrinth underground
"Down Once More/Track Down This Murderer" .... Full Company
Scene 9—Beyond the lake

"Sing, my angel of music!"

Jeweler
("Il Muto") ..... NATHAN PATRICK MORGAN
Monsieur Lefèvre/Firechief .. KENNETH KANTOR
Joseph Buquet .... RICHARD POOLE
Passarino
("Don Juan Triumphant") ..... JEREMY STOLLE
Slave Master ("Hannibal") .... ERIC OTTO
Solo Dancer
("Il Muto") .... NICHOLAS CUNNINGHAM
Page ("Don Juan
Triumphant") .... KELLY JEANNE GRANT
Porter/Fireman .... ANDREW DROST
Spanish Lady
("Don Juan Triumphant") ...... LYNNE ABELES
Wardrobe Mistress/Confidante
("Il Muto") .... SATOMI HOFMANN
Princess ("Hannibal") .... ELIZABETH WELCH
Madame Firmin .... SUSAN OWEN
Innkeeper's Wife
("Don Juan Triumphant") ..... HEATHER HILL
Marksman .... PAUL A. SCHAEFER
The Ballet Chorus
of the Opéra Populaire .... DARA ADLER,
AMANDA EDGE, JESSY HENDRICKSON,
GIANNA LOUNGWAY,
MARIA PHEGAN, JESSICA RADETSKY
Ballet Swing .... POLLY BAIRD
Swings .... SCOTT MIKITA,
GREG MILLS, JANET SAIA

UNDERSTUDIES

For the Phantom: LAIRD MACKINTOSH,
GREG MILLS, PAUL A. SCHAEFER,
JEREMY STOLLE
For Christine: SUSAN OWEN,
ELIZABETH WELCH
For Raoul: GREG MILLS, PAUL A. SCHAEFER,
JEREMY STOLLE, JIM WEITZER
For Firmin: KENNETH KANTOR,
SCOTT MIKITA, CARRINGTON VILMONT
For André: SCOTT MIKITA, GREG MILLS,
RICHARD POOLE, JIM WEITZER
For Carlotta: HEATHER HILL,
SATOMI HOFMANN, JANET SAIA
For Mme. Giry: KELLY JEANNE GRANT,
SATOMI HOFMANN, JANET SAIA
For Piangi: ANDREW DROST,
NATHAN PATRICK MORGAN,
JEREMY STOLLE
For Meg Giry: POLLY BAIRD, AMANDA EDGE,
CARLY BLAKE SEBOUHIAN
Dance Captain: POLLY BAIRD
Assistant Dance Captain: AMANDA EDGE

ORCHESTRA

Conductors: DAVID CADDICK,
KRISTEN BLODGETTE, DAVID LAI,
TIM STELLA, NORMAN WEISS

The Phantom of the Opera

Violins: JOYCE HAMMANN (Concert Master),
  CLAIRE CHAN, KURT COBLE,
  JAN MULLEN, KAREN MILNE,
  SUZANNE GILMAN
Violas: VERONICA SALAS,
  DEBRA SHUFELT-DINE
Cellos: TED ACKERMAN, KARL BENNION
Bass: MELISSA SLOCUM
Harp: HENRY FANELLI
Flute: SHERYL HENZE
Flute/Clarinet: ED MATTHEW
Oboe: MELANIE FELD
Clarinet: MATTHEW GOODMAN
Bassoon: ATSUKO SATO
Trumpets: LOWELL HERSHEY,
  FRANCIS BONNY
Bass Trombone: WILLIAM WHITAKER
French Horns: DANIEL CULPEPPER,
  PETER REIT, DAVID SMITH
Percussion: ERIC COHEN, JAN HAGIWARA
Keyboards: TIM STELLA, NORMAN WEISS

Norm Lewis
*The Phantom
of the Opera*

Sierra Boggess
Christine Daaé

Jeremy Hays
*Raoul, Vicomte
de Chagny*

Laird Mackintosh
Monsieur André

Tim Jerome
Monsieur Firmin

Michele McConnell
Carlotta Giudicelli

Ellen Harvey
Madame Giry

Christian Šebek
Ubaldo Piangi

Deanna Doyle
Meg Giry

Sara Jean Ford
*Christine Daaé
at certain
performances*

Lynne Abeles
Spanish Lady

Dara Adler
Ballet Chorus

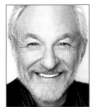

Polly Baird
*Dance Captain/
Ballet Swing*

Nicholas
Cunningham
Solo Dancer

Andrew Drost
Porter/Fireman

Amanda Edge
Ballet Chorus

Kelly Jeanne Grant
Page

Jessy Hendrickson
Ballet Chorus

Heather Hill
*Innkeeper's
Wife/Carlotta
Giudicelli at certain
performances*

Satomi Hofmann
*Wardrobe Mistress/
Confidante*

Kenneth Kantor
*Monsieur Lefèvre/
Firechief*

Gianna Loungway
Ballet Chorus

Scott Mikita
Swing

Greg Mills
Swing

Nathan Patrick
Morgan
Jeweler

Eric Otto
Slave Master

Susan Owen
Madame Firmin

Maria Phegan
Ballet Chorus

Richard Poole
Joseph Buquet

The Phantom of the Opera

Jessica Radetsky
Ballet Chorus

Janet Saia
Swing

Paul A. Schaefer
Marksman

Jeremy Stolle
Passarino

Carrington Vilmont
*Auctioneer/
Don Attilio*

Jim Weitzer
*Monsieur Reyer/
Hairdresser*

Elizabeth Welch
Princess

Andrew Lloyd
Webber
*Composer/Book/
Co-Orchestrator*

Harold Prince
Director

Charles Hart
Lyrics

Richard Stilgoe
*Book and Additional
Lyrics*

Gillian Lynne
*Musical Staging
and Choreography*

Maria Björnson
Production Design

Andrew Bridge
Lighting Designer

Mick Potter
Sound Designer

Martin Levan
*Original Sound
Designer*

David Cullen
Co-Orchestrator

David Caddick
*Musical Supervision
and Direction*

Kristen Blodgette
*Associate Musical
Supervisor*

Seth Sklar-Heyn
*Production
Supervisor*

Denny Berry
*Production
Dance Supervisor/
Associate
Choreographer*

Jake Bell
*Technical
Production
Manager*

David Lai
Conductor

Tara Rubin
Tara Rubin Casting
Casting

Alan Wasser
Foresight Theatrical
General Manager

Allan Williams
Foresight Theatrical
General Manager

Aaron Lustbader
Foresight Theatrical
General Manager

Cameron Mackintosh
Producer

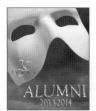
ALUMNI
2013-2014

Sarah Bakker
Madame Firmin

Kyle Barisich
Raoul

Jessica Bishop
Ballet Chorus

Marilyn Caskey
Madame Giry

Paloma Garcia-Lee
Ballet Chorus

David Michael Garry
*Don Attilio
("Il Muto")*

The Phantom of the Opera

Joelle Gates
Ballet Chorus

Samantha Hill
Christine Daaé

Arlo Hill
Swing

Peter Jöback
*The Phantom
of the Opera*

Ted Keegan
*Auctioneer/
Monsieur
Reyer/Hairdresser*

Gina Lamparella
Page

Dustin Layton
Solo Dancer

Kevin Ligon
Monsieur Firmin

Mabel Modrono
Ballet Chorus

Aubrey Morgan
Ballet Chorus

Bronson Norris
Murphy
Porter/Fireman

Hugh Panaro
*The Phantom
of the Opera*

Mary Michael
Patterson
Christine Daaé

Justin Peck
*Slave Master/
Solo Dancer*

Matthew Prescott
*Solo Dancer/
Slave Master*

Marni Raab
*Christine Daaé
alternate*

Rebecca Robbins
*Wardrobe Mistress/
Confidante*

Sean Rollofson
*Solo Dancer/
Slave Master*

Julie Schmidt
Page

Carly Blake
Sebouhian
Ballet Chorus

TRANSFER
STUDENTS
2013-2014

Gina Lamparella
Page

Bronson Norris
Murphy
Marksman

Matthew Prescott
Solo Dancer

Rebecca Robbins
Swing

Photo: Brian Mapp

MANAGEMENT
(L-R): Gregory T. Livoti (Stage Manager), Katherine McNamee (Assistant Company Manager), Steve Greer (Company Manager), Andrew Glant-Linden,
Jim Athens, Michael S. Borowski (Press Rep)

The Phantom of the Opera

MUSICIANS
Front Row (L-R): Atsuko Sato, Grace Paradise, Lowell Hershey
Back Row (L-R): Dean Plank, Richard Hagen, Norman Weiss, Francis Bonny, Karl Bennion

FRONT OF HOUSE
Sitting (L-R): Theresa Aceves, Lucia Cappelletti, Iftiaz Haroon, Matt Bosco, Luciana Lenihan, Lisa Bruno, Deidre Carroll
Standing (L-R): Kristin Zdonek, Brett Tubbs, Wade Walton, Perry Dell'Aquila, Cynthia Carlin, Grace Jones, Joan Thorn, Erich Loetterle, Lawrence Darden

The Phantom of the Opera

WARDROBE/HAIR/MAKE-UP
Front (L-R): Robert Strong Miller (Assistant Wardrobe Supervisor), Mary Czech, Sylvia Cappelli, Tiffany Bolick (Hairdresser), Sarah Snider, Jennifer Caruso
Back (L-R): George Sheer, Rosemary Taylor, Jennifer Arnold, Julie Ratcliffe (Wardrobe Supervisor), Ron Blakley, Michael Jacobs,
Pearleta N. Price (Assistant Make-up Supervisor)

CREW
Front: (L-R): Frank Dwyer, Jr., Ray Pesce, Frank Dwyer, Steve Clem
Back (L-R): Matthew Mezick (Head Props), Michael Girman (Automation Carpenter), Bill Kazden
Not pictured: Innumerable and all working!

The Phantom of the Opera

STAFF FOR *THE PHANTOM OF THE OPERA*

General Manager
FORESIGHT THEATRICAL
Aaron Lustbader   Alan Wasser
Allan Williams   Mark Shacket

General Press Representative
THE PUBLICITY OFFICE
Marc Thibodeau   Michael S. Borowski
Jeremy Shaffer

Assistant to Mr. Prince
RUTH MITCHELL

Production Supervisor
SETH SKLAR-HEYN

Production Dance Supervisor
DENNY BERRY

Associate Musical Supervisor
KRISTEN BLODGETTE

Casting
TARA RUBIN CASTING

Technical Production Manager ....JAKE BELL
Company Manager ....STEVE GREER
Production Stage Manager ....GREGORY T. LIVOTI
Stage Managers ....Bethe Ward, Jim Athens
Assistant Company Manager ....Katherine McNamee

U.S. Design Staff
Associate Scenic Designer ....DANA KENN
Associate Costume Designer ....SAM FLEMING
Associate Lighting Designer ....VIVIEN LEONE
Associate Sound Designer ....PAUL GATEHOUSE
Sculptures Consultant ....Stephen Pyle
Pro Tools Programmer ....Lee McCutcheon

Casting Associates ....Eric Woodall, CSA;
Merri Sugarman, CSA
Casting Assistants ....Kaitlin Shaw, Lindsay Levine
Dance Captain ....Polly Baird
Production Carpenter ....Joseph Patria
Production Electrician ....Robert Fehribach
Production Propertyman ....Timothy Abel
Production Sound Engineer ....Garth Helm
Production Wig Supervisor ....Leone Gagliardi
Production Make-up Supervisor ....Thelma Pollard
Assistant Make-up Supervisors ....Pearleta M. Price,
Shazia J. Saleem
Head Carpenter ....Russell Tiberio III
Automation Carpenters ..Santos Sanchez, Michael Girman
Assistant Carpenter ....Giancarlo Cottignoli
Flyman ....Daryl Miller
Head Electrician ....Alan Lampel
Pyro Technician ....JR Beket
Head Props ....Matthew Mezick
Asst. Props./Boat Captain ....Joe Caruso
Sound Operator ....Paul Verity
Asst. Sound Operator ....Rafe Carlotto
Wardrobe Supervisor ....Julie Ratcliffe
Assistant Wardrobe Supervisor ....Robert Strong Miller
Wardrobe Staff ....Jennifer Arnold, Ron Blakley,
Aaron Carlson, Jennifer Caruso, Eileen Casey,
Terence Doherty, Michael Jacobs, Annette Lovece,
Margie Marchionni, Ann McDaniel, Peter McIver,
Andrew Nelson, Elena Pellicciaro, Mary Lou Rios,
George Sheer, Sarah Snider, Rosemary Taylor
Hair Supervisor ....Leone Gagliardi
Hairdressers ....Tiffany Bolick, Sylvia Cappelli,
Charise Champion, Tyrel Limb

Conductor ....David Lai
Associate Conductor ....Tim Stella
Assistant Conductor ....Norman Weiss
Musical Preparation
Supervisor (U.S.) ....Chelsea Music Service, Inc
Synthesizer Consultant ....Stuart Andrews

Assistant to the Gen. Mgr. ....Jennifer O'Connor

Legal Counsel ....F. Richard Pappas
Accounting ....Marks, Paneth & Shron
Christopher A. Cacace
Logo Design and Graphics ....Dewynters Plc, London
Merchandising ....Dewynters Advertising Inc.
Advertising ....Serino/Coyne/Greg Corradetti,
Marci Kaufman Meyers, Tom Callahan, Peter Gunther,
Sarah Marcus, Jim Glaub, Crystal Chase, Brian DeVito
Marketing Direction .....Type A Marketing, Elyce Henkin
Displays ....King Displays, Wayne Sapper
Insurance (U.S.) .DeWitt Stern Group, Peter K. Shoemaker
Insurance (U.K.) ....Walton & Parkinson Limited
Richard Walton
Banking ....Signature Bank/Barbara von Borstel
Payroll Service ....Castellana Services, Inc.

Original Production Photographer ....Clive Barda
Additional Photography ....Joan Marcus,
Bob Marshak, Peter Cunningham
House Manager ....Hugh Barnett

CREDITS AND ACKNOWLEDGMENTS
Scenic construction and boat automation by Hudson Scenic Studios. Scenery automation by Jeremiah J. Harris Associates, Inc./East Coast Theatre Supply, Inc. Scenery painted by Nolan Scenery Studios. Set and hand properties by McHugh Rollins Associates, Inc. Sculptural elements by Costume Armour. "Opera Ball" newell post statues and elephant by Nino Novellino of Costume Armour. Proscenium sculptures by Stephen Pyle. Draperies by I. Weiss and Sons, Inc. Soft goods provided by Quartet Theatrical Draperies. Safety systems by Foy Lighting equipment and special lighting effects by Four Star Lighting, Inc. Sound equipment and technical service provided by Masque Sound and Recording Corp. Special effects designed and executed by Theatre Magic, Inc., Richard Huggins, President. Costumes executed by Barbara Matera, Ltd. Costumes for "Hannibal" and "Masquerade" executed by Parsons/Meares, Ltd. Costume crafts for "Hannibal" and "Masquerade" by Janet Harper and Frederick Nihda. Fabric painting by Mary Macy. Additional costumes by Carelli Costumes, Inc. Costume accessories by Barak Stribling. Hats by Woody Shelp. Millinery and masks by Rodney Gordon. Footwear by Sharlot Battin of Montana Leatherworks, Ltd. Shoes by JC Theatrical and Costume Footwear and Taffy's N.Y. Jewelry by Miriam Haskell Jewels. Eyeglasses by H.L. Purdy. Wigs by The Wig Party. Makeup consultant Kris Evans.

Furs by Christie Bros.

Shoes supplied by Peter Fox Limited

"The Phantom" character make-up created and designed by Christopher Tucker

Magic Consultant—Paul Daniels

CAMERON MACKINTOSH, INC.
Managing Director ....Nicholas Allott
Production Associate ....Shidan Majidi

THE REALLY USEFUL GROUP LTD.
Directors
Andrew Lloyd Webber   Madeleine Lloyd Webber
Mark Wordsworth   Barney Wragg
Jonathan Hull   Isobel Chester

Performance rights to *The Phantom of the Opera* are licensed by R&H Theatricals:
www.rnhtheatricals.com

To learn more about the production, please visit
www.PhantomBroadway.com
Find us on Facebook: PhantomBroadway
and Twitter: TheOperaGhosts

Energy-efficient washer/dryer courtesy of LG Electronics.

 THE SHUBERT ORGANIZATION, INC.
Board of Directors

Philip J. Smith   **Robert E. Wankel**
Chairman   President

Wyche Fowler, Jr.   **Diana Phillips**

Lee J. Seidler   **Michael I. Sovern**

Stuart Subotnick

Chief Financial Officer ....Elliot Greene
Sr. Vice President, Ticketing ....David Andrews
Vice President, Finance ....Juan Calvo
Vice President, Human Resources ....Cathy Cozens
Vice President, Facilities ....John Darby
Vice President, Theatre Operations ....Peter Entin
Vice President, Marketing ....Charles Flateman
Vice President, General Counsel ....Gilbert Hoover
Vice President, Audit ....Anthony LaMattina
Vice President, Ticket Sales ....Brian Mahoney
Vice President, Creative Projects ...........D.S. Moynihan
Vice President, Real Estate ....Julio Peterson

 The Shubert Organization is a proud member of the Broadway Green Alliance.

Pippin

First Preview: March 23, 2013. Opened: April 25, 2013.
Still running as of May 31, 2014.

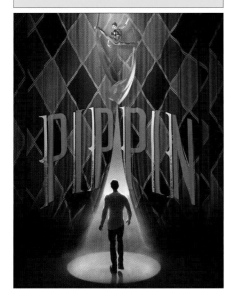

Tony Award winning revival of the 1972 musical about medieval emperor Charlemagne's heir-apparent who wants to do something wonderful and unique with his life—but isn't quite sure exactly what that might be. Egged on by the mysterious Leading Player and her minions, Pippin tries war, sex, politics, et cetera, before discovering the one thing that has the best chance of leading to his heart's content. This production is notable for director Diane Paulus' circus-style staging.

CAST

(in order of appearance)

Leading Player ....PATINA MILLER
Fastrada ....CHARLOTTE d'AMBOISE
Berthe ....TOVAH FELDSHUH
Lewis ....ERIK ALTEMUS
Charles ....TERRENCE MANN
Pippin ....MATTHEW JAMES THOMAS
Catherine ....RACHEL BAY JONES
Theo (Wed. Mat., Thurs. Eve., Sat. Mat.,
    Sun. Mat.) ....LUKE KOLBE MANNIKUS
Theo (Tues. Eve., Wed. Eve., Fri. Eve.,
    Sat. Eve.) ....ASHTON WOERZ
The Players ....GRÉGORY ARSENAL,
        LOLITA COSTET, COLIN CUNLIFFE,
       ANDREW FITCH, VIKTORIA GRIMMY,
    PRESTON JAMIESON, OLGA KARMANSKY,
          GABRIELLE McCLINTON,
       BETHANY MOORE, PHILIP ROSENBERG,
       YANNICK THOMAS, MOLLY TYNES,
            ANTHONY WAYNE

Continued on next page

☺ THE MUSIC BOX

239 W. 45th Street
A Shubert Organization Theatre

Philip J. Smith, *Chairman*   **Robert E. Wankel,** *President*

Barry and Fran Weissler   Howard and Janet Kagan

Lisa Matlin   Kyodo Tokyo   A&A Gordon/Brunish Trinchero   Tom Smedes/Peter Stern
Broadway Across America   Independent Presenters Network   Norton Herrick   Allen Spivak   Rebecca Gold
Joshua Goodman   Stephen E. McManus   David Robbins/Bryan S. Weingarten   Philip Hagemann/Murray Rosenthal
Jim Kierstead/Carlos Arana/Myla Lerner   Hugh Hayes/Jamie Cesa/Jonathan Reinis

Sharon A. Carr/Patricia R. Klausner   Ben Feldman   Square 1 Theatrics   Wendy Federman/Carl Moellenberg
Bruce Robert Harris/Jack W. Batman   Infinity Theatre Company/Michael Rubenstein   Michael A. Alden/Dale Badway/Ken Mahoney

PRESENT

The American Repertory Theater production of

PIPPIN

BOOK BY   MUSIC & LYRICS BY
Roger O. Hirson   **Stephen Schwartz**

STARRING

Matthew James Thomas   **Patina Miller**

Terrence Mann   **Charlotte d'Amboise**   **Rachel Bay Jones**

AND

Tovah Feldshuh

Erik Altemus   Grégory Arsenal   Lolita Costet   Colin Cunliffe   Andrew Fitch   Viktoria Grimmy   Sabrina Harper
Preston Jamieson   Olga Karmansky   Luke Kolbe Mannikus   Gabrielle McClinton   Bethany Moore
Brad Musgrove   Philip Rosenberg   Yannick Thomas   Billy Harrigan Tighe   Molly Tynes   Anthony Wayne   Ashton Woerz

SCENIC DESIGN BY **Scott Pask**	LIGHTING DESIGN BY **Kenneth Posner**	COSTUME DESIGN BY **Dominique Lemieux**	SOUND DESIGN BY **Jonathan Deans & Garth Helm**
	ILLUSIONS BY **Paul Kieve**	FIRE EFFECTS BY **Chic Silber**	FLYING EFFECTS BY **ZFX, Inc.**
TECHNICAL SUPERVISOR **Jake Bell**	DESIGN SUPERVISOR **Edward Pierce**	ADVERTISING **SpotCo**	PRESS REPRESENTATIVE **Boneau/Bryan-Brown**
MUSIC DIRECTOR **Charlie Alterman**	MUSIC COORDINATOR **John Miller**	CASTING **Duncan Stewart/Benton Whitley**	ASSOCIATE PRODUCER **James L. Simon**
ASSOCIATE DIRECTOR **Nancy Harrington**	ASSISTANT CHOREOGRAPHER **Brad Musgrove**	PRODUCTION STAGE MANAGER **Michael J. Passaro**	COMPANY MANAGER **Jeff Klein**
	EXECUTIVE PRODUCER **Alecia Parker**		GENERAL MANAGER **B.J. Holt**

ORCHESTRATIONS BY
Larry Hochman

MUSIC SUPERVISION AND ARRANGEMENTS BY
Nadia DiGiallonardo

CIRCUS CREATION BY
Gypsy Snider
of Les 7 doigts de la main

CHOREOGRAPHY BY
Chet Walker
in the style of Bob Fosse

DIRECTED BY
Diane Paulus

Special thanks to American Repertory Theater at Harvard University and Les 7 doigts de la main for their help in developing this production.
A.R.T. Artistic Director, Diane Paulus and Producer, Diane Borger, Les 7 doigts de la main Director General, Nassib el Husseini

9/24/13

Tovah Feldshuh as Berthe sings "No Time at All" to Matthew James Thomas as Pippin.

Pippin

MUSICAL NUMBERS

ACT I

Scene 1: THE OPENING
"Magic to Do" .... The Players
"Corner of the Sky" .... Pippin
Scene 2: HOME .... Leading Player, Charles, Pippin, Lewis and Fastrada
Scene 3: GLORY
"War Is a Science" .... Charles and The Players
"Glory" .... Leading Player and The Players
Scene 4: THE FLESH
"Simple Joys" .... Leading Player and The Players
"No Time at All" .... Berthe and The Players
"With You" .... Pippin and The Players
Scene 5: REVOLUTION
"Spread a Little Sunshine" .... Fastrada
"Morning Glow" .... Pippin and The Players

ACT II

"Entr'acte"
Scene 1: POLITICS
Scene 2: ENCOURAGEMENT
"On the Right Track" .... Leading Player and Pippin
Scene 3: ORDINARY LIFE
"Kind of Woman" .... Catherine
"Extraordinary" .... Pippin and The Players
"Love Song" .... Pippin and Catherine
Scene 4: THE FINALE .... Leading Player, Pippin and The Players

ORCHESTRA

Conductor/Keyboard: CHARLIE ALTERMAN
Associate Conductor/Keyboard:
SONNY PALADINO
Reeds: EDWARD JOFFE, RICK HECKMAN
Trumpet: DAVE TRIGG
Trombone: MICHAEL DAVIS
Violin/Viola: RICK DOLAN
Cello: PETER SACHON

Guitar: LARRY SALTZMAN
Bass: STEVE MILLHOUSE
Drums: JARED SCHONIG
Percussion: SEAN RITENAUER

Music Coordinator: JOHN MILLER
Music Preparation: DONALD OLIVER
& PAUL HOLDERBAUM/Chelsea Music, Inc.
Keyboard Programmer: RANDY COHEN

Cast Continued

ADDITIONAL PARTS AND SPECIALTIES

Noble: GABRIELLE McCLINTON
Peasant: ANDREW FITCH
The Manson Trio: ANDREW FITCH,
ANTHONY WAYNE
Head: COLIN CUNLIFFE
"With You" Hand Balancing:
GRÉGORY ARSENAL, PHILIP ROSENBERG
Á l'aveugle: GRÉGORY ARSENAL,
YANNICK THOMAS
Bolero: VIKTORIA GRIMMY
YANNICK THOMAS

UNDERSTUDIES

For Pippin: ERIK ALTEMUS,
BILLY HARRIGAN TIGHE
For Lewis: COLIN CUNLIFFE
BILLY HARRIGAN TIGHE
For Berthe: SABRINA HARPER
For Leading Player: GABRIELLE McCLINTON,
MOLLY TYNES
For Catherine: SABRINA HARPER,
BETHANY MOORE
For Fastrada: SABRINA HARPER,
MOLLY TYNES
For Charles: COLIN CUNLIFFE,
ANDREW FITCH

SWINGS

SABRINA HARPER, BRAD MUSGROVE,
BILLY HARRIGAN TIGHE
Dance Captains: BRAD MUSGROVE,
PHILIP ROSENBERG

Original Choreography for "Manson Trio"
by BOB FOSSE.
"Spread a Little Sunshine" Dance Arrangement
by ZANE MARK.
Special trapeze routine performed with
YANNICK THOMAS.

Matthew James Thomas is appearing with the permission of Actors' Equity Association pursuant to an exchange program between American Equity and UK Equity.

Matthew James
Thomas
Pippin

Patina Miller
Leading Player

Terrence Mann
Charles

Charlotte d'Amboise
Fastrada

Rachel Bay Jones
Catherine

Tovah Feldshuh
Berthe

Erik Altemus
Lewis; u/s Pippin

Pippin

Grégory Arsenal
Player

Lolita Costet
Player

Colin Cunliffe
Player; u/s Lewis

Andrew Fitch
Player; u/s Charles

Viktoria Grimmy
Player

Sabrina Harper
Player, Swing; u/s Berthe, Catherine, Fastrada

Preston Jamieson
Player

Olga Karmansky
Player

Luke Kolbe Mannikus
Theo

Gabrielle McClinton
Player; u/s Leading Player

Bethany Moore
Player; u/s Catherine

Brad Musgrove
Swing, Asst. Choreographer, Dance Captain

Philip Rosenberg
Player, Dance Captain

Yannick Thomas
Player

Billy Harrigan Tighe
Swing; u/s Pippin, Lewis

Molly Tynes
Player; u/s Leading Player, Fastrada

Anthony Wayne
Player

Ashton Woerz
Theo

Roger O. Hirson
Book

Stephen Schwartz
Music & Lyrics

Diane Paulus
Director

Chet Walker
Choreographer

Gypsy Snider
Circus Creation

Nadia DiGiallonardo
Music Supervisor and Arrangements

Larry Hochman
Orchestrations

Scott Pask
Scenic Design

Kenneth Posner
Lighting Design

Dominique Lemieux
Costume Design

Jonathan Deans
Sound Designer

Garth Helm
Sound Designer

Paul Kieve
Illusions

Jake Bell
Technical Supervisor

Edward Pierce
Design Supervisor

John Miller
Music Coordinator

Charlie Alterman
Music Director

Pippin

Michael J. Passaro
Production Stage
Manager

Duncan Stewart
Casting

Benton Whitley
Casting

Nancy Harrington
Associate Director

Mia Walker
Assistant Director

Fran & Barry Weissler
Producer

Howard & Janet Kagan
Producer

Lisa Matlin
Producer

Allan Gordon
Producer

Adam Gordon
Producer

Corey Brunish
Producer

Brisa Trinchero
Producer

Tom Smedes
Producer

Peter Stern
Producer

John Gore
Broadway Across
America
Producer

Norton Herrick
Producer

Allen Spivak
Producer

Rebecca Gold
Producer

Joshua Goodman
Producer

Bryan S. Weingarten
Producer

Philip Hagemann
Producer

Murray Rosenthal
Producer

Jim Kierstead
Producer

Carlos Arana
Producer

Myla Lerner
Producer

Hugh Hayes
Producer

Jamie Cesa
Producer

Jonathan Reinis
Producer

Ben Feldman
Producer

Sharon A. Carr
Producer

Patricia R. Klausner
Producer

Jay Leland Krottinger
Square 1 Theatrics
Producer

Ryan Tanner
Square 1 Theatrics
Producer

Pippin

Wendy Federman
Producer

Carl Moellenberg
Producer

Bruce Robert Harris
Producer

Jack W. Batman
Producer

Anna & Alan Ostroff
Infinity Theatre Co.
Producers

Michael Rubenstein
Producer

Michael A. Alden
Producer

Dale Badway
Producer

Ken Mahoney
Producer

James L. Simon
Associate Producer

Alecia Parker
Executive Producer

2013-2014 PIPPIN ALUMNI

Andrew Cekala
Theo

Orion Griffiths
Player

Kelsey Jamieson
Player

Andrea Martin
Berthe

Aidan O'Shea
Player

Stephanie Pope
Player; u/s Leading Player

Christopher Sieber
Charles

2013-2014 PIPPIN TRANSFER STUDENTS

Fernando Dudka
Player

Orion Griffiths
Player

Michelle K. Guy
Player

Kelsey Jamieson
Player

Kenneth Lindemann
Player

Richard Maguire
Player

Kyle Dean Massey
Pippin

Annie Potts
Berthe

Ciara Renée
Leading Player

Mirela Golinska Roche
Player

Christopher Sieber
Charles

Florian Zumkehr
Player

Pippin

2013-2014 AWARD

ACCA AWARD
Outstanding Broadway Chorus

MANAGEMENT
(L-R): Brad Musgrove
(Dance Captain),
Nancy Harrington
(Production Stage
Manager),
Stephen Gruse
(Assistant Stage Manager),
Julie Baldauff
(Stage Manager)

BOX OFFICE
(L-R): Tim Moran, Brian Cobb, Brendan Berberich

WARDROBE
Front (L-R): Michael Sancineto (Dresser), Marjorie Denton (Dresser),
Thomas Sharkey (Dresser), Meghan Carsella (Wardrobe Supervisor)
Stairs (From Top): David Thompson (Dresser),
Sara Foster (Dresser), Emily Ockenfels

CREW
Front Row (L-R): Reece Nunez (Deck Sound), Chris Pravata, John Carlotto,
Alan Schuster, William Rowland II, William K Rowland, Kevin Strohmeyer,
Marjorie Denton (Dresser), Michael Cecchini (Assistant Carpenter), Dennis Maher
Under the Stairs: Joseph "Dana" Gracey
Back Row (L-R): Kyle Garnett, Michael Sancineto (Dresser),
Worth Strecker (Production Props Coordinator)
Stairs (From Top): Sandy Paradise, Thomas Sharkey (Dresser), Kim Garnett

MUSICIANS
Front (L-R): Charlie Alterman (Music Director/Conductor),
Rick Dolan
Back (L-R): Michael Davis, Larry Saltzman,
Sean Ritenauer, Jared Schonig

Pippin
SCRAPBOOK

Correspondent: Molly Tynes, "Player"

Memorable Parties: Our first PSM Nancy Harrington threw a bowling party when she left the show that was awesome! We had a private party room with our own disco lit bowling lanes and an amazing spread of food and drink. Everyone had a blast. More recently, our producers, Howard and Janet Kagan, threw a holiday party for us and their other show, *Natasha, Pierre and the Great Comet of 1812* at Mari Vanna, a trendy Russian restaurant that is decorated like an eccentric Russian grandmother's living room. They rented out the entire place and invited a series of performers—belly dancers, palm readers, magicians, et cetera. The most exciting of these was a man who spun little sculptures out of melted sugar. He would dip a stick in the sugar and magically transform it into an intricate little creature such as a winged dragon, or a dog with a basket full of puppies. Many of us thought the sculptures were too beautiful to eat, but it seems many of the children disagreed and snacked away!

Most Exciting Celebrity Visitor: We've had so many fabulous visitors, but the title has to go to Liza Minnelli. She has come three times! The first time she saw the show, she came backstage and held court onstage. She spoke to each person one at a time and posed for photos. The second time she had a health issue and couldn't stay after the show. Instead she yelled to us all on the loudspeaker in her unmistakable Liza voice, "Darlings, it's Liza! I can't do the stairs because of my knee, you know. But I wanted to tell you that you were all effing fantastic!" The third time she waved to us and smiled from the audience throughout the entire show. Afterwards she passed on the message to all her "Babies," as she calls us, that we did a fabulous job and that she would be back yet again!

Actors Who Perform the Most Roles in This Show: Our swings definitely corner the market here. Sabrina Harper, our female swing, covers six female tracks AND three principals. Billy Harrigan Tighe, our male swing, covers Pippin, Lewis, and the entire male ensemble. But I'd have to say Brad Musgrove really takes the cake on this one. In addition to covering the entire male ensemble, he's also been on in several FEMALE ensemble tracks including a circus showgirl and a contortionist! The truth is he actually knows every part in the show. In understudy rehearsal he fills in for any absent roles (principal and ensemble alike) and is completely off book for all

---

MARKETING STRATEGY
Clint Bond, Jr.   Ken Sperr

GENERAL PRESS REPRESENTATIVE
BONEAU/BRYAN-BROWN
Adrian Bryan-Brown   Heath Schwartz   Amy Kass

Stage Manager ....Julie Baldauff
Assistant Stage Manager ....Stephen R. Gruse
Management Assistant ....Tyler Forrest
Casting Associate ....Andrea Zee
Assistant Director ....Mia Walker
Assistant to Stephen Schwartz ....Michael Cole
Assistant to Gypsy Snider ....Jeslyn Kelly
Associate Scenic Designer ....Jeff Hinchee
Assistant Scenic Designers ....Nick Francone,
    Jennifer Price-Fick
Apprentice Scenic Designer ....Stephen Davan
Assistant Costume Designer ....Jessica Worsnop
Costume Design Assistant ....Jason Bishop
"Fastrada" Costume Specialty ....Viktoria Grimmy
Associate Lighting Designer ....Anthony Pearson
Assistant Lighting Designer ....Jonathan Spencer
Production Carpenter ....Todd Frank
Assistant Carpenter ....Michael Cecchini
Production Electrician ....James Fedigan
Head Electrician ....Patrick Ainge
Production Props Coordinator ....Worth Strecker
Illusion Props ....Ron Bin Ion, Bill Smith
Props Artisan ....Bob Flanagan
Associate Sound Designer ....Drew Levy
Production Sound ....Nick Borisjuk
Sound Engineer ....Steve Henshaw
Sound Programmer ....Will Pickens
Deck Sound ....Reece Nunez
Automated Lighting Programmer ....Timothy F. Rogers
Wardrobe Supervisor ....Meghan Carsella
Dressers ..Marjorie Denton, David Thompson, Sara Foster,
    Thomas Sharkey, Laura Horner, Michael Sancineto
Hair/Make-up Supervisor ....Katie Beatty
Assistant Hair/Make-up ....Jonathan Sharpless
Make-up Artisan ....Hagen Linss
Dialect Coach ....Nancy Houfek
Associate Fire Specialist ....Aaron Waitz
Production Assistant ....Sharika Niles
Assistant to John Miller ....Nichole Jennino
Music Assistant ....Ben Rauhala
Music Intern ....Peter Hodgson

Legal Counsel ....Seth Gelblum/Loeb & Loeb
Accountant ....Marks Paneth & Shron LLP/
    Mark A. D'Ambrosi, Marina Flom
Advertising ....SpotCo/Drew Hodges, Ilene Rosen,
    Tom Greenwald, Nick Pramik, Stephen Sosnowski,
    Juliana Hannett, Chris Scherer,
    Kyle Young, Kristen Bardwil
Website Design ......ArtHouse Interactive/Sara Fitzpatrick
Production Photography ....Joan Marcus
Children's Supervisor ....Thomas Bradfield
Children's Teachers ....On Location Education
Banking ....City National Bank/
    Stephanie Dalton, Michele Gibbons
Insurance ....Aon/Albert G. Ruben Insurance Services, Inc.
Physical Therapy ....Sean Gallagher/
    Performing Arts Physical Therapy
Opening Night ....Foresight Events/
    Jennifer O'Connor, Connie Wilkin
Merchandising ....Broadway Merchandising, LLC
Payroll Services ....Castellana Services, Inc.
Theatre Displays ....BAM Signs, Inc.
Group Sales ....Group Sales Box Office
    Broadway.com/Groups

NATIONAL ARTISTS MANAGEMENT CO.
Head of Business Affairs/
    Associate Producer ....Daniel M. Posener
Chief Financial Officer ....Bob Williams
International Manager ....Nina Skriloff
General Management Associates ....Rina Saltzman,
    Stephen Spadaro
Associate to the Weisslers ....Brett England
Assistant to Mrs. Weissler ....Nikki Pelazza
Manager of Accounting/Admin. ....Marian Albarracin
Receptionist ....Michelle Coleman
Messenger ....Victor Ruiz
Executive Assistant ....Cristina Boccitto
Accounting Associate ....Marion Taylor

To learn more about the production, please visit
www.pippinthemusical.com

USE HASHTAG #ISAWPIPPIN TO TWEET YOUR THOUGHTS OF THE SHOW!

CREDITS
Show control and scenic motion control featuring stage command systems and scenery fabrication by PRG-Scenic Technologies, a division of Production Resource Group, LLC, New Windsor, NY. Lighting equipment from PRG Lighting. Sound equipment by Masque Sound®. Fire effects by Sunshine Studios. Costumes provided by Jennifer Love Costumes, Parsons-Meares, Studio Rouge, Martin Izquierdo, Rachel Navarro, David Thompson, John Furrow, Bra*Tenders. Shoes by LaDuca. Wigs by Tom Watson. Thanks to Gibson Guitar. Video equipment from PRG Video. Theo Ending originally conceived in 1998 by Mitch Sebastian.

SPECIAL THANKS
Diane Borger, Chris De Camillis, Haley Bennett, Nassib el Husseini, Gibson Guitars

THE SHUBERT ORGANIZATION, INC.
Board of Directors

Philip J. Smith	Robert E. Wankel
Chairman	President
Wyche Fowler, Jr.	Diana Phillips
Lee J. Seidler	Michael I. Sovern

Stuart Subotnick

Chief Financial Officer ....Elliot Greene
Sr. Vice President, Ticketing ....David Andrews
Vice President, Finance ....Juan Calvo
Vice President, Human Resources ....Cathy Cozens
Vice President, Facilities ....John Darby
Vice President, Theatre Operations ....Peter Entin
Vice President, Marketing ....Charles Flateman
Vice President, Audit ....Anthony LaMattina
Vice President, Ticket Sales ....Brian Mahoney
Vice President, Creative Projects ...........D.S. Moynihan
Vice President, Real Estate ....Julio Peterson

---

House Manager ....Jonathan Schulman

 The Shubert Organization is a proud member of the Broadway Green Alliance.

Pippin
SCRAPBOOK

of them! We are always amused by his spot-on portrayals, but our personal favorites are his Theo and his Fastrada.

Actors Who Have Done the Most Shows: Of the principals, Terrence Mann has done the most Broadway shows (12 or 13 by my count). In the ensemble, Stephanie Pope (from our original cast—she is now in the cast of *Chicago*) has done the most Broadway shows and subsequently received the Gypsy Robe. Her nine Broadway credits include the 1986 Revival of *Sweet Charity* with THE Bob Fosse himself. When we were putting the show together, she became famous for her "Ms. Pope" one-liner pearls of wisdom. Many of our cast members are much less experienced than she. We'd all be fussing around worrying about something, and she would just shake her head knowingly and speak the perfect witty one liner to quiet the fuss. It was brilliant. Now if only we could remember what she said!

Special Backstage Rituals: We have a special pre-show ritual which we do every single night without fail. When the lights dim onstage at the top of the show, Terry Mann leads the company in a group jam session. He bangs his prop juggling knives together, and people chime in with various harmony lines and rhythms. I can't give away all our secrets, so I can't actually name what song it is, but let's just say it's one of the finest dance hits of the 1990's. Hehehe. If you really want to know just come to the show; we have a tendency to get a little carried away during this ritual (despite the best efforts of Stage Management to shush us) and are often scolded for being so loud sometimes that the audience starts clapping along! Oops! The rhythmic shushing of our Stage Manager Stephen Gruse even become a part of the percussion section at one point. He's with another show now, but sometimes we shush ourselves in honor of him. This jam session has become such a part of the show that even when Terry goes on vacation, whoever is playing Charlemagne in his absence has to lead it. We even brought it with us to "Gypsy of the Year."

We also have a ritual for whenever someone leaves the show. After the curtain call of their final performance, we all gather around the departing actor cheering and pounding on the floor. We start chanting, "Through the chute! Through the chute!" They must then ceremoniously exit through the chute (a set piece used for many of the entrances and exits in the show), the curtain closes behind them, and we applaud them out.

Favorite Moment During Each Performance: Orion Griffiths performing his rolla bolla act at the top of Act II is truly a feat to behold. He places a board on top of five teetering metal

cylinders and miraculously balances on top of it all. Only a handful of people in the world can perform this trick. Even after hundreds of times seeing it, it is still astounding. (But Richie Maguire's reading of the line "extremely short" is a close second place.)

Favorite In-Theatre Gathering Places: Our theatre's backstage is very small. There is no greenroom. When the theatre was built I don't think it was intended to accommodate a company of this size. The men's dressing room on the fourth floor is the usual hangout spot after the show, but during the show there is not enough time to go up there. We usually find ourselves in our swing Brad Musgrove's offstage

The cast celebrates the 200th performance on stage.

Photo: Monica Simoes

dressing room—if you can even call it that. It's really just an alcove near the stage management office. And because of its close proximity to the stage, it winds up full of our water bottles, teas and coffees, hats and scarves, lipsticks, iPhones, lozenges, books, foam rollers, dance shoes, various potions and lotions people use to improve their performance, and anything else you can think of that an actor/dancer/acrobat might need—all in poor Brad's dressing room. There are usually a few posters that people want signed hanging on his mirror too. But he's a trouper about it all—a very grumpy trouper.

Favorite Snack Foods: The stage managment office has a bottomless candy jar. Sometimes our PSM Michael Passaro will put in almonds or something else healthy for us, but usually it's just full of Butterfingers and Snickers and such. We also have a hardcore baker in the company: our Head Carpenter Dennis! He makes cookies, brownies, pumpkin bread, banana bread, you name it. Almost every day he is baking something. The aroma often wafts onto the stage during Act I and makes the stage smell really good—and makes us all hungry!

Mascots: We have a couple of props that have taken on mascot-like roles. We have Horatio the Dead Body who levitates in Act I, and a baby doll prop who is probably the ugliest baby you've ever seen. One of our props guys, Kyle, gave him a prison tattoo. He also has a drawn-on mustache, but no one knows how it got there. We named him "Harv."

Favorite Therapy: Performing Arts Physical Therapy. Sean and his team come several days a week, but since this show is very demanding we are still always begging for more PT slots. What can we say? Sean and the whole team are amazing!

Memorable Ad-Libs: When you work with Terry Mann there is a memorable ad-lib at least once a week! He is known for his clever and humorous responses to just about anything going wrong onstage. He can make a bit out of any disaster. If an audience member sneezes during an awkwardly silent moment, he will turn right to them and say, "Bless you." Costume malfunctions have also been frequent fodder for Terry hilarity. But after conferring with the rest of the cast, I think we came to a consensus about our favorite Terry ad-lib. There is a pair of rolling stair units in the show that have exposed glass light bulbs lining each step. One day one of the bulbs shattered during "Magic To Do." There was glass EVERY-WHERE. During the following scene they sent out Rachel Bay Jones in her sad clown outfit with a giant broom to try to sweep it up (that was certainly a sight), but there was just too much glass for her to get it all. Just as the scene before Terry's number "War Is a Science" was about to begin, stage management decided we would have to stop the show. They told the soldiers on stage left not to enter, but unfortunately Terry and the soldiers on stage right entered before stage management could get the message to them. Usually the scene begins with Terry commanding, "Gentlemen! Be seated!" However upon encountering a half empty stage, he instead yelled, "Gentlemen! Don't be seated?" He then went on with his usual monologue inserting witty lines along the way in reference to the missing soldiers saying things like, "Tomorrow we go to battle against HALF the Visigoths!" Eventually he got the message that the show was stopping. He turned to the audience still completely in character and announced that we were having a bit of a technical difficulty and that the battle would just have to wait for a few minutes. He then dismissed the snickering soldiers and regally exited the stage. It was brilliant.

Technology Incidents During a Performance: Our audience is so close to the stage that we can see whenever they try to take cell phone photos or videos. It's hard to believe how many people ignore the announcement that it is prohibited. We've had people sit there holding up iPads to record the performance who are then mystified when ushers ask them to stop. One time in Act II, when Pippin exits through the audience after "Extraordinary," a woman on the aisle held up

Pippin
SCRAPBOOK

her glowing iPhone about a foot from Matthew's face and snapped a picture—like no one was going to notice that or think it was weird!

Memorable Publicity Event: We performed in front of Macy's as part of the 2013 Thanksgiving Day Parade. It was extremely cold! We performed "Magic To Do" which involves a lot of acrobatics, so we had everybody in parkas warming up inside Macy's until the last possible second. I will never forget our PSM Michael Passaro cheerfully announcing to us, "Please feel free to warm up in the purse aisle. We have mats!" We had been given flesh colored full body stockings to perform in, but when we saw the ladies of *Motown* performing with bare arms (and looking absolutely fantastic!) we decided to follow suit. We said, "If the *Motown* girls can do it, we can do it too!" So we took off our body stockings and danced on 34th Street in bare skin…and we were FREEZING.

Memorable Stage Door Fan Encounters: We definitely have some very loyal fans. There are quite a few faces that we see on a regular basis, and we are very thankful for their continued support!

Who Wore the Least: Two of the acrobat boys, Orion Griffiths and Kenneth Lindemann, wear teeny-tiny shorts with maybe a one-inch inseam and little bolero-style vests that are really more of a bra than a vest. And that's it! Hands-down they were the coldest at the Thanksgiving Day Parade.

Web Buzz: It has all been very good. Social media has been really important for us. From the very beginning we have had a lot of activity on Facebook, Instagram, et cetera. At one point there was an online fan page dedicated to the appreciation of Orion Griffiths's thighs. That was an interesting one.

Latest Audience Arrival: People are frequently seated after "Corner of the Sky." This means they missed "Magic To Do" and the scene that follows. This is a huge amount of tardiness! It happens several times a week. I mean really, how can you miss "Magic To Do?"

Catchphrases Only the Company Would Recognize: "Four more feet." "Where's Olga?" "Where's Rollah Boy?" "Go out if you need to go out. Go out if you need to go out." "Deeeeiiiiiiiaaaaaaack!" "Mind the Fitch Killers."

Best In-House Parody Lyric: "On the Right Track" has a whole alternate lyric involving the phrase "On My Ballsack." Example: "When you're on my ball sack, take it eeeeeasy sonny."

Memorable Directorial Notes: Our dance captain Brad Musgrove gives great notes. They are the perfect mix of teasing and informative instruction. He has some classic recurring notes that never fail to amuse including, "Walk like a normal person," "That's great, you can have your journey, just have it on 8," and "I want you to have that moment, sure, but I don't want to SEE it. Keep it inside. Actress inside."

Company In-Jokes: The flaccid crown, the many Horatio malfunctions, the time Yann made Molly levitate, the escape of the piggies, the Andrea Martin meerkat dance, Erik and his tribal prints, Pippin's many ladies' blouses,

Composer Stephen Schwartz with Leading Player Patina Miller at a CD-autographing event.

Rachel as the recurring onstage janitor, Andrew Fitch Day, Molly and Bethany's sexy dance, Gabby and Colin's foibles and fables, Anthony's occasional Alvin Ailey dance solo, the mad scramble to clear the table and stools, the grumpy marriage of Kyle and Brad, Olga's "He's crayyyyzy," and of course "Is this an audience or an oil painting?"

Tale From the Put-In: Two words: "Oooooh chile!"

Nicknames: Everyone in this company is called Erica. Except for the Jamiesons who are called the Prestons.

Embarrassing Moments: So many. The time Yann bit it when he ran out with the fire in the finale. Every time someone looks the wrong way in "War Is a Science." The time Charlotte lost her wig during "Spread a Little Sunshine" and then ripped off her entire wig prep and microphone and finished the number without amplification—actually that "embarrassing" moment was pretty badass, come to think of it. The time Patina lost the hoop she was twirling during "Simple Joys" and accidentally launched it at a lady in the front row. And not a minute later, Viktoria lost the hoop SHE was working with and launched it at the same exact lady! But my personal favorite has to be the time during the "talking" section in "Magic To Do" when Colin got so excited about the popcorn a woman in the front row was snacking on that he missed the cut off and ended up shouting in the clear, "Put it in my mouth!"

"Carols for a Cure" Carol: Matthew and Rachel did a beautiful duet called "The Cherry Tree Carol." Their voices are both so pure and lovely. It's really gorgeous.

"Gypsy of the Year" Presentation: "*Pippin* in Three Minutes," written, directed and choreographed by the gypsies of *Pippin*. Almost the entire ensemble participated as well as a few additional company members. It was a good group. We staged that sketch in about two hours total! It was a great bonding experience and a lot of fun.

Superstitions That Turned Out Not to Be True: We have a lot of people in the cast who are not from a theatre background and therefore don't know all the superstitions. I'm pretty sure at some point they wound up committing every

one of the no-nos. People have said the name of "The Scottish Play" without turning around and spitting. People have whistled backstage. It has all been done, and nothing bad has happened…yet.

Coolest Thing About Being in This Show: We always say, "It doesn't suck to be in a hit!" We got to go to the Tony Awards—and win! We got to perform on "Good Morning America," the Thanksgiving Day Parade, Letterman, and many more. We have gotten to do all this awesome stuff that people only dream of doing. It's pretty fabulous. I have to say it's also great to be in a company that legitimately gets along and legitimately wants to come to work every day. That is priceless.

Other Memories: It has been quite the journey together. It all started in 2012 with a summer in Cambridge, and now our *Pippin* family is ringing in 2014. Looking back: dorm room Olympics and wine, acrobatics at Walden Pond, watching the "French people" train in the backyard, Diane's "homework" at Union Square Theatre, Halloween with the Russian circus bears, Hurricane Sandy and rehearsing in deserted Union Square in parkas with no power, our Big Apple Circus field trip, Thanksgiving and New Year's Eve in Cambridge, Grafton Street oyster nights, "We're going to Broadway," seeing our marquee up at the Music Box for the first time, the hilarity of the barnyard improv, the many times Diane told us to "suck in," Chet's sound effects, the brilliance of Greg with that accordion, the amazingness of opening night on Broadway, the many press performances, recording the album, shooting the commercial, the Tonys, the Weissler summer party, Andrea's awesome BBQ, Olga's controversial Halloween party, the sad departures of many company members, the happy additions of many more, Tovah's crew dinner, freezing at Macy's, Gypsy of the Year, Yankee swap and Ashton's toilet paper, Colin's bday extravaganza, naps on Jaba, and snobs on the fourth floor. To all of it we raise a glass and say, "Oooohhhhhhhhhhhh Sante!!!!!!!!"

Matthew James Thomas and Andrea Martin at the CD event.

A Raisin in the Sun

First Preview: March 8, 2014. Opened: April 3, 2014.
Still running as of May 31, 2014.

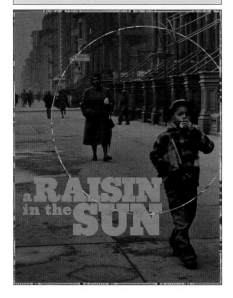

PLAYBILL®

Revival of Lorraine Hansberry's 1959 drama about a black family in 1950s Chicago that is torn over how to spend their deceased patriarch's $10,000 life insurance payout. The grown son (played by Denzel Washington) wants to use it to buy a partnership in a liquor store, but his mother wants to use it to buy the house in the suburbs she's always dreamed about. Things get complicated when the white neighbors of the house come around offering a bounty to keep the black folks from moving into their neighborhood.

CAST

(in order of appearance)

Ruth Younger	SOPHIE OKONEDO
Travis Younger	BRYCE CLYDE JENKINS
Walter Lee Younger	DENZEL WASHINGTON
Beneatha Younger	ANIKA NONI ROSE
Lena Younger	LATANYA RICHARDSON JACKSON
Joseph Asagai	SEAN PATRICK THOMAS
George Murchison	JASON DIRDEN
Karl Lindner	DAVID CROMER
Bobo	STEPHEN McKINLEY HENDERSON
Moving Men	KEITH ERIC CHAPPELLE, BILLY EUGENE JONES

Sophie Okonedo is appearing with the permission of Actors' Equity Association.

Continued on next page

⊕ **ETHEL BARRYMORE THEATRE**

243 West 47th Street
A Shubert Organization Theatre

Philip J. Smith, *Chairman*   **Robert E. Wankel,** *President*

SCOTT RUDIN   ROGER BERLIND   ELI BUSH   JON B. PLATT
SCOTT M. DELMAN   ROY FURMAN   STEPHANIE P. MCCLELLAND   RUTH HENDEL
SONIA FRIEDMAN/TULCHIN BARTNER   THE ARACA GROUP
HENI KOENIGSBERG   DARYL ROTH   JOAN RAFFE & JHETT TOLENTINO
EXECUTIVE PRODUCERS JOEY PARNES   S.D. WAGNER   JOHN JOHNSON

PRESENT

DENZEL WASHINGTON

IN

a RAISIN in the SUN

BY **LORRAINE HANSBERRY**

WITH **SOPHIE OKONEDO**
ANIKA NONI ROSE

DAVID CROMER   BRYCE CLYDE JENKINS
JASON DIRDEN   SEAN PATRICK THOMAS
KEITH ERIC CHAPPELLE   BILLY EUGENE JONES
STEPHEN MCKINLEY HENDERSON

AND **LATANYA RICHARDSON JACKSON**

SET DESIGN **MARK THOMPSON**   COSTUME DESIGN **ANN ROTH**   LIGHTING DESIGN **BRIAN MACDEVITT**   SOUND DESIGN **SCOTT LEHRER**
MUSIC CURATION **BRANFORD MARSALIS**   CASTING **HEIDI GRIFFITHS**   HAIR DESIGN **MIA M. NEAL**
PRODUCTION STAGE MANAGER **NARDA E. ALCORN**   COMPANY MANAGER **PENELOPE DAULTON**
PRESS REPRESENTATIVE **PHILIP RINALDI**   PRODUCTION MANAGER **AURORA PRODUCTIONS**   ASSOCIATE PRODUCER **JOI GRESHAM**

DIRECTED BY **KENNY LEON**

4/3/14

(L-R): David Cromer, Bryce Clyde Jenkins,
LaTanya Richardson Jackson, Anika Noni Rose,
Denzel Washington, Sophie Okonedo,

Photo: Brigitte Lacombe

A Raisin in the Sun

Cast Continued

UNDERSTUDIES

For Ruth Younger: MICHELLE WILSON
For Walter Lee Younger,
   Bobo: BILLY EUGENE JONES
For Travis Younger: DARIUS KALEB
For Beneatha Younger: MICHELLE BECK
For Joseph Asagai, Moving Men:
CHARLIE HUDSON III
For George Murchison:
KEITH ERIC CHAPPELLE
For Karl Lindner:
THOMAS MICHAEL HAMMOND
Standby for Lena Younger: MICHELE SHAY

The action of the play is set in Chicago's South Side, sometime between World War II and 1960.

ACT I

Scene 1. Friday morning.
Scene 2. Saturday morning.
Scene 3. Later, the same day.

ACT II

Scene 1. Friday night, a few weeks later.
Scene 2. Saturday, one week later. Moving day.
Scene 3. An hour later.

Lorraine Hansberry (1930-1965) is the author of the plays *A Raisin in the Sun*; *The Sign in Sidney Brustein's Window*, produced on Broadway shortly before her death in 1964; and *Les Blancs*, which premiered posthumously on Broadway in 1970. When *A Raisin in the Sun* premiered in 1959, it was the first play by an African-American woman to be produced on Broadway. Later that season, Miss Hansberry also became the youngest American playwright, the fifth woman, and the first African-American to win the New York Drama Critics Circle Award when *A Raisin in the Sun* was named Best Play. In 1961, the film version won a special award at the Cannes Film Festival, and Hansberry was nominated for a Writers Guild Award for her screenplay. *To Be Young, Gifted and Black,* an autobiographical portrait in her own words, adapted by her former husband and literary executor Robert Nemiroff, was the longest running Off-Broadway play of 1969. The author of many articles and essays on literary criticism, racism, sexism, homophobia, world peace, and other social and political issues, her published writings also include *The Drinking Gourd, What Use Are Flowers?,* and *The Movement,* a long essay written as text for a photojournalistic treatment of the Civil Rights Movement.

The recording heard before the performance is a radio conversation between Lorraine Hansberry and Studs Terkel as broadcast on Terkel's program "Almanac." The program, recorded in 1959, appears here courtesy of the Studs Terkel Radio Archive.

Photo: Courtesy of Lorraine Hansberry Literary Trust/lhlt.org

Denzel Washington
Walter Lee Younger

LaTanya Richardson Jackson
Lena Younger

Sophie Okonedo
Ruth Younger

Anika Noni Rose
Beneatha Younger

Stephen McKinley Henderson
Bobo

David Cromer
Karl Lindner

Bryce Clyde Jenkins
Travis Younger

Jason Dirden
George Murchison

Sean Patrick Thomas
Joseph Asagai

Keith Eric Chappelle
Moving Man; u/s George Murchison

Billy Eugene Jones
Moving Man; u/s Walter Lee Younger, Bobo

Michelle Beck
u/s Beneatha

Thomas Michael Hammond
u/s Karl Lindner

Charlie Hudson III
u/s Joseph Asagai, Moving Men

A Raisin in the Sun

Darius Kaleb
u/s Travis Younger

Michele Shay
*Standby for
Lena Younger*

Michelle Wilson
u/s Ruth Younger

Kenny Leon
Director

Mark Thompson
Set Design

Ann Roth
Costume Design

Brian MacDevitt
Lighting Design

Scott Lehrer
Sound Design

Branford Marsalis
Music Curation

Heidi Griffiths
Casting

Mia M. Neal
Hair Design

Gene O'Donovan
Aurora Productions
*Production
Management*

Ben Heller
Aurora Productions
*Production
Management*

Kate Wilson
Vocal Coach

Scott Lehrer

Rick Sordelet
Fight Direction

Scott Rudin
Producer

Roger Berlind
Producer

Jon B. Platt
Producer

Scott M. Delman
Producer

Roy Furman
Producer

Stephanie P.
McClelland
Producer

Ruth Hendel
Producer

Sonia Friedman
Producer

Norman Tulchin
Tulchin Bartner
Producer

Michael Rego, Hank Unger, Matthew Rego
The Araca Group
Producer

Heni Koenigsberg
Producer

Daryl Roth
Producer

Joan Raffe
Producer

Jhett Tolentino
Producer

Joey Parnes
Executive Producer

S.D. Wagner
Executive Producer

John Johnson
Executive Producer

Joi Gresham
Associate Producer

A Raisin in the Sun

SECURITY
(L-R): Doc Poland, DeLacy Tuff

Photos: Brian Mapp

BOX OFFICE
(L-R): Diane Heatherington, Karen Winer

FRONT OF HOUSE
Front (L-R): Anthony Wilkerson, Eric Rodriguez, Aileen Kilburn, John Dancy, Brian Gold
Back (L-R): Justin Roman, Heidi Giovine, Debra Vogel, Mercedes Carrasco, Sherry McIntyre, Audrey Terrell, Tracey Barnett

CREW
Front (L-R): Matthew Maloney (House Electrician), Narda E. Alcorn (Production Stage Manager), Karen Dickenson (Hair Supervisor)
Middle (L-R): Michael P. Zaleski (Stage Manager), Donna Holland (Dresser), Sarah Testerman (Sub. Stage Manager), Caroline O'Connor (Child Guardian), David Stollings (Head Sound), Penny Daulton (Company Manager)
Back (L-R): Joe Masucci (Head Carpenter), Paul Brydon (Flyman), Michael Hill (Sub. Electrician), Philip Feller (House Props), James Cariot (Head Props)

A Raisin in the Sun

Sophie Okonedo as Ruth Younger and Denzel Washington as her husband, Walter Lee Younger

2013-2014 AWARDS

TONY AWARDS
Best Revival of a Play
Best Performance by an Actress
in a Featured Role in a Play
(Sophie Okonedo)
Best Direction of a Play
(Kenny Leon)

THEATRE WORLD AWARD
(Sophie Okonedo)

A Raisin in the Sun
SCRAPBOOK

Correspondent: Jason Dirden, "George Murchison"

Opening Night Parties and/or Gifts: LaTanya Richardson Jackson gave everyone a Kangol hat with our *Raisin in the Sun* logo on the back.

Most Exciting Celebrity Visitor: I don't think anyone can top the President and First Lady coming to the show… but here are a few that have been pretty awesome to have as guests: Cicely Tyson, Lou Gossett Jr., Jamie Foxx, Whoopi Goldberg, Madam Justice Sotomayor.

What Was It Like Performing for the Obamas?: A dream. I don't think Disney could have written a more magical and surreal script. To have the first African-American President and First Lady come see Lorraine Hansberry's *A Raisin in the Sun* on Broadway—one of the finest examples of what can happen when

①

dreams are no longer deferred. I think this is a great tweet that puts it all into perspective: "8th Ave lined w/cops: The Obamas see #ARaisinInTheSun 2nite. Could Lorraine Hansberry have imagined such a dream deferred-but fulfilled" @lisaschwarzbaum.

Favorite In-Theatre Gathering Place: During the show: The couches in the basement. After the show: LaTanya's dressing room.

Special Backstage Rituals: Before every performance, the cast is invited to Denzel's room where we have a prayer circle giving thanks for the wonderful blessing of Lorraine Hansberry, *A Raisin in the Sun*, and the opportunity to relive this story every night. Also, to ask for strength, guidance, intention and clarity, so that we may touch and inspire those who have come to hear Ms. Hansberry's extraordinary words.

Worst Audience Behavior: CELL PHONES. CELL PHONES. CELL PHONES.

Memorable Ad-Libs: 1) Actual lines: RUTH: Where is it [the new house]? MAMA: Well—well—it's out there in Clybourne Park. What was said: RUTH: Where is it? MAMA:

Well—well—it's out there… in the park. 2) Actual line: WALTER: And I'll come up the steps of the house and the gardener will be clipping away at the hedges and he'll say, "Good evening, Mr. Younger." What was said: WALTER: And I'll come up the steps of the house and the gardener will be clipping away at the hedges and he'll say, "Good evening, Mr…Mr…" Travis, what's our name? TRAVIS: Younger. WALTER: Yeah, that's right.

Memorable Directorial Note: "This is an intimate performance of a big play."—Kenny Leon.

Company In-Jokes: The Fight Call Mama/ Beneatha April Fool's Prank: LaTanya swings back to slap Anika and hits her in the face. Pretty routine. But it's April 1st. Anika put a blood pellet in her mouth before fight call, so when LaTanya slaps her, Anika begins to bleed out of her mouth, saying she bit through her tongue. LaTanya is horrified and frozen. Anika looks up, grins and says, "April Fools!"

Embarrassing Moment: It was during a passionate argument with George, in which Beneatha exclaims, rather emphatically, her point of view. Once she finishes her argument, she is supposed to exit to her bedroom, open and slam the door with a ball of fury and great satisfaction. One night, she finishes her argument, turns with great passion, clearly too much, because she runs right smack into the bedroom door and bounces back. Hilarious!

Favorite Moment During Each Performance: Act I, Scene iii: The "Ocomogosiay/African Ritual" scene is an audience favorite. Beneatha

④

is embodying her newfound love for her African roots. Intoxicated, Walter becomes enamored by the music and movement, and is overcome by the spirit. Fully assimilated, wealthy George Murchison finds himself in the middle of it all. Also Act II, Scene ii: Just before we discover Walter has given away the money. Walter is dancing with Ruth, Beneatha is joking and laughing with the two of them, and they all have a gift for Lena. It's a beautiful portrait of the enormous amount of love the Youngers have for each other.

Favorite Off-Site Hangouts: Glass House, Bar Centrale.

Favorite Snack Foods: Whatever dessert someone decides to bring to the basement gets EATEN!

Favorite Therapy: Ricola, Grether's Pastilles.

②

Catchphrases Only the Company Would Recognize: "I feel a bit eggy" (must be said in a cockney dialect).

Understudy Anecdote: The understudies created a "Demerit." They self-police themselves, because it can get a little crazy on the fifth floor.

Nicknames: Anika Noni Rose a.k.a. Vitamin D. The three female understudies (Michele Shay, Michelle Wilson and Michelle Beck) a.k.a. The Michelles.

Coolest Thing About Being in This Show: This is one helluva a family! Everyone inside and outside of the Barrymore Theatre involved with this production has helped make this a wonderful journey.

1. Director Kenny Leon with members of Lorraine Hansberry's family on opening night.
2. Aonika Laurent Thomas and Sean Patrick Thomas.
3. Samuel L. Jackson and LaTanya Richardson Jackson.
4. Curtain call with (L-R): LaTanya Richardson Jackson, Denzel Washington and Sophie Okonedo.

The Realistic Joneses

First Preview: March 13, 2014. Opened: April 6, 2014.
Still running as of May 31, 2014.

PLAYBILL

A new American play by Will Eno about two neighboring suburban couples who discover they have far more in common than the fact that they share the same last name. The two husbands suffer from the same rare genetic disease that apparently causes them to take one another very literally and continually go off on conversational tangents. The wives are left to grapple with this as best they can, and to deal with emotional issues that arise from their quandary.

CAST

Jennifer Jones .... TONI COLLETTE
John Jones .... MICHAEL C. HALL
Bob Jones .... TRACY LETTS
Pony Jones .... MARISA TOMEI

UNDERSTUDIES

For Jennifer, Pony: ANNEY GIOBBE
For John, Bob: ANTONY HAGOPIAN

SETTING

A smallish town not far from some mountains.

TIME

Present

Toni Collette is appearing with the support of Actors' Equity Association.

2013-2014 AWARDS

DRAMA DESK AWARDS
Outstanding Ensemble Performance
Special Award
(Will Eno)

---

⑤ LYCEUM THEATRE
149 West 45th Street
A Shubert Organization Theatre

Philip J. Smith, *Chairman*   **Robert E. Wankel,** *President*

Jeffrey   Jerry   Jam   Stacey   Susan   Mary Lu
Richards   Frankel   Theatricals   Mindich   Gallin   Roffe

Andy Sandberg   Scott M. Delman   William Berlind   Caiola Productions
CandyWendyJamie Productions   Amy Danis & Mark Johannes   Finn Moellenberg Productions
Angelina Fiordellisi   Jay Franke   Gesso Productions   Grimaldi Astrachan Hello Entertainment
Meg Herman   Mara Smigel Rutter Productions   KM–R&D   Will Trice

In association with Yale Repertory Theatre

Present

TONI   MICHAEL C.   TRACY   MARISA
COLLETTE   HALL   LETTS   TOMEI

The Realistic
JONESES

BY
WILL ENO

Scenic Design	Costume Design	Lighting Design	Sound Design
DAVID ZINN	KAYE VOYCE	MARK BARTON	LEON ROTHENBERG

Technical Supervisor	Casting	Production Stage Manager
HUDSON THEATRICAL ASSOCIATES	DANIEL SWEE, C.S.A.	JILL CORDLE

General Manager	Advertising	Marketing/Press Representative	Associate Producers
BESPOKE THEATRICALS	SERINO/COYNE	IRENE GANDY/ALANA KARPOFF CHRISTOPHER PINEDA/THOMAS RAYNOR	MICHAEL CREA PJ MILLER

Directed By
SAM GOLD

The Realistic Joneses was commissioned by and premiered at Yale Repertory Theatre
James Bundy, Artistic Director; Victoria Nolan, Managing Director

4/6/14

(L-R): Toni Collette, Michael C. Hall and Tracy Letts

Photo: Joan Marcus

The Realistic Joneses

Toni Collette
Jennifer Jones

Michael C. Hall
John Jones

Tracy Letts
Bob Jones

Marisa Tomei
Pony Jones

Anney Giobbe
u/s Jennifer, Pony

Antony Hagopian
u/s John, Bob

Will Eno
Playwright

Sam Gold
Director

David Zinn
Scenic Design

Kaye Voyce
Costume Design

Mark Barton
Lighting Design

Leon Rothenberg
Sound Design

Daniel Swee
Casting Director

Neil A. Mazzella
Hudson Theatrical
Associates
Technical Supervisor

Maggie Brohn
Bespoke Theatricals
*General
Management*

Amy Jacobs
Bespoke Theatricals
*General
Management*

Devin Keudell
Bespoke Theatricals
*General
Management*

Nina Lannan
Bespoke Theatricals
*General
Management*

Jeffrey Richards
Producer

Jerry Frankel
Producer

Arny Granat
Jam Theatricals
Producer

Steve Traxler
Jam Theatricals
Producer

Stacey Mindich
Producer

Susan Quint Gallin
Producer

Mary Lu Roffe
Producer

Andy Sandberg
Producer

Scott M. Delman
Producer

Luigi and Rose Caiola
Caiola Productions
Producer

Candy Kosow Gold
Producer

Wendy Federman
Producer

Jamie deRoy
Producer

Amy Danis
Producer

Mark Johannes
Producer

The Realistic Joneses

Jeffrey Finn
Producer

Carl Moellenberg
Producer

Angelina Fiordellisi
Producer

Jay Franke
Jay Franke
Productions
Producer

Trish Whitehurst
Producer

Daniel Wallace
Producer

Dennis Grimaldi
Producer

Margot Astrachan
Producer

David Garfinkle
Producer

Meg Herman
Producer

John Mara, Jr.
Producer

Bellanca Smigel
Rutter
Producer

Rob Hinderliter
Producer

Dominick LaRuffa, Jr.
Producer

Ken Mahoney
Producer

Will Trice
Producer

James Bundy
Artistic Director
Yale Repertory
Theatre
Producer

Victoria Nolan
Managing Director
Yale Repertory
Theatre
Producer

Michael Crea
Associate Producer

PJ Miller
Associate Producer

Photos: Brian Mapp

BOX OFFICE
Shari Teitelbaum, Michael Taustine

FRONT OF HOUSE
Seated (L-R): Ryan Sprague (Concessions), Gerry Belitsis, Danielle Banyai, Kelly Brauer (Ushers)
Standing (L-R): William Pacheco, Tiffany Santucci, Nelson Hawkins (Ushers),
Thia Calloway (House Manager)

The Realistic Joneses

CREW

Seated (L-R): Leah Nelson (House Props), Laura Beattie (Dresser), Mike Pitzer (House Electrician), Morgan R. Holbrook (Stage Manager), Jill Cordle (Production Stage Manager)
Standing (L-R): Mark Diaz (House Carpenter), Wallace Flores (Sound), James Hodun (Dresser)

STAFF FOR *THE REALISTIC JONESES*

GENERAL MANAGEMENT
BESPOKE THEATRICALS
Maggie Brohn
Devin Keudell   Nina Lannan   Amy Jacobs
Associate General Manager ....Steve Dow

COMPANY MANAGER
Lizbeth Cone

GENERAL PRESS REPRESENTATIVES
JEFFREY RICHARDS ASSOCIATES
Irene Gandy   Alana Karpoff
Christopher Pineda   Thomas Raynor

PRODUCTION MANAGEMENT
HUDSON THEATRICAL ASSOCIATES
Neil A. Mazzella   Sam Ellis
Lindsey Turteltaub   Irene Wang

CASTING
Daniel Swee, C.S.A
Camille Hickman, Casting Associate

HAIR AND MAKEUP STYLIST
Jason Hayes

Production Stage Manager	Jill Cordle
Stage Manager	Morgan R. Holbrook
Assistant Director	Osheen Jones
Associate Set Designer	Tim McMath
Associate Costume Designer	Amy Jean Wright
Costume Shopper	Sarah Gosnell
Associate Lighting Designer	G. Benjamin Swope
Assistant Lighting Designer	Tess James
Moving Light Programmer	Marc Polimeni
Associate Sound Designer	Will Pickens
Props Coordinator	Kathy Fabian

Props Coordination Assistant	John Estep
Production Carpenter	Donnie Oberpriller
House Carpenter	Mark Diaz
Production Electrician	Michael Pitzer
Production Sound	Wallace Flores
House Props	Leah Nelson
Wardrobe Supervisor	Debbie Cheretun
Dressers	Laura Beattie, James Hodun
Hair Supervisor	Jason Hayes
Production Assistant	Alex Hajjar
General Management Interns	Tucker Delaney-Winn, Shana Ferguson
Advertising	Serino/Coyne/ Greg Corradetti, Tom Callahan, Robert Jones, Drew Nebrig, Ben Skinner, Jim Glaub, Mark Seeley
Interactive Marketing	Broadway's Best Shows/ Andy Drachenberg, Lindsay Hoffman
Press Assistant	Steven Strauss
Legal Counsel	Lazarus & Harris LLP/ Scott Lazarus, Esq.; Robert C. Harris, Esq.
Visa Consultant	Entertainment Visa Consultants/ David King
Accountant	FK Partners/ Robert Fried
Controller	Galbraith & Co./ Kenny Noth
Banking	City National Bank/ Michele Gibbons
Insurance	AON/Albert G. Ruben, Claudia Kaufman
Payroll Services	Checks and Balances/ Anthony Walker
Travel Agent	Tzell Travel/ The "A" Team, Andi Henig
Merchandising	Max Merchandise
Production Photographer	Joan Marcus
Company Mascots	Skye, Franco

CREDITS
Scenery built by Hudson Scenic Studio, Inc. Lighting equipment by Hudson Sound & Light, LLC. Sound equipment by PRG Sound. Special thanks to Bra*Tenders for undergarments and hosiery.

The Realistic Joneses rehearsed at the
New 42nd Street Studios.

 THE SHUBERT ORGANIZATION, INC.
Board of Directors

Philip J. Smith	**Robert E. Wankel**
Chairman	President
Wyche Fowler, Jr.	**Diana Phillips**
Lee J. Seidler	**Michael I. Sovern**

Stuart Subotnick

Chief Financial Officer	Elliot Greene
Sr. Vice President, Ticketing	David Andrews
Vice President, Finance	Juan Calvo
Vice President, Human Resources	Cathy Cozens
Vice President, Facilities	John Darby
Vice President, Theatre Operations	Peter Entin
Vice President, Marketing	Charles Flateman
Vice President, General Counsel	Gilbert Hoover
Vice President, Audit	Anthony LaMattina
Vice President, Ticket Sales	Brian Mahoney
Vice President, Creative Projects	D.S. Moynihan
Vice President, Real Estate	Julio Peterson

House Manager	Thia Calloway

The Shubert Organization is a proud member of the Broadway Green Alliance.

The Realistic Joneses
Scrapbook

Correspondent: Jill Cordle, Production Stage Manager, with input from the cast.

Memorable Note, Fax or Fan Letter: Michael received a fan letter with a hand drawn portrait of Dexter on the outside of the envelope.

Opening Night Parties and/or Gifts: We all received squirrel stuffed animals and small metal mailboxes (like on our poster) from our producers. The squirrels are very cute.

Favorite In-Theatre Gathering Place: The cast will gather backstage behind our giant wall and hang out starting at the five-minute call.

Special Backstage Rituals: Dance party backstage before the show!

Most Memorable Audience Reaction: We get some great reactions when the dead squirrel is picked up and when Michael throws out the rotten bag of produce from the fridge.

Worst Audience Behavior: Patrons in the front row resting their feet up on the front of the stage.

Unique Pre-Show Announcement: Will Eno wrote and recorded our pre-show announcement: "Hello and welcome to the historic Lyceum Theatre. Please take a moment to turn off your cellphones and eat all your candy and cough drops. Because we'll only be here for a short time, before we're gone forever, we ask that you refrain from photography and recording of any kind. This will add to the beauty of the whole thing. Architecture buffs and people who like leaving places will have already noted the exit doors, but everyone should take a look—they're located to the front, middle and rear of the auditorium. These doors may be used in the event of an emergency. I don't think there's going to be an emergency, though. I think everything's going to be fine, so you should just relax and feel good about yourselves, you know? You're at a play!"

Memorable Directorial Note: "Spikey-er." "Don't act."

Company In-Joke: "Who is it tonight, stiffy or limpy?"

Embarrassing Moment: During one preview, the light board malfunctioned at the top of the show. The cast had to exit the stage in the blackout and we made an announcement about the technical issue. Once we fixed the light board, we restarted the show.

Favorite Moment During Each Performance: Sitting around the fire pit during the final scene.

Favorite Off-Site Hangout: Bar Centrale or Bond 45.

Favorite Snack Food: Dark chocolate.

Favorite Therapy: Sugar-free Ricola and ginger Altoids. Marisa hula hoops backstage before she enters.

Mascot: Stiffy, the dead, stuffed squirrel.

Catchphrases Only the Company Would Recognize: "What are we doing, the play?"

Tales from the Put-In/Understudy Anecdote: Our female understudy, Anney Giobbe, had to go on early in previews. Anney only had one rehearsal or preparation before going on and was fantastic!

Nicknames: Tracy—Kid Lightning; Michael— Michael Chall.

Fastest Costume Change: Marisa—15 seconds.

Coolest Thing About Being in This Show: Being a very modern play in one of the oldest Broadway theatres.

1. Meeting the press prior to the start of rehearsals (L-R): Tracy Letts, Michael C. Hall, Marisa Tomei, Toni Collette, director Sam Gold and playwright Will Eno.
2. Sam Gold and wife and playwright Amy Herzog.
3. Actress Maria Dizzia and husband Will Eno.
4. Curtain call on opening night at the Lyceum Theatre (L-R): Tracy Letts, Toni Collette, Marisa Tomei and Michael C. Hall

Rock of Ages

First Preview: March 17, 2009. Opened: April 7, 2009.
Still running as of May 31, 2014.

Drew and Sherrie are two starry-eyed kids who arrive in Los Angeles with dreams of becoming long-haired head-banging rock stars, but they have to learn a lot about life—and help save a rock club destined for the wrecker's ball—before their dreams can come true. This musical has an original story but a score of classic 1980s rock hits.

CAST

Sherrie	KATE ROCKWELL
Drew	AARON C. FINLEY
Stacee Jaxx/Father	JOEY CALVERI
Lonny	GENSON BLIMLINE
Dennis	ADAM DANNHEISSER
Franz	CODY SCOTT LANCASTER
Regina/Candi	JOSEPHINE ROSE ROBERTS
Hertz	PAUL SCHOEFFLER
Justice/Mother	TERESA STANLEY
Waitress #1	TESSA ALVES
Sleazy Producer/Joey Primo	ANDREW CALL
Young Groupie	CASSIE SILVA
Mayor/Ja'Keith Gill/Strip Club DJ	ANDRE WARD
Reporter	NEKA ZANG

THE ENSEMBLE
TESSA ALVES, ANDREW CALL, CASSIE SILVA,
ANDRE WARD, NEKA ZANG

SWINGS
CRISTY CANDLER, TONY LePAGE,
MICHAEL MINARIK

Continued on next page

THE HELEN HAYES THEATRE

MARTIN MARKINSON   DONALD TICK

MATTHEW WEAVER   CARL LEVIN   JEFF DAVIS   BARRY HABIB   SCOTT PRISAND
MICHAEL COHL   REAGAN SILBER   JONATHAN LINDEN/S2BN ENTERTAINMENT   RELATIVITY MEDIA

in association with

JANET BILLIG RICH   HILLARY WEAVER
CORNER STORE FUND   RYAN KAVANAUGH   TONI HABIB
PAULA DAVIS   SIMON AND STEFANY BERGSON/JENNIFER MALONEY   CHARLES ROLECEK
SUSANNE BROOK   CRAIG COZZA   ISRAEL WOLFSON   SARA MERCER   JAYSON RAITT   MAX GOTTLIEB
MICHAEL MINARIK   DAVID KAUFMAN/JAY FRANKS   MICHAEL WITTLIN   PROSPECT PICTURES
LAURA SMITH/BILL BODNAR   WIN SHERIDAN   HAPPY WALTERS   MICHELE CARO   NEIL CANELL/JAY CANELL   MARIANO TOLENTINO
MARC BELL   and   THE ARACA GROUP

present

book by
CHRIS D'ARIENZO

starring
KATE ROCKWELL   AARON C. FINLEY   ADAM DANNHEISSER   CODY SCOTT LANCASTER
JOSEPHINE ROSE ROBERTS   PAUL SCHOEFFLER   TERESA STANLEY   *with* GENSON BLIMLINE *and* JOEY CALVERI

TESSA ALVES   ANDREW CALL   CRISTY CANDLER   TONY LePAGE
MICHAEL MINARIK   CASSIE SILVA   ANDRE WARD   NEKA ZANG

scenery based on an original design by BEOWULF BORITT	*costume design* GREGORY GALE	*lighting design* JASON LYONS	*sound design* PETER HYLENSKI	*projection design* ZAK BOROVAY

hair/wig design TOM WATSON	*make-up design* ANGELINA AVALLONE	*casting* TELSEY • COMPANY TIFFANY LITTLE CANFIELD, CSA	*production stage manager* MATTHEW DiCARLO

assistant director ADAM JOHN HUNTER	*associate choreographer* ROBERT TATAD	*associate producer* DAVID GIBBS

general management ROY GABAY	*press representative* THE HARTMAN GROUP	*advertising & marketing* aka	*technical supervisor* TECH PRODUCTION SERVICES

music director HENRY ARONSON	*music coordinator* JOHN MILLER	*original arrangements* DAVID GIBBS

music supervision, arrangements & orchestrations by
ETHAN POPP

choreographed by
KELLY DEVINE

directed by
KRISTIN HANGGI

10/1/13

Joey Calveri
as Stacee Jaxx
with the cast

Photo: Paul Kolnik

Rock of Ages

Cast Continued

OFFSTAGE VOCALS
TONY LePAGE

DANCE CAPTAIN
CRISTY CANDLER

UNDERSTUDIES
For Sherrie: TESSA ALVES, CASSIE SILVA
For Drew: ANDREW CALL, CODY SCOTT
LANCASTER, TONY LePAGE
For Franz/Stacee Jaxx:
ANDREW CALL, TONY LePAGE
For Hertz/Lonny/Dennis:
TONY LePAGE, MICHAEL MINARIK
For Regina: TESSA ALVES, NEKA ZANG
For Justice: TESSA ALVES, CRISTY CANDLER

BAND
Conductor/Keyboard: HENRY ARONSON
Guitar 1: JOEL HOEKSTRA
Guitar 2: TOMMY KESSLER
Drums: JON WEBER
Bass: WINSTON ROYE
Synthesizer Programmer: RANDY COHEN
Music Coordinator: JOHN MILLER
Copyist: Brian ALLAN HOBBS

Kate Rockwell
Sherrie

Aaron C. Finley
Drew

Joey Calveri
Stacee Jaxx/Father

Genson Blimline
Lonny

Adam Dannheisser
Dennis

Cody Scott Lancaster
Franz

Josephine Rose
Roberts
Regina/Candi

Paul Schoeffler
Hertz

Teresa Stanley
Justice/Moher

Tessa Alves
Ensemble

Andrew Call
Ensemble

Cristy Candler
*Swing, Dance
Captain*

Tony LePage
Swing

Michael Minarik
Swing

Cassie Silva
Ensemble

Andre Ward
Ensemble

Neka Zang
Ensemble

Henry Aronson
*Music Direction,
Keyboard*

Joel Hoekstra
Guitar

Tommy Kessler
Guitar

Winston Roye
Bass

Jon Weber
Drums

Chris D'Arienzo
Book

Kristin Hanggi
Director

Kelly Devine
Choreographer

Beowulf Boritt
*Original Scenery
Design*

Rock of Ages

Gregory Gale
Costume Design

Jason Lyons
Lighting Design

Peter Hylenski
Sound Design

Zachary Borovay
Projection Design

Tom Watson
Hair and Wig Design

Angelina Avallone
Make-up Design

Peter Fulbright
Tech Production
Services
Technical Supervisor

Ethan Popp
*Music Supervisor,
Arranger,
Orchestrator*

John Miller
Music Coordinator

David Gibbs
*Original
Arrangements*

Bernard Telsey
Telsey + Company
Casting

Robert Tatad
*Associate
Choreographer*

Roy Gabay
General Manager

Matthew Weaver
Producer

Carl Levin
Producer

Jeff Davis
Producer

Barry Habib
Producer

Scott Prisand
Producer

Michael Cohl
Producer

Ryan Kavanaugh
Relativity Media
Producer

Janet Billig Rich
Producer

Toni Habib
Producer

Paula Kaminsky
Davis
Producer

Stefany Bergson
Producer

Jennifer Maloney
Producer

Jayson Raitt
Producer

Bill Bodnar
Producer

Mariano Tolentino
Producer

Marc Bell
Producer

Michael Rego, Hank Unger, Matthew Rego
The Araca Group
Producer

Jake Boyd
Swing

Nick Cordero
*Dennis, Record
Company Man*

Ericka Hunter
Swing; u/s Sherrie

Rock of Ages

Lindsay Janisse
Swing

Lauralyn McClelland
Swing;
u/s Regina/Justice

Jennifer Rias
Swing, Dance
Captain;
u/s Regina/Justice

Justin Matthew
Sargent
Drew

Bret Tuomi
Hertz

Alyssa Herrera
Waitress #1,
Ensemble

Ericka Hunter
Sherrie

Lindsay Janisse
Young Groupie,
Ensemble

Lauralyn McClelland
Reporter, Ensemble

Rebecca Riker
Reporter, Ensemble

Josh Sassanella
Swing

Carrie St. Louis
Sherrie

Katie Webber
Waitress #1,
Ensemble; u/s
Sherrie, Justice

BOX OFFICE
(L-R): Tevy Bradley (Assistant Box Office Treasurer),
David Heveran (Box Office Treasurer)

STAGE MANAGEMENT
(L-R): Matthew DiCarlo (Production Stage Manager),
Francesca Russell (Assistant Stage Manager),
Justin Scribner (Stage Manager)

FRONT OF HOUSE
Front (L-R): Eleni Hadjiconstantinou (Usher), Berd Vaval (Ticket Taker),
Alan Markinson (House Manager)
Back (L-R): Linda Maley (Head Usher), Chiyo Sakai (Usher), Margaret Flanagan (Usher),
Susan Myerberg (General Manager)

CREW
(L-R):
Daryl Bornstein (Head Sound Mixer),
Robert Lindsay (Monitor Mixer),
Doug Purcell (Head Carpenter),
Dave Robinson (Props Sub),
Joseph Beck (Head Electrician)

Rock of Ages

Rock of Ages
SCRAPBOOK

Correspondent: Cody Scott Lancaster, "Franz"

Memorable Note, Fax or Fan Letter: There were a couple of months where every couple of days one or two cast members would get a fan letter asking for a signed headshot because they specifically were their "favorite actor on Broadway." There were about three different versions of the letter and the fan would send them in rotation. Eventually we all had the same letter. They didn't stop for months and it felt like some weird kind of scam. It went from flattering to creepy very quickly.

Milestone Parties, Celebrations and/or Gifts: We've had TONS of milestone celebrations. Just recently, *Rock of Ages* broke into the Top 30 longest-running Broadway shows in history. In April 2014 we celebrated both our 2,000th performance and our fifth anniversary on Broadway. We've been lucky enough to celebrate things that most shows don't get the chance to.

Most Exciting Celebrity Visitor and What They Did/Said: We've had tons, but Jimmy Fallon was a cast fave. He came (or rather, leaped) backstage afterwards, hung out for

doing and gathers for the tale.

Favorite In-Theatre Gathering Places: We have an EXTREMELY small backstage area so we bogart either the dressers' area, which we dub "the greenroom," or the stage manager's office. The latter has caused an "office hours" sign to be created. When the sign's up, we're not allowed in…but we all kindly ignore it and come in anyway.

Favorite Off-Site Hangout: Glass House Tavern has always been a favorite of the *Rock of Ages* family, but ever since Guy Fieri opened his restaurant next door (and did a walk-on role in the show!), we've become very close with him, his food, and his bar. :)

Favorite Snack Foods: We may be one of the most fit (and most naked) casts on Broadway, but that doesn't mean we're the healthiest. We have a snack table that is constantly loaded with treats (see picture at right). Schmackary's is bought quite often, cupcakes from Baked by Melissa, chips, bagels, beer, etc. It's amazing.

Mascot: Well… here's where the kiddies should skip to the next page. The *Rock of Ages* mascot is a big ol'—for censoring purposes—we'll say a silicone adult toy? It finds a new place to live every week and makes its way into every single RoA online video. It's been here at the Helen Hayes since the day we moved in.

Favorite Therapy: We are lucky enough to have Adept physical therapy come in every Tuesday and Saturday to work on our sore muscles.

Chris and Ali have saved our lives! And every corner you turn, you will find a giant bucket of Ricolas—Broadway's throat drop.

Memorable Ad-Lib: For some reason, the top of "Any Way You Want It" tends to throw off our understudies. The lyrics are, "She loves to dance, she loves to sing, she does everything. She loves to move, she loves to groove, she loves the loving thing." Renditions from three different understudies:
1. "She loves to sing, she loves to dance…SHE'S A FANCY PANTS."
2. "She loves to sing, SHE LOVES TO SING! She does everything."
3. "She loves to dance, she loves to move, SHE LOVES IT!"

Record Number of Cell Phone Rings, Cell Phone Photos or Texting Incidents During a Performance: Too many to count. Most of the time, our audience is drunk, so even though David Coverdale tells them to turn off their phones, they usually don't.

Memorable Press Encounter: We have one of the best publicity/marketing teams around

and have gotten so many cool opportunities. Some memorable ones this year are: performing at Six Flags and riding rollercoasters all day; performing at the official NFL tailgate party at MetLife Stadium for Super Bowl XLVIII, and having four NFL players make cameo appearances in our show; having Randi Zuckerberg join the cast as Regina for three weeks.

Memorable Stage Door Fan Encounter: My personal favorite was when two girls gave me their phone numbers and said, "You choose who you want, we're okay with whoever you pick." Needless to say, I picked neither. But the compliment put a smile on my face for days. Many of us have also gotten, "Were you in the show?" When you get a question like that after

about half an hour and pointed out at least one favorite joke, song, or bit for EVERY SINGLE cast member. A stand-up guy.

Actor Who Performed the Most Roles in This Show: Tony LePage is our Super Swing. He covers all EIGHT male roles in *Rock of Ages*, whether it's a principal or an ensemble track. Tessa Alves covers the most female roles. She covers every lead female and even plays more than one ensemble track in the same performance when times get rough!

Who Has Done the Most Shows: Josephine Rose Roberts ("Regina") had the most on-stage performances this year.

Special Backstage Rituals: We all gather in the greenroom before every show, have a prayer circle and our stage manager does a spiritual chant. But, for real? We have dance parties in our underwear a lot, and tell crass jokes.

Favorite Moment During Each Performance: Anytime the audience claps for me. I think that's the whole cast's favorite part…when I get applause. But for real? The last 30 seconds of the show during the "Don't Stop Believin'" dance party. We change it up every night and just have fun with each other. Also, anytime Andre Ward has a story to tell about his day, or an event from his past—the whole cast drops what they're

1. *Yearbook* correspondent Cody Scott Lancaster and Randi Zuckerberg (guest "Regina"). Is that a Roman Numeral "V" commemorating the show's fifth year anniversary on Broadway?
2. Jimmy Fallon sharing the love with the cast backstage at the Helen Hayes Theatre.
3. Munch a bunch of snack food: always in plentiful supply. No brown M&Ms.
4. Stage Management's feeble attempt to keep the cast away from his private space.

Rock of Ages

SCRAPBOOK

working your ass off for two and a half hours, the only realistic answer to give is "No" and to walk away. Haha!

What We Thought of the Web Buzz on Our Show: We have such an online presence. We have Twitter, Facebook, Instagram, everything. One website did a "Backstage with Kate Rockwell" series this year, and it was my mission to get into every episode...I ALMOST succeeded. Check out our Instagram (@rockofagesmusical) Adam Dannheisser likes to play around with that one.

Latest Audience Arrival: 8 p.m. at a 7 p.m. show.

Fastest Costume Change: At the end of Act I, Sherrie has about 30 seconds to change from a naive young girl from Kansas to a sultry stripper clad with leather skirt, corset, knee-high boots, and even a brand new wig.

Busiest Day at the Box Office: Saturdays.

Who Wore the Heaviest/ Hottest Costume: The heaviest costume in the show is worn by Drew (currently played by Aaron Finley) at the end of Act I. He wears a heavy leather jacket that has over 800 metal studs in it. Being a Drew understudy, I was SHOCKED by how heavy it is and how hard it is to DANCE in.

Who Wore the Least: Our ensemble ladies. Their simplest costume is just some bras and panties. They weigh about as much as they leave to the imagination: nothing.

Catchphrase Only the Company Would Recognize: "She loves to poo poo poo."

Sweethearts Within the Company: No one can say a single bad word about Jennifer Rias. Tony LePage showers everyone with love on

a daily basis. Cassie Silva doesn't even know the definition of "unhappy" or "cruel." I think she was a rainbow in a past life.

Which Orchestra Member Played the Most

Instruments and What Were They?: Tommy Kessler (who plays Guitar #2 and also is Blondie's full-time guitar player) has subbed in for Night Ranger's Joel Hoekstra on Guitar #1 a few times. He nails the opening guitar solo.

Best In-House Parody Lyrics: There are too

many to count, especially after running for five years. But I think a cast favorite is Joey Calveri's alternate lyrics to Carly Rae Jepsen's "Call Me Maybe": "And all the other boys/ Try to chaaaaase me/But they can't catch me/Cuz I'm too fast!!"

Memorable Directorial Note: "Too much tongue" is one we've gotten a few times. Also: "You could work the pole a bit more?"

Nicknames: Tony LePage: Tones. Tessa Alves: Bepsa Check. Cassie Silva: Cweetsie. Josephine Rose Roberts: Josey. Cody Scott Lancaster: Codes.

Embarrassing Moments: During "Harden My Heart"/"Shadows of the Night," Josey Roberts had some toilet paper hanging out of her tights. Classic.

"Carols for a Cure" Carol: This year was "O Holy Night" with Teresa Stanley bringing us to church on lead vocal.

"Gypsy of the Year" Skit and Who Wrote It: "*RoA* in Three Minutes." Tony LePage had the realization that every single song in our show could be sung to the music of "Don't Stop Believin'," so he composed it and we sang the whole show in three minutes.

1. Kate Rockwell and Aaron C. Finley celebrating five years and 2,000 performances of *Rock of Ages* on Broadway.
2. The *Rock of Ages* cast take part in Super Bowl XLVIII week with a performance on Super Bowl Boulevard (a.k.a. Broadway) in NYC.
3. Then, it's off to MetLife Stadium in New Jersey to continue the party.

Rocky

First Preview: February 13, 2014. Opened: March 13, 2014.
Still running as of May 31, 2014.

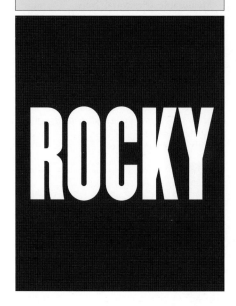

This new musical is based on the Oscar-winning 1976 film about a Philadelphia boxer nearing the end of an undistinguished career who, for a publicity stunt, is plucked out of obscurity and given a miraculous shot at the World Heavyweight Championship. Despite his chosen career, Rocky works out problems in his personal life with a boyish sweetness, including his romance with the nerdy girl Adrian whom he's loved since childhood. The production is notable for an Act II scenic effect in which part of the audience evacuates to the stage so the climactic slugfest can take place in a ring erected over the front section of the orchestra.

CAST

(in order of speaking)

Rocky Balboa ....ANDY KARL
Spider Rico/Boxer/
   Boom Operator ....ADAM PERRY
Announcer/Wysocki/
   Bob Dunphy ....NED EISENBERG
Fight Promoter/Apollo's Manager/
   Disc Jockey ....WALLACE SMITH
Sugar Jackson/Boxer/
   Cameraman ....JAMES BROWN III
Kid Rizzo/Boxer/
   Rocky's Cornerman ....LUIS SALGADO
Rocky's Cornerman/Gazzo/
   Tommy Crosetti ....ERIC ANDERSON
Buddy/Jimmy Michaels ....JOHN SCHIAPPA
Linda McKenna/
   Apollo Girl ....VASTHY MOMPOINT

Continued on next page

308

WINTER GARDEN

1634 Broadway

Ⓢ A Shubert Organization Theatre

Philip J. Smith, *Chairman*   **Robert E. Wankel,** *President*

Stage Entertainment USA & Sylvester Stallone
Metro-Goldwyn-Mayer
The Shubert Organization   Kevin King-Templeton
James L. Nederlander & Terry Allen Kramer   Roy Furman   Cheryl Wiesenfeld
Zane Tankel   Lucky Champions   Scott Delman   JFL Theatricals / Judith Ann Abrams
Latitude Link   Waxman / Shin / Bergère   Lauren Stevens / Josh Goodman

PRESENT

ROCKY

BOOK BY   MUSIC BY   LYRICS BY

Thomas Meehan and Sylvester Stallone   **Stephen Flaherty**   **Lynn Ahrens**

Based on the MGM / United Artists Motion Picture

STARRING

Andy Karl
Margo Seibert   **Terence Archie**

AND

Dakin Matthews   Danny Mastrogiorgio   Jennifer Mudge

WITH

Eric Anderson   Adrian Aguilar   Michelle Aravena   James Brown III   Sam J. Cahn   Vincent Corazza   Kevin Del Aguila
Ned Eisenberg   Bradley Gibson   Stacey Todd Holt   Sasha Hutchings   David Andrew Macdonald   Vasthy Mompoint
Vince Oddo   Okieriete Onaodowan   Adam Perry   Kristin Piro   Luis Salgado   John Schiappa   Samantha Shafer
Wallace Smith   Jenny Lee Stern   Dan'yelle Williamson   Mark Zimmerman

SCENIC DESIGN	COSTUME DESIGN	LIGHTING DESIGN	SOUND DESIGN
Christopher Barreca	David Zinn	Christopher Akerlind	Peter Hylenski

VIDEO DESIGN	SPECIAL EFFECTS DESIGN	WIG & MAKE-UP DESIGN	CASTING
Dan Scully Pablo N. Molina	Jeremy Chernick	Harold Mertens	Jim Carnahan, CSA Carrie Gardner, CSA

MUSIC SUPERVISOR
David Holcenberg

ORCHESTRATIONS	MUSIC DIRECTOR	VOCAL ARRANGEMENTS	MUSIC COORDINATOR
Stephen Trask Doug Besterman	Chris Fenwick	Stephen Flaherty	John Miller

PRODUCTION STAGE MANAGER	PRESS REPRESENTATIVE	ADVERTISING / MARKETING	ASSOCIATE PRODUCERS
Lisa Dawn Cave	Polk & Co.	SpotCo	Barbara Darwall Michael Hildebrandt

EXECUTIVE PRODUCERS	VP MARKETING & COMMUNICATIONS	PRODUCTION SUPERVISORS	GENERAL MANAGER
Adam Silberman Eric Cornell	Michele Groner	Jake Bell Lily Twining	Bespoke Theatricals

PRODUCERS
Joop van den Ende and Bill Taylor

CHOREOGRAPHY BY
Steven Hoggett & Kelly Devine

DIRECTED BY
Alex Timbers

World Premiere at the TUI Operettenhaus, Hamburg, Germany
The Producers wish to express their appreciation to Theatre Development Fund for its support of this production.

3/13/14

Rocky Balboa (Andy Karl) finally gets a date with his childhood crush Adrian (Margo Seibert).

Photo: Matthew Murphy

Rocky

MUSICAL NUMBERS

ACT I

"Ain't Down Yet"	Company, Fight Promoter, Gazzo, Buddy
"My Nose Ain't Broken"	Rocky Balboa
"Raining"	Adrian
"Patriotic"	Apollo Creed, Apollo's Manager, Miles Jergens, Apollo Girls, Ensemble
"My Nose Ain't Broken" (Reprise)	Rocky
"The Flip Side"	Rocky, Adrian
"Adrian"	Rocky
"Wanna Know Why"	Gazzo, Buddy, Rocky, Mickey
"Fight from the Heart"	Rocky
"One of Us"	Company

ACT II

"Training Montage 1"	Orchestra
"In the Ring"	Mickey
"Training Montage 2"	Company
"Happiness"	Rocky, Adrian
"I'm Done"	Adrian
"Southside Celebrity"	Company, Rocky, Apollo
"Adrian" (Reprise)	Adrian
"Keep on Standing"	Rocky
"Undefeated Man"	Apollo, Entourage
"The Fight"	Company

ORCHESTRA

Conductor: CHRIS FENWICK
Associate Conductor: PHILIP FORTENBERRY
Assistant Conductor: DANIEL GREEN
Guitars: ERIC J. STOCKTON, J.J. McGEEHAN, ANDREW ZINSMEISTER
Drums: WARREN ODZE
Bass: ALAN STEVENS HEWITT
Percussion: JAVIER DIAZ
Keyboards: CHRIS FENWICK, PHILIP FORTENBERRY, DANIEL GREEN
Reeds: GREG THYMIUS, MARC PHANEUF
Trumpets/Flugels: CRAIG JOHNSON, JOHN REID

Trombone/Bass Trombone: NATHAN MAYLAND
Concert Master: MARTIN AGEE
Violin: MONICA K. DAVIS
Viola: BETH MEYERS
Cello: STEPHANIE CUMMINS
Synthesizer Programmer: RANDY COHEN
Music Copyist: EMILY GRISHMAN
Music Coordinator: JOHN MILLER
Orchestration Associate: NEIL DOUGLAS REILLY
Additional Music Arrangements:
   STEPHEN FLAHERTY

(L-R) It's Apollo Creed (Terence Archie) up against Rocky Balboa (Andy Karl).

Photo: Matthew Murphy

Cast Continued

Apollo Creed	TERENCE ARCHIE
Apollo Girl/Ensemble	SASHA HUTCHINGS
Mike/Watchman/ Jack/Doctor	KEVIN DEL AGUILA
Mickey	DAKIN MATTHEWS
Dipper/Apollo's Cornerman	OKIERIETE ONAODOWAN
Boxer/Ensemble	VINCE ODDO
Adrian	MARGO SEIBERT
Gloria	JENNIFER MUDGE
Joanne/Ensemble	JENNY LEE STERN
Angie/Ensemble	MICHELLE ARAVENA
Paulie	DANNY MASTROGIORGIO
Miles Jergens/ Ensemble	DAVID ANDREW MACDONALD
Reporter/Boxer	ADRIAN AGUILAR
Boxer/Rocky Marciano/Referee	SAM J. CAHN
Apollo Girl/Shirley	KRISTIN PIRO

UNDERSTUDIES

For Rocky:
ADRIAN AGUILAR, VINCE ODDO
For Adrian:
MICHELLE ARAVENA, SAMANTHA SHAFER
For Apollo Creed:
BRADLEY GIBSON, OKIERIETE ONAODOWAN
For Mickey:
NED EISENBERG, MARK ZIMMERMAN
For Paulie:
STACEY TODD HOLT, JOHN SCHIAPPA
For Gloria:
KRISTIN PIRO, JENNY LEE STERN

SWINGS

VINCENT CORAZZA, BRADLEY GIBSON, STACEY TODD HOLT, SAMANTHA SHAFER, DAN'YELLE WILLIAMSON, MARK ZIMMERMAN

Newscaster: JONATHAN WALKER
Frank Carazza: VINCENT CORAZZA

DANCE CAPTAIN

JAMES BROWN III

FIGHT CAPTAIN

VINCE ODDO

PLACE

Philadelphia

TIME

1975

Rocky

Andy Karl
Rocky Balboa

Margo Seibert
Adrian

Terence Archie
Apollo Creed

Dakin Matthews
Mickey

Danny Mastrogiorgio
Paulie

Jennifer Mudge
Gloria

Adrian Aguilar
Reporter

Eric Anderson
Gazzo

Michelle Aravena
Angie

James Brown III
Sugar Jackson

Sam J. Cahn
Rocky Marciano

Vincent Corazza
Swing

Kevin Del Aguila
Mike

Ned Eisenberg
Wysocki

Bradley Gibson
Swing

Stacey Todd Holt
Swing

Sasha Hutchings
Apollo Girl

David Andrew
Macdonald
Miles Jergens

Vasthy Mompoint
Linda McKenna

Vince Oddo
Boxer

Okieriete
Onaodowan
Dipper Riley

Adam Perry
Spider Rico

Kristin Piro
Shirley

Luis Salgado
Kid Rizzo

John Schiappa
Buddy

Samantha Shafer
Swing

Wallace Smith
Apollo's Manager

Jenny Lee Stern
Joanne

Jonathan Walker
Newscaster

Dan'yelle Williamson
Swing

Mark Zimmerman
Swing

Sylvester Stallone
Book and Producer

Thomas Meehan
Book

Lynn Ahrens
Lyricist

Stephen Flaherty
*Composer/Vocal
Arrangements*

Rocky

Alex Timbers
Director

Steven Hoggett
Choreography

Kelly Devine
Choreography

Chris Barreca
Set Design

David Zinn
Costume Design

Christopher Akerlind
Lighting Design

Peter Hylenski
Sound Design

Dan Scully
Video Design

Pablo N. Molina
Video Design

Jeremy Chernick
*Special Effects
Design*

Harold Mertens
*Wig and Make-up
Design*

Kathy Fabian
Props Supervisor

Jim Carnahan
Casting

Carrie Gardner
Casting

David Holcenberg
Music Supervisor

Stephen Trask
Orchestrations

Doug Besterman
Orchestrations

Neil Douglas Reilly
*Orchestration
Associate*

John Miller
Music Coordinator

Jake Bell
Technical Supervisor

Devin Keudell
*Bespoke Theatricals
General
Management*

Amy Jacobs
*Bespoke Theatricals
General
Management*

Maggie Brohn
*Bespoke Theatricals
General
Management*

Nina Lannan
*Bespoke Theatricals
General
Management*

Kate Wilson
Dialect Coach

Lisa Dawn Cave
*Production Stage
Manager*

Charles Underhill
Stage Manager

Ian Unterman
Associate Director

Marcos Santana
*Associate
Choreographer*

Patrick McCollum
*Associate Fight
Choreographer*

Bill Taylor
*Stage Entertainment
USA
Producer*

Joop van den Ende
Producer

Philip J. Smith
*The Shubert
Organization
Producer*

Robert E. Wankel
*The Shubert
Organization
Producer*

James L. Nederlander
Producer

Rocky

Terry Allen Kramer
Producer

Roy Furman
Producer

Cheryl Wiesenfeld
Producer

Mary Beth O'Connor
Lucky Champions
Producer

Lou Spisto
Lucky Champions
Producer

Jim Kierstead
Lucky Champions
Producer

Wendy Federman
Lucky Champions
Producer

Carl Moellenberg
Lucky Champions
Producer

Scott M. Delman
Producer

Adam Blanshay
Just for Laughs
Theatricals
Producer

Gilbert Rozon
Just for Laughs
Theatricals
Producer

Judith Ann Abrams
Producer

Ralph Bryan
Latitude Link
Producer

Anita Waxman
Producer

Chunsoo Shin
Producer

Jane Bergère
Producer

Lauren Stevens
Producer

Joshua Goodman
Producer

Uschi Neuss
Stage Entertainment
GmbH
Original Production

Ulf Maschek
Stage Entertainment
GmbH
Original Production

Adam Silberman
Executive Producer

Photo: Brian Mapp

CREW
Front (L-R): Nick Irons, Phil Vetro, Christina Vargas, Brooke Rowzee, Abby Rowzee, Jennifer Brauer, Michael Cleary, Dennis Marion, Donnie Wright, Jeff Goodman, Dennis Wiener
Second Row (L-R): Bea Brauer, Gabby Hurley, Paris Nesbit, Denise DeMirjian, Craig Dawson, Mike Lanza, Renee Borys (Dresser), Michael Huller, Julio Lugo, Geoffrey Polischuk (Dresser), Ivan Lugo, Mai-Linh Stuhlbarg, Sabiel Almonte, Frank Lofgren, Glenn Russo
Third Row (L-R): Karen Zitnick, Reggie Carter, Kevin Bertolacci (Assistant Stage Manager), Kate Egan (Company Manager), Anna Perdita (Dresser), Samantha Lawrence (Dresser), Scott Harrington (Dresser), Moira Conrad (Wardrobe Supervisor), Chad Hewlitt, Richie Kirby
Fourth Row (L-R): Dave Brown, Kelly Stillwell (Assistant Stage Manager), Adam Jackson (Assoc. Company Manager), Rick Caroto, Victoria Tinsman (Hair Assistant), Brendan Whalen, Christen Edwards (Hair Assistant), Chris Lavin (Dresser), Dave Levenberg, Laura Ellington (Dresser), Keith Shaw (Dresser), Lonnie Goertz (Head Properties), Daniel Hochstine (Head Sound), John Maloney
Back Row (L-R): McBrien Dunbar (Head Carpenter), Joe Ianello, Chad Harlow (Hair Assistant), Charlie Hackett, Spencer Bell (Assistant Properties), Jeff Hahn, Robert Bass (Front of House Sound), Tommy Obermier

Rocky

Rocky
SCRAPBOOK

Photo: Courtesy of Eric Anderson

Correspondent: Eric Anderson "Gazzo"

Opening Night Party: Party at Roseland, complete with boxing ring photo-ops, cheesesteaks and "the steps."

Best Gifts: Dakin Matthews individually glued and painted model figurines of the entire cast of *Rocky*, swings included. Andy Karl received a meat piñata from the cast of *Jersey Boys*.

Most Exciting Celebrity Visitors: At the first preview, Tom Hanks started the crowd to chant, "Rock-y! Rock-y!" when Sylvester Stallone came into the ring at the end of the curtain call. Paul Rudd who was also there that night, later praised the show in depth to Fallon on "The Tonight Show." Will Smith literally said, "That's the most exciting time I've had at the theatre."

on three" circle. There are also lots of fist bumps, high fives backstage throughout the run.

Unique Pre-Show Announcement During Previews: "...because we're using a generator outside, the set can get a little grumpy."—Ian Unterman, associate director.

Memorable Ad-Libs During Previews: "Nothing works around here."—Andy Karl as Rocky—after the show stopped twice and he couldn't get the lock open on his locker. "Forgive the appearance of our office. We're remodeling."—David Macdonald as Mr. Jergens—after the house was held because the Jergens office couldn't come on stage.

Photo: Joseph Marzullo

Photo: Joseph Marzullo

could gauge the temperature of the audience before he hit the stage.

Coolest Thing About Being in This Show: "One day in rehearsal, I looked around the room and realized that I was working with a group of people who are the absolutely best at their jobs. I felt exhilarated and challenged. I am so proud to be a part of this company. And our collective desire to give this story away every night with integrity, is the COOLEST thing about being a part of *Rocky*!"—Margo Seibert

Other Memory: In the final week before previews, Alex Timbers rented a waffle truck, "Wafels and Dinges," for the entire cast and crew one night during dinner break.

Photo: Courtesy of Eric Anderson

Favorite In-Theatre Gathering Place: Female—Angie and Joanne's dressing room. Male—ensemble dressing room (halftime).

Actor Who Performs the Most Roles in This Show: I think I do. I play: Rocky's cornerman; Gazzo; Gym coach; "Raining" passerby; Rocky double; and Tommy Crosetti. Six roles; 10 changes.

Special Backstage Rituals: Before the show there are two circle-ups that happen upstage center in front of the ring. An inspirational circle-up, ending with an eyes closed, shouted, "HEY-OH...BOOM!," and directly afterwards, a "say the first thing that comes to your mind,

Favorite Moment During Each Performance: Riding the ring. And being at the Winter Garden. It was fun to think that I was making an entrance descending from Grizabella's Heavyside Layer every night (*Cats*).

Favorite Off-Site Hangout: Emmett O'Lunney's Irish Pub.

Favorite Snack Foods: Peanut butter pretzels, doughnuts, Girl Scout cookies and Scotch (after the show).

Favorite Therapy: Any PT toy that is invented—rollers, Thera bands, lacrosse balls, tennis balls...

Mascot: The turtles, Cuff & Link.

Favorite Show Catchphrases: "Boom." "You're bleeding, INSIDE!" "We're cluuuosed!"

Best In-House Parody Lyrics: "You wanna skate, I'm gonna f**k ya."

Fastest Costume Change: "Eye of the Tiger." Any of us into Rocky Double.

Who Wore the Heaviest/Hottest Costume?: Ned Eisenberg's Southside Celebrity Arctic wear.

Who Wore the Least?: The ring girls. And James Brown III in those tight blue shorts.

Superstitions That Turned Out to Be True: Al Jolson used the stage right quick change room, commonly referred to as "The Jolson Hole," as his dressing room, complete with a peephole installed that looked into the house so that he

1. *Yearbook* correspondent Eric Anderson, as an announcer, with Margo Seibert (Adrian) on opening night.
2. (L-R): The original Rocky, Sylvester Stallone, with Margo Seibert and Andy Karl (Rocky) at curtain call on opening night at the Winter Garden Theatre.
3. Also on opening night, Andy Karl tosses his towel (not to be confused with throwing in the towel!) into the audience—a nightly ritual.
4. Andy Karl with his opening night gift from the cast of *Jersey Boys*... a meat piñata!
5. Opening night gifts from Dakin Matthews (Mickey): handmade models of the cast.

Rodgers + Hammerstein's Cinderella

First Preview: January 25, 2013. Opened: March 3, 2013.
Still running as of May 31, 2014.

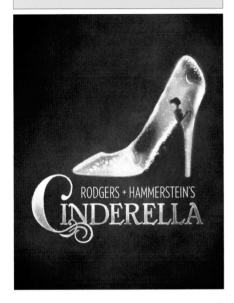

PLAYBILL

Originally written as a 1957 television special, this musical adaptation of the classic Grimm Brothers fairytale retells the story of a young woman's unhappy life with her evil stepmother and stepsisters, and how, with the help of a fairy godmother, she attends a dress ball at a palace where she meets a handsome prince who falls in love with her. For Broadway the show got a new libretto by Douglas Carter Beane with many innovative plot twists, magical costumes by William Ivey Long, and several Rodgers and Hammerstein trunk songs to beef up the score.

CAST OF CHARACTERS

(in order of appearance)

Ella .... CARLY RAE JEPSEN
Ella (Wed. mat. & Sat. eve.) .... ALESSA NEECK
Woodland Creature .... PETER NELSON
Topher .... JOE CARROLL
Lord Pinkleton .... PHUMZILE SOJOLA
Sebastian .... PETER BARTLETT
Marie .... VICTORIA CLARK
Jean-Michel .... TODD BUONOPANE
Madame .... FRAN DRESCHER
Gabrielle .... STEPHANIE GIBSON
Charlotte .... ANN HARADA
Fox .... JESSICA HERSHBERG, LAURA IRION
Raccoon .... LAURA IRION, CODY WILLIAMS
Footman .... ANDY MILLS
Driver .... CODY WILLIAMS
Lady of Ridicule .... JILL ABRAMOVITZ
Knights, Townspeople, Lords & Ladies of the Court,
Peasants .... JILL ABRAMOVITZ,
KRISTINE BENDUL, SHONICA GOODEN,

Continued on next page

⑤ BROADWAY THEATRE

1681 Broadway
A Shubert Organization Theatre

Philip J. Smith, *Chairman*   **Robert E. Wankel,** *President*

ROBYN GOODMAN   JILL FURMAN   STEPHEN KOCIS

EDWARD WALSON   VENETIAN GLASS PRODUCTIONS   THE ARACA GROUP
LUIGI CAIOLA & ROSE CAIOLA   ROY FURMAN   WALT GROSSMAN
PETER MAY/SANFORD ROBERTSON   GLASS SLIPPER PRODUCTIONS LLC/ERIC SCHMIDT
TED LIEBOWITZ/JAMES SPRY   BLANKET FORT PRODUCTIONS
IN ASSOCIATION WITH
CENTER THEATRE GROUP

PRESENT

RODGERS + HAMMERSTEIN'S CINDERELLA

MUSIC BY RICHARD RODGERS
LYRICS BY OSCAR HAMMERSTEIN II
NEW BOOK BY DOUGLAS CARTER BEANE
ORIGINAL BOOK BY OSCAR HAMMERSTEIN II

STARRING

CARLY RAE JEPSEN
FRAN DRESCHER

JOE CARROLL   PETER BARTLETT   TODD BUONOPANE
STEPHANIE GIBSON   ANN HARADA   PHUMZILE SOJOLA

AND

VICTORIA CLARK

JILL ABRAMOVITZ   KRISTINE BENDUL   CALLAN BERGMANN   LESLIE DONNA FLESNER
SHONICA GOODEN   KENDAL HARTSE   ROBERT HARTWELL   JESSICA HERSHBERG
LAURA IRION   BRANDON LEFFLER   SAM LIPS   NATHAN LUCREZIO
ANDY MILLS   SHINA ANN MORRIS   LINDA MUGLESTON   ALESSA NEECK   PETER NELSON
JEFF PEW   KIRSTIN TUCKER   CODY WILLIAMS   BRANCH WOODMAN

SCENIC DESIGN	COSTUME DESIGN	LIGHTING DESIGN	SOUND DESIGN
ANNA LOUIZOS	WILLIAM IVEY LONG	KENNETH POSNER	NEVIN STEINBERG

HAIR AND WIG DESIGN	MUSIC DIRECTOR AND CONDUCTOR	MUSIC COORDINATOR	PRODUCTION STAGE MANAGER
PAUL HUNTLEY	ANDY EINHORN	HOWARD JOINES	IRA MONT

CASTING	TECHNICAL SUPERVISION	FIGHT DIRECTOR	ASSOCIATE DIRECTOR	ASSOCIATE CHOREOGRAPHER
CINDY TOLAN ADAM CALDWELL	HUDSON THEATRICAL ASSOCIATES	THOMAS SCHALL	GINA RATTAN	LEE WILKINS

ASSOCIATE PRODUCER	PRESS REPRESENTATIVE	COMPANY MANAGER	GENERAL MANAGEMENT
CHARLES SALAMENO	SAM RUDY MEDIA RELATIONS	BRIG BERNEY	RICHARDS/CLIMAN, INC.

ORCHESTRATIONS
DANNY TROOB

MUSIC ADAPTATION, SUPERVISION AND ARRANGEMENTS
DAVID CHASE

CHOREOGRAPHED BY
JOSH RHODES

DIRECTED BY
MARK BROKAW

THE PRODUCERS WISH TO EXPRESS THEIR APPRECIATION TO THE THEATRE DEVELOPMENT FUND FOR ITS SUPPORT OF THIS PRODUCTION
PRODUCED BY ARRANGEMENT WITH RODGERS & HAMMERSTEIN: AN IMAGEM COMPANY
ORIGINAL BROADWAY CAST RECORDING ON GHOSTLIGHT RECORDS

2/3/14

Standing (L-R):
Fran Drescher,
Carly Rae Jepsen,
Stephanie Gibson.
Seated: Ann Harada

Photo: Carol Rosegg

Rodgers + Hammerstein's Cinderella

MUSICAL NUMBERS

ACT I

Overture	Orchestra

Prologue

Rocky Glen

"Me, Who Am I?" .... Topher, Sebastian, Lord Pinkleton, Knights, Pages

Outside the Cottage

"In My Own Little Corner" .... Ella

Throne Room of the Royal Palace

Town Square

"Now Is the Time" .... Jean-Michel

"The Prince Is Giving a Ball" .... Lord Pinkleton, Townspeople, Madame, Charlotte, Gabrielle, Ella, Marie

Inside the Cottage

"Cinderella March" .... Orchestra

Outside the Cottage

"In My Own Little Corner (Reprise)/Fol-De-Rol" .... Ella, Marie

"Impossible" .... Marie, Ella

Flight to the Castle

"It's Possible" .... Marie, Ella

Ballroom

"Gavotte" .... Sebastian, Topher, Lord Pinkleton, Madame, Charlotte, Gabrielle, Lords & Ladies of the Court

"Ten Minutes Ago" .... Topher, Ella

"Cinderella Waltz" .... Orchestra

"Ten Minutes Ago" (Reprise) .... Topher, Ella, Lords & Ladies of the Court

Palace Steps

ACT II

Entr'acte .... Orchestra

Palace Steps

"Stepsister's Lament" .... Charlotte, Ladies of the Court

Forest

"The Pursuit" .... Topher, Lord Pinkleton, Lords of the Court, Pages, Ella, Footman, Driver

Inside the Cottage

"When You're Driving Through the Moonlight" .... Ella, Madame, Charlotte, Gabrielle

"A Lovely Night" .... Ella, Madame, Charlotte, Gabrielle

"A Lovely Night" (Reprise) .... Ella, Gabrielle

Forest

"Loneliness of Evening" .... Topher, Ella

Throughout the Kingdom

"The Prince Is Giving a Ball" (Reprise) .... Sebastian, Lord Pinkleton, Heralds, Madame

Inside the Cottage

"There's Music in You" .... Marie

Palace Steps

"Now Is the Time" (Reprise) .... Jean-Michel, Gabrielle

"Do I Love You Because You're Beautiful?" .... Topher, Ella

Palace

"Ten Minutes Ago" (Reprise) .... Topher, Ella, The Company

Royal Gardens

"Finale" .... Marie, The Company

Cast Continued

KENDAL HARTSE, ROBERT HARTWELL, JESSICA HERSHBERG, LAURA IRION, SAM LIPS, NATHAN LUCREZIO, ANDY MILLS, LINDA MUGLESTON, PETER NELSON, JEFF PEW, CODY WILLIAMS, BRANCH WOODMAN

SWINGS
CALLAN BERGMANN,
LESLIE DONNA FLESNER,
BRANDON LEFFLER,
SHINA ANN MORRIS, ALESSA NEECK,
KIRSTIN TUCKER

DANCE CAPTAIN
KIRSTIN TUCKER

ASSISTANT DANCE CAPTAIN
BRANDON LEFFLER

UNDERSTUDIES
For Ella: JESSICA HERSHBERG,
ALESSA NEECK
For Woodland Creature: CALLAN BERGMANN,
BRANDON LEFFLER, NATHAN LUCREZIO
For Topher: SAM LIPS, JEFF PEW,
CODY WILLIAMS
For Lord Pinkleton: NATHAN LUCREZIO,
BRANCH WOODMAN
For Sebastian: PHUMZILE SOJOLA,
BRANCH WOODMAN
For Marie and Madame: JILL ABRAMOVITZ,
LINDA MUGLESTON
For Jean-Michel: NATHAN LUCREZIO,
CODY WILLIAMS
For Gabrielle: KENDAL HARTSE
For Charlotte: KENDAL HARTSE,
LAURA IRION
For Fox: LESLIE DONNA FLESNER,
SHINA ANN MORRIS, ALESSA NEECK,
KIRSTIN TUCKER
For Raccoon: CALLAN BERGMANN,
BRANDON LEFFLER,
SHINA ANN MORRIS, ALESSA NEECK,
KIRSTIN TUCKER
For Footman and Driver: CALLAN BERGMANN,
BRANDON LEFFLER
For Lady of Ridicule: LESLIE DONNA FLESNER,
SHINA ANN MORRIS, ALESSA NEECK,
KIRSTIN TUCKER

"Ten minutes ago I saw you"

Rodgers + Hammerstein's Cinderella

ORCHESTRA

Music Supervisor: DAVID CHASE
Music Director/Conductor: ANDY EINHORN
Associate Conductor/Keyboard: MATT PERRI
Piccolo/Flute/Alto Flute: KATHERINE FINK
Oboe/English Horn: LYNNE COHEN
Clarinet/E-flat Clarinet/Bass Clarinet: JONATHAN LEVINE
Bassoon/Flute/Clarinet: DANIEL SULLIVAN
French Horns: ADAM KRAUTHAMER, AARON KORN
Trumpet 1/Flugelhorn/Piccolo Trumpet: DOMINIC DERASSE
Trumpet/Flugelhorn: GARETH FLOWERS
Trombone/Bass Trombone: JOHN ALLRED
Percussion: BILL HAYES
Drums: RICH ROSENZWEIG
Harp: SUSAN JOLLES
Violin/Concertmaster: EMILY BRUSKIN YARBROUGH
Violins: LISA MATRICARDI, MAXIM MOSTON,
     MINEKO YAJIMA
Viola: JJ JOHNSON
Cello: SARAH SEIVER
Bass: MARK VANDERPOEL

Music Copying: Anixter Rice Music Service/RUSSELL ANIXTER
     and DONALD RICE

Synthesizer Programming: JEFF MARDER
Music Assistant: BRENDAN WHITING
Music Coordinator: HOWARD JOINES
Additional Orchestrations by BILL ELLIOTT,
     DOUG BESTERMAN and LARRY HOCHMAN

Additional lyrics by DOUGLAS CARTER BEANE
     and DAVID CHASE

Carly Rae Jepsen
Ella

Fran Drescher
Madame

Victoria Clark
Marie

Joe Carroll
Topher

Peter Bartlett
Sebastian

Todd Buonopane
Jean-Michel

Stephanie Gibson
Gabrielle

Ann Harada
Charlotte

Phumzile Sojola
*Lord Pinkleton;
u/s Sebastian*

Jill Abramovitz
*Lady of Ridicule,
Ensemble; u/s Marie,
Madame*

Kristine Bendul
*Ensemble/Assistant
Choreographer*

Callan Bergmann
Swing

Leslie Donna Flesner
Swing

Shonica Gooden
Ensemble

Kendal Hartse
*Ensemble;
u/s Gabrielle,
Charlotte*

Robert Hartwell
Ensemble

Jessica Hershberg
*Fox, Ensemble;
u/s Ella*

Laura Irion
*Raccoon, Fox,
Ensemble; u/s
Charlotte*

Brandon Leffler
*Swing/Assistant
Dance Captain*

Sam Lips
*Ensemble;
u/s Topher*

Nathan Lucrezio
*Ensemble;
u/s Jean-Michel,
Lord Pinkleton*

Andy Mills
Footman, Ensemble

Shina Ann Morris
Swing

Linda Mugleston
*Ensemble; u/s Marie,
Madame*

Alessa Neeck
Swing; u/s Ella

Peter Nelson
*Woodland Creature,
Ensemble*

Rodgers + Hammerstein's Cinderella

Jeff Pew
*Ensemble;
u/s Topher*

Kirstin Tucker
*Swing/Dance
Captain*

Cody Williams
*Raccoon, Driver,
Ensemble; u/s
Topher, Jean-Michel*

Branch Woodman
*Ensemble; u/s Lord
Pinkleton, Sebastian*

Richard Rodgers & Oscar Hammerstein II
Music, Lyrics, Original Book

Douglas Carter
Beane
New Book

Mark Brokaw
Director

Josh Rhodes
Choreographer

Anna Louizos
Scenic Design

William Ivey Long
Costume Design

Kenneth Posner
Lighting Design

Nevin Steinberg
Sound Design

Paul Huntley
Hair/Wig Design

David Chase
*Musical Supervisor/
Arranger*

Danny Troob
Orchestrations

Andy Einhorn
*Music Director/
Conductor*

Howard Joines
Music Coordinator

Thomas Schall
Fight Director

Gina Rattan
Associate Director

Lee Wilkins
*Associate
Choreographer*

Neil A. Mazzella
Hudson Theatrical
Associates
Technical Supervisor

Brig Berney
Company Manager

David R. Richards &
Tamar Haimes
Richards/Climan, Inc.
General Manager

Robyn Goodman
*Producer/
Aged In Wood*

Jill Furman
Producer

Stephen Kocis
Producer

Carl Moellenberg
Venetian Glass
Productions
Producer

Wendy Federman
Venetian Glass
Productions
Producer

Sharon A. Carr
Venetian Glass
Productions
Producer

Ricardo Hornos
Venetian Glass
Productions
Producer

Jamie deRoy
Venetian Glass
Productions
Producer

Richard Winkler
Venetian Glass
Productions
Producer

Van Dean
Venetian Glass
Productions
Producer

Kenny Howard
Venetian Glass
Productions
Producer

Rodgers + Hammerstein's Cinderella

Michael Filerman
Venetian Glass
Productions
Producer

Dan Frishwasser
Venetian Glass
Productions
Producer

(L-R): Stephanie Gibson, Fran Drescher and Ann Harada

Photo: Carol Rosegg

Michael Rego, Hank Unger, Matthew Rego
The Araca Group
Producer

Luigi Caiola and Rose Caiola
Producers

Roy Furman
Producer

Walt Grossman
Producer

Peter May
Producer

Michael Ritchie
Artistic Director
Center Theatre
Group
Producer

Edward L. Rada
Managing Director
Center Theatre
Group
Producer

Douglas C. Baker
Producing Director
Center Theatre
Group
Producer

CINDERELLA
2013 • 2014
ALUMNI

Paige Faure
Ensemble;
u/s Charlotte

Santino Fontana
Topher

Heidi Giberson
Fox, Ensemble;
u/s Ella

Harriet Harris
Madame

Greg Hildreth
Jean-Michel

Dan Horn
Swing

Adam Jepsen
Swing

Andy Jones
Ensemble;
u/s Topher

Rebecca Luker
Marie

Marla Mindelle
Gabrielle

Laura Osnes
Ella

Nick Spangler
Ensemble;
u/s Topher

Kevin Worley
Ensemble;
u/s Jean-Michel,
Lord Pinkleton

CINDERELLA
2013 • 2014
TRANSFER
STUDENTS

Kaitlyn Davidson
Ensemble; u/s Ella,
Gabrielle

Catherine Ricafort
Ensemble

Adam Rogers
Ensemble

Rodgers + Hammerstein's Cinderella

PRODUCTION STAGE MANAGER
Ira Mont

MANAGEMENT
(L-R): Zac Chandler (Assistant Stage Manager), Amy Steinman, Holli Campbell, Brig Berney (Company Manager)

FRONT OF HOUSE
Front Row (L-R):
Isaac Trujillo,
Svetlana Pinkhaus,
William Phelan, Marisol Lugo,
Mattie Robinson

Middle Row (L-R):
Mae Park,
Lori Bukun, Ismael Tirado,
Russ Ramsey (Theatre Manager)

Back Row (L-R):
Keri Grillo,
John Hall,
Nathaniel Wright

CREW
Front Row (L-R): Dyanna Hallick, Marissa Marlborough (Dresser), Casey Cameron (Dresser), Kelly Kasper, Caitlin Johnson (Dresser)
Middle Row (L-R): Justin Rathbun (Production Sound Engineer), Mo Leshley, Nanette Golia (Wardrobe Supervisor), Rick DalCortivo, Jr., Rick DalCortivo, Sr., Laura Shrewsbury, David Mitchell
Standing (L-R): Declan McNeil, Peter McNeil, Bob Beimers, Jeff Brewer (Head Electrician), Eric Castaldo (Assistant Properties), Pete Drummond (Head Properties), Jim Ernest, Jaymes Gill (Dresser), Chris Gossard, Herb Ouellette (Dresser), Scott Silvian (Assistant Sound)

Rodgers + Hammerstein's Cinderella

Rodgers + Hammerstein's Cinderella
SCRAPBOOK

Correspondent: Cody Williams, "Raccoon," "Driver," "Ensemble"; u/s "Topher," "Jean-Michel"

Memorable Note, Fax or Fan Letter: Douglas Carter Beane's daughter Gabby drew me a wonderful picture of a raccoon.

Most Exciting Celebrity Visitor and What They Did/Said: I was thrilled to have the entire Robertson Family from "Duck Dynasty"

at our show! About a week later, *GQ* wrote its infamous article about that show.

Actor Who Performed the Most Roles in This Show: I think this would have to be the delightful Alessa Neeck who has performed all eight female ensemble tracks AND Cinderella.

Who Has Done the Most Performances of This Show: Peter Bartlett and myself are tied for the most performances in 2013 with 375 each.

Special Backstage Rituals: There are so many! A few of my favorites include: the hip-hop dance to "What's a Matter With the Man?"; Laura Osnes exiting the stage with a cartwheel during "Loneliness of Evening"; Laura trying to break Andy Jones during "A Call to Arms"; having a dance duet with Ann Harada during the shoe-fitting scene; and watching Shonica Gooden and Heidi Giberson krump and freak dance as the wedding starts. (They make Phumzile Sojola laugh every time).

Favorite Moment During Each Performance: I love it whenever a small child in the audience has a big vocal reaction during a quiet moment. It makes everyone in the building smile.

Favorite In-Theatre Gathering Place: Laura Osnes' dressing room. Besides being one of the nicest people ever, she is an incredible baker with a comfortable couch.

Favorite Off-Site Hangout: Glass House Tavern. Greg Hildreth got us all down there and the risotto balls brought us all back.

Favorite Snack Foods: The Sour Patch Kids kept USR [upstage right], the dark chocolate Kit Kats in the hair room, and the Peanut Butter M&Ms in the wardrobe department.

Mascot: Willie the Raccoon

Favorite Therapy: Gotta love that sports massage. Take the pain!

"Carols for a Cure" Carol: "Happy Christmas, Little Friend."

Memorable Ad-Lib: During an early preview, Nick Spangler saved the day when the castle stairs malfunctioned. He heroically jumped over a giant gap dressed as a knight and stopped a mob of peasants by yelling, "Alright, disperse! I'm Captain Timson of the Royal Guard!"

Cell Phone Rings, Cell Phone Photos or Texting Incidents During a Performance: I'll

never forget an exchange between a rowdy audience member and our house manager. Usually Prince Topher has a line that reads "In one month (pause) let's all vote...." That particular night, it read "In one month [rowdy

1. *Yearbook* correspondent Cody Williams (R) with some of the cast of TV's "Duck Dynasty."
2. (L-R): Costumer William Ivey Long and Cody Williams at the Tony Awards.
3. (L-R): Steubuen, Prince Topher (Santino Fontana), Captain Timson, Francois.
4. (L-R): Victoria Clark and Harriet Harris at the CD signing at Barnes & Noble.
5. Also at Barnes & Noble (L-R): Ann Harada and Marla Mindelle.

audience guy: 'I'M GONNA PUNCH YOU IN THE FACE!'] let's all vote..."

Memorable Press Encounter: Ben Brantley started our review by calling me a "total studmuffin."

Fastest Costume Change: It would have to be Cinderella's change into the gold dress.

Who Wore the Heaviest/Hottest Costume?: Peter Nelson as the Woodland Creature (a.k.a. the Tree Giant).

Who Wore the Least?: I guess Andy Mills and I do. Respect the unitard or it won't respect you.

Catchphrases Only the Company Would Recognize: "It's.....!?!? IT'S?!?!?!?" "Hans, Christian, Lt. Brie reporting live...." "Duck Walk!"

Memorable Directorial Note: In the opening scene, Nick Spangler as Captain Timson would bark the order "To arms!" There once was a lot of confusion when he was reprimanded for being weird. Turns out people thought he was screaming "Two Arms!"

Nicknames: Robert Hartwell is the Muss.

Embarrassing Moment: For "The Prince Is Giving a Ball," Andy Mills enters wearing a backpack that has a bunch of different meat products hanging from it. The other day it got caught on the moving trees when he was bending over, and it pulled him to the ground. The sausage links looped over his head and caught his mouth like a bridle. Seeing him crawl onstage killed me.

Coolest Things About Being in This Show: It's a tie between listening to our 20-piece orchestra and making so many people happy.

Fan Club Information: The "Raccoders" are on Instagram and they are run by Cara Mackenzie.

Romeo and Juliet

First Preview: August 24, 2013. Opened: September 19, 2013.
Closed December 8, 2013 after 27 Previews and 93 Performances.

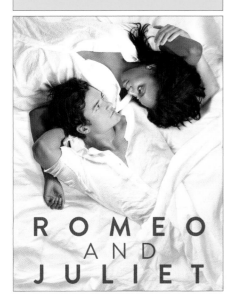

PLAYBILL®

ROMEO AND JULIET

William Shakespeare's classic tragic romance about doomed young love. In Verona the Montague and Capulet families carry on a longstanding murderous feud. But when Romeo Montague and Juliet Capulet meet by chance, they are instantly smitten. Faced with the implacable opposition of their families, they concoct a scheme to elope and escape Verona. But fate, murder and a misdelivered message lead to the untimely deaths of both lovers. This production is notable for having the Montagues played by white actors and the Capulets by African-Americans.

CAST

Romeo	ORLANDO BLOOM
Juliet	CONDOLA RASHAD
Friar Laurence	BRENT CARVER
Nurse	JAYNE HOUDYSHELL
Lord Capulet	CHUCK COOPER
Mercutio	CHRISTIAN CAMARGO
Lady Capulet	ROSLYN RUFF
Benvolio	CONRAD KEMP
Tybalt	COREY HAWKINS
Paris	JUSTIN GUARINI
Sampson	DONTÉ BONNER
Balthasar	JOE CARROLL
Citizen of Verona	DON GUILLORY
Juliet's Servant	SHERIA IRVING
Gregory	MAURICE JONES
Prince Escalus	GEOFFREY OWENS
Abraham/Apothecary	SPENCER PLACHY
Lord Montague	MICHAEL RUDKO

Continued on next page

RICHARD RODGERS THEATRE

UNDER THE DIRECTION OF JAMES M. NEDERLANDER AND JAMES L. NEDERLANDER

susan bristow llc   James L. Nederlander

Terry Allen Kramer   Merritt Forrest Baer   Paula Marie Black   Stephen C. Byrd
Alia Jones Harvey   Jon B. Platt   Stewart F. Lane/Bonnie Comley
in association with
Manny Bello   Peter May   Douglas Smith   Jonathan M. Tisch

present

ORLANDO CONDOLA
BLOOM | RASHAD

in

ROMEO AND JULIET

by

WILLIAM SHAKESPEARE

also starring

BRENT CARVER   JAYNE HOUDYSHELL   CHUCK COOPER   CHRISTIAN CAMARGO
and
ROSLYN RUFF   CONRAD KEMP   COREY HAWKINS   JUSTIN GUARINI
DONTÉ BONNER   JOE CARROLL   DON GUILLORY   SHERIA IRVING   MAURICE JONES
ERIC LOSCHEIDER   GEOFFREY OWENS   SPENCER PLACHY   MICHAEL RUDKO
TRACY SALLOWS   THOMAS SCHALL   CAROLYN MICHELLE SMITH   NANCE WILLIAMSON

scenic design	costume design	lighting design	original music & sound design
JESSE POLESHUCK	FABIO TOBLINI	DAVID WEINER	DAVID VAN TIEGHEM

hair design	movement direction	voice coach	casting director
DAVID BRIAN BROWN	NANCY BANNON	PATSY RODENBURG	JV MERCANTI

technical supervision	fight direction	associate producers	
HUDSON THEATRICAL ASSOCIATES	THOMAS SCHALL	MARVET BRITTO WILLETTE KLAUSNER
ANDREW CARLBERG DAVID & MICHELLE WILLIAMS	

press representative	production stage manager	company manager	general manager
THE HARTMAN GROUP	KRISTEN HARRIS	BOBBY DRIGGERS	101 PRODUCTIONS, LTD.

directed by

DAVID LEVEAUX

The producers wish to express their appreciation to the Theatre Development Fund for its support of this production.

9/19/13

Orlando Bloom (Romeo) and Condola Rashad (Juliet) peer into their future.

Photo: Carol Rosegg

Romeo and Juliet

Cast Continued

Lady Montague .... TRACY SALLOWS
Friar John .... THOMAS SCHALL
Prince's Attendant . CAROLYN MICHELLE SMITH
Citizen of Verona .... NANCE WILLIAMSON

MUSICIANS

Cello: TAHIRAH WHITTINGTON
Percussion: DAVID VAN TIEGHEM

UNDERSTUDIES

For Romeo/Balthasar/Abraham/Apothecary:
ERIC LOSCHEIDER
For Romeo/Benvolio/Abraham/Apothecary:
JOE CARROLL
For Juliet: SHERIA IRVING
For Friar Laurence/Lord Montague:
THOMAS SCHALL
For Nurse/Lady Montague:
NANCE WILLIAMSON
For Lord Capulet: GEOFFREY OWENS
For Mercutio/Friar John/Balthasar:
SPENCER PLACHY
For Lady Capulet:
CAROLYN MICHELLE SMITH
For Tybalt/Sampson: MAURICE JONES
For Paris/Gregory: DONTÉ BONNER
For Prince/Gregory/Sampson: DON GUILLORY

Orlando Bloom is appearing with the support of Actors' Equity Association. Conrad Kemp is appearing with the support of Actors' Equity Association pursuant to an exchange program between American Equity and UK Equity.

(L-R) Conrad Kemp (Benvolio) and Orlando Bloom (Romeo)

Photo: Carol Rosegg

Orlando Bloom
Romeo

Condola Rashad
Juliet

Brent Carver
Friar Laurence

Jayne Houdyshell
Nurse

Chuck Cooper
Lord Capulet

Christian Camargo
Mercutio

Roslyn Ruff
Lady Capulet

Conrad Kemp
Benvolio

Corey Hawkins
Tybalt

Justin Guarini
Paris

Donté Bonner
Sampson

Joe Carroll
Balthasar

Don Guillory
Citzen of Verona

Sheria Irving
Juliet's Servant

Maurice Jones
Gregory

Eric Loscheider
*u/s Romeo/
Balthasar/Abraham/
Apothecary*

Geoffrey Owens
Prince Escalus

Spencer Plachy
*Abraham/
Apothecary*

Romeo and Juliet

Michael Rudko
Lord Montague

Tracy Sallows
Lady Montague

Thomas Schall
*Friar John/
Fight Director*

Carolyn Michelle
Smith
Prince's Attendant

Nance Williamson
Citizen of Verona

William Shakespeare
Playwright

David Leveaux
Director

Jesse Poleshuck
Scenic Design

Fabio Toblini
Costume Design

David Weiner
Lighting Design

David Van Tieghem
*Original Music &
Sound Design*

David Brian Brown
Hair/Wig Design

JV Mercanti
*Casting/Associate
Director*

Patsy Rodenburg
Voice Coach

Elliot Zimet
Bird Training

Wendy Orshan
*101 Productions
General Manager*

James L.
Nederlander
Producer

Terry Allen Kramer
Producer

Paula Marie Black
Producer

Stephen C. Byrd
Producer

Alia Jones Harvey
Producer

Jon B. Platt
Producer

Stewart F. Lane/Bonnie Comley
Producer

Manny Bello
Producer

Peter May
Producer

Jonathan M. Tisch
Producer

Photo: Brian Mapp

FRONT OF HOUSE
Bottom Right (L-R):
Frank Holmes, Barbara Rodell
First Row (L-R):
Rosanne Kelly, Destiny Bivona,
Timothy Pettolina
(House Manager)
Second Row (L-R):
Brenda Schwarz, Russell Earle
Third Row (L-R):
Giovanny Lopez, Lori Miata,
Maureen Gonzalez
Top (L-R): Beverly Thornton,
Dorothy Darby

Romeo and Juliet

CREW

Front Row (L-R): Alex Rozansky, Susan Cook (Dresser), Paul Ludick (Dresser), Rick Caroto (Hair Supervisor), Robert Guy (Wardrobe Supervisor), Steve Carver (Electrician), Norm Ballard

Second Row (L-R): Suzanne Delahunt (Dresser), Sandy Binion (Orlando Bloom's Dresser), Chad Heulitt (Production Automation), Darin Stillman (Production Sound)

Third Row (L-R): Ronald Knox, Kevin Camus (Carpenter), Stephen DeVerna (Popertymaster), Larry Jennino, Eric Loscheider (Understudy), Justin Freeman (Production Electrician)

Back Row (L-R): Kristen Harris (Production Stage Manager), Tim Rossi, Brian Rizzo, Robert Witherow (Stage Manager)

STAFF FOR *ROMEO AND JULIET*

GENERAL MANAGEMENT
101 PRODUCTIONS, LTD.
Wendy Orshan   Jeffrey M. Wilson
Elie Landau   Ron Gubin   Chris Morey

COMPANY MANAGER
Bobby Driggers

GENERAL PRESS REPRESENTATIVE
THE HARTMAN GROUP
Michael Hartman   Whitney Holden Gore
Nicole Capatasto

TECHNICAL SUPERVISOR
HUDSON THEATRICAL ASSOCIATES
Sam Ellis

Production Stage Manager ....Kristen Harris
Stage Manager ....Robert Witherow
Associate Director ....JV Mercanti
Fight Captain ....Thomas Schall
Associate Scenic Designer ....Frank McCullough
Assistant Scenic Designers.................Lauren Alvarez,
  Jerome Martin, Veronica Spink
Assistant Costume Designer ....Holly Cain
Associate Lighting Designer......................Rob Ross
Assistant Lighting Designer..................David Sexton
Associate Sound Designer ....David Sanderson
Birds by ....Elliot Zimet
Assistant Hair Designer.........................Troy Beard
Production Carpenter ....Chris Kluth
Production Electrician ....Justin Freeman
Production Props ....Denise Grillo
Production Sound ....Darin Stillman
Production Automation ....Chad Heulitt
Moving Light Programmer ....Alex Fogel

Wardrobe Supervisor ....Robert Guy
Mr. Bloom's Dresser ....Sandy Binion
Dressers.................Suzanne Delahunt, Sara Darneille,
  Susan Cook, Paul Ludick
Hair Supervisor.................................Rick Caroto
Rehearsal Coach ....Danny Merritt
Production Assistants ....Luke Anderson,
  Elizabeth Goodman, Kelly Stillwell
Costume Shopper ....Nicole Delhomme
Assistant to Producer ....Elizabeth Auwaerter
Assistant to Mr. Lane ....Alyssa Renzi
Assistant to the General Managers ....Michael Rudd
Assistant to the Company Manager..........Richard Jones
101 Productions, Ltd. Staff.....................Beth Blitzer,
  Mark Gagliardi, Kathy Kim, Steve Supeck
101 Productions, Ltd. Interns ....Justin Coffman,
  Lionel Christian, Benjamin Lowy
Casting Assistant ....Felicia Rudolph
Legal Counsel ....Levine, Plotkin and Menin, LLP/
  Loren Plotkin, Daniel Watkins
Immigration Lawyer ....David King/
  Entertainment Visa Consultants
Accounting ....Marks, Paneth & Shron LLP/
  Christopher Cacace, Jana Jevnikar
Advertising ....Serino/Coyne
Banking ....Christina Ciniglio/Chase
Insurance ....DeWitt Stern
Merchandising ....Creative Goods
Payroll Services ....Castellana Services Inc.
Theatre Displays ....King Displays

MOTORCYCLE DESIGN
Shinya Kimura/Chabott Engineering.

CREDITS AND SPECIAL THANKS
Scenery and automation by Hudson Scenic, Inc. Lighting by Hudson Sound and Light LLC. Sound by Masque Sound. Costumes by Jennifer Love Costumes; Eric Winterling Inc.;

Carelli Costumes, Inc.; Jeff Fender Studios; Barbara Shaum Leather; Amy Ross. Select props by Gerard Studios, John Creech Design and Production. Special effects by Jauchem & Meeh Inc. Special thanks to Atelier New York, Cydwoq New York, Arai Helmets, the Scott Bodenner Studio, Manhattan Wardrobe Supply, Michael Golan, Bra*Tenders for hosiery and undergarments and to the Frye Company for footwear. Makeup provided by M•A•C. Denim provided by Ralph Lauren.

To learn more about the production, please visit
www.romeoandjulietbroadway.com

Chairman	**James M. Nederlander**
President	**James L. Nederlander**

Executive Vice President
Nick Scandalios

Vice President	Senior Vice President
Corporate Development	Labor Relations
Charlene S. Nederlander	**Herschel Waxman**

Vice President	Chief Financial Officer
Jim Boese	**Freida Sawyer Belviso**

HOUSE STAFF FOR
THE RICHARD RODGERS THEATRE
House Manager ....Timothy Pettolina
Box Office Treasurer ....Fred Santore Jr.
Assistant Treasurer ....Corinne Russ
Electrician ....Steve Carver
Carpenter ....Kevin Camus
Propertymaster ....Stephen F. DeVerna
Engineer ....Sean Quinn

Romeo and Juliet

SCRAPBOOK

Correspondent: Conrad Kemp, "Benvolio"

Memorable Note, Fax or Fan Letter: Joan Rivers' "I'll be your Juliet..." Correspondence ongoing. No confirmation of her being cast just yet.

Opening Night Party and/or Gifts: Condoms (one each) from 'The Slightly Slutty Citizen of Verona'. She got around the stage and when ANYBODY needed a dance partner. "Up, sir!"

Most Exciting Celebrity Visitor and What They Did/Said: Amongst the Denzel Washingtons and Ian McKellens, Liv Tylers, Joan Rivers and Leo DiCaprios of this world, we were very privileged to have Ed 'The Eagle' Vassano, a friend of Mercutio's, in the audience during his first public outing after a full bone-marrow transplant. Perhaps not a celebrity in the pure sense of the word, but worthy of true celebration.

Favorite In-Theatre Gathering Place: The Low Bars (Justin Guarini, Conrad Kemp and Corey Hawkins, sometimes collectively called 'Oreo') were often visited for toilet humor, low-brow repartee and bad improv. For a more discerning palate, Mike Rudko held stylishly grumpy court. Scrabble optional.

Special Backstage Rituals: There was always a lot of hugging. Each to their own ridiculous superstition. And Cannoli on Sundays... "Take ONE cannoli, leave the gun."

Favorite Backstage Photo and the Story That Goes with It: This is not Kenny. This is Corey Hawkins, between shows, exhausted by his Tybalt, and loving his desk.

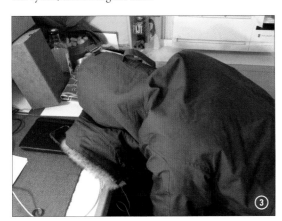

Most Memorable Audience Reaction: I think the ovation we received on first preview was special. It wasn't an audience loaded with friends and family and agents. They were punters who ate up the show and demonstrated their enjoyment with absolute abandon.

Worst Audience Behavior: Nothing terrible springs to mind. We had some cameras in row two, and some very late arrivals shuffling into the front row during Queen Mab, but nobody lobbed hemlock at us or called their broker as Romeo offered his prayers.

Unique Pre-Show Announcement: Metronomic consistency.

Memorable Ad-Lib: "Yikes!" a bone-dry Friar Laurence. Loved by the audience and a wonderful spur to the forgotten scene.

Memorable Press Encounter: Our first preview shut down W. 46th Street. In a good way.

Memorable Stage Door Fan Encounter: Panties rained down upon Benvolio at the stage door. It was cool until he realised his mother was involved.

Memorable Directorial Note: "Wag your tails."

Company In-Jokes: Maurice Jones... we still don't know what his real name is. And, of course, EPIC MUSIC... you had to be there, okay...

Embarrassing Moments: A potentially embarrassing moment was handled with aplomb by Juliet. Unable to find the knife with which to kill herself (kinda crucial), she opted for sleight of hand, fabric and a knack for miming a dagger ahead of throttling herself. Romeo's motorbike had a penchant for stalling at inopportune moments, and even toppled over once or twice, leaking petrol. Benvolio got a bloody nose from a boot tied to a balloon lobbed over a wall. But then that's happened to all of us. And occasionally the bell refused to ring despite the heavy exertions of the actor below.

Favorite Moment During Each Performance: Personally, the transition from 3.1 into 3.2.... "Gallop apace you fiery-footed steeds..." Juliet swinging towards the audience and into the light. I loved the rhythm and energy of the swing combining with the rhythm of the language and the energy of the imagery.

Favorite Snack Foods: Patzeria did a roaring trade in Grandmas. No, not your mom's mom. The slice.

Favorite Therapy: Water, painful leg massage, stitches and, in one hypochondriacal case, blackstrap molasses.

Best Story From the Ushers and Front-of-House Staff: Anything Fran said. About anything. This is Fran sitting in the house:

1. At the curtain call on opening night (L-R): Orlando Bloom, Condola Rashad, Brent Carver, Chuck Cooper, *Yearbook* correspondent Conrad Kemp, Justin Guarini.
2. Usher Fran Eppy keeping watch on the theatre.
3. Corey Hawkins, exhausted from his demanding role as Tybalt.

Romeo and Juliet
SCRAPBOOK

Photo: Joseph Marzullo

Photo: Joseph Marzullo

Photo: Courtesy of the production

Mascot: We had two doves in the show. Their names were Seventeen and Thirty-Eight. It was a toss-up between these consummate professionals and Corey Hawkins.

Tales from the Put-In: Ah, sure, with live animals, fire, a motorcycle, helium balloons and more blades than you can shake a stick at, what tales could we possibly have?

Nicknames: Rudders, OB/The Bloomdog/Captain Goldfish, Re-cast, Mexico... oh, and Chuck Cooper was called, wait for it... "Charles" by some of his guests.

Fastest Costume Change: Juliet had to do a bit of an Usain Bolt around the back-alley, in rain or snow, ice or no. Sounds dodgy, doesn't it? Well it isn't anything like that. Just a very quick exit and entrance whatever the weather.

Who Wore the Heaviest/Hottest Costume: We all looked pretty hot. Thanks.

Who Wore the Least?: Your momma. Sorry. Romeo, at a stage, provoked some flutter in the audience by wearing the least. For one hot minute.

What Did You Think of the Web Buzz on Your Show?: The Bloomdog (or Captain Goldfish as he was fondly known) was everywhere. He gives a ton of love to his fans, and the support he (and we) received was big.

Ghostly Encounters Backstage: Before our dress rehearsal, we created an Elizabethan bundle (including chocolate, tobacco, splashes of wine, red roses and white, polenta, some choice pieces of text, and some very good will), which we hung in the rafters as a distraction and plaything for all the little mischievous sprites and notions that might

Superstition That Turned Out to Be True: Beware the second performance. It's a difficult creature to rouse.

Coolest Thing About Being in This Show: The cast and crew. Closely followed by the fact that it was on Broadway. Broadway!

Who Heads Your Fan Club and What Is Their Website/Newsletter?: My mom. She's still battling with the inter-web. Give her a moment....

Any Other Stories or Memories You'd Like to Add: Two memories, amongst many, stand out for me, and both relate to particular human beings from whom much could be learned.

On August 28, 2013, the fiftieth anniversary of Martin Luther King Jr.'s "I Have a Dream" speech, Orlando paid tribute to the man and his courage in a brief and spontaneous acknowledgement during the curtain call.

On December 5, 2013, Nelson Mandela died. It was a very emotional evening for me in particular. I was given the opportunity and support to say a few tear-blurred words after the bows, something for which I am very grateful.

"The party's over, but I ain't cleaning up all this sh@$!"

— Chuck Cooper a.k.a. Lord Capulet.

Photo: Courtesy of the production

otherwise decide to play onstage and cause mishaps. As it turned out, we had quite a few bloody spells despite our bundle. But we all made it out the other end happily and healthily, so perhaps the bundle did keep the naughties mostly occupied.

1. "No autographs, please! Well, maybe one." Orlando and his fans after a performance.
2. Director David Leveaux (L) with his star-crossed lovers, Condola Rashad and Orlando Bloom.
3. In the dressing room with *Yearbook* correspondent Conrad Kemp.
4. Chuck Cooper taking a break on stage.

700 Sundays

First Preview: November 5, 2013. Opened: November 13, 2013.
Limited Engagement. Closed January 5, 2014 after 7 Previews and 46 Performances.

549

Return engagement of Billy Crystal's 2004 comic solo show recalling growing up at his home on suburban Long Island and at his father's Manhattan jazz record store. The title refers to the day of each week he got to spend with his dad, Jack Crystal, who died when Billy was 15.

Billy Crystal
Writer/Performer

Des McAnuff
Director

Alan Zweibel
*Additional
Material By*

Continued on next page

The Playbill Broadway Yearbook 2013-2014

⊛ IMPERIAL THEATRE

249 West 45th Street
A Shubert Organization Theatre
Philip J. Smith, *Chairman*   Robert E. Wankel, *President*

JANICE CRYSTAL   LARRY MAGID
and FACE PRODUCTIONS

Present

BILLY CRYSTAL
700 SUNDAYS

Written By
BILLY CRYSTAL

Additional Material by	Scenic Design	Lighting Design	Projection Design
ALAN ZWEIBEL	**DAVID F. WEINER**	**DAVID LEE CUTHBERT**	**MICHAEL CLARK**

Sound Design	Technical Supervisor	Production Stage Manager
STEVE CANYON KENNEDY	**DON GILMORE**	**LURIE HORNS PFEFFER**

General Manager	Company Manager	Press Representative	Advertising
NIKO COMPANIES	**JOLIE GABLER**	**THE HARTMAN GROUP**	**SERINO/COYNE**

Directed by
DES McANUFF

700 Sundays was originally produced by La Jolla Playhouse.

11/13/13

Billy Crystal tells the tales
of *700 Sundays*

Photo: Carol Rosegg

329

700 Sundays
Scrapbook

Correspondent: Conwell Worthington III, Stage Manager

Opening Night Party and Gifts: Party was at John's Pizzeria!! We received *700 Sundays* show jackets.

Most Exciting Celebrity Visitors: Basically the entire New York Yankees team!

Favorite In-Theatre Gathering Place: The green room...the TV is there.

Special Backstage Rituals: We have a Yankee on-deck circle upstage right. Right before the performance Billy will stand on it, and do a last minute costume check with his assistant.

Most Memorable Audience Interaction: We had an audience member sitting in the front row, who had brought an album of Billie Holiday's "Strange Fruit." The album is special to Billy because his family label, Commodore, produced it, and he spends a long time in the show discussing it. Billy was touched by the gesture, and invited the fan's group backstage. He met with them, autographed the album and gave it back to them as a gift. He also went a step further and posed for photos with them.

Unique Pre-Show Announcement: The late Bob Sheppard recorded our announcement over ten years ago. It is so great to hear this Yankee legend every night. He recorded many different understudy names for who would be going on for Billy that night...some highlights include: Denzel Washington, Derek Jeter, Carrot Top, and Jared the Subway guy. Billy loves to listen to the audience reaction when the "understudy" is announced.

Favorite Snack: Ricola!

Favorite Therapy: Yogi Throat Coat Tea.

David F. Weiner
Scenic Design

Steve Canyon Kennedy
Sound Design

Michael Clark
Projections Design

Manny Kladitis
Niko Companies, Ltd.
General Management

Janice Crystal
Producer

Larry Magid
Producer

Photos: Brian Mapp

BOX OFFICE
Jennifer Holze, John Zameryka

FRONT OF HOUSE
Front Row (L-R): Frances Barbaretti, Jaime Jacobs-Wilhelm, Lisette Lopez, Julia Gonzales, Mike Bush (Security), Judy Gilburt, Dennis Norwood, Larry Scheraldi, Marilyn Wasbotten
Back Row (L-R): Joann Swanson (House Manager), Ed Phillips, Michael Knowles, Joan Seymour, Lois Fernandez, Ron Albanese, Chris Caoili, Mary Sheehan

700 Sundays

Photo: Brian Mapp

CREW
Front Row (L-R): Walter Trarbach (Associate Sound Designer/Head Sound), Peter Donovan (Assistant Electrician), Timothy Altman, Heidi Brown, Nathan Winner (Head Electrician)
Back Row (L-R): Scott Farley (Hair Supervisor), German Pavon III, Conwell Worthington III (Stage Manager), Lurie Horns Pfeffer (Production Stage Manager), Walter Bullard, Jordan Gable

---

STAFF FOR *700 SUNDAYS*

GENERAL MANAGEMENT
NIKO COMPANIES, LTD.
Manny Kladitis
Justin Black   Jeffrey Chrzczon
Walter Milani   Becky Dole

COMPANY MANAGER
Jolie Gabler

GENERAL PRESS REPRESENTATIVE
THE HARTMAN GROUP
Michael Hartman
Matt Ross   Nicole Capatasto

Production Stage Manager	**Lurie Horns Pfeffer**
Stage Manager	Conwell Worthington III
Assistant to the Director	Hannah Ryan
Associate Scenic Designer	Christopher T. Borreson
Associate Lighting Designer	Patricia Nichols
Associate Sound Designer	Walter Trarbach
Production Carpenter	C. Mark Overton
Production Electrician	Brendan Quigley
Production Audio	Andrew Keister
Head Carpenter	Ken Fieldhouse
Head Electrician	Nathan Winner
Head Sound	Walter Trarbach
Video Programmer	Paul Vershbow
Assistant Electrician	Pete Donovan
Performance Photographs	Charles Peterson
Wardrobe Supervisor	Kendall Errair

Hair Supervisor	Scott Farley
Mr. Crystal's Personal Trainer	Dan Isaacson
Production Assistant	Jenny R. Brum
Assistant to Mr. Crystal	Kia Hellman
Assistant to Mr. Magid	Taylor Morganti
Assistant to Mr. McAnuff	Micah Frank
Advertising	Serino/Coyne/Angelo Desimini, Matt Upshaw, Tom Callahan
Legal Counsel	Franklin, Weinrib, Rudell & Vasallo/ Elliot Brown, Daniel Wasser
Accountant	Mark A. D'Ambrosi/Jana Jevnikar
Banking	City National Bank/ Michele Gibbons, Erik Piecuch
Insurance	Insurance Office of America/ Carol A. Bressi-Cilona, Gerrilynn Ashley
Travel/Housing	Road Concierge, An ALTOUR Company/Lisa Morris The Tzell Travel Group/Andi Henig, Jeanne Lafond
Payroll Services	Castellana Services, Inc.

CREDITS
Scenery by PRG Scenic Technologies. Lighting equipment from PRG Lighting. Sound equipment by Masque Sound. Projection equipment from Worldstage-Scharff Weisberg. Mr. Crystal's gym equipment provided by Gym Source. Fiberoptics by TPR Enterprises.

Mr. Crystal's tea provided by Yogi Tea.

The photo of Billy Crystal on the cover of the Playbill is by Andrew Eccles.

 THE SHUBERT ORGANIZATION, INC.
Board of Directors

Philip J. Smith	**Robert E. Wankel**
Chairman	President
Wyche Fowler, Jr.	**Diana Phillips**
Lee J. Seidler	**Michael I. Sovern**

Stuart Subotnick

Chief Financial Officer	Elliot Greene
Sr. Vice President, Ticketing	David Andrews
Vice President, Finance	Juan Calvo
Vice President, Human Resources	Cathy Cozens
Vice President, Facilities	John Darby
Vice President, Theatre Operations	Peter Entin
Vice President, Marketing	Charles Flateman
Vice President, General Counsel	Gilbert Hoover
Vice President, Audit	Anthony LaMattina
Vice President, Ticket Sales	Brian Mahoney
Vice President, Creative Projects	D.S. Moynihan
Vice President, Real Estate	Julio Peterson

House Manager	Joann Swanson

BROADWAY
green alliance   The Shubert Organization is a proud member of the Broadway Green Alliance.

The Snow Geese

First Preview: October 1, 2013. Opened: October 24, 2013.
Limited Engagement. Closed December 14, 2013 after 25 Previews and 60 Performances.

Sharr White's Chekhovian drama takes place in 1917 at the upstate New York country lodge of the upper middle class Gaesling family, which is still mourning the sudden death of its patriarch. When younger son Arnold goes over his late father's books, he finds that the once modestly wealthy family is actually flat broke due to the father's gross mismanagement. Despite Arnold's best efforts, his self-absorbed brother and feckless mother refuse to come to grips with what this means to their lives, and to the image they have of the revered father.

CAST
(in order of appearance)

Duncan Gaesling .... EVAN JONIGKEIT
Viktorya Gryaznoy .... JESSICA LOVE
Arnold Gaesling .... BRIAN CROSS
Max Hohmann .... DANNY BURSTEIN
Elizabeth Gaesling .... MARY-LOUISE PARKER
Clarissa Hohmann .... VICTORIA CLARK
Theodore Gaesling ...... CHRISTOPHER INNVAR

TIME
November 1, 1917
PLACE
The Gaesling family lodge outside of
Syracuse, New York

Stage Manager .... BRYCE McDONALD

Continued on next page

MANHATTAN THEATRE CLUB
SAMUEL J. FRIEDMAN THEATRE

ARTISTIC DIRECTOR
LYNNE MEADOW

EXECUTIVE PRODUCER
BARRY GROVE

AND

MCC THEATER

ARTISTIC DIRECTORS
ROBERT LuPONE, BERNARD TELSEY & WILLIAM CANTLER

EXECUTIVE PRODUCER
BLAKE WEST

PRESENT

THE
SNOW GEESE

BY
SHARR WHITE

WITH

MARY-LOUISE PARKER
DANNY BURSTEIN   VICTORIA CLARK

EVAN JONIGKEIT   BRIAN CROSS   CHRISTOPHER INNVAR   JESSICA LOVE

SCENIC DESIGN	COSTUME DESIGN	LIGHTING DESIGN	ORIGINAL MUSIC & SOUND DESIGN
JOHN LEE BEATTY	JANE GREENWOOD	JAPHY WEIDEMAN	DAN MOSES SCHREIER

PROJECTION DESIGN	HAIR & WIG DESIGN	FIGHT DIRECTOR
ROCCO DiSANTI	TOM WATSON	RICK SORDELET

DANCES	CASTING	PRODUCTION STAGE MANAGER
MIMI LIEBER	CAPARELLIOTIS CASTING & TELSEY + COMPANY	JAMES FITZSIMMONS

DIRECTED BY
DANIEL SULLIVAN

ARTISTIC PRODUCER
MANDY GREENFIELD

GENERAL MANAGER
FLORIE SEERY

DIRECTOR OF ARTISTIC DEVELOPMENT	DIRECTOR OF MARKETING	PRESS REPRESENTATIVE	PRODUCTION MANAGER
JERRY PATCH	DEBRA WAXMAN-PILLA	BONEAU/BRYAN-BROWN	JOSHUA HELMAN

DIRECTOR OF CASTING	ARTISTIC LINE PRODUCER	DIRECTOR OF DEVELOPMENT
NANCY PICCIONE	LISA McNULTY	LYNNE RANDALL

SPECIAL THANKS TO THE HAROLD AND MIMI STEINBERG CHARITABLE TRUST FOR SUPPORTING NEW AMERICAN PLAYS AT MANHATTAN THEATRE CLUB.
THE SNOW GEESE IS A RECIPIENT OF AN EDGERTON FOUNDATION NEW AMERICAN PLAYS AWARD.
MANHATTAN THEATRE CLUB WISHES TO EXPRESS ITS APPRECIATION TO THEATRE DEVELOPMENT FUND FOR ITS SUPPORT OF THIS PRODUCTION.

10/24/13

(L-R): Evan Jonigkeit, Victoria Clark, Danny Burstein, Brian Cross, Mary-Louise Parker, Jessica Love

Photo: Joan Marcus

The Snow Geese

UNDERSTUDIES

For Max Hohmann/Theodore Gaesling:
TONY CARLIN
For Arnold Gaesling/Duncan Gaesling:
EDMUND DONOVAN
For Elizabeth Gaesling/Clarissa Hohmann:
CATHERINE EATON
For Viktorya Gryaznoy:
ALEXANDRA HENRIKSON

DANCE CAPTAIN

VICTORIA CLARK

Christopher Innvar as Theodore Gaesling and Mary-Louise Parker as Elizabeth Gaesling are reunited in a flashback.

Photo: Joan Marcus

Mary-Louise Parker
Elizabeth Gaesling

Danny Burstein
Max Hohmann

Victoria Clark
Clarissa Hohmann

Evan Jonigkeit
Duncan Gaesling

Brian Cross
Arnold Gaesling

Christopher Innvar
Theodore Gaesling

Jessica Love
Viktorya Gryaznoy

Tony Carlin
u/s Max Hohmann, Theodore Gaesling

Edmund Donovan
u/s Duncan Gaesling, Arnold Gaesling

Catherine Eaton
u/s Elizabeth Gaesling/Clarissa Hohmann

Alexandra Henrikson
u/s Viktorya Gryaznoy

Sharr White
Playwright

Daniel Sullivan
Director

John Lee Beatty
Scenic Design

Jane Greenwood
Costume Design

Japhy Weideman
Lighting Design

Dan Moses Schreier
Original Music & Sound Design

Rocco DiSanti
Projection Design

Tom Watson
Hair & Wig Design

Rick Sordelet
Fight Director

Mimi Lieber
Dances

The Snow Geese

David Caparelliotis
Caparelliotis Casting
Casting

Bernard Telsey
Telsey + Company
Casting

Lynne Meadow
Manhattan Theatre
Club
Artistic Director

Barry Grove
Manhattan Theatre
Club
Executive Producer

Robert LuPone
MCC Theater
Artistic Director

William Cantler
MCC Theater
Artistic Director

Blake West
MCC Theater
Executive Producer

BOX OFFICE
Rachel James, Geoffrey Nixon

FRONT OF HOUSE
Front Row (L-R): Richard Ponce (Assistant House Manager), Wendy Wright, Patricia Polhill, Lyanna Alvarado, Taryn Wisky, Jacqui Kelliher
Back Row (L-R): Cindy Lopiano, John Wyffels, Jason Burgos, Jackson Ero, Ed Brashear, Jim Joseph (Theatre Manager), Dinah Glorioso

CREW
(L-R): Jeff Dodson (Master Electrician), Louis Shapiro (Sound Engineer), Matthew Abdelnour (Apprentice), James Fitzsimmons (Production Stage Manager), LeeAnn Lisella (Production Assistant), Natasha Steinhagen (Hair/Make-up Supervisor), Bryce McDonald (Stage Manager), Leah Redmond (Wardrobe Supervisor), Skye Bennett (Dresser), Andrew Braggs (Apprentice), Timothy Walters (Head Propertyman)

Photos: Brian Mapp

The Snow Geese

MANHATTAN THEATRE CLUB STAFF

Artistic Director	**Lynne Meadow**
Executive Producer	**Barry Grove**
General Manager	**Florie Seery**
Artistic Producer	**Mandy Greenfield**
Director of Artistic Development	Jerry Patch
Director of Artistic Operations	Amy Gilkes Loe
Artistic Line Producer	Lisa McNulty
Artistic Associate/	
Assistant to the Artistic Director	Nicki Hunter
Assistant to the Executive Producer	Melanie Sovern
Assistant to the Artistic Producer	Abby Lee
Director of Casting	**Nancy Piccione**
Associate Casting Director	Kelly Gillespie
Casting Assistant	Darragh Garvey
Literary Manager/Sloan Project Manager	Annie MacRae
Associate Director of	
Artistic Development	Elizabeth Rothman
Artistic Development Assistant	Scott Kaplan
Artistic Consultant	**Daniel Sullivan**

Bank of America/
US Trust Commissions ....Richard Greenberg,
Neil LaBute, Matthew Lopez, John Patrick Shanley
Alfred P. Sloan Foundation Commissions...April de Angelis,
Nathan Jackson, Nick Jones, Juliana Nash &
Courtney Baron, Melissa Ross, Heidi Schreck,
Sarah Treem, Bess Wohl
The Writer's Room Commissions ....Adam Bock &
Justin Levine, Thomas Bradshaw,
Samuel D. Hunter, Sharyn Rothstein
Mary Mill Commission ....Molly Smith Metzler

Director of Development	**Lynne Randall**
Director, Individual Giving & Major Gifts	Emily Fleisher
Director, Institutional Giving	Patricia Leonard
Director, Special Events	Stephanie Mercado
Associate Director of	
Individual Giving	Josh Martinez-Nelson
Manager, Individual Giving	Aubrie Fennecken
Development Associate/Individual Giving	Laura Petrucci
Development Associate/Special Events	Molly Clarke
Institutional Giving Manager	Heather Gallagher
Patrons' Liaison	Emily Yowell
Database Associate	Katie Fergerson
Director of Marketing	**Debra Waxman-Pilla**
Assistant Marketing Director	Caitlin Baird
Marketing Accounts Manager	Cody Andrus
Director of Finance	**Jessica Adler**
Director of Human Resources	**Stephanie Dolce**
Business Manager	Ryan Guhde
Business & HR Associate	Mallory Triest
Business Assistant	Josiah Grimm
IT Manager	Mendy Sudranski
Systems Analyst	Jason Fritzsch
Studio Manager/Receptionist	Thatcher Stevens
Associate General Manager	**Lindsey Sag**
Company Manager/NY City Center	Samantha Kindler
General Management Assistant	Derrick Olson
Director of Subscriber Services	**Robert Allenberg**
Subscriber Services Manager	Kevin Sullivan
Subscriber Services Representatives	Mark Bowers,

Tim Salamandyk, Rosanna Consalvo Sarto, Paul Winkler

Director of Education	**David Shookhoff**
Assistant Education Director/	
Coordinator, Paul A. Kaplan Theatre	
Management Program	Amy Harris
MTC Teaching Artists	Stephanie Alston,

David Auburn, Chris Ceraso, Charlotte Colavin,

Danny Burstein as Max Hohmann and Victoria Clark as Clarissa Hohmann

Dominic Colon, Allison Daugherty, Andy Goldberg,
Kel Haney, Elise Hernandez, Jeffrey Joseph, Julie Leedes,
Kate Long, Victor Maog, Andres Munar, Melissa Murray,
Angela Pietropinto, Carmen Rivera, Judy Tate,
Candido Tirado, Liam Torres, Joe White

Theatre Management Interns ....Allyson Capetta,
Amara Fehring, Aislinn Frantz, Matthew Glasner,
Natalie Hratko, Jacqui Kelliher, Kelly McCready,
Emily MacLeod, Gabriella Napoli,
Megan Patterson, Julia Sears, Rebecca Smithee

Production Manager	**Joshua Helman**
Associate Production Manager	Bethany Weinstein
Assistant Production Manager	Steven Dalton
Properties Supervisor	**Scott Laule**
Assistant Properties Supervisor	Lily Fairbanks
Props Carpenter	Peter Grimes
Costume Supervisor	**Erin Hennessy Dean**

GENERAL PRESS REPRESENTATION
BONEAU/BRYAN-BROWN
Chris Boneau   Aaron Meier
Christine Olver   Emily Meagher

Script Readers ....Mirella Cheeseman, Aaron Grunfeld,
Clifford Lee Johnson III, Thomas Park,
Elizabeth Sharpe-Levine

SERVICES

Accountants	Fried & Kowgios CPAs, LLP
Advertising	SpotCo/Drew Hodges, Tom Greenwald,

Ilene Rosen, Tim Falotico, Laura Fraenkel

Web Design	SpotCo Interactive
Legal Counsel	Charles H. Googe, Jr.;

Caroline Barnard; Carolyn J. Casselman;
Paul, Weiss, Rifkind, Wharton and Garrison LLP

Real Estate Counsel	Marcus Attorneys
Labor Counsel	Harry H. Weintraub/

Glick and Weintraub, P.C.

Immigration Counsel	Theodore Ruthizer/

Kramer, Levin, Naftalis & Frankel, LLP

Media Counsel	Cameron Stracher
Insurance	DeWitt Stern Group, Inc./Anthony Pittari
Maintenance	Reliable Cleaning
Production Photographer	Joan Marcus
Event Photography	Bruce Glikas
Cover Design	SpotCo
Cover Photograph	Jason Bell
Theatre Displays	King Displays
Merchandise	Creative Goods Merchandise/Pete Milano

For more information visit
www.ManhattanTheatreClub.com

PRODUCTION STAFF FOR *THE SNOW GEESE*

Company Manager	**Erin Moeller**
Production Stage Manager	**James Fitzsimmons**
Stage Manager	Bryce McDonald
Assistant Director	Jess Chayes
Make-Up Designer	Angelina Avallone
Dialect Coach	Charlotte Fleck
German Language Consultant	Björn Technau
Associate Scenic Designer	Kacie Hultgren
Associate Costume Designer	Daniel Urlie
Associate Lighting Designer	Yael Lubetzky
Assistant Sound Designer	Joshua Reid
Assistant Production Designer	Hana Sooyeon Kim
Associate Fight Director	Christian Kelly-Sordelet
Hair/Make-Up Supervisor	Natasha Steinhagen
Lighting Programmer	John Wilson
Automation Operator	Vaughn Preston
Dresser	Skye Bennett
Costume Shopper	Mary Margaret Powers
Production Assistants	LeeAnn Lisella, Katie Kavett

CREDITS

Scenery fabrication by PRG Scenic Technologies. Lighting equipment provided by PRG Lighting. Sound equipment provided by Masque Sound. Projection equipment provided by PRG. Built costumes by Eric Winterling, Inc. Rented costumes by Cosprop. Custom shirts by CEGO. Makeup provided by M·A·C. Special thanks to Viva De Concini and Kristen Reoch.

MANHATTAN THEATRE CLUB
SAMUEL J. FRIEDMAN THEATRE STAFF

Theatre Manager	**Jim Joseph**
Assistant House Manager	Richard Ponce
Box Office Treasurer	**David Dillon**
Assistant Box Office Treasurers	Rachel James,
	Geoffrey Nixon
Head Carpenter	Chris Wiggins
Head Propertyman	Timothy Walters
Sound Engineer	Louis Shapiro
Master Electrician	Jeff Dodson
Wardrobe Supervisor	Leah Redmond
Apprentices	Matthew Abdelnour, Andrew Braggs
Chief Engineer	Deosarran
Maintenance Engineers	Ricky Deosarran, Maximo Perez
Security	Allied Barton
Lobby Refreshments	Sweet Hospitality Group

MCC THEATER STAFF

Artistic Directors	Robert LuPone, Bernard Telsey,
	William Cantler
Executive Director	Blake West
General Manager	Pamela Adams
Assistant Company Manager/	
Assistant General Manager	Megan Ringeling
Manager of Artistic Development/	
Company Manager	Jessica Chase
Literary Manager/Resident Dramaturg	Stephen Willems
Development Associate Individual Giving	Glenn Grieves
Development Associate Special Events	Kathryn Banas
Grant Writer	Jessica Goldberg
Director of Marketing	Michael Crowley
Marketing Associate	Joyelle Cabato
Director of Education & Outreach	Caroline Azano
Education & Outreach Assistant	Lyssa Deehan

The Snow Geese
SCRAPBOOK

Correspondent: Jessica Love, "Viktorya Gryaznoy"

Opening Night Parties and/or Gifts: MLP [Mary-Louise Parker] gave (customized) champagne and a beautiful book of photographs of the rehearsal process and Evan Jonigkeit gave a liberty coin from 1917, the year of our play.

Most Exciting Celebrity Visitor and What They Did/Said: Susan Sarandon came and suggested that my character could be pregnant in the last scene, and that her water should break when she is kissed.

Favorite In-Theatre Gathering Place: Boys' dressing room.

Memorable Ad-Lib: On the first or second night our automation broke between the first scene (which is in the living room) and the second (which is on a birding blind). It took about fifteen minutes to fix, and when the boys finally entered the birding blind, Evan said, "I don't remember that being

such a long walk...."

Company In-Jokes: There is a stuffed fox on our set. We named her Stephanie and we like to say horrible things about her performance, i.e. "I mean, she isn't really listening, she's performing listening, but it's completely hollow." Mary-Louise and I like to ask one another, "Does this intention make me look fat?" or "Is my subtext making my neck droopy?" I also sometimes pretend I'm a crazy, old regional theatre grande dame and scream down the stairs for my dresser. But I only do it when she's standing right next to me.

Embarrassing Moments: My bloomers fell off on stage once. And one time Danny Burstein forgot his German line, and substituted it with the super authentic, "gibba gabba."

Favorite Moment During Each Performance: The most consistent laugh in our show is during Danny's Broadway Cares speech. Now MLP and I can't watch him do it without losing it.

Favorite Off-Site Hangout: We like the Hour Glass...which MLP still might think is called The Glass Slipper.

Mascot: Stephanie the Prop Fox. Or Bryce McDonald, our ASM.

Catchphrases Only the Company Would Recognize: "It's not your grandmother's 1917."

Coolest Thing About Being in This Show: The new friends.

1. (L-R): *Yearbook* Correspondent Jessica Love, Danny Burstein, Mary-Louise Parker at curtain call on opening night.
2. Mary-Louise Parker (L) with her mom, Caroline Louise Parker.
3. Playwright Sharr White and Evelyn Carr White.
4. The entire cast takes a bow on opening night (L-R): Christopher Innvar, Jessica Love, Danny Burstein, Mary-Louise Parker, Victoria Clark, Brian Cross and Evan Jonigkeit.

Soul Doctor

First Preview: July 17, 2013. Opened: August 15, 2013.
Closed October 13, 2013 after 32 Previews and 66 Performances.

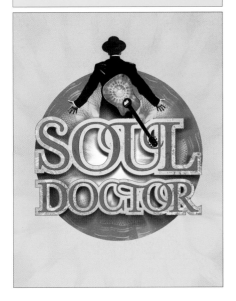

This musical biography tells the Jazz Singer-*like true story of Shlomo Carlebach, who starts as a conservative rabbi on the run from Nazi Austria, but who falls in love with the pop music of the 1960s and becomes something of a rock star. The score includes more than three dozen of his songs, many of which combine traditional liturgical texts with an infectious backbeat. Along the way Carlebach acquires a devoted fan following and forms a lifelong friendship with black singer Nina Simone—but becomes estranged from his religious family and community.*

CAST

(in order of appearance)

Nina	AMBER IMAN
Shlomo	ERIC ANDERSON
Reb Pinchas	RON ORBACH
Young Shlomo	ETHAN KHUSIDMAN or TEDDY WALSH
Young Eli Chaim	ETHAN KHUSIDMAN or TEDDY WALSH
Father	JAMIE JACKSON
Mother	JACQUELINE ANTARAMIAN
Moisheleh	MICHAEL PATERNOSTRO
Eli Chaim	RYAN STRAND
Chassidim	ETHAN KHUSIDMAN, TEDDY WALSH
Rebbe	JAMIE JACKSON
Joel	ETHAN KHUSIDMAN or TEDDY WALSH
Ira	ETHAN KHUSIDMAN or TEDDY WALSH

Continued on next page

CIRCLE IN THE SQUARE

UNDER THE DIRECTION OF
PAUL LIBIN and THEODORE MANN (1924–2012)
SUSAN FRANKEL, General Manager

JEREMY CHESS   JEROME LEVY
ROBERT BECKWITT   EDWARD STEINBERG   JOEL KAHN   DANNY BOY PRODUCTIONS

PRESENT

SOUL DOCTOR

WITH

ERIC ANDERSON

JACQUELINE ANTARAMIAN   DIANNA BARGER   RICHARD CERATO
TARA CHAMBERS   MARIA CONTI   ALEXANDRA FROHLINGER
AFRA HINES   AMBER IMAN   ABDUR-RAHIM JACKSON   JAMIE JACKSON
ETHAN KHUSIDMAN   DILLON KONDOR   ZARAH MAHLER   VASTHY MOMPOINT
RON ORBACH   IAN PAGET   HEATHER PARCELLS   MICHAEL PATERNOSTRO
JC SCHUSTER   ERIC STOCKTON   RYAN STRAND   TEDDY WALSH

MUSIC AND ADDITIONAL LYRICS	BOOK	LYRICS
SHLOMO CARLEBACH	**DANIEL S. WISE**	**DAVID SCHECHTER**

BASED ON THE REAL LIFE STORY OF RABBI SHLOMO CARLEBACH. GRANT OF RIGHTS BY NESHAMA & NEDARA CARLEBACH
CONCEIVED BY JEREMY CHESS. CREATED & DEVELOPED BY DAVID SCHECHTER AND DANIEL S. WISE. ADDITIONAL MATERIAL BY NESHAMA CARLEBACH

SCENIC DESIGN	COSTUME DESIGN	LIGHTING DESIGN	SOUND DESIGN
NEIL PATEL	MAGGIE MORGAN	JEFF CROITER	JOHN SHIVERS & DAVID PATRIDGE

WIG & HAIR DESIGN	CASTING	CREATIVE ADVISOR	PRODUCTION CONSULTANT
CHARLES G. LaPOINTE	JOY DEWING CASTING	WENDY GOLDBERG	PRODUCTION CORE

ORCHESTRATIONS & ADDITIONAL ARRANGEMENTS	MUSIC SUPERVISION & ARRANGEMENTS	MUSIC DIRECTION & ARRANGEMENTS
STEVE MARGOSHES	BRIAN KOONIN	SETH FARBER

ADVERTISING & MARKETING	PRESS REPRESENTATIVE	PROMOTIONS
SPOTCO	RICHARD KORNBERG	LEANNE SCHANZER PROMOTIONS

GENERAL MANAGER	EXECUTIVE PRODUCER	PRODUCTION MANAGEMENT	PRODUCTION STAGE MANAGER
BESPOKE THEATRICALS	RED AWNING	AURORA PRODUCTIONS	PETER WOLF

ASSOCIATE DIRECTOR/DRAMATURG	ASSOCIATE CHOREOGRAPHER/CREATIVE CONSULTANT
GINA RATTAN	MICHAEL BALDERRAMA

CHOREOGRAPHED BY
BENOIT-SWAN POUFFER

DIRECTED BY
DANIEL S. WISE

ASSOCIATE PRODUCERS: ELAINE PRAGER, BRIAN MURRAY, DAVID HAFT, BERNARD MICHAEL

ORIGINAL NEW YORK WORKSHOP PRODUCTION PRESENTED BY THE NATIONAL YIDDISH THEATER-FOLKSBIENE
ORIGINAL 2008 OFF-BROADWAY PRODUCTION DIRECTED BY DAVID SCHECHTER

THE PRODUCERS WISH TO EXPRESS THEIR APPRECIATION TO THEATRE DEVELOPMENT FUND FOR ITS SUPPORT OF THIS PRODUCTION.

8/15/13

(L-R): JC Schuster, Eric Anderson, Ian Paget, Alexandra Frohlinger sing "Ode Yishama."

Photo: Carol Rosegg

Soul Doctor

MUSICAL NUMBERS

ACT I

Concert in Vienna City Square, 1972
"Return Again" ....Nina
"Brothers & Friends (Leman Achai*/(Ein K'Elokeinu*)" ....Shlomo and Holy Beggars
Carlebach Home/Vienna City Square, 1938
"Good Shabbos" ....Moisheleh, Young Shlomo
"Once in a Garden (Essa Einai/Leshana Haba*)" ....Moisheleh, Young Shlomo, Vienna Beggars
"I Will Sing Your Song (Pischu Li)" ....Young Shlomo
Brooklyn, 1940
"Keep the Fire Burning (Uvnei Ossah*)" ....Father, Young Shlomo, Young Eli Chaim, Yeshiva Boys
"Torah Song (Lulei Torascha*)" ....Father, Young Shlomo, Young Eli Chaim, Shlomo, Eli Chaim, Yeshiva Boys
"Shlomo's Dream" ....Moisheleh and Vienna Beggars
Chassidim in Brooklyn, 1957
"Arise! (Uforatztah)" ....Eli Chaim and Chassidim
"Let Our Joy Be the Spark" ....The Rebbe
Columbia University
"Rosh Hashanah Rock" ....Shlomo, Eli Chaim, Band Leader, Columbia Students
A Smoky Piano Bar
"I Put a Spell on You" ....Nina
"You Know How I Feel" ....Nina
"Ki Va Moed" ....Nina, Shlomo
The Cantor From Hell; Father's Synagogue
"Ein K'Elokeinu" (Ki Va Moed*)" ....Ira, Joel
"He's Just a Child (Ana Hashem*)" ....Shlomo
A Storefront Gospel Church
"Ki Va Moed" ....Nina, Shlomo, Minister, Sinner, Churchgoers
"Show Me the Way (Ana Hashem*)" ....Shlomo
Washington Square Park
"Elijah Rock" ....Blind Guitarist
"Where Am I to Turn? (Pischu Li/Schifchie*)" ....Ruth, Shlomo, Holy Beggars
"Somebody Is Lonely (Hashmi'ini*)" ....Shlomo, Holy Beggars
Recording Studio, 1959
"Ode Yishama*" ....Shlomo and Backup Singers

Continued on next page

Photo: Carol Rosegg

(L-R): Heather Parcells, Abdur-Rahim Jackson, Vasthy Mompoint and Dianna Barger, some of the "Holy Beggars."

Cast Continued

Ruth ....ZARAH MAHLER
Milt ....MICHAEL PATERNOSTRO
Recording Engineer ....RON ORBACH
The Holy Hippie ....RYAN STRAND
Announcer ....RON ORBACH
Timothy Leary ....MICHAEL PATERNOSTRO
The Holy Beggars ....DIANNA BARGER, TARA CHAMBERS, MARIA CONTI, ALEXANDRA FROHLINGER, ABDUR-RAHIM JACKSON, DILLON KONDOR, VASTHY MOMPOINT, IAN PAGET, HEATHER PARCELLS, JC SCHUSTER, ERIC J. STOCKTON

SWINGS
RICHARD CERATO, AFRA HINES

UNDERSTUDIES
For Shlomo: RICHARD CERATO, JAMIE JACKSON
For Eli Chaim/The Holy Hippie: IAN PAGET
For Nina: VASTHY MOMPOINT
For Reb Pinchas/Recording Engineer/ Announcer: MICHAEL PATERNOSTRO
For Father/Rebbe: MICHAEL PATERNOSTRO
For Mother: HEATHER PARCELLS
For Young Eli Chaim/Chassid/Ira: ALEXANDRA FROHLINGER
For Ruth: DIANNA BARGER
For Moisheleh/Milt/ Timothy Leary: JC SCHUSTER

DANCE CAPTAIN
AFRA HINES

THE HOLY BEGGAR BAND
SETH FARBER: Conductor/Keyboards
FRANCISCO CENTENO: Associate Conductor
ERIC J. STOCKTON: Guitar
DILLON KONDOR: Guitar
MARIA CONTI: Violin
TARA CHAMBERS: Cello
CLINT DE GANON: Drums
FRANCISCO CENTENO: Bass

Music Contractor: ANTOINE SILVERMAN
Music Preparation: DONALD OLIVER and PAUL HOLDERBAUM/Chelsea Music, Inc.

Soul Doctor

MUSICAL NUMBERS

ACT II

The King of Kosher Music
  "Shlomo Medley (Asher Bara, Yiboneh, Simcha L'Artzecha*)" ....Shlomo,
  Eli Chaim, Young Jewish Fans

Bleecker Street/The Village Gate, 1963
  "Sinnerman" ....Nina, Shlomo, Eli Chaim and Ensemble

Washington Square Park
  "Where Am I to Turn?" (Reprise) ....Ruth, Holy Beggars
  "I'm Always With You (V'Hayu*)" ....Nina, Shlomo

Berkeley Folk Festival, 1966
  "Sing Shalom (Sim Shalom*)" ....Shlomo, Ruth, The Holy Hippie, Holy Beggars

The House of Love and Prayer, 1968
  "We'll Build a House" (Leman Achai*)" ....Shlomo, Holy Beggars
  "Song of Shabbos" ....Shlomo, Ruth, The Holy Hippie, Dr. Joel, Holy Beggars
  "Family Legacy (Ana Hashem/Haneshama Lach*)" ....Shlomo and Father

Shlomo's Parents' Home, 1968
  "The Sun Is Sinking Fast (Hinei*)" ....Mother, Father, Holy Beggars

The House of Love and Prayer
  "Lord Get Me High*" ....Ruth, Timothy Leary, Holy Beggars
  "I Tried to Guide Them (Ana Hashem*)" ....Shlomo
  "Yerushalyim" ....Shlomo, Ruth and Holy Beggars

Jerusalem, The Wailing Wall
  "Adam Was Alone (Mimkomcha*)" ....Holy Beggars

Shlomo's Home
  "I Was a Sparrow (Schifchie*)" ....Ruth

Concert in Vienna City Square, 1972
  "Return Again (Reprise)" ....Nina and Holy Beggars
  "Am Yisrael Chai" ....Shlomo and Holy Beggars

*Title of original Shlomo Carlebach melody

Amber Iman as Nina Simone
and Eric Anderson as Shlomo.

Eric Anderson
Shlomo

Jacqueline
Antaramian
Mother

Dianna Barger
*Holy Beggar;
u/s Ruth*

Richard Cerato
Swing; u/s Shlomo

Tara Chambers
Holy Beggar/Cellist

Maria Conti
Holy Beggar/Violinist

Alexandra Frohlinger
*Holy Beggar; u/s
Young Eli Chaim/Ira*

Afra Hines
*Swing/Dance
Captain*

Amber Iman
Nina

Abdur-Rahim
Jackson
Holy Beggar

Jamie Jackson
*Father/Rebbe;
u/s Shlomo*

Ethan Khusidman
*Young Shlomo/
Chassid/Joel, Young
Eli Chaim/Chassid/
Ira*

Dillon Kondor
*Holy Beggar/
Guitarist*

Zarah Mahler
Ruth

Soul Doctor

Vasthy Mompoint
Holy Beggar;
u/s Nina

Ron Orbach
Reb Pinchas/
Engineer/Announcer

Ian Paget
Holy Beggar;
u/s Eli Chaim/
The Holy Hippie

Heather Parcells
Holy Beggar;
u/s Mother

Michael Paternostro
Moisheleh/Milt/
Timothy Leary;
u/s Father/Rebbe,
Reb Pinchas

JC Schuster
Holy Beggar; u/s
Moisheleh/Milt/
Timothy Leary

Eric J. Stockton
Holy Beggar/
Guitarist

Ryan Strand
Eli Chaim/
The Holy Hippie

Teddy Walsh
Young Shomo/Joel,
Young Eli Chaim/Ira

Daniel S. Wise
Director/Book

David Schechter
Lyricist/Co-Creator

Neshama Carlebach
Additional Material

Benoit-Swan Pouffer
Choreographer

Neil Patel
Scenic Design

Maggie Morgan
Costume Design

Jeff Croiter
Lighting Design

John Shivers
Sound Design

David Patridge
Sound Design

Charles G. LaPointe
Hair Design

Steve Margoshes
Orchestrations

Brian Koonin
Music Supervision/
Arrangements

Seth Farber
Music Director/
Conductor/
Arrangements

Gina Rattan
Associate Director/
Dramaturg

Michael Balderrama
Associate
Choreographer/
Creative Consultant

Antoine Silverman
Music Coordinator

Joy Dewing, CSA
Casting Director

Maggie Brohn
Bespoke Theatricals
Theatrical
Management

Amy Jacobs
Bespoke Theatricals
Theatrical
Management

Devin Keudell
Bespoke Theatricals
Theatrical
Management

Nina Lannan
Bespoke Theatricals
Theatrical
Management

Richard Kornberg
Richard Kornberg &
Associates
General Press
Representative

Nicole Kastrinos
Red Awning
Executive Producer

James E. Cleveland
Production Core
Production
Consultant

Adrian White
Production Core
Production
Consultant

David Upton
Production Core
Production
Consultant

Soul Doctor

Ron Grimshaw
Production Core
*Production
Consultant*

Chasmin Hallyburton
Production Core
*Production
Consultant*

Julie Shelton
Production Core
*Production
Consultant*

Lauren Libretti
Production Core
*Production
Consultant*

Eric Anderson
as Shlomo

Photo: Carol Rosegg

Amber Mathis
Production Core
*Production
Consultant*

Gene O'Donovan
Aurora Productions
*Production
Management*

Ben Heller
Aurora Productions
*Production
Management*

Dr. Jerome Levy
Producer

Paul Libin
Circle in the Square
Theatre and
Theatre School
President

Theodore Mann
(1924-2012)
Circle in the Square
Theatre and
Theatre School
Artistic Director

Susan Frankel
Circle in the Square
General Manager

Photos: Brian Mapp

CREW
(L-R): Stewart Wagner (Head Electrician),
Jane Masterson (Light Board Operator),
Owen E. Parmele (Prop Master),
German Pavon, III (Follow Spot),
Tony Menditto (House Carpenter),
Stephanie Vetter (Deck Audio),
Rob Dagna (Properties Assistant)

MUSICIANS
Front Row (L-R): Maria Conti (Violin), Seth Farber (Music Director),
Tara Chambers (Cello)
Back Row (L-R): Francisco Centeno (Bass), Dillon Kondor (Guitar),
Eric J. Stockton (Guitar)

MANAGEMENT/CHILD GUARDIAN
Front Row (L-R): Rebecca Azenberg (Assistant Company Manager),
Lisa Buxbaum (Assistant Stage Manager)
Back Row (L-R): Rachel Maier (Child Guardian),
Kate Egan (Company Manager), Brian Bogin (Stage Manager),
Peter Wolf (Production Stage Manager)

Soul Doctor

Photos: Brian Mapp

FRONT OF HOUSE
Front Row (L-R): Susan Frankel (General Manager), Cheryl Dennis (House Manager),
Dan Gallagher, Kelly Varley, Xavier Young
Back Row (L-R): Laurel Brevoort, Patricia Kennedy, Joe Guice, Sophie Koufakis,
Barbara Zavilowicz, John Lovett

WARDROBE/HAIR
Front Row (L-R): Amanda Zane, Samantha Wiener (Hair Supervisor)
Second Row (L-R): Elizabeth Ensminger, Bonnie Prather, Brandalyn Fulton (Assistant Hair Supervisor)
Third Row (L-R): Jake Fry, Liz Brady, Angela Lehrer, Jason Bishop (Assistant Wardrobe Supervisor)
Fourth Row: Jessica Worsnop (Wardrobe Supervisor)

STAFF FOR *SOUL DOCTOR*

GENERAL MANAGEMENT
BESPOKE THEATRICALS
Amy Jacobs Steve Dow
Nina Lannan Maggie Brohn Devin Keudell

COMPANY MANAGER
Kate Egan
Assistant Company Manager ....Rebecca Azenberg

EXECUTIVE PRODUCER
RED AWNING
Nicole Kastrinos

GENERAL PRESS REPRESENTATIVES
RICHARD KORNBERG & ASSOCIATES
Richard Kornberg Billy Zavelson
Don Summa Danielle McGarry

PRODUCTION MANAGEMENT
AURORA PRODUCTIONS
Gene O'Donovan   Ben Heller
Chris Minnick, Anita Shah, Jarid Sumner,
Anthony Jusino, Liza Luxenberg,
Rachel London, David Cook, Bridget Van Dyke,
Cat Nelson, Melissa Mazdra

CASTING
JOY DEWING CASTING
Joy Dewing
Casting Assistant ....Nikki Grillos
Casting Interns ....Josh Del Brandt, Bronwyn Whittle

Production Stage Manager ....Peter Wolf
Stage Manager ....Brian Bogin
Assistant Stage Manager ....Lisa Buxbaum
Creative Consultant ....Mindy Cooper
Assistant Director ....Chris McCoy
Dance Captain ....Afra Hines
Associate Music Director ....James Morgan

Associate Scenic Designer ....Caleb Levengood
Assistant Scenic Designer ....Stephen Dobay
Associate Costume Designer ....Angela Kahler
Assistant Costume Designers............Amy Pedigo-Otto,
Maggie Chan
Costume Shopper ....Sydney Gallas
Costume Intern ....Kara Branch
Associate Lighting Designer ....Joel Shier
Assistant Lighting Designer ....Kenneth Wills
Moving Light Programmer ....Sean Beach
Assistant Hair Designer ....Gretchen Androsavitch
Associate to the Hair Designer ....Glenna Williamson
Dialect Consultant ....Stephen Gabis
Vocal Coach ....Andrea Green
Production Carpenter ....Lemoncello
Production Electrician ....Dan Coey
Production Sound ....Kevin Kennedy
Deck Audio ....Stephanie Vetter
Sound Board Operator ....George Huckins
Light Board Operator ....Jane Masterson
Follow Spot ....German Pavon, III
Production Properties ....Pete Sarafin
Properties Assistant ....Rob Dagna
Wardrobe Supervisor ....Jessica Worsnop
Assistant Wardrobe Supervisor ....Jason Bishop
Dressers ....Elizabeth Brady, Tracey Diebold,
Jake Fry, John Furrow, Amanda Zane
Hair Supervisor ....Pat Marcus
Assistant Hair Supervisor ....Samantha Wiener
Synthesizer Programmer ....Randy Cohen
Children's Guardian ....Rachel Maier
Costume Construction/Stitchers ....Bonnie Prather,
Erin Roth
Production Assistants .....Sarah Testerman, Trisha Henson
Stage Manager Intern ....Emily Cates
General Management
Associates...........Margaret Skoglund, Jimmy Wilson
General Management Interns ...Alex Hajjar, Reeve Pierson
Press Interns ....Allison Lembo, Lisa Prywes
Assistant to Mr. Wise....................Matthew Dunivan

Soul Doctor Interns ....Rachel Kastner, Rina Schiller,
Zoe Silver, Ethan Stein
Advertising ....SpotCo/Drew Hodges, Tom Greenwald,
Stephen Sosnowski, Caraline Sogliuzzo, Cletus McKeown
Marketing ....SpotCo/Nick Pramik, Kristen Rathbun,
Emily Hammerman, Sara Barton
Website/Interactive Marketing ....SpotCo/Kyle Young,
Marisa Delmore, Callie Goff
Promotions ....Leanne Schanzer Promotions, Inc./
Leanne Schanzer, Justin Schanzer, Kara Laviola,
Michael Schanzer, Kim Gorman, Brynn Mosello
Director of Investor Relations ....Joyce Friedmann
Production Photography ....Carol Rosegg
Archival Photography ....Matthew Dunivan
Supervising Orthopedist ....Phillip Bauman, MD
Physical Therapy ....Sean P. Gallagher, PT/
Performing Arts Physical Therapy
Legal Counsel ....Zell & Co./Marc Zell, Esq.
Controller ......Marks Paneth & Shron LLP/Floyd Sklaver
Banking ....Chase Commercial Services/
Christina Ciniglio, Helene Simon
Insurance ....DeWitt Stern Insurance & Risk Services/
Anthony Pittari
Payroll Services ......Checks and Balances/Anthony Walker
Travel Agent ....Tzell Travel/The "A" Team, Andi Henig
Housing Services ....ABA IDEAL/Elizabeth Helke
Merchandising ....Max Merchandise
Music Clearances ....CR Music & Media Consulting/
Chris Robertson

CREDITS
Scenery and scenic effects built, painted and electrified by
ShowMotion Inc. Lighting by Production Resource Group.
Sound equipment by Masque Sound. Costume construction
by Tricorne, Eric Winterling Studios and Artur & Tailors.
Undergarments provided by Bra*Tenders. Costume
dyeing by Jeff Fender Studio. Millinery by Arnold Levine.
Footwear construction by T.O. Dey. Guitars courtesy of
Gibson Brands. Energy efficient washer/dryer courtesy of
LG Electronics.

Soul Doctor
SCRAPBOOK

Correspondent: Vasthy Mompoint, "Holy Beggar"

Opening Night Parties and/or Gifts: Opening night was at the Liberty Theatre and included Kosher food and lots of dancing and singing. We had a full concert at the end by Neshama Carlebach, Shlomo Carlebach's daughter, complete with gospel backup singers.

Most Exciting Celebrity Visitors: I thought it was cool to meet the Carlebach family. His wife and kids and grand-children. It felt very special that they were able to be there while we paid him tribute.

Favorite In-Theatre Gathering Place: There's a little area stage-left backstage where we like to congregate. We also have group therapy, strip dancing (JC Schuster), and it is the birth place of *Soul Doctor* Bits.

Actor Who Performed the Most Roles in This Show: Alex Fro 100 percent! She is the Holy Angel (Calpurnia), a Yeshiva boy, a Brooklyn boy, an Hasidic Jewish Man (LOL), the Production Assistant, the Lost Soul. And she understudies Young Eli Chaim.

Special Backstage Ritual: Before every show we put our hands in and chant "OY Oy Oy

Amber Iman (C), and fellow cast members (L-R): Jacqueline Antaramian, Ian Paget, Michael Paternostro, Jamie Jackson, Zarah Mahler, Eric Anderson and Ron Orbach, shuffle the *Soul Doctor* deck.

Gevalt!" Started by the talented Eric Anderson.

Favorite Backstage Photo (and the Story That Goes With It): I am obsessed with headshots. I think they are so funny for so many reasons. For my birthday the cast gave me their headshots all with notes on them such as: Please, stare at my Chocolate Beauty (Amber Iman) or I'm giving this to you so that if you are

ever looking around and wonder: "Are there any pretty people out there?," you'll have your answer (Ian Paget).

Memorable Audience Reaction: From Jacqueline Antaramian: When Amber comes on for the curtain call seeing all the sweet little Jewish ladies and men stumble—and I mean truly and sweetly stumble!—to get to their feet to give her a standing ovation. And then, when Eric comes on for the curtain call, well, forget about it. It is a great moment in why we do what we do. Mustn't be under-appreciative.

Worst Audience Behavior: From Ron Orbach: Texting is bad, but snoring is worse.

Memorable Ad-Lib: When Heather Parcells flashes Shlomo and JC Schuster screams "show me, show me" as we exit. They laugh every time.

Memorable Press Encounter: From Ron Orbach, who plays Reb Pinchas: Press: "Who is Reb Pinchas?"

Memorable Stage Door Fan Encounters: All of the people that come to the stage door with photos of Shlomo, or stories of how he introduced them to their husbands or wives. How he married them and played at their

MUSIC CREDIT

"I Put a Spell on You" written by Jalacy J. Hawkins. Published by EMI Unart Catalog Inc. Used by permission

SPECIAL THANKS

Michael Rain, Gerry McIntyre, Hilda Willis, Rabbi Sam Intrator, Zalmen Mlotek, R'Schneur & Devorah Kaplan, Sandy Divack Moss, Kenneth Anderson, Nesanel Druxman, Eli Kaplan Wildmann, Linda Fine

New Orleans production sponsored in part by Louisiana Economic Development Office of Entertainment Industry.

Soul Doctor rehearsed at Playwrights Horizons Studios.

Soul Doctor
SCRAPBOOK

weddings. It's amazing to see first-hand the influence he had/has.

Memorable Directorial Note: "Some of you don't know how to smoke a joint properly... uh... figure it out... somehow."

Cast Hangout: Natsumi's and Jamie Jackson's dressing room.

Company In-Jokes: Eric Anderson does this thing, LOL, where you are talking to him (serious talk/non-serious talk) and all of a sudden he'll start falling AS he's saying "I trust you." He fully goes for a real trust fall without ANY warning. It's HILARIOUS.

Embarrassing Moment: Ryan Strand: Saying "Cool it, homo" instead of "Cool it, Shlomo." LOL.

Favorite Moment During Each Performance: For me it's the Nina/Shlomo Scene. No matter what kind of house we have that is the scene that always brings them in. Eric and Amber are magic in the scene.

Favorite Snack Foods: Alcohol, M&M's, pretzels, animal crackers, alcohol.

Favorite Therapies: Physical therapy! And Singer's Saving Grace. Tiger Balm is almost always wafting through the air.

"Carols for a Cure" Carol: "The Chanukah Song" by Adam Sandler.

Catchphrase Only the Company Would Recognize: "Eez eet possseeble?" ("Is it possible?") from our hot French choreographer. He says that before he teaches us anything. To make it seem as though we had a choice! LOL.

Best In-House Parody Lyrics: When Eric Anderson takes his bows some cast members sing: "Eric Anderson, Eric Anderson, he plays Shlomo and is the lead of our show!" It's actually a beautiful song...like Tony-worthy.

Understudy Anecdote: The cast is very small. We almost all understudy one another! It's a good thing we all get along and love each other. :))

Nicknames: All the hippies have named themselves but Ferret is probably the best one to describe Heather Parcells. LOL.

Heaviest/Hottest Costume: It might be Amber Iman's Robe. It's heavy and thick but she manages to twirl it around with ease!

What Did You Think of the Web Buzz on Your Show? I love the description that it's "*Hair* meets *Fiddler on the Roof*" LOL! So right-on.

Coolest Thing About Being in This Show: I love the Jewish faith. There are so many parts of it that are beautiful. I love that as we leave the theatre there are rabbis blessing the stage and blessing the theatre. You can feel it in the air. :)

Other Memory of Working on the Show: Our Musical Director will yell "Shut up!" when we start singing after he's told us not to sing. That doesn't sound funny but, trust me, it is. LOL. It's fast and sharp and you always hit yourself for not listening in the first place.

1. *Yearbook* correspondent Vasthy Mompoint, recipient of the Gypsy Robe, takes a spin.
2. At intermisson with more card-playing cast members (L-R): Jacqueline Antaramian, Michael Paternostro, Jamie Jackson, Ron Orbach.
3. During tech on the show (L-R clockwise from the top): Dianna Barger, Vasthy Mompoint, Ian Paget, Heather Parcells, JC Schuster, Alexandra Frohlinger, Gina Rattan, Daniel Wise.
4. Vasthy with all those photos up on the wall, a gift for her birthday.

Spider-Man Turn Off the Dark

First Preview: November 28, 2010. Opened: June 14, 2011.
Closed January 4, 2014 after 182 Previews and 1,066 Performances.

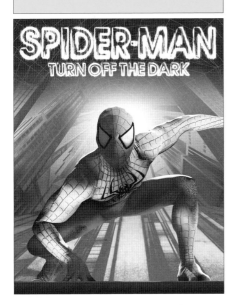

PLAYBILL®

Given extraordinary powers by the bite of a genetically enhanced spider, Peter Parker resolves to do battle with the forces of evil and his nemesis, the Green Goblin, as Spider-Man in this musical based on the comic book character of the same name.

CAST
(in order of appearance)

Peter Parker/ Spider-Man	JUSTIN MATTHEW SARGENT
Arachne	CHRISTINA DeCICCO
Mary Jane Watson	REBECCA FAULKENBERRY
Mrs. Gribrock	ISABEL KEATING

The Bullies

Flash	JAKE ODMARK
Kong	AARON LaVIGNE
Meeks	KEVIN DeJESUS-JONES
Boyle	DWAYNE CLARK
Uncle Ben	KEN MARKS
Aunt May	ISABEL KEATING
MJ's Father	DAN SHARKEY
Norman Osborn/ Green Goblin	ROBERT CUCCIOLI
Emily Osborn	LAURA BETH WELLS
Danny, Lab Assistant	DAN SHARKEY
Ring Announcer	DAN SHARKEY
Ring Girl	HETTIE BARNHILL
Trainer	EMMANUEL BROWN
First Gangster	AARON LaVIGNE
Second Gangster	DWAYNE CLARK
Third Gangster	JAKE ODMARK
Hero Flyer	KEVIN DeJESUS-JONES

Continued on next page

The Playbill Broadway Yearbook 2013-2014

FOXWOODS THEATRE
Operated by Lyric Theatre LLC

Michael Cohl & Jeremiah J. Harris, Land Line Productions, Hello Entertainment/David Garfinkle/Tony Adams
Sony Pictures Entertainment, Norton Herrick and Herrick Entertainment, Billy Rovzar & Fernando Rovzar, Stephen Bronfman
Jeffrey B. Hecktman, Omneity Entertainment/Richard G. Weinberg James L. Nederlander, Terry Allen Kramer
S2BN Entertainment, Jam Theatricals, The Mayerson/Gould/Hauser/Tysoe Group, Patricia Lambrecht, and Paul McGuinness
by arrangement with
Marvel Entertainment
present

SPIDER-MAN
TURN OFF THE DARK

Music and Lyrics by	Book by
Bono and The Edge	**Julie Taymor, Glen Berger & Roberto Aguirre-Sacasa**

Starring

Justin Matthew Sargent   Rebecca Faulkenberry   Christina DeCicco and Robert Cuccioli as Norman Osborn/Green Goblin

Featuring

Michael Mulheren   Ken Marks   Isabel Keating   Dan Sharkey   Matt Wilkas
Laura Beth Wells   Jake Odmark   Dwayne Clark   Aaron LaVigne

with

Ashley Adamek   David Armstrong   Gerald Avery   Kevin Aubin   Hettie Barnhill   Emmanuel Brown   Julius C. Carter   Cass Christopher
Michelle Dawson   Kevin DeJesus-Jones   Adam Ray Dyer   Drew Heflin   Dana Marie Ingraham   Ari Loeb   Kevin C. Loomis   Kristen Martin
Jodi McFadden   Paul McGill   Monette McKay   Jessica McRoberts   Kristen Faith Oei   Maxx Reed   Adam Roberts
Josh Sassanella   Jennifer Savelli   Whitney Sprayberry   Alex Michael Stoll

Scenic Design	Lighting Design	Costume Design	Sound Design
George Tsypin	**Donald Holder**	**Eiko Ishioka**	**Jonathan Deans**
Projection Design	Mask Design	Hair Design	Make-up Design
Kyle Cooper	**Julie Taymor**	**Campbell Young Associates**	**Judy Chin**
		Luc Verschueren	
Aerial Design	Aerial Rigging Design	Media Design	Prosthetics Design
Scott Rogers	**Jaque Paquin**	**Howard Werner**	**Louie Zakarian**
Arrangements & Orchestrations	Music Supervision	Music Producer	Music Direction
David Campbell	**Teese Gohl**	**Paul Bogaev**	**Kimberly Grigsby**
Music Coordinator	Vocal Arrangements		Additional Arrangements / Vocal Arrangements
Antoine Silverman	**David Campbell, Teese Gohl**		**Dawn Kenny & Rori Coleman**
	Kimberly Grigsby		
Associate Scenic Design	Associate Director	Associate Choreographer	Production Stage Manager
Rob Bissinger	**Keith Batten**	**Jason Snow**	**Kathleen E. Purvis**
Casting Director	Marketing Director	Marketing	Associate Producer
Telsey + Company	**Len Gill**	**Keith Hurd**	**Anne Tanaka**
Press Representation	Production Management	General Management	Executive Producers
O & M Co.	**Juniper Street Productions & MB Productions**	**Foresight Theatrical Aaron Lustbader Allan Williams**	**Glenn Orsher Stephen Howard Martin McCallum Adam Silberman**

Choreography and Aerial Choreography by
Daniel Ezralow

Additional Choreography by
Chase Brock

Direction by
Julie Taymor

Additional Direction by
Philip Wm. McKinley

TM and © 2013 Marvel Entertainment, LLC

10/1/13

Reeve Carney (R) hands off the Spidey mask to Justin Matthew Sargent

Spider-Man Turn Off the Dark

MUSICAL NUMBERS

ACT I

"The Myth of Arachne" ....Peter
"Behold and Wonder" ....Arachne, Ensemble
"Bullying by Numbers" ....Peter, Bullies, High School Students
"No More" ....Peter, Mary Jane
"D.I.Y. World" ....Norman, Emily, Peter, Mary Jane,
High School Students, Lab Assistants
"Venom" ....Bullies
"Bouncing Off the Walls" ....Peter, High School Students
"Rise Above" ....Peter, Arachne, Ensemble
"Pull the Trigger" ....Norman, Emily, Viper Executives, Soldiers
"Picture This" ....Peter, Mary Jane, Norman, Emily

ACT II

"A Freak Like Me Needs Company" ....Green Goblin, Ensemble
"If the World Should End" ....Mary Jane, Peter
"Sinistereo" ....Reporters
"Spider-Man!" ....Citizens of New York
"Turn Off the Dark" ....Arachne, Peter
"I Just Can't Walk Away" ....Mary Jane, Peter
"Boy Falls From the Sky" ....Peter
"I'll Take Manhattan" ....Green Goblin
"Finale – A New Dawn" ....Full Company

Cast Continued

Purse Lady ....ISABEL KEATING
Purse Snatcher ....JULIUS C. CARTER
J. Jonah Jameson ....MICHAEL MULHEREN
Reporters
   Buttons ....KEN MARKS
   Bud ....JAKE ODMARK
   Stokes ....DAN SHARKEY
   Maxie ....ISABEL KEATING
   Travis ....AARON LaVIGNE
   Robertson ....DWAYNE CLARK
Viper Executives ....DWAYNE CLARK,
   AARON LaVIGNE, KEN MARKS,
   DAN SHARKEY
The Sinister Six
   Swarm ....DREW HEFLIN
   The Lizard ....JULIUS C. CARTER
   Electro ....MAXX REED
   Kraven the Hunter .....KEVIN DeJESUS-JONES
   Carnage ....ALEX MICHAEL STOLL
   Swiss Miss ....ADAM ROBERTS
Marbles ....LAURA BETH WELLS
Exterminator Flyer ....DAVID ARMSTRONG
Receptionist ....LAURA BETH WELLS
Newsboy ....JAKE ODMARK
MJ's Friend ....LAURA BETH WELLS
Green Goblin Flyer ....ADAM ROBERTS
Citizens, Weavers, Students, Lab Assistants,
   Reporters, Puppeteers, Spider-Men,
   Secretaries, Soldiers ......DAVID ARMSTRONG,
   GERALD AVERY, HETTIE BARNHILL,
   EMMANUEL BROWN, JULIUS C. CARTER,
   CASS CHRISTOPHER, DWAYNE CLARK,
   KEVIN DeJESUS-JONES, DREW HEFLIN,
   DANA MARIE INGRAHAM, ISABEL KEATING,

AARON LaVIGNE, KEN MARKS,
KRISTEN MARTIN, JODI McFADDEN,
MONETTE McKAY, JAKE ODMARK,
KRISTEN FAITH OEI, MAXX REED,
ADAM ROBERTS, DAN SHARKEY,
WHITNEY SPRAYBERRY,
ALEX MICHAEL STOLL, LAURA BETH WELLS
Ensemble Aerialists ....ASHLEY ADAMEK,
DAVID ARMSTRONG, KEVIN AUBIN,
GERALD AVERY, HETTIE BARNHILL,
EMMANUEL BROWN, JULIUS C. CARTER,
CASS CHRISTOPHER, KEVIN DeJESUS-JONES,
ADAM RAY DYER, DREW HEFLIN,
DANA MARIE INGRAHAM, ARI LOEB,
KRISTEN MARTIN, JODI McFADDEN,
PAUL McGILL, MONETTE McKAY,
JESSICA McROBERTS, KRISTEN FAITH OEI,
ADAM ROBERTS, JOSH SASSANELLA,
JENNIFER SAVELLI, WHITNEY SPRAYBERRY,
ALEX MICHAEL STOLL

At certain performances, the role of Peter Parker/
Spider-Man will be played by MATT WILKAS.

UNDERSTUDIES

For Peter Parker/Spider-Man: JAKE ODMARK
For Mary Jane Watson: KRISTEN MARTIN,
   KRISTEN FAITH OEI
For Norman Osborn/Green Goblin:
   DAN SHARKEY
For Arachne: MICHELLE DAWSON,
   JODI McFADDEN
For J. Jonah Jameson: KEVIN C. LOOMIS,
   KEN MARKS, DAN SHARKEY

For Mrs. Gribrock: MICHELLE DAWSON,
   JESSICA McROBERTS, LAURA BETH WELLS
For Flash: AARON LaVIGNE,
   JOSH SASSANELLA
For Boyle: JULIUS C. CARTER,
   AARON LaVIGNE, JOSH SASSANELLA
For Kong: ADAM RAY DYER,
   JOSH SASSANELLA
For Meeks: ADAM RAY DYER,
   AARON LaVIGNE, JOSH SASSANELLA
For Uncle Ben: KEVIN C. LOOMIS,
   DAN SHARKEY
For Aunt May: MICHELLE DAWSON,
   JESSICA McROBERTS,
   LAURA BETH WELLS
For MJ's Father: AARON LaVIGNE,
   KEVIN C. LOOMIS
For Emily Osborn: MICHELLE DAWSON,
   JESSICA McROBERTS
For First Gangster: KEVIN AUBIN,
   ADAM RAY DYER, ARI LOEB,
   PAUL McGILL, JOSH SASSANELLA
For Second Gangster: KEVIN AUBIN,
   ADAM RAY DYER, AARON LaVIGNE,
   ARI LOEB, PAUL McGILL,
   JOSH SASSANELLA
For Third Gangster: KEVIN AUBIN,
   ADAM RAY DYER, AARON LaVIGNE,
   ARI LOEB, PAUL McGILL,
   JOSH SASSANELLA
For Purse Lady: ASHLEY ADAMEK,
   MICHELLE DAWSON,
   JESSICA McROBERTS
For Purse Snatcher: KEVIN AUBIN,
   ADAM RAY DYER, ARI LOEB,
   ADAM ROBERTS, JOSH SASSANELLA
For Buttons: KEVIN C. LOOMIS,
   JOSH SASSANELLA
For Bud: GERALD AVERY, AARON LaVIGNE,
   KEVIN C. LOOMIS, JOSH SASSANELLA
For Stokes: KEVIN C. LOOMIS,
   JOSH SASSANELLA
For Maxie: MICHELLE DAWSON,
   JESSICA McROBERTS,
   LAURA BETH WELLS
For Travis: KEVIN C. LOOMIS, JAKE ODMARK,
   JOSH SASSANELLA
For Robertson: JULIUS C. CARTER,
   AARON LaVIGNE, KEVIN C. LOOMIS,
   JOSH SASSANELLA
For Viper Executives: AARON LaVIGNE,
   KEVIN C. LOOMIS, JAKE ODMARK,
   JOSH SASSANELLA
For Danny, Lab Assistant:
   KEVIN C. LOOMIS, JOSH SASSANELLA
For Ring Announcer: KEVIN C. LOOMIS,
   JOSH SASSANELLA
For Ring Girl: ASHLEY ADAMEK,
   JESSICA McROBERTS, JENNIFER SAVELLI,
   WHITNEY SPRAYBERRY
For Trainer: KEVIN AUBIN, ADAM RAY DYER,
   DREW HEFLIN, ARI LOEB, PAUL McGILL

Continued on next page

Spider-Man Turn Off the Dark

Justin Matthew
Sargent
*Peter Parker/
Spider-Man*

Robert Cuccioli
*Norman Osborn/
Green Goblin*

Rebecca
Faulkenberry
Mary Jane Watson

Christina DeCicco
Arachne

Michael Mulheren
J. Jonah Jameson

Ken Marks
*Uncle Ben, Buttons,
Viper Executive,
Ensemble*

Cast Continued

For Carnage: KEVIN AUBIN, ADAM RAY DYER,
ARI LOEB, ADAM ROBERTS
For Electro: DAVID ARMSTRONG,
EMMANUEL BROWN, ADAM RAY DYER,
ARI LOEB, PAUL McGILL
For Kraven the Hunter: KEVIN AUBIN,
EMMANUEL BROWN, ADAM RAY DYER,
DREW HEFLIN, ARI LOEB,
JOSH SASSANELLA
For The Lizard: KEVIN AUBIN,
ADAM RAY DYER, ARI LOEB,
PAUL McGILL
For Swarm: GERALD AVERY,
DANA MARIE INGRAHAM, ARI LOEB,
PAUL McGILL
For Swiss Miss: KEVIN AUBIN
For Marbles: MICHELLE DAWSON,
JESSICA McROBERTS
For Receptionist: MICHELLE DAWSON,
JESSICA McROBERTS
For Newsboy: GERALD AVERY,
AARON LaVIGNE, JOSH SASSANELLA
For MJ's Friend: MICHELLE DAWSON,
JESSICA McROBERTS

DANCE CAPTAIN
ASHLEY ADAMEK

ASSISTANT DANCE CAPTAIN
DREW HEFLIN

SWINGS
ASHLEY ADAMEK, KEVIN AUBIN,
MICHELLE DAWSON, ADAM RAY DYER,

ARI LOEB, KEVIN C. LOOMIS, PAUL McGILL,
JESSICA McROBERTS, JOSH SASSANELLA,
JENNIFER SAVELLI

ORCHESTRA
Conductor: KIMBERLY GRIGSBY
Associate Conductor: CHARLES duCHATEAU
Guitars: ZANE CARNEY, MATT BECK,
BEN BUTLER
Basses: AIDEN MOORE,
RICHARD HAMMOND
Drums: JON EPCAR
Keyboards: BILLY JAY STEIN,
CHARLES duCHATEAU
Percussion: JOHN CLANCY
Hammered Dulcimer/Percussion: BILL RUYLE
Concertmaster: ANTOINE SILVERMAN
Viola/Violin: CHRISTOPHER CARDONA
Cello: ANJA WOOD
Trumpets: DON DOWNS, TONY KADLECK
French Horn: THERESA MacDONNELL
Trombone/Tuba: MARCUS ROJAS
Reeds: AARON HEICK

Electronic Music Design: BILLY JAY STEIN
Music Coordination: ANTOINE SILVERMAN
Music Copying Supervisor: STEVEN M. ALPER
Music Copyists: BETTIE ROSS,
RUSSELL ANIXTER, STEVEN COHEN,
JODY JAROWEY, DON RICE,
ROY WILLIAMS, DAVID WOLFSON
Piano Vocal Score Coordination: MARK BAECHLE

Isabel Keating
*Aunt May, Mrs.
Gribrock, Maxie,
Purse Lady*

Dan Sharkey
*MJ's Father, Danny,
Ring Announcer,
Stokes, Viper
Executive*

Matt Wilkas
*Peter Parker/
Spider-Man
Alternate*

Laura Beth Wells
*Emily Osborn,
Marbles,
Receptionist, MJ's
Friend, Ensemble*

Jake Odmark
*Flash, Third
Gangster, Bud,
Newsboy, Ensemble;
u/s Peter Parker/
Spider-Man*

Dwayne Clark
*Boyle, Second
Gangster, Robertson,
Viper Executive,
Ensemble*

Aaron LaVigne
*Kong, First Gangster,
Travis, Viper
Executive, Ensemble*

Ashley Adamek
*Dance Captain,
Swing*

David Armstrong
*Exterminator Flyer,
Ensemble*

Kevin Aubin
Swing

Gerald Avery
Ensemble

Hettie Barnhill
Ring Girl, Ensemble

Emmanuel Brown
Trainer, Ensemble

Julius C. Carter
The Lizard, Ensemble

Spider-Man Turn Off the Dark

Cass Christopher
Ensemble

Michelle Dawson
u/s Arachne, Swing

Kevin DeJesus-Jones
Meeks, Hero Flyer, Kraven the Hunter, Ensemble

Adam Ray Dyer
Swing

Drew Heflin
Swarm, Ensemble, Assistant Dance Captain

Dana Marie Ingraham
Ensemble

Ari Loeb
Swing

Kevin C. Loomis
u/s J. Jonah Jameson, Swing

Kristen Martin
Ensemble; u/s Mary Jane Watson

Jodi McFadden
Ensemble; u/s Arachne

Paul McGill
Swing

Monette McKay
Ensemble

Jessica McRoberts
Swing

Kristen Faith Oei
Ensemble; u/s Mary Jane Watson

Maxx Reed
Electro, Ensemble

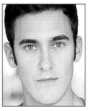

Adam Roberts
Swiss Miss, Green Goblin Flyer, Ensemble

Josh Sassanella
Swing

Jennifer Savelli
Swing

Whitney Sprayberry
Ensemble

Alex Michael Stoll
Carnage, Ensemble

Julie Taymor
Co-Book Writer, Director, Mask Designer

Bono
Music & Lyrics

The Edge
Music & Lyrics

Philip Wm. McKinley
Additional Direction

Glen Berger
Co-Book Writer

Roberto Aguirre-Sacasa
Co-Book Writer

Daniel Ezralow
Choreographer, Aerial Choreographer

Chase Brock
Additional Choreography

George Tsypin
Scenic Designer

Donald Holder
Lighting Designer

Eiko Ishioka
Costume Designer

Jonathan Deans
Sound Designer

Kyle Cooper
Projections Designer

Campbell Young
Campbell Young Associates
Hair Designers

Luc Verschueren
Campbell Young Associates
Hair Designers

Spider-Man Turn Off the Dark

Judy Chin
Make-up Designer

Scott Rogers
Aerial Designer

Jaque Paquin
Aerial Rigging Designer

Howard Werner
Media Design

Rob Bissinger
Associate Scenic Designer

Keith Batten
Associate Director

Jason Snow
Resident Director/ Choreographer

Jim Athens
Assistant Stage Manager

Sandra M. Franck
Assistant Stage Manager

Valerie Lau-Kee Lai
Assistant Stage Manager

Jenny Slattery
Assistant Stage Manager

Michael Wilhoite
Assistant Stage Manager

David Campbell
Arrangements and Orchestrations, Vocal Arrangements

Teese Gohl
Music Supervisor

Paul Bogaev
Music Producer

Kimberly Grigsby
Music Director

Antoine Silverman
Music Coordinator

Rori Coleman
Additional Arrangements/Vocal Arrangements

Dawn Kenny
Additional Arrangements/Vocal Arrangements

Billy Jay Stein
Electronic Music Designer

Bernard Telsey
Telsey + Company Casting

Keith Hurd
Marketing

Alexandra Paull, Ana Rose Greene, Joseph DeLuise, Hillary Blanken, Kevin Broomell, Guy Kwan, Juniper Street Productions
Production Management

Mike Bauder
MB Productions
Production Management

Fred Gallo
Technical Director

Alan Wasser
Foresight Theatrical
General Manager

Allan Williams
Foresight Theatrical
General Manager

Aaron Lustbader
Foresight Theatrical
General Manager

Michael Cohl
Producer

Jeremiah J. Harris
Producer

David Garfinkle
Hello Entertainment
Producer

Norton Herrick
Producer

Billy Rovzar
Producer

Fernando Rovzar
Producer

Spider-Man Turn Off the Dark

Stephen Bronfman
Producer

Jeffrey B. Hecktman
Producer

Richard G. Weinberg
Omneity
Entertainment
Producer

**James L.
Nederlander**
Producer

Terry Allen Kramer
Producer

Arny Granat
Jam Theatricals
Producer

Steve Traxler
Jam Theatricals
Producer

**Frederic H.
Mayerson**
The Mayerson/
Gould/Hauser/
Tysoe Group
Producer

James M. Gould
The Mayerson/
Gould/Hauser/
Tysoe Group
Producer

Ron Tysoe
The Mayerson/
Gould/Hauser/
Tysoe Group
Producer

Paul McGuinness
Producer

Glenn Orsher
Executive Producer

Stephen Howard
Executive Producer

Adam Silberman
Executive Producer

Collin Baja
Carnage, Ensemble

Reeve Carney
*Peter Parker/
Spider-Man*

Daniel Curry
*Ensemble Aerialist,
Swing*

Jake Epstein
*Peter Parker/
Spider-Man
Alternate*

Reed Kelly
*Swiss Miss,
Ensemble*

Kourtni Lind
Ring Girl, Ensemble

Natalie Lomonte
Swing

Jennifer Sanchez
Swing; u/s Arachne

Robert Cuccioli as
The Green Goblin
with one of his victims.

Photo: Jacob Cohl

Spider-Man Turn Off the Dark

Jamison Scott
Swing

Emily Shoolin
Swing

Cassandra Taylor
Ensemble

Brett Thiele
Trainer, Ensemble

Christopher W. Tierney
Meeks, Hero Flyer, Kraven the Hunter, Ensemble

Timothy Warmen
MJ's Father, Danny, Ring Announcer, Stokes, Viper Executive

Darius Barnes
Swing

Jason Gotay
Peter Parker/ Spider-Man Alternate

Elizabeth Judd
Ensemble; u/s Mary Jane Watson

Jamison Scott
Swing

Brett Thiele
Trainer, Ensemble

Timothy Warmen
MJ's Father, Danny, Ring Announcer, Stokes, Viper Executive

STAFF FOR
SPIDER-MAN TURN OFF THE DARK

GENERAL MANAGEMENT
FORESIGHT THEATRICAL
Alan Wasser   Allan Williams
Aaron Lustbader   Mark Shacket

PRODUCTION MANAGEMENT
JUNIPER STREET PRODUCTIONS
Hillary Blanken   Kevin Broomell
Guy Kwan   Ana Rose Greene   Alexandra Paull
Joseph DeLuise

MB PRODUCTIONS
Mike Bauder
Sonya Duveneck

TECHNICAL DIRECTOR
Fred Gallo

CASTING
TELSEY + COMPANY
Bernard Telsey CSA, Will Cantler CSA,
David Vaccari CSA,
Bethany Knox CSA, Craig Burns CSA,
Tiffany Little Canfield CSA, Rachel Hoffman CSA,
Justin Huff CSA, Patrick Goodwin CSA,
Abbie Brady-Dalton CSA, David Morris, Cesar A. Rocha

COMPANY MANAGER
Ryan Conway

GENERAL PRESS REPRESENTATIVE
O&M CO.
Rick Miramontez   Andy Snyder
Ryan Ratelle   Michael Jorgensen

Production Stage Manager .... Kathleen E. Purvis

Stage Manager .... Andrew Neal
Assistant Stage Managers .... Jim Athens,
Sandra M. Franck, Valerie Lau-Kee Lai,
Jenny Slattery, Michael Wilhoite
Sub Stage Managers .... Theresa A. Bailey,
Samantha Preiss, Jeffrey Rodriguez
Associate Company Manager .... Thom Mitchell
Assistant Company Manager .... Tammie L. Ward
Assistant Director .... Eileen F. Haggerty
Resident Director/Choreographer .... Jason Snow
Assistant Original Direction .... Dodd Loomis
Assistant Choreographer .... Cherice Barton
Production Aerial Supervisor .... Angela Phillips
Flight Instructor .... Gonzalo Brea
UK Casting .... Gillian Hawser

Set Design Creative Team:
Associate Scenic Designer .... Rob Bissinger
Pop-up and Dimensional Design .... Arturs Virtmanis
Illustration and Graphics .... Baiba Baiba
Cityscape Graphics .... Sergei Goloshapov

Assistant Set Design Team:
First Assistant Set Design .... Anita La Scala
Graphic Art .... Sia Balabanova, Rafael Kayanan
Pop-ups .... Nathan Heverin
Model Makers .... Eric Beauzay, Catherine Chung,
Rachel Short Janocko, Damon Pelletier,
Daniel Zimmerman
Draftsmen .... Robert John Andrusko, Toni Barton,
Larry W. Brown, Mark Fitzgibbons,
Jonathan Spencer, Josh Zangen
Assistant Set Design ....Tijana Bjelajac, Szu-Feng Chen,
Heather Dunbar, Mimi Lien, Qin (Lucy) Lu,
Robert Pyzocha, Chsato Uno, Frank McCullough
Previsualization .... Lily Twining
Associate Costume
    Designer .... Mary Nemecek Peterson
Assistant Costume Designers .... Angela M. Kahler,
Katie Irish, Michael Hannah

Costume Shoppers .... Jennifer Adams, Dana Burkart,
Cathy Parrott, Jen Raskopf
Associate Makeup Designer .... Angela Johnson
Associate Lighting Designer .... Vivien Leone
Assistant Lighting Designers .... Caroline Chao,
Carolyn Wong, Michael Jones
Assistant to the
    Lighting Designer .... Porsche McGovern
Automated Lighting Programmer .... Richard Tyndall
Assistant Video Designer .... Sarah Jakubasz
Video Programmer .... Phil Gilbert
Associate Sound Designers ...Brian Hsieh, Keith Caggiano
Puppet and Mask
    Production Supervisor .... Louis Troisi
Assistant Puppet and
    Mask Coordinator .... Curran Banach
Automated Flying Programmer .... Jason Shupe
Production Carpenter .... Jack Anderson
Assistant Carpenters .... Andrew Elman, Dave Fulton,
Hugh Hardyman, Kris Keene, Matthew J. Lynch,
Mike Norris, Geoffrey Vaughn
Production Electricians ..... Randall Zaibek, James Fedigan
Head Electrician .... Ron Martin
Production Video Electricians .... Jason Lindahl,
Chris Herman
Production Sound Engineer .... Simon Matthews
Head Sound Engineer .... John Sibley
Assistant Sound Engineer .... Scott Sanders
Production Properties
    Supervisor .... Joseph P. Harris, Jr.
Associate Properties Supervisor .... Timothy M. Abel
E-Stop Personnel .... Gonzalo Brea
Production Wardrobe Supervisor ......Michael D. Hannah
Assistant Wardrobe Supervisors .... Christel Murdock,
Sonya Wysocki
Dressers .... Robert Belopede, Dana Burkart,
Diana Calderazzo, Jackie Freeman, Lyle Jones,
Carrie Kamerer, Rosemary Keough, Shannon McDowell,
Leslie Moulton, Daniel Mura, Evelina Nervil,

Spider-Man Turn Off the Dark

Kyle O'Connor, Michael Piscitelli, Lacie Pulido, Jack Scott, Kyle Stewart, Ron Tagert, Cheryl Widner

Seamstress .... Alejandra Rubinos

Laundry .... David Gilleo

Hair Supervisor .... Ruth Carsch

Assistant Hair Supervisor .... Lisa Weiss

Assistant Hair Designer .... Cory McCutcheon

Hairstylists .... Brian Hennings, Stacy Schneiderman

Production Makeup Supervisor .... Angela Johnson

Assistant Makeup Supervisor .... Tiffany Hicks

Production Photographer/
   Videographer .... Jacob Cohl

Video Crew ... Ben Nabors, Matt Kazman, Nora Tennessen

Cover Photo .... Jacob Cohl

Lead Guitar Technician .... Dallas Schoo

Additional Guitar Technician .... Mike Vegas

Workshop Audio Engineers ...... Carl Glanville, Angie Teo

Vocal Coach .... Don Lawrence

Dialect Coach .... Deborah Hecht

Acting Coach .... Sheila Grey

Technical Production Assistants .... Sue Barsoum, Steve Chazaro, Kate DellaFera, Sonya Duveneck, Ania Parks, Alexandra Paull, Melissa Spengler, Kim Straatemeier

Production Assistants .... Allison Cottrell, Hannah Dorfman, Amanda Johnson, Gregory Murray, Samantha Preiss, Danya Taymor, Raynelle Wright

Costume Interns .. Yingshi June Lin, Tomke Von Gawinski

Orthopedist .... David S. Weiss, MD

Physical Therapist .... Heidi Green

Official Athletic Trainer .. Prime Blueprint/Dr. Edyth Heus

Consulting Producer .... Jeffery Auerbach

Producing Consultant .... Carl Pasbjerg

Producing Associate .... Jamie Forshaw

Executive Assistant to Michael Cohl .... Sofia Axtmayer

Executive Assistant to
   Jeremiah J. Harris .... Stella Morelli

Executive Assistant to Glenn Orsher .... Tricia Olson

Marketing Director .... Len Gill

Marketing .... Keith Hurd

Marketing Associate .... Mary Caitlin Barrett

Advertising & Marketing .. aka/Scott Moore, Pippa Bexon, Danielle Barchetto, Kyle Hall, Adam Jay, Jacob Matsumiya, Janette Roush, Trevor Sponseller

Website Design &
   Internet Marketing .... Situation Interactive/
      Damian Bazadona, John Lanasa, Jeremy Kraus, Victoria Gettler, Chris Powers

National Public Relations .... Ken Sunshine/ Sunshine, Sachs & Associates

Sponsorship Consultant .... Cary Chevat

Press Associates .... Sarah Babin, Molly Barnett, Scott Braun, Jaron Caldwell, Philip Carrubba, Jon Dimond, Joyce Friedmann, Yufen Kung, Chelsea Nachman, Marie Pace, Pete Sanders

Press Interns .... Nancy Alligood, Patrick Lazour, Kevin O'Malley

Legal Counsel .... Levine Plotkin & Menin LLP/ Ron Feiner, Esq., Beigelman, Feiner & Feldman/ Joseph T. Moldovan, Esq., Jack Levy, Esq., Joshua D. Saviano, Esq., Morrison Cohen LLP/Dale Cendali, Esq.; Courtney Farkas, Esq. Kirkland & Ellis LLP

Accounting .... Marks Paneth & Shron/Chris Cacace, Marina Flom, Kirill Baytalskiy

General Management Associates ... Mark Barna, Jake Hirzel

General Management Office .... Julia Barnett, Kaitlin Boland, Lauren Friedlander, Nina Lutwick

Insurance .... DeWitt Stern Group/Pete Shoemaker

Banking .... Signature Bank/Barbara von Borstel, Margaret Monigan, Mary Ann Fanelli, Janett Urena

Payroll .... Castellana Services, Inc.

Transportation and
   Housing .... Road Rebel Touring and Travel Services, Alternative Business Accommodations, The Mansfield Hotel

Dry Cleaners .... Winzer Cleaners

Group Sales
1-800-Broadway

CREDITS AND ACKNOWLEDGMENTS

Scenery and scenic effects built and electrified by PRG Scenic Technologies, New Windsor, NY. Scenery painted by Scenic Art Studios, Cornwall, NY. Show control and scenic motion control featuring Stage Command Systems® by PRG Scenic Technologies, New Windsor, NY. Aerial effects equipment provided by Fisher Technical Services Inc. Video projection equipment, lighting equipment and sound equipment provided by PRG, Secaucus, NJ. Special effects executed by Excitement Technologies, Addison, TX. Softgoods built by I. Weiss and Sons Inc., Fairview, NJ. Props executed by the Spoon Group, Rahway, NJ; the Rollingstock Company, Sarasota, FL; the Paragon Innovation Group Inc., Toronto, ON; Illusion Projects, Las Vegas, NV; Beyond Imagination, Newburgh, NY; Cigar Box Studios Inc., Newburgh, NY; Czinkota Studios, Gardiner, NY; and Hamilton Scenic Specialty Inc., Dundas, ON. Media content created by Prologue Films. Puppets executed by Nathan Heverin, New Paltz, NY; Michael Curry Design Inc., Portland, OR; the Paragon Innovation Group Inc., Toronto, ON; Igloo Projects/Philip Cooper, Brooklyn, NY. Puppet assistance by Ilya Vett. Hauling by Clark Transfer Inc.; Michael O'Brien & Sons, Bronx, NY; and Prop Transport, New York, NY. Excerpt from "Manhattan" written by Richard Rodgers, Lorenz Hart, used by permission of Piedmont Music Company, publisher. "The Boy Falls From the Sky" lyrics by Bono and The Edge, music by U2, used by permission.

Costumes constructed by Parsons-Meares Ltd.

Additional costumes by Bill Hargate Costumes; Tom Talmon Studios; Artur & Tailors Ltd.; Danielle Gisiger; Valentina Kozhecksy; Arel Studio; Costume Armour, Cornwall, NY; Maria Ficalora Knitwear; and Jon Gellman Designs. Millinery by Monica Vianni, Arnold Levine. Costume crafts by Paragon Innovation Group Inc., Toronto, ON; James Chai, Philip Cooper, New York, NY; Signs and Shapes International. Custom shirts by L. Allmeier. Custom shoes by Jitterbug Boy, LaDuca Shoes, Montana Leather, Capri Shoes and World Tone. Digital printing and screen printing by Gene Mignola. Costume painting by Parmalee Welles-Tolkan, Mary Macy, Margaret Peot, Virginia Clow, Claudia Dzundza. Additional printing by Jeff Fender. Development painting by Hochi Asiatico.

IN MEMORY OF
Tony Adams

SPECIAL THANKS

Stan Lee, Anne Runolfsson, Thomas Schumacher, William

Court Cohen, Trevor Bowen, Keryn Kaplan, Shan Lui, Liz Devlin, Catriona Garde, Susan Hunter, Missy Iredell, Michelle Lieu, Jennifer McManus, Principle Management Dublin and New York, Steve Lillywhite, David Toraya, Allen Grubman, Gil Karson, Larry Shire, Paul Wachter, Seth Gelblum, Michael West, Elliot Goldenthal, Rick Rubin, Jon Kilik, Michael Arndt, Bill Flanagan, Jennifer Lyne, Colin Farrell, Susan Stroman, Eoin Colfer, Jake Bell, Don Lasker, Darryl Scherba, William Dailey, Michael O'Brien and Sons, Derek Mouton of MCD, Vox Amplification, Fender Guitars, Rickenbacker Guitars, to NS Design for the loan of the electric violin and cello, Roland, Tekserve, James Jones Hammered Dulcimers, Bruce Glikas

---

The Chrysler Building and its image are trademarks of Tishman Speyer Properties, LP and its affiliates and is used herein with permission.

Makeup provided by M·A·C Cosmetics

Rehearsed at the New 42nd Street Studios

Souvenir merchandise designed and created by
S2BN Entertainment
Norman Perry   Brahma Jade   Pete Milano
www.SpiderManOnBroadwaystore.com

Energy efficient washer/dryer courtesy of
LG Electronics

To learn more about the production please visit
www.SpiderManOnBroadway.com

HISTORY OF THE FOXWOODS THEATRE

The Foxwoods Theatre combines architectural preservation with state-of-the-art construction and technology. The spirit and character of New York's grandest historic theatres has been maintained and united with the technical amenities of a modern facility.

In 1997 the Ford Center for the Performing Arts was erected on the site of the legendary Lyric Theatre (1903; 1,261 seats) and Apollo Theatre (1920; 1,194 seats). The auditorium's interior design is based on historic elements from the Apollo Theatre. The Apollo's original ceiling dome, proscenium arch, and side boxes were removed, restored and re-installed (upon expansion for the larger scale of the new theatre) in the new auditorium. The side wall panels were created for acoustical considerations and designed to complement the historic features. New murals were commissioned to form a frieze over the new side boxes. Informally titled "Wings of Creativity," they were inspired by ancient Greek myths of Apollo, patron god of musicians and poets.

The lobby's design is based on historical elements of the Lyric Theatre. An elliptical dome from the Lyric was reproduced as the centerpiece of a new two-story atrium. The grand limestone staircase was designed to provide the flow and spirit of a grand theatre or opera house. The staircase railings feature lyre designs that were recreated from the original 43rd Street façade balcony rails. In the floor is a magnificent mosaic featuring comedy and tragedy masks inspired by sculptures on the historic 43rd St. façade. The 650-sq.-ft. mosaic includes 172,800 hand-cut pieces of marble from all over the world. At the top of the stairs is a medallion with the head of Zeus, taken from the Lyric's auditorium, and on the dress circle level, cold-painted windows (a stained glass technique) featuring a cupid design have been restored. The lighting in the lobby features the bare

Spider-Man Turn Off the Dark
SCRAPBOOK

Correspondent: Adam Roberts, "Swiss Miss," "Green Goblin Flyer," "Ensemble"

Memorable Note/Fax/Fan Letter: The thank-you note we received from the Autism-Friendly Performance audience members.

Opening Night Party/Gifts: Leather *Spider-Man* bag/umbrellas with the opening date scratched out multiple times due to multiple postponements. Party at Bowlmor Lanes.

Most Exciting Visitor: Bill Clinton opening night and John Harbaugh right after the Ravens had won the Super Bowl. He stayed afterwards and was very gracious with his time.

Favorite In-theatre Gathering Place: PT room that doubles as greenroom and gym.

Actor with the Most Roles: Onstage: Isabel Keating; Swing: Jessica McRoberts.

Special Backstage Ritual: Group huddle and name chant after someone makes a debut or goes on for a first time when curtain drops.

Favorite Backstage Photo or Story: Cutout paper replicas of Reeve Carney's face all over the backstage area, valid for one free drink when brought to the bar after his final performance.

Memorable Audience Reaction: 700 children from local homeless shelters—the excitement and noise level was through the roof.

Worst Audience Behavior: A nanny allowed a child to vomit over the balcony ledge onto the innocent patrons in the orchestra below during a show.

Unique Pre-Show Announcement: Spider-Man creator Stan Lee was the voice heard in version 1.0.

Memorable Ad-lib: Patrick Page forgetting lines and instead summarizing them saying, "I have no idea" at the beginning of "D.I.Y. World."

Memorable Press Encounters: Macy's Thanksgiving Day Parade, Letterman performance, and Spidey's appearance atop a skyscraper in Times Square for the New Year's Ball Drop.

Memorable Stage Door/Fan Encounter: Our most loyal and beloved fans Nami (mother)

Photo: Monica Simoes

Photo: Joseph Marzullo

and her adorable daughter Szu Szu.

Memorable Directorial Note: We were all required to make character bios for all roles performed in show, which were bound into a book. We were then asked to speak to one another as those characters 15 minutes prior to the show.

Company In-Jokes: The rate of returning company members is very high, so a popular quote around the building is: "I ain't EVER leaving *Spider-Man*."

Embarrassing Moments: Too many to count. It's *Spider-Man*!

Favorite Moment During Each Performance: The flying and seeing the expression on the kids' faces.

Favorite Hangout: Reunion Surf Bar.

Favorite Snack Food: Green Symphony and Lucky Star Deli on 43rd St.

Therapy: Foam rollers and lacrosse balls.

Pit Stop (Orchestra Story): All four members of the band Carney were hired to work on the show, and two of the musicians played on stage during the first incarnation.

Public Relations: An older man complained after the show about the exorbitant price of the movie he had just watched and that he was distracted by the dancing through the screen.

Mascot: Spidey.

"Gypsy of the Year" Sketch: "Spider-Man Overcomes Demons" directed and choreographed by Kristine Covillo and Adam Dyer.

Carols for a Cure: "A Savior Is Born," written by Josh Sassanella and Jamison Scott.

Catchphrase: "Take it to the Tick."

Fastest Costume Change: Peter Parker's "Boy Falls From The Sky" into Spider-Man costume.

Who Wore Heaviest/Hottest Costumes: Heaviest: Adam Roberts 70-pound Green Goblin wings. Hottest: Any supervillain.

Who Wore the Least?: Hettie Barnhill as the Ring Girl.

Coolest Thing About Being in This Show: The message and the company's unwavering acknowledgement to "everyday heroes" in the world around us.

1. The final Spider-Man, Justin Matthew Sargent, gets his final kiss at the final curtain call from Rebecca Faulkenberry's Mary Jane Watson.
2. Curtain call on closing night.
3. (L-R): Reeve Carney and Robert Cuccioli use Buca di Beppo pasta sauce to paste their handprints on autographed placards.

---

carbon filament light bulb, utilized in the early 20th century, to create a warm candlelight glow.

At 1,932 seats, the new theatre is one of Broadway's largest. The Ford Center opened with the acclaimed musical *Ragtime*, followed by the Broadway revival of *Jesus Christ Superstar* and the award-winning revival of *42nd Street*. In 2005, the Ford Center was renamed the Hilton Theatre. Its premiere production was the musical *Chitty Chitty Bang Bang*, followed by the dance-inspired musical *Hot Feet*, the holiday spectacular *Dr. Seuss' How the Grinch Stole Christmas: The Musical*, *The Pirate Queen* and the new Mel Brooks musical *Young Frankenstein*. In 2010, the Hilton Theatre was renamed the Foxwoods Theatre. We are

pleased to welcome *Spider-Man Turn Off The Dark* to the Foxwoods stage.

FOXWOODS THEATRE

C.O.O., Lyric Theatre/ General Manager	Erich Jungwirth
Assistant General Manager	Sue Barsoum
House Manager	Eric Paris
Facility Manager	Jeff Nuzzo
Assistant Facility Manager	David Dietsch
Box Office Treasurer	Spencer Taustine
Assistant Box Office Treasurer	Michelle Smith
Head Carpenter	James C. Harris
Head Electrician	Art J. Friedlander
Head of Properties	Joseph P. Harris Jr.
Head of Sound	John R. Gibson
Staff Accountant	Joyia Bradley
Office Manager	Brian Mahoney
Shipping/Receiving	Dinara Kratsch

FOXWOODS THEATRE
Operated by Lyric Theatre LLC

A Time to Kill

First Preview: September 28, 2013. Opened: October 20, 2013.
Closed November 17, 2013 after 23 Previews and 33 Performances.

PLAYBILL®

Based on John Grisham's best-selling novel, this courtroom drama follows the rural Mississippi trial of a penniless black man facing the death penalty for killing two white men who raped his 10-year-old daughter. Treating the audience as the jury, his white lawyer faces the seemingly hopeless task of fighting an open-and-shut case against a prosecution with all the resources of the state attorney general's office. But, with the help of a drunk and disbarred older attorney and a smart young law clerk, the defendent's lawyer gradually starts to turn the case around. The production is notable for having prominent film, TV and stage stars in supporting roles.

CAST
(in order of appearance)

Jake Brigance, *attorney* ......SEBASTIAN ARCELUS
Vernon Pate, *court deputy*................J.R. HORNE
Ozzie Walls,
   sheriff of Ford County ....CHIKÉ JOHNSON
Omar Noose, *circuit judge for*
   Ford County .....FRED DALTON THOMPSON
Drew Tyndale,
   a public defender ....JOHN PROCACCINO
Carl Lee Hailey...JOHN DOUGLAS THOMPSON
Rufus R. Buckley, *district attorney*
   for Polk County.....................PATRICK PAGE
Norma Gallo, *court reporter* .....TIJUANA T. RICKS
DeWayne Looney, *a deputy* JEFFREY M. BENDER
Billy Ray Cobb ....LEE SELLARS
Pete Willard ....DASHIELL EAVES
Lucien Wilbanks ....TOM SKERRITT

Continued on next page

354

DARYL ROTH EVA PRICE

JONATHAN MANN MARTIAN ENTERTAINMENT PETER MAY SQUARE 1 THEATRICS
JUDITH ANN ABRAMS/JAYNE SHERMAN DAVID BRYANT/ROCK CANDY PRODUCTIONS BRYAN K.L. BYRD III/THE STORYLINE PROJECT
MARY BETH DALE/AVRAM FREEDBERG ELLIOTT MASIE/SARA BETH ZIVITZ PHILIP MEISSNER/SLOSBERG PRODUCTIONS
present

A TIME TO KILL
A NEW COURTROOM DRAMA

BASED ON THE CLASSIC BEST SELLER BY
JOHN GRISHAM

adapted for the stage by
RUPERT HOLMES

starring

SEBASTIAN ARCELUS   JOHN DOUGLAS THOMPSON   ASHLEY WILLIAMS
TOM SKERRITT
TONYA PINKINS   CHIKÉ JOHNSON
PATRICK PAGE
JEFFREY M. BENDER DASHIELL EAVES J.R. HORNE JOHN PROCACCINO TIJUANA T. RICKS LEE SELLARS
PHILIP KERR MOROCCO OMARI BRENNA PALUGHI
and
FRED DALTON THOMPSON

SCENIC DESIGN	COSTUME DESIGN	LIGHTING DESIGN	ORIGINAL MUSIC AND SOUND DESIGN
JAMES NOONE	DAVID C. WOOLARD	JEFF CROITER	LINDSAY JONES

PROJECTION DESIGN	FIGHT DIRECTOR	HAIR & WIG DESIGN	CASTING
JEFF SUGG	DAVID S. LEONG	PAUL HUNTLEY	TARA RUBIN CASTING

PRESS REPRESENTATIVE	DIALECT COACH	ADVERTISING & MARKETING	TECHNICAL SUPERVISOR
O&M CO.	STEPHEN GABIS	SERINO/COYNE	PETER FULBRIGHT

PRODUCTION STAGE MANAGER	COMPANY MANAGER	GENERAL MANAGER
JAMES LATUS	JENNIFER KEMP	101 PRODUCTIONS, LTD.

DIRECTED BY
ETHAN MCSWEENY

Originally presented by Arena Stage
Molly Smith, Artistic Director   Edgar Dobie, Managing Director

The producers wish to express their appreciation to the Theatre Development Fund for its support of this production.

10/20/13

(Center, L-R) Patrick Page and Sebastian Arcelus with the cast of *A Time to Kill*

Photo: Carol Rosegg

A Time to Kill

Cast Continued

D.R. Musgrove, *co-counsel*
   to the district attorney ....DASHIELL EAVES
Ellen Roark ....ASHLEY WILLIAMS
Gwen Hailey, *Carl Lee's wife* ......TONYA PINKINS
Dr. W.T. Bass ....JOHN PROCACCINO
Terrell Grist................................LEE SELLARS
Dr. Wilbert Rodeheaver, *head of staff at*
   Whitfield Mental Hospital ....LEE SELLARS

UNDERSTUDIES
For Carl Lee, Ozzie, Looney:
MOROCCO OMARI
For Ellen Roark, Court Reporter:
BRENNA PALUGHI
For Rufus R. Buckley: LEE SELLARS
For Jake: DASHIELL EAVES
For Judge Noose: J.R. HORNE
For Gwen: TIJUANA T. RICKS
For Rodeheaver, Pete Willard:
JEFFREY M. BENDER
Standby for Lucien: PHILIP KERR

TIME
The Early 1980s

PLACE
In and around the Clanton courthouse in
Ford County, Mississippi

Photo: Carol Rosegg

(L-R): Tonya Pinkins,
John Douglas Thompson
and Sebastian Arcelus

Sebastian Arcelus
Jake Brigance

John Douglas
Thompson
Carl Lee Hailey

Ashley Williams
Ellen Roark

Tom Skerritt
Lucien Wilbanks

Patrick Page
Rufus R. Buckley

Tonya Pinkins
Gwen Hailey

Chiké Johnson
Ozzie Walls

Fred Dalton
Thompson
Judge Noose

Jeffrey M. Bender
*Deputy Looney;
u/s Rodeheaver,
Pete Willard*

Dashiell Eaves
*Pete Willard/D.R.
Musgrove; u/s Jake*

J.R. Horne
Mr. Pate

John Procaccino
*Drew Tyndale/
W.T. Bass*

Tijuana T. Ricks
*Court Reporter;
u/s Gwen*

Lee Sellars
*Cobb/Rodeheaver/
Grist*

Philip Kerr
Standby Lucien

Morocco Omari
*u/s Carl Lee, Ozzie,
Looney*

Brenna Palughi
*u/s Ellen, Court
Reporter*

John Grisham
Original Novel

Rupert Holmes
Playwright

Ethan McSweeny
Director

James Noone
Scenic Designer

David C. Woolard
Costume Designer

Jeff Croiter
Lighting Designer

A Time to Kill

Lindsay Jones
*Original Music &
Sound Designer*

Jeff Sugg
Projection Designer

Paul Huntley
Hair Designer

David Leong
Fight Director

Stephen Gabis
Dialect Coach

Tara Rubin
Tara Rubin Casting
Casting

Wendy Orshan
101 Productions, Ltd.
General Manager

Peter Fulbright
Tech Production
Services
Technical Supervisor

Daryl Roth
Producer

Eva Price
Producer

Judith Ann Abrams
Co-Producer

David Bryant
Co-Producer

Avram C. Freedberg
Co-Producer

Mary Beth Dale
Co-Proudcer

Carl D. White
Martian
Entertainment
Co-Producer

Gregory Rae
Martian
Entertainment
Co-Producer

Elliott Masie
Co-Producer

Peter May
Co-Producer

John B. Yonover
Rock Candy
Theatricals
Co-Producer

Remmel T. Dickinson
Rock Candy
Theatricals
Co-Producer

Jayne Baron
Sherman
Co-Producer

R.K. Greene
The Storyline Project
Co-Producer

Jay Leland Krottinger
Square 1 Theatrics
Co-Producer

Ryan Tanner
Square 1 Theatrics
Co-Producer

Molly Smith
Arena Stage
Artistic Director

Edgar Dobie
Arena Stage
Executive Producer

Photo: Carol Rosegg
(L-R): Ashley Williams,
Sebastian Arcelus
and Tom Skerritt

A Time to Kill

DAY DOORMAN
Joe Kasper

MANAGEMENT
(L-R): Jeff Brancato (Production Assistant), James Latus (Production Stage Manager), David Sugarman (Stage Manager)

EVENING DOORMAN
John Green

Photos: James Latus

FRONT OF HOUSE
Front Row (L-R): Helen Bentley (Chief Usher), Patricia Byrne (Usher), Melissa Jorgensen (Asst. Treasurer), Mae Smith (Directress), Sheila Staffney (Usher)
Back Row (L-R): Andrew McKay (Usher), Julia Gonzalez (Usher), Carolyne Jones-Barnes (House Manager), Rita Russell (Ticket Taker), Yuri Fernandez (Assistant Porter)

CREW
Front Row (L-R): Adam Girardet (Wardrobe), Scotty Westervelt (Wardrobe Supervisor), AraBella Fischer (Wardrobe)
Back Row (L-R): Dave Horowitz (Sound), Hugh Freeland (Electrics), Allison Rogers (Wardrobe), Rob Presley (Props), Emilia Martin (Hair and Make-up), Justin Sanok (Flys), Terry McGarty (Carpenter), Doug "Pablo" Moscinski, Sylvia Yoshioka (Electrics)
Not pictured: Tommy Mitchell (Props), Tom Lawrey (Electrics), Stacey Sarmiento (Wardrobe)

A Time to Kill
SCRAPBOOK

Correspondent: James Latus, Production Stage Manager

Memorable Note, Fax or Fan Letter: From Ben Rodenmeyer, from Mississippi: "…I am also a huge fan of Tonya Pinkins (*Caroline or Change*? More like Caroline or work sister!)…."

Opening Night Parties and/or Gifts: The opening night party was at Bryant Park Grill. Opening night gifts ranged from leather bound journals, gavel key chains from the stage managers and Dixie Grits to contributions to the Southern Poverty Law Center. Most notable: a joke addendum to the *Playbill* cast list, bios and accompanying celebrity photos of additional characters named in the show but not seen on stage, authored by J.R. Horne.

Most Exciting Celebrity Visitor and What They Did/Said: Loretta Swit came to see the show three times. The first time she was white head to toe: hair, sweater, pants, jacket and shoes. Glenn Close also came backstage after the show and said how much she "Loved" actors!!!

Favorite In-Theatre Gathering Place: Wardrobe Room or top floor hospitality room where there is a shower that nobody seemed to use. You don't get very dirty in a courtroom. It is always open and available. Because it's so far up, there is danger from low-flying planes.

Special Backstage Rituals: "*Time to Kill* a Bottle Thursdays," with a different show-related themed drink each week. Also: incessant chanting of "rubber baby buggy bumper"; John Douglas Thompson's eclectic selection of music, which runs from opera to rap to Louis Armstrong and back again; Lee Sellars touching up his spider tattoo on his head; Patrick Page's rumbling vocal warm-ups, which sound like the R train coming through the theatre; Sebastian

Continued on next page

A Time to Kill
SCRAPBOOK

Arcelus' vocal warm-ups, which sound strangely like a threatening bird of prey; extra guest pages from the doorman to accommodate all of Tonya Pinkins' friends.

Favorite Backstage Photo: The photo taken by S.M. Jeff Brancato of Fred Dalton Thompson's size 24EEE feet, sticking out from under his cubby hole on stage left.

Most Memorable Audience Reaction: The kiss between Ellen and Jake usually gets gasps. And snorts from backstage. And one night, an enthusiastic audience member yelled out, "Huh, huh, nice…" at least three times per scene.

Most Memorable Audience Behavior: The young woman in the balcony who removed her tights during the show.

Unique Pre-Show Announcement: "Places please for the top of our story." – James Latus.

Memorable Ad-Lib: "If Carl Lee was black… I mean white… if he was white…" —Tonya Pinkins (Gwen Hailey). And Tom's friend "Tommy LEE Wilbanks."

Memorable Stage Door Fan Encounter: The gentleman who had his wife film Fred Thompson sign about 30 pictures of himself; the young man from Houston who had come all the way just to see the show; a mother and

daughter from Mississippi in town to tour colleges who loved the show.

Memorable Directorial Note: To Ashley Williams (Ellen Roark): "Do it as if it's really happening." To J.R. Horne (Mr. Pate): "Let's pre-set the vodka." "Pour the vodka earlier." "Is there a way to show off the bottle more? Maybe you can shift it out front a bit?" "Try moving the chair and pouring the vodka second." "Can you try sniffing the vodka before pouring it?" "Might you pour a little earlier? I think Ozzie's entrance is pulling focus from it."

Nickname: "Corn on the cob" for the character "Cora Cobb."

Embarrassing Moments: Sebastian making his entrance into the courtroom, then falling. Various water spillages and the occasional prop vodka spill.

Favorite Moment During Each Performance: When Jeff Bender (Deputy Looney) pops his fake tooth out when he knows he is out of audience sightline, but in clear sightline of those onstage; "I'm fine, Your Honor" Rufus Buckley.

Favorite Off-Site Hangouts: Glass House, Hurley's.

Favorite Snack Foods: James Latus' famous baked goods during Sunday night's "Wine and Unwind" after the show. And Staci's drinks.

Favorite Therapy: Whiskey and gossip. Several dressing rooms offered relaxing tonics after the show.

Best Story from the Ushers and Front-of-House Staff: See story of pulling tights off in the balcony.

Mascot: Black Burt Reynolds Scarecrow

Catchphrases Only the Company Would Recognize: "Ragweed is the culprit." "Rodeheaver" to the tune of "Goldfinger."

Understudy Anecdote: Jeff Bender (u/s Dr. Rodeheaver) forgets the line "I can't recall."

Nicknames: Sebastian Arcelus—"Michael Cera" or "Doughnuts"; Chiké Johnson—"Black Burt Reynolds"; J.R. Horne—"Mr. Pate"; Ashley Williams—"Smashley."

Fastest Costume Change: Sebastian going into Act II, Scene 4.

Who Wore the Least?: Ashley Williams (Ellen Roark) during previews—the shortest shorts

in one scene and no pants in another.

What Did You Think of the Web Buzz on Your Show? No comment.

Coolest Thing About Being in This Show: J.R. Horne demanding to be put in a dress and called Lin.

1. Author John Grisham (C) joins (L-R): director Ethan McSweeny, Sebastian Arcelus, playwright Rupert Holmes and John Douglas Thompson for the curtain call on opening night.
2. Ashley Williams sharpening her skills backstage.
3. Production mascot Black Burt Reynolds Scarecrow.
4. The entire cast at curtain call on opening night.

The Trip to Bountiful

First Preview: March 30, 2013. Opened: April 23, 2013.
Limited Engagement. Closed October 9, 2013 after 27 Previews and 187 Performances.

A revival of Horton Foote's 1953 play about elderly widow Carrie Watts who is sick of living in the city with her bossy daughter-in-law and milquetoast son, and longs to return once more to Bountiful, Texas, the small town where she grew up. Carrie boards a bus with the help of a sympathetic young woman who appears to her as the daughter she never got to have. A coming-of-age story for an octogenarian, the odyssey satisfies Carrie's yearnings in ways she did not expect.

CAST

(in order of appearance)

Mrs. Carrie Watts	CICELY TYSON
Ludie Watts	CUBA GOODING JR.
Jessie Mae Watts	VANESSA WILLIAMS
Thelma	CONDOLA RASHAD
Houston Ticket Agent	DEVON ABNER
Second Houston Ticket Agent	CURTIS BILLINGS
Roy	ARTHUR FRENCH
Sheriff	TOM WOPAT

Travelers and
Houston Bus Station Employees ..DEVON ABNER, CURTIS BILLINGS, PAT BOWIE, LEON ADDISON BROWN, SUSAN HEYWARD, BILL KUX, LINDA POWELL, CHARLES TURNER

UNDERSTUDIES

For Mrs. Carrie Watts: PAT BOWIE
For Ludie Watts: LEON ADDISON BROWN
For Jessie Mae Watts: LINDA POWELL

Continued on next page

STEPHEN SONDHEIM THEATRE

NELLE NUGENT   KEVIN LILES   PAULA MARIE BLACK
DAVID R. WEINREB   STEPHEN C. BYRD   ALIA M. JONES   KENNETH TEATON
CAROLE L. HABER/PHILIP GEIER   WENDY FEDERMAN/CARL MOELLENBERG/RICARDO HORNOS
FIFTY CHURCH STREET PRODUCTIONS/HALLIE FOOTE/ TYSON AND KIMBERLY CHANDLER

IN ASSOCIATION WITH

JOSEPH SIROLA   HOWARD AND JANET KAGAN/CHARLES SALAMENO   SHARON A. CARR/PATRICIA R. KLAUSNER
RAYMOND GASPARD/ANDRÉA M. PRICE   WILLETTE MURPHY KLAUSNER/REGINALD M. BROWNE

PRESENT

CICELY TYSON   CUBA GOODING JR.   VANESSA WILLIAMS

IN

THE TRIP TO BOUNTIFUL

BY

HORTON FOOTE

ALSO STARRING

CONDOLA RASHAD

AND

TOM WOPAT

WITH

DEVON ABNER   CURTIS BILLINGS   ARTHUR FRENCH
PAT BOWIE   LEON ADDISON BROWN   SUSAN HEYWARD   BILL KUX   LINDA POWELL   CHARLES TURNER

SCENIC DESIGN **JEFF COWIE**	COSTUME DESIGN **VAN BROUGHTON RAMSEY**	LIGHTING DESIGN **RUI RITA**	ORIGINAL MUSIC AND SOUND DESIGN **JOHN GROMADA**
HAIR DESIGN **PAUL HUNTLEY**	MAKE-UP DESIGN **ANGELINA AVALLONE**	ADVERTISING & MARKETING **AKA**	CASTING **CAPARELLIOTIS CASTING**
TECHNICAL SUPERVISION **HUDSON THEATRICAL ASSOCIATES**	PRESS REPRESENTATIVE **THE HARTMAN GROUP**	COMPANY MANAGER **JENNIFER HINDMAN KEMP**	PRODUCTION STAGE MANAGER **ROBERT BENNETT**

ASSOCIATE PRODUCERS
FRANCESCA ZAMBELLO   FAITH GAY   MARVET BRITTO   RANDOLPH STURRUP

ASSOCIATE DIRECTOR
DAVID ALPERT

GENERAL MANAGER
PETER BOGYO

DIRECTED BY

MICHAEL WILSON

GO N'SYDE 'Carrie's Bountiful Tea' is the official beverage of *THE TRIP TO BOUNTIFUL*.
The Producers wish to express their appreciation to Theatre Development Fund for its support of this production.

6/3/13

(L-R): Vanessa Williams, Cicely Tyson and Cuba Gooding Jr. at the homestead in Bountiful.

Photo: Joan Marcus

The Trip to Bountiful

Cast Continued

For Thelma: SUSAN HEYWARD
For Roy: CHARLES TURNER
For Sheriff: DEVON ABNER
For Houston Ticket Agent: BILL KUX
For Second Houston Ticket Agent: BILL KUX

SETTING

Houston, Harrison and a country place in Texas
March, 1953

MUSICIANS

Conductor and Piano: LYNNE SHANKEL
Cello: DANIEL MILLER
Clarinet, Flute: RICHARD HECKMAN
Trumpet: ROBERT MILLIKAN
Bass: DAVID PHILLIPS
Vocals: AISHA de HAAS

Cicely Tyson
Mrs. Carrie Watts

Cuba Gooding Jr.
Ludie Watts

Vanessa Williams
Jessie Mae Watts

Condola Rashad
Thelma

Tom Wopat
Sheriff

Devon Abner
Houston Ticket Agent; u/s Sheriff

Curtis Billings
Second Houston Ticket Agent

Pat Bowie
Ensemble; u/s Mrs. Carrie Watts

Leon Addison Brown
Ensemble; u/s Ludie Watts

Arthur French
Roy

Susan Heyward
Ensemble; u/s Thelma

Bill Kux
Ensemble; u/s Houston Ticket Agent

Linda Powell
Ensemble; u/s Jessie Mae Watts

Charles Turner
Ensemble; u/s Roy

Horton Foote
Playwright

Michael Wilson
Director

Rui Rita
Lighting Design

John Gromada
Composer/ Sound Design

Paul Huntley
Wig Design

Kate Wilson
Voice Coach

David Caparelliotis
Caparelliotis Casting Casting

Neil A. Mazzella
Hudson Theatrical Associates Technical Supervision

Peter Bogyo
General Manager

David Alpert
Associate Director

Kevin Liles
Producer

Paula Marie Black
Producer

Stephen C. Byrd
Producer

Alia M. Jones
Producer

Carole Haber
Producer

The Trip to Bountiful

Philip H. Geier
Producer

Wendy Federman
Federman/
Moellenberg/Hornos
Producer

Carl Moellenberg
Federman/
Moellenberg/Hornos
Producer

Ricardo Hornos
Federman/
Moellenberg/Hornos
Producer

Rick Costello
Fifty Church Street
Productions
Producer

Hallie Foote
Producer

Tyson Chandler
Producer

Kimberly Chandler
Producer

Joseph Sirola
Producer

Howard & Janet Kagan
Producers

Sharon A. Carr
Producer

Patricia R. Klausner
Producer

Raymond Gaspard
Producer

Reginald M. Browne
Producer

Faith Gay
Associate Producer

Francesca Zambello
Associate Producer

Pascale Armand
*Ensemble;
u/s Thelma*

Billy Eugene Jones
*Ensemble; u/s Ludie
Watts*

Adepero Oduye
Thelma

BOX OFFICE
(L-R): Ronnie Tobia,
Jaime Perlman

STAGE MANAGEMENT
Front:
Jereme Kyle Lewis
(Production Asst.)
Back (L-R):
Robert Bennett
(Production Stage Manager),
Diane DiVita
(Stage Manager)

Photos: Brian Mapp

FRONT OF HOUSE
Left Side (Bottom to Top): Diana Trent Vargas, Molly McQuilkin, Karen Murray,
Kristopher Kaye, Roger Darbaise, Trevor Rex, Travis Navarra, Justin Brown
Right Side (Bottom to Top): Johannah-Joy Magyawe, Candice Schnurr,
Linda Gjonbalaj, Brian Nicholas Rossi, Nicole Ramirez, Jessica Alverson

The Trip to Bountiful

GOTHAM SECURITY
Front (L-R): Joe Lopez, Brandon Blakes
Back (L-R): Keith Edwards, Carlos Ortiz

HAIR/WARDROBE
(L-R): Katherine Sorg (Dresser), Eileen Miller (Wardrobe Supervisor), Daniel Koye (Hair & Makeup Supervisor), Mary Ann Lewis-Oberpriller (Dresser)

CREW
Front (L-R): Alex Neumann (Associate Sound Designer), Paul Ashton, Jocelyn Smith, Ed Chapman (Sound Engineer), Andrew Sullivan
Back (L-R): Eileen Miller, William Craven, Rebecca Heroff, Steve Beers, Josh Weitzman, Andrew Forste, Donald "Buck" Roberts

---

STAFF LISTING FOR *THE TRIP TO BOUNTIFUL*

GENERAL MANAGER
Peter Bogyo

COMPANY MANAGER
Jennifer Hindman Kemp

GENERAL PRESS REPRESENTATIVE
THE HARTMAN GROUP
Michael Hartman   Tom D'Ambrosio   Frances White

CASTING
CAPARELLIOTIS CASTING
David Caparelliotis and Lauren Port

PRODUCTION STAGE MANAGER ....Robert Bennett
Stage Manager ....Diane DiVita
Associate Director ....David Alpert
Associate Set Designer ....Aimee B. Dombo
Associate Costume Designer ....Leon Dobkowski
Associate Lighting Designer ....John Viesta III
Associate Sound Designer ....Alex Neumann
Production Coordinator ....Patrick Mediate
Automated Light Programmer ....Jay Penfield
Assistant to the
    General Manager ....Anthony McDonald
Production Assistants ....Jereme Kyle Lewis, Wade Dooley
SDC Foundation Observer ....Sydney Chatman
Assistant to Lighting Designer ....Mandi Effpie
Sound Design Intern ....Kristin Rizzo
Production Carpenter.......................Geoffrey Quart
Production Electrician ....James Maloney
Production Sound Engineer ....Ed Chapman
Production Assistant Sound ....Alex Neumann
Production Properties Coordinator ....Propaganda LLC
Wardrobe Supervisor ....Eileen Miller
Dressers ......Mary Ann Lewis-Oberpriller, Katherine Sorg
Hair & Makeup Supervisor ....Daniel Koye
Voice Coach ....Kate Wilson
Singing Consultant ....Deborah Lapidus
Movement Consultants ....Mark Olsen, Hope Clark
Scenery Graphics Designer ....Aimee Dombo

Advertising/Marketing/Digital ....AKA/
    Elizabeth Furze, Scott A. Moore, Bashan Aquart,
    Melissa Marano, Danielle Barchetto, Sarah Borenstein,
    Ryan Greer, Adam Jay, Jamaal Parham, Flora Pei,
    Janette Roush, Sara Rosenzweig
Marketing Consultants ....The Britto Agency
Grassroots Marketing ....Abigail Rose Solomon
Web Design/Maintenance ....AKA
Special Promotions ....Jeffrey Solis
Accountant ....Fried & Kowgios CPA's LLP/
    Robert Fried, CPA
Controller ....Galbraith & Company, Inc./Tabitha Falcone
Banking ....First Republic Bank/Marianne Johnson
Insurance ....DeWitt Stern/Peter Shoemaker
Legal Counsel ....David H. Friedlander, Esq.
Production Photography ....Joan Marcus
Inhouse Photography ....Lisa Pacino
Opening Night Coordination ....Serino/Coyne LLC/
    Suzanne Tobak
Payroll Service ....Castellana Services Inc.
Rehearsal Space ....Chelsea Studios
Theatre Displays ....BAM Signs, Inc./Adam Miller

THE FOXBORO COMPANY, INC.
Nelle Nugent ....President and CEO
Kenneth Teaton ....SVP Production and Creative Affairs
Patrick Mediate ....Development Manager

CREDITS
Scenery fabrication by Hudson Scenic Studio, Inc. Lighting equipment from PRG Lighting. Sound equipment by Sound Associates. Costumes for Miss Tyson, Miss Williams and Miss Rashad by Eric Winterling, Inc. Uniforms and costumes by Western Costume Co. Custom shoes by Western Costume Co. Millinery by Lynne Mackey Studio. Custom shirts by Cego. Additional costumes from the Costume House and Hellen Uffner Vintage Clothing.

MUSIC CREDITS
"Satin Doll" written by Duke Ellington. Courtesy of Sony/ATV Music Publishing, LLC. **"Blue Moon"** written by Richard Rodgers and Lorenz Hart. Courtesy of Sony/

ATV Music Publishing, LLC. **"Don't Let the Stars Get in Your Eyes"** written by Slim Willet, Kenneth Burns and Henry Haynes. Courtesy of Sony/ATV Music Publishing, LLC. **"I Apologize"** written by Al Hoffman, Al Goodhart and Ed Nelson. Courtesy of Warner/Chappell Music, Inc. Music clearance by BZ/Rights & Permissions, Inc.

SPECIAL THANKS
Charles Davis, Myrtis Outlar, Betty Joyce Sikora, Rosa and Spencer Green, Reverend Ruiel Taylor, Robert Garcia, Robert Nelson, Josh Fitts, Diane Woods, Mary Nelle Wiley, Betty Jo Dickerson, Frankie Mangum, Dorothy Randle, Millard McQueen, Mr. and Mrs. Dale McCrohan, David Woolard, Russell Martin, Robert Garcia, Millard McQueen & Cynthia Franco of the Horton Foote Papers at Southern Methodist University's DeGolyer Library. Bra*Tenders for undergarments and hosiery.

For all tickets, including groups, please contact
Telecharge.com: (212) 239-6200
Outside of New York: 1-800- 432-7250
or www.telecharge.com

STEPHEN SONDHEIM THEATRE
SYDNEY BEERS   GREG BACKSTROM
General Manager   Associate Managing Director
VALERIE SIMMONS
Operations Manager

STEPHEN SONDHEIM THEATRE STAFF
House Manager ....Johannah-Joy G. Magyawe
Assistant House Manager ....Molly McQuilkin
Treasurer ....Jaime Perlman
House Carpenter ....Steve Beers
House Electrician ....Josh Weitzman
House Properties ....Andrew Forste
Assistant Treasurers ....Andrew Clements,
    Carlos Morris, Ronnie Tobia
Engineer ....Deosarran
Security ....Gotham Security
Maintenance ....Juan Hernandez
Lobby Refreshments by ....Sweet Hospitality Group

Twelfth Night/Richard III

First Preview: October 15, 2013. Opened: November 10, 2013. Closed February 16, 2014. Limited Engagement.
Twelfth Night played 18 Previews and 82 Performances in repertory with *Richard III*, which played 10 Previews and 31 Performances.

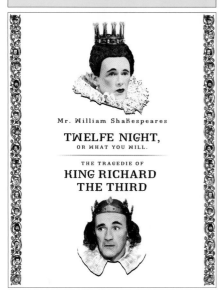

PLAYBILL®

Two Shakespeare classics presented in repertory in a period production that transferred from a hit London run. "Twelfe Night" (using spelling from the original printed version) is a romantic comedy of disguised gender and identity. Richard III is a history of the physically and spiritually twisted Yorkist prince who murders his royal relatives to seize the throne of England for himself. Aside from the two plays being performed on alternating nights by the same cast, the production is notable for having all the female parts played by males, as in Shakespeare's day. This makes for some interesting twists in Twelfth Night, *in which some of the female characters disguise themselves as men.*

TWELFTH NIGHT CAST
(in order of speaking)

Orsino .... LIAM BRENNAN
Curio/Officer/
   Olivia's Servant .... MATT HARRINGTON
Valentine/Officer .... KURT EGYIAWAN
Viola .... SAMUEL BARNETT
Sea Captain/Priest .... TERRY McGINITY
Sir Toby Belch .... COLIN HURLEY
Maria .... PAUL CHAHIDI
Sir Andrew Aguecheek .... ANGUS WRIGHT
Feste .... PETER HAMILTON DYER
Olivia .... MARK RYLANCE
Malvolio .... STEPHEN FRY
Antonio .... JOHN PAUL CONNOLLY
Sebastian .... JOSEPH TIMMS
Fabian .... JETHRO SKINNER
Servant/Officer .... BRYAN PATERSON
Continued on next page

Continued on next page

---

⑤ BELASCO THEATRE
111 West 44th Street
A Shubert Organization Theatre

Philip J. Smith, *Chairman*   **Robert E. Wankel,** *President*

SONIA FRIEDMAN PRODUCTIONS SCOTT LANDIS ROGER BERLIND
GLASS HALF FULL PRODUCTIONS/JUST FOR LAUGHS THEATRICALS 1001 NIGHTS PRODUCTIONS
TULCHIN BARTNER PRODUCTIONS JANE BERGÈRE PAULA MARIE BLACK RUPERT GAVIN
STEPHANIE P. McCLELLAND SHAKESPEARE'S GLOBE CENTRE USA
MAX COOPER TANYA LINK PRODUCTIONS and SHAKESPEARE ROAD

present

SHAKESPEARE'S GLOBE
PRODUCTIONS OF

Mr. William Shakespeares

TWELFE NIGHT,
OR WHAT YOU WILL.

THE TRAGEDIE OF

KING RICHARD THE THIRD

MARK RYLANCE
and
(in alphabetical order)
SAMUEL BARNETT LIAM BRENNAN PAUL CHAHIDI
JOHN PAUL CONNOLLY PETER HAMILTON DYER KURT EGYIAWAN
MATT HARRINGTON COLIN HURLEY TERRY McGINITY
JETHRO SKINNER JOSEPH TIMMS ANGUS WRIGHT
MATTHEW SCHECHTER HAYDEN SIGNORETTI
DOMINIC BREWER DYLAN CLARK MARSHALL TONY WARD
with STEPHEN FRY as MALVOLIO

Musicians
EMILY BAINES SAMUEL BUDISH ARNGEIR HAUKSSON
PRISCILLA HERREID EDWARD HILTON GREG INGLES NICHOLAS PERRY

Lighting Design	Production Stage Manager	UK Casting	US Casting
STAN PRESSNER	ARTHUR GAFFIN	CHARLOTTE BEVAN	JIM CARNAHAN, CSA

US General Management	UK General Management	US Technical Supervision
BESPOKE THEATRICALS	DIANE BENJAMIN and FIONA STEWART for SONIA FRIEDMAN PRODUCTIONS	HUDSON THEATRICAL ASSOCIATES

Press Representatives	Advertising & Marketing
BONEAU/BRYAN-BROWN	SPOTCO

Designer	Music
JENNY TIRAMANI	CLAIRE van KAMPEN

Director
TIM CARROLL

11/10/13

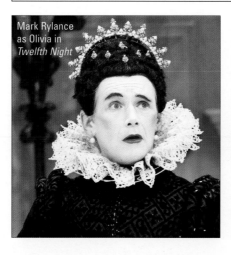

Mark Rylance as Olivia in *Twelfth Night*

Mark Rylance as Richard III

Photos: Simon Annand

Twelfth Night/Richard III

Cast Continued

UNDERSTUDIES

For Curio, Olivia's Servant,
Officer, Olivia, Maria: DOMINIC BREWER
For Valentine, Priest, Captain,
Officer, Fabian: TONY WARD
For Sir Toby Belch: JOHN PAUL CONNOLLY
For Malvolio, Antonio: TERRY McGINITY
For Feste: KURT EGYIAWAN
For Orsino,
Sir Andrew Aguecheek: JETHRO SKINNER
For Viola, Sebastian: MATT HARRINGTON

RICHARD III CAST

(in order of speaking)

Richard, Duke of Gloucester,
Later King Richard III ....MARK RYLANCE
Clarence/Lord Mayor ....LIAM BRENNAN
Brakenbury/Catesby ...PETER HAMILTON DYER
Hastings/Tyrrell ....PAUL CHAHIDI
Lady Anne/Grey ....JOSEPH TIMMS
Rivers/Scrivener/Blunt ....TERRY McGINITY
Queen Elizabeth ....SAMUEL BARNETT
Dorset/Bishop of Ely/
Guard ....MATT HARRINGTON
Duke of Buckingham ....ANGUS WRIGHT

1st Murderer/Cardinal/Ratcliff/
Halberdier ....JOHN PAUL CONNOLLY
2nd Murderer/Messenger/
Halberdier/Guard ....JETHRO SKINNER
King Edward IV/Stanley ....COLIN HURLEY
Duchess of York/Richmond .....KURT EGYIAWAN
Prince Edward ....MATTHEW SCHECHTER
Duke of York ....HAYDEN SIGNORETTI
Servant/Officer ....BRYAN PATERSON

UNDERSTUDIES

For Clarence, Lord Mayor, Rivers, Scrivener,
Guard, Cardinal, Ratcliff, Halberdier, Messenger,
Guard, Brakenbury: TONY WARD
For Brakenbury, Tyrrell, Blunt, Dorset,
Bishop of Ely, Guard, 1st Murderer,
Halberdier, Messenger: DOMINIC BREWER
For Hastings, Catesby, Grey: JETHRO SKINNER
For Lady Anne, Queen Elizabeth, Richmond,
2nd Murderer: MATT HARRINGTON
For King Edward IV,
Stanley: JOHN PAUL CONNOLLY
For Duchess of York,
Buckingham: TERRY McGINITY
For Prince Edward,
Duke of York: DYLAN CLARK MARSHALL

MUSICIANS

Shawms, Curtal,
Rauschpfeife, Recorder: EMILY BAINES
Drum, Tambourine,
Baroque Timpani: SAM BUDISH
Lute, Theorbo, Cittern,
Hurdy Gurdy: ARNGEIR HAUKSSON
Shawms, Curtal, Recorders: PRISCILLA HERREID
Tenor Sackbut, Bass Sackbut,
Recorders: ED HILTON
Alto Sackbut, Tenor Sackbut,
Natural Trumpet, Recorders: GREG INGLES
Shawms, Curtal, Rauschpfeife, Recorders,
Pipe and Tabor, Natural Trumpet,
Bagpipes: NICK PERRY

Samuel Barnett, Liam Brennan, Paul Chahidi, John
Paul Connolly, Peter Hamilton Dyer, Kurt Egyiawan,
Stephen Fry, Colin Hurley, Terry McGinity, Mark
Rylance, Jethro Skinner, Joseph Timms, Angus
Wright, Dominic Brewer and Bryan Paterson are
appearing with the permission of Actors' Equity
Association.

Samuel Barnett
12N: Viola;
RIII: Queen Elizabeth

Liam Brennan
12N: Orsino;
RIII: Clarence/
Lord Mayor

Paul Chahidi
12N: Maria;
RIII: Hastings/Tyrrell

John Paul Connolly
12N: Antonio; u/s Sir
Toby Belch; RIII: 1st
Murderer/Cardinal/
Ratcliff/Halberdier;
u/s King Edward IV

Peter Hamilton Dyer
12N: Feste;
RIII: Brakenbury/
Catesby

Kurt Egyiawan
12N: Valentine/
Officer; u/s Feste;
RIII: Richmond/
Duchess of York

Stephen Fry
12N: Malvolio

Matt Harrington
12N: Curio/Officer/
Olivia's Servant; u/s
Viola/Sebastian;
RIII: Dorset/Bishop
of Ely/Guard

Colin Hurley
12N: Sir Toby Belch;
RIII: King Edward IV/
Stanley

Terry McGinity
12N: Sea Captain/
Priest; u/s Malvolio/
Antonio; RIII: Rivers/
Scrivener/Blunt; u/s
Duchess of York

Mark Rylance
12N: Olivia;
RIII: Richard III

Jethro Skinner
12N: Fabian; u/s
Orsino/Sir Andrew
Aguecheek; RIII: 2nd
Murderer/Messenger/
Halberdier/Guard

Joseph Timms
12N: Sebastian;
RIII: Lady Anne/Grey

Angus Wright
12N: Sir Andrew
Aguecheek;
RIII: Duke of
Buckingham

"If music be the food of love, play on..."

Twelfth Night/Richard III

Matthew Schechter
RIII: Prince Edward

Hayden Signoretti
RIII: Duke of York

Dominic Brewer
12N: u/s Curio/Olivia's Servant/Officer/Olivia/ Maria; RIII: u/s Guard/Halberdier/ Messenger

Dylan Clark Marshall
RIII: u/s Prince Edward/Duke of York

Tony Ward
12N: u/s Valentine/ Priest/Officer/; RIII: u/s Clarence/Lord Mayor/Rivers/ Scrivener/Cardinal

Emily Baines
Musician

Samuel Budish
Musician

Arngeir Hauksson
Musician

Priscilla Herreid
Musician

Greg Ingles
Musician

Tim Carroll
Director

Jenny Tiramani
Designer

Jim Carnahan, CSA
U.S. Casting

Maggie Brohn
Bespoke Theatricals
U.S. General Management

Amy Jacobs
Bespoke Theatricals
U.S. General Management

Devin Keudell
Bespoke Theatricals
U.S. General Management

Nina Lannan
Bespoke Theatricals
U.S. General Management

Neil A. Mazzella
Hudson Theatrical Associates
U.S. Technical Supervision

Sonia Friedman
Sonia Friedman Productions
Producer

Scott Landis
Producer

Roger Berlind
Producer

Adam Blanshay
Glass Half Full Productions/Just for Laughs Theatricals
Producer

Gilbert Rozon
Just for Laughs Theatricals
Producer

Norman Tulchin
Tulchin Bartner Productions
Producer

Jane Bergère
Producer

Stephen Fry as Malvolio in *Twelfth Night*

Photo: Simon Annand

Paula Marie Black
Producer

Stephanie P. McClelland
Producer

Max Cooper
Producer

Twelfth Night / Richard III

Photos: Brian Mapp

2013-2014 AWARDS

TONY AWARDS
Outstanding Performance by a
Featured Actor in a Play
(Mark Rylance / *Twelfth Night*)
Outstanding Costume Design of a Play
(Jenny Tiramani / *Twelfth Night*)

NY DRAMA CRITICS' CIRCLE AWARD
Special Citation

DRAMA DESK AWARDS
Outstanding Revival of a Play
(*Twelfth Night*)
Outstanding Director of a Play
(Tim Carroll / *Twelfth Night*)

OUTER CRITICS CIRCLE AWARD
Outstanding Director of a Play
(Lucille Lortel Award)
(Tim Carroll / *Twelfth Night*)

THEATRE WORLD AWARD
(Paul Chahidi / *Twelfth Night*)

FRONT OF HOUSE
Front Row (L-R): Roland Andrews, Deborah Nesbit, Shuwanda Nzikou-Ilagou, Maria Lugo,
Stephanie Wallis (House Manager)
Second Row: Jennifer Stock
Third Row (L-R): Michele Moyna, Craig Dawson, Laura Kaye, Pamela Loetterle
Fourth Row (L-R): Edytha Harlin, Philip Escobedo
Back Row (L-R): Michael Cleary, Kathleen Dunn, Joseph Pittman (Ticket-Taker)

STAGE MANAGEMENT
(L-R): Arthur Gaffin (Production Stage Manager),
Bryan Paterson (Stage Manager), Lee Micklin (Stage Manager), Jill Cordle
(Production Stage Manager)

GENERAL MANAGEMENT/COMPANY MANAGEMENT
(L-R): Danielle Saks (Associate General Manager),
Lizbeth Cone (Company Manager), Amy Jacobs (General Management)

CREW
Sitting (L-R): Kristina Wagner (Assistant Carpenter),
Carlos Martinez (Production Electrician), Carlos Jaramillo (House Properties),
Steve Loehle (Production Properties)
Standing (L-R): John Kenny (Assistant House Carpenter), George Dummitt

WARDROBE
(L-R): Dora Bonilla (Dresser),
Maureen George (Dresser)

DOORMAN
Enrico "Rick" Bozzacco

Twelfth Night/Richard III

Samuel Barnett
as Queen Elizabeth
in *Richard III.*

Twelfth Night/Richard III
SCRAPBOOK

Correspondent: Dominic Brewer, understudy "Olivia," "Maria," "Brakenbury," and others.

Memorable Faxes: The flood of faxed messages from all the other Broadway companies was heart-warming on opening night. This tradition has yet to reach the UK, but it's a brilliant idea, speaking volumes about the friendliness and support of the Broadway community.

Opening Night Party: Our opening night party was in the opulent Gotham Hall, but Bruce Wayne failed to attend. A memorable moment happened en route to an apartment block party-after-the-after-party where nine of the company got trapped in a lift until some kind firemen and women came to rescue us.

Most Exciting Celebrity Visitors: For the excitement their respective visits inspired in the company, it's probably an even split between Daniel Day-Lewis and Steven Spielberg and their families. The memorable quotes around their visits came from the cast: "DDL is in? I'm going to sh*t my pants off" and "Does anyone mind if Steven Spielberg comes down to say hello?" It has been nothing less than astonishing to meet a wish-list of brilliant actors throughout this whole run.

Favorite In-Theatre Gathering Place: The communal dressing room is the hangout of choice for most of the company during the show, and afterwards "the pub" directly beneath the stage (aka "The Elephant") for some highly competitive ping pong and foosball.

Special Backstage Ritual: There is a unique "ritual" that literally hangs backstage: a bundle, or offering, inspired by Mayan rituals made of flowers, food, coins and other items to offer as a gift to the spirits and ancestors of the theatre and all associated with these productions—from the author and original casts, to the people from history who inspired the characters, to other actors and crew who have trod the boards of the theatre before us. It's an offering, a memorial and a protective charm. Helping to

1. Stephen Fry, in the role of Santa Claus, delivers presents for those who were nicely naughty.
2. Pretending to pass off an American custom as a benefit, management jokingly grants the cast an extra hour "to sleep, perchance to dream."

Belasco Theatre
111 West 44th Street
New York, NY 10019

MEMORANDUM

To: The Company of Twelfth Night/Richard III

From: Artie, Lee, Bryan, Mitch & Lizz

Re: Daylight Savings

Date: November 3, 2013

To thank you, and in consideration of your hard work over the last several weeks, an extra hour of sleep has been arranged for the entire company. On Saturday night, please set your clocks back one hour

There are rumors circulating that this is an annual event that is observed by everyone in the country. This is not true. *This is something that we've arranged especially for you.*

**Daylight Savings ends
Saturday night
November 3
"fall back" one hour**

create the bundle for this run at the Belasco was a fascinating and moving experience.

Favorite Backstage Photo: Stephen Fry as Santa Claus. (See photo at left.) Stephen made a splendid Santa for our Christmas party, doling out the Secret Santa presents the company had bought each other. As an alternative Santa he promised to only give gifts to those boys and girls who had been naughty this year instead of nice. Luckily, every single one of us had been bad.

Most Memorable Audience Behavior: The couple who dressed in full Elizabethan costume and who truly looked the part in the onstage seating for our show on Halloween.

Most Memorable Audience Reaction: There have been several fainters onstage during both shows; one instance during *Twelfth Night* was quite dramatic. The play stopped while an impressive number of doctors stepped up from the audience to offer their assistance while paramedics were called to the theatre. Fortunately the ailing gentleman made a full recovery.

Unique Pre-Show Announcement: Our delightful and unfailingly optimistic stage manager Artie makes every announcement unique, but his "Saturday Night on Broadway" call is a company favourite.

Memorable Ad-Lib: Colin's superb post-show announcement during our three weeks of fundraising for Broadway Cares was a masterclass in stand-up comedy, which grew into what affectionately became known as "Act Six." The evening Ghiv pulled out a pair of rubber gloves in response to one of Colin's jokes was a highlight.

Memorable Stage Door Fan Encounter: Heading out for dinner between shows I spotted the actor Sam Rockwell hovering by the pass gate. He was keen to meet some of the cast, but rather than announce he was there he was just waiting to see who he could catch. I was excited to be able to walk him in and introduce him to the cast.

Memorable Directorial Note: "Kill your babies."

Embarrassing Moment: Angus opening a very memorable Secret Santa gift, and the reaction of his visiting wife and son. Embarrassing...but also hilarious.

Favorite Moment During Each Performance: As understudy,

Twelfth Night/Richard III
SCRAPBOOK

I have no specific onstage moment, but coming together as a company at the start of our working day to practice the respective jigs that end both shows is great fun, and singing *Twelfth Night*'s top of Act Two song "Hey Robin" in beautiful harmony is a pleasure. Watching Mark and Kurt practice the climactic sword fight before each performance of *Richard III* is always exciting too.

Favorite Off-Site Hangout: Soho House has been a great place to have a post-show drink, play pool and even have a late night swim on a few occasions. I've also spent a good deal of time in our local cinemas, catching up with all the award season hopefuls.

Favorite Snack Foods: It's not really a snack food, but the excellent meals from the Kwik Meal cart on W. 45th are a company favourite and a perfect dinner between shows. Then there has been a steady supply of birthday cakes, cheesecake, cupcakes, sweets, cookies, brownies....

Favorite Therapy: Ping-Pong can be a great stress reliever, or stress producer depending on who you are playing against. Also the arrival of the "Max" handheld massager, if you'll pardon the pun, caused a buzz.

Mascot: It must be Apache, Mark's Jack Russell who pops in to guard us all from time to time, and who also made a memorable one-off appearance on our opening night, and then refused to leave.

Catchphrases Only the Company Would Recognize: "The House is OH-pen." "Hey, you beshrew me? I'll beshrew you!" "There were twelve, but now there are only nine." "I fell over."

Understudy Anecdote: My most memorable moment to date as understudy wasn't actually during one of the shows, instead it was taking on the role of the "Green Man," a pre-Christian forest spirit and god of fertility, who made an appearance in a one-off post-show celebration on the feast of Epiphany; the actual Twelfth Night that gives Shakespeare's play its title. Suitably made up (in "Elphaba" green), and decked out in a

costume covered in real foliage, I sang a traditional wassailing song, blessed the theatre, cast and audience and abducted a virgin maid, well...Maria.

Fastest Costume Change: There are a lot of fast changes during both shows for several cast members. The fastest is probably Sam's change from Viola into the disguised Cesario.

Who Wore the Heaviest/Hottest Costume?: A lot of the cast have to deal with some extraordinary clothes, made authentically to the period, which can prove uncomfortable and take some getting used to, including wearing a sword and dagger for many of the men, and corsets for the men playing women. Amongst the men, Liam's false beard for the Mayor of London in *Richard III* may be the hottest piece of costume.

Who Wore the Least?: The most revealing costume must be Maria's. He dazzles (and confuses) the *Twelfth Night* audience every day with his ample cleavage. (See photo at left.)

Ghostly Encounters Backstage: We've not spotted Mr. Belasco or any of the theatre's reported spooks to date, but with the white make-up several of the cast wear for *Twelfth Night*, along with the eerie gliding of the female characters, you'd be forgiven for thinking you'd spotted a ghost backstage. However, we have had a strange happening onstage: one evening the candles on one of our six hanging candelabras completely burnt down, probably twice as quickly as all the others, without any perceptible draft or obvious external influence. An unsolved mystery.

Coolest Thing About Being in This Show: That our audiences clearly adore the shows, and have wholeheartedly welcomed us to New York.

1. Methinks they doth pro-text too much! (L-R): Matt Harrington and Kurt Egyiawan.
2. Paul Chahidi (*Twelfth Night*'s Maria) eating cake to keep up his girlish figure.
3. Angus Wright (as Sir Andrew Aguecheek) reading *Vanity Fair* backstage.

Vanya and Sonia and Masha and Spike

First Preview: March 5, 2013. Opened: March 14, 2013.
Limited Engagement. Closed August 25, 2013 after 11 Previews and 189 Performances.

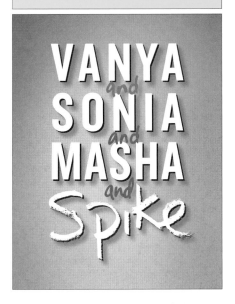

PLAYBILL®

Christopher Durang pokes fun at both Anton Chekhov and modern showbiz in this comedy about two grown siblings who welcome a visit from their movie-star sister at their country house, only to find she has brought along her buff boy-toy—and her epic ego. The characters and situations are contemporary, yet manage to echo those from Chekhov plays The Seagull, The Three Sisters, The Cherry Orchard *and* Uncle Vanya. *The play is notable for its series of show-stopping comic speeches for each of the characters.*

CAST
(in order of appearance)

Vanya	DAVID HYDE PIERCE
Sonia	KRISTINE NIELSEN
Cassandra	SHALITA GRANT
Masha	JULIE WHITE
Spike	BILLY MAGNUSSEN
Nina	LIESEL ALLEN YEAGER

TIME and PLACE
Set in the present, in a lovely farmhouse
in Bucks County

UNDERSTUDIES
For Vanya: KEITH REDDIN
For Sonia and Masha: LINDA MARIE LARSON
For Cassandra: HEATHER ALICIA SIMMS
For Spike: CREED GARNICK
For Nina: AMELIA McCLAIN

⑤ GOLDEN THEATRE
A Shubert Organization Theatre
Philip J. Smith, *Chairman*   **Robert E. Wankel,** *President*

JOEY PARNES   LARRY HIRSCHHORN

JOAN RAFFE & JHETT TOLENTINO   MARTIN PLATT & DAVID ELLIOTT   PAT FLICKER ADDISS   CATHERINE ADLER   JOHN O'BOYLE
JOSHUA GOODMAN   JAMIE DEROY / RICHARD WINKLER   CRICKET HOOPER JIRANEK / MICHAEL PALITZ
MARK S. GOLUB & DAVID S. GOLUB   RADIO MOUSE ENTERTAINMENT   SHADOWCATCHER ENTERTAINMENT   MARY COSSETTE / BARBARA MANOCHERIAN
MEGAN SAVAGE / MEREDITH LYNSEY SCHADE   HUGH HYSELL / RICHARD JORDAN   CHERYL WIESENFELD / RON SIMONS
S.D. WAGNER   JOHN JOHNSON

IN ASSOCIATION WITH
McCARTER THEATRE CENTER   LINCOLN CENTER THEATER

PRESENT

DAVID HYDE PIERCE   **KRISTINE NIELSEN**   **JULIE WHITE**

IN

VANYA and **SONIA**
and **MASHA** and **Spike**

A NEW COMEDY BY
CHRISTOPHER DURANG

WITH
BILLY MAGNUSSEN

SHALITA GRANT   **LIESEL ALLEN YEAGER**

SCENIC DESIGN	COSTUME DESIGN	LIGHTING DESIGN	ORIGINAL MUSIC & SOUND DESIGN
DAVID KORINS	EMILY REBHOLZ	JUSTIN TOWNSEND	MARK BENNETT

CASTING	PRODUCTION STAGE MANAGER	PRESS REPRESENTATIVE	ADVERTISING & MARKETING
DANIEL SWEE	DENISE YANEY	O&M CO.	SPOTCO

DIRECTED BY
NICHOLAS MARTIN

ORIGINALLY COMMISSIONED AND PRODUCED BY McCARTER THEATRE CENTER, PRINCETON, N.J. EMILY MANN, ARTISTIC DIRECTOR; TIMOTHY J. SHIELDS, MANAGING DIRECTOR; MARA ISAACS, PRODUCING DIRECTOR
AND PRODUCED BY LINCOLN CENTER THEATER, NEW YORK CITY, UNDER THE DIRECTION OF ANDRÉ BISHOP AND BERNARD GERSTEN, IN 2012.

THE PRODUCERS WISH TO EXPRESS THEIR APPRECIATION TO THEATRE DEVELOPMENT FUND FOR ITS SUPPORT OF THIS PRODUCTION.

7/30/13

David Hyde Pierce (Vanya) and Julie White (Masha)
as Snow White and one of her dwarfs.

Photo: Carol Rosegg

Vanya and Sonia and Masha and Spike

David Hyde Pierce
Vanya

Kristine Nielsen
Sonia

Julie White
Masha

Billy Magnussen
Spike

Shalita Grant
Cassandra

Liesel Allen Yeager
Nina

Creed Garnick
u/s Spike

Linda Marie Larson
u/s Sonia, Masha

Amelia McClain
u/s Nina

Keith Reddin
u/s Vanya

Heather Alicia
Simms
u/s Cassandra

Christopher Durang
Playwright

Nicholas Martin
Director

David Korins
Sets

Emily Rebholz
Costumes

Justin Townsend
Lighting

Mark Bennett
*Original Music
and Sound*

Daniel Swee
Casting Director

Leah J. Loukas
Wig Designer

Joey Parnes
Producer

Larry Hirschhorn
Producer

Joan Raffe
Producer

Jhett Tolentino
Producer

Martin Platt
Producer

David Elliott
Producer

Pat Flicker Addiss
Producer

Catherine Adler
Producer

John O'Boyle
Producer

Joshua Goodman
Producer

Jamie deRoy
Producer

Richard Winkler
Producer

Cricket Hooper
Jiranek
Producer

Michael Palitz
Producer

Mark S. Golub
Producer

David S. Golub
Producer

Vanya and Sonia and Masha and Spike

M. Kilburg Reedy
Radio Mouse
Entertainment
Producer

Jason E. Grossman
Radio Mouse
Entertainment
Producer

Mary Cossette
Producer

Barbara
Manocherian
Producer

Megan Savage
Producer

Meredith Lynsey
Schade
Producer

Hugh Hysell
Producer

Richard Jordan
Producer

Cheryl Wiesenfeld
Producer

Ron Simons
Producer

S.D. Wagner
Producer

John Johnson
Producer

Emily Mann
*Artistic Director
McCarter Theatre
Center*

Timothy J. Shields
*Managing Director
McCarter Theatre
Center*

André Bishop
*Artistic Director
Lincoln Center
Theater*

Bernard Gersten
*Executive Producer
Lincoln Center
Theater*

2013-2014
ALUMNA

Sigourney Weaver
Masha

2013-2014
TRANSFER
Student

Walter Belenky
u/s Spike

Photo: Brian Mapp

CREW
Sitting on Floor (L-R): Esther Vasquez (Usher), Sylvia Yoshioka (Head Electrician), Jeannie Naughton (Dresser), Ruddi Almonte (Usher), Edytha Harlin (Usher)
Sitting in Chairs (L-R): Rita Russell (Ticket Taker), Denise Yaney (Stage Manager)
Standing (L-R): Dylan Foley (Production Props), Patricia Byrne (Usher), Margie Howard (Asst. Stage Manager), Sheila Staffney (Usher), Terry McGarty (Head Carpenter), Deborah McIntyre (Usher), Carolyne Jones-Barnes (House Manager), Thomas Mitchell (Head Props), Yolanda Ramsay (Hair/Wigs Supervisor), Wayne Smith (Sound), Julia Gonzalez (Usher), Yuri Fernandez (Porter), Helen Bentley (Chief Usher), Mae Smith (Asst. Chief Usher), Audrey Maher (Dresser)

Vanya and Sonia and Masha and Spike

Julie White in a light moment with Billy Magnussen.

Julie White and Kristine Nielsen prepare for a costume party.

STAFF FOR
VANYA AND SONIA AND MASHA AND SPIKE

GENERAL MANAGEMENT
JOEY PARNES PRODUCTIONS
Joey Parnes
John Johnson   S.D. Wagner

COMPANY MANAGER
Kit Ingui

PRESS REPRESENTATIVE
O&M CO.
Rick Miramontez   Andy Snyder
Marie Pace

Production Stage Manager	Denise Yaney
Stage Manager	M.A. Howard
Associate Company Manager	Kim Sellon
Management Associate	Jillian Robbins
Assistant Director	Bryan Hunt
Associate Set Designer	Rod Lemmond
Assistant Costume Designer	Ren LaDassor
Associate Lighting Designer	Chris Thielking
Associate Sound Designer	Josh Liebert
Associate Sound Designer	Charles Coes
Wig Designer	Leah J. Loukas
Production Carpenter	Larry Morley
Production Properties	Mike Smanko
Production Electrician	Dan Coey
Audio Engineer	Wayne Smith
Head Props	Dylan Foley
Wardrobe Supervisor	Lynn Bowling
Dressers	Audrey Maher, Jean Marie Naughton
Hair/Wig Supervisor	Yolanda Ramsay
Outside Props	James Keane
Casting Associate	Camille Hickman
Advertising/Marketing/Interactive	SpotCo/

Drew Hodges, Jim Edwards, Tom Greenwald, Nick Pramik, Stephen Sosnowski, Stephen Santore, Ryan Zatcoff, Kristen Rathbun, Julie Wechsler, Kyle Young

Press Associates	Sarah Babin, Molly Barnett, Scott Braun, Philip Carrubba, Jon Dimond, Joyce Friedmann, Michael Jorgensen, Yufen Kung, Chelsea Nachman, Ryan Ratelle, Pete Sanders
Press Interns	Nancy Alligood, Brian Falduto, Kevin O'Malley
Management Interns	Bianca Crudo, Jeneve Dube
Legal Counsel	Lazarus & Harris LLP/ Scott Lazarus, Esq., Robert Harris, Esq.
Accountants	Marks Paneth & Shron LLP/ Mark A. D'Ambrosi, Patricia M. Pedersen, Petrina Moritz
Banking	City National Bank/ Stephanie Dalton, Michele Gibbons
Insurance	AON/Albert G. Ruben/ George Walden, Claudia B. Kaufman
Payroll	Castellana Services Inc./ Lance Castellana, James Castellana, Norman Sewell
Orthopedist	David S. Weiss, MD/ NYU Langone Medical Center
Physical Therapy	PhysioArts
Physical Therapy	Performing Arts Physical Therapy
Production Photographer	Carol Rosegg
Production Videographer	Fresh Produce Productions/ Frank Basile
Opening Night Coordination	The Lawrence Company/ Michael Lawrence

CREDITS
Scenery fabricated and painted by Global Scenic Services, Inc., Bridgeport, CT. Lighting equipment by PRG. Sound equipment by Masque Sound. Car service by IBA Limousine. Natural herb cough drops by Ricola, USA. "Here Comes the Sun" written by George Harrison, published by Wixen Music Publishing, Inc. Music recorded at Second Story Studios, Scott Lehrer, engineer. Antoine Silverman, violin. Simon Kafka, guitar. Special thanks to Yamaha Pianos. Make-up provided by M•A•C.

Souvenir merchandise provided by Encore Merchandising, Inc.

Rehearsed at the New 42nd Street Rehearsal Studios.

Additional rehearsals took place at the Playwrights Horizons Rehearsal Studios.

SPECIAL THANKS
Mara Isaacs, Adam Siegel, Patrick Herold, Julian Christenberry, Jane Pfeffer, Louise Foisy, Barry Rosenberg, Stuart Levy

THE SHUBERT ORGANIZATION, INC.
Board of Directors

Philip J. Smith	**Robert E. Wankel**
Chairman	President
Wyche Fowler, Jr.	**Diana Phillips**
Lee J. Seidler	**Michael I. Sovern**

Stuart Subotnick

Chief Financial Officer	Elliot Greene
Sr. Vice President, Ticketing	David Andrews
Vice President, Finance	Juan Calvo
Vice President, Human Resources	Cathy Cozens
Vice President, Facilities	John Darby
Vice President, Theatre Operations	Peter Entin
Vice President, Marketing	Charles Flateman
Vice President, Audit	Anthony LaMattina
Vice President, Ticket Sales	Brian Mahoney
Vice President, Creative Projects	D.S. Moynihan
Vice President, Real Estate	Julio Peterson
House Manager	Carolyne A. Jones-Barnes

 The Shubert Organization is a proud member of the Broadway Green Alliance.

BOX OFFICE TREASURERS
(L-R): Diane Lettieri, Gary Powers

Vanya and Sonia and Masha and Spike

Scrapbook

Correspondent: Shalita Grant, "Cassandra"

Final Performance, August 25, 2013: I woke up feeling very anxious. A whole year and so much has happened! I rolled over to finish my farewell cards, some harder to write than others. I spent the morning doing errands and trying hard not to get all "doomsday" about the day.

Walking to the theatre I was fretting about the cards. Did I say everything I wanted? Did I miss anyone? All along I knew it wasn't about the cards but I allowed myself to think it was. I arrived before most of the cast and gave everyone their cards. Once I was back in my now sterile-looking dressing room, I felt a weight lifted and smiled. I realized I was saying goodbye to the show but it didn't mean the relationships I developed were gone! Those friendships can continue and memories are forever as long as you don't get brain damage.

When Kristine got to the theatre I went to her room and chatted. We started the journey together and it was wonderful to touch base one last time. David stopped in with his cards and a quick word. Kristine said, "I caught myself getting misty-eyed about today, but I'll make sure not to on stage. It's not therapy!" Love her.

The show began just like it always had. There was very little evidence that this was the last one. Walking out onstage I received my first full entrance applause. Staring into David's eyes, about to say my first line, I knew this one would be a good one.

We made it through the first act, then the second and we were electric. The audience felt so right there with us. It was a celebration of the playwright, of the work that was happening before them. It was truly my favorite show. Then, we got to the play-within-the-play scene. And David took us all in for the last time. Each of us greedily staring at him in anticipation of hearing his play. And he choked up.

That's when it hit me like a ton of bricks. The stubborn denial of this being our last time on stage together saying the brilliant words of a playwright I've admired for ten years, and sharing in the comedic genius of every person on stage. My eyes welled with tears as I silently encouraged a man I had come to admire and adore. I couldn't help but share in what he was experiencing but also hoping him through it. It took him some time. For a moment I thought he wouldn't get through it, seeing him try and fail again and again. But then he made it. And we all exhaled and went on.

Curtain call: All the covers, the playwright, we all, on stage said "thank you" to Broadway.

Backstage we were all wet with tears and joy for ourselves and for each other, hugging and kissing and congratulating.

When I left the theatre it was with a surprising lack of sentimentality. Everything I needed to say, everything I needed to feel, I had said and felt. I walked out head held high, heart full.

Photo: Joseph Marzullo

1. David Hyde Pierce (C) and Kristine Nielsen (R) lead the audience in applauding Julie White (L), who stepped into the role of Masha July 30 for the final month of the run, replacing Sigourney Weaver.

2. *Yearbook* correspondent Shalita Grant addresses the lunchtime crowd as part of the summer concert series Broadway in Bryant Park.

3. Grant and Billy Magnussen horse around backstage at Broadway in Bryant Park.

Photo: Monica Simoes

Photo: Monica Simoes

The Velocity of Autumn

First Preview: April 1, 2014. Opened: April 21, 2014.
Closed May 4, 2014 after 22 Previews and 16 Performances.

Threatened by her grown children with forcible removal to an old folks' home, spirited old lady Alexandra barricades herself inside her Brooklyn brownstone with dozens of Molotov cocktails, threatening to blow the house and herself to kingdom come if the kids don't leave her alone. Her favorite son Chris climbs in a window hoping to talk sense into her. Instead, they wind up having the honest conversation about life, parenthood and childhood that so many people dream of having, but never quite find the time for—until it's too late.

CAST

Alexandra ....ESTELLE PARSONS
Chris ....STEPHEN SPINELLA

PLACE

Brooklyn, NY

TIME

Now

STANDBYS

For Alexandra: LIBBY GEORGE
For Chris: STEVEN HAUCK

Production Stage Manager: BONNIE L. BECKER
Stage Manager: SCOTT ROWEN

---

⑤ BOOTH THEATRE

222 West 45th Street
A Shubert Organization Theatre

Philip J. Smith, *Chairman*   Robert E. Wankel, *President*

LARRY KAYE & HOP THEATRICALS   VAN DEAN & THE BROADWAY CONSORTIUM
JOAN RAFFE & JHETT TOLENTINO
MICHAEL J. MORITZ, JR.   CATHERINE & FRED ADLER
ROB HINDERLITER & DOMINICK LARUFFA, JR. and KIRN PRODUCTIONS

in association with

NEAL RUBINSTEIN   JAMES L. SIMON & STEPHEN GANNS/JONATHAN DEMAR
R. ERIN CRAIG & SEILER-SMITH/FRANKLIN THEATRICAL & JAMES VALLETTI and TONY McANANY

present

ESTELLE PARSONS   STEPHEN SPINELLA

in

the Velocity OF AUTUMN

by **ERIC COBLE**

Scenic Design	Costume Design	Lighting Design
EUGENE LEE	**LINDA CHO**	**RUI RITA**
Sound Design	Associate Director	Production Stage Manager
DARRON L. WEST	**MATT LENZ**	**BONNIE L. BECKER**
Advertising & Marketing	Press Representative	Company Manager
AKA	**POLK & CO.**	**CAROL M. OUNE**
Casting Director	Technical Supervisor	General Management
GEOFF JOSSELSON	**JUNIPER STREET PRODUCTIONS**	**FORESIGHT THEATRICAL**
		MARK SHACKET

Associate producers
JOAN & MARVIN ROSENBERG
SHARLEEN COOPER COHEN/JOHN PERKOFF & MICHELLE SCHAAP   KIMBERLY LOREN EATON
LAUREN CLASS SCHNEIDER and **CRAIG J. HORSLEY/MICHAEL RUBENSTEIN**

Directed by

MOLLY SMITH

The Producers wish to express their appreciation to Theatre Development Fund for its support of this production.

4/21/14

Stephen Spinella and
Estelle Parsons

The Velocity of Autumn

Estelle Parsons
Alexandra

Stephen Spinella
Chris

Libby George
Alexandra Standby

Steven Hauck
Chris Standby

Eric Coble
Playwright

Molly Smith
Director

Matt Lenz
Associate Director

Eugene Lee
Scenic Design

Linda Cho
Costume Design

Rui Rita
Lighting Design

Darron L. West
Sound Design

Paul Huntley
Hair and Wig Design

Bonnie L. Becker
Production Stage Manager

Alan Wasser
Foresight Theatrical
General Manager

Allan Williams
Foresight Theatrical
General Manager

Aaron Lustbader
Foresight Theatrical
General Manager

Ana Rose Green, Guy Kwan, Joseph DeLuise, Hillary Blanken
Juniper Street Productions
Production Manager

Larry Kaye/
HOP Theatricals
Producer

Van Dean/
The Broadway Consortium
Producer

Joan Raffe
Producer

Jhett Tolentino
Producer

Michael J. Moritz, Jr.
Producer

Catherine Adler
Producer

Rob Hinderliter
Producer

Dominick LaRuffa, Jr.
Producer

James L. Simon
Producer

Lauren Class Schneider
Associate Producer

Michael Rubenstein
Associate Producer

The Velocity of Autumn

Stephen Spinella and Estelle Parsons

Photo: Joan Marcus

STAFF FOR *THE VELOCITY OF AUTUMN*

GENERAL MANAGEMENT
FORESIGHT THEATRICAL
Mark Shacket
Aaron Lustbader   Allan Williams   Alan Wasser

COMPANY MANAGER
Carol M. Oune

GENERAL PRESS REPRESENTATIVE
POLK & CO.
Matt Polk   Wayne Wolfe
Colgan McNeil   Sasha Pensanti

CASTING
Geoff Josselson

PRODUCTION MANAGEMENT
JUNIPER STREET PRODUCTIONS
Hillary Blanken   Joseph DeLuise
Guy Kwan   Ana Rose Greene

Production Stage Manager ....Bonnie L. Becker
Stage Manager ....Scott Rowen
Associate Director ....Matt Lenz
Associate Scenic Designers ....Edward Pierce,
Nick Francone, Jen Price
Associate Costume Designer ....Nancy A. Palmatier
Assistant Lighting Designer ....Amanda Zieve
Associate Sound Designer ....Charles Coes
Assistant Sound Designer ....Beth Lake
Production Carpenter ....Fred Gallo
Production Electricians .....James Fedigan, Randall Zaibek
Production Properties Supervisor ....Michael Pilipski
Production Sound Engineer ....Gabriel Bennett

Advance Carpenter ....Dave Fulton
Advance Electrician/Lighting Programmer ...Alan Schuster
Wardrobe Supervisor ....Ryan Rossetto
Ms. Parsons' Dresser ....Rose Keough
Hair Dresser ....Robert Lugo

Advertising & Marketing ....AKA/Elizabeth Furze,
Scott A. Moore, Bashan Aquart, Jamaal Parham,
Melissa Marano, Kyle Hall, Janette Roush, Ryan Greer,
Sara Rosenzweig, Valentina Berger
Special Promotions ....Jeffrey Solis
Theatre Displays ....King Displays
Website Design & Internet Marketing ....AKA
Legal Counsel ....Eric Goldman, Esq.
Accounting ....Marks Paneth LLC
General Management Associates ....Lane Marsh,
Mark Barna, Nina Greene
General Management Office...........Jennifer O'Connor,
Kaitlin Boland
Production Photographer ....Joan Marcus
Insurance ....DeWitt Stern/Peter Shoemaker
Banking ....Signature Bank/
Thomas Kasulka, Margaret Monigan
Payroll ....Castellana Services Inc.
Travel and Housing Coordination ....Lisa Morris

CREDITS AND ACKNOWLEDGEMENTS
Scenery built by Stiegelbauer Associates Inc. Tree by American Foliage. Additional scenery provided by PRG Scenic Technologies. Softgoods provided by I. Weiss Theatrical Solutions.

SPECIAL THANKS
Patricia Masera

Makeup provided by M•A•C Cosmetics.

 THE SHUBERT ORGANIZATION, INC.
Board of Directors

Philip J. Smith Chairman	**Robert E. Wankel** President
Wyche Fowler, Jr.	**Diana Phillips**
Lee J. Seidler	**Michael I. Sovern**

Stuart Subotnick

Chief Financial Officer ....Elliot Greene
Sr. Vice President, Ticketing ....David Andrews
Vice President, Finance ....Juan Calvo
Vice President, Human Resources ....Cathy Cozens
Vice President, Facilities ....John Darby
Vice President, Theatre Operations..............Peter Entin
Vice President, Marketing ....Charles Flateman
Vice President, General Counsel ....Gilbert Hoover
Vice President, Audit ....Anthony LaMattina
Vice President, Ticket Sales ....Brian Mahoney
Vice President, Creative Projects ...........D.S. Moynihan
Vice President, Real Estate ....Julio Peterson

House Manager ....Laurel Ann Wilson

 The Shubert Organization is a proud member of the Broadway Green Alliance.

Violet

First Preview: March 28, 2014. Opened: April 20, 2014.
Limited Engagement. Still running as of May 31, 2014.

Broadway debut of the 1997 musical about Violet, a North Carolina backwoods woman who has lived since childhood with a hideous facial scar. Violet sets out on an odyssey across the South in 1964 to find the television faith healer whom she believes will fix her face and redeem her life. Along the way she meets a variety of characters, including two soldiers who find that this headstrong and determined woman exerts a strange fascination on them both. This production, seen previously for one night as part of the 2013 Encores! Off-Center series, is notable for Sutton Foster's performance in the title role.

CAST

(in order of appearance)

Young Violet	EMERSON STEELE
Violet	SUTTON FOSTER
Father	ALEXANDER GEMIGNANI
Leroy Evans/Radio Soloist/Bus Driver 3/ Bus Passenger	CHARLIE POLLOCK
Preacher/Radio Singer/ Bus Driver 1/Bus Driver 4	BEN DAVIS
Old Lady/Hotel Hooker	ANNIE GOLDEN
Flick	JOSHUA HENRY
Music Hall Singer/ Bus Passenger	ANASTAĆIA McCLESKĒY
Virgil/Billy Dean/Bus Driver 2/ Radio Singer/Bus Passenger	AUSTIN LESCH
Lula Buffington/Almeta/ Bus Passenger	REMA WEBB
Monty	COLIN DONNELL

Continued on next page

AMERICAN AIRLINES THEATRE

ROUNDABOUT THEATRE COMPANY

Todd Haimes, Artistic Director
Harold Wolpert, Managing Director
Julia C. Levy, Executive Director
Sydney Beers, General Manager

in association with

Amy Sherman-Palladino and Daniel Palladino   David Mirvish   Barry and Fran Weissler
Elizabeth Armstrong   Mary Jo and Ted Shen

presents

Sutton Foster

Colin Donnell   Alexander Gemignani   Joshua Henry

VIOLET

Based on the New York City Center *Encores!* Off-Center concert production

Music by
Jeanine Tesori

Book and Lyrics by
Brian Crawley

Based on "The Ugliest Pilgrim" by Doris Betts

with

Ben Davis   Annie Golden   Emerson Steele

Austin Lesch   Anastaćia McCleskēy   Charlie Pollock
Jacob Keith Watson   Rema Webb   Virginia Ann Woodruff

Set Design	*Costume Design*	*Lighting Design*	*Sound Design*	
David Zinn	Clint Ramos	Mark Barton	Leon Rothenberg	
Orchestrations	*Musical Coordinator*	*Hair & Wig Design*	*Dialect Coach*	*Production Stage Manager*
Rick Bassett Joseph Joubert Buryl Red	Seymour Red Press	Charles G. LaPointe	Kate Wilson	Kristen Harris
Casting	*Violet General Manager*	*Production Management*	*Press Representative*	
Jim Carnahan, C.S.A. Carrie Gardner, C.S.A. Stephen Kopel, C.S.A.	Denise Cooper	Aurora Productions	Polk & Co.	
Associate Managing Director	*Director of Marketing & Audience Development*	*Director of Development*		
Greg Backstrom	Tom O'Connor	Lynne Gugenheim Gregory		
Founding Director	*Adams Associate Artistic Director**			
Gene Feist	Scott Ellis			

Music Direction by
Michael Rafter

Choreography by
Jeffrey Page

Directed by
Leigh Silverman

Roundabout gratefully acknowledges partial underwriting support from Gina and David Boonshoft.

Playwrights Horizons, Inc., New York City, produced *Violet* Off-Broadway in 1997, and it was initially developed at the O'Neill Theatre Center during the 1994 National Music Theatre Conference.

*Generously underwritten by Margot Adams, in memory of Mason Adams.

Roundabout Theatre Company is a member of the League of Resident Theatres.   www.roundabouttheatre.org

4/20/14

(L-R): Joshua Henry, Colin Donnell and Sutton Foster

Photo: Joan Marcus

Violet

MUSICAL NUMBERS

"Water in the Well"	Violet, Young Violet and Father
"Surprised"	Violet
"On My Way"	Violet and Company
"M&Ms"	Company
"Luck of the Draw"	Father, Young Violet, Violet, Monty and Flick
"Question 'n Answer"	Monty and Violet
"All to Pieces"	Violet, Monty and Flick
"Let It Sing"	Flick
"Anyone Would Do"	Hotel Hooker
"Who'll Be the One (If Not Me)"	Radio Trio
"Last Time I Came to Memphis"	Monty and Violet
"Lonely Stranger"	Music Hall Singer
"Lay Down Your Head"	Violet
"Anyone Would Do" (Reprise)	Music Hall Singer, Almeta and Hotel Hooker
"Hard to Say Goodbye"	Violet and Flick
"Promise Me, Violet"	Violet, Monty and Flick
"Raise Me Up"	Preacher, Lula Buffington and Choir
"Down the Mountain"	Violet, Young Violet, Father and Virgil
"Look at Me"	Violet
"That's What I Could Do"	Father
"Surprised" (Reprise)	Violet
"Promise Me, Violet" (Reprise)	Flick and Violet
"Bring Me to Light"	Company

Photo: Joan Marcus

(R-L): Annie Golden, Sutton Foster and the cast of *Violet*

Cast Continued

SWINGS
JACOB KEITH WATSON,
VIRGINIA ANN WOODRUFF

STANDBYS/UNDERSTUDIES
Standby for the role of Violet: HAVEN BURTON
For Young Violet: EMMA HOWARD
For Monty: AUSTIN LESCH
For Flick: AZUDI ONYEJEKWE
For Father, Preacher/Radio Singer/Bus Driver 1/
   Bus Driver 4: CHARLIE POLLOCK

Production Stage Manager ...... KRISTEN HARRIS
Stage Manager .... ROBERT WITHEROW
Dance Captain .... ANASTAĆIA McCLESKĒY

TIME
September 1964

PLACE
Across the American South

ORCHESTRA
Conductor: MICHAEL RAFTER
Associate Conductor,
   Synthesizer: JASON MICHAEL WEBB
Cello: EMILY BRAUSA
Guitars: SEAN DRISCOLL, MATT HINKLEY
Synthesizer: SHAWN GOUGH
Bass: LEO HUPPERT
Drums: SEAN McDANIEL
Violin: JUSTIN SMITH
Synthesizer Programmer: RICK BASSETT
Additional arrangement for the
   Healing Sequence: JASON MICHAEL WEBB.
Music Preparation:
   Emily Grishman Music Preparation/
   KATHARINE EDMONDS,
   EMILY GRISHMAN

Sutton Foster
Violet

Colin Donnell
Monty

Alexander
Gemignani
Father

Joshua Henry
Flick

Ben Davis
*Preacher, Radio
Singer, Bus Driver 1,
Bus Driver 4*

Annie Golden
*Old Lady,
Hotel Hooker*

Emerson Steele
Young Violet

Violet

Austin Lesch
*Virgil, Billy Dean,
Bus Driver 2,
Radio Singer,
Bus Passenger;
u/s Monty*

Anastacia McCleskëy
*Music Hall Singer,
Bus Passenger*

Charlie Pollock
*Leroy Evans, Radio
Soloist, Bus Driver 3,
Bus Passenger;
u/s Father, Preacher*

Jacob Keith Watson
Swing

Rema Webb
*Lula Buffington,
Almeta, Bus
Passenger*

Virginia Ann
Woodruff
Swing

Haven Burton
Standby Violet

Emma Howard
u/s Young Violet

Azudi Onyejekwe
u/s Flick

Jeanine Tesori
Composer

Brian Crawley
Lyrics & Book

Doris Betts
Original Story

Leigh Silverman
Director

Jeffrey Page
Choreographer

Michael Rafter
Musical Director

David Zinn
Set Design

Clint Ramos
Costume Design

Leon Rothenberg
Sound Design

Joseph Joubert
Co-Orchestrations

Buryl Red
Co-Orchestrations

Seymour Red Press
Music Coordinator

Charles G. LaPointe
Hair & Wig Design

Kate Wilson
Dialect Coach

Gene O'Donovan
Aurora Productions
*Production
Management*

Ben Heller
Aurora Productions
*Production
Management*

Jim Carnahan, C.S.A.
Casting

Carrie Gardner,
C.S.A.
Casting

Stephen Kopel, C.S.A.
Casting

Arlene Shuler
President & CEO
New York City Center

Amy
Sherman-Palladino
Associate Producer

Emerson Steele
as Young Violet
and Ben Davis
as Preacher

Violet

Daniel Palladino
Associate Producer

David Mirvish
Associate Producer

Fran and Barry Weissler
Associate Producers

Ted and
Mary Jo Shen
Associate Producers

Gene Feist
*Founding Director
Roundabout Theatre
Company*

Todd Haimes
Roundabout Theatre
Company
Artistic Director

Photos: Brian Mapp

SECURITY
Carl Meade

BOX OFFICE
(L-R): Ted Osborne (Box Office Manager), Solangel Bido, Mead Margulies

FRONT OF HOUSE
(L-R): Michael Nach, Chester Hawkins, Jim Lynch, Sauda Moultrie, Zipporah Aguasvivas (Associate House Manager), Crystal Suarez (Head Usher)

Violet

CREW

Seated (L-R): Robert W. Dowling II (House Properties), Elizabeth Coleman (Production Audio Engineer), Ksenia Vanyan (Dresser), Hannah Overton (Assistant Audio Engineer/House Sound), Emile Metcalf (IA Apprentice), Susan J. Fallon (Wardrobe Supervisor), Barb Bartel (Front Light Operator), Carly DiFulvio Allen (Company Manager)

Standing (L-R): Glenn Merwede (Production/House Carpenter), Kristen Harris (Production Stage Manager), Manuela LaPorte (Hair and Wig Supervisor), Brian Carfi, Susan Heart (Dresser), Alexandra Marsh (Make-up Assistant), Robert Witherow (Stage Manager), Jennifer Fisher (Wardrobe Dayworker), Julien Havard (Ms. Foster's Dresser), Dale Carman (Dresser), Brian Maiuri (Production/House Electrician), Beth DuBon (Dresser), Will King (Front Light Operator), Bobby Tacoma (Front Light Operator)

ROUNDABOUT THEATRE COMPANY STAFF
ARTISTIC DIRECTOR ....TODD HAIMES
MANAGING DIRECTOR ....HAROLD WOLPERT
EXECUTIVE DIRECTOR ....JULIA C. LEVY
ADAMS ASSOCIATE
   ARTISTIC DIRECTOR ....SCOTT ELLIS
DIRECTOR OF ARTISTIC
   DEVELOPMENT ....JIM CARNAHAN
GENERAL MANAGER................SYDNEY BEERS
ASSOCIATE MANAGING
   DIRECTOR ....GREG BACKSTROM

ARTISTIC STAFF
DIRECTOR OF CASTING ....Jim Carnahan
Artistic Consultant ....Robyn Goodman
Resident Directors ....Doug Hughes, Sam Gold
Associate Artists ....Mark Brokaw, Evan Cabnet,
     Bill Irwin, Pam MacKinnon, Joe Mantello,
       Kathleen Marshall, Theresa Rebeck
Literary Manager ....Jill Rafson
Senior Casting Director ....Carrie Gardner
Casting Director ....Stephen Kopel
Casting Associate ....Jillian Cimini
Casting Assistants ....Lain Kunin, Alexandre Bleau
Artistic Associate ....Amy Ashton
Literary Associate ....Josh Fiedler
Educational Foundation of
   America Commission ....Lydia Diamond
Roundabout Commissions.............Helen Edmundson,
   Adam Gwon & Michael Mitnick, Joshua Harmon,
   Andrew Hinderaker, Stephen Karam, Steven Levenson,
     Matthew Lopez, Kim Rosenstock
Laurents/Hatcher Foundation
   Commission ....Meghan Kennedy

Casting Interns ....Caitlin Morrison, Emma Miller,
   James Scully, Heather Washburn, Claire Yenson
Script Readers ....Shannon Deep, Michael Perlman,
     Alexis Roblan, Nicole Tingir
Artistic Apprentice ....Olivia O'Connor

EDUCATION STAFF
DIRECTOR OF EDUCATION ....Jennifer DiBella
Assistant Director of Education ....Mitch Mattson
Education Program Manager ....Paul Brewster
Education Program Manager ....Kimberley Oria
Education Assistant ....Julia Borowski
Education Dramaturg ....Ted Sod
Teaching Artists ....Cynthia Babak, Victor Barbella,
   LaTonya Borsay, Mark Bruckner, Chloe Chapin,
   Michael Costagliola, Joe Doran, Mathilde Dratwa,
   Elizabeth Dunn-Ruiz, Sarah Ellis, Carrie Ellman-Larsen,
   Theresa Flanagan, Deanna Frieman, Geoffrey Goldberg,
   Sheri Graubert, Adam Gwon, Creighton Irons,
   Devin Haqq, Carrie Heitman, Karla Hendrick,
   Jason Jacobs, Alana Jacoby, Tess James,
   Hannah Johnson-Walsh, Lisa Renee Jordan,
   Boo Killebrew, Anya Klepikov, Sarah Lang, John Lavigne,
   Erin McCready, James Miles, Nick Moore,
   Meghan O'Neil, Nicole Press, Leah Reddy,
   Amanda Rehbein, Nick Simone, Heidi Stallings,
   Daniel Sullivan, Carl Tallent, Vickie Tanner,
   Laurine Towler, Jennifer Varbalow, Kathryn Veillette,
   Leese Walker, Christopher Weston, Gail Winar,
     Jamie Kalama Wood, Chad Yarborough
Teaching Artist Emeritus ....Reneé Flemings
Education Apprentices ...Rachel Friedman, Rebecca Powell

MANAGEMENT/ADMINISTRATIVE STAFF
ASSOCIATE MANAGING
   DIRECTOR ....Greg Backstrom
General Manager,
   American Airlines Theatre ....Denise Cooper
General Manager, Steinberg Center ....Nicholas J. Caccavo
Operations Manager ....Valerie D. Simmons
Associate General Manager ....Maggie Cantrick
Assistant Managing Director ....Katharine Croke
Rentals Manager ....Nancy Mulliner
Archivist ....Tiffany Nixon
Assistant to the Executive Director &
   Manager, Government Relations ....Nicole Tingir
Assistant to the Managing Director ....Christina Pezzello
Management Apprentice ....Jeesun Choi

FINANCE STAFF
DIRECTOR OF FINANCE.................Susan Neiman
Payroll Director ....John LaBarbera
Accounts Payable Manager ....Frank Surdi
Payroll Benefits Administrator ....Yonit Kafka
Manager Financial Reporting ....Joshua Cohen
Business Office Assistant.....................Jackie Verbitski
Lead Receptionist ....Kyle Stockburger
Receptionists ....Jessie Malone, Michael Valentine
Messenger ....Darnell Franklin
Business Office Apprentice ....Gregory Shepard

DEVELOPMENT STAFF
DIRECTOR OF
   DEVELOPMENT ....Lynne Gugenheim Gregory
Assistant to the
   Director of Development ....Jonathan Sokolow
Associate Director of Development ....Christopher Nave

Violet

INFORMATION TECHNOLOGY STAFF

MARKETING STAFF

AUDIENCE SERVICES STAFF

SERVICES

Sutton Foster
as Violet

Photo: Joan Marcus

MANAGING DIRECTOR EMERITUS....Ellen Richard

Roundabout Theatre Company
231 West 39th Street, New York, NY 10018
(212) 719-9393.

GENERAL PRESS REPRESENTATIVE
POLK & CO.
Matt Polk   Michelle Bergmann
Jessica Johnson   Layne McNish

STAFF FOR *VIOLET*

CREDITS

Scenery constructed and automated by Hudson Scenic Studio, Inc. Lighting equipment from PRG Lighting. Audio equipment from PRG Audio. Menswear constructed by Jennifer Love Costumes. Womenswear constructed by Tricorne, Inc. Millinery by Arnold S. Levine, Inc. Costume painting and distressing by Hochi Asiatico Studio. Custom badges by Gloria Sun. Ms. Foster's shoes by LaDuca. Ms. Foster's sweater by Maria Ficalora. Exclusive stock and amateur stage performing rights are represented by Music Theatre International.

SPECIAL THANKS

Greyhound, Bra*Tenders for undergarments and hosiery, Christopher Sieber, Van Hughes, Paul Whitty, Chris Sullivan

AMERICAN AIRLINES THEATRE STAFF

Wicked

First Preview: October 8, 2003. Opened: October 30, 2003.
Still running as of May 31, 2014.

This imaginative "prequel" to The Wizard of Oz traces the friendship of two young women of Oz, Elphaba and Glinda, and how events beyond their control transform them into the familiar Wicked Witch of the West and Good Witch of the North. Dorothy, the Scarecrow and other beloved Oz characters don't arrive until nearly the end, but reveal fascinating backstories of their own. The show also offers a surprise from the early life of the Wizard himself, and explores what it really means to be "wicked."

THE CAST
(in order of appearance)

Glinda	ALLI MAUZEY
Witch's Father	MICHAEL DeVRIES
Witch's Mother	KRISTEN GORSKI-WERGELES
Midwife	KATHY SANTEN
Elphaba	LINDSAY MENDEZ
Nessarose	CATHERINE CHARLEBOIS
Boq	MICHAEL WARTELLA
Madame Morrible	CAROL KANE
Doctor Dillamond	JOHN SCHIAPPA
Fiyero	DEREK KLENA
Ozian Official	MICHAEL DeVRIES
The Wonderful Wizard of Oz	TOM McGOWAN
Chistery	CHRISTOPHER KING

Monkeys, Students, Denizens of the Emerald City,
Palace Guards and
Other Citizens of Oz ....IOANA ALFONSO,
LARKIN BOGAN, JERAD BORTZ,
MICHAEL DeVRIES,
MAIA EVWARAYE-GRIFFIN,
KRISTEN GORSKI-WERGELES,

Continued on next page

⇒N⇐ GERSHWIN THEATRE

UNDER THE DIRECTION OF
JAMES M. NEDERLANDER AND JAMES L. NEDERLANDER

Marc Platt
Universal Pictures
The Araca Group   and   Jon B. Platt
David Stone

present

WICKED

Music and Lyrics   Book
Stephen Schwartz   **Winnie Holzman**

Based on the novel by Gregory Maguire

starring

Lindsay Mendez   **Alli Mauzey**

also starring

Derek Klena

Catherine Charlebois   John Schiappa   Michael Wartella

Alicia L. Albright Ioana Alfonso Todd Anderson Larkin Bogan Jerad Bortz
Michael DeVries Maia Evwaraye-Griffin Kristen Gorski-Wergeles Spencer Jones Christopher King
Kelly Lafarga Colby Q. Lindeman Emily Mechler Brian Munn Eddie Pendergraft
Casey Quinn Alexander Quiroga Amanda Rose Michael McCorry Rose Adam Sanford
Kathy Santen Heather Spore Carla Stickler Ron Todorowski Brian Wanee Betsy Werbel
Michael Williams Lindsay Wood Briana Yacavone

and

Carol Kane   **Tom McGowan**

Settings	Costumes	Lighting	Sound
Eugene Lee	Susan Hilferty	Kenneth Posner	Tony Meola
Projections	Wigs & Hair	Production Supervisor	Technical Supervisor
Elaine J. McCarthy	Tom Watson	Thom Widmann	Jake Bell
Music Arrangements	Music Director	Dance Arrangements	Music Coordinator
Alex Lacamoire & Stephen Oremus	Bryan Perri	James Lynn Abbott	Michael Keller
Associate Set Designer	Special Effects	Associate Choreographer	Associate Director
Edward Pierce	Chic Silber	Corinne McFadden Herrera	Lisa Leguillou
Casting	Production Stage Manager	General Management	Press
Telsey + Company Craig Burns, CSA	Marybeth Abel	321 Theatrical Management	The Hartman Group

Executive Producers
Marcia Goldberg
& Nina Essman

Orchestrations
William David Brohn

Music Supervisor
Stephen Oremus

Musical Staging by
Wayne Cilento

Directed by
Joe Mantello

Grammy Award-winning Original Cast Recording on DECCA BROADWAY

10/1/13

Derek Klena as Fiyero
and Lindsay Mendez
as Elphaba.

Photo: Joan Marcus

Wicked

MUSICAL NUMBERS

ACT I

"No One Mourns the Wicked"	Glinda and Citizens of Oz
"Dear Old Shiz"	Students
"The Wizard and I"	Morrible, Elphaba
"What Is This Feeling?"	Galinda, Elphaba and Students
"Something Bad"	Dr. Dillamond and Elphaba
"Dancing Through Life"	Fiyero, Galinda, Boq, Nessarose, Elphaba and Students
"Popular"	Galinda
"I'm Not That Girl"	Elphaba
"One Short Day"	Elphaba, Glinda and Denizens of the Emerald City
"A Sentimental Man"	The Wizard
"Defying Gravity"	Elphaba, Glinda, Guards and Citizens of Oz

ACT II

"No One Mourns the Wicked" (reprise)	Citizens of Oz
"Thank Goodness"	Glinda, Morrible and Citizens of Oz
"The Wicked Witch of the East"	Elphaba, Nessarose and Boq
"Wonderful"	The Wizard and Elphaba
"I'm Not That Girl" (reprise)	Glinda
"As Long As You're Mine"	Elphaba and Fiyero
"No Good Deed"	Elphaba
"March of the Witch Hunters"	Boq and Citizens of Oz
"For Good"	Glinda and Elphaba
"Finale"	All

ORCHESTRA

Conductor: BRYAN PERRI

Associate Conductor: DAVID EVANS
Assistant Conductor: BEN COHN
Concertmaster: CHRISTIAN HEBEL
Violin: VICTOR SCHULTZ
Viola: KEVIN ROY
Cello: DANIEL MILLER
Harp: LAURA SHERMAN
Lead Trumpet: JON OWENS
Trumpet: TOM HOYT
Trombones: DALE KIRKLAND,
    DOUGLAS PURVIANCE
Flute: HELEN CAMPO
Oboe: TUCK LEE

Clarinet/Soprano Sax: JOHN MOSES
Bassoon/Baritone Sax/Clarinets: CHAD SMITH
French Horns: THEO PRIMIS,
    CHAD YARBROUGH
Drums: MATT VANDERENDE
Bass: KONRAD ADDERLEY
Piano/Synthesizer: BEN COHN
Keyboards: PAUL LOESEL, DAVID EVANS
Guitars: RIC MOLINA, GREG SKAFF
Percussion: ANDY JONES
Music Coordinator: MICHAEL KELLER

Wicked uses Yamaha Pianos exclusively.

Cast Continued

CHRISTOPHER KING,
COLBY Q. LINDEMAN, EMILY MECHLER,
EDDIE PENDERGRAFT, CASEY QUINN,
ALEXANDER QUIROGA,
MICHAEL McCORRY ROSE,
ADAM SANFORD, KATHY SANTEN,
HEATHER SPORE, CARLA STICKLER,
RON TODOROWSKI, BRIAN WANEE,
BETSY WERBEL, MICHAEL WILLIAMS,
LINDSAY WOOD

STANDBY
For Glinda: TIFFANY HAAS

UNDERSTUDIES
For Elphaba: CARLA STICKLER
For Glinda: EMILY MECHLER,
    HEATHER SPORE
For Fiyero: JERAD BORTZ,
    MICHAEL McCORRY ROSE
For The Wizard and Dr. Dillamond:
    MICHAEL DeVRIES, BRIAN MUNN
For Madame Morrible: KATHY SANTEN,
    BETSY WERBEL
For Boq: LARKIN BOGAN,
    EDDIE PENDERGRAFT
For Nessarose/Midwife: ALICIA L. ALBRIGHT,
    AMANDA ROSE, BRIANA YACAVONE
For Chistery: TODD ANDERSON,
    SPENCER JONES, BRIAN WANEE
For Witch's Father and Ozian Official:
    BRIAN MUNN, ALEXANDER QUIROGA
For Witch's Mother: ALICIA L. ALBRIGHT,
    KELLY LAFARGA, LINDSAY WOOD
For Midwife: KELLY LAFARGA,
    LINDSAY WOOD

SWINGS
ALICIA L. ALBRIGHT, TODD ANDERSON,
SPENCER JONES, KELLY LAFARGA,
BRIAN MUNN, AMANDA ROSE,
BRIANA YACAVONE

DANCE CAPTAINS
ALICIA L. ALBRIGHT, SPENCER JONES,
LINDSAY WOOD

Lindsay Mendez
Elphaba

Alli Mauzey
Glinda

Carol Kane
Madame Morrible

Tom McGowan
The Wizard

Derek Klena
Fiyero

Catherine Charlebois
Nessarose

John Schiappa
Dr. Dillamond

Wicked

Michael Wartella
Boq

Tiffany Haas
Glinda Standby

Alicia L. Albright
*Dance Captain,
Swing; u/s
Nessarose/Midwife/
Witch's Mother*

Ioana Alfonso
Ensemble

Todd Anderson
Swing; u/s Chistery

Larkin Bogan
Ensemble; u/s Boq

Jerad Bortz
Ensemble; u/s Fiyero

Michael DeVries
*Witch's Father/
Ozian Official;
u/s Wizard/
Dillamond*

Maia
Evwaraye-Griffin
Ensemble

Kristen
Gorski-Wergeles
*Witch's Mother,
Ensemble*

Spencer Jones
*Dance Captain,
Swing; u/s Chistery*

Christopher King
Chistery/Ensemble

Kelly Lafarga
*Swing; u/s Witch's
Mother/Midwife*

Colby Q. Lindeman
Ensemble

Emily Mechler
Ensemble; u/s Glinda

Brian Munn
*Swing; u/s
Wizard/Dillamond/
Witch's Father/
Ozian Official*

Eddie Pendergraft
Ensemble; u/s Boq

Casey Quinn
Ensemble

Alexander Quiroga
*Ensemble; u/s
Witch's Father/
Ozian Official/Fiyero*

Amanda Rose
*Swing; u/s
Nessarose/Midwife*

Michael
McCorry Rose
Ensemble; u/s Fiyero

Adam Sanford
Ensemble

Kathy Santen
*Midwife;
u/s Morrible*

Heather Spore
*Ensemble;
u/s Glinda*

Carla Stickler
*Ensemble;
u/s Elphaba*

Ron Todorowski
Ensemble

Brian Wanee
*Ensemble;
u/s Chistery*

Betsy Werbel
*Ensemble;
u/s Morrible*

Michael Williams
Ensemble

Lindsay Wood
*Ensemble, Dance
Captain; u/s Witch's
Mother/Midwife*

Briana Yacavone
*Swing;
u/s Nessarose/
Midwife*

Stephen Schwartz
Music and Lyrics

Winnie Holzman
Book

Joe Mantello
Director

Wayne Cilento
Musical Staging

Wicked

Eugene Lee
Scenic Designer

Susan Hilferty
Costume Designer

Kenneth Posner
Lighting Designer

Tony Meola
Sound Designer

Elaine J. McCarthy
Projection Designer

Tom Watson
Hair and Wig Design

Joe Dulude II
Make-up Designer

Thom Widmann
*Production
Supervisor*

Jake Bell
Technical Supervisor

Stephen Oremus
*Music Supervisor/
Arranger*

William David Brohn
Orchestrations

Alex Lacamoire
Music Arrangements

Bryan Perri
*Music Director/
Conductor*

James Lynn Abbott
*Dance
Arrangements*

Michael Keller
Music Coordinator

Edward Pierce
*Associate Scenic
Designer*

Chic Silber
Special Effects

Corinne McFadden
Herrera
*Associate
Choreographer*

Lisa Leguillou
Associate Director

Stephen Sposito
Resident Director

Bernard Telsey
Telsey + Company
Casting

Gregory Maguire
*Author of Original
Novel*

Marcia Goldberg, Nancy Nagel Gibbs
and Nina Essman
321 Theatrical Management
General Management

Marc Platt
Producer

Michael Rego, Hank Unger and
Matthew Rego
The Araca Group
Producer

Jon B. Platt
Producer

David Stone
Producer

Clyde Alves
Swing; u/s Chistery

James Brown III
Ensemble

Katie Rose Clarke
Glinda

Randy Danson
Madame Morrible

Tess Ferrell
*Swing;
u/s Nessarose/
Midwife*

Wicked

Adam Grupper
The Wonderful Wizard of Oz

F. Michael Haynie
Boq

Kevin Jordan
Swing

Rhea Patterson
Ensemble

Justin Guarini as Fiyero

Photo: Joan Marcus

Jonathan Ritter
Ensemble

Mark Shunkey
Chistery

Travis Waldschmidt
Ensemble

Jonathan Warren
Swing, Dance Captain, Fight Captain; u/s Chistery

TRANSFER STUDENTS 2013-2014

Clyde Alves
Swing; u/s Chistery

Jenni Barber
Glinda

Kelli Barrett
Nessarose

PJ Benjamin
The Wonderful Wizard of Oz

Anne Brummel
Standby for Elphaba

Christine Dwyer
Elphaba

Anna Eilinsfeld
Ensemble; u/s Elphaba

Emily Ferranti
Swing; u/s Nessarose/Midwife

Tess Ferrell
Swing; u/s Nessarose/Midwife

K. Todd Freeman
Doctor Dillamond

Justin Guarini
Fiyero

Ryan Patrick Kelly
Ensemble

Kyle Dean Massey
Fiyero

Lindsay K. Northen
Ensemble; u/s Glinda

Jonathan Ritter
Ensemble

Mary Testa
Madame Morrible

Jonathan Warren
Swing, Dance Captain, Fight Captain; u/s Chistery

Robin Wilner
Ensemble; u/s Witch's Mother/Midwife

Laura Woyasz
Standby for Glinda

Lauren Linville
Ensemble

Wicked

Photos: Brian Mapp

FRONT OF HOUSE
Front Row (L-R): Heather Farrell, Michele Belmond, James Madden, Penny Bonacci, Freddy Rivera
Second Row (L-R): Richard D. Kaye (Manager), Kirth Crawford, Jeremy Bohmstein, Siobhan Dunne, Jacob Korder
Third Row (L-R): Carmen Rodriguez, Philippa Koopman, Eileen Roig, Joe Ortenzio, David Pena
Fourth Row (L-R): Jose Rodriguez, Ivan Rodriguez, Brenda Denaris, Alex Kehr, Leonila Guity, Chris Bonilla

MANAGEMENT
Front (L-R): Jennifer Marik (Stage Manager), Susan Sampliner (Company Manager), Gregg Kirsopp
Back (L-R): Susan Keappock, Christy Ney (Assistant Stage Manager), Marybeth Abel (Production Stage Manager)

WARDROBE
Front (L-R): Barbara Rosenthal, Kathe Mull (Dressers)
Back (L-R): Cate Goetschius (Dresser), Douglas MacArthur (Dresser), Bobbye Sue Albrecht (Dresser), Joy Idowu, Alyce Gilbert (Production Wardrobe Supervisor), Michael Michalski (Dresser), Christina Cocchiara, Kevin Hucke (Assistant Wardrobe Supervisor), Karen Lloyd

HAIR AND MAKE-UP
(L-R): Ron Harmon, Ryan P. McWilliams (Assistant Hair Supervisor), Mary Kay Yezerski (Hair Supervisor), Craig Jessup, Cheri Tiberio (Hair Dresser)

STAFF FOR *WICKED*

GENERAL MANAGEMENT
321 THEATRICAL MANAGEMENT
Nina Essman   Nancy Nagel Gibbs
Marcia Goldberg

GENERAL PRESS REPRESENTATIVE
THE HARTMAN GROUP
Michael Hartman
Tom D'Ambrosio   Frances White

CASTING
TELSEY + COMPANY
Bernard Telsey CSA, Will Cantler CSA,
David Vaccari CSA,
Bethany Knox CSA, Craig Burns CSA,
Tiffany Little Canfield CSA, Rachel Hoffman CSA,
Justin Huff CSA, Patrick Goodwin CSA,

Abbie Brady-Dalton CSA,
David Morris, Cesar A. Rocha CSA, Andrew Femenella,
Karyn Casl CSA, Kristina Bramhall,
Jessie Malone, Conrad Woolfe

TECHNICAL SUPERVISION
JAKE BELL PRODUCTION SERVICES LTD.

COMPANY MANAGER ....SUSAN SAMPLINER

PRODUCTION
    STAGE MANAGER ....MARYBETH ABEL

Stage Manager ....Jennifer Marik
Assistant Stage Managers ....Julie DeVore, Christy Ney
Associate Company Manager ....Adam Jackson
Resident Director...........................Stephen Sposito
Dance Supervisor ....Mark Myars
Associate Music Supervisor ....Adam Souza

Assistant to Mr. Schwartz ....Michael Cole
Assistant Scenic Designer ....Nick Francone
Dressing/Properties ....Kristie Thompson
Scenic Assistant ....Christopher Domanski
Oz Map Design ....Francis Keeping
Draftsman ....Ted LeFevre
Set Model Construction ....Miranda Hardy
Associate Costume Designers ....Michael Sharpe,
                                          Ken Mooney
Assistant Costume Designers ....Maiko Matsushima,
                                          Amy Clark
Costume Coordinator ....Amanda Whidden
Wig Coordinator ....J. Jared Janas
Associate Lighting Designer ....Karen Spahn
Associate Lighting Designer/
    Automated Lights ....Warren Flynn
Assistant Lighting Designer ....Ben Stanton
Lighting Assistant ....Jonathan Spencer

Wicked

CREW
Kneeling (L-R): George Wagner (Production Properties), Kevin Anderson, Harold Shea, Dennis Fox (Flyman), C. Mark Overton (Head Carpenter), Josh Kinsella, John Curvan, Craig Aves (Deck Electrician/Moving Light Operator)
Standing (L-R): John Riggins (Carpenter), Rodney McKenna, Mark Illo (Property Master), Larry Doby, Brendan Conroy, Bruce Moore, Steve Caputo, Jess Ferrera, Jeff Sigler, Jordan Pankin, Valerie Menz (Follow Spot Operator), Mike Szymanski, James Connelly, Brendan Quigley (Head Electrician), Bill Nimmo, Josh Maszle (Sound Engineer), Neil McShane (Electrician), Steve Shea, Dennis Peters

Associate Sound Designer ....Kai Harada
Sound Assistant ....Shannon Slaton
Projection Programmer ....Mark Gilmore
Assistant Projection Designer ....Anne McMills
Projection Animators ....Gareth Smith, Ari Sachter Zeltzer
Special Effects Associate ....Aaron Waitz
Associate Hair Designer ....Charles G. LaPointe
Fight Director ....Thomas Schall
Flying Effects ....ZFX Flying Illusions
Production Carpenter ....Rick Howard
Head Carpenter ....C. Mark Overton
Deck Automation Carpenter ....Joshua Kinsella
Production Electrician ....Robert Fehribach
Head Electrician ....Brendan Quigley
Deck Electrician/Moving Light Operator ....Craig Aves
Follow Spot Operator ....Valerie Menz
Production Properties ....George Wagner
Property Master ....Joe Schwarz
Production Sound Engineer ....Douglas Graves
Sound Engineer ....Josh Maszle
Production Wardrobe Supervisor ....Alyce Gilbert
Assistant Wardrobe Supervisor ....Kevin Hucke
Dressers ...Bobbye Sue Albrecht, James Byrne, Mindy Eng,
Catherine Goetschius, Dianne Hylton,
Douglas MacArthur, Michael Michalski, Kathe Mull,
Laurel Parrish, Teresa Pruitt, Barbara Rosenthal,
Jason Viarengo, Randy Witherspoon
Hair Supervisor ....Mary Kay Yezerski
Assistant Hair Supervisor ....Ryan P. McWilliams
Hairdressers ....Brittnye Batchelor, Cheri Tiberio
Makeup Design ....Joe Dulude II
Makeup Supervisor ....Craig Jessup
Music Preparation Supervisor ....Peter R. Miller,
Miller Music Service
Synthesizer Programming ....Andrew Barrett for
Lionella Productions, Ltd.
Rehearsal Drummer ....Gary Seligson
Music Intern ....Joshua Salzman
Production Assistants .....Timothy R. Semon, David Zack
Advertising ...Serino Coyne/Greg Corradetti, Robert Jones
Marketing .....bdb marketing/Betsy Bernstein, Julie Kruger
Online Marketing ....Situation Interactive
Website ....Istros Media Corporation
Merchandise ....The Araca Group
Theatre Display ....King Displays
Group Sales ....Haley Ward (646-289-6885)
Banking ....JP Morgan Chase Bank/Christina Ciniglio
Payroll ....Checks & Balances
Director of Finance ....John DiMeglio
Production Administrator ....Robert Brinkerhoff

Accountant................Fried & Kowgios Partners CPAs
Insurance ....AON/Albert G. Ruben Insurance
Legal Counsel ....Loeb & Loeb/Seth Gelblum
Legal Counsel for Universal Pictures ....Keith Blau
Physical Therapy ....Encore Physical Therapy, P.C.
Orthopaedist ....David S. Weiss, MD
Onstage Merchandising ....George Fenmore, Inc.

Makeup provided by MAC Cosmetics

MARC PLATT PRODUCTIONS
Adam Siegel, Greg Lessans, Joey Levy,
Jared LeBoff, Claire Wihnyk, Jonathan Ahdout

STONE PRODUCTIONS
David Stone   Patrick Catullo   Aaron Glick

321 THEATRICAL MANAGEMENT
Amy Merlino Coey, Mattea Cogliano-Benedict,
Veronica Decker, Tara Geesaman, Tracy Geltman,
Andrew Hartman, Ryan Lympus, Brent McCreary,
Alex Owen, Rebecca Peterson, Ken Silverman

UNIVERSAL PICTURES
Vice Chairman, NBCUniversal ....Ron Meyer
Chairman,
Universal Filmed Entertainment ....Jeff Shell
Chairman, Universal Pictures ....Donna Langley
President, Universal Pictures ....Jimmy Horowitz
SVP, CFO Productions ....Arturo Barquet
Executive, Live Theatricals ....Chris Herzberger
Vice President, Legal Affairs ....Keith Blau
Sr. Finance Manager ....Stan Zaidinski

 Wicked is a proud member of the Broadway Green Alliance

To find out more about the world of *Wicked*
and to take our Broadway survey,
visit www.wickedthemusical.com.

CREDITS
Scenery built by F&D Scene Changes, Calgary, Canada. Show control and scenic motion control featuring Stage Command Systems© and scenery fabrication by Scenic Technologies, a division of Production Resource Group, New Windsor, NY. Lighting and certain special effects equipment from Fourth Phase and sound equipment from ProMix, both divisions of Production Resource Group LLC. Other special effects equipment by Sunshine Scenic Studios and Aztec Stage Lighting. Video projection system provided by Scharff Weisberg Inc. Projections by Vermilion Border Productions. Costumes by Barbara Matera Ltd., Parsons-Meares Ltd., Scafati, TRICORNE New York City and Eric Winterling. Millinery by Rodney Gordon and Lynne Mackey. Shoes by T.O. Dey, Frederick Longtin, Pluma, LaDuca Shoes NYC, and J.C. Theatrical. Flatheads and monkey builds built by Michael Curry Design Inc. Masks and prosthetics by W.M. Creations, Inc., Matthew W. Mungle and Miyo Yamamoto; lifecasts by Todd Kleitsch. Fur by Fur & Furgery. Undergarments and hosiery by Bra*Tenders, Inc. Antique jewelry by Ilene Chazanof. Specialty jewelry and tiaras by Larry Vrba. Custom Oz accessories by LouLou Button. Custom screening by Gene Mignola. Certain props by John Creech Designs and Den Design Studio. Energy-efficient washers courtesy of LG Electronics. Additional hand props courtesy of George Fenmore. Confetti supplied by Artistry in Motion. Puppets by Bob Flanagan. Musical instruments from Manny's and Carroll Musical Instrument Rentals. Drums and other percussion equipment from Bosphorus, Black Swamp, PTECH, D'Amico and Vater. Emergen-C provided by Alacer Corp. Rehearsed at the Lawrence A. Wien Center, 890 Broadway, and the Ford Center for the Performing Arts.

NEDERLANDER

Chairman ....**James M. Nederlander**
President ....**James L. Nederlander**

Executive Vice President
Nick Scandalios

Vice President   Senior Vice President
Corporate Development   Labor Relations
Charlene S. Nederlander   **Herschel Waxman**

Chief Financial Officer
Freida Sawyer Belviso

STAFF FOR THE GERSHWIN THEATRE
Manager ....**Richard D. Kaye**
Assistant Manager ....Susan Sunday
Treasurer ....John Campise
Assistant Treasurer ....Anthony Rossano
Carpenter ....John Riggins
Electrician ....Neil McShane
Property Master ....Mark Illo
Flyman ....Dennis Fox
Fly Automation Carpenter ....Michael J. Szymanski
Head Usher ....Martha McGuire Boniface

Wicked
SCRAPBOOK

Correspondent: Michael McCorry Rose, Ensemble, understudy "Fiyero"

Most Exciting Celebrity Visitor: Diane Keaton came backstage to visit her good friend Carol Kane, our Madame Morrible. It was in the middle of July and about 157 degrees outside and she still wore an impeccable black leather pantsuit that had people's heads turning the moment she entered the stage door. She was bursting with life and had a wonderful curiosity about what we do and what our daily routines are like in the show. It was heartening to see someone of her stature so genuinely interested in knowing about what goes into an eight-show week at a Broadway musical.

Actor Who Performed the Most Roles in This Show: Brian Munn has performed ten roles: The Wizard, Doctor Dillamond and eight separate ensemble tracks.

Who Has Done the Most Performances: Original cast member Kristen Gorski-Wergeles, who plays "Witch's Mother."

Special Backstage Ritual: There is a moment in the show after the ensemble exits from The Ozdust Ballroom where many of us cross to the opposite side of the stage in the backstage cross over. Every night we give high-fives as we pass one another in the dark. It's a simple ritual, but it feels good, as if we're part of a team.

Favorite Moment: Mine was March 5, 2013, because that was the night I made my Broadway debut in *Wicked*.

Coolest Thing About Being in This Show: The coolest thing about being in *Wicked* is being part of "The 'For Good' Group" that my fellow cast member Emily Mechler and I started this year, under the guidance of our Company Manager Susan Sampliner. "The 'For Good' Group" gives fans who are suffering from terminal or life-threatening illnesses an opportunity to meet cast members backstage after the show. The time we were able to spend with those inspiring young people and their families in 2013 was a highlight of my year.

Memorable Fan Note: "I just wanted to say thank you for taking the time to meet with Julia yesterday after your performance of *Wicked*. Since seeing *Wicked* for the first time in February, it has become her favorite show. Julia is always singing to the CD. Getting to see it in person again was wonderful, but meeting with you after the performance was a special treat. I can't thank you enough for taking the time to brighten Julia's life. Since getting her prognosis, we are thankful for each day and try to make every day special. You did that for her yesterday. I have attached the photo we took of all of you together. Julia wanted to see it today and said the she would 'cherish it forever.'"

Favorite In-Theatre Gathering Place: I usually arrive at the theatre and head up to Lindsay Mendez's dressing room and we chat while she's being fussed over by a small army of make-up, hair and wardrobe experts (Craig, Mary Kay and Kathe).

1. Members of the cast gather to perform on NBC-TV's "The Today Show" marking *Wicked*'s tenth anniversary October 30, 2013. Top Row (L-R): Alli Mauzey, Jonathan Warren, Michael Williams, Betsy Werbel, Ron Todorowski, Maia Evwaraye-Griffin, Casey Quinn, Emily Mechler, Michael McCorry Rose, Lindsay Mendez.
Middle Row (L-R): Larkin Bogan, Christopher King, Ioana Alfonso, Kristen Gorski-Wergeles, Carla Stickler, Colby Q. Lindeman, Michael Wartella. Bottom: Alexander Quiroga.
2. In costume for the broadcast. Top Row (L-R): Ron Todorowski, Alexander Quiroga, Michael Williams, Alicia L. Albright. Middle Row (L-R): Eddie Pendergraft, Kristen Gorski-Wergeles, Maia Evwaraye-Griffin, Betsy Werbel, Carla Stickler Bottom Row (L-R): Ioana Alfonso, Casey Quinn, Emily Mechler
3. Juan Pablo the Year-Round Christmas Bear.
4. Lindsay Mendez and *Yearbook* Correspondent Michael McCorry Rose.

Favorite Off-Site Hangout: Without question: Azalea.

Favorite Snack Foods: Kind Bars

Mascot: Juan Pablo the Year-Round Christmas Bear (see photo, above). He lives in Alli Mauzey's dressing room, except for the time he was bear-napped and held for ransom. That was a tense couple of days at the Gershwin Theatre.

Favorite Therapy: Knob Creek Manhattan on the rocks.

Milestone Celebration: October 30, 2013, *Wicked*'s tenth anniversary on Broadway.

Memorable Press Encounter: The morning of the 10 Year Anniversary the cast did a rehearsal and sound check for our performance of "What Is This Feeling" and "The Wizard and I" on "The Today Show" outside at Rockefeller Plaza. It was so early that the sun hadn't come up yet. Singing and dancing that early in the morning was, in a word: surreal. Well maybe a few words:

Wicked
Scrapbook

1. The cast gathers on the Gershwin theatre stage June 18, 2013 to mark the show's 4,000th Broadway performance.
2. The cast in costume on the Rockefeller Center plaza for the October 30, 2013 "Today Show" broadcast.
3. The women of *Wicked* (L-R): Emily Mechler, Lindsay Northen, Maia Evwaraye-Griffin, Robin Wilner, Casey Quinn, Kristen Gorski-Wergeles, Carla Stickler, Alicia L. Albright.

surreal and really fun.

Memorable Stage Door Fan Encounter: A few months ago I was signing autographs at the stage door when I met a woman from Charleston, West Virginia whose mother performed in a production of *Hello, Dolly!* with my father and grandfather at the Charleston Civic Light Opera Guild in 1969. #smallworld

Web Buzz: To call it a "buzz" would be an understatement. I am amazed by the many examples of *Wicked* inspiring and galvanizing large communities of people both on and off the web.

Fastest Costume Change: Elphaba and Glinda's "One Short Day" costume change into Emerald City: it lasts 17 seconds. It's executed by two dressers, one prop person and a hair person. According to Kathe Mull (Elphaba's dresser) it took nearly two months to get the change finessed down to 17 seconds.

Busiest Week at the Box Office: During the week ending December 29, 2013 *Wicked* grossed $3,201,333 during a nine-show week and became the first Broadway show in history to surpass the $3 million dollar mark for a single week of shows.

Heaviest Costume: The Beefeater Coat in "Emerald City" is the heaviest costume. According to its wearer, Michael DeVries, "it weighs 45 pounds on the first show of the week and about 750 pounds by the end of the week."

Catchphrase Only the Company Would Recognize: "Kah-KAW!"

Sweethearts Within the Company: Marybeth Abel and Gregg Kirsopp, who are both part of our stage management team and recently celebrated their 30th wedding anniversary.

Orchestra Member Who Played the Most Instruments: Andy Jones, percussion, 59 instruments. I couldn't name them all, but I think many of them look suspiciously like medieval torture devices.

Best In-House Parody Lyrics: In support of the 10 Year Anniversary Michael Wartella and I shot and edited together a video of the cast lip-synching to Mika's "Popular Song." Check it out: www.youtube.com/watch?v=uDEZ5qXqEzg

Memorable Directorial Note: As said to Lindsay Mendez by Resident Director Lisa Leguillou about Lindsay's blocking in the song "No Good Deed": "Why are you pulling your skirt up like Chita Rivera singing 'America'?"

Embarrassing Understudy Anecdote: The time I was on as Fiyero in front of an audience of nearly 2,000 people and rather than saying the line "I've been thinking about that lion cub and everything," as it reads in the script, I said "I've been thinking about that Lion King and everything." My blocking is to run offstage about a minute later and was therefore able to explode in riotous laughter shortly after my unfortunate (and very public) line flub. Poor Christine Dwyer and Tiffany Haas (Elphaba and Glinda, respectively) had to keep it together for the rest of Act I. Sorry ladies.

Nickname: Mine is "Rosey."

"Carols for a Cure" Carol: "The Holly and The Ivy."

Ghostly Encounters Backstage: According to sources in the know about these things, we have three ghosts. Drew (a.k.a. Dennis) is the only one we know by name. The other two ghosts who are regularly seen haven't been named, but one dresses in a 19th century blue suit and the other wears a white t-shirt. I merely report.

Superstitions That Turned Out to Be True: One night we were chatting before the show and the name of "The Scottish Play" was said out loud by a cast member who shall remain nameless (but it rhymes with Terek Flena) and at that performance multiple people reported sustaining seriously minor injuries. These reports could not be independently verified at time of print.

The Winslow Boy

First Preview: September 20, 2013. Opened: October 17, 2013.
Limited Engagement. Closed December 1, 2013 after 32 Previews and 53 Performances.

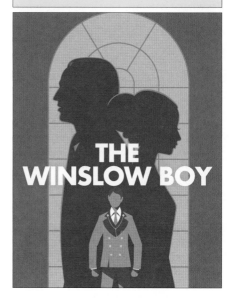

A revival of Terence Rattigan's 1946 drama about a young man who is expelled from an English military academy on the eve of World War I when falsely accused of stealing a five-shilling money order. The seemingly minor issue blows up into a national cause célèbre. Based on a true story, the drama focuses less on the court proceedings and more on the effects that the controversy and ensuing trial have on the boy's family. The boy discovers that his imperious father is more devoted than he dreamed and will do anything, including ruining the family's finances and his own health, to see that the boy's name is cleared.

CAST

(in order of appearance)

Ronnie Winslow .....SPENCER DAVIS MILFORD
Violet ....HENNY RUSSELL
Arthur Winslow ....ROGER REES
Grace Winslow ....MARY ELIZABETH
                          MASTRANTONIO
Dickie Winslow.................ZACHARY BOOTH
Catherine Winslow ....CHARLOTTE PARRY
John Watherstone ....CHANDLER WILLIAMS
Desmond Curry ....MICHAEL CUMPSTY
Miss Barnes................MEREDITH FORLENZA
Fred ....STEPHEN PILKINGTON
Sir Robert Morton ....ALESSANDRO NIVOLA

The action passes in the drawing room of a house in Kensington and extends over two years of a period preceding the war of 1914-1918.

Continued on next page

AMERICAN AIRLINES THEATRE

ROUNDABOUT THEATRE COMPANY

Todd Haimes, Artistic Director
Harold Wolpert, Managing Director
Julia C. Levy, Executive Director
Sydney Beers, General Manager

presents

Michael Cumpsty   Mary Elizabeth Mastrantonio   Alessandro Nivola   Roger Rees

in The Old Vic production of

THE WINSLOW BOY

By
Terence Rattigan

with
Zachary Booth   Spencer Davis Milford   Charlotte Parry   Chandler Williams
Meredith Forlenza   Stephen Pilkington   Henny Russell

Set & Costume Design Peter McKintosh	*Lighting Design* David Lander	*Sound Design* Drew Levy
Original Music Michael Bruce	*Hair & Wig Design* Paul Huntley	*Dialect Coach* Stephen Gabis	*Production Stage Manager* Nevin Hedley
Production Management Aurora Productions	*Casting* Jim Carnahan, C.S.A. Stephen Kopel, C.S.A.	*The Winslow Boy General Manager* Denise Cooper	*Press Representative* Polk & Co.
Associate Managing Director Greg Backstrom	*Director of Marketing & Audience Development* Tom O'Connor	*Director of Development* Lynne Gugenheim Gregory	
Founding Director Gene Feist	*Adams Associate Artistic Director** Scott Ellis		

Directed by
Lindsay Posner

The original Old Vic production of *The Winslow Boy* was first performed on March 8, 2013 at The Old Vic, London (Artistic Director Kevin Spacey, Chief Executive Sally Greene, Producer John Richardson)

*Generously underwritten by Margot Adams, in memory of Mason Adams.

Roundabout Theatre Company is a member of the League of Resident Theatres.
www.roundabouttheatre.org

10/17/13

The Interrogation (L-R): Spencer Davis Milford, Zachary Booth, Alessandro Nivola, Roger Rees, Mary Elizabeth Mastrantonio, Charlotte Parry

Photo: Joan Marcus

The Winslow Boy

Act I: A Sunday morning in July.
Act II: Nine months later.
Six o'clock of a spring evening.
Act III: Nine months later. Ten-thirty p.m.
Act IV: Five months later. An afternoon in June.

UNDERSTUDIES

For Grace Winslow, Violet, Miss Barnes:
GLYNIS BELL
For Desmond Curry, Sir Robert Morton, Fred:
ANTHONY CRANE
For Catherine Winslow:
MEREDITH FORLENZA
For Arthur Winslow:
ANTHONY NEWFIELD
For John Watherstone, Dickie Winslow:
STEPHEN PILKINGTON
For Ronnie Winslow: RYAN QUIGLEY

Production Stage Manager: NEVIN HEDLEY
Stage Manager: JANET TAKAMI

Welcome to Terence Rattigan's *The Winslow Boy* at the American Airlines Theatre. I have wanted to produce *The Winslow Boy* for some time now, and when I saw Lindsay Posner's production at the Old Vic, I knew I'd found the production I had been dreaming of. This play hasn't been seen on Broadway since its premiere in 1947, but Lindsay's fresh vision has breathed new life into this story of a family in turmoil at the beginning of the 20th century.

Rattigan based *The Winslow Boy* on the true story of the trial of young George Archer-Shee, who becomes a subject of public and political debate as his case is taken to London's High Court. Similarly, *Machinal*, the next play in this theatre, is inspired by the even more sensational real-life trial of accused murderess Ruth Snyder. I am excited to offer these plays in counterpoint here at the American Airlines Theatre.

Also at Roundabout, the Steinberg Center for Theatre is filled from the Underground up with new plays this fall. A return engagement of last season's Underground hit *Bad Jews* is not to be missed at the Laura Pels Theatre, and the world premiere of *Too Much, Too Much, Too Many* marks our eighth production in the Black Box Theatre. Please share your thoughts by emailing me at artisticoffice@roundabouttheatre.org. Thank you again for joining us, and I hope that you enjoy *The Winslow Boy*.

Sincerely,
Todd Haimes, Artistic Director

Michael Cumpsty
Desmond Curry

Mary Elizabeth Mastrantonio
Grace Winslow

Alessandro Nivola
Sir Robert Morton

Roger Rees
Arthur Winslow

Zachary Booth
Dickie Winslow

Spencer Davis Milford
Ronnie Winslow

Charlotte Parry
Catherine Winslow

Chandler Williams
John Watherstone

Meredith Forlenza
Miss Barnes

Stephen Pilkington
Fred

Henny Russell
Violet

Glynis Bell
u/s Grace Winslow, Violet, Miss Barnes

Anthony Crane
u/s Desmond Curry, Sir Robert Morton, Fred

Ryan Quigley
u/s Ronnie Winslow

Anthony Newfield
u/s Arthur Winslow

Terence Rattigan
Playwright

Lindsay Posner
Director

Peter McKintosh
Set and Costume Design

David Lander
Lighting Design

Drew Levy
Sound Design

Michael Bruce
Original Music

The Winslow Boy

Paul Huntley
Hair and Wig Design

Stephen Gabis
Dialect Coach

Frank Ventura
*Period Movement
& Choreography*

Gene O'Donovan
Aurora Productions
*Production
Management*

Ben Heller
Aurora Productions
*Production
Management*

Jim Carnahan, C.S.A.
Casting

Stephen Kopel, C.S.A.
Casting

Sally Greene
Old Vic
Chief Executive

Gene Feist
Roundabout Theatre
Company
Founding Director

Todd Haimes
Roundabout Theatre
Company
Artistic Director

Charlotte Parry
and Roger Rees

Photo: Joan Marcus

BOX OFFICE
(L-R): Heather Seibert, Solangel Bido,
Ted Osborne (Box Office Manager)

FRONT OF HOUSE
Front Row (L-R): Dominga Veloz, Sheila Portorreal, Rachel Graf Evans
Back Row (L-R): Martin Ortiz, Zipporah Aguasvivas (Associate House Manager),
Oscar Castillo, Crystal Suarez (Head Usher)

Photos: Brian Mapp

CREW
Sitting (L-R):
Carly DiFulvio Allen (Company Manager),
Dann Wojnar (Sound Operator),
Brian Maiuri (Production Electrician),
Emile Metcalf (IA Apprentice)
Standing (L-R):
Dale Carman (Dresser),
Susan Fallon (Wardrobe Supervisor),
Nevin Hedley (Production Stage Manager),
Manuela LaPorte (Hair/Wig Supervisor),
Ksenia Vanyan (Wardrobe Dayworker),
Pam Short (Dresser), Michael Day,
Janet Takami (Stage Manager),
Robert W. Dowling II (Running Properties)

The Winslow Boy

ROUNDABOUT THEATRE COMPANY STAFF

ARTISTIC DIRECTOR . . . . .TODD HAIMES
MANAGING DIRECTOR . . . . .HAROLD WOLPERT
EXECUTIVE DIRECTOR . . . . .JULIA C. LEVY
ADAMS ASSOCIATE
   ARTISTIC DIRECTOR . . . . .SCOTT ELLIS
GENERAL MANAGER . . . . .SYDNEY BEERS

ARTISTIC STAFF

DIRECTOR OF ARTISTIC DEVELOPMENT/
   DIRECTOR OF CASTING . . . . .Jim Carnahan
Artistic Consultant . . . . .Robyn Goodman
Resident Directors . . . . .Doug Hughes, Sam Gold
Associate Artists . . . . .Mark Brokaw, Scott Elliott,
        Bill Irwin, Pam MacKinnon, Joe Mantello,
        Kathleen Marshall, Theresa Rebeck
Literary Manager . . . . .Jill Rafson
Senior Casting Director .Carrie Gardner
Casting Director . . . . .Stephen Kopel
Casting Associate . . . . .Jillian Cimini
Casting Assistants . . . . .Lain Kunin, Logan Reid
Artistic Associate . . . . .Amy Ashton
Literary Associate . . . . .Josh Fiedler
Educational Foundation of
   America Commissions . . . . .Bekah Brunstetter,
        Lydia Diamond
Roundabout Commissions . . . . .Helen Edmundson,
        Adam Gwon & Michael Mitnick,
        Joshua Harmon, Andrew Hinderaker,
        Stephen Karam, Matthew Lopez, Kim Rosenstock
Casting Interns . . . . .Joyah Spangler, Steven Laing,
        Ragan Rhodes
Script Readers . . . . .Shannon Deep, Michael Perlman,
        Alexis Roblan, Nicole Tingir
Artistic Apprentice . . . . .Olivia O'Connor

EDUCATION STAFF

Director of Education . . . . .Jennifer DiBella
Assistant Director of Education . . . . .Mitch Mattson
Education Program Manager . . . . .Paul Brewster
Education Dramaturg . . . . .Ted Sod
Teaching Artists . . . . .Cynthia Babak, Victor Barbella,
        LaTonya Borsay, Mark Bruckner, Chloe Chapin,
        Michael Costagliola, Joe Doran, Mathilde Dratwa,
        Elizabeth Dunn-Ruiz, Sarah Ellis, Carrie Ellman-Larsen,
        Theresa Flanagan, Deanna Frieman, Geoffrey Goldberg,
        Sheri Graubert, Adam Gwon, Creighton Irons,
        Devin Haqq, Carrie Heitman, Karla Hendrick,
        Jason Jacobs, Alana Jacoby, Tess James,
        Hannah Johnson-Walsh, Lisa Renee Jordan, Boo Killebrew,
        Anya Klepikov, Sarah Lang, John Lavigne, Erin McCready,
        James Miles, Nick Moore, Meghan O'Neil, Nicole Press,
        Leah Reddy, Amanda Rehbein, Nick Simone,
        Heidi Stallings, Daniel Sullivan, Carl Tallent,
        Vickie Tanner, Laurine Towler, Jennifer Varbalow,
        Kathryn Veillette, Leese Walker, Christopher Weston,
        Gail Winar, Jamie Kalama Wood, Chad Yarborough
Teaching Artist Emeritus . . . . .Reneé Flemings
Education Apprentices . . .Rachel Friedman, Rebecca Powell

EXECUTIVE ADMINISTRATIVE STAFF

ASSOCIATE MANAGING
   DIRECTOR . . . . .Greg Backstrom
Assistant Managing Director . . . . .Katharine Croke
Assistant to the Managing Director . . . . . .Christina Pezzello
Assistant to the Executive Director . . . . .Nicole Tingir

---

MANAGEMENT/ADMINISTRATIVE STAFF

General Manager,
   American Airlines Theatre . . . . .Denise Cooper
General Manager,
   Steinberg Center . . . . .Nicholas J. Caccavo
Operations Manager . . . . .Valerie D. Simmons
Associate General Manager . . . . .Maggie Cantrick
Archivist . . . . .Tiffany Nixon
Management Apprentice . . . . .Jeesun Choi

FINANCE STAFF

DIRECTOR OF FINANCE . . . . .Susan Neiman
Human Resources Director . . . . .Stephen Deutsch
Payroll Director . . . . .John LaBarbera
Accounts Payable Manager . . . . .Frank Surdi
Payroll Benefits Administrator . . . . .Yonit Kafka
Manager Financial Reporting . . . . .Joshua Cohen
Business Office Assistant .Jackie Verbitski
Office Manager . . . . .Scott Kelly
Receptionists . . . . .Dee Beider, Elisa Papa, Allison Patrick
Messenger . . . . .Darnell Franklin
Business Office Apprentice . . . . .Gregory Shepard

DEVELOPMENT STAFF

DIRECTOR OF
   DEVELOPMENT . . . . .Lynne Gugenheim Gregory
Associate Director of Development . . . . . . .Christopher Nave
Director, Special Events .Lane Hosmer
Director, Institutional Giving . . . . .Erica Raven
Associate Director, Individual Giving . . . . .Tyler Ennis
Manager, Telefundraising . . . . .Gavin Brown
Manager, Special Events .Natalie Corr
Manager, Donor Information Systems . . . . .Lise Speidel
Institutional Giving Officer,
   Solicitations and Special Projects . . . . .Brett Barbour
Individual Giving Officer,
   Stewardship . . . . .Jordan Frausto
Individual Giving Officer,
   Patron Services . . . . .Toni Rosenbaum
Special Events Assistant . . . . .Genevieve Carroll
Development Assistant . . . . .Martin Giannini
Development Apprentice . . . . .Rachel Starnes

INFORMATION TECHNOLOGY STAFF

DIRECTOR OF
   INFORMATION TECHNOLOGY . .Daniel V. Gomez
Systems Administrator . . . . .Jim Roma
Tessitura &
   Applications Administrator . . . . .Yelena Ingberg
Web Administrator . . . . .Robert Parmelee
DBA/Developer . . . . .Ruslan Nikandrov
IT Associate . . . . .Cary Kim

MARKETING STAFF

DIRECTOR OF MARKETING &
   AUDIENCE DEVELOPMENT . . . . . . .Tom O'Connor
Senior Marketing Manager . . . . .Rani Haywood
Manager, Design & Production . . . . .Eric Emch
Digital Content Producer . . . . .Mark Cajigao
Marketing Associate . . . . .Rachel LeFevre-Snee
Digital Marketing Associate . . . . .Alex Barber
Marketing Assistant . . . . .Dayna Johnson
Telesales Manager . . . . .Patrick Pastor
Telesales Office Coordinator . . . . .Adam Unze
Marketing Apprentices . . . . .Alyssa DeAlesandro,
        Jamie Gottlieb
Digital Marketing Apprentice . . . . .Jennifer Marinelli

---

AUDIENCE SERVICES STAFF

DIRECTOR OF AUDIENCE
   SERVICES . . . . .Wendy Hutton
Associate Director of Audience Services . . . . .Bill Klemm
Customer Care Manager . . . . .Robert Kane
Box Office Managers . . . . .Edward P. Osborne,
   Jaime Perlman, Krystin MacRitchie, Catherine Fitzpatrick
Assistant Box Office Managers . . . . .Robert Morgan,
        Andrew Clements, Nicki Ishmael
Assistant Audience
   Services Managers .Lindsay Ericson,
        Jessica Pruett-Barnett, Kaia Lay Rafoss, Joe Gallina
Customer Care Associate . . . . .Thomas Walsh
Audience Services . . . . .Jennifer Almgreen, Solangel Bido,
        Josh Boscarino, Eric Bridle, Lauren Cartelli,
        Adam Elsberry, Alanna Harms, Kara Harrington,
        Blair Laurie, Rebecca Lewis-Whitson, Michelle Maccarone,
        Mead Margulies, Laura Marshall, Chuck Migliaccio,
        Carlos Morris, Katie Mueller, Sarah Olsen, Josh Rozett,
        Austin Ruffer, Heather Seibert, Nalane Singh,
        Ron Tobia, Hannah Weitzman
Audience Services Apprentice . . . . .Natalie Donohue

SERVICES

Counsel . . . . .Paul, Weiss,
        Rifkind, Wharton and Garrison LLP,
        Charles H. Googe Jr., Carol M. Kaplan
Counsel . . . . .Rosenberg & Estis
Counsel . .Andrew Lance/Gibson, Dunn, & Crutcher, LLP
Counsel . .Harry H. Weintraub/Glick and Weintraub, P.C.
Counsel . . . . .Stroock & Stroock & Lavan LLP
Counsel . . . .Daniel S. Dokos/Weil, Gotshal & Manges LLP
Counsel . .Claudia Wagner/Manatt, Phelps & Phillips, LLP
Immigration Counsel . . . . .Mark D. Koestler and
        Theodore Ruthizer
House Physicians . . .Dr. Theodore Tyberg, Dr. Lawrence Katz
House Dentist . . . . .Neil Kanner, D.M.D.
Insurance . . . . .DeWitt Stern Group, Inc.
Accountant . . . . .Lutz & Carr CPAs, LLP
Advertising . . . . .Spotco/Drew Hodges, Tom Greenwald,
   Ilene Rosen, Josh Fraenkel, Kara Carothers, Chris Blondel
Interactive Marketing . . . . .Situation Interactive/
        Damian Bazadona, Eric Bornemann,
        Elizabeth Kandel, Danielle Migliaccio
Events Photography . . . . .Anita and Steve Shevett
Production Photographer .Joan Marcus
Theatre Displays . . . . .King Displays, Wayne Sapper
Lobby Refreshments . . . . .Sweet Hospitality Group

MANAGING DIRECTOR
   EMERITUS . . . . .Ellen Richard

GENERAL PRESS REPRESENTATIVE
POLK & CO.
Matt Polk
Jessica Johnson   Layne McNish

STAFF FOR *THE WINSLOW BOY*

Company Manager . . . . .Carly DiFulvio Allen
Production Stage Manager . . . . .Nevin Hedley
Stage Manager . . . . .Janet Takami
Production Management . . . . .Aurora Productions Inc./
        Gene O'Donovan, Ben Heller, Chris Minnick,
        Anthony Jusino, Jarid Sumner, Anita Shah,
        Liza Luxenberg, Rachel London, David Cook,
        Bridget Van Dyke, Melissa Mazdra, Cat Nelson
Assistant Director . . . . .Gabriel Weissman

The Winslow Boy
SCRAPBOOK

Curtain call on opening night (L-R): Mary Elizabeth Mastrantonio, Spencer Davis Milford, Roger Rees, Alessandro Nivola, Charlotte Parry, Zachary Booth, Henny Russell and Stephen Pilkington.

Correspondent: Stephen Pilkington, "Fred"

Opening Night Gift: Chandler Williams and I gave the cast t-shirts for opening night gifts. They have become quite the fashion item backstage.

Most Exciting Celebrity Visitor: We've had a lot of wonderful guests, but in particular, Victor Garber saw the show on opening night and took the time to visit us backstage. He took the time to introduce himself to as many cast as he came upon.

Favorite In-Theatre Gathering Place: You will find most of the cast gathering each night in Mary Elizabeth's dressing room during the last 10 minutes of the show for friendly gossip and general debauchery. Well, I can't talk too much more about that.

Special Backstage Ritual: I share a dressing room with Chandler Williams and so Dressing Room 7 is probably the loudest, as no night is complete without hearing the immortal words of Peter O'Toole as Henry II in the wonderful film *Becket*. ("Alright gentlemen, the council is open!") It's become our warm-up routine.

Most Memorable Audience Reaction: Just last night actually, a gentleman in the front row got to his feet and just kept yelling "Thank you! Thank you!" during the curtain call, which was very sweet. At least I think it was "thank you." He did look at me strangely when I told him "You're welcome."

Favorite Therapy: Throat Coat has become quite the hot commodity amongst the cast. As soon as it appears, we're suddenly out again.

Fastest Costume Change: Charlotte Parry seems to be in a different dress every time

I see her backstage. I'm not sure where or how she does it, but somewhere backstage there's magic happening. That, or an amazing team of dressers.

Catchphrase Only the Company Would Recognize: "Of course I did it!" (Ronnie Winslow)

Unique Pre-Show Announcement: We have the unique thrill of hearing the dulcet tones of the wonderful Roger Rees before our show goes up. *The Winslow Boy* is a British drama, so it's great to have Roger and all his Britishisms serenade us before we begin our journey each night.

Understudy Anecdote: "I'm very famous, you know!" Yelled by an actor during understudy rehearsal. Handsome, talented chap.

Coolest Thing About Being in This Show: Working with wonderful seasoned actors at Roundabout. What could be better? Every night is an acting class for me.

Who Heads Your Fan Club: My mom. I'm very famous, you know.

Mary Elizabeth Mastrantonio and Chandler Williams at the cast party.

Makeup Design	Ashley Ryan
Assistant Set Designer	Rachel Nemec
UK Assistant Set Designer	Simon Wells
Associate Costume Designer	Brian J Bustos
UK Costume Assistant	Yvonne Milnes
Associate Lighting Designer	Travis McHale
Original UK Sound Design	Fergus O'Hare
Assistant Sound Designer	Stephanie Celustka
Production Properties Supervisor	Jessica Provenzale
UK Properties Assistant	Maggie Nottage
Period Movement & Choreography	Frank Ventura
Original UK Etiquette	Jack Murphy
Production Carpenter	Glenn Merwede
Production Electrician	Brian Maiuri
Running Properties	Robert W. Dowling II
Sound Operator	Dann Wojnar
Wardrobe Supervisor	Susan Fallon
Dressers	Dale Carman, Pamela Short
Wardrobe Dayworker	Ksenia Vanyan
Hair and Wig Supervisor	Nellie LaPorte
IA Apprentice	Emile Metcalf
Production Assistant	Sara Sahin
Children's Tutoring provided by	On Location Education
Press Intern	Drew Factor

THE OLD VIC STAFF

Artistic Director	Kevin Spacey
Chief Executive	Sally Greene
Producer	John Richardson
Development Director	Vivien Wallace
Finance Director	Conor Marren
Marketing Director	Catrin John
Director, Old Vic New Voices	Steve Winter
Chief Operating Officer	Kate Varah
General Manager	Ros Brooke-Taylor
Production Manager	Dominic Fraser
Director, American Associates	Gina Napoli

The American Associates of The Old Vic, Inc.

Board ...... Dina DeLuca Chartouni (Chair), Alan Banes, Susan Gilchrist, Anne Keating, Marsha Lee, Conor Marren, Frank Selvaggi

Old Vic Associates ...... Rob Ashford, Edward Hall, David Liddiment, Anthony Page, Thea Sharrock, Matthew Warchus

CREDITS

Scenery constructed and painted by Capital Scenery, Lowfield Heath, UK. Lighting equipment by PRG. Sound equipment by Masque Sound. Costumes constructed by Tricorne Costumes. Additional costumes supplied by Cosprop and Angels the Costumiers. Special effects equipment by Jauchem & Meeh, Inc. Props supplied by The Old Vic and the Royal National Theatre. Petitions of Right Act 1860 courtesy of Parliamentary Archives. Shipping by

Jackie Jupp Project Management Ltd. Special thanks to Bra*Tenders for hosiery and undergarments.

Makeup provided by M•A•C Cosmetics.

AMERICAN AIRLINES THEATRE STAFF

Company Manager	Carly DiFulvio Allen
House Carpenter	Glenn Merwede
House Electrician	Brian Maiuri
House Properties	Robert W. Dowling II
House Sound	Dann Wojnar
IA Apprentice	Emile Metcalf
Wardrobe Supervisor	Susan J. Fallon
Box Office Manager	Ted Osborne
Assistant Box Office Manager	Robert Morgan
House Manager	Stephen Ryan
Associate House Manager	Zipporah Aguasvivas
Head Usher	Crystal Suarez
House Staff	Oscar Castillo, Anne Ezell, Rebecca Knell, Jim Lynch, Enrika Nicholas, Sheila Portorreal, Celia Torres, Dominga Veloz
Security	Julious Russell
Additional Security	Gotham Security
Maintenance	Jason Battle, Jerry Hobbs

Summary Closings

First Preview: February 18, 2013
Opened: March 7, 2013
Closed: June 30, 2013 after
19 Previews and
132 Performances

PLAYBILL

THE BIG KNIFE

Limited Engagement
First Preview: March 22, 2013
Opened: April 16, 2013
Closed: June 2, 2013 after
29 Previews and
56 Performances

Limited Engagement
First Preview: April 5, 2013
Opened: April 24, 2013
Closed: June 30, 2013 after
18 Previews and
71 Performances

These shows closed shortly after the start of the 2013-2014 season with virtually no changes to their casts from the previous year's Playbill Broadway Yearbook. *For complete details and photographs from these shows, please consult the 2012-2013 edition.*

Limited Engagement
First Preview: April 7, 2013
Opened: April 21, 2013
Closed: July 14, 2013 after
12 Previews and
73 Performances

Limited Engagement
First Preview: March 21, 2013
Opened: April 15, 2013
Closed: August 11, 2013 after
28 Previews and
136 Performances

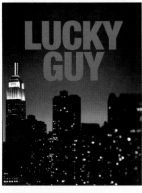

Limited Engagement
First Preview: March 1, 2013
Opened: April 1, 2013
Closed: July 3, 2013 after
33 Previews and
104 Performances

First Preview: March 29, 2012
Opened: April 24, 2012
Closed: June 15, 2013 after
27 Previews and
478 Performances

Events

Photo: Joseph Marzullo

Photo: Monica Simoes

Broadway Bares XXIII: "United Strips of America"

June 23, 2013 at Roseland Ballroom

Broadway Bares XXIII: "United Strips of America," featured 220 of New York's sexiest dancers and raised a record high $1,430,241 to benefit Broadway Cares/Equity Fights AIDS.

This year's edition of the Burlesque-style revue was directed by Nick Kenkel and produced by BC/EFA led by producing director Michael Graziano.

In "United Strips of America," Max von Essen and Michael Cusumano portrayed a bi-coastal couple who set out on separate, sexy journeys through a dozen states.

The evening also included appearances by Christopher Sieber, Lesli Margherita, Jim Newman, Billy Porter, Alan Cumming, Kate Rockwell, Eric LaJuan Summers and Charl Brown as well as "American Idol" finalist Adam Lambert, who delivered a rousing rendition of "The Star-Spangled Banner" at the midnight performance. A pre-show performance by The Skivvies (Nick Cearley and Lauren Molina) provided a mash-up of more than a dozen Americana-themed songs.

1. Hosts Lesli Margherita (*Matilda the Musical*) and Christopher Sieber (*Shrek the Musical*) set the tone of the evening with a strip tease of their own.
2. Proving Texas grows 'em big are cowboy Marty Lawson (*How to Succeed...*) and his cheerleaders.
3. Meeting up in Nebraska, Michael Cusumano (*Chicago*) (L) and Max von Essen (*Evita*) (R) lend helping hands to drum major Timothy Hughes (*Chaplin*).
4. Allyson Carr (*Mamma Mia!*) is rescued by lifeguard Daniel Robinson (*Hairspray*) off the coast of California.

Broadway Meows 5

July 22, 2013 at Don't Tell Mama

Broadway Meows 5, held at Don't Tell Mama night-club, presented the songs of composer-lyricist Seth Bisen-Hersh, who was joined on stage by Karmine Alers, Justin Barnette, Elyse Beyer, Brian Childers, Dana Costello, Lara Janine, Aaron Keller, Miriam Kushel, Melissa Mitchell, Rori Nogee, David Perlman, Adam Shapiro, Stacy Shirk and Haley Swindal. All the proceeds from the evening went to the Humane Society of New York. The evening was directed by Melissa Meli.

Also lending their voices to the cause:
1. Seth Bisen-Hersh.
2. Aaron Keller.
3. Westley Todd Holiday.
4. Cassie Okenka.
5. Kimberly Faye Greenberg.
6. Teresa Hui.

Broadway Barks 15

July 13, 2013 in Shubert Alley

Broadway Barks, which benefits New York City animal shelters, marked its 15th year with a parade of Broadway stars showcasing dogs and cats available for adoption. The event was produced by Broadway Cares/Equity Fights AIDS and sponsored by the ASPCA (The American Society for the Prevention of Cruelty to Animals) with additional sponsorship by *The New York Times*. Co-Founder Bernadette Peters and Hilary Knight, who designed this year's Barks poster and PLAYBILL cover, were on hand to autograph copies of each. In addition to those pictured, others on hand to parade the pets included Annaleigh Ashford, Matt Bogart, Bertie Carvel, Bryan Terrell Clark, Lilla Crawford, Robert Cuccioli, Charlotte d'Amboise, John Dossett, Gabriel Ebert, Harvey Fierstein, Drew Gehling, Ann Harada, Morgan James, Andy Karl, Isabel Keating, Terrence Mann, Lesli Margherita, Andrea Martin, Judy McLane, Michael Mulheren, Bebe Neuwirth, Laura Osnes, Billy Porter, Andrew Rannells, Stark Sands, Matthew James Thomas, Clarke Thorell, Sigourney Weaver, Joanna Christie, Corey Cott, LaVon Fisher-Wilson, Carol Kane, Kara Lindsay, Jane Lynch, Dominic Scaglione, Felicia Finley and Liesel Allen Yeager.

1. *Motown*'s Brandon Victor Dixon, Charl Brown and Valisia LeKae.
2. Michael Urie (*How to Succeed...*).
3. David Hyde Pierce (*Vanya and Sonia and Masha and Spike*).
4. Harvey Fierstein and Bernadette Peters.
5. *Cinderella*'s Victoria Clark.
6. From *Matilda* (L-R): Bailey Ryon, Milly Shapiro, Lauren Ward, Sophia Gennusa and Oona Laurence.

Broadway in Bryant Park

Summer Thursdays 2013 in Bryant Park

Photos: Joseph Marzullo

Cast members from Broadway and Off-Broadway shows stepped outside for some fun, sun and fresh air in Bryant Park Thursdays mid-July to mid-August performing at free concerts sponsored by 106.7 Lite FM. Lunchtime crowds were treated to songs from *Annie, Avenue Q, Big Fish, Chicago, The Fantasticks, First Date, Forever Tango, Kinky Boots, Mamma Mia!, Motown, Once, The Phantom of the Opera, Pippin, Rodgers + Hammerstein's Cinderella, Rock of Ages, Soul Doctor, Spider-Man, Stomp, Wicked* and others.

(L-R): Tonya Wathen, Brian Spitulnik and Michael Cusumano from the cast of *Chicago*.

(L-R): Saycon Sengbloh and Rebecca E. Covington from the cast of *Motown: The Musical*.

Broadway Show League Championship

September 5, 2013 at Hecksher Fields in Central Park

Photos: Joseph Marzullo

The 2013 Broadway Softball League champs were crowned when *Motown: The Musical* defeated *Rock of Ages* 10-4 to win the championship in the Broadway Show League's Effrat Division. With a score of 10-0, Atlantic Theater Company trounced Davenport Theatrical in the Lewin Division, while Actors' Equity beat Barrow Street 7-5 in the Koehler Division. MVPs in each division were: Brianna Moore (*Rock of Ages*) and Jim Maresca (*Motown The Musical*)—Effrat; Miriam Baron (*The Book of Mormon*) and Pat Dabdoub (Atlantic Theater Company)—Lewin; Juana Okayama and Greg Salata (both Actors' Equity)—Koehler.

(L): Members of the *Motown: The Musical* team—on the bench, but in the game.
(R): *Motown*'s Charl Brown heads for home, helping to keep his team in the groove and on the way to winning the 2013 championship.

American Theatre Wing Gala

September 16, 2013 at the Plaza Hotel

The "Prince of Broadway"—Harold Prince, that is—was feted by The American Theatre Wing at a starry gala honoring the director/producer. The evening raised $700,000 for the organization's education and outreach programs. "With Hal Prince, how could we not make money?" asked the Wing's chairman of the board, William Ivey Long. "Everybody wants to come and kiss him." During a long career as producer and director, Prince has won 21 Tony Awards, more than anyone else. Hearing the plaudits for Prince, Santino Fontana, *Cinderella*'s prince, entered to sing a mashup of nearly 30 hit songs from Prince's shows, arranged by music director Rob Berman. Angela Lansbury recited a roll call of classic Prince achievements. Other performers included Sierra Boggess, Emily Skinner, Richard Kind, LaChanze and Jim Wann.

Photo: Joseph Marzullo

(L-R): William Ivey Long (ATW's board chairman), Hal Prince, Heather Hitchens (ATW's executive director).

Chita: A Legendary Celebration

October 7, 2013 at the August Wilson Theatre

Chita Rivera celebrated her 80th birthday in style with a one-night-only sold-out event that raised $413,660 for Broadway Cares/Equity Fights AIDS. Directed by Graciela Daniele and written by Terrence McNally, with musical direction by Michael Croiter, the legendary artist was joined on stage by Tommy Tune and Ben Vereen. Composer John Kander offered a special tribute on video. Also taking part were several of Chita's dancers from *Kiss of the Spider Woman* and *The Dancer's Life*.

Photos 1 & 2: Daniel Roberts; 3: Monica Simoes

1. A little "Class" (*Chicago*) with Ben Vereen and Chita.
2. Chita and her boys singing "Where You Are" from *Kiss of the Spider Woman*.
3. Everything is "Rosie" (*Bye Bye Birdie*) with Chita and Tommy Tune.

Dramatists Guild: Great Writers Thank Their Lucky Stars

October 21, 2013 at the Edison Ballroom

Photos: Joseph Marzullo

Jason Robert Brown, Marsha Norman

Ben Vereen, Stephen Schwartz

Michael John LaChiusa, Kate Baldwin

Bernadette Peters, Stephen Sondheim

The Dramatists Guild Fund benefit paired great writers with great performers. Hosted by Michael Urie and directed by Noah Himmelstein the evening began with Dramatists Guild president Stephen Schwartz introducing Ben Vereen who sang "Magic to Do" (*Pippin*). Next, Alan Menken introduced Jeremy Jordan singing "Santa Fe" (*Newsies*). Sherie Rene Scott sang "Hey, Stay Awhile" (*Landscape of the Body*), with John Guare acting as an angry cyclist in an ill-fitting bicycle helmet. Michael John LaChiusa introduced Kate Baldwin, who sang "Stranger" (*Giant*), and George C. Wolfe brought on Tonya Pinkins and Julian Fleisher for "The Last Chance Blues" (*Jelly's Last Jam*). Andrew Lippa introduced Norbert Leo Butz for "Fight the Dragons" (*Big Fish*). Theresa Rebeck brought on Julie White to perform an excerpt from her 2003 play *Bad Dates*. Next came presentations to the evening's two honorees, donors Roe Green and Don Loftus. Adam Guettel brought along Kelli O'Hara to introduce a new song, "Take Me There" (*Days of Wine and Roses*). Lynn Ahrens and Stephen Flaherty, celebrating their 30th year of collaboration, saluted Marin Mazzie, who performed "Back to Before" from *Ragtime*. Composer Jason Robert Brown and librettist Marsha Norman introduced their incoming show *The Bridges of Madison County* with O'Hara and Steven Pasquale singing "Falling into You." Bernadette Peters ended the proceedings with "Move On" (*Sunday in the Park with George*).

25th Annual "Gypsy of the Year"

December 9 and 10, 2013 at the Minskoff Theatre

Photos: Monica Simoes

T he 25th Annual "Gypsy of the Year" fundraiser for Broadway Cares/Equity Fights AIDS collected a grand total of $4,343,234, up sharply from last year's $3.9 million.

"Bound to the Playground," a nimble dance number in which the gypsies of *The Lion King* skipped, leaped and whirled over sets of thick jump ropes, earned that show the Best Stage Presentation honor, for the second year in a row. First runner-up went to "Cosmic Love" by the cast of *Newsies*.

The show's untitled opening number, directed and choreographed by Devanand Janki and Robert Tatad, offered Klea Blackhurst doing her patented impression of Broadway *diva assoluta* Ethel Merman, upbraiding the corps of modern-day gypsies that they have it so much easier than gypsies did in the old days, to the tune of "You Gotta Get a Gimmick" from *Gypsy*. The youngsters (one of whom paused to take a "selfie" with the Merm) then proceeded to demonstrate how much harder it is today to be a triple-threat dancer-singer-actor who has to commute from Queens on the R train.

Top Broadway musical fundraiser was *Kinky Boots*, which brought in

$377,301. Top Broadway play fundraisers were *The Glass Menagerie* with $161,218 and *Twelfth Night/Richard III* with $116,653. The top fundraisers among Off-Broadway shows were *Avenue Q* with $27,066 and *Peter and the Starcatcher* with $23,360.

Other top Broadway fundraisers were *Wicked* with $273,940, *The Book of Mormon* with $209,943, *Newsies* with $125,469 and *The Phantom of the Opera* with $125,373.

1. The opening number with Klea Blackhurst (top), Tyne Daly and Jonathan Hadary (C) and dancers dressed as the cast of *Newsies*.
2. The cast of *Avenue Q* in its tribute to the late Michael Jeter.
3. *Newsies* cast members perform "Cosmic Love," for which they received first runnner-up for Best Stage Presentation.
4. Desmond Richardson and Bahiyah Hibah from the cast of *After Midnight* in "The Sepia Beauty."
5. *The Lion King* wins Best Stage Presentation for "Bound to the Playground," directed and choreographed by Ray Mercer.
6. Dancers Responding to AIDS in "Only the Beginning," choreographed by Jeremy McQueen.

43rd Annual Theater Hall of Fame Ceremony

January 27, 2014 in the Gershwin Theatre's North Rotunda

Photos: Aubrey Reuben

The 43rd Annual Theater Hall of Fame Ceremony was held in the Gershwin Theatre's North Rotunda. The 2013 inductees: actors Cherry Jones and Ellen Burstyn; directors Jerry Zaks, George C. Wolfe and Lynne Meadow; producer Cameron Mackintosh (not in attendance); designer David Hays; and, posthumously, playwright Lorraine Hansberry. Tony Award winner Joel Grey hosted the ceremony, which was produced by Terry Hodge Taylor. Introducing the honorees were, respectively, Zachary Quinto, Betty Buckley, Jack Viertel, John Guare, Sarah Jessica Parker, Robert Wankel, Julia Hays and Phylicia Rashad.

At the dinner reception in the New York Friars Club:
1. Cherry Jones and Lee Roy Reams.
2. Director George C. Wolfe and the Broadway League's Seth Gelblum.
3. Manhattan Theatre Club's Lynne Meadow and Barry Grove.
4. Director Jerry Zaks.
5. Estelle Parsons and Pia Lindström.
6. Ellen Burstyn and Betty Buckley.
7. Diane Varga and scenic designer David Hays.

The Gypsy Robe

Presented on the opening night of a new musical

Photos: Walter McBride 1, 3-8, 10, 11, 13, 14; Stephanie Masucci 2, 9, 12

The ritual of the Gypsy Robe began in 1950 when Bill Bradley, in the chorus of *Gentlemen Prefer Blondes*, persuaded Florence Baum, a chorus member, to let him have her dressing gown. He sent it to a friend in the chorus of *Call Me Madam*, Arthur Partington, on opening night, telling him it had been worn by all of the *Ziegfeld Follies* beauties. Arthur added a rose from Ethel Merman's gown and sent it to a chorus member in the next show to open, *Guys and Dolls*. It continued this way, passing from show to show, until a specific ceremony was begun with rules on how the Robe is to be presented, worn and paraded onstage. The Robe goes only to a musical with a chorus and to the chorus member with the most Broadway Chorus credits. An artifact from the show is attached to the Robe, which is signed by the recipient and cast members. The recipient attends the next musical opening and presents the Robe to the most experienced gypsy in that show. Numerous robes have been filled and retired over the years. Here are this season's recipients.

1. Jennifer Allen, *The Bridges of Madison County*.
2. Taprena Michelle Augustine, *A Night with Janis Joplin*.
3. Andrea Goss, *Cabaret*.
4. Stacey Todd Holt, *Rocky*.
5. Rosena M. Hill Jackson, *After Midnight*.
6. Curtis Holbrook, *If/Then*.
7. Kevin Ligon, *Bullets Over Broadway*.
8. Anastacia McCleskey, *Violet*.
9. Vasthy E. Mompoint, *Soul Doctor*.
10. Arbender J. Robinson, *Beautiful–The Carole King Musical*.
11. Arbender J. Robinson, *Les Misérables*.
12. Angie Schworer, *Big Fish*.
13. Jennifer Smith, *A Gentleman's Guide to Love & Murder*.
14. Dennis Stowe, *Aladdin*.

Roundabout Theatre Company Gala: In Here, Life Is Beautiful

March 10, 2014 at the Hammerstein Ballroom

Academy Award, Olivier and Golden Globe winner Sam Mendes received the Jason Robards Award for Excellence in Theatre at RTC's 2014 gala. Mendes' association with RTC began in 1998 by directing the Tony Award-winning *Cabaret*, which returned this season. The tribute featured performances by Jenni Barber, Kevin Chamberlin, Alan Cumming, Katie Finneran, Brian d'Arcy James, Rebecca Naomi Jones, Aaron Krohn,

Erin Mackey, Bernadette Peters, Marc Shaiman, Scott Wittman. Also making appearances were Dylan Baker, Jonathan Cake, Jeremy Irons, Helen Mirren, Liam Neeson, Cynthia Nixon, and Juliet Rylance. All proceeds from the event benefited Roundabout Theatre Company's Musical Theatre Fund and Education programs.

1. Alan Cumming.   3. Sam Mendes.   5. Liam Neeson.
2. Helen Mirren.   4. Cynthia Nixon.

9th Annual Broadway Backwards

March 24, 2014 at the Al Hirschfeld Theatre

The ninth annual *Broadway Backwards* concert—featuring male singers performing songs traditionally sung by women and females singing tunes written for men—raised a record-breaking $423,182 to benefit Broadway Cares/Equity Fights AIDS and The Lesbian, Gay, Bisexual & Transgender Community Center (The Center). Created and directed by Robert Bartley, this edition was hosted by Julie White and child actress Bebe Wood (TV's *The New Normal*).

The musical highlight of the evening was Patricia Morison, the original Kate in *Kiss Me, Kate* (who celebrated her 99th birthday March 19), performing "Brush Up Your Shakespeare" from that show. Others who participated included Uzo Aduba, Bryan Batt, Michael Berresse, Stephen Bienske, Stephanie J. Block, Robin De Jesus, Rick Elice, Anthony Festa, Jonathan Groff, Colin Hanlon, Rachel Bay Jones, Andrew Keenan-Bolger, Andy Kelso, Beth Leavel, Norm Lewis, Jose Llana, Kyle Dean Massey, Sean McGee, Debra Monk, Cass Morgan, Ken Page, Billy Porter, Andrew Rannells, Roger Rees, John Tartaglia, Brandon Uranowitz, Max von Essen and Tony Yazbeck.

1. Patricia Morison: "Brush Up Your Shakespeare" from *Kiss Me, Kate*.
2. Robin De Jesus: "Prehistoric Man" from *On the Town*.
3. (L-R): Michael Berresse and Tony Yazbeck: "Nowadays/Hot Honey Rag" from *Chicago*.
4. (L-R): Cass Morgan and Debra Monk: "I Still Get Jealous" from *High Button Shoes*.
5. (L-R): Andy Kelso and Andrew Keenan-Bolger: "The History of Wrong Guys" from *Kinky Boots*.
6. Bryan Batt and ensemble: "I Can Hear the Bells" from *Hairspray*.

Stars in the Alley

May 21, 2014 in Shubert Alley

The Broadway League presented *Stars in the Alley*, a free outdoor concert in Shubert Alley. Hosted by Tony-nominated *The Phantom of the Opera* star Norm Lewis, the concert featured appearances and performances from more than 20 shows currently running on Broadway and two from next season, accompanied by a live 12-piece orchestra.

1. Saul Williams and Tonya Pinkins (*Holler If Ya Hear Me*).
2. Host Norm Lewis (*The Phantom of the Opera*).
3. Kelli O'Hara (*The Bridges of Madison County*).
4. Justin Guarini & Christine Dwyer (*Wicked*).
5. Lena Hall (*Hedwig and the Angry Inch*).
6. Clyde Alves, Tony Yazbeck, Jay Armstrong Johnson (*On the Town*).

Photos: Monica Simoes

27th Annual Broadway Flea Market and Grand Auction

September 22, 2013 in Shubert Alley and on West 44th Street

Photos: Joseph Marzullo

1. Some of the men from the movie of *West Side Story* (L-R): Harvey Evans, David Bean, Eddie Verso, Bert Michaels.
2. The girls of *Matilda The Musical* (L-R): Bailey Ryon, Milly Shapiro, Oona Laurence, Sophia Gennusa.
3. (L-R): *The Glass Menagerie*'s Celia Keenan-Bolger, Cherry Jones (on vocal rest), Brian J. Smith.

Broadway Cares/Equity Fights AIDS raised $631,222 at its annual Flea Market and Grand Auction, bringing the 27-year grand total to more than $10.3 million. More than 60 actors donated their time to signing autographs and taking photos. Of the 56 tables, the top ten fundraisers were: *Wicked* ($19,244); United Scenic Artists Local 829 ($18,206); *The Phantom of the Opera* ($15,887); *Newsies* ($13,353); TDF ($13,099); *Kinky Boots* ($12,326); Creative Goods Merchandise ($9,739); Reel Time Video Production ($9,508); Association of Theatrical Press Agents and Managers (ATPAM) ($9,056); and *Matilda The Musical* ($8,102).

The Grand Auction, including both live and silent auctions, saw the top-selling live auction—the chance for a walk-on in *Kinky Boots*—sell for $8,250. The mask worn by Hugh Panaro in the 25th anniversary Broadway performance of *Phantom* fetched $7,500, while tickets to *Wicked*'s 10th anniversary performance/after-party brought in $7,000. Other auction items and the amounts they raised included: a private lunch with Angela Lansbury ($5,500); a day at *Phantom*, including an appearance in the show's opening number ($5,750); opening night tickets and VIP party passes to *Hedwig and the Angry Inch* ($6,500), to *If/Then* ($6,000), to *Betrayal* ($5,300) and to *Aladdin* ($4,600); and the chance to be a judge at BC/EFA's *Gypsy of the Year* and *Easter Bonnet* competitions which went to two bidders ($5,500 each).

At the silent auction, Elphaba's broom from *Wicked*, used and signed by Idina Menzel, sold for $9,000, and a script from the TV pilot of "Smash," autographed by Megan Hilty, Katharine McPhee, Debra Messing, Christian Borle and Anjelica Huston, went for $3,800.

Born for Broadway

September 30, 2013 at 54 Below

The fourth annual celebrity cabaret, *Born for Broadway*, was held at 54 Below and raised money for paralysis-based organizations. Directed by Marcia Milgrom Dodge, with musical direction by Lawrence Yurman, the event was hosted by Harriet Harris and featured performances by Karen Akers, Annaleigh Ashford, Adrian Bailey, Jim Brochu, Carmen Ruby Floyd, Annie Funke, Carole Lasser, Aaron Lazar, Timothy McDevitt, Howard McGillin, Kathleen Monteleone, Marissa Perry, Chris Pinnella, Steve Rosen, Graham Rowat, Andrew Samonsky, Peter Scolari, Ali Stroker, John Tartaglia and Betsy Wolfe.

Born for Broadway was created ten years ago as a student-sponsored cabaret at Marymount Manhattan College, where founder and executive producer Sarah Galli was enrolled as a performance major. Galli created the show as a way to give back after her brother, Jeff, suffered a spinal cord injury in 1998 in a diving accident.

1. Howard McGillin.
2. Marissa Perry and Annie Funke.
3. Ali Stroker.
4. Annaleigh Ashford and Kathleen Monteleone.

Broadway Salutes

September 24, 2013 at Times Square Visitor Center

Holland Taylor was the master of ceremonies for the fifth annual *Broadway Salutes* event, which paid tribute to over 400 theatre professionals, including stagehands, wardrobe workers, hair and makeup artists, theatre owners, actors, producers, playwrights, casting directors, general managers, publicists, ushers, designers, musicians, directors, choreographers and more, especially those who have worked 25, 35 and 50 years within their crafts.

The event, once again directed by Marc Bruni, featured performances by Annaleigh Ashford ("Don't Rain on My Parade," marking the 50th anniversary of *Funny Girl*'s Broadway debut), Hugh Panaro ("The Music of the Night" celebrating *The Phantom of the Opera*'s 25th anniversary), and Lillias White ("Keepin' Out of Mischief Now," in honor of *Ain't Misbehavin*'s debut 35 years ago).

1. Holland Taylor.
2. Annaleigh Ashford.
3. Hugh Panaro.
4. Lillias White.

Broadway on the Hudson

September 27, 2013 in Brookfield Place Waterfront Plaza, World Financial Center

Sponsored by United Airlines, the free afternoon concert, *Broadway on the Hudson*, took place at Brookfield Place Waterfront Plaza. The event included performances by cast members from *Annie*, *Chicago*, *Newsies*, *The Phantom of the Opera*, *Pippin*, *Rock of Ages*, *Rodgers + Hammerstein's Cinderella*, *Spider-Man Turn Off the Dark*, as well as Justin Guarini from *Romeo and Juliet* and *First Date* star Krysta Rodriguez.

The cast of *Broadway on the Hudson*.

Drama League's Musical Celebration of Broadway

February 3, 2014 at the Pierre Hotel

Emmy Award winner and frequent host of the Tony Award telecast Neil Patrick Harris was honored at the Drama League's 30th Anniversary Musical Celebration of Broadway. A stellar cast of 42 co-workers and friends made the tribute highly entertaining and sometimes quirky through a streamlined 80 minutes. The evening began with introductory remarks from Marc Kudisch and Becky Ann Baker. Tributes, live and filmed, and performances were provided by Jesse Tyler Ferguson, Victor Garber, Christina Hendricks and John Cameron Mitchell, David Hyde Pierce and Michael Mayer (who directed Harris in *Hedwig and the Angry Inch* on Broadway this season).

The entertainment began with Zachary Levi and dancers performing a parody of *Beauty and the Beast*'s "Be My Guest" called "Be My Host." Additional entertainment included: Erin Davie, Paige Price and Chryssie Whitehead ("You Could Drive a Person Crazy"); Norm Lewis ("I Got Plenty o' Nuttin'"); Dan Finnerty singing a vocal version of the theme from "Doogie Howser, M.D." (here called "Doogie Howser, M.C."); Kate Jennings Grant ("With So Little To Be Sure Of"); Lawrence Clayton and James Barbour ("Bring Him Home"); Kal Penn; Cady Huffman, Krysta Rodriguez, Eddie

Korbich and Malcolm Gets ("Side by Side by Side"); Audra McDonald ("Can't Stop Talking About Him"); Katie Finneran, Erin Davie and Drew Gehling ("Getting Married Today"). Then came David Burtka (Harris' longtime partner, and the co-parent of their twins) who serenaded the honoree with "Marry Me a Little." The event was directed by Mayer and Johanna McKeon, with script and special material by Stephen Cole and choreography by JoAnn Hunter. Roger T. Danforth and Trevor Tamashiro produced, with music director David Evans leading three pieces from the piano.

1. Neil Patrick Harris and David Burtka.
2. (L-R): Cady Huffman, Eddie Korbich, Paige Price, James Barbour and Marc Kudisch.
3. (L-R): David Evans and Stephen Cole.
4. Zachary Levi.
5. Becky Ann Baker.
6. Norm Lewis.
7. Kal Penn.

Photos: Joseph Marzullo

Theatre Development Fund Gala

March 3, 2014 at the Edison Ballroom

Theatre Development Fund's (TDF) gala, which celebrated the 35th season of TDF's Accessibility Programs (TAP), was held March 3 at the Edison Ballroom, hosted by Tovah Feldshuh. Feld Entertainment, Inc. executive vice presidents Nicole Feld, Alana Feld and Juliette Feld were honored. Entertainment was provided by Melissa Errico (accompanied by pianist Tedd Firth), the singing string quartet Well-Strung (Edmund Bagnell, Christopher Marchant, Daniel Shevlin and Trevor Wadleigh), Ringling Bros. and Barnum & Bailey Circus ringmaster Johnathan Lee Iverson and husband-and-wife hand-balancing act Duo Fusion. The evening was directed by Donna Drake.

1. (L-R): Nicole Feld, Tovah Feldshuh, Melissa Errico, Alana Feld and Juliette Feld.
2. Duo Fusion: Ihosvanys (pronounced Giovani) Perez and Virginia Tuells.
3. Johnathan Lee Iverson.
4. Well-Strung (L-R): Edmund Bagnell, Daniel Shevlin, Trevor Wadleigh, Christopher Marchant.

Photos: Joseph Marzullo

The New 42nd Street Gala

November 18, 2013 at the New Victory Theater

Michael D. Eisner, former Disney CEO who helped usher the Disney catalogue to Broadway, was honored at The New 42nd Street's gala held at the New Victory Theater. Barry Diller and Thomas Schumacher served as honorary co-chairs for the event that honored Eisner "for bringing kids to the arts and the arts to kids." The evening included musical performances, remarks from Tony Award winner Julie Taymor, Bill Haber and Robert A.M. Stern, and appearances from members of the Disney on Broadway family. A gala dinner followed on stage at the New Amsterdam Theatre.

1. (L-R) Alton Fitzgerald White (*The Lion King*), Heather Headley (*The Lion King*), Josh Strickland (*Tarzan*), Ashley Brown (*Mary Poppins*), who entertained at the gala.
2. Thomas Schumacher (President, Disney Theatrical Group), Julie Taymor, Michael D. Eisner and Cora Cahan (President, The New 42nd Street).

The Actors Fund: Lorna's Pink Party

October 14 & 21, 2013 at Birdland

Birdland hosted *Lorna's Pink Party*, the Actors Fund's 2013 edition of *Nothing Like a Dame*, which raised $120,000 to benefit The Actors Fund's Phyllis Newman Women's Health Initiative and the Dr. Philomena McAndrew Fund of Tower Cancer Research Foundation.

Hosted by actress, recording artist and author Lorna Luft, the evening also featured Liza Minnelli, who performed with a broken wrist. The legendary entertainer broke her wrist in three places while rehearsing at home Oct. 13. Although her doctors requested Minnelli stay at the hospital, she insisted on performing alongside her sister; the daughters of Judy Garland re-created the "Sisters Medley" they first performed at the 1993 Tony Awards. "Nothing was going to stop me from coming here tonight," Minnelli said backstage beforehand. "Lorna asked me to be here and I wouldn't let her down."

Luft, who had recently gone public with her battle against breast cancer, said, "This event means the world to me. I'm so grateful to be feeling so well and performing again. These two Birdland nights are the perfect opportunity for me to gather some friends—including my sister—to raise money to help two essential organizations."

1. There were never such devoted sisters: Lorna Luft and Liza Minnelli raise their voices to raise funds for The Actors Fund's Phyllis Newman Women's Health Initiative and the Dr. Philomena McAndrew Fund of Tower Cancer Research Foundation.
2. Others on hand to lend their voices to these worthy causes: Front (L-R): Trevor McQueen Eaton, Kelly King, Lorna Luft, Liz Callaway, Nick Adams, Phyllis Newman Back (L-R): Norm Lewis, Ann Hampton Callaway, Marcia Strassman, Jim Caruso

The 28th Annual Easter Bonnet Competition

April 21-22, 2014 at the Minskoff Theatre

The 28th annual Broadway Cares/Equity Fights AIDS Easter Bonnet Competition raised an all-time record $4,532,129 in six weeks of nightly curtain-call appeals. That total eclipsed the previous $4.25 million record set one year ago.

This year's top fundraising award went to the national tour of *The Book of Mormon* (Latter Day Company), which raised a stunning $405,009, nearly one tenth of this year's total for 57 participating Broadway, Off-Broadway and touring shows.

Special guests Idina Menzel, Denzel Washington, Bryan Cranston and Fran Drescher presented the performance and bonnet awards at the Minskoff.

The winner for Outstanding Bonnet Design was the Broadway musical *Once*, which created a hat that incorporated several musical instruments from the show that were played during the bonnet presentation. Frequent winner, *The Lion King*, once again took the top prize in the Outstanding Bonnet Presentation category with its *Flashdance*-inspired

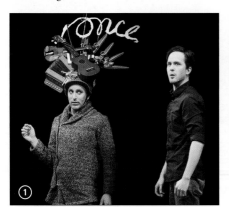

"Momentum." Runner-up in the category was *After Midnight*'s "Snatched," in which a man danced with a series of beautiful women who picked his pockets. Their bonnet featured a spray of feathers and a New York city skyline.

The Broadway musicals that raised the most were *Kinky Boots* ($284,170), *Beautiful* ($208,697), *Rodgers + Hammerstein's Cinderella* ($206,941) and *The Book of Mormon* ($181,065). Broadway plays that raised the most were *All the Way* ($186,424) and *Mothers and Sons* ($100,102). The Off-Broadway shows that raised the most were *Avenue Q* ($28,577) and *Heathers* ($24,363).

1. Eric Love and Ryan McCurdy representing *Once*, winner of Outstanding Bonnet Design.
2. *The Lion King*'s Ben Jeffrey (L) and Fred Berman in "Momentum," which won for Outstanding Bonnet Presentation.
3. The *After Midnight* entry, runner-up for Outstanding Bonnet Presentation.
4. The cast of *Avenue Q* gets an extra-added prize by receiving its honor from Denzel Washington!

5. (L-R): Jarrod Spector, Anika Larsen, Jessie Mueller and Jake Epstein from *Beautiful*.
6. Bryan Cranston, LBJ in *All the Way*, celebrates his show raising the most among Broadway plays.
7. Presenters Bryan Cranston and Fran Drescher, here showing her enthusiasm for being a part of the show.
8. Tyne Daly of *Mothers and Sons* offering advice to *A Couple of Stage Dads Seeking Help*.

The Antoinette Perry (Tony) Awards

June 8, 2014 at Radio City Music Hall

A Gentleman's Guide to Love & Murder, All the Way, Hedwig and the Angry Inch and A Raisin in the Sun won the major production categories at the 2014 Antoinette Perry "Tony" Awards.

The 68th annual awards, representing excellence in Broadway theatre for the 2013-2014 season, were presented at Radio City Music Hall in a ceremony hosted by Hugh Jackman and broadcast on CBS-TV.

The nominees and recipients of the 68th Annual Tony Awards follow. Winners are listed in boldface, with an asterisk (*).

Best Performance by an Actor in a Leading Role in a Musical
*Neil Patrick Harris, *Hedwig and the Angry Inch*
Ramin Karimloo, *Les Misérables*
Andy Karl, *Rocky*
Jefferson Mays, *A Gentleman's Guide to Love & Murder*
Bryce Pinkham, *A Gentleman's Guide to Love & Murder*

Photos: Joseph Marzullo

Best Musical
After Midnight
Aladdin
Beautiful: The Carole King Musical
***A Gentleman's Guide to Love & Murder**

Best Play
Act One, James Lapine
***All the Way**, Robert Schenkkan
Casa Valentina, Harvey Fierstein
Mothers and Sons, Terrence McNally
Outside Mullingar, John Patrick Shanley

Best Revival of a Musical
***Hedwig and the Angry Inch**
Les Misérables
Violet

Best Revival of a Play
The Cripple of Inishmaan
The Glass Menagerie
***A Raisin in the Sun**
Twelfth Night

Best Performance by an Actress in a Leading Role in a Musical
Mary Bridget Davies, *A Night with Janis Joplin*
Sutton Foster, *Violet*
Idina Menzel, *If/Then*
*Jessie Mueller, *Beautiful: The Carole King Musical*
Kelli O'Hara, *The Bridges of Madison County*

Best Performance by an Actor in a Leading Role in a Play
Samuel Barnett, *Twelfth Night*
***Bryan Cranston, *All the Way**
Chris O'Dowd, *Of Mice and Men*
Mark Rylance, *Richard III*
Tony Shalhoub, *Act One*

1. Neil Patrick Harris (Best Performance by an Actor in a Leading Role in a Musical, *Hedwig and The Angry Inch*).

2. Sophie Okonedo (Best Performance by an Actress in a Featured Role in a Play, *A Raisin in the Sun*).

3. Jessie Mueller (Best Performance by an Actress in a Leading Role in a Musical, *Beautiful: The Carole King Musical*).

4. Lena Hall (Best Performance by an Actress in a Featured Role in a Musical, *Hedwig and the Angry Inch*).

5. Mark Rylance (Best Performance by an Actor in a Featured Role in a Play, *Twelfth Night*).

6. Bryan Cranston (Best Performance by an Actor in a Leading Role in a Play, *All the Way*).

7. James Monroe Iglehart (Best Performance by an Actor in a Featured Role in a Musical, *Aladdin*).

8. Audra McDonald (Best Performance by an Actress in a Leading Role in a Play, *Lady Day at Emerson's Bar & Grill*).

The Tony Awards

Best Performance by an Actress in a Leading Role in a Play
Tyne Daly, *Mothers and Sons*
LaTanya Richardson Jackson, *A Raisin in the Sun*
Cherry Jones, *The Glass Menagerie*
*Audra McDonald, *Lady Day at Emerson's Bar & Grill*
Estelle Parsons, *The Velocity of Autumn*

Best Performance by an Actor in a Featured Role in a Musical
Danny Burstein, *Cabaret*
Nick Cordero, *Bullets Over Broadway*
Joshua Henry, *Violet*
*James Monroe Iglehart, *Aladdin*
Jarrod Spector, *Beautiful: The Carole King Musical*

Best Performance by an Actress in a Featured Role in a Musical
Linda Emond, *Cabaret*
*Lena Hall, *Hedwig and the Angry Inch*
Anika Larsen, *Beautiful: The Carole King Musical*
Adriane Lenox, *After Midnight*
Lauren Worsham, *A Gentleman's Guide to Love & Murder*

Best Performance by an Actor in a Featured Role in a Play
Reed Birney, *Casa Valentina*
Paul Chahidi, *Twelfth Night*
Stephen Fry, *Twelfth Night*
*Mark Rylance, *Twelfth Night*
Brian J. Smith, *The Glass Menagerie*

Best Performance by an Actress in a Featured Role in a Play
Sarah Greene, *The Cripple of Inishmaan*
Celia Keenan-Bolger, *The Glass Menagerie*
*Sophie Okonedo, *A Raisin in the Sun*
Anika Noni Rose, *A Raisin in the Sun*
Mare Winningham, *Casa Valentina*

Best Direction of a Musical
Warren Carlyle, *After Midnight*
Michael Mayer, *Hedwig and the Angry Inch*
Leigh Silverman, *Violet*
*Darko Tresnjak, *A Gentleman's Guide to Love & Murder*

Best Direction of a Play
Tim Carroll, *Twelfth Night*
Michael Grandage, *The Cripple of Inishmaan*
*Kenny Leon, *A Raisin in the Sun*
John Tiffany, *The Glass Menagerie*

Best Choreography
*Warren Carlyle, *After Midnight*
Steven Hoggett & Kelly Devine, *Rocky*
Casey Nicholaw, *Aladdin*
Susan Stroman, *Bullets Over Broadway*

Best Scenic Design of a Musical
*Christopher Barreca, *Rocky*
Julian Crouch, *Hedwig and the Angry Inch*
Alexander Dodge, *A Gentleman's Guide to Love & Murder*
Santo Loquasto, *Bullets Over Broadway*

Best Scenic Design of a Play
*Beowulf Boritt, *Act One*
Bob Crowley, *The Glass Menagerie*
Es Devlin, *Machinal*
Christopher Oram, *The Cripple of Inishmaan*

Best Costume Design of a Musical
*Linda Cho, *A Gentleman's Guide to Love & Murder*
William Ivey Long, *Bullets Over Broadway*
Arianne Phillips, *Hedwig and the Angry Inch*
Isabel Toledo, *After Midnight*

Best Costume Design of a Play
Jane Greenwood, *Act One*
Michael Krass, *Machinal*
Rita Ryack, *Casa Valentina*
*Jenny Tiramani, *Twelfth Night*

Best Lighting Design of a Musical
*Kevin Adams, *Hedwig and the Angry Inch*
Christopher Akerlind, *Rocky*
Howell Binkley, *After Midnight*
Donald Holder, *The Bridges of Madison County*

Best Lighting Design of a Play
Paule Constable, *The Cripple of Inishmaan*
Jane Cox, *Machinal*
*Natasha Katz, *The Glass Menagerie*
Japhy Weideman, *Of Mice and Men*

Best Sound Design of a Musical
Peter Hylenski, *After Midnight*
Tim O'Heir, *Hedwig and the Angry Inch*
Mick Potter, *Les Misérables*
*Brian Ronan, *Beautiful: The Carole King Musical*

Best Sound Design of a Play
Alex Baranowski, *The Cripple of Inishmaan*
*Steve Canyon Kennedy, *Lady Day at Emerson's Bar & Grill*
Dan Moses Schreier, *Act One*
Matt Tierney, *Machinal*

Best Book of a Musical
Aladdin, Chad Beguelin
Beautiful: The Carole King Musical, Douglas McGrath
Bullets Over Broadway, Woody Allen
*A Gentleman's Guide to Love & Murder, Robert L. Freedman

1. Jason Robert Brown (Best Original Score and Best Orchestrations, *The Bridges of Madison County*).
2. Kenny Leon (Best Direction of a Play, *A Raisin in the Sun*).
3. Warren Carlyle (Best Choreography, *After Midnight*).

The Tony Awards

Best Original Score (Music and/or Lyrics) Written for the Theatre
Aladdin, Music: Alan Menken; Lyrics: Howard Ashman, Tim Rice and Chad Beguelin
***The Bridges of Madison County,* Music & Lyrics: Jason Robert Brown**
A Gentleman's Guide to Love & Murder, Music: Steven Lutvak;
Lyrics: Robert L. Freedman & Steven Lutvak
If/Then, Music: Tom Kitt; Lyrics: Brian Yorkey

Tony Honors for Excellence in the Theatre
Joseph P. Benincasa
Joan Marcus
Charlotte Wilcox

Isabelle Stevenson Award
Rosie O'Donnell

Regional Theatre Tony Award
Signature Theatre, New York, N.Y.

Best Orchestrations
Doug Besterman, *Bullets Over Broadway*
Jason Robert Brown, The Bridges of Madison County
Steve Sidwell, *Beautiful: The Carole King Musical*
Jonathan Tunick, *A Gentleman's Guide to Love & Murder*

Special Tony Award for Lifetime Achievement in the Theatre
Jane Greenwood

Here's a tally of the 2014 Tony Award winners:
A Gentleman's Guide to Love & Murder 4
Hedwig and the Angry Inch 4
A Raisin in the Sun 3
All the Way 2
Beautiful—The Carole King Musical 2
The Bridges of Madison County 2
Lady Day at Emerson's Bar & Grill 2
Twelfth Night 2
Act One 1
Aladdin 1
After Midnight 1
The Glass Menagerie 1
Rocky 1

1. Jenny Tiramani (Best Costume Design of a Play, *Twelfth Night*)

2. Brian Ronan (Best Sound Design of a Musical, *Beautiful: The Carole King Musical*).

3. Natasha Katz (Best Lighting Design of a Play, *The Glass Menagerie*); Kevin Adams (Best Lighting Design of a Musical, *Hedwig and the Angry Inch*).

4. Christopher Barreca (Best Set Design of a Musical, *Rocky*).

5. Steve Canyon Kennedy (Best Sound Design of a Play, *Lady Day at Emerson's Bar & Grill*).

6. Linda Cho (Best Costume Design of a Musical, *A Gentleman's Guide to Love & Murder*)

7. Beowulf Boritt (Best Set Design of a Play, *Act One*).

8. Team *Gentleman's Guide* (L-R): John Johnson (Producer), Sue Wagner (Producer), Joey Parnes (Producer), cast members—Lauren

Worsham, Bryce Pinkham, Lisa O'Hare, Jefferson Mays—Robert L. Freedman (Book & Lyrics; Best Book of a Musical), Steven Lutvak (Music & Lyrics), Darko Tresnjak (Director; Best Direction of a Musical).

9. Team *Hedwig and the Angry Inch* (Best Revival of a Musical) (L-R): John Cameron Mitchell (Book), Michael Mayer (Director), Stephen Trask (Music & Lyrics), David Binder (Producer)

Photos: Joseph Marzullo

Other Theatre Awards
Covering the 2013-2014 Broadway Season

PULITZER PRIZE FOR DRAMA
The Flick by Annie Baker (Off-Broadway)

NY DRAMA CRITICS' CIRCLE AWARDS
Best American Play: *All the Way*
Best Play: *The Night Alive* (OB)
Best Musical: *Fun Home* (OB)
Special Citations: *Twelfth Night* and *Richard III*; Richard Nelson and the company of *The Apple Family Plays* (OB)

DRAMA DESK AWARDS
Outstanding Play: *All the Way*
Outstanding Musical: *A Gentleman's Guide to Love & Murder*
Outstanding Revival of a Play: *Twelfth Night*
Outstanding Revival of a Musical: *Hedwig and the Angry Inch*
Outstanding Actor in a Play: Bryan Cranston, *All the Way*
Outstanding Actress in a Play: Audra McDonald, *Lady Day at Emerson's Bar & Grill*
Outstanding Actor in a Musical: (Tie) Neil Patrick Harris, *Hedwig and the Angry Inch*; Jefferson Mays, *A Gentleman's Guide to Love & Murder*
Outstanding Actress in a Musical: Jessie Mueller, *Beautiful: The Carole King Musical*
Outstanding Featured Actor in a Play: Reed Birney, *Casa Valentina*
Outstanding Featured Actress in a Play: Celia Keenan-Bolger, *The Glass Menagerie*
Outstanding Featured Actor in a Musical: James Monroe Iglehart, *Aladdin*
Outstanding Featured Actress in a Musical: (Tie) Anika Larsen, *Beautiful: The Carole King Musical*; Lauren Worsham, *A Gentleman's Guide to Love & Murder*
Outstanding Director of a Play: Tim Carroll, *Twelfth Night*
Outstanding Director of a Musical: Darko Tresnjak, *A Gentleman's Guide to Love & Murder*
Outstanding Choreography: Warren Carlyle, *After Midnight*

Veanne Cox (see Drama Desk Awards)

Outstanding Music: Jason Robert Brown, *The Bridges of Madison County*
Outstanding Lyrics: Robert L. Freedman and Steven Lutvak, *A Gentleman's Guide to Love & Murder*
Outstanding Book of a Musical: Robert L. Freedman, *A Gentleman's Guide to Love & Murder*
Outstanding Orchestrations: Jason Robert Brown, *The Bridges of Madison County*
Outstanding Music in a Play: Nico Muhly, *The Glass Menagerie*
Outstanding Revue: *After Midnight*
Outstanding Set Design: Christopher Barreca, *Rocky*
Outstanding Costume Design: William Ivey Long, *Bullets Over Broadway: The Musical*
Outstanding Lighting Design: Christopher Akerlind, *Rocky*
Outstanding Projection Design: Aaron Rhyne, *A Gentleman's Guide to Love & Murder*
Outstanding Sound Design in a Musical Brian Ronan, *Beautiful: The Carole King Musical*
Outstanding Sound Design in a Play: Matt Tierney, *Machinal*
Outstanding Solo Performance: John Douglas Thompson, *Satchmo at the Waldorf* (OB)
Unique Theatrical Experience: *Cirkopolis* (OB)
Special Award: The casts of *The Realistic Joneses* (Toni Collette, Michael C. Hall, Tracy Letts and Marisa Tomei) and *The Open House* (Hannah Bos, Michael Countryman, Peter Friedman, Danny McCarthy and Carolyn McCormick) (OB)
Special Award to Soho Rep (OB)
Special Award to Will Eno
Special Award to Veanne Cox (OB)
Sam Norkin Off-Broadway Award to Ed Sylvanus Iskandar (OB)

OUTER CRITICS CIRCLE AWARDS
Outstanding New Broadway Play: *All the Way*
Outstanding New Broadway Musical: *A Gentleman's Guide to Love & Murder*
Outstanding New Off-Broadway Play: *The Explorer's Club* (OB)
Outstanding New Off-Broadway Musical: *Fun Home* (OB)
Outstanding Book of a Musical (Broadway or OB): Robert L. Freedman, *A Gentleman's Guide to Love & Murder*
Outstanding New Score (Broadway or OB): Jason Robert Brown, *The Bridges of Madison County*
Outstanding Revival of a Play (Broadway or OB): *The Glass Menagerie*
Outstanding Revival of a Musical (Broadway or OB): *Hedwig and the Angry Inch*
Outstanding Director of a Play (Lucille Lortel Award): Tim Carroll, *Twelfth Night*

(L-R): Anika Larsen and Lauren Worsham (see Drama Desk Awards)

Photos: Joseph Marzullo

Outstanding Director of a Musical: Darko Tresnjak, *A Gentleman's Guide to Love & Murder*
Outstanding Choreographer: Warren Carlyle, *After Midnight*
Outstanding Set Design (Play or Musical): Christopher Barreca, *Rocky*
Outstanding Costume Design (Play or Musical): William Ivey Long, *Bullets Over Broadway*
Outstanding Lighting Design (Play or Musical): Kevin Adams, *Hedwig and the Angry Inch*
Outstanding Actor in a Play: Bryan Cranston, *All the Way*
Outstanding Actress in a Play: Cherry Jones, *The Glass Menagerie*
Outstanding Actor in a Musical: Jefferson Mays, *A Gentleman's Guide to Love & Murder*
Outstanding Actress in a Musical: Audra McDonald, *Lady Day at Emerson's Bar & Grill*
Outstanding Featured Actor in a Play: Brian J. Smith, *The Glass Menagerie*
Outstanding Featured Actress in a Play: (Tie) Andrea Martin, *Act One* Mare Winningham, *Casa Valentina*
Outstanding Featured Actor in a Musical: Nick Cordero, *Bullets Over Broadway*
Outstanding Featured Actress in a Musical: Marin Mazzie, *Bullets Over Broadway*
Outstanding Solo Performance: John Douglas Thompson, *Satchmo at the Waldorf* (OB)
John Gassner Award (New American Play): (Tie) Eric Dufault, *Year of the Rooster* (OB) Madeleine George, *The (Curious Case of the) Watson Intelligence* (OB) Steven Levenson, *The Unavoidable Disappearance of Tom Durnin* (OB)
Special Achievement Award: Bill Berloni

THE DRAMA LEAGUE AWARDS
Outstanding Production of a Play: *All the Way*
Outstanding Production of a Musical: *A Gentleman's Guide to Love & Murder*
Outstanding Revival of a Play: *The Glass Menagerie*
Outstanding Revival of a Musical: *Hedwig and the Angry Inch*
Distinguished Performance Award: Neil Patrick Harris, *Hedwig and the Angry Inch*

Other Theatre Awards

Covering the 2013-2014 Broadway Season

Pat Birch (see Astaire Awards)

Distinguished Achievement in Musical Theatre: Barbara Cook

Founders Award for Excellence in Directing: John Tiffany
Unique Contribution to the Theatre Award: Key Brand Entertainment/Broadway Across America: John Gore

THEATRE WORLD AWARDS
For Outstanding Broadway or Off-Broadway debuts:
Paul Chahidi, *Twelfth Night, or What You Will*
Nick Cordero, *Bullets Over Broadway*
Bryan Cranston, *All the Way*
Mary Bridget Davies, *A Night with Janis Joplin*
Sarah Greene, *The Cripple of Inishmaan*
Rebecca Hall, *Machinal*
Ramin Karimloo, *Les Misérables*
Zachary Levi, *First Date*
Chris O'Dowd, *Of Mice and Men*
Sophie Okonedo, *A Raisin in the Sun*
Emerson Steele, *Violet*
Lauren Worsham, *A Gentleman's Guide to Love & Murder*
Dorothy Loudon Award for Excellence in the Theatre: Celia Keenan-Bolger, *The Glass Menagerie*
John Willis Award for Lifetime Achievement in the Theatre: Christopher Plummer

CLARENCE DERWENT AWARDS
From Actors' Equity for "most promising female and male performers on the New York metropolitan scene."
Whitney Bashor, *The Bridges of Madison County*
Stephen Boyer, *Hand to God* (OB)

RICHARD SEFF AWARDS
From Actors' Equity, to "female and male character actors 50 years of age or older."
Peter Maloney, *Outside Mullingar*
Mare Winningham, *Casa Valentina*

OTHER ACTORS' EQUITY AWARDS
Joe A. Callaway Award for best performances in a classic play in the New York metropolitan area: Jonathan Cake, *Much Ado About Nothing* (OB) and J. Smith-Cameron, *Juno and the Paycock* (OB)
St. Clair Bayfield Award for the best supporting performance by an actor in a Shakespearean play in the New York metropolitan area: Tina Benko, *A Midsummer Night's Dream* (OB)
ACCA Award for Outstanding Broadway Chorus: the cast of *Pippin*
Paul Robeson Award for "a person who best exemplifies the principles by which Mr. Robeson lived": Director/playwright/author/actor/educator: Shauneille Perry

FRED EBB AWARD
Michael Kooman and Christopher Dimond

THE TDF/IRENE SHARAFF AWARDS
From the Theatre Development Fund, for outstanding costume design
Lifetime Achievement Award for Costume Design: Deborah M. Dryden
Robert L.B. Tobin Award for Sustained Excellence in Theatrical Design: Marjorie Bradley Kellogg
Artisan Award: Marianne Krostyne
Young Master Award: Linda Cho
Special Memorial Tribute: Sam Kirkpatrick

FRED AND ADELE ASTAIRE AWARDS
Outstanding Choreography of a Broadway Show: Warren Carlyle, *After Midnight*
Outstanding Female Dancer in a Broadway Show: (Tie) Dormeshia Sumbry-Edwards, *After Midnight;* Karine Plantadit, *After Midnight;*
Outstanding Male Dancer in a Broadway Show: Jared Grimes, *After Midnight*
Douglas Watt Lifetime Achievement Award: Pat Birch
Outstanding Achievement in the Preservation of Musical Theatre Award: Luigi

HENRY HEWES DESIGN AWARDS
Presented in October 2013 for work in the 2012-2013 Season
Scenic Design: Mimi Lien, *Natasha, Pierre and the Great Comet of 1812* (OB)
Costume Design: Ann Roth, *The Nance*
Lighting Design: Jane Cox, *The Flick* (OB)
Notable Effects: Peter Nigrini for projection design for *Here Lies Love* (OB)

KLEBAN PRIZE IN MUSICAL THEATRE
Promising Musical Theatre Lyricist: Nathan Tysen
Promising Musical Theatre Librettist: Arthur Perlman

BROADWAY BEACON AWARDS
Laura Osnes, Condola Rashad, Michael Urie

LILLY AWARDS
Kristen Anderson-Lopez
Susan Bernfield
Johanna Day
Joyce Ketay
Mary-Mitchell Campbell
Rebecca Naomi Jones
Dominique Morrisseau
Kelli O'Hara
Jen Silverman
Jeanine Tesori
Liesl Tommy
Lifetime Achievement Award
Winnie Holzman

ARTIOS AWARDS/ CASTING SOCIETY OF AMERICA
New York Broadway Theatre – Comedy
Vanya and Sonia and Masha and Spike, Daniel Swee
New York Broadway Theatre – Drama
Golden Boy, Daniel Swee
New York Broadway Theatre – Musical
Kinky Boots, Bernard Telsey, Justin Huff
New York Theatre – Comedy or Musical
The Madrid, David Caparelliotis
New York Theatre – Drama
If There Is I Haven't Found It Yet, Jim Carnahan
Regional Theatre East
The Glass Menagerie, Jim Carnahan, Stephen Kopel
Regional Theatre West
Pygmalion, David Caparelliotis
Los Angeles Theatre
Joe Turner's Come and Gone, Joanne DeNaut, Andy Crocker (Associate)
Special Theatrical Performance East
Carousel, Jay Binder, Jack Bowdan
Special Theatrical Performance West
The Book of Mormon, Carrie Gardner
HONORARY AWARDS
Career Achievement Award
Nina Tassler
Hoyt Bowers Award
Linda Lowy
New York Apple Award
Michael J. Fox

GRAMMY AWARD
Best Musical Theatre Album: *Kinky Boots*

Ramin Karimloo (see Theatre World Awards)

Faculty

The Playbill Broadway Yearbook | 2013 • 10 • 2014

Top: Celebrating the launch of Playbill's education website PlaybillEDU.com on July 23, 2013.
(L-R): Jill Boriss, Nick Viagas, Robert Viagas, Jon Goldman, Sarah Jane Arnegger, Kelechi Ezie

***Matilda*'s New Teachers This Season:**
Middle: Jill Paice (Miss Honey)
Bottom: Christopher Sieber (Miss Trunchbull)

Faculty

The Shubert Organization

Philip J. Smith
Chairman and co-CEO

Robert E. Wankel
President and co-CEO

Photos: Ben Strothmann

Coalition of Broadway Unions and Guilds (COBUG)

Photo: Brian Mapp

Seated (L-R): Carol Bokun (Local 306), Tony DePaulo (IATSE), Gene McElwain (Local 751), Kimberly Rimbold (AEA), K.C. Boyle (Local 802 AFM)
Standing (L-R): Theresa Couture (Local 802), Deborah Allton-Maher (AGMA), Mauro Melleno (SDC), Laura Penn (SDC), Pat White (Local 764 Wardrobe), Leah Okin (IATSE Local 764), Lawrence Paone (IATSE Local 751), David Faux (Dramatists Guild), Ira Mont (AEA), Carl Mulert (USA 829), Elizabeth Nelson (SDC)

Faculty

The Nederlander Organization

James M. Nederlander
Chairman

James L. Nederlander
President

Nick Scandalios
Executive Vice President

Photo: Courtesy Nederlander Organization

All photos by Anita & Steve Shevett except where otherwise noted.

Freida Belviso
*Chief Financial
Officer*

Bill Register
*Vice President
Operations*

Herschel Waxman
*Senior Vice
President
Labor Relations*

Jack Meyer
*Vice President
Programming*

Charlene S.
Nederlander
*Vice President
Corporate
Development*

Susan Lee
*Brand
Development
Strategist*

Tony Awards Staff

Photo: Brian Mapp

Seated (L-R): Carl Levin (Tony Awards Business and Operations Manager), Shawn Purdy (Tony Awards Press Representative, Slate PR), Heather Hitchens (Executive Director, American Theatre Wing), Jan Friedlander Svendsen (Director, Tony Awards Sponsorship), Jean Kroeper Murphy (Manager, Tony Awards Administration)
Second Row (L-R): Elisa Shevitz (Director of Communications, The Broadway League), Ian Weiss (Producer, Serino/Coyne), Charlotte St. Martin (Executive Director, The Broadway League), Rachel Schwartz (Office Administrator, American Theatre Wing), Will Beech (Intern, Tony Awards), Marielle Young (Intern, The Broadway League)
Third Row (L-R): Ben Pesner (Digital Content Producer, Tony Awards), Lindsey Brown (Slate PR), Noelle Llewellyn (Director, Entertainment Publicity, CBS), Mel Lauer (Assistant to the Executive Director, The Broadway League), Suzanne Tobak (Senior Director of Events, Serino/Coyne)
Back Row (L-R): Chrissann Gasparro (Events Manager, Serino/Coyne), Joanna Sheehan (Tony Awards Licensing and Clearances, ATW), Erica Ryan (Communications/Government Relations Manager, The Broadway League), Nick Pramik (Director of Marketing, SpotCo), Kendra Srebro (Marketing Coordinator, The Broadway League)

Faculty

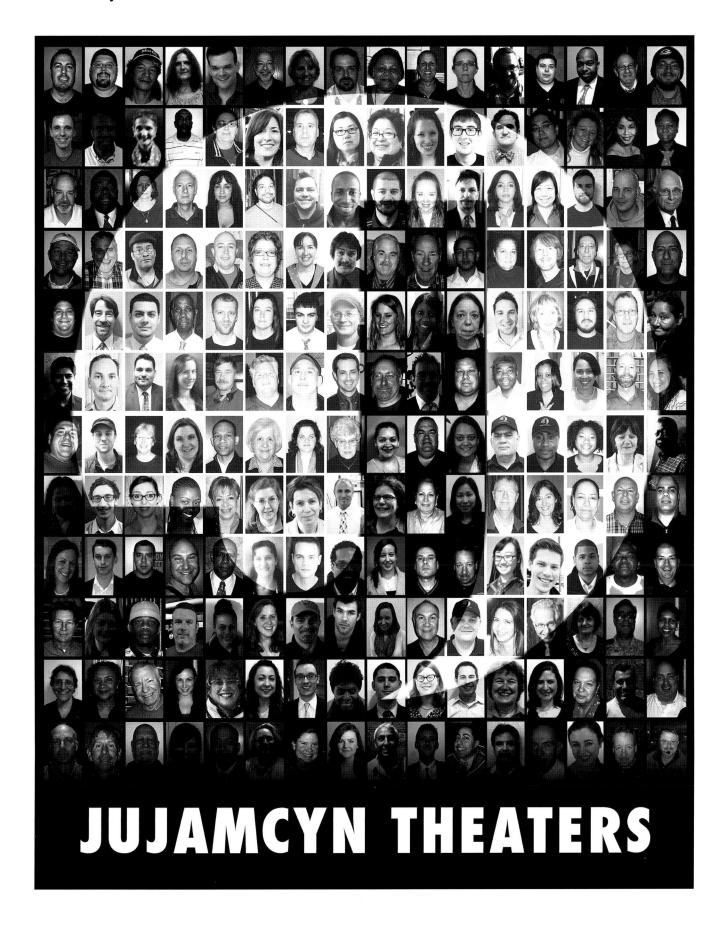

JUJAMCYN THEATERS

Faculty

The Broadway League

Seated (L-R): Kendra Srebro, Elisa Shevitz, Mel Lauer, Leslie Dock, Laura Fayans, Lindsay Florestal, Kayla Kreidell, Jan Friedlander Svendsen
Middle Row (L-R): Julia Davis, Ben Pesner, Ed Sandler, Jason Laks, Jennifier Stewart, Josh Cacchione, Rachel Reiner,
Charlotte St. Martin (Executive Director), Karen Hauser
Back Row (L-R): Erica Ryan, Jessica Zenou, Zenovia Varelis, Mark Smith, Neal Freeman, Chris Brucato, Colin Gibson, Seth Popper, Matt Finnerty,
Jean Kroeper Murphy, Elizabeth Rublein
Not pictured: Chris Brockmeyer, Tom Ferrugia, Robin Fox

Manhattan Theatre Club

First Row (L-R): Mandy Greenfield, Lynne Meadow (Artistic Director), Barry Grove (Executive Producer), Florie Seery, Nancy Piccione
Second Row (L-R): Stephanie Mercado, Caitlin Baird, Melanie Sovern, Jillian Ruben, Emily Yowell, Josiah Grimm
Third Row (L-R): Debra Waxman, Ben Ferber, Scott Kaplan, Elizabeth Rothman, Annie MacRae, Lisa McNulty, Jessica Adler,
Amy Harris, Josh Martinez-Nelson
Fourth Row (L-R): Ryan Guhde, Will DeCamp, Kelly Gillespie, Mallory Triest, Patricia Leonard, Molly Clarke, Aubrie Fennecken,
Thatcher Stevens, Samantha Kindler
Back Row (L-R): Mark Bowers, Cody Andrus, Vincent Losito, Jerry Patch, Barclay Stiff, Lindsey Sag, Jason Fritzsch, Nicki Hunter, Amy Loe

Faculty

The Roundabout Theatre Company

Seated (L-R): Sydney Beers, Julia Levy (Executive Director), Todd Haimes (Artistic Director), Harold Wolpert (Managing Director), Tom O'Connor
Standing (L-R): Daniel V. Gomez, Jennifer DiBella, Jill Rafson, Susan Neiman, Nicholas Caccavo, Valerie Simmons, Greg Backstrom, Denise Cooper, Wendy Hutton

Dodgers

Front Row (L-R): Michael Altbaum, Flora Johnstone, Jessica Morris, Tony Lance, Courtney Sachs, Andrew Serna, Lauren Freed
Middle Row (L-R): Daniel Kogan, Mariann Fresiello, Laurinda Wilson, Annie Van Nostrand, Anne Ezell, Paula Maldonado, Ashley Tracey, Bayleigh, Sandra Carlson, Jessica Ludwig
Back Row (L-R): Lyndsey Goode, Linda Wright, Richard Hester, Dana Sherman, Jennifer Vaughan, John Haber, Priya Iyer, Abigail Kornet, Tim Sulka, Pamela Lloyd, Edward Strong, Christina Aguilar, Lauren Mitchell, Michael David, John Gendron, Kimberly Kelley
Not pictured: Benjamin Cohen, Jeff Parvin, Claire Yenson

Faculty

IATSE Local One, Stagehands

EXECUTIVE BOARD
Seated (L-R): Dan Terrill, Jr. (Chairman, Board of Trustees), Robert C. Score (Secretary), James J. Claffey, Jr. (President), John M. Diaz, Sr. (Vice President), Robert McDonough (Treasurer)
Standing (L-R): Paul F. Dean, Jr. (Business Manager), Edward J. McMahon III (Business Manager), Robert C. Nimmo (Business Manager), Kevin McGarty (Business Manager), William Ngai (Trustee)

OFFICERS
Edmond Supple, Sr. (Administrative Secretary), Anthony Manno (Financial Secretary), Dan Thorn (Replacement Room Chairman)

Stage Directors and Choreographers Society

Seated (L-R): John Rando (Executive Vice President), Laura Penn (Executive Director), Susan H. Schulman (President), Robert Moss, Ethan McSweeny (Treasurer), Marcia Milgrom Dodge
Standing Front Row (L-R): Leigh Silverman (Vice President), Barbara Wolkoff, Meredith McDonough, Sharon Ott, Seret Scott, Elizabeth Miller Nelson, Evan Yionoulis, Tom Moore, Michelle Sokolowski, Michele Holmes
Standing Back Row (L-R): Mark Duncan, Christopher Ashley, Mauro Melleno, Dan Knechtges, Pam MacKinnon, Randy Anderson, Kim Rogers, Kristy Cummings, Linda Hartzell, Cole Jordan, Adam Levi

Faculty

Actors' Equity Association

Nick Wyman
President

Mary McColl
Executive Director

NATIONAL COUNCIL

Paige Price
1st Vice President

Rebecca Kim Jordan
2nd Vice President

Ira Mont
3rd Vice President

Sandra Karas
Secretary-Treasurer

Melissa Robinette
Eastern Regional Vice President

Dev Kennedy
Central Regional Vice President

Doug Carfrae
Western Regional Vice President

AEA STAFF
Front Row (L-R): Louise Foisy, Kathleen Munroe, Michelle Lehrman, Hope Bowman, Toni Stanton, Diane Raimondi
Middle Row (L-R): William Dreyer, Pearl Brady, Kaitria Resetar, Jillian Moss, Jeffrey Bateman, Mary Kate Gilrein
Back Row (L-R): Tatiana Kouloumbis, Barry Rosenberg, David Westphal, Buckly Stephens, Walt Kiskaddon

AEA STAFF
Front Row (L-R): Anne Fortuno, Matthew Arthur, Thomas Miller, Andrea Murray, Jen Hills, Joe Chiplock
Middle Row (L-R): Adriana Douzos, Sierra Pasquale, Doug Beebe, Stephanie Schwartz, John Fasulo, Chris Williams, Calandra Hackney, Timothy Try
Back Row (L-R): Heather Peterson, Perry Jones, Flora Stamatiades, David Thorn, Courtney Godan, Jennifer Michaud
Not pictured: Steve DiPaola (Asst. Executive Director), Thomas Carpenter (Eastern Regional Director)

AEA STAFF
Front Row (L-R): Catherine Jayne, Sylvina Persaud, Laura Schuman, Kathy Mercado, Joanna Spencer
Middle Row (L-R): Gary Dimon, Tripp Chamberlain, Dragica Dabo, Beverly Sloan, Frank Stancati, Russell Lehrer
Back Row (L-R): Robert Druitt, Matthew Conti, Debbie Johnson, Megan Rogers, Jonathan Donahue, Chris Bennett

Faculty

Dramatists Guild

STAFF
Front (L-R): Amy VonVett, Rebecca Stump, Rachel Routh, Gary Garrison, Roland Tec, Brandon Piper, Deborah Murad, Seth Cotterman
Back (L-R): Ralph Sevush, David Faux, Caterina Bartha, Tari Stratton, Patrick Shearer, Jenn Bushinger, Joey Stocks

DRAMATISTS GUILD COUNCIL/STEERING COMMITTEE
Seated (L-R): Doug Wright (Secretary), Theresa Rebeck (Treasurer)
Middle Row (L-R): Julia Jordan, Stephen Schwartz (President), John Weidman, Marsha Norman, David Lindsay-Abaire, Peter Parnell (Vice President)
Back Row (L-R): David Auburn, David Ives, Craig Carnelia
Not pictured: Daniel Goldfarb

Association of Theatrical Press Agents and Managers

Seated (L-R): Robert Nolan, Nick Kaledin (Secretary-Treasurer), Penny Daulton (Vice President), Philip Rinaldi (Press Agent Chapter Chair)
Standing (L-R): Gregg Arst, Jeremy Shaffer, Maria Somma, Rina Saltzman, Matthew Markoff, Steve Greer, David Gersten, Kevin McAnarney
Not pictured: David Calhoun (President), Susan Elrod (Managers Chapter Chair), Barbara Carroll

Faculty

Theatrical Teamsters, Local 817

EXECUTIVE BOARD
(L-R): James Leavey (Recording Secretary), Charles Spillane, Jr. (Trustee), James Fanning (Vice President), Francis J. Connolly, Jr. (Secretary Treasurer), Thomas J. O'Donnell (President), Michael Hyde (Trustee), Gene O'Neill (Trustee)

OFFICE STAFF
(L-R): Tina Gusmano, Christine Harkerss, Margie Vaeth, Allison Hammond, Marg Marklin

Local 829 United Scenic Artists

Seated (L-R): Levonne Barry, Cathy Santucci Keator, Beverly Miller, Cecilia Friederichs
Standing (L-R): Carl Mulert, Carl Baldasso, F. Mitchell Dana, Ed Pierce

Faculty

IATSE Local 751, Treasurers & Ticket Sellers Union

OFFICERS AND STAFF
Sitting (L-R): Patricia Quiles, Stephanie Swisher-Lajoie
Standing (L-R): James Sita, Gene McElwain (President),
Lawrence Paone (Secretary-Treasurer/Business Agent)

EXECUTIVE COUNCIL
Front Row (L-R): Noreen Morgan, Karen Winer, Gene McElwain (President), Patricia DeMato
Middle Row (L-R): John Nesbitt, Harry Jaffie, Lawrence Paone (Secretary-Treasurer/Business Agent),
Dave Heveran, Stanley Shaffer
Back Row (L-R): Robert Begin, Peter Attanasio Jr., Matthew Fearon, John Toguville,
Michael Loiacono

Theatrical Wardrobe Union, IATSE Local 764

First Row (L-R): Shannon Koger (Secretary/Treasurer), Barbara Palmer, Angela Lehrer, Adam Adelman, Nicole Baker, James Kabel, Alexa Burt
Second Row (L-R): Shelly Friedman (Trustee), Dennis Birchall, Susan Heart, Bobby Condon, Barbara Hladsky, Joe Dehn, Peggy Danz Kazdan,
Sue Stepnik, Paul Drost
Third Row (L-R): Karen Winer, Paula Cohen (Trustee), Susan Frances Schaffel, Gregg Simmons, Mark Klein, Maureen Leshley, Pat Sullivan (Trustee)
Fourth Row (L-R): Jenna Krempel (Vice-President), Ryann Lynch, Jim Collum, Courtney Alfrey, Bill Hubner, John Corbo, Victoria Tjoelker,
Vera Chow, Colleen Ehrlich, Dolores Jones, Patricia White (President), Alejandra Rubinos
Back Row (L-R): Vangeli Kaseluris (Trustee), Martha Smith (Trustee), AraBella Fischer, Frank Gallagher (Business Representative),
Leah Okin (Business Representative)

Faculty

American Federation of Musicians, Local 802

Sitting (L-R): John O'Connor (Recording Vice President), Tino Gagliardi (President), Tom Olcott (Financial Vice President),
Pat Dougherty (Executive Board member)
Standing (L-R): Executive Board members Jay Brandford, Sara Cutler, Clint Sharman, Martha Hyde, Andy Schwartz, Bob Cranshaw, Bud Burridge
Not pictured: Gail Kruvand

IATSE Local 306 Motion Picture Projectionists, Video Technicians and Allied Crafts (Ushers)

Sitting (L-R): Lorraine Lowrey (Vice President), Margie Blair, Helen Bentley, Lea Lefler,
Rita Russell (President)
Standing (L-R): Barry Garfman (Business Rep/Projectionist), Andrew Nagy, John Seid (Secretary-Treasurer), Joe Rivierzo, Donna Vanderlinden, Kenny Kelly (Sergeant-at-Arms)

International Union of Operating Engineers Local 30

BUSINESS MANAGER
John T. Ahern

Faculty

American Theatre Wing

Front Row (L-R): LaTanya Richardson Jackson (Board of Trustees), Dasha Epstein (Board of Trustees), Heather A. Hitchens (Executive Director), William Ivey Long (Chairman), Pia Lindström (Board of Trustees), David Brown (Board of Trustees)
Middle Row (L-R): Raisa Ushomirsky (Comptroller), Phil Getter (Board of Trustees), David Henry Hwang (Board of Trustees), Michael Price (Treasurer), Enid Nemy (Secretary), Rachel Schwartz (Office Administrator), Mark Abrahams (Board of Trustees), Nicole Gardner (Director of Development), Kenny Gallo (Director of Digital Media and Technology)
Back Row (L-R): Joanna Sheehan Bell (Director of Programs), James Higgins (Board of Trustees), Peter Schneider (Vice-Chairman), Patricia Crown (Board of Trustees), Ted Chapin (Vice-Chairman), Jeffrey Eric Jenkins (Board of Trustees), Sally Susman (Board of Trustees), Megan Kolb (Program Associate), Jeremiah Hernandez (Development and Events Coordinator)

Broadway Cares/Equity Fights AIDS

Front Row (L-R): Valerie Lau-Kee Lai (Producer), Frank Conway (Associate Director of Corporate Sponsorship and Production Services), Andy Halliday (Retail Outreach Assistant), Angelica Franklin (Associate Graphics Designer), Anna Troiano (Intern), Yvonne Ghareeb (Print & Catering Manager), Ngoc Bui (Associate Director of Finance), Keith Bullock (Office Manager), Denise Roberts Hurlin (Founder, DRA), Michael Graziano (Producing Director), Tom Viola (Executive Director)
Middle Row (L-R): Trisha Doss (Associate Producer), Lane Beauchamp (Marketing Manager), Sarah Cardillo (Development Officer), Ed Garrison (Database Manager), Rose James (Associate Director of Finance), Chris Gizzi (Shipping Manager), Chris Davis (Producer, DRA), Chris DeLuise (Associate Production Manager)
Back Row (L-R): Dex Ostling (Associate Web Developer), Nathan Hurlin (Production Manager), Madeline Reed (Data Entry Assistant), Larry Cook (Director of Finance & Administration), Dennis Henriquez (Courier), Gary Damiano (Volunteer), Ryan Walls (Senior Development Officer), Scott T. Stevens (Producer, Special Projects), Joe Norton (Associate Director of Education & Outreach), Jason Daunter (Producer), Danny Whitman (Director of Communications & Development), Aaron Waytkus (Art Director/Graphics Manager), Skip Lawing (Event Ticketing), Roy Palijaro (Associate Director of Internet Marketing and Data Systems), Peter Borzotta (Retail Outreach Manager)

Faculty

Theatre Development Fund and TKTS

TKTS TREASURERS
Front (L-R): Ann Ramirez, Rajesh Sharma, Gale Spyridon, Michael McCarthy
Back (L-R): John Cinelli, John Palumbo, William Castellano (Head Treasurer), Brian Roeder

TDF COSTUME COLLECTION
Front (L-R): Joanne Haas (Associate Director), Stephen Cabral (Director), Joey Haws (Rental Assistant)
Back (L-R): Mark Runion (Administrator), Debbi Hobson (Staff Designer), Craig Stekeur (Receptionist)

TDF STAFF
Front Row (L-R): Michael Buffer, Craig Stekeur, David LeShay, Debbi Hobson, Joey Haws
Second Row (L-R): Christina Trivigno, Lisa Carling, Michael Naumann, Victoria Bailey, Daniel Renner, Stephen Cabral
Third Row (L-R): Joann Guerilus, Allie Relihan, Connie Hall, Allison Taylor, Philip Dallmann, Jane Pfeffer, Eric Sobel, Erin Winchester, Kim Midkiff
Fourth Row (L-R): Catherine Lizima, Paula Torres, Christophe Mentor, Jonathan Calindas, Richard Price, JoAnn Gall, Vickie Alvarez, Lea Wülferth, Julie Williams, Sal Polizzi, Fran Polino, Tymand Staggs, Tina Kirsimae, Tom Westerman, Michael Yaccarino
Fifth Row (L-R): Michelle St. Hill, Joseph Cali, Joyce Hinds, George Connolly, Donald Beale
Back Row (L-R): Julian Christenberry, Ginger Bartkoski Meagher, Mark Blankenship, Sarah Aziz, Thomas Adkins

Faculty

The Actors Fund

Photo: Brian Mapp

BOARD OF TRUSTEES
Seated (L-R): Teresa Eyring, Nancy Coyne, Kristen Madsen, Nick Wyman, Joyce Gordon, Roberta Reardon
Standing (L-R): Tom Viola, Michael Kerker, Janice Reals Ellig, Jeff Bolton, Thomas Schumacher, Stewart F. Lane, Martha Nelson, Chris Keyser, Brian Stokes Mitchell (Chairman), Joseph P. Benincasa (President & CEO)

On screen—Western Council: Front (L-R): Sharon Lieblein (Looking Ahead Advisory Committee Vice-Chair), Ilene Graff (Western Council Co-Vice Chair)
Back (L-R): Keith McNutt (Actors Fund Western Region Director), David Rambo (Western Council Member), Meg Thomas (Major Gifts Officer)
Trustees not pictured: Alec Baldwin, Annette Bening, Philip S. Birsh, John Breglio, Ebs Burnough, James J. Claffey, Jr., Merle Debuskey, Rick Elice, Marc Grodman, Mark Hostetter, Ken Howard, David Henry Hwang, Anita Jaffe, Kate Edelman Johnson, Steve Kalafer, Paul Libin, Matthew Loeb, Kevin McCollum, Lin-Manuel Miranda, James L. Nederlander, Bebe Neuwirth, Phyllis Newman, Lee H. Perlman, Harold Prince, Abby Schroeder, Philip J. Smith, Charlotte St. Martin, David Steiner, Edward D. Turen, Jomarie Ward, Joseph H. Wender, David White, BD Wong, George Zuber

Photo: Brian Mapp

NEW YORK STAFF
Front (L-R): Jay Haddad, Lillian Wasserman, Allison Hooban, Jessica Siegel, Joy Pascua-Kim, Jean Lee, Matthew Whitenack, Dale Daley, Allison Abrams, Erica Chung, Elizabeth Avedon
Middle Row (L-R): Amy Wilder, Connie Yoo (Chief Financial Officer), Barbara Davis (Chief Operating Officer), Alayna George, Patricia Schwadron, Barbara Toy, Tamar Shapiro, Amy Picar, Holly Wheeler, Billie Levinson, Judy Fish, Gloria Jones, Marjorie Roop, Joseph P. Benincasa (President & CEO)
Back Row (L-R): Thomas Exton (Chief Advancement Officer), Xaq Webb, Rebecca Sauer, Susan Latham, Robyn Cucurullo, Samuel A. Smith, Tim Pinckney, Stephen Joseph, Paul Riedel, Matthew Kovach, Denise Poirier, Kent Curtis, David Engelman

Photo: Nina Prommer

WESTERN COUNCIL
Front (L-R): John Acosta, Pam Dixon, Kate Edelman Johnson, John Holly, Ilene Graff, Ilyanne Morden Kichaven
Middle (L-R): Meg Thomas, John Bowab, Martin Wiviott, Barbara Allyne Bennet, Bridget Hanley, Jomarie Ward, David Rambo, Keith McNutt
Back (L-R): Scott Mauro, William Thomas, Ken Werther, Hollace Davids, Daniel Henning, James Karen

Photo: Ted Abenheim

WESTERN REGION OFFICE
Front (L-R): Robin LaBorwit, Keith McNutt, Joanne Webb, Ina Williams
Middle (L-R): Angelique Prahalis, Joy Tribble, Emmanuel Freeman, Brigid Sweeney, Tina Hookom, Magen Senen, Laura Campbell, Venus Tarkington
Back (L-R): Stuart Berkowitz, Caitlin Sorenson, Amanda Steele, Dan Kitowski, Natasha Missick, Amy Hammond, Frank Salamone, Joey Shanley, John Cao, Meg Thomas, Louie Anchondo

Faculty

Boneau/Bryan-Brown

Chris Boneau

Adrian Bryan-Brown

Photos: Joan Marcus

Jim Byk   Michelle Farabaugh   Jackie Green   Kelly Guiod   Linnae Hodzic   Kevin Jones   Amy Kass

Holly Kinney   Emily Meagher   Aaron Meier   Christine Olver   Joe Perrotta   Amanda Sales   Heath Schwartz   Susanne Tighe

Make-Up Artists and Hair Stylists, IATSE Local 798

Photo: Courtesy of Local 798

Front: Rose Chatterton
Seated (L-R): Angela Johnson, Sunday Englis, Eve Morrow, Cindy Gardner, Leslie Fuller, Charles McKenna, Rosemarie Levy (Business Rep.), Cynthia O'Rourke
Standing (Middle, L-R): Tonya Bodison, Daniel Dashman (Business Rep.), Seidah Nichols, Michelle Kearns, Debbie Peiser, Christine Domaniecki, Linda Grimes, Stephen Bishop, Milton Buras, Stephanie Wise
Standing (Back, L-R): Daniel Green, Christopher Milone, Kristin Ryals, Jill Astmann-Karol, Jorge Vargas, John James

Faculty

Lincoln Center Theater

Front Row (L-R): Mike Assalone, Alexandra Lopez, Ira Weitzman, Rebecca Leshin, Susan Knox
Second Row (L-R): Kristen Parker, Kati Koerner, Ashley Dunn, Jessica Niebanck, Adam Siegel
Third Row (L-R): Steve Spears, Emily McGill, David Cannon, Mike Adank, Sydney Rais-Sherman, David Brown, Allotey Peacock
Back Row (L-R): Neal Brilliant, Amanda Kaus, Julia Judge, Alex Mustelier, Meghan Lantzy, Linda Mason Ross, Laura Stuart, Jennifer Wintzer

The Hartman Group

Front Row (L-R): Tom D'Ambrosio, Michael Hartman, Colgan McNeil
Back Row (L-R): Emily McGill, Bethany Larsen, Wayne Wolfe, Frances White, Nicole Capatasto, Whitney Holden Gore, Matt Ross

Faculty

Richard Kornberg & Associates

(L-R): Billy Zavelson, Richard Kornberg, Don Summa, Conor Greene
Not pictured: Danielle McGarry

The Publicity Office

Seated (L-R): Marc Thibodeau, Michael Borowski
Standing: Jeremy Shaffer

Jeffrey Richards Associates

Front Row (L-R):
Lindsay Hoffman, Irene Gandy,
Jeffrey Richards, Franco,
Alana Karpoff, Michael Crea, Skye
Back Row (L-R):
Will Trice, Steven Strauss,
Christopher Pineda, Thomas Raynor,
Andy Drachenberg, PJ Miller

Polk & Company

Sitting (L-R): Tom D'Ambrosio,
Matt Polk, Colgan McNeil
Standing (L-R): Katie Reed,
Layne McNish, Jessica Johnson,
Michelle Bergmann, Frances White,
Sasha Pensanti, Wayne Wolfe,
Jason Snow

Faculty

J. AQUINO
GOSPEL CHOIR

A. AYVAZYAN
HALL MONITOR

A. BAKER
BRUNCH CLUB

S. BARTON
CHEERLEADING

T. BEDDOE
PROM COMMITTEE

W. BEISHIR
DETENTION

A. BIZJAK
JAZZ TEAM

J. BODLEY
ROCK BAND

A. BOND
SANDWICH CLUB

J. BOOR
STUDENT COUNCIL

A. BRODER
YOGI & MEDITATOR

N. BUDNYK
BEAUTY SCHOOL DROPOUT

J. CARBONELLA
WOOD SHOP

K. CAROTHERS
HEAD OF THE PLASTICS

K. CARTER
TEAM EDWARD

E. CERDEIROS
POP CULTURE CLUB

J. COOPER
COMIC BOOK CLUB

J. COOPER
BANJO CLUB

T. COPPOLA
BREAKFAST CLUB

D. COX
HISTORICAL SOCIETY

G. CRADDOCK
EAGLE SCOUTS

B. CRAWFORD
STUDENT PAPER EDITOR

T. CREWS
VALEDICTORIAN

A. CRUZ
GLEE CLUB

M. CURRY
URBAN ACHIEVER

A. DAVIS
BLACK HISTORY CLUB

M. DELMORE
BABYSITTERS CLUB

A. EISENHOWER
SWIM TEAM

J. FAERBER
WARREN FAN CLUB

T. FALOTICO
WATER POLO

J. FOX
A.M. ANNOUNCEMENTS

K. FOX
COMPETITIVE JAZZ DANCE

L. FRAENKEL
SMALL PEOPLE CLUB

T. FRANCIS
STUDY CLUB

S. FROST
QUIDDITCH CLUB

SpotCo Class of 2014

F. GARGIULO
MOCK TRIAL

R. GASKINS
DRILL TEAM

C. GOFF
MOST TALKATIVE

G. GREEN
PEP SQUAD

D. HODGES
PRINCIPAL

N. PRAMIK
LINGUISTICS

B. BERK
DEAN OF STUDENTS

T. GREENWALD
AV SQUAD

I. ROSEN
GUIDANCE COUNSELOR

E. HAMMERMAN
DEAD POETS SOCIETY

J. HANNETT
DRAMA SOCIETY

H. HILL
RECYCLING CLUB

J. HUBBELL
COMPUTER CLUB

L. JOHNSON
DANCE TEAM

M. JOHNSON
VARSITY BASKETBALL

J. KOCH
RAP GENIUS

S. KINGETT
DUMBLEDORE'S ARMY

S. LADD
TEACHER'S PET

B. LAURIE
MARCHING BAND

L. LEWIS
ASTROLOGY CLUB

N. LINDEMAN
PING PONG

L. MACHLICA
THE PINK LADIES

M. McCRACKEN
NERD

J. McGOWAN
A CAPPELLA

C. McKEOWN
RESIDENT EXTERMINATOR

J. McNICHOLAS
BROADCAST CLUB

B. MORAN
CABER TOSS

T. MOSER
BRAVO CLUB

S. MUNOZ
NO CLUB CLUB

J. PERRI
WATER BOY

L. PREGOSIN
ROOKIE OF THE YEAR

D. PRESTON
MATHLETES

S. PRINCE
ARTS AND CRAFTS

K. RATHBUN
QUIZ BOWL CAPTAIN

C. RICE
CLASS PREZ

A. ROTHENBERG
COLOR GUARD

S. SANTORE
CROSS COUNTRY

C. SCHERER
RESIDENT DJ

B. SCHULTZ
HOME ECONOMICS

C. SCHWITZ
FIRST TEAM ALL-STATE

D. SELLERS
JAZZ BAND

C. SHALOIKO
SKI CLUB

D. SNYPE
BALLET FOLKLORICO

C. SOGLIUZZO
TEAM SPIRIT

S. SOSNOWSKI
FENCING

K. SUER
SOCIAL COMMITTEE

S. TARTICK
JR. MAGICIANS ASSOC.

H. TROY
UNICORN COMMITTEE

J. VANDERWOUDE
BEST WHEELS

B. WATSON
YOUNG DEMOCRATS

J. WECHSLER
SPEED-WALKING CLUB

R. WEISS
ACADEMIC DECATHLON

H. WILSON
BEST DRESSED

K. YOUNG
MASCOT

R. ZATCOFF
HOMEROOM REP

Faculty

2013–2014

SERINO/COYNE

Faculty

438   The Playbill Broadway Yearbook 2013-2014

Faculty

Playbill

Philip S. Birsh
CEO & President

Arthur T. Birsh
Chairman

Bruce Hallett
Publisher

Clifford S. Tinder
*Senior Vice
President/Publisher,
Classic Arts Division*

Joan Alleman
Vice President

Blake Ross
Editor in Chief

Photo: Courtesy of Playbill

ONLINE EDITORIAL/PLAYBILL.COM
Sitting (L-R): Adam Hetrick, Andrew Gans, Blake Ross, Robert Viagas
Standing (L-R): Mark Ezovski, Joseph Marzullo, David Gewirtzman, Andrew Ku, Carey Purcell, Michael Gioia, Matt Blank, Jon Goldman
Not pictured: Monica Simoes

Photo: Brian Mapp

OFFICE MANAGEMENT
Sitting (L-R): Wanda Young, Oldyna Dynowska, Tiffany Feo
Standing (L-R): Esvard D'Haiti, Arturo Gonzalez, Dolly Reyes,
Anderson Peguero

Photo: Brian Mapp

PRODUCTION / ARTISTIC / EDITORIAL
Sitting (L-R): Diana Leidel, Clifford S. Tinder, Maude Popkin
Standing (L-R): Harry Haun, Alex Near, Brian Libfeld, Damian Fowler
Not pictured: Kesler Thibert

Faculty

Playbill

SALES
Sitting (L-R): Clara Barragán, Yadira Mitchell, Ellen Kamhi
Standing (L-R): Max Silverstein, Talaura Harms, Nicholas Foster, Jim Cairl, Glenn Asciutto, Ari Ackerman, Glenn Shaevitz
Not pictured: Jolie Schaffzin

PLAYBILL EDU / VIP / VAULT / MEMORY BANK / PRO
Sitting (L-R): Sarah Jane Arnegger, Brad Gumbel, Robert Viagas, Megan Dekic
Standing (L-R): Jon Goldman, Steven McCasland, Robbie Rozelle, Frank Dain, David Gewirtzman, Andrew Ku

Harry Haun
Columnist

Jennifer Lanter
Columnist

Ben Rimalower
Columnist

Mervyn Rothstein
Columnist

Seth Rudetsky
Columnist

Mark Shenton
London Correspondent

Robert Simonson
Senior Correspondent

Steven Suskin
Columnist

Faculty

Playbill

ACCOUNTING
Sitting (L-R): John LoCascio, Lewis Cole, Andrew Montero
Standing (L-R): Theresa Bernstein, Jim Eastman, JoAnn D'Amato

Regional Advertising Salespersons

Kenneth R. Back
Sales Manager
Indianapolis and
Cincinnati

Elaine Bodker
Sales
St. Louis

Bob Caulfield
Sales
San Francisco

Margo Cooper
Sales Manager
St. Louis

Louis Doucette
Sales
San Antonio

Leslie J. Feldman
Senior Vice
President
Regional Sales

Ron Friedman
Sales Manager
Columbus

Tom Green
Sales Manager
Florida, Texas,
New Orleans

Betsy Gugick
Sales Manager
Dallas

Ed Gurien
Sales
Florida/Dallas

Karen Kanter
Sales Manager
California

Brantley
Manderson
Sr. Acct. Mgr.
Atlanta/Charlotte

Michel Manzo
Sales Manager
Philadelphia

Marilyn A. Miller
Sales Manager
Minneapolis

Judy Pletcher
Sales Manager
Washington, DC

Donald Roberts
Sales Manager
Florida

Kenneth Singer
Sales Manager
Houston

Suzy Wagner
Sales
Washington, DC

Jill Wettersten
Sales Manager
Chicago

Not
pictured:
Jeff Ross

Faculty

Playbill / Woodside Offices

PROGRAM EDITORS AND PRODUCTION
Sitting (L-R): Amy Asch, Bill Reese, Patrick Cusanelli (Production Director), Sean Kenny
Standing (L-R): Ben Hyacinthe, Pam Karr, Diane Kolack, Judy Samelson, Claire Mangan, Scott Hale, Matt Bonanno, Khadijah Rentas

PLAYBILLSTORE.COM
(L-R): Bruce Stapleton, Craig Fogel,
Yajaira Marrero, Phil Newsom

NIGHT SHIFT MANUFACTURING
(L-R): Ana Rincon, Juan Burgos, Lennox Worrell, Sneider Cahuana, Pablo Yagual,
Rodrigo Garcia, Steve Ryder

DAY SHIFT MANUFACTURING
(L-R): Tony Constantino, Lidia Yagual, Nancy Galarraga, Larry Przetakiewicz, Steve Ramlall, Scott Cipriano, James Anticona, Frank Dunn, John Matthews, Janet Moti, Francisco Montero, Arnold Jacklitsch, Jose Ortiz (obscured), Ray Sierra, Frank Divirgilio, Robert Cusanelli

In Memoriam

June 1, 2013 to May 31, 2014

Jack Aaron
Cosmo Allegretti
Georgia Allen
Lynn Clifton Allen
Richard Allen
Maya Angelou
Luis Avalos
Ivor David Balding
Amiri Baraka (a.k.a.
    LeRoi Jones)
Anna Marie Barlow
Jack Beaber
Francine Beers
Walter Roy Beery
Mark Bendo
Donald Bevan
G. James Beyer
Karen Black
Jordan Bowers
Peter Boyden
Marc Breaux
Eileen Brennan
Tom Brennan
D.J.R. Bruckner
Hank Brunjes
Perry Bruskin
Sid Caesar
Mary Grace Canfield
Glen Cannon
Clifford Carpenter
Mary Carver
Patrice Chereau
Robert Christen
Sybil Christopher
Marilyn B. Coleman
Robert Colston
David Connell
Jane Connell
Richard Coogan
Ralph Cook
Charles Cooper
Roy Cooper
Clayton Corzatte
Jere Couture
Matthew Cowles
Sage Fuller Cowles
Richard Creamer
Harold "Stumpy"
    Cromer
Anna E. Crouse
Philip Cusack
Nigel Davenport
Ann B. Davis
Garry Davis
Jack Davison
Phillip Hayes Dean

Broadway Dims Its Lights

Broadway theatres dimmed their marquee lights this season upon the passing of the following theatre personalities, listed here along with the date the honor was accorded: Actress Jean Stapleton, June 5, 2013. Actor James Gandolfini, June 26, 2013. Producer Ashton Springer, July 24, 2013. Publicist Shirley Herz, August 14, 2013. Actress Julie Harris, August 28, 2013. Actor Philip Seymour Hoffman, February 5, 2014. Composer Mitch Leigh, March 19, 2014. Director Nicholas Martin, May 2, 2014.

Mickey Deems
B.J. DeSimone
William Dodds
Ralph Drischell
Ruth Duccini
Marta Eggerth
Anne Einhorn
Mark Enis
Mitchell Erickson
Charlotte Fairchild
Dennis Farina
Franz Fazakas
Gene Feist
Felix Febich
Michael Filerman
Patrice Wymore Flynn
Joan Fontaine
Juliet Forbes
Steve Forrest
Phyllis Frelich
Peggy Ann Ellis Fried
Laurie Frink
Bonnie Gallup
James Gandolfini
Gary Gardner
Kelly Garrett
Faith Geer
Jeremy Geidt
Frank Gero
Arthur Gelb
Martin Gold
Ernesto Gonzalez
Eydie Gormé
Arthur Gorton
Richard "Bick" Goss
Martin Gottfried
Henry Guettel
Marjorie Gunner
Sheila Guyse
Laurence Haddon
Lawrence Hamilton
Sam Harkness
Julie Harris

Jane Harvey
Roy Hausen
Seamus Heaney
Marta Heflin
Shirley Herz
Roger Hill
Philip Seymour
    Hoffman
Denis Holmes
Bob Howard
David Howard
Ronald Hunter
Damon Intrabartolo
Leonard Jackson
Mitchell Jason
Louise Jenkins
Christopher Jones
Irene Kane (a.k.a.
    Chris Chase)
Stanley Kauffmann
Jane Kean
Clinton King
Gloria Lambert
Rev. Sidney Lanier
Jay Lanin
Ed Lauter
Barbara Lawrence
Leslie Lee
Eddie Lawrence
Mitch Leigh
Jacques le Sourd
David LeVine
Joan Lorring
Mary Lum
Paul Lyday
Pirie MacDonald
Sheila Mac Rae
Neveen Mahmoud
Ruth Maleczech
Arthur Malet
Nancy Malone
Angelo Mango
Charles Marowitz

Gabriel García
    Márquez
Anthony Marriott
Sarah Marshall
Angela Martin
Nicholas Martin
Virginia Mattis
Curtis McClarin
Ellen McCowen
Daniel McClung
David McDaniel
Charles McGowan
Allan McKeown
Marian McPartland
Jack Merigold
Roy Miller
Wynne Miller
Juanita Moore
Betty Munro
Tony Musante
Byron Nease
Terry Nicholson
Patricia Noto
Peter O'Toole
Eleanor Parker
Chuck Patterson
Margaret Pellegrini
Lazaro Perez
Rob Peters
Stowe Phelps
John Pinette
Marc Platt (a.k.a.
    Marc Platoff
    and Marcel Leplat)
Henry Polic II
Seth Popper
Stephen Porter
Louise Quick
Erv Raibel
Kathleen Raitt
James Rebhorn
Elliott Reid
June Reimer

Joseph Ruskin
Regina Resnik
Paul Robeson Jr.
Jay Robinson
Joe Rocco
Dotty Rogan
David Rogers
Paul Rogers
George Rondo
Mickey Rooney
Ronald Roston
Bernard Sahlins
Michele Savoia
Maximilian Schell
Eda Seasongood
Lorenzo Semple Jr.
Victor Spinetti
Ashton Springer
Thomas Stanton
Jean Stapleton
J.D. Steel
James Stevenson
Ben Stewart
June Eve Story
Maxine Stuart
Conrad Susa
Donald L. Symington
Paul Szilard
Frances Tannehill
Richard S. Thomas
J. Michael Travis
Francine L. Trevens
Sybil Trubin
Ed Vassallo
Virginia Vincent
David Vogel
Maria Von Trapp (Jr.)
Ralph Waite
Honey Waldman
Louis W. Waldon
Jerry Ward
Laura Waterbury
Don Weissmuller
Christopher Evan
    Welch
Tony Wells
Richard Wendley
Ned Wertimer
Andrew James "Snoo"
    Wilson
Walt Witcover
Dee Dee Wood
Miller Wright
Patrice Wymore
Carmen Zapata
Efrem Zimbalist Jr.

Index

Index

Index

Index

Index

Index

Index

Index

Index

Index

Index

Index

Index

Index

Index

Index

Index

Index

Index

Index

Index

Index

Index

Borough of Manhattan

The Playbill Broadway Yearbook Map

Broadway-related places mentioned in the 10th edition of *The Playbill Broadway Yearbook*

Theatres
1. Al Hirschfeld Theatre
2. Ambassador Theatre
3. American Airlines Theatre
4. August Wilson Theatre
5. Belasco Theatre
6. Bernard B. Jacobs Theatre
7. Booth Theatre
8. Broadhurst Theatre
9. Broadway Theatre
10. Brooks Atkinson Theatre
11. Circle in the Square Theatre
12. Cort Theatre
13. Ethel Barrymore Theatre
14. Eugene O'Neill Theatre
15. Foxwoods Theatre
16. Gerald Schoenfeld Theatre
17. Gershwin Theatre
18. Helen Hayes Theatre
19. Imperial Theatre
20. John Golden Theatre
21. Longacre Theatre
22. Lunt-Fontanne Theatre
23. Lyceum Theatre
24. Majestic Theatre
25. Marquis Theatre
26. Minskoff Theatre
27. Music Box Theatre
28. Nederlander Theatre
29. Neil Simon Theatre
30. New Amsterdam Theatre
31. Palace Theatre
32. Richard Rodgers Theatre
33. Samuel J. Friedman Theatre
34. Shubert Theatre/ Shubert Organization Offices
35. St. James Theatre
36. Stephen Sondheim Theatre
37. Studio 54 Theatre
38. Vivian Beaumont Theater
39. Walter Kerr Theatre
40. Winter Garden Theatre
41. Avery Fisher Hall
42. Carnegie Hall
43. Kazino
44. New Victory Theatre
45. Radio City Music Hall
46. The Town Hall Theatre
47. Hudson Theatre
48. Joe's Pub
49. NYU Skirball Center
50. Playwrights Horizons
51. Liberty Theatre
52. Theatre Row

Other Significant Points of Interest
34. Shubert Organization
53. Nederlander Organization
35. Jujamcyn Theaters
54. Actors' Equity Association
55. Playbill/Playbill Books
56. American Theatre Wing
57. Bowlmor Lanes
58. Brill Building
59. Gansevoort Park Hotel
60. Heckscher Ball Fields
61. Metropolitan Museum of Art
62. Pierre Hotel
63. The Players Club
64. Plaza Hotel
65. Roseland Ballroom
17. Theater Hall of Fame
66. Times Square Museum and Visitors Center
67. Times Square Statues
68. TKTS Booth
69. Shubert Alley
70. Waldorf-Astoria Hotel

Eateries and Clubs
71. Angus McIndoe
72. Atlantic Grill
73. Azalea
74. Bar Centrale
75. Beer Culture
76. Birdland
77. Bocca di Bacco
78. Bond 45
79. Brickyard
80. Brookfield Place
81. Bryant Park Grill
82. BXL Café
83. Characters
84. Chipotle
85. Convo Bar
86. Copacabana
87. The Cosmic Diner
88. Don't Tell Mama
89. Edison Ballroom
37. 54 Below
90. Frames
91. Glass House Tavern
92. Gotham Hall
93. Guy's American Kitchen and Bar
94. Harley's Smokeshack
95. Haven Rooftop
96. Hammerstein Ballroom
97. Hourglass Tavern
98. Hurley's
99. Ça va
100. Iron Bar
101. Ivy
102. Joe Allen
103. John's Pizzeria
104. Langan's
105. Lillie's
106. The Long Room
107. Lucky Star Deli
108. Mari Vanna
109. Market Diner
110. Num Pang
111. O'Flaherty's Ale House
112. Reunion Surf Bar
113. Sardi's Restaurant
114. Schmackary's
115. Schnippers
116. Skylark
117. Soho House
118. Sosa Borella
119. St. Andrews
120. Star Lite Deli
121. Toloache

Boxes with arrows indicate the general direction of locations that are outside the borders of this map.